The Psychology
of Entrepreneurship

The Psychology of Entrepreneurship

Edited by

J. Robert Baum
Robert H. Smith School of Business
University of Maryland

Michael Frese
Department of Work and Organizational Psychology
University of Giessen, Germany

Robert A. Baron
Lally School of Management and Technology
Rensselaer Polytechic Institute

LAWRENCE ERLBAUM ASSOCIATES, PUBLISHERS
2007   Mahwah, New Jersey   London

Lawrence Erlbaum Associates, Inc., Publishers
10 Industrial Avenue
Mahwah, New Jersey 07430
www.erlbaum.com

Cover design by Kathryn Houghtaling Lacey

Library of Congress Cataloging-in-Publication Data

Baum, J. Robert.
The psychology of entrepreneurship J. Robert Baum, Michael Frese, Robert A. Baron.
    p. cm. — (SIOP organizational frontier series).
Includes bibliographical references and index.
ISBN 0-8058-5062-7 (alk. paper)
1. Entrepreneurship. 2. Entrepreneurship—Psychological aspects. I. Frese, Michael, 1949–   II. Baron, Robert A.   III. Title.   IV. Organizational frontiers series.
HB615.B388   2006
338′.04019—dc22   2006040523
                                                                            CIP

Books published by Lawrence Erlbaum Associates are printed on acid-free paper, and their bindings are chosen for strength and durability.

Printed in the United States of America
10 9 8 7 6 5 4 3 2 1

The Organizational Frontiers Series

The Organizational Frontiers Series is sponsored by The Society for Industrial and Organizational Psychology (SIOP). Launched in 1983 to make scientific contributions to the field, the series has attempted to publish books on cutting edge theory, research, and theory-driven practice in industrial/organizational psychology and related organizational science disciplines.

Our overall objective is to inform and to stimulate research for SIOP members (students, practitioners, and researchers) and people in related disciplines including the other subdisciplines of psychology, organizational behavior, human resource management, and labor and industrial relations. The volumes in the Organizational Frontiers Series have the following goals:

1) Focus on research and theory in organizational science, and the implications for practice.
2) Inform readers of significant advances in theory and research in psychology and related disciplines that are relevant to our research and practice.
3) Challenge the research and practice community to develop and adapt new ideas and to conduct research on these developments.
4) Promote the use of scientific knowledge in the solution of public policy issues and increased organizational effectiveness.

The volumes originated in the hope that they would facilitate continuous learning and a continuing research curiosity about organizational phenomena on the part of both scientists and practitioners.

SIOP Organizational Frontiers Series

SIOP Organizational Frontiers Series

Series Editor
Robert Pritchard
University of Central Florida

Baum/Frese/Baron: (2007) *The Psychology of Entrepreneurship.*

Weekly/Ployhart: (2006) *Situational Judgement Tests: Theory, Measurement and Application.*

Dipboye/Colella: (2005) *Discrimination at Work: The Psychological and Organizational Bases.*

Griffin/O'Leary-Kelly: (2003) *The Dark Side of Organizational Behavior.*

Hofmann/Tetrick: (2003) *Health and Safety in Organizations.*

Jackson/Hitt/DeNisi: (2003) *Managing Knowledge for Sustained Competitive Knowledge.*

Barrick/Ryan: (2003) *Personality and Work.*

Lord/Klimoski/Kanfer: (2002) *Emotions in the Workplace.*

Drasgow/Schmitt: (2002) *Measuring and Analyzing Behavior in Organizations.*

Feldman: (2002) *Work Careers.*

Zaccaro/Klimoski: (2001) *The Nature of Organizational Leadership.*

Rynes/Gerhart: (2000) *Compensation in Organizations.*

Klein/Kozlowski: (2000) *Multilevel Theory, Research and Methods in Organizations.*

Ilgen/Pulakos: (1999) *The Changing Nature of Performance.*

Earley/Erez: (1997) *New Perspectives on International I-O Psychology.*

Murphy: (1996) *Individual Differences and Behavior in Organizations.*

Guzzo/Salas: (1995) *Team Effectiveness and Decision Making.*

Howard: (1995) *The Changing Nature of Work.*

Schmitt/Borman: (1993) *Personnel Selection in Organizations.*

Zedeck: (1991) *Work, Families and Organizations.*

Schneider: (1990) *Organizational Culture and Climate.*

Goldstein: (1989) *Training and Development in Organizations.*

Campbell/Campbell: (1988) *Productivity in Organizations.*

Hall: (1987) *Career Development in Organizations.*

For a complete list of LEA titles, please contact
Lawrence Erlbaum Associates, Publishers, at www.erlbaum.com

To the many colleagues, especially Robert Jones, whose
outstanding work "on the interface" made this book possible
(J. Robert Baum, Michael Frese, Robert A. Baron)

And to:
Edwin A. Locke, Rudy Lamone, and Jo Ann Baum,
who made my late-in-life academic career possible and
productive, and to Hank Sims, Cindy Stevens, Ken G. Smith,
and Anil Gupta, whose counsel and support have sustained
me (J. Robert Baum)

The many colleagues who have supported my career from
early on (among others, Norbert Semmer, Siegfried Greif,
Nico Hoffmann, Walter Volpert, Eberhard Ulich, Dieter Zapf,
Martin Seligman, and the late John Sabini) and to my wife
Sharon and my kids (Michael Frese)

The friends who, "way back when," first made me aware of
the value and appeal of I/O psychology and made me a part
of it: James C. Naylor, Robert Pritchard, Dan Ilgen,
and Howard Weiss (Robert A. Baron)

Contents

Series Foreword

This is the twenty-fourth book in the Organizational Frontiers Series of books initiated by the Society for Industrial and Organizational Psychology. The overall purpose of the Series volumes is to promote the scientific status of the field. Ray Katzell first edited the Series. He was followed by Irwin Goldstein, Sheldon Zedeck, and Neal Schmitt. The topics of the volumes and the volume editors are chosen by the editorial board or individuals propose volumes to the editorial board. The series editor and the editorial board then work with the volume editor(s) in planning the volume.

The success of the series is evident in the high number of sales (now over 50,000). Volumes have also received excellent reviews and individual chapters as well as volumes have been cited very frequently. A symposium at the SIOP annual meeting examined the impact of the Series on research and theory in industrial and organizational psychology. The conclusion of most symposium participants was that the volumes have exerted a significant impact on research and theory in the field and are regarded as being representative of the best the field has to offer.

This volume, edited by J. Robert Baum, Michael Frese, and Robert A. Baron, reflects thinking and research on a relatively new topic, entrepreneurship. The volume also enlarges our understanding of this topic and integrates a large body of information using a uniquely psychological focus. The volume also offers an international perspective on the topic which enriches our understanding and appreciation of the different perspectives available.

There are several other strengths of this volume. It starts with three fundamental research questions about how and why some people recognize opportunities, start new ventures, and grow these into successful ventures. These questions serve to focus the other chapters. A good deal of attention is also given to the conceptualization of entrepreneurship. This is especially valuable for a topic which is in the early stages of development. Another major strength of the volume is how it identifies research needs. These are noted in many of the chapters and the concluding chapter discusses specific improvements that future research could make.

The editors and chapter authors deserve our gratitude for clearly communicating the nature, application, and implications of the theory and research described in this book. Production of a volume such as this involves the hard work and cooperative effort of many individuals. The editors, the chapter authors, and the editorial board all played important roles in this endeavor. As all royalties for the Series volume are used to help support SIOP, none of the editors or authors received any remuneration. The editors and authors deserve our appreciation for engaging a difficult task for the sole purpose of furthering our understanding of organizational science. We also want to express our gratitude to Anne Duffy, our editor at Lawrence Erlbaum Associates, who has been a great help in the planning and production of the volume.

January 12, 2006
—Robert D. Pritchard
University of Central Florida
Series Editor

Preface

J. Robert Baum
Michael Frese
Robert A. Baron

The purpose of this book is to inspire and guide the search for understanding the psychology of entrepreneurship. Entrepreneurship is essential for international social and economic well-being because new ventures are the dominant source of job creation, market innovation, and economic growth in many societies at this time (Aldrich, 1999; Kirchhoff, 1997). Those of us who are interested in entrepreneurship research have much work to do because the psychological factors and relationships that play a role in successful entrepreneurship are not clear.

To guide the search for understanding, Robert A. Baron (2002) derived three fundamental research questions:

1. How and why do some people, but not others, recognize opportunities?
2. How and why do some people, but not others, decide to (a) become entrepreneurs, (b) start new ventures, and (c) exploit opportunities?
3. How and why do some people, but not others, organize new ventures that grow rapidly and are successful?

In pursuit of answers to these fundamental research questions, the authors of chapters in *The Psychology of Entrepreneurship* review existing entrepreneurship research and point to the accumulated, *and limited*, conclusions about the causes of successful entrepreneurship. Most importantly, each author identifies research opportunities to guide future research.

Chapter 1 introduces the variety of definitions of entrepreneurship, describes the setting, and provides a history of entrepreneurship research. The chapters that follow the introduction explore entrepreneurs' individual differences in terms of personality, human capital, intrapsychic processing, and behaviors. Subsequent chapters present existing knowledge about external factors such as social networks and cultures. The four final chapters review and summarize the opportunities and challenges of research about entrepreneurs beginning with a discussion of methodology. Specific advice is offered about research design, including subject selection and data collection—all with the goal of understanding the causes of *successful* entrepreneurship.

CHAPTER SUMMARIES

Chapter 1, Entrepreneurship as an Domain of Psychology Study: An Introduction

The editors and Jerome A. Katz introduce the subject of entrepreneurship with a discussion of the social and economic importance of entrepreneurship and the psychological roots of entrepreneurship research. Six benefits for industrial/organizational (I/O) psychologists who study entrepreneurship are identified. The authors explain the multiple definitions of entrepreneurship and review the situational extremes that appear in the entrepreneurship setting.

The importance of deciding the boundaries of "entrepreneur" and "entrepreneurship" for research sampling is emphasized. This decision is complex because the various types of entrepreneurship (e.g., mom-and-pop small businesses, community businesses, high-potential technology ventures, and venturing within established organizations) present situational extremes in terms of uncertainty/risk, resources, and urgency (Baum, Locke, & Smith, 2001). To assist readers with the complexity, the authors offer eight sampling dimensions which should be addressed by empirical researchers of the entrepreneurship phenomenon. Finally, a history of entrepreneurship research is presented to orient would-be I/O psychology/entrepreneurship researchers.

The following summaries of chapters 2 through 16 are specific about content to help readers make choices about the sequence and focus of their reading. The summaries also identify some of the research opportunities and questions that chapter authors pose. We hope our inclusion of a research agenda stimulates your interest, because the opportunity to make a difference in the understanding of entrepreneurship is great. We firmly believe that research based on the principles, methods, and findings of IO psychology will be extremely beneficial.

Chapter 2, Entrepreneurship: A Process Perspective

Robert A. Baron describes the entrepreneurship process (phases/stages) and suggests that research adopting a process perspective is needed. He presents the array of stage models that are used by current researchers [Some entrepreneurship stage models utilize three categories (e.g., opportunity search, resource gathering, and exploitation); others use up to seven categories]. Baron recommends a six-phase model, and he describes the actions that entrepreneurs take and the alternative outcomes in each phase. He also discusses specific multilevel variables (personal, group, and societal) that affect outcomes, and he identifies specific areas where further study is needed. For example, he notes that we know little about the skills that are most important for successful entrepreneurship (or their importance across phases). Baron identifies several relevant macro (external or societal level) variables that are also candidates for research attention as controls in micro models.

Baron notes that the importance of specific entrepreneurship variables may well vary across phases, but that little is known about how and why the impact of these variables changes. Thus, Baron notes that I/O psychology researchers are particularly well prepared to improve knowledge about the entrepreneurship phenomenon because longitudinal studies, comprising an area of expertise in I/O psychology, are needed. He offers a complete discussion of the challenges (and solutions) implicit in such longitudinal studies.

In addition to the general suggestions just noted, Baron focuses on the need for cross-phase research about whether entrepreneurs are more, or less, risk-prone than other persons. He also suggests that researchers should study failure as a phase phenomenon and include analysis of the relation of skills and knowledge to failure. Put simply, Baron sees a need to understand how behaviors change across phases of the entrepreneurial process and which individual differences are important during which stages.

Chapter 3, Born to Be an Entrepreneur? Revisiting the Personality Approach to Entrepreneurship

Andreas Rauch and Michael Frese begin with a thorough review of past entrepreneurship personality research. The authors recall the early dominance and eventual decline of personality research in entrepreneurship, but they point to renewed interest. The authors blame the decline in research interest on poor results from studies that were based on scant theory and flawed methodologies. Nine reasons for the current rebirth in interest in personality effects in entrepreneurship are offered, including prescriptions for better methodologies.

Drawing on the meta-analyses and Rauch and Frese (2000), they offer a research model to guide entrepreneurs' personality research. It includes KSAs (knowledge, skill, and ability), broad and specific traits, and action strategies, as well as environmental controls. "Old and new" personality traits are reviewed and considered in light of the entrepreneur's environment. Rauch and Frese conclude that there are small to moderate relationships between personality (high need for achievement [nAch], risk propensity, passion, innovativeness, autonomy, locus of control, and self-efficacy) and successful entrepreneurship and suggest that those who called for the end of doing research on personality traits for lack of important relationships are clearly wrong.

Rauch and Frese strongly encourage I/O psychology researchers to (a) use differentiating hypotheses for general vs. specific personality traits and (b) match the focus of independent and dependent variables. Further, they suggest that (c) interaction should be utilized to better explain the relation between personality and entrepreneurship outcomes.

The research model presented captures a whole set of research questions, including the authors' call for better personality theory and for research that included mediation and interaction. Research questions such as "Do the Big Five personality traits matter for entrepreneurship success?" and "Do midlevel theories and interactional models offer better explanations of personality trait effects?" are embedded in the model.

Chapter 4, Entrepreneurs' Competencies

Gideon Markman discusses a set of entrepreneurial KSAs (knowledge, skill, and ability) that have demonstrated the ability to predict entrepreneurship success, and a second set that are likely predictors. His discussion of competencies (KSAs that work) begins with a complete discussion of the difference between weak and strong situations, because Markman emphasizes that the entrepreneur's situation is sufficiently weak that individual differences express themselves in terms of venture outcomes.

Markman suggests that entrepreneurs' knowledge competencies reflect unique relevant industry and venturing experience and information. These competencies are discussed in terms of specificity, complexity, cumulativeness, tacitness, and codification. Entrepreneurs' skill competencies, which are specific task proficiencies, involve specific technical, organizational, management, product/service, industry, and human skills. Markman proposes that general ability to overcome adversity (perseverance) and general cognitive ability are entrepreneurial ability competencies. The discussion of knowledge, skill, and ability repeatedly refers to the interaction among KSAs and points to shared attributes. For example, it is unlikely that much knowledge or skill would be accumulated without relevant ability. Markman reminds us that ability is a general characteristic.

Markman offers a list of issues to inspire research about competencies. For example: Which competencies are most important for raising venture capital? How can the reciprocal causality among KSAs be measured? Is industry tacit knowledge a competency, and can it be measured? These questions, together with Markman's research review of psychology based work about entrepreneurs' competencies, should enable I/O psychologists to develop useful studies about entrepreneurs' competencies.

Chapter 5, Entrepreneurial Motivation

Edwin A. Locke and J. Robert Baum open with a reminder that entrepreneurial motivation is an inner drive toward entrepreneurship goals. It energizes, directs, and sustains new venture creation and growth. Six psychology-based theories of motivation are reviewed (needs, reinforcement, equity, expectancy, goal, and social-cognitive), and the authors note that only needs (nAch, etc.), goal, and social-cognitive (self-efficacy) theories have received attention from entrepreneurship researchers. In addition to goals and self-efficacy, Locke and Baum discuss an array of motivating factors that are relevant in entrepreneurship (intentions, perseverance, vision, independence, achievement motivation, drive, and egoistic passion).

The authors concluded that vision, goals, and self-efficacy deserved further attention. They developed and tested three models that included vision, goals, and self-efficacy as situationally specific motivation concepts that mediate traits, competencies, values, and motives (independence, self-confidence, achievement motive, passion, new resource skill, and drive). Results indicate that motivation is a partial mediator of relevant general personal characteristics. The results also shed light on the relevance of traits and values for predicting entrepreneurship performance when the distal general forces are mediated by situationally specific motivation concepts.

The authors offer four research questions for study by I/O psychologists. Among these are "How important is nonconscious motivation vs. conscious motivation for entrepreneurship success?", and "Does the importance of traits depend on the stage of new venture creation?"

Chapter 6, Entrepreneurs as Organization Products Revisited

Pino Audia and Christopher Rider remind readers of the importance of a social orientation for a full understanding of entrepreneurship. The title is derived from the notion that new ventures are frequently created as a reaction to employment experiences and with resources that are gained as an employee. That is, organization contexts provide entrepreneurs with opportunities to develop psychological and social resources that are necessary for new venture creation. Furthermore, political turbulence, market concentration, and organization dissolution may motivate entrepreneurs to leave their home organization to establish their own. In other words, entrepreneurs are often organization products.

Audia and Rider provide research evidence that employees gain insight about self-employment opportunities and develop social ties that are essential for self-employment as they work. Researchers have found that as entrepreneurs gain psychological, social, and economic resources, they gain confidence to start a company. Although there has been significant entrepreneurship research about networking and other social process, the authors point to many research opportunities. For example, little is known about exactly how work experiences create psychological assets that are useful for venture creation. We also need to know about the importance of weak tie networks for entrepreneurship, and we have an urgent need to understand the structure and processes of the venture capital networks.

Chapter 7, Cognition and Capabilities in Entrepreneurial Ventures

Lowell Busenitz and Jonathan Arthurs focus on cognition in entrepreneurship with attention to the thinking processes that build entrepreneurs' entrepreneurial and dynamic capabilities (ability to deal with change). They explain that understanding cognitive processes helps researchers understand the forces and likely outcomes that are involved in entrepreneurial information processing and decision making.

Busenitz and Arthurs note that entrepreneurs tend to use a heuristic-based decision style more extensively than others and that they tend to have high-level learning styles that involve abstraction from little codifiable information. The authors take us through discussions of the relation and impact of this style of entrepreneurial cognition on opportunity recognition, social resource gathering, and capital resource gathering.

The authors note that as ventures mature, more resources, systems, and people become involved, leading to very different decision dynamics and alternatives. The authors suggest that these changes in the gravity of decisions require a change in decision style, which may be difficult for some entrepreneurs to make. The ability to make the change in decision style is a dynamic capability.

In summary, this chapter is about the characteristics of entrepreneurs' thinking styles, and it suggests that decision styles must fit the characteristics of the decision at hand and that heuristic decision making, although effective in early venture stages, may have limited usefulness in more mature businesses. The authors' theory presents interesting challenges that may be addressed by I/O psychologists. Questions raised are: "Is there empirical evidence that the shift in need for 'entrepreneurial capabilities to dynamic capabilities' actually occurs?" "Can cognitive psychology theory expand the current view that entrepreneurs cognition is primarily heuristic?" "Are there situations in which successful early stage entrepreneurs should adopt a more rational decision style?" "If so, are heuristics-oriented entrepreneurs able to adapt?" "Are dynamic capabilities only available as a team resource?"

Chapter 8, Psychological Actions and Entrepreneurial Success: An Action Theory Approach

Michael Frese draws on "action theory" (e.g., action regulation theory) (Frese & Zapf, 1994) to explore the sequence, structure, and focus of entrepreneurs' actions. Action theory provides a three dimensional framework for evaluating human action (sequence, structure, and focus). "Sequence" reflects the path from goals to feedback, and "structure" indicates the level of regulation of action (skill to metacognitive–heuristic). "Focus" ranges from task to self. The theory is explained in detail in the chapter and is subsequently linked with entrepreneurial action to provide an explanation for entrepreneurs' performance.

Frese draws on the theory to propose several relationships. For example, he explores the planning component of the sequence dimension of action theory. Here, "plans" is used in the psychological sense that one has some kind of order of operations for the next few seconds, minutes, months, or years, and Frese indicates that it follows from action theory that more successful entrepreneurs have more ready-made plans available. The application of action theory to entrepreneurship is best developed in terms of plans. Four action processes are offered to explain entrepreneurial planning behavior: complete planning, critical-point planning, opportunistic, and reactive. The most successful process is identified as complete planning.

Reviewing the characteristics of the structure of action, Frese notes that new tasks appear repeatedly for early-stage entrepreneurs as the firm emerges, so conscious regulation of action is likely to exist for several years in contrast to most other jobs. This leads to the action theory conclusion that cognitive ability is thereby more important for early stage entrepreneurs than for most occupations.

Additional conclusions are drawn, and an array of research questions is offered to guide I/O psychologists who are interested in an action theory approach to understanding entrepreneurs' performance. For example, the action orientation of mental models has not been explicitly developed, and the role of training in developing an ability to move between levels of regulation has not been explored.

Chapter 9, Entrepreneurship and Leadership

John Antonakis and Erko Autio point to gains for researchers of entrepreneurship who study past and current leadership methods and findings. There are commonalities across the two research domains in terms of the importance of individual characteristics, social relationships, and performance orientation. For example, (a) both are involved with innovation and change, (b) both attempt to influence others, (c) both attempt to exploit opportunities, and (d) entrepreneurs are leader/managers throughout the firm startup process. Antonakis and Autio encourage entrepreneurship researchers to focus on individual behavior and to include context in performance models.

The authors provide a review of contemporary leadership thinking in terms of typologies, behaviors, and outcomes. They point to the importance of process theories in current thinking and offer a process model for entrepreneurship. They finish with three prescriptions for entrepreneurship researchers: (a) Use process models, (b) Include context, and (c) Use taxonomic trait structures for study.

In addition, we editors suggest that I/O psychologists also try to find answers to "Can business founders become business leaders?" and "Do the core social dynamics of entrepreneurial action operate differently than the social dynamics of leadership action?" We also recommend a review of followership literature for insights about how entrepreneurs might lead external constituencies (financiers, customers, and suppliers) (Fernandez & Vecchio, 1997; Pearce, Kramer, & Robbins, 1997).

Chapter 10, Education and Training in Entrepreneurship

Jerome A. Katz explores the background, track record, and delivery methods of entrepreneurship education. In response to the question "Can entrepreneurship be taught?" he points to substantial research that points to the efficacy of university education programs. He notes that entrepreneurship education has grown in importance for universities. Furthermore, government and commercial providers are heavily involved in entrepreneurship education.

Most entrepreneurship education programs involve formation of a business plan, and Katz addresses the key question, "Are business plans necessary for successful entrepreneurship?" His answer is complex and we recommend a thorough reading.

Taking these aspects together, Katz suggests, I/O psychologists have much to add and much to gain from a study of entrepreneurship education and training. He points to the abundance of research opportunities that exist for psychologists in academic entrepreneurship, and he compliments the openness of the community of entrepreneurship scholars.

Chapter 11, Intrapreneurship and Innovation

Tom Lumpkin describes entrepreneurial behavior in established businesses. Intrapreneurship is variously called corporate entrepreneurship, corporate venturing, and entrepreneurial strategy/culture; it is related to business innovation in that both involve newness of product, market, or business model. However, *intrapreneurship* is an organization-level (or team) concept that sometimes simply reflects acceptance of change, and *innovation* is an individual or organization-level process that involves newness, not just change.

Lumpkin discusses the link between intrapreneurship and innovation, and he identifies the barriers to both and offers prescriptions for effective intrapreneurship and innovation. He reviews "entrepreneurial orientation" (EO), the strategy-making practices and processes that managers engage in to identify and create venture opportunities. EO has five dimensions—autonomy, innovativeness, proactiveness, competitive aggressiveness, and risk taking. There is quantitative evidence that firms that are high in entrepreneurial orientation will more effectively pursue innovation than others.

Lumpkin presents a plethora of research questions for I/O psychologists and entrepreneurship researchers. He notes that assistance in terms of validating the "entrepreneurial orientation" concept would be much appreciated. It should be tested in multiple settings and with a variety of research designs. He also noted that it would be interesting and useful to understand the cognitive factors that create barriers to innovation. As mentioned in Gartner's chapter 14, organizational psychologists offer sophisticated advice about developing and measuring team and organization-level individual difference concepts from knowledge of group decision making.

Chapter 12, Cross-Cultural Entrepreneurship: The Case of China

Rosalie L. Tung, Jan Walls, and Michael Frese discuss the challenge of conducting cross-cultural entrepreneurship studies. They present a rich array of research questions and offer methodological advice. Most cross-cultural studies are based on Hofstede's seminal cultural research, and this chapter is not different; however, the focus on Chinese entrepreneurship through three case studies and the comparison with entrepreneurship in Japan, Korea, and Israel add understanding that is not generally available.

Analysis of Chinese entrepreneurship draws on the GLOBE study in an extensive section that compares and contrasts the effects of cultural dimensions (performance orientation, assertiveness, collectivism, gender egalitarianism, humane orientation, power distance, and uncertainty avoidance) across multiple cultures. The cross-cultural research methodology discussion includes specific suggestions for improvement of questionnaires. Research issues include: "Is entrepreneurship simply a subculture in all cultures, so that there are no differences among entrepreneurs across cultures?" "Does a culture have to provide a good match with entrepreneurs' tendencies for entrepreneurship to thrive?" In other words, "Entrepreneurs seem to thrive as outliers, so is it true that the differences between a culture and its entrepreneurs matters more than the culture itself?" Fundamental research questions are: "Why are founding rates so different across countries?" "How can large Chinese ventures remain nimble?"

Chapter 13, Method Challenges and Opportunities in the Psychological Study of Entrepreneurship

Per Davidsson discusses the methodological advantages and challenges involved in studying entrepreneurs and their companies. Archival studies, survey and case research, and laboratory experiments are discussed in terms of the advantages and disadvantages of each. Davidsson begins by pointing to the two fundamental research conceptions of entrepreneurship: (a) individual entrepreneurship and (b) entrepreneurship as a role (the role of new venture creator). The second conception appears in a variety of settings, including established firms. Davidsson encourages psychologists to include the second conception of entrepreneurship in their thinking. This conception focuses on the creative, opportunity-oriented nature of the entrepreneurship process.

Davidsson offers prescriptions for appropriate study design in term of levels of analysis, sampling practices (homogeneity vs. heterogeneity), and aggregation. With regard to sampling practices, Davidsson recommends that samples should be drawn from a general population, not just a population of entrepreneurs. With regard to aggregation of individual level measures to the firm level (the upward direct effects model), he points to the value that I/O psychologists can add to entrepreneurship research through application of sophisticated methods of measurement of team characteristics.

Davidsson notes that secondary data are not rich sources of information for entrepreneurship researchers; however, several studies have extracted meaningful information. He discusses the limitations of direct survey research (questionnaires), but notes its usefulness, efficiency, and acceptability. Davidsson points to the exceptional data that are available to all entrepreneurship researchers through the longitudinal Panel Study of Entrepreneurial Dynamics (PSED) study of nascent entrepreneurs. He offers a thorough description and prescriptions for its use. Davidsson's chapter ends with a discussion of case (ethnographic) studies, laboratory research, and intriguing suggestions for psychologists who wish to utilize either methodology.

Chapter 14, Psychology, Entrepreneurship, and the "Critical Mess"

Author Bill Gartner encourages entrepreneurship scholars to go beyond narrow disciplinary perspectives as they begin to understand the entrepreneurship phenomenon. He encourages qualitative research that creates a "critical mess" of knowledge derived from practitioners and academics from diverse disciplines. He suggests that such knowledge may lead to new insights, as useful patterns of thinking and behavior are uncovered from analysis of the mess.

Gartner encourages descriptive research that focuses on (a) the *process* of starting a business and (b) the personal actions that cause new venture success. He emphasizes the inherent practical value of such research and calls for the use of autobiographies, public press, and personal interviews. In closing, Gartner encourages future Society of Industrial and Organizational Psychology (SIOP) thinkers to draw upon existing work from multiple academic orientations and multiple sources to guide their focused research. The editors hope that readers find that *The Psychology of Entrepreneurship* offers a good beginning point for a review of the multiple perspectives about entrepreneurship.

Chapter 15, As Long as We're Going to the Trouble, Why Not Do it Right?

[This chapter description was written by the author, Kelly G. Shaver.] I argue that only some psychological contributions have been embraced by entrepreneurship researchers. Others, primarily of the methodological nature, have been notable by their absence. Concepts have been imported piecemeal with insufficient attention to the larger psychological context from which they arose. Comparisons between entrepreneurs and others, when they have been made at all, have often been overinterpreted.

Rather than following the data-intensive strategies of traditional psychological researchers, entrepreneurship scholars have produced a literature that is model heavy and data-impoverished. And finally, entrepreneurship research has too frequently avoided the clear operational definitions that could help the field disentangle conflicting research-based claims. To advance our understanding of entrepreneurial behavior, I suggest that psychological and organizational researchers should bring their entire methodological toolkits when they show up for work in the entrepreneurship laboratory.

Chapter 16, Research Gains: Benefits of Closer Links Between I/O Psychology and Entrepreneurship

In this chapter, we editors revisit the core entrepreneurship research questions and summarize the opinions offered throughout *The Psychology of Entrepreneurship*. The Giessen–Amsterdam model of entrepreneurship (Rauch & Frese, 2000) is used to organize the review of the book chapters. Specific ways in which the findings, concepts, and theories of I/O psychology can be useful in answering the research questions and specific ways in which I/O psychology can, in turn, benefit from closer links to the field of entrepreneurship, are examined.

We hope *The Psychology of Entrepreneurship* will inspire a new generation of I/O psychology researchers, entrepreneurship researchers, and students who are interested in the entrepreneurship phenomenon. Entrepreneurship is critically important for international well-being, and we believe there is much to be gained by adding to existing knowledge about the adventuresome pioneers who establish new businesses, introduce new products or processes, and enter new markets. Join this search for answers about the psychology of entrepreneurship and consider the multiple concepts and research tools that fit the unique entrepreneurship situation.

We close with these words, written in 1931 by the novelist E. L. Doctorow (as quoted by Plimpton, 1988): "Creativity is like driving a car at night. You never see further than your headlights, but you can make the whole trip that way." We hope that the chapters in this book help extend the glow of entrepreneurship's headlights and in this way contribute significantly to progress in this new but rapidly growing field.

REFERENCES

Aldrich, H. E. (1999). *Organizations evolving*. London: Sage

Baron, R. A. (2002). OB and entrepreneurship: The reciprocal benefits of closer conceptual links. In B. M. Staw & R. Kramer (Eds.), *Research in organizational behavior* (pp. 225 269). Greenwich, CT: JAI Press.

Baum, J. R., Locke, E. A., & Smith, K. G. (2001). A multidimensional model of venture growth. *Academy of Management Journal, 44*, 292–303.

Fernandez, C., & Vecchio, R. P. (1997). Situational leadership theory revisited: A test of an across jobs perspective. *Leadership Quarterly, 8*, 67–84.

Frese, M., & Zapf, D. (1994). Action as the core of work psychology: A German approach. In. H. C. Triandis, M. D. Dunnette, & J. M. Hough (Eds.), *Handbook of industrial and organizational psychology* (Vol. 4, 2nd ed., pp. 271–340). Palo Alto, CA: Consulting Psychology Press.

Kirchhoff, B. (1997). Entrepreneurship economics. In W. B. Bygrave (Ed.), *The portable MBA in entrepreneurship* (pp. 450–471). New York, Wiley.

Pearce, J. A., Kramer, T. R., & Robbins, D. K. (1997). The effects of managers' entrepreneurial behavior on subordinates. *Journal of Business Venturing, 12*(2), 147–160.

Plimpton, G. (1988). *Writers at work: The Paris review interviews* (seventh series). New York: Penguin Books.

Rauch, A., & Frese, M. (2000). Psychological approaches to entrepreneurial success: A general model and an overview of findings. *International Review of Industrial and Organizational Psychology, 15*, 101–142.

Contributors

John Antonakis is Professor of Organizational Behavior in the Faculty of Economics and Business Administration (HEC) of the University of Lausanne. His research centers on predictors of effective leadership, the contextualized nature of leadership, the links among leadership, work design, and motivation. His research has appeared in a variety of scientific outlets, including an edited book (with A. T. Cianciolo & R. J. Sternberg) titled *The Nature of Leadership* (2004, Sage Publications). He is on the editorial board two major leadership journals (*Leadership* and *The Leadership Quarterly*).

Jonathan D. Arthurs is Assistant Professor of Strategic Management and Entrepreneurship at Washington State University. His research is focused on the relationship of entrepreneurs with their venture capitalists, initial public offerings, and governance of bankrupt firms. He is published in *The Journal of Business Venturing, Venture Capital,* and *Entrepreneurship Theory and Practice.*

Pino Audia is an Assistant Professor in the Organizational Behavior and Industrial Relations Group at the Haas School of Business, University of California, Berkeley. His research focuses on micro explanations of macro phenomena such as organizational inertia and the emergence of industrial clusters. Pino is published in *The Annual Review of Sociology, Management Science, Human Resource Management Review, Academy of Management Journal,* and the *Journal of Sociology.* Pino was the recipient of the Outstanding Publication in Organizational Behavior award from the Academy of Management for his article 'The Paradox of Success'.

Erkko Autio is Professor in Technology-Based Venturing and Director at the Instut Stratège of HEC Lausanne where he directs the Institute's research, teaching, and applied activities. His research focuses on venture growth, alliance strategies, and rapid international growth of new technology-based firms. He has published in *The Academy of Management Journal, Strategic Management Journal, Research Policy, Journal of Business Venturing,* and *Venture Capital Journal.* Professor Autio has been on the faculty at Jönköping International Business School and London Business School where he helped launch the Global Entrepreneurship Monitor (GEM) initiative.

Robert A. Baron is the Dean R. Wellington Professor of Management and Psychology at Rensselaer Polytechnic Institute. His current research focuses primarily on social and cognitive factors that play a role in entrepreneurs' success. Baron is a Fellow of both the American Psychological Association and the American Psychological Society. He has published more than one hundred articles and thirty-eight chapters in edited volumes. He is the author or co-author of more than forty books in the fields of psychology and management, including *Social Psychology* (11th edition), *Psychology: From Science to Practice; Behavior in Organizations* (9th ed.; in press), and *Entrepreneurship: A Process Perspective.* Professor Baron currently serves on the Editorial Boards of the Journal of Applied Psychology and the Academy of Management Journal, and is an Associate Editor for Management Science.

J. Robert Baum is Associate Professor of Entrepreneurship at the Smith School of Business, University of Maryland. His research interests include nascent entrepreneurship, new venture growth, quantitative methods, and entrepreneurial strategic decision-making. He has published in *The Journal of Applied Psychology, The Academy of Management Journal, The Journal of Business Venturing, Strategic Management Journal,* and *Frontiers of Entrepreneurship Research.* Baum has chapters in three books, and he is a member of the Editorial Board of the *Journal of Business Venturing.* Baum founded three companies and created two rollups. He is a member of three corporate boards, including a venture capital firm, and he is chairman of a national health care company.

Lowell W. Busenitz is Associate Professor of strategic management and entrepreneurship at the University of Oklahoma. His research focuses on entrepreneurs' strategic decision making, risk in entrepreneurial ventures, international entrepreneurship and the relationship between venture capitalists and entrepreneurs. Professor Busenitz has published in the *Academy of Management Journal, Academy of Management Review, Journal of Business Venturing, Journal of Management, Entrepreneurship Theory and Practice, Academy of Management Executive* and *Journal of High Technology Management Research.* He serves on the editorial review boards of the *Journal of Business Venturing, Entrepreneurship Theory and Practice* and the *Journal of Management.*

Per Davidsson is Professor of entrepreneurship at Brisbane Graduate School of Business. His research deals with the start-up and growth of small firms and the social benefits of entrepreneurship, including job creation. His research has appeared in *Strategic Management Journal, Journal of Business Venturing, Small Business Economics, Regional Studies, Entrepreneurship and Regional Development,* and *Journal of Economic Psychology*. He has been editor of *Entrepreneurship Theory & Practice* and a member of the five editorial review boards. Professor Davidsson is director of the JIBS Program on Entrepreneurship and Growth in SMEs (PEG).

Michael Frese, University of Giessen and London Business School, holds a chair for work and organizational psychology at the University of Giessen and is Visiting Professor at the London Business School. He has taught at the University of Berlin, was Associate Professor at the University of Pennsylvania, and professor at the Universities of Munich and Amsterdam. His research is focused on organizational psychology, including unemployment, stress, personal initiative, and the psychological success factors of entrepreneurs. He is author of more than 200 articles and editor/author of more than 20 books and special journal issues. Prof. Frese is President of the International Association of Applied Psychology and Editor of *Applied Psychology: An International Review*.

William B. Gartner is the Arthur M. Spiro Professor of Entrepreneurship at Clemson University. His research focuses on entrepreneurship and small business development. His research about nascent entrepreneurs explores how they find and identify opportunities, recognize and solve startup problems, and undertake actions to successfully launch new ventures. He is co-founder of the Entrepreneurship Research Consortium which initiated, developed, and managed the Panel Study of Entrepreneurial Dynamics. Professor Gartner has published in the *Academy of Management Review, Journal of Management, Journal of Business Venturing, Entrepreneurship Theory and Practice,* and the *Journal of Small Business Management*. He holds editorial board memberships at four journals.

Jerome A. Katz is Professor of Management and holder of the Coleman Foundation Chair in Entrepreneurship at Saint Louis University. He is recognized internationally as an expert on entrepreneurship and e-commerce. His research in these areas has been funded by the ILO, America's NSF and NFIB, the Soros, Kauffman and Coleman Foundations, and Sweden's ESBRI. He is editor of two book series in entrepreneurship, including *Advances in Entrepreneurship, Firm Emergence, and Growth,* and sits on the editorial boards of several entrepreneurship journals, including *Journal of Business Venturing, Entrepreneurship Theory & Practice,* and the *Journal of Small Business Management*.

Edwin A. Locke is Dean's Professor (Emeritus) of Leadership and Motivation at the R. H. Smith School of Business at the University of Maryland. He has published over 260 chapters, notes, and articles in professional journals on such subjects as work motivation, job satisfaction, incentives, and the philosophy of science. He is also the author or editor of 10 books, including *Goal Setting: A Motivational Technique That Works* and *A Theory of Goal Setting and Task Performance*. Dr. Locke has been elected a Fellow of the American Psychological Association, the Academy of Management, and has been a consulting editor for leading journals and recipient of the Lifetime Achievement Award from the Academy of Management.

G. Tom Lumpkin is the Kent Hance Regents Endowed Chair and Professor of Entrepreneurship at Texas Tech University in Lubbock, Texas. His primary research interests include entrepreneurial orientation, opportunity recognition, entrepreneurial learning, new venture strategies, and strategy making processes. His research has been published in the *Academy of Management Review, Academy of Management Journal, Entrepreneurship Theory and Practice, Journal of Business Venturing, Journal of Management, Organizational Dynamics,* and *Strategic Management Journal.* Recently, Tom co-authored a textbook entitled *Strategic Management: Creating Competitive Advantages* with Greg Dess and Alan Eisner. Tom received his PhD in Business Administration from the University of Texa at Arlington and MBA from the University of Southern California.

Gideon D. Markman is Assistant Professor of Innovation Management and Entrepreneurship at the University of Georgia. His research interests include innovation management and technological entrepreneurship. His work was published in the *Academy of Management Journal, Journal of Applied Psychology, Journal of Business Venturing,* and *Academy of Management Executive.* His research on entrepreneurs' social skills and adversity quotient was featured in Business Week, Inc. Magazine, Entrepreneur Magazine, and Self Magazine. Markman has published several book chapters in edited volumes.

Andreas Rauch is a research fellow at the University of Giessen, Department of Work and Organizational Psychology. He received his PhD at the University of Amsterdam, Department of Work and Organizational Psychology. His main research interest is entrepreneurship, and he has focused on individual differences of business owners, the impact of entrepreneurship on economic growth, cross-cultural differences, and the success-factors of entrepreneurs. Andreas is published in *International Review of Industrial and Organizational Psychology, Journal of Small Business Management,* and *Applied Psychology: An International Review.*

Chris Rider is a PhD student at the Walter A. Haas School of Business, University of California, Berkeley. His research spans micro and macro levels of analysis. He examines how organizational accountability systems may promote "good" (and prevent "bad") judgment and decision making and how existing organizations prepare (or do not prepare) employees for entrepreneurship. His current research projects include empirical studies of the effects of various organizational decision making styles on multiple performance metrics, firm entry rates and individual entrepreneurial transitions in the venture capital industry, and founding and mortality rates of U.S. footwear manufacturers.

Kelly G. Shaver is Professor of Entrpreneurial Studies at the College of Charleston. He is the author of seven books, co-author or co-editor of five others, and he is author or co-author of over 140 papers and research articles on attribution processes and entrepreneurship. Dr. Shaver was Editor of *Entrepreneurship Theory and Practice* and has served on the editorial boards of the *Journal of Personality and Social Psychology* and the *Journal of Personality*. He currently serves on the editorial boards of the Journal of Applied Social Psychology, Entrepreneurship and Regional Development, and the *Journal of Developmental Entrepreneurship*. Prof. Shaver is a Fellow of the American Psychological Society, a member of the Society of Experimental Social Psychology, and is past Chair of the Entrepreneurship Division of the Academy of Management.

Rosalie Tung is the Ming and Stella Wong Professor of International Business at Simon Fraser University (Canada). She has been elected as a Fellow of the Royal Society of Canada and as a Fellow of the Academy of Management. Dr. Tung also held the position of Director, International Business Center, at the University of Wisconsin-Milwaukee. She has served as a visiting professor at Harvard University, the University of California-Los Angeles, the University of Manchester Institute of Science and Technology (U.K.), and the Chinese University of Hong Kong. Dr. Tung is one of the world's five most cited authors in international business. She is the author or editor of nine books and has published widely on the subjects of international management and organizational theory in journals. Dr. Tung has been President of the Academy of Management.

Jan Walls is Director of the David Lam Centre for International Communication at Simon Fraser University. He has taught Chinese language and culture courses and contributed to Asia-focused program development at the University of British Columbia, University of Victoria and SFU. From 1981 to 83, he served as First Secretary for Cultural and Scientific Affairs in the Canadian Embassy in Beijing, and from 1985 to 87 he was Senior Vice President of the Asia Pacific Foundation of Canada, where he developed their first programs in cultural and educational affairs. He specializes in the theory and practice of cross-cultural translation and communication.

1

Entrepreneurship as an Area of Psychology Study: An Introduction

J. Robert Baum
Michael Frese
Robert A. Baron
Jerome A. Katz

THE NEED TO UNDERSTAND *THE ENTREPRENEUR*

Entrepreneurship is fundamentally personal. Although entrepreneurship research has shown that there are multiple personal, organizational, and external causes of successful new venture creation (Baum, Locke, & Smith, 2001; Rauch & Frese, 2000), it takes *human* vision, intention, and work to conceive and convert business ideas to successful products and services. Through their thinking and action, entrepreneurs themselves integrate human and financial resources to organize, produce, and market products and services that yield value for customers and workers.

According to venture financiers, entrepreneurs' personal characteristics (individual differences) are the most important factors for business success—even more important than the business idea or industry setting (Shepherd, 1999; Zopounidis, 1994). Entrepreneurs themselves claim that their decisions and actions are the most important reasons for their company's survival (even as they complain about external challenges and resource shortages) (MacMillan, Siegel, & SubbaNarasimha, 1985; Sexton, 2001).

Despite the belief that entrepreneur's personal characteristics are important for new venture success, the psychology of the entrepreneur has not

1

been thoroughly studied. We believe that industrial/organizational (I/O) psychology researchers have much to offer the dynamic field of entrepreneurship research—particularly in terms of general theoretical knowledge about human psychology and research technique sophistication. In turn, I/O psychology theory will be enriched, and I/O psychology researchers will gain professionally from the study of entrepreneurs.

BENEFITS FOR I/O PSYCHOLOGISTS: THE INTERSECTION OF I/O PSYCHOLOGY AND ENTREPRENEURSHIP

The Psychology of Entrepreneurship addresses the many points of intersection between traditional I/O psychology and entrepreneurship. First, organizations are the central phenomenon of organizational psychology, and organizations only come about through entrepreneurs and entrepreneurship. This implies that to be interested in the development of organizations, I/O researchers need to be interested in the entrepreneurial process.

Furthermore, the founders of organizations typically influence the development and culture of the units that they start, and their influence persists throughout and beyond their lives (Schein, 1987). The relationship between the entrepreneur and the organization that he or she founded can be quite complicated, as discussed by Baron in chapter 2 of this book. Thus, organizational psychologists ought to be interested in entrepreneurship if they take the roots of the phenomenon that they are studying—the organization—seriously.

Second, there are interesting issues involving multiple levels of analysis and multiple stages of business in entrepreneurship:

1. In the beginning, the solitary entrepreneur has an enormous influence on the start-up firm (Schein, 1983, van Gelderen, Frese, & Thurik, 2000).
2. As the new venture grows, influence shifts to the entrepreneurial team and key employees (Savage, 1979).
3. Subsequently, organizational factors dominate the established firm.

Not all business founders are good managers of their businesses and therefore it makes sense to search for differential predictors of the emergence and success of organizations. We think this is similar to the importance of the differentiation of effective and ineffective leadership in leadership research (Lord, de Vader, & Alliger, 1986).

Third, industrial organizational research and entrepreneurship research both focus on performance outcomes. Industrial and organizational psychologists evaluate performance in terms of supervisory judgements; however, entrepreneurship research measures performance more completely and more objectively in terms of market performance (e.g., organizational survival, growth, and profitability). Although there are problems with such measures of growth and profitability in entrepreneurship, clearly, such a performance concept is not just a function of individual behaviors. Environmental factors and luck clearly play a part. Thus, performance as measured in entrepreneurship research is a much more meaningful performance concept than the one related to supervisor rating of performance. I/O performance concepts are often confounded with organizational politics and communication issues (impression management). Thus, we think that it would be beneficial to routinely test whether certain theories of performance, developed in the area of employee performance and performance assessment of supervisors, generalize to the area of entrepreneurial performance.

Fourth, the direct personal implications of performance are typically higher for entrepreneur–business owners than for employees; thus, characteristics that support coping, including knowledge, skills, ability, and motivation, are relevant for understanding entrepreneurs and the entrepreneurship process. We also believe that I/O psychologists may gain from testing established psychological theories in the relatively simple, but extreme, entrepreneurship setting (Eden, 1973). The setting is simple in the sense that one or a few persons start new organizations; for a time, the young organization and its products and processes provides a compact, low-complexity laboratory for I/O psychologists. Furthermore, the entrepreneurship setting is extreme in the sense that it is dominated by high uncertainty, time pressure, and resource shortages. According to Dov Eden (1973), these conditions provide an attractive, time-compressed setting for studies of human cognition and behavior under trying conditions.

Fifth, by its very nature, entrepreneurship research has been more cross-cultural because differential founding rates have been shown to exist across different countries (Reynolds, Bygrave, Autio, Cox, & Hay, 2002). Cross-cultural management and cross-cultural entrepreneurship should be much more strongly related to each other and should be used to test each other's hypotheses (House, Hanges, Javidan, Dorfman, & Gupta, 2004). Fit to culture and misfit (niche) are both adequate hypotheses about entrepreneurial success. So again, this is an interesting area to explore and summarize.

Sixth, recent entrepreneurship research may guide I/O psychologists to focus on personal abilities such as opportunity recognition, which has received much attention from entrepreneurship researchers but little attention from general psychologists. Psychologists may be interested in entrepreneurship research about new personality trait concepts such as passion for work (Baum & Locke, 2004) and renewed attention to old personality concepts, such as achievement motivation and the "Big Five" personality attributes (Ciavarella, Buchholtz, Riordan, Gatewood, & Stokes, 2004). I/O psychologists who study knowledge and expertise may also benefit from entrepreneurship studies that have explored entrepreneurs' complex requirements for domain, management, and marketing knowledge in the entrepreneurship setting.

PSYCHOLOGISTS BEGAN ENTREPRENEURSHIP RESEARCH

Like so many other social sciences, entrepreneurship's legitimization came from the efforts of psychologists. It's not uncommon in academic disciplines for a single work to galvanize attention and respect for an emerging field, and David McClelland's (1961) book *The Achieving Society* did this for the field of entrepreneurship.

Unfortunately, 30 years of personality research following McClelland's lead yielded scant knowledge that financiers, practitioners, and entrepreneurship researchers considered useful for predicting entrepreneurship outcomes (Gartner, Shaver, Gatewood, & Katz, 1994). For example, associations between achievement motivation and choice of entrepreneurship as a career and between achievement motivation and new venture success in 20 studies yielded significant correlations, but the explained variance was less than 5% (Johnson, 1990). However, a new cohort of psychology-based researchers has broadened and deepened the search for the individual differences that cause entrepreneurship. Many of these cutting-edge researchers have successfully uncovered personality traits, competencies, cognitions, behaviors and environmental conditions that impact new venture creation and success. Much of this work is included in this book.

ENTREPRENEURSHIP FUNDAMENTALS

We now briefly introduce a few fundamentals of entrepreneurship. First, we elaborate our statement that entrepreneurship is socially and economically important. Second, we explain the challenge caused by the unresolved definition of entrepreneur and entrepreneurship. [There are multiple definitions of "entrepreneur" in terms of (a) business stages (Shane, 2003), (b) types of businesses (Timmons, 2000), (c) business goals (Smith & Smith, 2000), (d) levels of innovation (Shane, 2001), (e) degrees of independence (Bird, 1989), and (f) management roles (Bird, 1989).] Third, we review the characteristics and importance of the entrepreneur's situation (entrepreneurship environments present high uncertainty, high risk, urgency, and resource scarcity). Together, the "definition" and "situation" sections of this chapter point to data collection and measurement challenges and opportunities. Finally, we present a brief history of research about the psychology of entrepreneurship from the 1930s to the early 1990s.

IMPORTANCE OF ENTREPRENEURSHIP

Entrepreneurship is important because it is the economic mechanism through which inefficiencies in economies are identified and mitigated. Furthermore, entrepreneurs convert technological and organizational innovation into better products and services (Schumpeter, 1911 and subsequent editions) and motivate established competitors to improve products and processes. The Organization for Economic Cooperation and Development (OECD) has stated, "Entrepreneurship is central to the functioning of market economies" (OECD, 1998). The U.S. Small Business Administration went even further, to declare, "In short, the crucial barometer of economic freedom and well-being is the continued creation of new and small firms in all sectors of the economy by all segments of society" (Small Business Association, 1998).

Entrepreneurship through establishment of new independent businesses was so successful in the United States during the 1980s and 1990s in creating new jobs that it overcame the elimination of over 5 million jobs in established big business (Kirchhoff, 1997). On the other hand, more than 50% of new ventures fail within 5 years in the United States. (Aldrich, 1999; *The State of Small Business: A Report to the President*, 1995) and in other countries (Bruederl, Preisendoerfer, & Ziegler, 1992); thus, it is important to understand the factors that influence new venture creation and growth.

A few entrepreneurs such as Bill Gates, Michael Dell, Sergey Brin, and Larry Page have created companies that disturb, shape, and improve important business domains. Ultimately they have made outsized contributions to society and the economy. These entrepreneurs represent the "ideal type" that informs our conception of entrepreneurship. However, not all new ventures grow to make large differences in products, markets, or national economies. Indeed, most founders establish ventures that continue as small businesses for life. But even these new permanently small businesses are a major economic force. Taken together, U.S. firms with fewer than 500 employees are identified as small businesses, and they account for 51% of private sector output, employ 51% of private sector workers, and constitute 99% of all employers (Small Business Association, 2001). The big contributors mentioned (Gates, Dell, etc.) were small businesses during the time from their emergence as promising new ventures until they grew beyond "small." In summary, those who found and operate the categories of businesses referred to as new promising ventures and new small businesses are important research subjects in terms of their impact on absolute gross national product (GNP) and employment and their potential for social and economic impact.

ENTREPRENEURSHIP DEFINED

There are hundreds of definitions of *entrepreneur, entrepreneurship,* and *entrepreneurial.* The root word apparently has sex appeal because many people want to be labeled as entrepreneurs or want their thinking and behavior described as "entrepreneurial"—even in established firms. Many attempts have been made to capture the meaning of *entrepreneur* and to create useful definitions, and we offer past and current thinking. We point to the current dominant definition of *entrepreneurship* (Shane & Venkataraman, 2000); however, empirical researchers are left to struggle with selection of appropriate subjects for study because current definitions are very general. Thus, it is probably best to (a) offer clear descriptions of samples, and (b) remember that readers understand entrepreneurship through dynamic ideal types and personal experiences. Thus, today's dominant definition may be temporary.

Cantillon (1680–1734) defined entrepreneurs as "those who are willing to buy at a certain price and sell at an uncertain price" (quoted in Blaug, 2000, p. 379). Weber in 1898 suggested, "Entrepreneurship means the taking over and organizing of some part of an economy in which people's needs are satisfied through exchange for the sake of making a profit and at one's own economic risk" (as quoted in Swedberg, 2000, p 26). Schumpeter (1911 and later editions) suggested that entrepreneurship occurs under five conditions of newness: new goods, new production methods, new markets, new sources of materials, or new organizations.

Gartner (1988) offered a simple and empirically useful definition of entrepreneurship that drove many entrepreneurship researchers to restrict their studies to founder-only samples. He suggested that entrepreneurs are those who create new independent organizations. Some theorists add that the purpose of a new organization that qualifies as "entrepreneurship" must also create value through a product or service (Aldrich & Wiedenmayer, 1993). Taken together, profit-making exchange, personal risk, opportunity, newness, and added value are explicit or implied in most researchers' conceptions of entrepreneur and entrepreneurship (Bhide, 2000).

A generally accepted, and now popular, process and people oriented definition of entrepreneurship has emerged. The definition is, "Entrepreneurship is a process that involves the discovery, evaluation, and exploitation of opportunities to introduce new products, services, processes, ways of organizing, or markets" (Shane & Venkataraman, 2000; Venkataraman, 1997).

Accepting the Shane and Venkataraman definition, entrepreneurship researchers are thereby interested in explanations for why, when, and how some people discover and exploit opportunities. This entails a psychology-centered search for which individual differences explain the human behaviors that are necessary for recognizing potential opportunities for successful startup, emergence, and new venture growth. In part, researchers must explain the causes of, and types of, strategic thinking, new resource acquisition, organizing, motivating, and marketing behaviors that lead to success throughout the entrepreneurship process.

Katz (2003) pointed to the diversity of interpretation of the Shane and Venkataraman (2000) definition and reminded readers of the diversity of subspecialties within the entrepreneurship academic domain. He proposed a "prairie populist" definition of entrepreneurship as the subject of a collection of academic disciplines including entrepreneurship, new venture creation, entrepreneurial finance, small business, family business, free enterprise, private enterprise, high-technology business, new product development, microenterprise development, applied economic development, professional practice studies, women's entrepreneurship, minority entrepreneurship, and ethnic entrepreneurship. The advantage of this inclusive viewpoint is that it yields conceptions of entrepreneurship that are similar to the way the general public views entrepreneurship.

Even with the clarity of the Shane and Venkataraman (2000) definition and the Katz (2003) recognition of multiple legitimate perspectives, we have practical problems involving identification of subjects. The general definitions help us think about what we mean when we say entrepreneur, entrepreneurship, entrepreneurial behavior, or new venture creation, but they do not give us sufficient boundaries for sample selection. Choices remain for the entrepreneurship researcher. For example:

1. Will subjects include individuals who are solitary founders, founder teams, purchasers of established businesses, franchisees, and those who aspire to be founders?
2. Will subjects include only recent founders or purchasers? (Will people who were founders 25 years ago be included?)
3. Must subjects be active founder–managers to qualify for the sample?
4. If a new venture fails, will the founder–manager still be included in the entrepreneur sample?
5. Will subjects include only those who dream of rapid growth and significant ultimate scale (vs. mom-and-pop startups)?
6. Must the subject's behavior or intentions include an orientation to high technology or disruptive innovation?
7. Do employees who establish new ventures within established firms qualify as entrepreneurs? In other words, does entrepreneurship occur in established firms?
8. Will the subject's business stage (nascent, started, emerged, initial growth, rapid growth) figure in the collection of the sample?

In light of the possibility of large sample definition variances across studies, it is best for researchers to offer clear descriptions of the subjects studied.

THE ENTREPRENEUR'S SITUATION

Ever since Lewin, psychologists have talked about the importance of the environment. The concept of situation figures in the determination of cognition and behavior in modern psychology as well (Bandura, 1986; Endler, 1983; House, Shane, & Herold, 1996; Lewin, 1951; Mischel, 1968). Situation may be very important in entrepreneurship psychology research because new venture finance and entrepreneurship theorists suggest that entrepreneurs function within extremes of complexity, uncertainty, personal risk, urgency, surprise, and resource scarcity (Baum, 2004; Funder & Ozer, 1983; Smith & Smith, 2000). Furthermore, entrepreneurs' task demands are complex because they must fill multiple roles that address needs in terms of technology, service, leadership, and differentiation from others. Of course, researchers who associate extreme uncertainty and personal risk with entrepreneurship adopt a definition of entrepreneur that excludes lower risk business roles. Other researchers may include lower risk roles in their definition of "entrepreneur" (e.g., self-employed small business operators and business buyers). Whatever the definition of entrepreneur employed, the entrepreneur's situation deserves special attention in the search for personal characteristics that predict startup and new venture operating success.

As conceived by Schumpeter, entrepreneurs face extreme situations because their work involves disruptive change.[1] They create new markets, disturb established markets, introduce new processes, and form new organizations (Schumpeter, 1911 and later editions). Newness causes information deficits and follow-on uncertainty. Little or no information is available to guide entrepreneurs' expectations about new marketing and organizational outcomes. High uncertainty impacts the pace of decision making (faster) and may drive entrepreneurs to conduct experiments and to maintain vigilant monitoring with continuous strategic adaptation. Unless intellectual property is protected, competitive advantages may be temporary as competitors with valuable substitutes emerge. High-speed continuous development is required for success (Baum, 2004; Eisenhardt, 1989).

Furthermore, few entrepreneurs have sufficient financial resources to acquire complete facilities, process systems, equipment, and professional talent, and few can support startup losses alone. The financing challenge is

---

[1] As noted earlier in the discussion of entrepreneurship definitions, current definitions are general, subjects studied are not homogeneous, and some wannabe entrepreneurs never achieve their goals. Thus, some research conceptions and operationalizations of "entrepreneur" do not fit the Schumpeterian viewpoint.

heightened in rapidly growing new ventures as investment demands accelerate and cash dwindles. Entrepreneurs are frequently forced to accept capital from financiers who negotiate from aggressive and powerful positions and who minimize their investors' risk by setting high goals for the entrepreneurs and offering just-in-time cash. Thus, entrepreneurs who manage high-potential startups with outside financing confront a threatening array of continuous demands for high performance, and they experience a continuous and stressful sense of urgency as they worry about survival (Smith & Smith, 2000).

Entrepreneurs who start high-potential companies operate in the midst of communities of big dreamers. In Silicon Valley and other technology centers, networking presents a competitive marketplace for personal achievement, which appears to heighten personal tension (and achievement) (Eisenhardt, 1989). Not all entrepreneurs experience the level of dynamism present in new high-tech venture communities, but most are intimately involved with direct personal financial risks and most confront competitive outcomes and barriers personally. The link between the experience of founders and founding teams with their organizations is tight. Indeed, the near absence of organizational hierarchy in new ventures causes entrepreneurs to experience organization conditions personally.

The entrepreneur's extreme situation presents challenges and opportunities for psychology researchers. First, opportunities arise for researchers because weak general relationships between variables may be uncovered under specific extreme situations. Of course, if resultant findings from the special situation simply reflect weak general relationships, the findings may not be very useful. Second, and in contrast, research variables that reflect specific common situations tend to yield significant predictors that are more useful within the specific setting. Finally, extreme situations may be more difficult to reflect as situationally specific measures when the focal concepts are generalizations (need for achievement of what was not of interest in McClelland's original conception of nAch [need for achievement]). Whatever the benefits and challenges for generalizability and measurement, at least the entrepreneur's situation presents psychology researchers with the opportunity to study human cognition and behavior under higher uncertainty and greater resource scarcity than can be found in established business populations.

RESEARCH ROOTS OF THE PSYCHOLOGY OF ENTREPRENEURSHIP

Although psychology was central to the legitimization and even the popularization of entrepreneurship, the roots of entrepreneurship are based in economics. The first quarter of the 20th century brought about a wave of theorizing among economists regarding how economic growth happens. The prevailing *zeitgeist* was one of tremendous economic growth, brought about by one of the most concentrated periods of technological change in history. Economists rightly were trying to understand how this happened, and one of the avenues pursued was the idea that individuals—entrepreneurs—were the agents or focal points of change. Under these models proposed by Schumpeter (1911 and later editions), Taussig (1915) and Knight (1921), entrepreneurs translated inventions into businesses and, in many cases, wealth.

Some economists suggested that the impact of individuals was more important than had been believed, and they pointed to personal characteristics that they thought were important for successful entrepreneurship. For example, Schumpeter (1934 edition, p. 93) described the archetypical entrepreneur as one who had

> the dream and the will to found a private kingdom, usually, though not necessarily, also a dynasty, ... the will to conquer: the impulse to fight, to prove oneself superior to others, to succeed for the sake, not of the fruits of success, but of success itself ... [and] the joy of creating, of getting things done, or simply of exercising one's energy and ingenuity.

Schumpeter, Taussig, and Knight proposed that entrepreneurs had the power to identify, operationalize, and market technological innovations that could markedly change the directions of societies. In 1946, Schumpeter started the Research Center for Entrepreneurial History at Harvard, and the theoretical underpinning of the center set the standard for "Great Man" approaches to the study of the entrepreneur, which were institutionalized when *Explorations in Entrepreneurial History* began publication at Harvard in 1949 under H. G. J. Aitken. The influence of Schumpeter's choice of the "Great Man" model was important for the development of the field, because it suggested that potential entrepreneurs might be identified and supported in order to speed economic development.

Schumpeter's focus on the individual found a willing audience in a new psychology professor at Harvard, David McClelland. McClelland's interest in achievement motivation led to the publication of *The Achieving Society* in 1961, and *Motivating Economic Achievement* in 1969 with David Winter. The book details how potential entrepreneurs can be helped through training—in this case, in training the behaviors of people with high achievement motivation—and shows the difference such training can make. A carefully performed psychological quasi-experiment done in India provided the proof of the potential of entrepreneur training and became the gold standard for outcomes assessment in entrepreneurship education and training. The first ongoing program for academic provision of services to entrepreneurs, the Small Business Institute program of the US Small Business Administration, built on McClelland's ideas when it started in 1972. In what turned out to be an important variation, those first 20 programs of 1972 were housed not in psychology departments, as were McClelland's, but in business schools. This set the stage for the growth of entrepreneurship as a business discipline instead of a specialty in psychology.

Schumpeter and the Great Man tradition influenced not only McClelland, but also the fledgling generation of academic entrepreneurship researchers. Started in 1953, the U.S. Small Business Administration turned to academics in the late 1950s with that most persuasive of arguments, grant money, to study entrepreneurship. The resulting works included psychologically driven research such as Hal Pickle's (1964) early stakeholder assessment of entrepreneurial potential or Hoad and Rosko's (1964) Great Man analyses.

With McClelland's success using achievement motivation to assess entrepreneurial potential, a flood of research emerged using trait theory to identify potential entrepreneurs. Population level studies also emerged from McClelland's work, and Mayer and Goldstein (1964) conducted a qualitative study of all the businesses started in Rhode Island in 1 year. The approach used was drawn from a mixture of anthropology and, as it was called then, ecological psychology (Barker, 1968), developed from Kurt Lewin's approach. Mayer and Goldstein continued their studies, looking at blue-collar workers' aspirations for betterment via entrepreneurship (Mayer & Goldstein, 1964). Along the same lines, sociologists such as Hagen (1962) identified the more widely distributed potential for entrepreneurship in the population among people who see themselves as marginalized, whereas Dooley (1972) did the same for Harvard MBAs of the period, and Fine (1970) among the wage-employed in general. This was reintegrated into mainstream psychology through the works of Al Shapero (1975), a psychologist who held one of the first chairs of entrepreneurship at the Ohio State University.

In the end, the field was ambivalently served by the early trait approach. On one hand, the trait approach was easily pursued (Jencks, 1950), with potential respondents of that era willing to take long psychological tests, and the number of potential trait or trait profiles was nearly infinite, giving substantial opportunity to plow new ground and publish heretofore-unseen combinations. For example, Litzinger (1965) found relationships between entrepreneur's performance and risk preferences and independence. Schrage (1965) conducted studies of achievement and power motivation, and Hornaday and Aboud (1971) explored the relationship between entrepreneurs' and managers' intelligence, creativity, energy, and tolerance of uncertainty. However, few of the research studies from the time replicated the rigor or theoretical depth of McClelland's work. The only other work to have a sustained impact on the field was a broad-ranging descriptive study of Michigan manufacturers undertaken by Collins, Moore, and Umwalla (1964). This study used a variety of techniques including in-depth interviews, psychological tests, and work histories to describe the people who were successful in that industry and locale. The study became one of the definitive descriptions of the solo small businessperson.

Institutionally, the major elements of the infrastructure for the academic discipline of entrepreneurship were set in place during this period. This included courses (starting at Harvard in 1947), majors (1968 for undergraduates at Babson), endowed positions (Georgia State University, 1963), and journals (*Journal of Small Business Management*, 1963). Virtually all of these were located outside of psychology departments, making the involvement of psychologists more difficult as the field matured.

During the 1970s and 1980s, entrepreneurship and psychology had an exceedingly unsteady relationship. Part of this came from the emergence, growth, and stabilization of entrepreneurship in schools of business, an arena in which few psychologists were willing to venture or felt welcome. Part came from a focus on (a) the economic development model, which dealt with how community resources could be organized to optimize economic growth, and (b) the wealth creation model. Economists recognized that being oriented toward wealth creation is a special mind-set and required the entrepreneur and the firm to pursue particular approaches. From this mind-set, the strategic planning approach to entrepreneurship emerged (Weisman, 1945). Popularized by Christensen's *Management Succession in Small and Growing Enterprises* (1953), this approach came into its own during the 1970s and 1980s, powering the second phase of growth of the intellectual discipline of entrepreneurship, much as psychology had powered the first phase in the prior two decades. During this period, the proportion of economist–strategy scholars in the entrepreneurship field grew to roughly 60% of active entrepreneurship faculty and researchers.

Just as McClelland's (1961) *The Achieving Society* became one of the bellwether books for defining a period of entrepreneurship, Hal Livesay's (1979) *American Made* defined the period of the 1970s and 1980s. It has been argued that Livesay's book, influencing policymakers in the United States and United Kingdom, led to the "entrepreneurial decade," as Ronald Reagan and Margaret Thatcher declared the 1980s (Katz, 2003). Unlike the early entrepreneurial historians, Livesay considered the strategies pursued by entrepreneurs and their fit to the opportunities and resources of the times. His approach encapsulated the strategic approach to entrepreneurship, and strategy itself was very much the province of business school professors.

In practice, the strategic approach of entrepreneurship typically falls into one of two foci. The less psychological focus is on the strategies themselves, which are largely based on analyses at the firm, industry, and economy levels. Perhaps some of the most classic examples of this are the studies of Charles Hofer and his colleagues (Hofer & Charan, 1984; Hofer & Sandberg, 1987; Sandberg, 1986).

The more psychological focus is on the strategic decision-making process, in which the strategist and the methods of strategic thinking become material for which a psychological approach is suitable. This approach was put forth most consistently by Arnold Cooper and his associates (Cooper & Dunkelberg, 1981, 1986; Cooper, Folta, & Woo, 1995). Cooper looked at both the entrepreneur's decision process and the decision setting, showing how each contributed to the creation and success of new firms.

As the proportion of strategy-oriented professors grew during the 1980s, the percentage of psychology-based professors in the field of entrepreneurship slowly began to decline, replaced by faculty from sociology, finance, and engineering, among other disciplines. Current estimates put the percentage of psychology-based faculty in entrepreneurship in the 20% to 30% range. Even so, psychology represents the second largest contributing discipline to entrepreneurship—still larger than entrepreneurship itself, which has only recently begun to have its own PhDs.

From a field that became entrepreneurship's "second fiddle" during the 1970s and 1980s, psychological concepts actually gained ground through a series of well-conceived studies and thought-provoking conceptual pieces. During this period, the Harvard Business School became the world's center for psychoanalytic organizational theory. Abraham Zaleznik and Harry Levinson were there. Eliot Jaques came through repeatedly from England, as did Charles deVillieres Mertens from Belgium. Manfred Kets deVries was a protégée of Zaleznik, who in turn mentored Danny Miller. Invariably, their works included explicit considerations of entrepreneurs, providing a constant reminder and a thoughtful comparison with salaried big business managers. Works such as Zaleznik and Kets deVries (1975), Kets deVries (1977), and Kets deVries and Miller (1984) considered the entrepreneur through a highly distinctive lens—that of the driven outsider, the individual who succeeded, despite strong psychological drives and conflicts. This approach paralleled the theme of marginality theorists in sociology, such as Bonjean (1966) and Hagen (1962), who even coined the term "rage hypothesis" to explain the motivation behind entrepreneurship. These efforts built on works such as Collins et al., (1964), Eden (1973, 1975) and Shapero (1975) to create one portrait of the entrepreneur as a type of manager emotionally and psychologically different from salaried managers. Under these models, the entrepreneur might not have been a Great Man, but he or she was clearly a different one.

During the 1980s, social network theory emerged as a second psychology-oriented viewpoint that impacted thinking about entrepreneurship. The key point of contact was the introduction of social psychological elements by Howard Aldrich, a professor at the University of North Carolina who received his doctorate in sociology from the University of Michigan, a program with strong ties to the social psychology programs of the Institute for Social Research at Michigan. His works during this period (Aldrich, 1979; Aldrich, Reese, & Dubini, 1989; Aldrich, Rosen, & Woodward, 1987; Aldrich & Whetten, 1981; Aldrich & Zimmer, 1986) built from the concept of weak and strong network ties, eventually moving toward more ecological and institutional models of entrepreneurship in the 1990s.

Even as social network theory grew in importance for explanations of entrepreneurship, trait studies of entrepreneurs continued, but at a much-reduced level compared with the 1970s. Bill Gartner (1988) dealt a decisive blow to entrepreneurship trait research with his 1988 article "Who is an Entrepreneur? Is the Wrong Question." Gartner (1988, p. 21) explained:

> A startling number of traits and characteristics have been attributed to the entrepreneur, and a "psychological profile" of the entrepreneur assembled from these studies would portray someone larger than life, full of contradictions, and conversely, someone so full of traits that (s)he would have to be a sort of generic "Everyman."

Interestingly, Gartner's complaint was narrower than the research community's interpretation of it. Gartner criticized *personality trait* research, not *personal characteristics* research. Gartner tried to refocus attention on a broad conception of the psychology of entrepreneurship with his special issue of *Entrepreneurship Theory and Practice* titled "Finding the Entrepreneur in Entrepreneurship" (Gartner, Shaver, Gatewood, & Katz, 1994). Nevertheless, his 1988 article dominated and accelerated the drift from study of the psychology of entrepreneurship to study of new venture strategies and externalities. Recently, a growing cohort of psychology-based researchers has renewed interest in entrepreneurs' personal characteristics as predictors of success by moving beyond the past focus on traits. These researchers have found significant individual differences (e.g., traits, skills, attitudes, cognitions, values, motives, goals, and even personal health) between entrepreneurs and other persons, and they have discovered that successful entrepreneurs may differ from less successful entrepreneurs as well. Meta-analyses, more complex models, better research tools, and concepts that are closer to performance in terms of causality have been used (Baron, 1998, 1999; Baum & Locke, 2004; Busenitz & Barney, 1997; Frese, Brantjes, & Hoorn, 2002; Frese, van Gelderen, & Ombach, 2000; Mitchell, Smith, Seawright & Morse, 2000).

The history of entrepreneurship research reveals the great contribution that psychologists made to early understanding of the entrepreneur. We believe that I/O psychologists are prepared once again to make important research contributions that will create knowledge about the economically, socially, and technologically important entrepreneurship process. Through I/O psychology, the entrepreneurship research field may reconnect with the living nexus of organizational creation, the entrepreneur as a psychological being.

Many business schools have recognized the value of I/O psychologists' orientation and training for enrichment of management departments. Increasingly, I/O psychologists populate business school entrepreneurship faculties, which tend to be well supported by entrepreneurship practitioners (Katz, 2003). We hope *The Psychology of Entrepreneurship* will inspire I/O psychologists to explore the interesting world of entrepreneurship research and to take advantage of the many attractive professional opportunities available in the entrepreneurship academic community.

REFERENCES

Aldrich, H. E. (1979). *Organizations and environments*. Englewood Cliffs, NJ: Prentice Hall.

Aldrich, H. E. (1999). *Organizations evolving*. London: Sage.

Aldrich, H. E., Reese, P. R., & Dubini, P. (1989). Women on the verge of a breakthrough?: Networking among entrepreneurs in the United States and Italy. *Entrepreneurship and Regional Development, 1*(4), 339–356.

Aldrich, H. E., Rosen, B., & Woodward, W. (1987). The impacts of social networks on business foundings and profit: A longitudinal study. In N. C. Churchill, J. A. Hornaday, B. A. Kirchhoff, O. J. Krasner, & K. H. Vesper (Eds.), *Frontiers of entrepreneurship research, 1987* (pp. 154–168). Babson Park, MA: Babson College.

Aldrich, H. E., & Whetten, D. A. (1981). Organization-sets, action-sets, and networks; Making the most of simplicity. In P. C. Nystrom & W. H. Starbuck (Eds.), *Handbook of Organizational Design* (Vol. 2, pp. 385–408). London: Oxford University Press.

Aldrich, H. E., & Wiedenmayer, G. (1993). From traits to rates: An ecological perspective on organizational foundings. In J. A. Katz & R. H. Brockhaus, Sr. (Eds.), *Advances in entrepreneurship, firm emergence, and growth* (pp. 45–195). Greenwich, CT: JAI Press.

Aldrich, H. E., & Zimmer, C. (1986). Entrepreneurship through social networks. In D. L. Sexton & R. W. Smilor (Eds.), *The art and science of entrepreneurship* (pp. 3–23). Cambridge, MA: Ballinger.

Bandura, A. (1986). *Social foundations of thought and action*. Englewood Cliffs, NJ: Prentice Hall.

Barker, R. G. (1968). *Ecological psychology: Concepts and methods for studying the environment of human behavior*. Stanford, CA: Stanford University Press.

Baron, R. A. (1998). Cognitive mechanisms in entrepreneurship: Why and when entrepreneurs think differently than other people. *Journal of Business Venturing, 13*, 275–294.

Baron, R. A. (1999). Counterfactual thinking and venture formation: The potential effects of thinking about "what might have been." *Journal of Business Venturing, 15*, 79–91.

Baron, R. A. (2002). OB and entrepreneurship: The reciprocal benefits of closer conceptual links. In B. M. Staw & R. Kramer (Eds.), *Research in organizational behavior* (pp. 225–269). Greenwich, CT: JAI Press.

Baum, J. R. (2004 August). *Cognitions and behaviors of successful nascent entrepreneurs: A three-year panel study*. Presented at the Academy of Management Meeting, New Orleans, LA.

Baum, J. R., & Locke, E. A. (2004). The relationship of entrepreneurial traits, skill, and motivation to subsequent venture growth. *Journal of Applied Psychology, 89*, 622–634.

Baum, J. R., Locke, E. A., & Smith, K. G. (2001). A multidimensional model of venture growth. *Academy of Management Journal, 44*(2), 292–303.

Bhide, A. V. (2000). *The origin and evolution of new businesses.* New York: Oxford University Press.

Bird, B. J. (1989). *Entrepreneurial behavior.* Glenview, IL: Scott, Foresman.

Blaug, R. (2000). Blind hierarchism and radical organizational forms. *New Political Science, 22*(3), 379–396.

Bonjean, C. M. (1966). Mass, class, and the industrial community: A comparative analysis of managers, businessmen, and workers. *American Journal of Sociology, 72*(2), 149–162.

Bruederl, J., Preisendoerfer, P., & Ziegler, R. (1992). Survival chances of newly founded business organizations. *American Sociological Review, 57,* 222–242.

Busenitz, L. W., & Barney, J. B. (1997). Differences between entrepreneurs and managers in large organizations: Biases and heuristics in strategic decision-making. *Journal of Business Venturing, 12,* 9–30.

Christensen, R. (1953). *Management succession in small and growing enterprises.* New York: Harper and Row.

Ciavarella, M. A., Buchholtz, A. K., Riordan, C. M., Gatewood, R. D., & Stokes, G. S. (2004). The big five and venture survival: Is there a linkage? *The Journal of Business Venturing, 19*(4), 465–484.

Collins, O. F., Moore, D. G., & Umwalla, D. B. (1964). *The enterprising man.* East Lansing, MI: MSU Business Studies, Bureau of Business and Economic Research.

Cooper, A. C., & Dunkelberg, W. C. (1981). A new look at business entry: Experience of 1805 entrepreneurs. In K. H. Vesper (Ed.), *Frontiers of Entrepreneurship Research* (pp. 1–20). Wellesley, MA: Babson College.

Cooper, A. C. & Dunkelberg, W. C. (1986). Entrepreneurship and paths to business ownership. *Strategic Management Journal, 7*(1), 53–68.

Cooper, A. C., Folta, T. B., & Woo, C. (1995). Entrepreneurial information search. *Journal of Business Venturing, 10,* 107–120.

Dooley, A. R. (1972). Graduate student views on entrepreneurship and courses in entrepreneurship. In A. C. Cooper & J. L. Komives (Eds.), *Technical entrepreneurship: A symposium* (pp. 210–230). Milwaukee, WI: Center for Venture Management.

Eden, D. (1973). Self-employed workers: a comparison group for organizational psychology. *Organizational Behavior and Human Performance, 9,* 186–214.

Eden, D. (1975). Organizational membership vs. self-employment: Another blow to the American dream. *Organizational Behavior and Human Performance, 13,* 79–94.

Eisenhardt, K. M. (1989). Making fast strategic decisions in high-velocity environments. *Academy of Management Journal, 32*(3), 543–576.

Endler, N. S. (1983). Interactionism: A personality model but not yet a theory. In M. M. Page & D. Dienstbier (Eds.), *Personality—Current theory and research* (pp. 155–200). 1982 Nebraska Symposium on Motivation. Lincoln: University of Nebraska Press.

Fine, B. D. (1970). *Comparison of organizational membership and self-employment.* Ann Arbor, MI: University of Michigan (Microfilms No. 71-23, 751).

Frese, M., Brantjes, A., & Hoorn, R. (2002). Psychological success factors of small-scale businesses in Namibia: The roles of strategy, entrepreneurial orientation and the environment. *Journal of Developmental Entrepreneurship, 7*(3), 259–282.

Frese, M., van Gelderen, M., & Ombach, M. (2000). How to plan as a small-scale business owner: Psychological process characteristics of action strategies and success. *Journal of Small Business Management, 38*(2), 1–18.

Funder, D. C., & Ozer, D. J. (1983). Personality processes and individual differences. *Journal of Personality and Social Psychology, 44*(1), 107–112.

Gartner, W. B. (1988). "Who is an entrepreneur?" is the wrong question. *American Journal of Small Business, 12*(4), 11–32.

Gartner, W. B., Shaver, K. G., Gatewood, E., & Katz, J. A. (1994). Finding the entrepreneur in entrepreneurship. *Entrepreneurship Theory and Practice, 18*(3), 5–10.

Hagen, E. E. (1962). *On the theory of social change: How economic growth begins.* Homewood, IL: Dorsey Press.

Hoad, W. M., & Rosko, P. (1964). *Management factors contributing to the success or failure of new small manufacturers.* Michigan Business Reports No. 44. Ann Arbor, MI: Bureau of Business Research, Graduate School of Business Administration, University of Michigan.

Hofer, C. W., & Charan, R. (1984, Summer). The transition to professional management: Mission impossible? *American Journal of Small Business,* pp. 3–12.

Hofer, C. W., & Sandberg, W. R. (1987, Summer). Improving new venture performance: Some guidelines for success *American Journal of Small Business,* pp. 11–25.

Hornaday, J. A., & Aboud, J. (1971). Characteristics of successful entrepreneurs. *Personal Psychology, 24,* 141–153.

House, R. J., Shane, S. A., & Herold, D. (1996). Rumors of the death of dispositional research have been greatly exaggerated. *Academy of Management Review, 21*(1), 203–224.

House, R. J., Hanges, P. J., Javidan, M., Dorfman, P. W., & Gupta, V. (Eds.). (2004). *Cultures, leadership and organizations: A 62 nation global study.* Thousand Oaks, CA: Sage.

Jencks, L. H. (1950). Approaches to entrepreneurial personality. *Explorations in entrepreneurial history, 3*(2), 91–99.

Johnson, B. R. (1990). Toward a multidimensional model of entrepreneurship: The case of achievement motivation and the entrepreneur. *Entrepreneurship Theory and Practice, 14,* 39–54.

Katz, J. A. (2003). The chronology and intellectual trajectory of American entrepreneurship education. *Journal of Business Venturing, 18,* 283–300.

Kets deVries, M. F. R. (1977). The entrepreneurial personality: A person at the crossroads. *The Journal of Management Studies, 14*(1), 34–75.

Kets deVries, M. F. R., & Miller, D. (1984). *The neurotic organization.* San Francisco: Jossey-Bass.

Kirchhoff, B. (1997). Entrepreneurship economics. In W.B. Bygrave (Ed.), *The portable MBA in entrepreneurship* (pp. 450–471). New York, Wiley.

Knight, F. (1921). *Risk, uncertainty, and profit.* New York: Augustus Kelly.

Lewin, K. (1951). In D. Cartwright (Ed.), *Field theory in social science: Selected theoretical papers by Kurt Lewin.* Edited by Dorwin Cartwright. New York: Harper and Row.

Litzinger, W. (1965). The motel entrepreneur and the motel manager. *Academy of Management Journal, 8,* 268–281.

Livesay, H. (1979). *American made.* Boston: Little, Brown.

Lord, R. G., de Vader, C. L., & Alliger, G. M. (1986). A meta-analysis of the relation between personality traits and leadership perceptions: An application of validity generalization procedures. *Journal of Applied Psychology, 71,* 402–10.

MacMillan, I. C., Siegel, R., & SubbaNarasimha, P. N. (1985). Criteria used by venture capitalists to evaluate new venture proposals. *Journal of Business Venturing, 1,* 119–128.

Mayer, K. B., & Goldstein, S. (1964). Manual workers and small businessmen. In A. B. Shostak & W. Gomberg (Eds.), *Blue-collar world: Studies of the American worker* (pp. 537–549). Englewood Cliffs, NJ: Prentice Hall.

McClelland, D. (1961). *The achieving society.* New York: Free Press.

McClelland, D. C., & Winter, D. G. (1969). *Motivating economic achievement.* New York: Free Press.

Mitchell, R. K., Smith, B., Seawright, L. W., & Morse, E. A. (2000). Cross-cultural cognitions and the venture creation decision. *Academy of Management Journal, 43,* 974–993.

Mischel, W. (1968). *Personality and assessment.* New York: Wiley.

Organization for Economic Co-operation and Development. (1998). *Entrepreneurship— PolicyBrief 1244.* Paris, France: OECD. www.oecd.org, accessed May 22, 2004.

Pickle, H. B. (1964). *Personality and success: An evaluation of personal characteristics of successful small business managers.* Washington: Small Business Administration.

Rauch, A., & Frese, M. (2000). Psychological approaches to entrepreneurial success: A general model and an overview of findings. In C. L. Cooper & I. T. Robertson (Eds.), *International re-*

view of industrial and organizational psychology (Vol. 15, pp. 101–142). New York: John Wiley & Sons.

Reynolds, P. D., Bygrave, W. D., Autio, E., Cox, L. W., & Hay, M. (2002). *Global entrepreneurship monitor—2002 Executive report*. London: London Business School.

Sandberg, W. R. (1986). *New venture performance: The role of strategy and industry structure*. Lexington, MA: D. C. Heath.

Savage, D. (1979). *Founders, heirs, and managers*. Beverly Hills, CA: Sage.

Schein, E. H. (1983). The role of the founder in creating organizational culture. *Organizational Dynamics, 12*, 13–28.

Schein, E. H. (1987). *Organizational culture and leadership*. San Francisco, CA: Jossey-Bass.

Schrage, H. (1965). The R&D entrepreneur: Profile of success. *Harvard Business Review, 43*, 56–69.

Schumpeter, J. (1911). *The theory of economic development*. Cambridge, MA: Harvard University Press. (Revised editions in 1934 and 1961)

Sexton, D. L. (2001). Wayne Huizenga: Entrepreneur and wealth creator. *Academy of Management Executive, 1*, 40–48.

Shane, S. A. (2001). Technology opportunities and new firm creation. *Management Science, 47*, 200–220.

Shane, S. A. (2003). *A general theory of entrepreneurship: The individual-opportunity nexis approach to entrepreneurship*. Aldershot, UK: Eward Elgar.

Shane, S. A., & Venkataraman, S. (2000). The promise of entrepreneurship as a field of research. *Academy of Management Review, 25*(1), 217–226.

Shapero, A. (1975). The displaced, uncomfortable entrepreneur. *Psychology Today, 9*(November), 83–88.

Shepherd, D. A. (1999). Venture capitalists' assessment of new venture survival. *Management Science, 45*(5), 621–632.

Small Business Administration (1998). *The new American evolution: The role and impact of small firms*. Washington, DC: Government Printing Office.

Small Business Administration. (2001). *New and small firm creation*. Washington, DC: Government Printing Office.

Smith, J. K., & Smith, R. L. (2000). *Entrepreneurial Finance*. New York: Wiley.

Swedberg, R. (2000). *Entrepreneurship: The social science view*. Oxford: Oxford University Press.

Taussig, F. W. (1915). *Principles of economics* (rev. ed., Vol. II). New York: Macmillan.

The state of small business: A report to the President. (1995). Washington, DC: U.S. Government Printing Office.

Timmons, J. A. (2000). *New venture creation: Entrepreneurship 2000* (5th ed.). Homewood, IL: Irwin.

van Gelderen, M., Frese, M., & Thurik, R. (2000). Strategies, uncertainty and performance of small business startups. *Small Business Economics, 15*, 165–181.

Venkataraman, S. (1997). The distinctive domain of entrepreneurship research: An editor's perspective. In J. Katz & R. Brockhaus (Eds.), *Advances in entrepreneurship, firm emergence, and growth* (pp. 119–138). Greenwich, CT: JAI Press.

Weber, M. (1946). *The theory of social and economic organization*, Eds. A. H. Henderson & T. Parsons. Glencoe, IL: Free Press. (Original work published 1924)

Weisman, R. (1945). *Small business and venture capital*. New York: Harper and Row.

Zaleznik, A., & Kets deVries, M. F. R. (1975). *Power and the corporate mind*. Boston: Houghton Mifflin.

Zopounidis, C. (1994). Venture capital modeling: Evaluation criteria for the appraisal of investments. *Financier, 1*(May), 54–64.

2

Entrepreneurship:
A Process Perspective

Robert A. Baron

> Wisdom lies neither in fixity nor in change, but in the dialectic between the two. (Octavio Paz, London Times, June 1989, p. 12)

Although these words were written in a context far removed from entrepreneurship, they echo important themes included in a widely accepted definition of the field (Shane & Venkataraman, 2000). These scholars define entrepreneurship as

> a field of business that seeks to understand how opportunities to create something new (e.g., new products or services, new markets, new production processes or raw materials, new ways of organizing existing technologies) *arise* and are *discovered* or created by specific persons, who then use various means to *exploit or develop* them, thus producing a wide range of *effects*. (p. 218) (italics added)

This definition encompasses virtually every central aspect of entrepreneurship as a domain of management science. From the perspective of this chapter, however, its most salient feature is its clear suggestion that entrepreneurship should be viewed as a continuous, evolving *process* rather than a single event or a series of unrelated events. In other words, consistent with Paz's words, the definition offered by Shane and Venkataraman (2000) suggests that in order to fully understand the nature of entrepreneurship, we must focus not solely on conditions existing at specific points in time (fixity), but also on *change*—how this process unfolds and develops over time.

This approach—which is referred to here as a *process perspective*—has gained increasing acceptance in the field. For example in a recent book,

Shane (2003) states: "The purpose of this book is to offer an overarching conceptual framework for entrepreneurship that explains *the different parts of the entrepreneurial process* in a coherent way" (p. 3, italics added). Similarly, Jack and Anderson (2002) note that "in order to understand entrepreneurship, we need to move away from considering the entrepreneur in isolation and look at the *entrepreneurial process*" (p. 467, italics added). Many other authors have echoed these thoughts, (e.g., Aldrich, 1999; Harvey & Evans, 1995; Low & Abrahamson, 1997), so it seems clear that a process perspective is currently one central theme of modern entrepreneurship theory.

Although existing process models of entrepreneurship differ in many respects, all appear to agree on three important issues. First, they offer largely consistent views concerning the major phases of this process (e.g., Bygrave, 1989; Shane, 2003; Venkataraman, 1997). For instance, Shane (2003) suggests that these phases proceed as follows: (a) the emergence of opportunities (which derive from changing economic, technological, and social conditions), (b) recognition of these opportunities by specific persons, (c) evaluation of these opportunities coupled with an active decision to pursue them, (d) assembly of required resources, (e) development of a strategy for using these resources to exploit the opportunity, and (f) actual exploitation. Other authors (e.g., Bygrave, 1989) propose a similar sequence of events, moving gradually from innovation through an active decision by nascent entrepreneurs to start new ventures, and then to actual implementation and subsequent growth of the companies they create.

Second, process models are also in general agreement concerning the major categories of variables that play a role in each phase of the entrepreneurial process. Specifically, all recognize that at least three major groups of variables are relevant: *individual-level factors*—factors relating to the experience, skills, motives, cognitions, and characteristics of potential or actual entrepreneurs; *group* or *interpersonal factors*—factors involving entrepreneurs' relations with other persons, such as their exposure to role models of entrepreneurship and the size and quality of their social networks; and *societal-level variables*—factors relating to the social, economic, and political environments in which entrepreneurs operate.

Third, current process models of entrepreneurship also agree on the following crucial point: *The relative importance of specific variables may fluctuate across different phases of the process.* For example, Shane (2003) notes that factors that explain one part of the entrepreneurial process do not necessarily explain other parts. Similarly, Baron (2002) suggests: "Three groups of factors [individual-level, interpersonal-level, societal-level] influence entrepreneurs' behavior and thought during all phases of the entrepreneurial process .... However, *the relative importance of variables in these three categories may vary significantly across these phases*" (p. 232, italics added).

This chapter seeks to expand on earlier theory and research by offering an integrated and comprehensive process model of entrepreneurship. To accomplish this task, it proceeds as follows. First, major phases of the entrepreneurial process are identified and for each, individual-level, group-level, and societal-level variables previously found to exert significant effects on dependent variables relevant to that phase are reviewed. Next, the possibility that the impact of specific variables may change over the course of the entrepreneurial process is carefully examined. Third, several research methods potentially useful in testing a process model and its corollaries are considered (e.g., longitudinal designs; longitudinal-sequential designs). Finally, implications and potential benefits of a process model are reviewed.

A PROCESS MODEL OF ENTREPRENEURSHIP: PHASES, INDEPENDENT VARIABLES, AND DEPENDENT MEASURES

Although all processes are, in a sense, continuous in nature, it is often useful to divide them into specific segments or phases for purposes of systematic analysis. This appears to be true for entrepreneurship, primarily because entrepreneurs must perform different activities and accomplish different tasks at different points during their efforts to start and develop new ventures (e.g., Gartner, 1989; Reynolds & White, 1997). These activities can serve as useful "markers" for dividing the entrepreneurial process into several major phases. In this initial section, one such division is suggested. For each phase identified, both *independent variables*—factors that may influence the activities performed by entrepreneurs during that phase—and key *dependent* measures—indices of their effectiveness in performing these activities—are described. (An overview of the process model described in this and subsequent sections is presented in Fig. 2.1.)

Major Phases of the Entrepreneurial Process: An Overview

In a sense, entrepreneurship has no clear or definite beginning; rather, the idea of starting a new venture and adopting the role of "entrepreneur" often develops gradually in the minds and actions of specific persons so that retrospectively, they cannot clearly identify a point in time at which it emerged. For purposes of this discussion, however, the entrepreneurial process will be divided into three major phases: *prelaunch*—the period that encompasses activities occurring prior to the launch of a new venture; *launch* or *startup*—the phase that includes activities related to the actual launch of a new venture and its initial period of operation (e.g., 12 to 18 months), and *postlaunch*—the period that involves activities occurring after the startup period (beyond 18 months, to 24 months of operation). The rela-

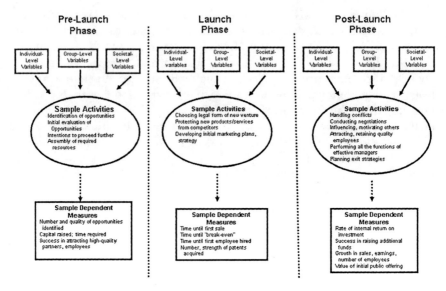

Figure 2.1.   A process model of entrepreneurship.

tive length of these periods can vary tremendously; for instance, some entrepreneurs may spend several years in the prelaunch period, whereas others may move from an idea to an actual company in a matter of months. In general, though, the prelaunch and launch phases are shorter in duration than the postlaunch phase, which can extend for years or even decades.

These major phases of the entrepreneurial process can be further divided into smaller segments on the basis of the specific activities performed by entrepreneurs. For instance, the prelaunch period encompasses recognition of opportunities, initial evaluation of these opportunities, and the development of intentions to proceed further along the road leading to launch of a new venture (e.g., Mitchell et al., 2002). These activities, in turn, are followed (also during the prelaunch phase) by efforts to assemble the required resources—financial, human, informational, and otherwise (Baron & Shane, 2004).

Once sufficient resources have been assembled, the *launch* period begins, and entrepreneurs shift their attention to tasks such as choosing a legal form for their new companies, developing initial marketing plans and an overall strategy for exploiting the recognized opportunities. Another consideration, which can occupy entrepreneurs' attention during both the prelaunch and launch phases, involves activities designed to protect new products or services from competitors (e.g., by securing intellectual property rights or quickly building *complementary assets*—assets required to provide the new product or service to potential customers that cannot be quickly or readily duplicated by competitors). The launch or startup period is often viewed as occurring during the first 12 to 18 months of a new venture's existence.

After a new venture is launched and has been operating for a period of time (12 to 18 months), it enters the third major phase, the *postlaunch* period. During this phase, entrepreneurs shift from dealing mainly with ideas and plans to running a functioning company. They must deal with an increasing range of people both inside and outside the new venture, and this often involves exercising or acquiring important interpersonal skills, such as those useful in handling conflicts, conducting negotiations, and influencing and motivating others. In addition, because growing businesses require an expanding labor force, entrepreneurs must be able to successfully recruit, motivate, and retain high-quality employees. In other words, during the postlaunch phase, entrepreneurs must learn to function as effective managers, at least to a degree, and this constitutes a major shift in their activities. Ultimately, many entrepreneurs must consider and enact various *exit strategies*—procedures through which they can transfer ownership of their businesses to other persons.

Please note that there is no intention here of suggesting that boundaries between each of these major phases are clear or firm; on the contrary, activities performed in one phase can and often do spill over into another. For example, following launch of a new venture, entrepreneurs are often still actively involved in assembling needed resources (e.g., arranging for successive waves of financing). Similarly, during the launch or startup phase, entrepreneurs often direct at least part of their attention to securing orders, in some instances even before the companies' products or services are officially available for sale. Once again, therefore, it is important to emphasize that entrepreneurship is a *process*, and that dividing it into discrete segments or phases, although useful in many respects, also suggests the existence of definite boundaries that, in most cases, do not actually exist.

Variables That Influence Important Outcomes During Each Phase

Because it involves a very wide range of activities performed over an extended period of time, it is only reasonable to expect that entrepreneurship, as a process, is influenced by a multitude of variables. In fact, the extant literature in entrepreneurship suggests that this is certainly the case (e.g., Katz & Shepherd, 2003; Shane, 2003). However, as noted earlier, all these variables may be viewed as falling into three major categories: *individual-level variables*, *group* or *interpersonal-level variables*, and *societal-level variables*. Assembling an exhaustive list of these factors is beyond the scope of this chapter; in fact, perhaps such a list could never be complete. However it may be useful for purposes of the present discussion to provide key examples of variables falling into each category—variables that have been found, in recent research, to play an important role in the entrepreneurial process. Discussion of the specific phases during which these factors exert their primary effects is reserved for a subsequent section.

Individual-Level Variables.   Factors in this category relate to the behavior, cognitions, characteristics, knowledge, skills, and abilities of specific entrepreneurs (e.g., Baum & Locke, 2004; Krueger, 2003). At one point in the past, entrepreneurship researchers were reluctant to focus on such factors because early investigations of the impact of these variables yielded inconsistent and often contradictory results. This led some scholars to conclude that studying individual-level variables in the context of entrepreneurship was largely a waste of time (e.g., Shaver & Scott, 1991). More recently, however, the pendulum of scientific opinion has swung noticeably in the other direction, primarily because of growing recognition of three important points:

1. Early investigations of individual-level factors often lacked a strong theoretical basis and this virtually doomed them to failure.
2. Initial investigations of individual-level variables needlessly restricted the scope of such factors, focusing almost exclusively on several aspects of personality (e.g., need for achievement, locus of control); in fact, individual-level variables are far broader in scope and include the cognitions, knowledge base, skills and even the health and stress tolerance of specific entrepreneurs.
3. Early investigations employed measures that were often low in reliability and of uncertain validity; this, of course, made it difficult for these studies to yield strong and informative results.

As recognition of these important points has increased, a growing number of researchers have turned their attention to conducting theory-based investigations of the impact of a wide range of individual-level variables. Among these, various aspects of entrepreneurs' cognition have received by far the greatest attention (e.g., Mitchell et al., 2004). This research has examined many aspects of *entrepreneurial cognition* (e.g., Krueger, 2003), including the specific cognitions formed by entrepreneurs (e.g., Mitchell, Smith, Seawright, & Morse, 2000; Mitchell et al., 2002), entrepreneurial *intentions* (i.e., form a new venture; e.g., Krueger, 2003), entrepreneurs' attributions (e.g., Gatewood, Shaver, & Gartner, 1995), and their tendency to engage in counterfactual thinking (imagining "what might have been"; Baron, 2000; Gaglio, 2004). The findings of these studies have added much to our understanding of how entrepreneurs think, reason, and make decisions; this, in turn, offers important insights into the nature of the entrepreneurial process.

Additional research on entrepreneurial cognition has focused on the question of whether entrepreneurs are subject to the same cognitive biases and errors as other persons. Research in the field of entrepreneurial cognition suggests that they are (Baron, 1998). For example, several studies suggest that entrepreneurs may be especially susceptible to such errors as *overconfidence*—unrealistically high belief in the accuracy of one's own judgments (e.g., Amit, MacCrimmon, Zietsma, & Oesch, 2001; Busenitz & Barney, 1997). Similarly, additional studies indicate that entrepreneurs are subject to other forms of cognitive bias, such as the *illusion of control*—unjustified belief in the capacity to influence one's outcomes (Simon, Houghton, & Aquino, 2000).

Finally, other research has examined the cognitive bases of opportunity recognition (e.g., Baron, 2006; Gaglio & Katz, 2001; Shane, 2000, 2001). Detailed discussion of this work is beyond the scope of this chapter, but it seems clear that this, too, has examined many variables that fit into the category of individual-level factors.

Although cognitive factors have clearly received the greatest amount of recent attention, they are not the only individual-level variables that have been found to play a role in important aspects of entrepreneurship. For example, several recent studies (e.g., Ciavarella, Bucholtz, Riordan, Gatewood, & Stokes, 2004) indicate that certain aspects of personality also influence important outcomes such as the survival of new ventures. These studies, in contrast to early ones, focused on aspects of personality for which strong theoretic foundations exist (e.g., the "Big Five" dimensions; Hurtz & Donovan, 2000; Mount & Barrick, 1995) and have employed measures of these factors that are known to be both reliable and valid. It is not surprising, then, that theory-based predictions have been verified in this work. Other research on individual-level variables has examined the role of emotional and practical intelligence (e.g., Sternberg, 2004), and these factors, too, appear to be relevant to many of the activities and tasks entrepreneurs perform. In short, it is clear that individual-level variables play an important role in entrepreneurship and should be included in efforts to develop an accurate and comprehensive model of the entrepreneurial process.

Group or Interpersonal-Level Variables.   Although entrepreneurs may sometimes formulate ideas for new products, services, or markets in isolation, virtually everything else they do involves either direct or indirect interactions with other persons. Once they generate an idea, they must persuade others of its potential value in order to secure the resources needed for its development. And once they actually launch their new venture, they must interact with many different persons—potential customers, employees, suppliers, and so on. Clearly, then, variables that influence entrepreneurs' relations with others—group or interpersonal-level factors—play a key role in many aspects of the entrepreneurial process. Among these variables, *social capital*—the ability of individuals to extract benefits from their social structures, networks, and memberships, or, alternatively, the actual benefits themselves—has received the greatest amount of attention (Baron, in press; Nahapiet & Ghoshal, 1998; Portes, 1998). Research on the effects of this important variable suggests that entrepreneurs can obtain a wide range of benefits from their social ties with others, from support, advice, and encouragement on the one hand, through the acquisition of tangible financial resources on the other. Additional benefits include increased cooperation and trust from others and enhanced access to information— especially to information that is accurate and potentially useful. Viewed in this light, social capital is definitely worth possessing: although it is an intangible asset, it can yield highly beneficial outcomes to the persons who possess it (e.g., Adler & Kwon, 2002; Davidsson & Honig, 2003).

It is important to distinguish social capital from *human capital*, which refers primarily to the knowledge individuals possess—especially, knowledge that can contribute to more productive and efficient entrepreneurial activity. This includes formal education, past experience in a given field, and specific training that is not part of formal degree programs. In short, human capital is focused more on what individuals *know*—the skills and knowledge they have acquired and bring to any work setting—whereas social capital refers more directly to *whom they know*, and the depth, intensity, and positive nature of these relationships.

Another social or group-level variable that often plays a key role in entrepreneurship is *social competence*—an array of skills that assist individuals in interacting effectively with others (e.g., Baron & Markman, 2003). Social competence, which includes such skills as the ability to perceive others accurately, to express one's own emotions and reactions clearly, to be persuasive, and to make a good first impression on others, is closely related to social capital. Social capital, which reflects, at least in part, individuals' reputations as well as the breadth and depth of their social networks, often serves as a *necessary* condition for entrepreneurs in terms of gaining access to capital and other resources is concerned. To the extent they have high social capital, they "get through the door," so to speak, and can then meet, and interact with, potential investors, customers, and employees. However, once access to others has been gained through social networks, reputation, and related aspects of social capital, it is entrepreneurs' *social competence*—their skills in interacting with others—that then determines the nature of their relationships with these persons and, ultimately, their success (e.g., Baron & Markman, 2000). Research on the effects of social competence suggests that it is highly advantageous to entrepreneurs: The better their standing with respect to this variable, the greater is the success of their new ventures (e.g., Baron & Markman, 2003).

Social competence and social capital are also related in an additional manner: It is partly through social competence that individuals build their social networks. In other words, the higher their social competence, the broader are entrepreneurs' social networks likely to be, and the greater are the benefits they can obtain from them (e.g., Baron & Markman, 2000).

Other group-level variables that play a role in the entrepreneurial process include exposure to models of entrepreneurial activities, support and influence from friends and family, cultural or group values and attitudes concerning the role of entrepreneur, and size of social network (see Shane, 2003). All of these factors have been found to affect the outcomes entrepreneurs experience during various phases of the entrepreneurial process and, ultimately, their success in starting new venture. Additional factors for which empirical evidence is currently lacking, but which seem highly likely to exert such effects, include conflict-handling and negotiating skills, leadership skills (e.g., Vecchio, 2003), and the capacity to generate trust and confidence in others (e.g., Lewicki & Wiethoff, 2000). In sum, it seems clear that group or social-level variables, too, must be included in a comprehensive process model of entrepreneurship.

Societal-Level (Macro) Variables.   When entrepreneurs start new ventures, they do so against a backdrop of societal conditions. What is the current state of capital markets and the local economy? Is there a shortage or surplus of qualified potential employees? What are current government policies concerning taxation, regulation, and special programs designed to assist entrepreneurs? Are demographics favorable or unfavorable to the new venture's products or services? Are societal norms favorable or unfavorable to new ventures and their activities (e.g., is there a strong cultural bias in favor of established, well-known companies)? These and many other factors influence the outcomes that entrepreneurs experience (e.g., Shane, 2003). Again, detailed discussion of these important factors is beyond the scope of this chapter. However, they too must be carefully incorporated into a comprehensive process model of entrepreneurship.

The model proposed here suggests that entrepreneurship involves a continuous process that moves, over time, through a series of major phases. These phases are not demarcated by the passage of specific amounts of time, but rather by shifts in the activities and tasks performed by entrepreneurs— that they actually *do* as part of their efforts to develop new ventures. The model also suggests that throughout the process, three major categories of variables play a role (or, more accurately, ever-changing roles): factors relating to the cognitions, skills, motives, abilities, and characteristics of entrepreneurs (individual-level variables), factors relating to entrepreneurs' relations within others (group or interpersonal-level variables), and factors relating to the political, economic, and social environments in which entrepreneurs operate (societal-level variables). It is suggested here that this model (refer to Fig. 2.1) may provide a framework useful for gaining fuller and more comprehensive understanding of the entrepreneurial process.

It should quickly be added that although this model is meant to be comprehensive in nature, it almost certainly does not include all activities performed by entrepreneurs or all variables that may influence their performance of these activities and, ultimately, the outcomes they experience. However, the model shown in Fig. 2.1 does at least suggest the broad outlines of what a comprehensive process model of entrepreneurship might include, and it remains for future research to fill in the blanks and to refine this or subsequent process models into the complete and accurate representation of entrepreneurship that is a key goals of the field.

A Note on Dependent Measures

If entrepreneurs perform different activities and tasks at different times during the entrepreneurial process, this suggests that measures of their success, too, should reflect these changes. In other words, financial measures such as return on investment, rate of growth in sales or earnings, or growth in number of employees are not necessarily reasonable or useful indices during earlier phases of the process—for instance, in the prelaunch period when there is no company and no profit-and-loss statement in the traditional sense of this term. For this reason, a process model of entrepreneurship suggests that different metrics are required during different phases of new venture development. In fact, as a general principle, these measures should carefully reflect the activities and tasks being performed during each phase. Perhaps some concrete illustrations will help to clarify this important point.

During the prelaunch period, entrepreneurs are, in a sense, not quite entrepreneurs; indeed, during the earliest periods, many have not yet formed the clear intention of starting a new company. Rather, they are focused on identifying and evaluating opportunities. During this phase, appropriate measures of success might involve number and quality of opportunities identified—perhaps as rated by experts in fields relevant to each opportunity or idea. Later, once entrepreneurs have decided to proceed, they focus on assembling the required resources. Financial measures may be meaningful at this point in time. For instance, such measures as (a) the amount of money raised by entrepreneurs, (b) the proportion of the amount sought that was actually obtained, and (c) and how much time was required to raise these funds may all be relevant. In fact, such measures are often employed as indices of success during this phase of the process. However, other measures, too, may be relevant: Are the entrepreneurs successful in attracting high-quality partners or employees? In obtaining intellectual property protection? Do they formulate effective initial plans for exploiting the opportunity they have identified? None of these outcomes can be assessed in purely financial terms. However, they *can* be assessed quantitatively, in terms of such measures as the length of time required to hire key employees, the rated quality of these persons, the number and strength of patents obtained, and the rated completeness and quality of strategic plans for marketing and gaining competitive advantage (e.g., Shane, 2003).

Turning to the launch period (generally defined as encompassing the period from legal establishment of a new venture until 12 or 18 months later), other measures are more appropriate. For instance, time of first sale may be useful. Similarly, time until the break-even point was reached can be informative. Other useful measures of effectiveness can be provided by the number and strength of patents and trademarks, and by when the first employees were hired. These and other measures are related to the activities performed by entrepreneurs during this period, and may be informative for this reason.

Finally, during the postlaunch period, traditional financial measures of success become both appropriate and revealing. What is the rate of growth in sales? Earnings? Number of employees? What is the internal rate of return on investment? How successful was the company in raising additional funds necessary for continued growth? When did the company go public, and what was its valuation? In addition, measures relating to the retention of employees, their productivity, and costs associated with employee benefits and hiring all become increasingly relevant as the startup venture changes, gradually, into a viable, growing business.

The purpose of this discussion is certainly not that of providing a complete list of all potential measures of entrepreneurs' performance or success. Rather, the main goal is merely to emphasize, once again, that because entrepreneurs perform different activities over time and focus on an ever-changing array of tasks, different measures are appropriate during different phases of the entrepreneurial process. This point has, of course, been recognized in previous research in the field of entrepreneurship. However, making it explicit and including it as a basic part of the model offered here may be helpful from the point of view of assisting researchers to choose measures most reflective of the activities and tasks on which they wish to focus.

A KEY COROLLARY: THE CHANGING ROLE OF VARIABLES
OVER VARIOUS PHASES OF THE PROCESS

If entrepreneurship is indeed a process during which entrepreneurs perform an ever-changing array of activities, and if a wide range of individual-level, group-level, and societal-level variables influence entrepreneurs behavior, cognitions, and performance throughout the process, then a key corollary follows logically: *The impact of specific variables may change appreciably over different phases of the process.* In other words, specific variables that play a key role during one phase may play a smaller or even an insignificant role during other phases. This deduction has important implications for the field of entrepreneurship. First, it is consistent with suggestions offered by Gartner (1989) that entrepreneurship researchers should direct careful attention to what entrepreneurs actually *do*—the activities they perform. Focusing on these activities will help researchers to select variables that, for clear theoretical reasons, are relevant to these activities and may, potentially, affect them. Second, this corollary suggests that there is no reason to assume that specific variables will play the same role throughout the process. On the contrary, it implies that the magnitude, and even the direction, of such effects may change greatly over time, in the context of different tasks and changing foci for entrepreneurs. Third, this corollary helps explain why inconsistent findings have often been obtained in past research with respect to the impact of specific variables. If different studies examined the impact of these factors during different phases of the entrepreneurial process, then contrasting or even contradictory results would not be at all surprising; on the contrary, they would merely reflect the changing role of these variables across different phases and across different activities performed by entrepreneurs during these phases.

Perhaps, at this point, a specific illustration of these points may be useful. Consider efforts to examine the question of whether entrepreneurs are more risk-prone (i.e., more accepting of risk or actually risk seeking) than other persons. This basic idea did not originally derive from strong theoretical considerations, but rather, it appears, from general "commonsense" beliefs about entrepreneurs—for instance, the view that they *must* be more risk-prone than persons who choose full-time employment in large organizations (e.g., Knight, 1921; Rees & Shah, 1986).

Initial studies designed to test this proposition reported results consistent with it: Entrepreneurs did, indeed, appear to be more accepting of risk than other individuals (e.g., Begley & Boyd, 1987; Caird, 1991). However, subsequent investigations called this conclusion into question, suggesting, instead, that entrepreneurs are not "riskier" than other persons; rather, they simply tend to perceive lower levels of risk in various situations than do nonentrepreneurs (e.g., Simon et al., 2000), and in fact may strongly seek to manage risk rather than to seek or prefer it. Perhaps the inconsistent nature of research findings on this topic is underscored most clearly by two recent meta-analyses. The first, by Stewart and Roth (2001), concluded that across many different studies, entrepreneurs are indeed more accepting of risk than other persons. The second, by Miner and Raju (2004), reached precisely the opposite conclusion. Although the authors of the second meta-analysis (Miner & Raju, 2004) attribute these contrasting findings to differences in the measures of risk-taking propensity employed in different studies (and included in the two meta-analyses), another explanation also seems plausible: Perhaps different studies of the risk-taking propensities of entrepreneurs have examined these tendencies during different phases of the entrepreneurial process. Studies reporting that entrepreneurs are indeed more risk-prone than other individuals may have focused on *early* phases of the process—a time when, indeed, acceptance or tolerance of risk may be required. After all, most new ventures do indeed fail, so choosing to give up secure employment to start one is definitely "risky business." Such differences in risk acceptance may tend to disappear during later phases of the process, however, when efforts to maximize profitability and to preserve the new venture's limited resources literally require entrepreneurs to manage risk very carefully. Similar arguments concerning changes in acceptance of risk over time—and across different phases of the entrepreneurial process—have been made by Levesque, Shepherd, and Douglas (2002). These researchers note that people generally seek to maximize the overall utility of their career choices, and that factors that enter into the decision to become self-employed or remain in a current job may change over time. For instance, the utility weight for income decreases with age, while the disutility weight for risk increases with age. As a result of these and related changes, entrepreneurs' willingness to accept risk may well shift considerably over the course of the entrepreneurial process. It appears, then, that the correct question to pose is not "Are entrepreneurs more or less accepting of risk than other persons?" but rather "*When,* during the process, are they more or less accepting of risk?" In short, a process perspective may help to sharpen the focus of the key questions addressed in ongoing research—and to facilitate the attainment of useful and accurate answers to them.

Other instances of inconsistent findings in the entrepreneurship literature, too, may stem from the same basic source: relatively little attention to *when,* during the entrepreneurial process, specific factors are more or less likely to exert significant effects and on which dependent measures are being considered. As another example, consider *self-efficacy,* a motivational variable that has recently received growing attention from entrepreneurship researchers (Chen, Greene, & Crick, 1998; Markman, Baron, & Balkin, 2003). In general terms, this variable relates to individuals' belief that they can accomplish whatever they set out to accomplish. When would this aspect of motivation be expected to play an important role? Perhaps primarily during early phases of the process, when individuals first conclude that they can, indeed, convert their ideas into viable companies and when they must generate enthusiasm for the new venture in others. As a result, entrepreneurs' self-efficacy may be highly predictive of entrepreneurial intentions and of success during relatively early phases (e.g., in obtaining financial support, and in recruiting partners and prospective employees). However, it may be of somewhat less importance during later phases, when such tasks as developing strong strategies for marketing and growth become increasingly important, and when the entrepreneur has less and less direct control over daily operations and must delegate increasing authority to others. Some empirical findings are consistent with these suggestions (e.g., Chen et al., 1998). For example, Markman, Balkin, and Baron (2002) found that patent recipients high in self-efficacy are more likely to use their inventions to start new ventures than patent recipients low in self-efficacy. Do the effects of self-efficacy decrease during later phase as suggested here? A recent study by Baron and Markman (2005) suggests that this, too, may be so.

These researchers founds that *creative self-efficacy*—individuals' confidence in their own creativity and the ability to perform creative tasks such as generating ideas or formulating patentable inventions (Tierney & Farmer, 2002)—is significantly related to the number of patents sought and actually obtained by entrepreneurs. In contrast, this aspect of self-efficacy was not significantly related to other dependent measures relating to later phases of the entrepreneurial process (e.g., income generated by new ventures or their survival). Overall, it appears that at least early in the process, self-efficacy may play an important role in the activities performed by entrepreneurs

In sum, it is suggested here that one corollary of a process model of entrepreneurship—the suggestion that the impact of specific variables may change considerably over phases of the process—is important and worthy of careful attention. Indeed, investigation of this prediction seems essential for the development of a truly comprehensive model of the entrepreneurial process, one that will be useful in training future entrepreneurs and in contributing to their success.

METHODS OF INVESTIGATING A PROCESS MODEL

The central theme of the process model presented in this chapter can be stated in a single word: *change*. The model assumes that entrepreneurship unfolds over time and that during different phases of the process, entrepreneurs are engaging in somewhat different activities. Because they are, different measures of their performance, too, are appropriate (e.g., measures of intentions or success in assembling resources during early phases; traditional financial measures of performance during later ones). The model further suggests that as a result of these shifts in activities and outcomes, variables that influence the entrepreneurial process may also change, so that factors that play a role during one phase may play a greater or lesser role during other phases.

Although this process model appears to offer important benefits (discussed later), it also poses complex issues for researchers. In the past, most research in the field has been *cross-sectional* in nature: Data have been collected from one or more groups of persons (e.g., entrepreneurs, non-entrepreneurs) or from one or more groups of companies at a single point in time (or over a limited period of time). Then, differences between the groups have been examined. A number of exceptions to this generalization exist, and in some instances, the activities or outcomes experienced by entrepreneurs have been studied over a longer period of time (e.g., Abetti, 2003). However, it seems reasonable to suggest that a large proportion of research conducted in the field of entrepreneurship to date has adopted a cross-sectional approach. Such research is very useful for answering many important questions—"Do entrepreneurs think differently than other persons?" (Mitchell et al, 2002); "On what basis do venture capitalists' make funding decisions?" (Shepherd & Zacharakis, 2002); "What is the role of human or social capital in the decision to become an entrepreneur?" (e.g., Carter, Gartner, Shaver, & Gatewood, 2003; Davidsson & Honig, 2003); and "What differences, if any, exist between women and men entrepreneurs?" (e.g., Baron, Markman, & Hirsa, 2001; DeMartino & Barbato, 2003). However, it cannot directly address the question of *change*: how the behavior, cognitions, activities, attitudes, vision, and goals of entrepreneurs shift over time. Nor can cross-sectional research fully address the possibility that the role of various factors in the success of new ventures may shift considerably over time.

To fully address these and related issues, it will be necessary for entrepreneurship researchers to adopt *longitudinal* research designs, in which entrepreneurs, and the new ventures they found, are studied over extended periods of time. Data collected in this manner would then enable researchers to address questions pertaining to how the behavior, cognitions, and goals of entrepreneurs change over time, and how the process of starting new ventures actually unfolds and develops.

Unfortunately, longitudinal designs are easier to describe than to implement: They require long-term commitments from researchers and long-term cooperation from entrepreneurs. In addition, longitudinal research involves many complexities. For instance, changes over time may be confounded with what are known as *cohort effects*. That is, entrepreneurs who start businesses at one point in time may be different in many ways from ones who start them at other times, so that differences or trends that appear over time may be due, at least in part, to this factor rather than to central aspects of the entrepreneurial process itself. Similarly, new ventures started at one point in time may develop in different ways and along different lines than ones started at later times, because they are launched under different sociohistorical conditions.

Another issue raised by longitudinal research is *subject attrition*—shrinkage in the initial sample: Some participants lose interest, close their businesses, or become unable or unwilling to continue in the research for varied reasons. Although this problem can be addressed, at least to some degree, by comparing persons who continue in the study with ones who drop out, it cannot be totally eliminated. Still another complex issue is raised by *time-of-measurement effects*—effects stemming from the social, political, and economic environment existing at the time a study is conducted.

Several research methods designed to deal with these and other issues relating to longitudinal research exist, but none provides s fully satisfactory solution. Rather, each offers data on some aspects of development while ignoring others. For instance, consider *time-lag* studies. In this research design, age (i.e., length of time new ventures have existed) is held constant, but cohort effects (e.g., the specific years in which they were started) are varied. With respect to entrepreneurship, this would involve obtaining data about new ventures started at different points in time (e.g., new ventures started in 1980, 1990, 2000), and several years later (e.g., in 1982, 1992, and 2002). Time-lag designs provide information on how the specific times at which new ventures were founded affects their subsequent growth. For instance, it might indicate that new ventures started in 1980 and 1990, when capital was relatively difficult to obtain, show slower initial growth than those started in 2000, at the height of the previous bull market. Because all the ventures included in such research designs would be of the same age (in this instance, 2 years old), time-lag studies provide no information on how new ventures actually change over time.

In contrast, an alternative design, known as *sequential* research, combines various features of cross-sectional and longitudinal research. For instance, *cohort-sequential* designs study two or more different cohorts (new ventures founded at different points in time; e.g., 1990 and 2000), and follow their development over specific periods of time (e.g., 2 or 3 years). *Cross-sequential* designs, on the other hand, perform cross-sectional studies at different historical times. For example, new ventures founded at different points in time (e.g., 1990–1995, 1996–2000) could be studied in 2002, 2004, and 2006. In this way, cohort effects (when the companies were founded) can be disentangled from age (how long they have been in existence), to see if the various cohorts develop in similar or different ways.

Although these and other research designs are useful for reducing confounding between cohort effects, changes that occur to entrepreneurs and new ventures over time, and time-of-measurement effects (i.e., when specific companies are studied), they all present a mixed picture of advantages and disadvantages. Thus, most experts in fields that have long used longitudinal methods (e.g., human development) recommend a combination of methods as the best means of obtaining informative data (e.g,. Lemme, 1999). Because relatively little longitudinal research has been conducted in the field of entrepreneurship to date, increased use of any of these methods by entrepreneurship researchers might well contribute significantly to our understanding of entrepreneurship as an ongoing, ever-changing process.

IMPLICATIONS OF A PROCESS PERSPECTIVE ON ENTREPRENEURSHIP

If this chapter had appeared in print 10 or perhaps even 5 years ago, it might well have been viewed as somewhat controversial in nature. At present, though, the opposite is true: The ideas offered here represent a growing consensus in the field of entrepreneurship (e.g., Shane & Venkataraman, 2000). Most current research in entrepreneurship acknowledges the basic usefulness of a process perspective, even if it does not take active steps to test it. Thus, the model offered here represents more of an extension and refinement of previous views than a clarion call for something new and truly radical. Despite this, fact, however, it offers several important benefits.

First, it provides a unified framework within which to conduct future research on entrepreneurship. Such an overarching model has been lacking in the field, although the basic premises and scope of the model presented here are clearly visible in earlier, sophisticated papers (e.g., Venkataraman, 1997).

Second, it is a basic fact that in most fields, advances in theory—in basic understanding of the phenomena of interest—occur prior to advances in practice. For instance, rapid progress in medicine did not occur until relatively powerful microscopes that revealed the existence of dangerous disease-producing organisms had been developed. Similarly, major advances in applied geology (e.g., location of fossil fuels) occurred after the theory of plate tectonics ("continental drift") was proposed and verified. It seems reasonable to suggest that the same principle may apply to the field of entrepreneurship. Development of a comprehensive theoretical framework of the entrepreneurial process may provide a firm foundation for development of useful techniques for assisting entrepreneurs in their efforts to found new ventures.

Third, as noted in an earlier section, a comprehensive process model may help entrepreneurship to resolve several persistent empirical puzzles.

Are entrepreneurs more, or less, risk-prone than other persons? Do their personal characteristics matter in any meaningful way? Why do some promising new ventures grow and prosper whereas others somehow "get off the track" and fail? A comprehensive process model, with its recognition of the fact that different variables or combinations of variables may play contrasting roles in shaping important outcomes during different phases of the process, may facilitate resolution of these complex issues.

Similarly, the model offered here calls attention to the importance of including variables at all levels of analysis—individual, group, and societal. In this sense, it may help to resolve an underlying tension between "micro" and "macro" approaches to the study of entrepreneurship. Researchers in the field come from many different disciplines (economics, management, strategy, industrial/organizational psychology, organizational behavior), and they bring these contrasting perspectives to bear on important research questions. The model offered here suggests that variables at all levels are important, and emphasizes the fact that the impact of these variables may well differ depending on the phase of the process being considered and the outcomes (dependent measures) of primary interest. Adoption of this perspective may well enhance development of a more unified and inclusive view of entrepreneurship.

Finally, by emphasizing the fact that entrepreneurship is a process, the present model may facilitate the development of closer conceptual ties between entrepreneurship and related fields. Many fields closely linked to entrepreneurship (e.g., organizational behavior, human resource management, strategy, economics, sociology) recognize that the questions they study relate, at least in part, to ongoing and ever-changing processes. Learning (both individual and organizational), conflict, motivation, decision making, careers, organizational development and change, organizational politics, leadership—these are just a few of the processes studied by such fields. To the extent that entrepreneurship, too, adopts a process perspective, it will be in a better position to create stronger conceptual links to these fields—and hence to benefit from their large body of their well-established empirical findings and well-developed theories. As noted by the present author elsewhere (Baron, 2002), this can confer important benefits upon entrepreneurship and facilitate its development as a field.

In sum, a process perspective appears to offer several important advantages to entrepreneurship. Until now, the field has lacked an inclusive framework that would allow individual researchers to place their own work, and that of others, within the context of a single theoretical structure. A comprehensive process perspective may help to provide such a framework and that, in turn, may prove beneficial to the field of entrepreneurship in several respects. But please note: There is no intention here of suggesting that such a framework was totally lacking in the past. On the contrary, a strong case can be made for the view that a process perspective has been present in the field of entrepreneurship for quite some time—it was simply not recognized or clearly articulated as such. As Henry Miller, a noted author, once put it (1938), "Confusion is a word we have invented for an order which is not yet understood" (*Tropic of Capricorn*, p. 132) In conclusion, it is the primary assertion of this chapter that adoption of a comprehensive process perspective will greatly facilitate progress toward full understanding of the entrepreneurial process—and that, it can be argued, is the key and defining goal of the field of entrepreneurship.

REFERENCES

Abetti, P. A. (2003). Case study: the entrepreneurial control imperative: A case history of Steria (1969–2000). *Journal of Business Venturing, 18,* 125–143.

Adler, P., & Kwon, S. (2002). Social capital: Prospects for a new concept. *Academy of Management Review, 27,* 17–40.

Aldrich, H. (1999). *Organizational evolving.* London: Sage.

Amit, R., MacCrimmon, K. R., Zietsma, C., & Oesch, J. M. (2001). Does money matter? Wealth attainment as the motive for initiating growth-oriented technology ventures. *Journal of Business Venturing, 16,* 119–143.

Baron, R. A. (1998). Cognitive mechanisms in entrepreneurship: Why and when entrepreneurs think differently than other people. *Journal of Business Venturing, 12,* 275–294.

Baron, R. A. (2000). Counterfactual thinking and venture formation: The potential effects of thinking about what might have been. *Journal of Business Venturing, 15,* 79–92.

Baron, R. A. (2002). OB and entrepreneurship: The reciprocal benefits of closer conceptual links. In B. M. Staw & R. Kramer (Eds.), *Research in organizational behavior* (pp. 225–269). Greenwich, CT: JAI Press.

Baron, R. A. (2006). Opportunity recognition as pattern recognition: How entrepreneurs "connect the dots" to identify new business opportunities. *Academy of Management Perspectives, 20,* 104–119.

Baron, R. A., & Markman, G. D. (2000). Beyond social capital: How social skills can enhance entrepreneurs' success. *Academy of Management Executive, 14,* 106–116.

Baron, R. A., & Markman, G. D. (2003). Beyond social capital: The role of entrepreneurs' social competence in their financial success. *Journal of Business Venturing, 18,* 41–60.

Baron, R. A., & Markman, G. D. (2005). Toward a process view of entrepreneurship: The changing impact of individual level variables across phases of new venture development. In M. A. Rahim, R. T. Golembiewski, & K. D. Mackenzie (Eds.), *Current topics in management* (Vol. 9, pp. 45–64). New Brunswick, NJ: Transaction.

Baron, R. A., Markman, G. D., & Hirsa, A. (2001). Perceptions of women and men as entrepreneurs: Evidence for differential effects of attributional augmenting. *Journal of Applied Psychology, 86,* 923–292.

Baron, R. A., & Shane, S. A. (2004). *Entrepreneurship: A process perspective.* Cincinnati, OH: Thompson/South-West.

Baum, J. R., & Locke, E. A. (2004). The relationship of entrepreneurial traits, skill, and motivation in subsequent venture growth. *Journal of Applied Psychology, 89,* 587–598.

Begley, T., & Boyd, D. (1987). A comparison of entrepreneurs and managers of small business firms. *Journal of Management, 13,* 99–108.

Busenitz, L. W., & Barney, J. B. (1997). Differences between entrepreneurs and managers in large organizations: Biases and heuristics in strategic decision-making. *Journal of Business Venturing, 12,* 9–30.

Bygrave, W. D. (1989, Fall). The entrepreneurship paradigm: A philosophical look at its research methodologies. *Entrepreneurship Theory and Practice*, pp. 7–26.

Caird, S. (1991). The enterprising tendency of occupational groups. *International Small Business Journal, 9*, 75–81.

Carter, N. M., Gartner, W. B., Shaver, K. G., & Gatewood, E. J. (2003). The career reasons of nascent entrepreneurs. *Journal of Business Venturing, 18*, 13–39.

Chen, C. C., Greene, P. G., & Crick, A. (1998). Does entrepreneurial self-efficacy distinguish entrepreneurs from managers? *Journal of Business Venturing, 13*, 395–316.

Ciavarella, M. A., Bucholtz, A. K., Riordan, C. M., Gatewood, R. D,. & Stokes, G. S. (2004). The big five and venture success: Is there a linkage? *Journal of Business Venturing, 19*, 465–464.

Davidsson, P., & Honig, B. (2003). The role of social and human capital among nascent entrepreneurs. *Journal of Business Venturing, 18*, 301–331.

DeMartino, R., & Barbato, R. (2003). Differences between women and men MBA entrepreneurs: Exploring family flexibility and wealth creation as career motivators. *Journal of Business Venturing, 18*, 815–832.

Gaglio, C. M. (2004). The role of mental simulations and counterfactual thinking in the opportunity identification process. *Entrepreneurship Theory and Practice, 28*, 533–552.

Gaglio, C. M., & Katz, J. A. (2001). The psychological basis of opportunity identification: Entrepreneurial alertness. *Small Business Economics, 16*, 95–1110.

Gartner, W. B. (1989). "Who is an entrepreneur?" is the wrong question. *Entrepreneurship Theory and Practice, 13*, 47–68.

Gatewood, E. K., Powers, J. B., Shaver, K. G., & Gartner, W. (2001). *The effects of perceived entrepreneurial ability on task effort, performance, and expectancy.* Working paper.

Harvey, M., & Evans, R. (1995). Strategic windows in the entrepreneurial process. *Journal of Business Venturing, 10*, 331–347.

Hurtz, G. M., & Donovan, J. J. (2000). Personality and job performance: The big five revisited. *Journal of Applied Psychology, 85*, 869–879.

Jack, S. L., & Anderson, A. R. (2002). The effects of embedded ness on the entrepreneurial process. *Journal of Business Venturing, 17*, 467–487.

Katz, J., & Shepherd, D. A. (Eds.). (2003). *Cognitive approaches to entrepreneurship research.* New York: Elsevier Science.

Knight, F. (1921). *Risk, uncertainty, and profit.* New York: Augustus Kelly.

Krueger, N. F., Jr. (2003). The cognitive psychology of entrepreneurship. In Z. Acs & D. B. Audrestsch, (Eds.), *Handbook of entrepreneurial research* (pp. 105–140). London: Kluwer Law International.

Lemme, B. H. (1999). *Development in adulthood* (2nd ed.). Boston: Allyn & Bacon.

Levesque, M., Shepherd, D. A., & Douglas, E. J. (2002). Employment or self-employment; A dynamic utility-maximizing model. *Journal of Business Venturing, 17*, 189–210.

Lewicki, R. J., & Wiethoff, C., (2000). Trust, trust development, and trust repair. In M. Deutsch & P. T. Coleman (Eds.)., *The handbook of conflict resolution* (pp. 86–107). San Francisco: Jossey-Bass.

Low, M., & Abrahamson, E. (1997). Movements, bandwagons, and clones: Industry evolution and the entrepreneurial process. *Journal of Business Venturing, 12*, 435–458.

Markman, G. D., Balkin, D. B., & Baron, R. A. (2002, Winter). Inventors and new venture formation: The effects of general self-efficacy and regretful thinking. *Entrepreneurship Theory & Practice*, pp. 149–165.

Markman, G. D., Baron, R. A., & Balkin, D. B. (2003). The role of regretful thinking, perseverance, and self-efficacy in venture formation. In J. Katz & D. A. Shepherd (Eds.), *Cognitive approaches to entrepreneurship research* (pp. 73–104). New York: Elsevier Science.

Miller, H. (1938). *Tropic of Capricorn*, "On the ovarian trolley: An interlude." New York: Grove Press.

Miner, J. B., & Raju, N. S. (2004). When science divests itself of its conservative stance: The case of risk propensity differences between entrepreneurs and managers. *Journal of Applied Psychology. 89*, 3–13.

Mitchell, R. K., Smith, B., Seawright, K. W., & Morse, E. A. (2000). Cross-cultural cognitions and venture creation decisions. *Academy of Management Journal, 43*, 974–993.

Mitchell, R. K., Smith, J. B., Morse, E. A., Seawright, K. W., Peredo, A. M.,& McKenzie, B. (2002, Summer). Are entrepreneurial cognitions universal? Assessing entrepreneurial cognitions. *Entrepreneurship Theory & Practice*, pp. 9–32.

Mitchell, R. K., Busenitz, L., Lant, T., McDougall, P. P., Morse, E. A., & Smith, J. B. (2004). The distinctive and inclusive domain of entrepreneurial cognition research. *Entrepreneurship Theory and Practice, 28*, 505–518.

Mount, M. K., & Barrick, M. R. (1995). The Big Five personality dimensions: Implications for research and practice in human resources management. In K. M. Rowland & G. Ferris (Eds.), *Research in personnel and human resources management*, (Vol. 13, pp. 153–200). Greenwich, CT: JAI Press.

Nahapiet, J., & Ghoshal, S. (1998). Social capital, intellectual capital, and the organizational advantage. *Academy of Management Review, 23*, 242–266.

Portes, A. (1998). Social capital. *Annual Review of Sociology, 23*, 1–24.

Rees, H., & Shah, A. (1986). An empirical analysis of self-employment in the UK. *Journal of Applied Econometrics, 1*, 95–108.

Reynolds, P., & White, S. (1997). *The entrepreneurial process: economic growth, men, women, and minorities.* Westport, CT: Quorum Books.

Shane, S. (2000). Prior knowledge and the discovery of entrepreneurial opportunities. *Organization Science, 11*, 448–469.

Shane, S. (2001). Technology opportunities and new firm creation. *Management Science, 47*, 20–220.

Shane, S. (2003). *A general theory of entrepreneurship: The individual-opportunity nexus approach to entrepreneurship.* Aldershot, UK: Edward Elgar.

Shane, S., & Venkataraman, S. (2000). The promise of entrepreneurship as a field of research. *Academy of Management Review, 25*, 217–226.

Shaver, K. G., & Scott, L. R. (1991). Person, process, choice: The psychology of new venture creation. *Entrepreneurship Theory and Practice, 16*, 23–42.

Shepherd, D. A., & Zacharakis, A. (2002). VCs' expertise: A call for research into decision aids and cognitive feedback. *Journal of Business Venturing, 17*, 1–20.

Simon, M., Houghton, S. M., & Aquino, K. (2000). Cognitive biases, risk perceptions, and venture formation: How individuals decide to start companies. *Journal of Business Venturing, 15*, 113–134.

Sternberg, R. J. (2004). Successful intelligence as a basis for entrepreneurship. *Journal of Business Venturing, 19*, 189–202.

Stewart, W., & Roth, P. (2001). Risk taking propensity differences between entrepreneurs and mangers: A meta-analytic review. *Journal of Applied Psychology, 86*, 145–153.

Tierney, P., & Farmer, S. M. (2002). Creative self-efficacy: Potential antecedents and relationship to creative performance. *Academy of Management Journal, 45*, 1137–1148.

Vecchio, R. P. (2003). Entrepreneurship and leadership: Common trends and common threads. *Human Resource Management Review, 13*, 303–328.

Venkataraman, S. (1997). The distinctive domain of entrepreneurship research: An editor's perspective. In J. Katz & R. Brockhaus (Eds.), *Advances in entrepreneurship, firm emergence, and growth* (pp. 119–138). Greenwich, CT: JAI Press.

3

Born to Be an Entrepreneur? Revisiting the Personality Approach to Entrepreneurship

Andreas Rauch
Michael Frese

> I believe that … a focus on the traits and personality characteristics of entre-
> preneurs will never lead us to a definition of the entrepreneur nor help us to
> understand the phenomenon of entrepreneurship. (Gartner, 1989, p. 48)

The personality approach is one of the classical and early approaches to entrepreneurship. At the same time, it is one of the more controversial areas of
research. The personality approach to entrepreneurship has been criticized
in the entrepreneurship literature with the following arguments (Aldrich &
Wiedenmayer, 1993; Brockhaus & Horwitz, 1985; Gartner, 1989; Low &
MacMillan, 1988): Entrepreneurship requires too varied behaviors to be related to specific personality traits; personality traits are not strongly
enough related to entrepreneurship to warrant further studies; and alternative views, such as ecological approaches, have been proposed that concentrate on environmental accounts. These arguments were quite effective and
led to the dominant position in entrepreneurship research that works on
personality traits should be discontinued (Low & MacMillan, 1988). A similar position seemed to exist for a while in organizational behavior and in-
dustrial/organizational psychology, as well: Here similar arguments on
the lack of usefulness of personality prediction of performance (and leadership) were voiced (Guion & Gottier, 1965). Much of this started out with the
book by Mischel (1968) arguing that results on personality constructs were
limited by $r = .30$ to explain meaningful behaviors and that there was lack of

cross-situational consistency in personality variables. However, over time, the tide changed and there is now a revival of personality research in performance and leadership research and in many other areas of industrial/organizational psychology too. There is now the consensus that there is ample evidence for the validity of certain personality variables for organization behavior (Barrick & Mount, 1991) and for leadership (Judge, Bono, Ilies, & Gerhardt, 2002).

This revival of personality research became possible because a number of solutions to the challenge by Mischel (1968) were proposed: First, personality dispositions need to be sampled across different situations and occasions and can then predict reasonably well a class of behaviors; however, personality traits are not able to predict a single behavioral act: "As broad dispositions, traits cannot be expected to be very good predictors of individual acts" (Epstein & O'Brien, 1985, p. 532).

Second, the predictive power of personality traits becomes higher, if one takes the interaction of personality and situational parameters into account (Magnusson & Endler, 1977). For example, if the task requirements of the industry imply a high degree of direct customer access with different customers, then extraversion should be a more important predictor of success within this setting than in other settings (Vinchur, Schippmann, Switzer, & Roth, 1998). Also, the difference between strong situations (personality has little impact) and weak situations (personality effects are strong) is important here (Mischel, 1968).

Third, the predictive power of personality traits becomes more transparent when differentiating between proximal and distal variables. In other words, personality research should model both process and general traits, and more specific traits might lead to more specific processes (Kanfer, 1992b). Proximal individual differences (such as goal orientation and self-efficacy; Baum & Locke, 2004) are nearer to behavior and more powerful predictors of behavior than distal individual differences (such as conscientiousness) (Rauch & Frese, 2000).

Fourth, in a groundbreaking article, Mischel and Shoda (1998) went one step beyond the proximal/distal differentiation and argued that it is possible and necessary to develop a unitary approach integrating personality traits and personality dynamics—the latter looking at variables, such as encoding, expectancies and beliefs, affects, goals and values, competencies, and self-regulatory plans. We should not reify individual differences: They may not be causal agents, even if they predict behavior; we need to be able to describe the dynamics of how individual differences have an influence on behavior. A good understanding of individual differences "requires an integrated conceptual scheme that classifies not only behaviors, but specifies their determinants and key mechanisms through which they operate" (Bandura, 1999, p. 200).

Fifth, it is surprising that the one individual difference that has been shown to be the highest predictor of performance, cognitive ability (Hunter & Hunter, 1984), which is also one of the best studied individual difference variables in psychology, has not been researched much within entrepreneurship (with a few exception, e.g., Frese et al., 2004; Ray & Singh, 1980). We do not concentrate on cognitive ability within this chapter, because we focus on personality-related individual differences. However, we suggest that cognitive ability needs to be considered in entrepreneurship research. This may be done in a way similar to performance research within industrial/organizational psychology, where it is considered a baseline factor.

Sixth, many personality advocates assume that there are linear relationships between a personality variable and success (or performance). However, it is necessary to test in all cases whether there are nonlinear relationships. For example, people may be too ambitious, too risk oriented, too achievement oriented, to self-efficacious, or too optimistic. In contrast to achievement tests (such as cognitive ability), more of the same thing may not be a good thing at all. Thus, we urge future researchers to test for nonlinear relationships and editors to insist on such tests.

Seventh, the method of meta-analysis—the quantitative review of articles—has dramatically changed our view of the function of personality. Beginning with Barrick and Mount's (1991) meta-analysis, the relationship between personality traits and performance became obvious; in addition, meta-analyses showed that personality traits can add explained variance in performance over and above intelligence (Schmidt & Hunter, 1998).

Eighth, one function of meta-analysis has been that people started to take small correlations more seriously again. Hunter and Schmidt (1990) explicated that any individual study invariably exhibits methodological problems that weaken the relationship between constructs, such as sampling biases, lack of reliability of measurements, and lack of statistical power. When several studies are taken together and when appropriate corrections for some of the methodological problems are used, the correlations become clearer and higher. With the use of meta-analysis, Barrick and Mount's (1991) result that conscientiousness was related to job performance, with an adjusted $r = .22$, could be compared to other areas of inquiry. Many relationships in medicine (Meyer et al., 2001) and physics (Hedges, 1987) are small as well, and these sciences take them seriously. Moreover, the importance of small correlations for practical purposes has been discussed in more detail elsewhere (Abelson, 1985; Rosenthal & Rubin, 1982).

Finally, differentiation in the dependent variables—performance—has led to new insights and more differentiated prediction models. Research on personality and performance quickly showed that relationships between personality and performance varied depending on what kind of class of performance was researched. The differentiation between task and contextual performance was most important. With contextual performance contributing "to organizational effectiveness in ways that shape the organizational, social, and psychological context that serves as the catalyst for task activities and processes," for example, by helping each other in a work group, it became obvious that personality factors contributed more strongly to contextual performance than to task performance (Borman & Motowidlo, 1997, p. 100).

We argue in this chapter that entrepreneurship should be an active participant in the revival of personality research, although it should use more sophisticated theories and methodological approaches, as implied in the nine points just discussed. Personality traits, individual differences, or dispositions are defined by their propensity to act (Baron, 1981), by being consistent across various situations, and by being stable over time (Caprana & Cervone, 2000). Thus, personality characteristics are enduring dispositions that show a high degree of stability across time (Roccas, Sagiv, Schwartz, & Knafo, 2002), although there is no question that there are quickly changing personality factors (the states) as well as slowly changing parts of personality (Nesselroade, 1991). It is a common misunderstanding to assume that all behavior is determined by a trait. This is definitely not the case: A personality trait is a disposition, not a determination. Only broad classes of behaviors are predicted by personality traits (Epstein & O'Brien, 1985). A person can chose to behave against his or her disposition, and it is a common experience of entrepreneurs that they have to manage their personality. Thus, it makes very little sense to expect a high relationship between any one personality trait and specific decisions by an entrepreneur (Epstein & O'Brien, 1985).

In the following, we attempt to summarize the literature on personality traits and entrepreneurship. However, we are not able to do justice to all of the new developments within both personality (e.g., a real integration of trait research and personality dynamics) and entrepreneurship; for example, we do not describe individual differences that have been newly developed for entrepreneurship (e.g., passion for work) or that have opened up new and fascinating areas of inquiry of individual differences within entrepreneurship research (e.g., cognitive individual differences or action strategies); they are discussed in other chapters of this volume (cf. Baron, chap. 2; Markman, chap. 4; Locke & Baum, chap. 5; Busenitz & Arthurs, chap. 7; Frese, chap. 8; and Baron, Frese, & Baum, chap. 16).

We base our chapter on recent meta-analyses of personality factors, among others one that we have performed (Collins, Hanges, & Locke, 2004; Rauch & Frese, 2005; Stewart & Roth, 2004[1]). A meta-analysis allows one to do a quantitative review of individual differences. This is advantageous be-

---

[1]We report r = sample size weighted mean correlation. Corrected r = corrected for unreliability.

cause each individual study has power problems (lack of statistical significance may be related to a small sample size), sample problems, reliability problems, and idiosyncratic problems of this study. Often narrative reviews rely on statistical significance as the most important indicator of the size of a relationship and inappropriately weight studies equally. Moreover, narrative reviews tend to conform to biases that have become commonplace in an area of science. For these reasons, meta-analyses often lead to surprising results. They have changed medicine and within medicine many thousand of meta-analyses have been done. However, a meta-analysis has to rely on the articles published on each personality trait and a minimum number of articles forms the basis of meta-analysis. Because new areas often have too few studies in these areas, a meta-analysis falls short of summarizing that part of the literature that is particularly new and challenging but that has not been tested in several articles. This is one reason why we cannot do justice to all the eight points discussed earlier and do not discuss some new developments that have taken place in entrepreneurship research (but compare the other chapters of this book).

We first present a very short historical account of the relevant literature, then present a general model of the relationship between personality and entrepreneurship, differentiating between broad (general and distal) constructs and more specific (more proximal) traits, and, finally, present some conclusions of this literature review.

PERSONALITY AND ENTREPRENEURSHIP: HISTORICAL BACKGROUND

Personality characteristics of entrepreneurs had already been included in classical economic theorizing. For example, Schumpeter (1935) incorporated concepts similar to innovativeness, achievement orientation, dominance, and other personality factors of the entrepreneur into theories of economic development. Knight (1921) viewed entrepreneurship as risk taking under uncertainty, and Hayek (1941) conceptualized knowledge and entrepreneurial discovery as driving forces for economic development. McClelland (1961) took up these economic ideas and explained economic wealth of nations as due, at least in part, to differences in achievement motivation. His theory received widespread attention in entrepreneurship research. McClelland (1961) related the concept of achievement motivation to entrepreneurship and economic development, although not all replications found the same significant effect (e.g., Frey, 1984). In entrepreneurship research, the interest in achievement motivation shifted from economic/societal level to the level of the individual business owner, and achievement motivation became the personality theory probably most frequently studied, reaching a peak level during the 1980s.

In addition, a high number of different traits of entrepreneurs were studied as well (Hornaday & Aboud, 1971; Timmons, Smollen, & Dingee, 1985). Unfortunately, this high diversity of traits that were studied seemed to indicate that there was no theoretical consensus about the basic "entrepreneurial" dispositions in the relevant literature. Moreover, a number of different narrative reviews reported inconsistent and conflicting empirical evidence for the relationship between personality traits and entrepreneurship and, as a consequence, the personality approach was heavily criticized during the 1990s (e.g., Brockhaus & Horwitz, 1985; Chell, Haworth, & Brearley, 1991; Cooper & Gimeno-Gascon, 1992; Davis-Blake & Pfeffer, 1989; Gartner, 1989). The arguments and consequences were: First, most studies on entrepreneurs' characteristics were purely descriptive without providing a theoretical framework for their study (Low & MacMillan, 1988). A conceptual link between the personality, business creation, and success was not established (Low & MacMillan, 1988). Surprisingly, one of the consequences was, however, that true effects may have been under- rather than overestimated (Johnson, 2003; Tett, Steele, & Beaurgard, 2003) because the relationship of relevant traits with entrepreneurship may have drowned in the noise of unimportant trait–entrepreneurship relationships. Second, nearly all the traditional research and reviews utilized simplified assumptions and ignored potential mediating processes as well as situational contingencies. Third, methodologically, the quality in entrepreneurship research was (and still is) weak (Low & MacMillan, 1988; Smith, Gannon, & Sapienza, 1989). A consequence may be that true effects of personality traits are underestimated, for example, when power deficits of individual studies are generalized wrongly as evidence for rejecting the hypothesis (beta error).

No wonder that narrative reviews have most often come to negative results. Only very recently, meta-analytic evidence (Collins et al., 2004; Rauch & Frese, 2005; Stewart & Roth, 2004) has been accumulated, challenging the narrative reviews of the 1990s.

A PROPOSED MODEL OF ENTREPRENEURS' PERSONALITY CHARACTERISTICS

A variant of our Giessen-Amsterdam model (Rauch & Frese, 2000) is presented in Fig. 3.1. It describes pathways through which individual differences affect business success. The model is compatible with the proximal/distal distinction (Johnson, 2003; Kanfer, 1992a) as well as with empirically established entrepreneurship growth models (Baum, Locke, & Smith, 2001). The model describes how general (broad) personality traits may affect the personality dynamics of setting goals and developing strategies that, in turn, affect business creation and success. The model assumes that the effects of broad personality traits are not directly related to business

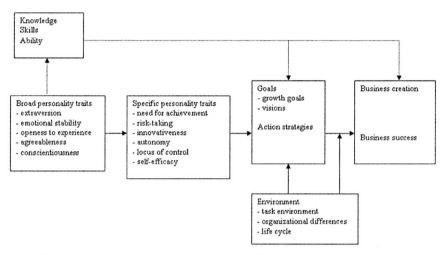

Figure 3.1. A model of entrepreneurs' personality characteristics and success.

outcomes but because they influence traits that are more specific/proximal to entrepreneurship, for example, need for achievement, risk taking, and innovativeness. These more specific traits, in turn, affect goals and action strategies and, as a result, business success. Moreover, the effects of these specific traits are dependent on environmental variables. Although the model includes nonpersonality variables, our review in this chapter concentrates on personality variables. Obviously, there are many nonexplained constructs that may play a role, such as cognitive styles, biases, heuristics, self-regulation, and so on, which we have not described in this model. The model relies on constructs that have been studied within entrepreneurship literature and constitutes a convenient summary of our approach in this chapter; it does not aspire to be complete.

Broad Personality Traits of Entrepreneurs

We argue in this chapter that broad traits should be less strongly related to business creation and success than more specific personality traits. Broad trait taxonomies do not address those behaviors most important for entrepreneurship and therefore lead to low correlations at best. However, we also argue that there are meaningful relationships between some broad personality traits and business creation and success, because otherwise, we could not maintain a mediator model as described in Fig. 3.1, which hypothesizes broad personality traits to have an effect on business creation and success via specific personality traits and even more specific dynamic parameters of the person, such as goals and strategies.

One of the most frequently used broad trait taxonomies is the Big Five personality taxonomy (Costa & McCrae, 1988). Such taxonomies have been extensively studied in organizational behavior. Meta-analyses indicated consistent positive relationships with employees' job performances. Extraversion, agreeableness, and openness to experience correlate differentially with job performance in different occupations, whereas emotional stability and conscientiousness are the most important variables predicting performance across different occupations (Barrick, Mount, & Judge, 2001).

In entrepreneurship research such broad taxonomies have been less frequently studied and with varying success. One article (Brandstätter, 1997) found no differences between business owners and nonowners, and emotional stability and independence were positively correlated with success; a second one (Wooton & Timmerman, 1999) indicated that openness to experience was negatively related to business startup; and a third one (Ciaverella, Buchholtz, Riordan, Gatewood, & Stokes, 2004) reported a negative relationship between openness to experience and survival and a positive relationship between conscientiousness and survival.

In spite of this disappointing contradictory evidence, a meta-analysis showed that general and broad traits related significantly to entrepreneurial success with $r = .151$ (Rauch & Frese, 2005). Although this relationship is smaller than for more specific traits (where r was .231), it would be premature to conclude that broad personality measures are not at all useful in the prediction of entrepreneurial success. The difference between broad personality traits and specific ones was even more pronounced when considering the question of business creation, with broad measures not being significantly related to business creation whereas there was $r = .244$ for specific personality measures (Rauch & Frese, 2005).

Specific Personality Traits of Entrepreneurs

Broad traits, such as the Big Five, are distal and aggregated constructs, and they may predict aggregated classes of behavior but not specific behaviors (Epstein & O'Brien, 1985). Therefore, the Big Five traits are well related to aggregated classes of performance, such as overall supervisor ratings for employees (Barrick & Mount, 1991). Entrepreneurship research frequently uses more specific performance concepts, such as sales growth and accounting-based criteria. Therefore, the predictive validity of Big Five traits should be lower in entrepreneurship research than in research on employees.

Starting a business or business growth may be driven by more specific behaviors, and therefore more proximal constructs should be more closely related to the tasks of entrepreneurs than the broad traits (Baum & Locke, 2004). Particularly, these specific traits should be related to the tasks of entrepreneurship. However, there was no attempt to do a "task analysis" of

what entrepreneurs have to do well to succeed in developing a business.[2]
The vast majority of studies on entrepreneurs' personality used criterion
validated concepts of personality rather than broad trait measures. Rauch
and Frese (2005) classified studies on entrepreneurs' traits according to the
specificity of personality assessment. The meta-analysis indicated that specific traits produced higher relationships with both business creation and
business success than global trait measures. These were the specific personality traits: need for achievement, risk-taking, innovativeness, autonomy,
locus of control, and self-efficacy.

Need for Achievement.   Owners with high need for achievement prefer moderately challenging tasks rather than routine or very difficult
tasks, take personal responsibility for their performance, seek feedback
about their performance, and search for new and better ways to improve
their performance. The validity of achievement motivation is surprisingly
well established: Two meta-analyses indicate that business owners, as
compared to other populations, have a higher need for achievement (corrected $r = .227$ and $r = .242$; Rauch & Frese, 2005, and Collins et al., 2004, respectively). Additionally, entrepreneurs' need for achievement is
positively correlated with business success (corrected $r = .314$ and $r = .260$,
Rauch & Frese, 2005, and Collins et al., 2004, respectively). These effect
sizes are as high as the effects of sleeping pills on the improvement of in-
somnia (which is $r = .30$; Meyer et al., 2001). These data suggest that need
for achievement is an important characteristic of successful entrepreneurs. We recommend that need for achievement be included in studies
that want to understand the process of how success develops. Newer concepts, such as passion for work, that are related to the achievement motive
and that were developed specifically for entrepreneurship should be
shown to add explained variance in comparison to measures of achievement motives (Baum & Locke, 2004; cf. Locke & Baum, chap. 5).

Risk Taking.   Risk taking was included in early economic theorizing
(Knight, 1921) and received a considerable amount of empirical attention.
Risk taking is usually defined either as a probability function or as an individual disposition towards risk. Combining both aspects, Chell et al. (1991)
described a risk taker as someone "who in the context of a business venture,
pursues a business idea when the probability of succeeding is low" (p. 42).
There are two competing theoretical positions regarding the effects of risk-
taking propensity on entrepreneurship and success (Stewart & Roth, 2004):

---

[2]In fairness to this literature we should add that a better and more precise understanding of
what entrepreneurs need to do, for example, detection and exploitation of opportunities, has
only recently been elaborated (cf. Baum et al., chap. 1; Baron, chap. 2; Busenitz, chap. 7; Baron
et al., chap. 16).

direct linear relationship of risk taking with creation and success, or a curvilinear relationship. The first position hypothesizes that entrepreneurs have a higher risk-taking propensity than other people because entrepreneurship is concerned with decision making under uncertainty (e.g. Knight, 1921). As a consequence, risk-tolerant individuals are more likely to start a business than risk-averse people. The vast majority of studies actually attempted to test such direct relationships (and, therefore, meta-analyses have only looked at this aspect). The second position of a curvilinear relationship between risk taking and entrepreneurship can be, for example, based on McClelland's (1961) need for achievement theory. Entrepreneurs are high in need for achievement (discussed earlier), and need for achievement leads to moderate risk taking (Timmons et al., 1985). The effect of risk-taking propensity is unfortunately linked to different perspectives; a nonowner might view a particular behavior as highly risky, whereas a business owner might see the same behavior as an attempt to minimize risk (Chell et al., 1991).

Two meta-analyses reported on the direct linear relationship of risk-taking on entrepreneurship and came to essentially the same results in spite of slight differences in methodologies. Stewart and Roth (2004) analyzed 18 studies on differences in risk-taking propensity of entrepreneurs and managers and reported an average relationship of $r = .11$, whereas we found a corrected $r = .118$ (Rauch & Frese, 2005). In addition, Rauch and Frese (2005) analyzed risk-taking propensity–success relationships and reported a corrected $r = .092$. The overall relationships between risk taking, entrepreneurship, and success were heterogeneous, indicating the presence of moderators. It is important to note that Miner and Raju's (2004) meta-analysis reported the opposite conclusions. We do, however, concur with Stewart and Roth's (2004) reply that the Miner and Raju (1994) study incorrectly included effect sizes from studies not relevant for to the research question, effects sizes from dependent samples, and effect sizes from studies that confused constructs. Thus, we believe that this study is not a good indication for contradicting findings, but rather an example of how wrongly included effect sizes affect meta-analytic outcomes.

Thus, we conclude that the effect of risk-taking propensity on entrepreneurship and business success is positive and significant, but small. It is also smaller in comparison to other personality characteristics (Rauch & Frese, 2005). Therefore, we suggest to test in the future, whether the curvilinear relationship between entrepreneurs' risk taking, business creation, and success appears to be true and to use alternative (and possibly more objective) approaches to assessing risk-taking propensity—as in simulated environments, in decision making (cf. use of heuristics in Busenitz, chap. 7) or scenario techniques.

Innovativeness.   Similar to need for achievement and risk-taking, innovativeness has been one of the core concepts of Schumpeter's approach to entrepreneurship (e.g., Drucker, 1993; Schumpeter, 1935). Innovativeness assumes a person's willingness and interest to look for novel ways of action (e.g., Patchen, 1965). It implies that a business owner tends to introduce new products, new services, new markets, new processes of production, new technologies, and new research into the firm. Innovativeness can be described as a person characteristic; however, the implementation of innovations cannot usually be done by one person alone and usually needs to be studied on the level of the firm (Klein & Sorra, 1996).

Cumulative evidence indicates entrepreneurs are more innovative than other people (corrected r = .235) and innovativeness is positively correlated with success (corrected r = .220; Rauch & Frese, 2005). The latter effect is homogeneous, indicating that the innovativeness of business owners is directly related to business success, and that an additional search for moderators may not be useful. Note, however, that we concentrated in this meta-analysis on the personality variable innovativeness. Entrepreneurship research has also studied the innovativeness of the firm on the firm level (not the owner's level). We assume that firm-level characteristics are affected by an owner's personality, and thus, firm-level innovativeness assesses how far the owner was successful in making innovativeness a common approach of the whole firm and not just of the owner. Interestingly, innovativeness at the level of the individual business owner produces correlations with success similar to those of innovativeness at the level of the firm (corrected r = .209; Rauch, Wiklund, Frese, & Lumpkin, 2005). Environmental demands moderated the effect of innovativeness on the firm level (in spite of the fact that there was no indication for moderator effects on the firm owner's level): Innovativeness is more important in new-technology firms than in firms working within traditional industries.

Thus, the innovativeness of the individual entrepreneur is directly related to business creation and to business success. This relationship is of moderate size (Cohen, 1977). By the way, it is surprising that as far as we know, traditional measures of creativity (or divergent intelligence) have rarely been studied in entrepreneurship research (an exception is, e.g., Heunks, 1996).

Autonomy.   The popular literature is full of anecdotal evidence of entrepreneurs leaving their secure positions in established organizations to start their independent venture. In contrast to employees, entrepreneurs have to make decisions in the absence of supervisors, they have to independently set goals and develop plans of actions, and they have to control goal achievement themselves. People high in autonomy are uniquely suited to this type of job. They want to be in control; they avoid the restrictions and rules of established organizations and thus choose the entrepreneurial role (Brandstätter, 1997; Cromie, 2000). Some scholars have even described entrepreneurs as deviant, psychopathic, and unable to adapt to rules and norms of an established organization (e.g., Collins & Moore, 1970). Although personality differences in autonomy between entrepreneurs and nonentrepreneurs are plausible, the relationship between need for autonomy and success is not as easily developed on a theoretical basis. Need for autonomy may actually obstruct venture growth because it may hamper effective cooperation with others, even though this is one of the prerequisites of getting high (venture) capital investments. On the other hand, need for autonomy may contribute to survival because the entrepreneur tries hard to maintain an independent business because he or she is very motivated not to have a boss above him or her.

The empirical literature indicates some support for differences in autonomy between entrepreneurs and nonentrepreneurs (corrected r = .144; Rauch & Frese, 2005). A number of studies analyzed autonomy–success relationships, and the overall effect is positive and significant (corrected r = .162, Rauch & Frese, 2005). Unfortunately, none of the studies used growth as the dependent variable, making it impossible to answer the hypothesis that need for autonomy may hamper growth.

Locus of Control.   The concept of internal locus of control implies that one believes in controlling one's destiny and future (Rotter, 1966). People with an external locus of control believe that they are controlled by others or outside (often chance) events. The construct is supposed to be important for entrepreneurs because believing in one's own active influence helps to increase the motivation to reach success. In contrast, externally controlled people may be more passive. If one believes that one is not able to control business outcomes, one has no reasons to actively change one's environment.

Earlier narrative reviews reported inconsistent and conflicting evidence between internal locus of control, entrepreneurship, and success (e.g., Chell et al., 1991; Cooper & Gimeno-Gascon, 1992). A meta-analysis on 20 studies demonstrated, however, small, positive, and significant differences between owners' and nonowners' internal locus of control (corrected r = .199), as well as positive correlations between internal locus of control and success (corrected r = .108; Rauch & Frese, 2005). Both effects are small, significant, and heterogeneous, indicating the presence of moderators. The use of different scales—mainly Rotter's (1966) and Levenson's (1974) scales—may have contributed to increase error variance. On the other hand, some studies are quite conservative, because locus of control should be similarly high in managers; however, it was often managers that were compared to entrepreneurs. Managers, like entrepreneurs, should believe that they control outcomes, and therefore other comparison groups may produce higher differences in locus of control.

Self-Efficacy.   Self-efficacy is the belief to be able to perform a certain action effectively. People with high self-efficacy are likely to persevere when problems arise and search for opportunities to take actions to ameliorate problems (Bandura, 1982, 1997); they also show a higher degree of personal initiative (Speier & Frese, 1997); they have higher hopes for success and, therefore, take a long-term perspective (Heckhausen & Schulz, 1995); they also actively search for information (Ashford & Tsui, 1991), which leads to a better knowledge. Self-efficacy has been shown to be related to performance in employees (Stajkovic & Luthans, 1998). Evidence for the importance of self-efficacy in entrepreneurship begin to mount more recently. Most studies in entrepreneurship use a self-efficacy measure that is of medium generality; thus, it is not as general as a general trait but not as specific as the belief that one can do one task well. Empirical studies indicate that entrepreneurs are higher in self-efficacy than nonentrepreneurs (Markman, Baron, & Balkin, 2005; Utsch, Rauch, Rothfuss, & Frese, 1999). Moreover, self-efficacy showed the highest correlation with success in a meta-analysis (corrected $r = .419$; Rauch & Frese, 2005). Such a correlation is as a high as the correlation between weight and height in U.S. adults, one of the highest medical relationships (Meyer et al., 2001).

CONCLUSION

There are small to moderate relationships between personality traits, business creation, and business success. Business owners as compared to other populations are higher in need for achievement, risk propensity, innovativeness, and internal locus of control (Collins et al., 2004; Rauch & Frese, 2005; Stewart & Roth, 2004). These personality traits are additionally related to business success. Thus, the empirical evidence reviewed in this chapter leads to the conclusion that all those who have called for the end of doing research on personality traits for lack of important relationships with entrepreneurship are clearly wrong.

Why have these theoreticians and narrative reviews been so wrong? The answer is that there simply is lots of distracting "noise" in the data: Some relationships are, indeed, very small—for example, the relationship of risk taking with both business creation and success or the relationship between business creation and broad personality measures. Also, whenever people throw in all sorts of personality variables and correlate them with all sorts of dependent variables, the correlations appear to be quite small. Moreover, there are large variations in the size of the reported relationships and many studies are based on small samples. All of this made it difficult to detect the "true" relationships of personality with entrepreneurship as long as only narrative reviews were used. Meta-analyses have helped to show that there are clear and important relationships that have been easy to overlook in those narrative interviews. But it is also an issue of interpretation. Smaller correlations are now interpreted to be more meaningful because as meta-analyses have been utilized in various sciences and as results become comparable across disciplines, scholars see more clearly that medium sized correlations dominate in most disciplines, not just in personality research but also in other areas of psychological research, as well as in physics (Hedges, 1987) and medicine (Meyer et al., 2001). This is not so surprising. The entrepreneurial decision to really go ahead, start the firm, keep up the spirit, and make the first sales or entrepreneurial success are multiply determined. This means any *one* predictor of success is unlikely to determine success. Only a complete set of multiple determinants functions in some additive (and sometimes multiplicative) way to predict success. Entrepreneurship is multiply determined; therefore, high correlations should be a cause of concern because methodological problems often produce artificial relationships. In contrast, in such an area, we should expect only small or moderate correlations. Thus, the criterion is *not* the size of the correlation per se any longer, but the size of the increment that variables show above and beyond a basic set of variables.

Entrepreneurship research should develop a set of variables that have been shown in careful meta-analyses to be important. In order to be able to do this, a number or primary studies still have to be done. We think that the number of studies on the achievement motive is adequate (we found more than 30 useable studies for our meta-analysis) to draw this conclusion at this point in time, whereas we are hesitant to draw a similar conclusion on self-efficacy, although this variable showed a higher degree of relationship with success (but there were fewer studies that could be included into a meta-analysis). Given current knowledge, and based on the three meta-analyses discussed in this chapter, we suggest that entrepreneurship research should prove that future constructs show added explanation of variance on top of some measure of the achievement motive (and, similarly, a set of economic predictors). Probably future studies and meta-analyses will also show that entrepreneurship needs to include cognitive ability into such a basic set of variables—at least, performance research in the employee setting suggests that this might be an important variable. However, to our knowledge, there are as yet only a few studies that included cognitive ability into entrepreneurship research (e.g., Frese et al., 2005; Ray & Singh, 1980), but research on education as an important predictor of success suggests that cognitive ability may be an important basic variable in entrepreneurship research as well.

Thus, personality traits relate to business creation and success in general. More specific conclusions relate to the issue of specificity and broadness of personality traits, the match between independent and dependent variable, the level-of-analysis problems, mediator and contingency approaches, and quality issues.

The Issue of Specificity and Broadness of Personality Traits and Criterion Measures

It has helped to differentiate between broad and specific personality traits. The specific traits should follow from a rudimentary task analysis of entrepreneurship. Specific traits showed higher relationships with business creation and success than the broad traits (Rauch & Frese, 2005). Broad personality traits are highly aggregated across time and situations and therefore do not predict specific behaviors in specific situations. Therefore, there is only a weak although significant relationship between broad personality traits and entrepreneurial success (Rauch & Frese, 2005). A similar effect of specificity was found for employee performance as well (Tett, Steele, & Beaurgard, 2003).

It is noteworthy that the specificity issue just discussed is not restricted to the personality variable but also to the criterion variable (Hattrup & Jackson, 1996). However, most studies of the personality approach to entrepreneurship ignore the level of specificity issue. Global traits as aggregated characteristics are likely to be related to aggregated classes of behavior but not to specific behaviors (Epstein & O'Brien, 1985). Thus, independent and dependent variables should be at the same level of generality to produce high and meaningful relationships (Wittmann, 2002). Entrepreneurship for good reasons is not forced to use overall success rating (e.g., by a supervisor or peer) but rather uses some more specific measures of success, such as growth in sales or in the number of employees, number of new products introduced, or profit rate. More specific personality variables should correlate with specific criterion variables (e.g., innovativeness with number of introduced innovations).

It follows from Fig. 3.1 that if the specificity of traits and their proximity to behavior are important, then even more proximal constructs, namely, processes related to personality, such as cognitive or self-regulatory processes, can lead to even stronger relationships. In fact, research on such proximal constructs has recently started, and some of the studies found strong predictors of success for goal setting and goal communication (Baum et al., 1998), specific self-efficacy (Baum et al., 2001; Chen et al., 1998), personal initiative (Koop, De Reu, & Frese, 2000), action strategies (Frese, van Gelderen, & Ombach, 2000), and cognitive processes and biases

(Baron, 2004). These proximal individual difference constructs are often not defined as consistent behavior across time and situation and are therefore not discussed in this review about the effects of personality traits on entrepreneurship (see, however, many of the other chapters in this book).

The Match Between Independent and Dependent Variables

Future work might want to be more specific with regard to the match between independent and dependent variables: Match hypothesis assumes higher correlations if the dependent variable is highly relevant for the independent variable. Match hypothesis has, for example, been useful in the area of social support and stress at work (Cohen & Wills, 1985; Frese, 1999). Whenever social support matched to the social nature of the stressors (independent variable) and the social nature of the stress reaction (dependent variable), there were high effects for social support (Frese, 1999). The match hypothesis for entrepreneurship research would suggest that visions and goals that are explicitly related to growth might be related to the dependent variable growth of the firm (Baum et al., 1998). Similarly, the achievement motive is likely to be related to a keen interest in the task of what is produced or serviced (e.g., a programmer who has founded a firm and who loves to do programming); this leads to the hypothesis that the dependent variable most highly related to the achievement motive is whether an entrepreneurial unit stays innovative in the area. In contrast, we do not suggest that achievement motive should be highly related to growth, because the entrepreneur may fear that he or she will become a general manager and cannot be involved in the task of programming any longer if the firm becomes too large.

Thus, we suggest that we should develop differential hypotheses on the relationship between specific traits with specific dependent variables. It may pay off to differentiate various success measures, for example, survival and firm stability, growth, being at the forefront of innovations, and profit rate. Matching independent and dependent variables would suggest that achievement motives should be less related to profit rate than rate of innovation, because profit is not what high achievement is after; need for autonomy may be related more to survival than to growth; risk taking may be negatively related to survival but positively (among the survivors) to profit rate; and so on.

The Level-of-Analysis Problem in Entrepreneurship Research

Personality is usually assessed at the level of the individual business owner, whereas success is often assessed at the level of the firm. This poses another thorny issue of the level of analysis (Klein, Dansereau, & Hall, 1994). Most studies of entrepreneurs' personality do not discuss this issue explicitly; we therefore suggest that it needs to be explicated. In microbusinesses (up to 10 employees), it makes sense that the personality of entrepreneurs has a direct relationship with business success—the individual owner is probably making most of the important decisions and his or her actions are most important for the success of the company. However, already in small companies (up to 50 employees) it is unclear whether this is still the right level of analysis. For larger companies—for example, for midsize companies above 50 employees—a simple relationship between the entrepreneur's personality and business success makes little conceptual sense. Here the following causal chain is more likely: The personality of the founder influences the culture of the company at some time, and it is then the culture or climate of the company that leads to higher or lower success rates. In general, the correspondence of the level of analysis issue suggests that personality characteristics should be more highly related to individual-level outcomes than to firm-level outcomes variables and that these relationships should be higher in small firms than in large ones.

Mediator Approaches to the Effects of Personality Traits on Entrepreneurship

Most researchers of the personality approach agree that distal personality traits are not directly related to success, but their effects are mediated by more specific, proximal processes, such as motives, cognitive processes, or self-regulatory processes (Barrick, Mitchell & Steward, 2003; Epstein & O'Brien, 1985; Johnson, 2003; Kanfer, 1992a). We similarly assume that mediators explain the effect of personality traits on entrepreneurship. Broad personality traits are related to success because they impact specific traits, goals, and strategies, which, in turn, affect business success.

In entrepreneurship research, such mediating processes are rarely studied and therefore there is too little literature here to summarize mediating processes in a meta-analysis. Examples of empirical studies are those of Baum and Locke (2004), who showed that motivation mediates personality–success relationships in small enterprises, and of Frese et al. (2005), who provided evidence for active planning of action strategies to mediate personality–success relationships. Two additional studies showed that business strategy mediates between personality traits and business success (Baum, 1995; Rauch, Frese, & Sonnentag, 2000).

Contingency Approaches to the Effects of Personality on Entrepreneurship

The high variation in the correlations between personality traits and entrepreneurship reported in the literature is an indication for the presence of moderator effects. The function of moderator effects on the relationship between entrepreneur's personality and business success has been rarely studied, and therefore there are not enough empirical studies in this area to cumulate the empirical evidence by using a meta-analytical approach. However, we believe that personality traits have an influence on entrepreneurship, depending on contingencies. Such contingencies affect the function of broad traits but may become even more important when studying specific traits. For example, self-efficacy can be general but it can also be task specific. Task specificity of self-efficacy might be a moderator of the relationship between trait self-efficacy and entrepreneurship. Including such contingencies into a model of the effects of personality traits of entrepreneurs should increase the predictive power of the model.

Many personality psychologists argue that the interaction between individuals' traits and situational conditions predicts behavior better than any one of these factors alone (Bandura, 1986; Magnusson & Endler, 1977). Personality traits can affect behavior only if the situational constraints allow their expression (Mischel, 1968). Unfortunately, there is a lack of research and theory on the relevant context conditions (Barrick et al., 2003). Mischel (1968) conceptualized situations according to their strengths. A strong situation determines behavior because of well-established expectations and incentives. Thus, in strong situations people behave similarly, regardless of individual differences. Weak situations, on the other hand, provide greater possibilities for individual interpretation and action. Hattrup and Jackson's (1996) review of the strength of situations identified four situational categories relevant for the expression of individual differences in organizations: information attributes, task attributes, physical attributes, and social attributes. For example, situations with little and ambiguous information are weaker than situations with better information and less ambiguity. Tasks with low structure and high autonomy are weak and therefore allow the expression of individual differences. This classification suggests that entrepreneurship may be a weak situation in general because entrepreneurs have to maneuver in a situation with high autonomy and low structure and they have to make decisions based on uncertain and ambiguous information. Thus, personality traits should relate to business creation and success. Another classification of situations can be developed based on the favorability of the task environment of organizations, for example, environmental complexity, dynamism, and munificence (Dess & Beard, 1984). Unfavorable environments may constrain the expression of individual traits. Favorable environments (e.g., growing markets and demands) may allow the expression of individual traits. Clearly, these are just a few ideas; we need better theoretical conceptualizations of the situational/environmental variables that interact with the effects of personality traits.

Contingencies are rarely studied. One problem may be that we do not have good and valid classifications of potential situational variables. Also, moderator analyses are invariably conservative because of power and methodological issues (McClelland & Judd, 1993). One moderator frequently discussed in entrepreneurship research is business creation versus success (Begley & Boyd, 1987). Different personality traits may affect these two situations differently. For example, people high in risk propensity may be more likely to start a business because they do not fear losing the incentives of employed work. However, running a business in a risky way may not be related to positive business outcomes. Two meta-analyses tested this moderator effect but did not find support for the hypothesis that personality traits in general are more important for business creation than for business success (Collins et al., 2004, Rauch & Frese, 2005). Until future studies directly address this issue, we have to conclude that the same traits (particularly specific traits) that are correlated with business creation are also correlated with business success, at least for a certain time period (we should probably restrict this time period to approximately 5 years). It is thus very possible that the life cycle of the business is another moderator in entrepreneurship. One study directly addressed the effects of different personality traits on success at different phases of the business development (Baron & Markman, 2004) and found that extraversion is important in early phases of new venture creation, whereas conscientiousness is related to long-term survival. Future research needs to take a more developmental and longitudinal approaches to study these effects and take time into account.

A number of methodological moderators have been evaluated in meta-analyses. Such moderators are type of assessment used for measuring risk-taking propensity (Stewart & Roth, 2004), type of criterion assessment (subjective criteria produce higher relationships than organizational criteria or survival; Rauch & Frese, 2005), type of comparison group (smaller effects when using managers as comparison groups than other ones; Collins et al., 2004). Thus, it is likely that there are important contingencies that impact on the size of relationships between personality, business creation, and success. Rather than neglecting personality effects, entrepreneurship research needs to address such interactions more carefully and to specify conditions to which the empirical evidence may be generalized.

Quality Issues

It behooves a chapter such as this one to make a few remarks on the methodology of the relevant literature because many methodological problems may have weakened the relationship between entrepreneurs' personality and both business creation and success. For example, the Brockhaus and Nord (1979) study is frequently cited as providing evidence for nonsignificant relationships between personality variables and entrepreneurship. The problem is that the study is based on a sample of only 31 business owners. Given the small sample size and the small effects expected in general, there is a high risk of rejecting the hypothesis wrongly (beta error). Actually, the effect of risk taking in the Brockhaus and Nord (1979) study is exactly within the confidence interval reported in meta-analyses (Rauch & Frese, 2005; Stewart & Roth, 2004). Thus, more sophisticated generalizations can be drawn from quantitative reviews, which compare evidence across studies and control for methodological problems, such as sampling error variance.

Moreover, roughly a third of the articles identified for our own meta-analysis (Rauch & Frese, 2005) did not report the relevant descriptive statistics (r or d statistics, standard deviations, means, and reliabilities were not depicted). This does not just appear in unsophisticated studies but also in otherwise methodologically sophisticated studies (thus, we sometimes saw only beta weights being described but no intercorrelation table). Lack of such descriptive information makes it difficult to interpret empirical results, particularly if sample sizes are small and expected effects are small in general (e.g., between risk taking and success).

Interestingly, publication practices also biased the correlations between entrepreneurs' personality traits and both business creation and success: Unpublished articles in the area of personality show higher correlations (Rauch & Frese, 2005), whereas unpublished articles in the area of entrepreneurial orientation show lower correlations (each time compared to the published articles) (Rauch et al., 2005). This shows that a bias (both by authors and reviewers) has operated: The biases were that there are no significant correlations between personality and success but that there clear correlations between entrepreneurial orientation and success.

Thus, one of our conclusions is that entrepreneurship research needs to improve the methodological quality of studies in the area of personality to be able to depict the "true effects" of such variables on business creation and success.

Additionally, it is important to note that most studies in the area of entrepreneurs' personality traits are still cross-sectional. More specific traits can probably be changed more easily than global traits. Thus, we cannot rule out reverse causality, so that success leads to changes (van Gelderen, Frese, & Thurik, 2000). Also third variable interpretations need to be ruled out— for example, that in certain subcultures, certain personality traits are found more frequently, and that these subcultures are also related to success. To deal with alternative hypotheses, entrepreneurship scholars should employ more longitudinal studies.

Finally, our chapter did not address different operationalizations of personality traits. There is, however, evidence that the predictive validities are different for different instruments. Stewart and Roth (2004), for example, found Jackson's risk-taking measure (Jackson, 1976) to produce higher relationships with entrepreneurship than measures based on the Kogan–Wallach (1964) Choice Dilemma Questionnaire. Collins et al. (2004) did not find different effects sizes for different instruments for achievement motivation. In principle, meta-analyses provide an excellent tool for testing predictive validities of different instruments relevant in the entrepreneurship literature.

Personality and Other Predictors of Success in Entrepreneurship

Finally, a model of the effects of personality traits on business creation and business success must include other individual differences variables as well as nonpersonality variables, such as action strategies, cognitive ability, and environment, which are additional predictors of performance (Campbell, McCloy, Oppler, & Sager, 1993; Kanfer, 1992a). Given the large body of empirical findings suggesting that factors other than characteristics of business owners affect small business performance, the proponents of the personality approach should account for these effects, both theoretically and empirically (Davis-Blake & Pfeffer, 1989). On the other hand, economic models of entrepreneurial success need to include owners` personality characteristics as extraneous variables. Otherwise, their models are misspecified and potential spurious correlations may appear and cannot be controlled (e.g., that achievement motive produces the correlation between innovation and success or between receiving enough venture capital and success). In other words, we cannot develop a consistent theory about entrepreneurship if we do not take into consideration personality variables as well.

REFERENCES

Abelson, R. P. (1985). A variance explanation paradox: When a little is a lot. *Psychological Bulletin, 97,* 129–133.

Aldrich, H. E., & Wiedenmayer, G. (1993). From traits to rates: An ecological perspective on organizational foundings. In J. A. Katz & R. H. Brockhaus (Eds.), *Advances in entrepreneurship, firm emergence, and growth* (Vol. 1, pp. 145–195). Greenwich, CT: JAI Press.

Ashford, S. J., & Tsui, A. S. (1991). Self-regulation for managerial effectiveness: The role of active feedback seeking. *Academy of Management Journal, 34*(2), 251–280.

Bandura, A. (1982). Self-efficacy mechanism in human agency. *American Psychologist, 37,* 122–147.

Bandura, A. (1986). *Social foundations of thought and action.* Englewood Cliffs, NJ: Prentice Hall.

Bandura, A. (1997). *Self-efficacy: The exercise of control.* New York: Freeman.

Bandura, A. (1999). Social-cognitive theory of personality. In D. Cervonce & Y. Shoda (Eds.), *The coherence of personality: Social-cognitive bases of consistency, variability, and organization* (pp. 185–241). New York: Guilford Press.

Baron, J. (1981). Reflective thinking as a goal of education. *Intelligence, 5,* 291–309.

Baron, R. A. (2004). The cognitive perspective: A valuable tool for answering entrepreneurship's basic "why" questions. *Journal of Business Venturing, 19,* 221–240.

Baron, R. A., & Markman, G. D. (2004). Toward a process view of entrepreneurship: The changing impact of individual-level variables across phases of new firm development. In M. A. Rahim, R. T. Golembiewski, & K. D. McMackenzie (Eds.), *Current topics in Management* (Vol. 9, pp. 45–64). New Brunswick, NJ: Transaction.

Barrick, M. R., Mitchell, T. R., & Steward, G. L. (2003). Situational and motivational influences on trait-behavior relationships. In M. R. Barrick & A. M. Ryan (Eds.), *Personality and work: Reconsidering the role of personality an organizations* (pp. 60–82). San Francisco, CA: Jossey-Bass.

Barrick, M. R., & Mount, M. K. (1991). The big five personality dimensions and job performance: A meta-analysis. *Personnel Psychology, 41*(1), 1–26.

Barrick, M. R., Mount, M. K., & Judge, T. A. (2001). The FFM personality dimensions and job-performance: Meta-analysis of meta-analyses. *International Journal of Selection and Assessment, 9,* 9–30.

Baum, J. R. (1995). The relation of traits, competencies, motivation, strategy and structure to venture growth. In W. D. Bygrave, B. J. Bird, S. Birley, N. C. Churchill, M. G. Hay, R. H. Keeley, & W. E. Wetzel, Jr. (Eds.), *Frontiers of entrepreneurship research.* Wellesley Park, MA: Boston College.

Baum, J. R., & Locke, E. A. (2004). The relation of entrepreneurial traits, skill, and motivation to subsequent venture growth. *Journal of Applied Psychology, 89*(4), 587–598.

Baum, J. R., Locke, E. A., & Kirkpatrick, S. A. (1998). A longitudinal study of vision and vision communication to venture growth in entrepreneurial firms. *Journal of Applied Psychology, 83,* 43–54.

Baum, J. R., Locke, E. A., & Smith, K. G. (2001). A Multidimensional model of venture growth. *Academy of Management Journal, 44*(2), 292–303.

Begley, T. M., & Boyd, D. P. (1987). Psychological characteristics associated with performance in entrepreneurial firms and smaller businesses. *Journal of Business Venturing, 2,* 79–93.

Borman, W. C., & Motowidlo, S. J. (1997). Task performance and contextual performance: The meaning for personnel selection research. *Human Performance, 10,* 99–109.

Brandstätter, H. (1997). Becoming an entrepreneur—A question of personality structure? *Journal of Economic Psychology, 18,* 157–177.

Brockhaus, R. H., & Horwitz, P. S. (1985). The psychology of the entrepreneur. In D. L. Sexton & R. W. Smilor (Eds.), *The art and science of entrepreneurship* (pp. 25–48). Cambridge, MA: Ballinger.

Brockhaus, R. H., & Nord, W. R. (1979). An exploration of factors affecting the entrepreneurial decision: Personality conditions versus environmental conditions. *Academy of Management Proceedings of the 39th Annual Meeting,* pp. 364–368.

Campbell, J. P., McCloy, R. A., Oppler, S., & Sager, C. E. (1993). A theory of performance. In N. Schmitt, W. C. Borman (Eds.), *Personnel selection in organizations* (pp. 35–79). San Francisco: Jossey-Bass.

Caprana, G. V., & Cervone, D. (2000). *Personality: Determinants, dynamics, and potentials.* New York: Cambridge University Press.

Chell, E., Haworth, J. M., & Brearley, S. (1991). *The entrepreneurial personality.* London: Routledge.

Chen, C. C., Greene, P. G., & Crick, A. (1998). Does entrepreneurial self-efficacy distinguish entrepreneurs from managers? *Journal of Business Venturing, 13*(4), 295–316.

Ciaverella, M. A., Buchholtz, A. K., & Riordan, C. M., Gatewood, R. D., & Stokes, G. S. (2004). The big five and venture survival: Is there a linkage? *Journal of Business Venturing, 19,* 465–483.

Cohen, J. (1977). *Statistical power analysis for the behavioral science.* New York: Academic Press.

Cohen, S., & Wills, T. A. (1985). Stress, social support, and the buffering hypothesis. *Psychological Bulletin, 98,* 310–357.

Collins, C. J., Hanges, P. J., & Locke, E. A. (2004). The relationship of achievement motivation to entrepreneurial behavior: A meta-analysis. *Human Performance, 17*(1), 95–117.

Collins, O. F., & Moore, D. G. (1970). *The organization makers*. New York: Appelton-Century-Crofts.

Cooper, A. C., & Gimeno-Gascon, F. J. (1992). Entrepreneurs, process of founding, and new firm performance. In D. L. Sexton & J. D. Kasarda (Eds.), *The state of the art of entrepreneurship* (pp. 301–340). Boston: PSW.

Costa, P. T., & McCrae, R. R. (1988). From catalog to classification: Murray–s needs and the five-factor model. *Journal of Personality and Social Psychology, 55*, 258–265.

Cromie, S. (2000). Assessing entrepreneurial intentions: Some approaches and empirical evidence. *European Journal of Work and Organizational Psychology, 9*(1), 7–30.

Davis-Blake, A., & Pfeffer, J. (1989). Just a mirage: The search for dispositional effects in organizational research. *Academy of Management Review, 14*(3), 385–400.

Dess, G. G., & Beard, D. W. (1984). Dimensions of organizational task environments. *Administrative Science Quarterly, 29*, 52–73.

Drucker, P. F. (1993). *Innovation and entrepreneurship*. New York: Harper Business.

Epstein, S., & O'Brien, E. J. (1985). The person-situation debate in historical and current perspective. *Psychological Bulletin, 98*, 513–537.

Frese, M. (1999). Social support as a moderator of the relationship between stress at work and psychological dysfunctioning: A longitudinal study with objective measures. *Journal of Occupational Health Psychology, 4*, 179–192.

Frese, M., Krauss, S., Escher, S., Grabarkiewicz, R., Friedrich, C., & Keith, N. (2004). *Micro business owners characteristics and their success: The role of psychological action strategy characteristics in an African environment*. Giessen: Department of Psychology, submitted for publication.

Frese, M., Krauss, S. I., Keith, N., Escher, S., Grabarkiewicz, R., Luneng, S. T., Heers, C., Unger, J. M., Friedrich, C. (2005). *Business owners' action planning and its relationship to business success in three African countries*. Giessen: Department of Psychology, submitted for publication.

Frese, M., van Gelderen, M., & Ombach, M. (2000). How to plan as a small scale business owner: Psychological process characteristics of action strategies and success. *Journal of Small Business Management, 38*(2), 1–18.

Frey, R. S. (1984). Does n-Achievement cause economic development? A cross lagged panel analysis of the McClelland thesis. *Journal of Social Psychology, 122*, 67–70.

Gartner, W. B. (1989). "Who is an entrepreneur?" is the wrong question. *Entrepreneurship Theory and Practice, 12*(2), 47–68.

Guion, R. M., & Gottier, R. F. (1965). Validity of personality measures in personnel selection. *Personnel Psychology, 27*, 409–421.

Hattrup, K., & Jackson, S. E. (Eds.). (1996). *Learning about individual differences by taking situations seriously*. San Francisco, CA: Jossey-Bass.

Hayek, F. (1941). *The pure theory of capital*. Chicago: University Press.

Heckhausen, J., & Schulz, R. (1995). A life-span theory of control. *Psychological Review, 102*, 284–304.

Hedges, L. V. (1987). How hard is hard science, how soft is soft science? The empirical cumulativeness of research. *American Psychologist, 42*, 443–455.

Heunks, F. J. (1996). Innovation, creativity, and success. *Small Business Economics, 8*, 263–272.

Hornaday, J. A., & Aboud, J. (1971). Characteristics of successful entrepreneurs. *Personnel Psychology, 24*, 141–153.

Hunter, J. A., & Schmidt, F. L. (1990). *Methods of meta-analysis*. Newbury Park, CA: Sage.

Hunter, J. E., & Hunter, R. F. (1984). Validity and utility of alternative predictors of job performance. *Psychological Bulletin, 96*, 72–98.

Jackson, D. N. (1976). *Personality Inventory manual*. Goshen, NY: Research Psychologists.

Johnson, J. W. (2003). Toward a better understanding of the relationship between personality and individual job performance. In M. R. Barrick & A. M. Ryan (Eds.), *Personality and work: Reconsidering the role of personality in organizations* (pp. 83–120). San Francisco, CA: Jossey-Bass.

Judge, T. A., Bono, J. E., Ilies, R., & Gerhardt, M. W. (2002). Personality and leadership: A qualitative and quantitative review. *Journal of Applied Psychology, 87*(4), 765–780.

Kanfer, R. (1992a). Work motivation: New directions in theory and research. In C. L. Cooper & I. T. Robertson (Eds.), *International Review of Industrial and Organizational Psychology* (Vol. 7, pp. 1–53). London: John Wiley & Sons.

Kanfer, R. (1992b). Work motivation: New directions in theory and research. In C. L. Cooper & I. T. Robertson (Eds.), *International review of industrial and organizational psychology, 1992* (Vol. 7, pp. 1–54). Chichester: Wiley.

Klein, K. J., Dansereau, F., & Hall, R. J. (1994). Levels issues in theory development, data collection, and analysis. *Academy of Management Review, 19*(2), 195–229.

Klein, K. J., & Sorra, J. S. (1996). The challenge of innovation implementation. *Academy of Management Review, 21*(4), 1055–1080.

Knight, F. H. (1921). *Risk, uncertainty, and profit.* New York: Kelly and Millman.

Kogan, N., & Wallach, M. A. (1964). *Risk, uncertainty, and profit.* New York: Holt, Rinehart, & Winston.

Koop, S., De Reu, T., & Frese, M. (2000). Sociodemographic factors, entrepreneurial orientation, personal initiative, and environmental problems in Uganda. In M. Frese (Ed.), *Success and failure of microbusiness owners in Africa: A psychological approach* (pp. 55–76). Westport, CT: Quorum.

Levenson, H. (1974). Activism and powerful others: Distinctions within the concept of internal–external control. *Journal of Personality Assessment, 38,* 377–383.

Low, M. B., & MacMillan, B. C. (1988). Entrepreneurship: Past research and future challenges. *Journal of Management, 14*(2), 139–162.

Magnusson, D., & Endler, N. S. (1977). Interactional psychology: Present status and future prospects. In D. Magnusson & N. S. Endler (Eds.), *Personality at the crossroads: Current issues in interactional psychology* (pp. 3–36). Hillsdale, NJ: Lawrence Erlbaum Associates.

Markman, G. D., Baron, R. A., & Balkin, D. B. (2005). Are perseverance and self-efficacy costless? Assessing entrepreneurs' regretful thinking. *Journal of Organizational Behavior, 26*(1), 1–19.

McClelland, D. C. (1961). *The achieving society.* New York: Free Press.

McClelland, G. H., & Judd, C. M. (1993). Statistical difficulties of detecting interactions and moderator effects. *Psychological Bulletin, 114,* 376–390.

Meyer, G. J., Finn, S. E., Eyde, L. D., Kay, G. G., Moreland, K. L., Dies, R. R., et al. (2001). Psychological testing and psychological assessment: A review of evidence and issues. *American Psychologist, 56,* 128–165.

Miner, J. B., & Raju, N. S. (2004). Risk propensity differences between managers and entrepreneurs and between low- and high-growth entrepreneurs: A reply in a more conservative vein. *Journal of Applied Psychology, 89*(1), 3–13.

Mischel, W. (1968). *Personality and assessment.* New York: Wiley.

Mischel, W., & Shoda, Y. (1998). Reconciling processing dynamics and personality dispositions. *Annual Review of Psychology, 49,* 229–258.

Nesselroade, J. R. (1991). Interindividual differences in intraindividual change. In L. M. Collins & J. L. Horn (Eds.), *Best methods for the analysis of change: Recent advances, unanswered questions, future directions* (pp. 95–105). Washington: American Psychological Association.

Patchen, M. (1965). *Some questionnaire measures of employee motivation and morale.* Ann Arbor: Institute of Social Research, University of Michigan.

Rauch, A., & Frese, M. (2000). Psychological approaches to entrepreneurial success: A general model and an overview of findings. In C. L. Cooper & I. T. Robertson (Eds.), *International Review of Industrial and Organizational Psychology* (Vol. 15, pp. 101–141). New York: John Wiley & Sons.

Rauch, A., & Frese, M. (2005). *Let's put the person back into entrepreneurship research: A meta-analysis on the relationship between business owners' personality and business creation and success.* Manuscript submitted for publication.

Rauch, A., Frese, M., & Sonnentag, S. (2000). Cultural differences in planning-success relationships: A comparison of small enterprises in Ireland, West Germany, and East Germany. *Journal of Small Business Management, 38*(4), 28–41.

Rauch, A., Wiklund, J., Frese, M., & Lumpkin, G. T. (2005). *Entrepreneurial orientation and business performance: Cumulative empirical evidence.* Univ. of Giessen: submitted.

Ray, J. J., & Singh, S. (1980). Effects of individual differences on productivity among farmers in India. *The Journal of Social Psychology, 112,* 11–17.

Roccas, S., Sagiv, L., Schwartz, S. H., & Knafo, A. (2002). The big five personality factors and personal values. *Personality and Social Psychological Bulletin, 28*(6), 789–801.

Rosenthal, R., & Rubin, D. B. (1982). A simple, general purpose display of magnitude of experimental effect. *Journal of Educational Psychology, 74,* 166–169.

Rotter, J. B. (1966). Generalized expectancies for internal versus external control of reinforcement. *Psychological Monographs, 80*(1), 1–28.

Schmidt, F. L., & Hunter, J. E. (1998). The validity and utility of selection methods in personnel psychology: Practical and theoretical implications of 85 years of research findings. *Psychological Bulletin, 124,* 262–274.

Schumpeter, J. (1935). *Theorie der wirtschaftlichen Entwicklung* (Theory of economic growth). München: Von Duncker Und Humbolt.

Smith, K. G., Gannon, M. J., & Sapienza, H. J. (1989). Selecting methodologies for entrepreneurship research: Trade-offs and guidelines. *Entrepreneurship Theory and Practice, 13,* 39–49.

Speier, C., & Frese, M. (1997). Generalized self-efficacy as a mediator and moderator between control and complexity at work and personal initiative: A longitudinal field study in East Germany. *Human Performance, 10,* 171–192.

Stajkovic, A. D., & Luthans, F. (1998). Self-efficacy and work-related performance: A meta-analysis. *Psychological Bulletin, 124,* 240–261.

Stewart, W. H., & Roth, P. L. (2004). Data-quality affects meta-analytic conclusions: A response to Miner and Raju (2004) concerning entrepreneurial risk propensity. *Journal of Applied Psychology, 89*(1), 14–21.

Tett, R. P., Steele, J. R., & Beaurgard, R. S. (2003). Broad and narrow measures on both sides of the personality-job performance relationship. *Journal of Organizational Behavior, 24,* 335–356.

Timmons, J. A., Smollen, L. E., & Dingee, A. L. M. (1985). *New venture creation.* Homewood, IL: Irvine.

Utsch, A., Rauch, A., Rothfuss, R., & Frese, M. (1999). Who becomes a small scale entrepreneur in a post-socialistic environment: On the differences between entrepreneurs and managers in East Germany. *Journal of Small Business Management, 37*(3), 31–42.

van Gelderen, M., Frese, M., & Thurik, R. (2000). Strategies, uncertainty and performance of small business startups. *Small Business Economics, 15,* 165–181.

Vinchur, A. J., Schippmann, J. S., Switzer, F. S. I., & Roth, P. L. (1998). A meta-analytic review of predictors of job performance for salespeople. *Journal of Applied Psychology, 83,* 586–597.

Wittmann, W. W. (2002, July). *Work motivation and level of performance: A disappointing relationship? Integrative Approaches to Work Motivation: Ability and Non-ability Determinants of Regulatory Processes, Learning, and Performance.* Paper presented at the XXV International Congress of Applied Psychology, Singapore.

Wooton, K. C., & Timmerman, T. A. (1999). The use of personality and the five factor model to predict business ventures: From outplacement to start-up. *Journal of Vocational Behavior, 58,* 82–101.

4

Entrepreneurs' Competencies

Gideon D. Markman

The field of entrepreneurship captures how enterprising individuals dis-cover and appropriate opportunities to create new wealth. Focusing on the entrepreneur, this chapter advances the view that starting a new ven-ture requires an assemblage of many individual-level factors, most broadly aggregated into knowledge, skills, and abilities (KSAs)—collec-tively, henceforth branded *entrepreneurs' competencies*. Assuming all else equal,[1] the stronger the competencies, the greater is the success of enter-prising individuals[2] (Baum, Locke, & Smith, 2001; Bird, 1988; Boyatzis, 1982; Chandler & Jansen, 1992; McClelland, 1961; Spencer & Spencer, 1983). This chapter builds on and extends existing research based on the reasoning that personal competencies do indeed play an important role in the entrepreneurial process. Although past literature on individual differ-ences in entrepreneurship is instructive, it offers neither an inclusive the-ory nor practical guidance regarding what competencies are needed to start a new company. The framework of entrepreneurs' competencies be-gins to address this issue. Developing a broader theory is important, given the substantial increase in entrepreneurial activity of the past decades and given the high failure rate of young ventures (and thus mounting costs). Put differently, new ventures are the product of individ-ual-level action, and advancing a theory—however broad and rudimen-tary—on individual-level competencies may enhance our understanding of entrepreneurship.

---

[1] Assuming all else equal, includes traits, motivation, strategies, and so forth.

[2] Consistent with strategic management and entrepreneurship literature, *success* refers to financial gains.

THEORETICAL BACKGROUND

People are naturally gifted in different ways, and thus when thinking about entrepreneurs and competencies it is useful to make a distinction between "weak" and "strong" situations (Mischel, 1973). *Weak situations* refer to contextual conditions that cultivate or pose low barriers to the expression of individual differences and their subsequent influence on situations (House & Aditya, 1997). These conditions include dense communication networks (Granovetter, 1985), a compressed single hierarchy, highly centralized decision making, and narrow offerings. Firm smallness and a sense of informality make ties among members more cohesive, whereas newness requires centralized decision making where limited capital commands narrow offerings. Over and above smallness and newness, young ventures also reflect weak situations because they are firms-in-the-making in the process of developing organizational protocols, culture, routines, and capabilities. In such contexts, individual differences can readily influence a wide range of outcomes, perhaps even initial venture performance.

Strong situations, in contrast, are contexts that raise formidable barriers to the expression of individual differences on their environment. Such contexts are the result of well-defined roles based on prescribed job descriptions and organizational charts with protracted hierarchies that hamper direct communications between a chief executive officer (CEO) and frontline employees. Strong situations are also the result of decentralized decision making, professionalization and specialization (e.g., research and development [R&D], marketing, sales, human resources [HR], business development, etc.), and multiple lines of offerings. Strong situations characterize established organizations, as they have formal norms, rules, and regulations that define and reward acceptable behavior and censor, sanction, and even punish inappropriate action. Because mature or large firms follow well-established (at times even entrenched) aggregations of norms, culture, values, rules, protocols, and routines, the expression of individual differences are less likely to exert dramatic influences on firm-level outcomes. Put simply, the constraints of strong situations minimize the effects of individual differences.

The theoretical model presented in this chapter is restricted to weak situations, then, and it is based on three broad and overlapping entrepreneurs' competencies, including knowledge, skills, and abilities. Despite overlapping attributes, these three competencies are further broken down into subcategories that are highly relevant to entrepreneurial activities. For instance, the knowledge competence may include access to unique information and experience, and it is discussed later in terms of its specificity, complexity, cumulativeness, tacitness, and codification (Marsili, 2002). The skill competence may entail technical skills (e.g., organizational, management, product/service, and industry skills) and human skills (e.g., human and social capital and social skills). Finally, the ability competence could consist of the capability to cope with and overcome adversity and the cognitive ability to discover opportunities. Because entrepreneurship is by definition voluntary and the majority of new ventures are discontinued within 5 years, it is evident that motives and motivation and even traits (Ciavarella, Buchholtz, Riordan, Gatewood, & Stokes, 2004) are important determinants of venture creation, but they are the focal topic of a different chapter in this volume.

The model discussed here does not argue that entrepreneurs' competencies will inevitably cause individuals to pursue new venture formation. First, such competencies might be invaluable in diverse professional pursuits and sundry career options, including but not limited to general management and top management teams. Second, the model merely suggests that—ceteris paribus—the stronger the competencies, the higher is the likelihood that, if and when such persons pursue entrepreneurship, they will attain some advantage relative to those who lack such competencies. It should also be noted that as in most emerging theories, the model is in no way exclusive: Additional dimensions of individual differences, including the fashioning of other competencies, motivation, traits, situations, and opportunities, may also play a role. However, to keep the chapter within reasonable bounds while acknowledging that all possible predictors of entrepreneurship are not confined to competencies, the dimensions examined here appear to be ones that are especially relevant to the entrepreneurial process.

Developing a theory of entrepreneurs' competencies is needed because it may clarify and advance previous paradigms. For example, Alvarez and Busenitz (2001) reason that when entrepreneurs are able to use heuristics to capitalize on insights and decisions that are concurrently valuable, rare, difficult to imitate, and yet exploitable, these "insights and decisions" might "lead to a competitive advantage" (p. 759). Such paradigm is certainly correct, and applying a resource-based view to entrepreneurship is, by itself, a valuable ongoing contribution (Doh, 2000; Eisenhardt, Schoonhoven, & Bird, 1996; Guillen, 2000). However, the focus on "insights and decisions" as source of competitive advantage without specifying who can and who cannot make such "insights and decisions" (and why or how) leaves much to be desired in terms of theoretical contributions. Such conceptualization suffers from four limitations. First, this and similar frameworks give little specificity as to what kinds of insights are valuable, rare, difficult to imitate, yet exploitable, and even less is stated about who can make such insights. Second, it is an ex post view that makes attributes retroactively, based on outcomes. For instance, this view presumes that a venture succeeded because entrepreneurs made insightful decisions. If on the other hand the new venture failed, then the paradigm construes that failure was due to entrepreneurs' inability to make insightful decisions. Third, in the absence of specificity on *why* or *how* some persons but not others make insightful decisions, one is obliged to divide the world into two dichotomous categories: entrepreneurs and nonentrepreneurs. As past research illustrates, including among university life scientists or other "entrepreneurial scholars," "entrepreneurship is not an either or condition" (Louis, Blumenthal, Gluck, & Soto, 1989, p. 128). Moreover, individuals may be aware of the existence of an opportunity but may not possess the competencies to exploit the opportunity (Kogut & Kulatilaka, 2004). Finally, in the parlance of real option theory, economic agents must not only recognize and adequately valuate "insightful" opportunities, but they must also have the competencies to exploit such opportunities.

Evidently, even the most insightful opportunities can and will turn impractical, unattractive, or flat-out destructive to entrepreneurs when they are not married with abilities and skills to put into practice or when they are bolted onto an unsuitable business model. Given that about one in five persons seeks an entrepreneurial career sometimes during his or her life span (Reynolds, Carter, Gartner, & Greene, 2004), and because entrepreneurship is an ongoing process (Baron & Markman, in press), developing a framework of entrepreneurs' competencies seems timely.

The rest of the chapter is organized sequentially around the three competencies of knowledge, skills, and abilities. The section on knowledge as an entrepreneur's competency highlights several dimensions of knowledge, but focuses primarily on tacit and codified knowledge. The section on skills as an entrepreneur's competency focuses mainly on human skills, which includes human and social capital. The section on abilities highlights the importance of perseverance and cognitions. Finally, the chapter concludes with a brief summary of the main points regarding entrepreneurs' competencies and makes broad suggestions for future research.

KNOWLEDGE

At the broadest level possible, knowledge is an important competency in the context of entrepreneurship in at least three ways. First, any discovery of an opportunity is knowledge. Second, if all opportunities must be identified before being assessable and put into use then knowledge can assist not only with additional discoveries, but also with the valuations and fit assessments of opportunities. Third, knowledge can support implementation in building and organizing venture's capabilities for carrying out tasks to exploit and appropriate opportunities. Knowledge, then, allows entrepreneurs to solve a wide array of problems and address irregularities inherent in the development of ventures. New or uniquely recombined old knowledge allow entrepreneurs to enter or create markets and compete with varying degrees of success with established firms or other entrepreneurs. Entrepreneurs disrupt economic equilibrium when they identify and combine resources—at times in the absence of a clear market for their offerings (Venkataraman, 1997). Economic theory suggests that, in general, the application of common information leads to normal or average economic profit, which hinders entrepreneurial action (Kirzner, 1997). In contrast, the deployment of specific or unique knowledge may yield above normal returns and create new wealth to those who possess such specialized knowledge (Hayek, 1945). Indeed, when an opportunity is based on specific knowledge and is deployed in a market that is not widely traded, new wealth might be produced.

Theoretical and empirical studies confirm that knowledge is an important ingredient in diverse areas related to entrepreneurship. To name just a few, Ardichvili, Cardozo, and Ray (2003) propose that prior knowledge is an important antecedent of entrepreneurial alertness to opportunity identification. Sarasvathy, Simon, and Lave (1998) used verbal protocols to illustrate that entrepreneurs evaluate and process information differently from bankers. Research on business failure notes that "entrepreneurs with more experience possess the *knowledge* to perform the roles and tasks necessary for success more effectively" (Shepherd, 2003, p. 318). Others suggest that entrepreneurs rely on their knowledge of intellectual property law to protect their new discoveries, R&D, products, and services, while fending off resourceful rivals (Markman, Balkin, & Baron, 2002). A final example regarding the link between knowledge and entrepreneurship is illustrated by a study of life scientists in research-intensive universities. Controlling for university policies and structures, Louis et al. (1989) report that individual differences predict the appeal of large-scale science grants and supplemental income, whereas group norms predict involvement in commercialization. Naturally, the creation, dissemination, appropriation, and protection of new knowledge are crucial in any knowledge-intensive business regardless of sectors, markets, and industries, but the view advanced here is that they are keenly important in entrepreneurial contexts, where unique knowledge (new or old but uniquely recombined) may be the only difference between new entrants and incumbents.

Entrepreneurship scholars tend to conceptualize knowledge as important to the extent that it facilitates discovery of opportunities (Shane, 2001), but if entrepreneurship is a process (cf. Baron & Markman, in press) then knowledge is surely important during advanced stages of venture formation as well. For example, entrepreneurs rely on unique knowledge to interpret market dynamics—how to overcome entry barriers originating in established firms' scale economies (Bain, 1956). Knowledge also defines the modal properties of learning processes, sources of competitive advantage, and the qualitative nature of opportunities that are associated with discovery and innovation processes (Dosi, 1982). For example, technology-related entry barriers are a function of the knowledge underlying such technologies, which in turn influences the extent to which new opportunities accrue. Information gathering and processing represents an important aspect of successful project completion, especially for ventures with projects hinging on innovation (Hansen, 1999). Through networking, individuals can accumulate valuable knowledge, understanding, and skills (Arora & Gambardella, 1990).

Knowledge: An Entrepreneur's Competency

The general view that knowledge provides entrepreneurs with opportunities to create new wealth is not new. Hence, in an effort to advance theory, the view advanced in this chapter is that we now need to understand what knowledge is, what dimensions are relevant to entrepreneurs, and how it leads to new knowledge, learning, and wealth creation. This will allow us to see why, when, and how knowledge can become an entrepreneurs' competency.

Recent studies suggest that the nature of knowledge varies across technologies and market contexts in displaying different degrees of specificity, complexity, cumulativeness, tacitness, and codification (Marsili, 2002). To briefly explain, specificity refers to an asymmetry in knowledge applicability or usability, for example, when knowledge is aptly applied to a variety of services or production processes but has no or little applicability in a different context. Knowledge complexity refers to the intricacy level of information. Consider the complexity of knowledge entrepreneurs face when they try to distinguish alternative courses of action: Identifying and selecting the optimal resources and best strategy to overcome barriers to entry into a certain technology space or market requires entrepreneurs to disentangle and analyze highly complex contingencies. Cumulativeness refers to the extent to which new knowledge builds on existing knowledge. Finally, tacit knowledge defines the degree to which knowledge is inaccessible, whereas codification refers to knowledge that becomes easier to organize, transmit, use, and separate.

In practice, distinctions between the various dimensions of knowledge remain somewhat indefinite and indistinct, but in order to advance theory and enhance our understanding of actions taken by economic agents, scholars must seek greater specificity of knowledge. For instance, ignoring the various dimensions of knowledge, as defined earlier, might lead to an underspecified view of entrepreneurial undertakings. Entrepreneurs use knowledge and capabilities that are not fully or even adequately understood precisely because they hinge on information that is not codified or highly idiosyncratic. Thus, the equifinality principle suggests that entrepreneurs endowed with different knowledge may well end up doing different things with equal consequences, because they codify, process, and utilize that knowledge differently. Alternatively, entrepreneurs endowed with the same knowledge may end up doing different things with different or equal consequences, because, again, they codify, process, and utilize that knowledge differently. With these caveats in mind, the next sections highlight some of the interrelationship among the dimensions of knowledge, with special attention given to tacit and codified knowledge. Questions for future research in this promising area are presented toward the end of the chapter.

One way to look at codified knowledge and tacit knowledge (as well as the other dimensions) is to note that they constitute complimentary modes of conceptualizing the role of knowledge and its link to entrepreneurial action. Codification is important because it allows repeatability; entrepreneurs can conceptualize the role of their unique knowledge, describe its contribution to a process of production of goods or services, and perhaps in the process achieve even further knowledge and learning. The problem to entrepreneurs, however, is that once repeatability of a certain action or process becomes known, it is easily imitated and thus befalls its capability of generating superior rents. Tacitness too may encumber repeatability or routinization and thus entrepreneurial action, but because it is inherently unspecified and unstated, it yields causal ambiguity to those who try to ascertain the link between entrepreneurs' actions and consequences. In this respect, tacit knowledge is raising barriers to imitators while widening the window of opportunity. Causal ambiguity hinders imitation because it is exceedingly challenging for rivals to imitate products or services that hinge on ambiguous elements and features. However, when tacit knowledge is understood without difficulty, it may become common and codified and thus unable to delay imitation by rivals or less qualified entrepreneurs.

Resources that generate above-normal returns are rare, valuable, and difficult to imitate (Barney, 1991; Peteraf, 1993). This implies that knowledge may become an entrepreneurs' competency when it allows the discovery and utilization of rare, valuable, and difficult to imitate resources. Entrepreneurs may also harness some advantage when their knowledge assists them in neutralizing threats or attacks by others in their task environment. Knowledge, then, may become a competency when it allows entrepreneurs, but not incumbents, to combine or bundles other resources and assets in a crafty way, while remaining immobile or costly to understand by others (Barney, 1991). Imperfectly immobile knowledge includes idiosyncratic information for which codification is not well defined or when it is highly specific or private to an entrepreneur. Also, if sustaining a competitive advantage requires isolating means that prevent imitation

(Lippman & Rumelt, 1982), then knowledge that can yield limits to competition is certainly a valuable competency. This is important because once entrepreneurs gain a market foothold, they must seek and find additional resources or means to block or freeze out competitors, which would allow them earn rents for a period of time (Peteraf, 1993).

Consistent with the knowledge-based view, knowledge accumulates through a recursive process of creativity, exploration, and exploitation. However, knowledge accumulation is limited by one's absorptive capacity—the capacity to recognize, assimilate, and apply information to commercial ends (Cohen & Levinthal, 1990; Lane & Lubatkin, 1998). This concept suggests that entrepreneurs' expanding absorptive capacities and knowledge bases set a certain limit on how successful they can be in obtaining and processing additional knowledge and subsequently, additional rents. Similarly, it appears that prior knowledge helps entrepreneurs to recognize and exploit opportunities. For example, the notion of cumulativeness was captured by a study in which individuals from diverse scientific and industry backgrounds who assessed the same invention (i.e., 3DP) recognized, and then developed, very different business opportunities (Shane, 2000). Thus, a founder's cumulative knowledge in one domain enhances the probability that the founder's discoveries will reside within the respective domain or "knowledge corridor." This also hints that cumulative knowledge may produce some tunnel vision or barriers to discovery in domains others than where entrepreneurs developed their cumulative knowledge. Thus, different types and forms of knowledge exert quite different effects on entrepreneurs—on their proclivity to discover and on their likelihood to achieve technological and innovation progress.

The key point of this section is that certain dimensions of knowledge are important components of entrepreneurs' competencies. The consideration of such and other dimensions of knowledge enriches our understanding of individual differences among entrepreneurs. For example, once we distinguish between knowledge codification, tacit knowledge, and so on and the actual exploitability or utility of knowledge, we may begin to see that successful entrepreneurs vary from less successful ones by (a) what they know, (b) how much knowledge they can absorb and access, (c) how effectively they can distinguish between relevant and irrelevant knowledge (e.g., valuable, rare, inimitable, executable), and (d) how quickly and effectively they can learn, reabsorb, disseminate, and appropriate their knowledge insights.

Nonetheless, knowledge, however unique and advantageous, has no economic impact unless entrepreneurs have the skills and abilities to use it to create new wealth. Hence, the importance of skills and ability as parts of entrepreneurs' competencies is the subject of the next section. Human capital—what entrepreneurs know—also has limited meaning if it is not linked to skills or abilities; it is therefore referenced in the next section, rather than under knowledge.

SKILLS

As a short prelude to this and following sections and in an effort to elucidate the theory behind entrepreneurs' competencies, it is important to stress two points. First, it should be recognized from the preceding discussion that knowledge is inherently interrelated to and reciprocally dependent on skills and abilities. Second, skills and abilities are also inherently interrelated constructs, which may explain why, despite decades of research, many studies make either no effort to distinguish between the two or in fact treat them interchangeably. Indeed, because skills and abilities are derivatives of knowledge (Piazza-Georgi, 2002), separating them is challenging. Occasionally, a skill is defined as expertness acquired or developed through training and practice, whereas ability is defined as dexterity acquired or developed through learning and experience (e.g., intelligence, reasoning, verbal, and perceptual). Naturally, such distinctions are blurred in management as the development of skills—through active and passive learning, training, and experience—leads to the development of abilities and vice versa. Work and organizational psychologists, however, sought a clearer demarcation between the two. For example, these disciplines define skills as proficiency on tasks, whereas abilities as more general traits. Both skills and abilities depend on the phase of learning and the nature of the task (Ackerman, 1988). To echo Matthews and his colleagues (Matthews, Jones, & Chamberlain, 1992, p. 406), "ability may be related to individual differences in the rate of progression through the phases of skill acquisition, as well as to overall performance levels." Thus, the development of a skill on a given task is predicated, at least in part, on the possession of abilities (Fleishman & Quaintance, 1984).

It is important to identify the distinct differences between skills and abilities, but it is equally relevant to recognize their overlap, particularly in the context of other constructs. One interesting observation about skills and abilities vis-à-vis general knowledge is that the former are the product of lifelong education, experience, and talent, and may require recurring practice so as not to be lost. Another distinction is that skills and abilities seem more difficult to transfer to other individuals or contexts. Indeed, codified knowledge such as may be found in books, libraries, databanks, media, blueprints, and other accessible documents is obviously transferable (although at a cost). Still, it is certain that knowledge is critical to the development of skills and abilities, while at the same time skills and abilities influence one's absorbent capacity of additional knowledge.

This chapter recognizes that skills and ability are distinct and that skill acquisition hinges on ability. At the same time, the chapter is also cognizant of the fact that skills and ability share many attributes in common. In the interest of parsimony, yet clarity and ease, skills and abilities are discussed mainly under different headings despite the overlap in their conceptualization. With these observations in mind, the next subsections intend to specify what skills might be considered as entrepreneurs' competencies.

Skills: An Entrepreneurs' Competency

Although studies address diverse issues regarding individual differences in entrepreneurship, very few studies focus on skills per se. For example, some note that entrepreneurial teams with diverse skills make strategic choices that improve venture performance (Roure & Madique, 1986). Others explain that entrepreneurs who possess a range of skills can handle chaotic situations better than those who have a narrow set of skills (Eisenhardt & Schoonhoven, 1990). Building on top management team research, others suggest that entrepreneurs benefit from technical, conceptual, and human skills (e.g., Ensley, Carland, & Carland, 2000). Technical skills capture the extent to which entrepreneurs capitalize on processes to yield products or services that advance their venture. These skills are the result of professional experience such as scientific and applied research, and because they allow entrepreneurs to initiate competitive changes in price, supply, and business location, they are a fundamental source of growth and wealth creation (Baum et al., 2001). Similarly and consistent with the discussion on knowledge, conceptual skills may include "knowledge skills"—the skills to discover and recognize opportunities; to spot and process trends in consumers' taste, markets, and industries; to evaluate and quickly modify organizational functions; and to plan, organize, and strategize. Technical skill and conceptual skills—respectively, the extent to which entrepreneurs capitalize on their venture, products, services, or technology, and the extent to which entrepreneurs exploit administrative and managerial skills—are interrelated, and to an extent both hinge on entrepreneurs' accumulated experience (including learning and training). In essence, technical and conceptual skills are key competencies because even with optimal market conditions, superior resources, and insightful discoveries, entrepreneurs must have the skills to manage these resources and effectively exploit their discoveries (Bruederl, Preisendoerfer, & Ziegler, 1992; Watson, Stewart, & BarNir, 2003).

Human skills capture the extent to which individuals leverage on human relationships inside and outside their venture, including skills in leading and motivating employees, and networking with outsiders. Human skills hinge heavily on, and essentially aggregate, human and social capital. For example, social capital refers to resources that can be accessed and utilized through relationships. These stocks of accumulated resources include "information, ideas, leads, business opportunities, financial capital, power, emotional support, goodwill, trust, and cooperation" (Baker, 2000, p. 25). Human capital refers to skills attained primarily through education, practice, and work training and experiences. This suggests again that skills are driven, at least in part, by ability. Hence, although these constructs are distinct in theory, many scholars, including in entrepreneurship recognize their conceptual overlap, at times even including the concept of social skills (Davidsson & Honig, 2003; Simon & Hitt, 2003). It is also important to note that when research views knowledge as what entrepreneurs know, knowledge is frequently aggregated under human capital. For example, a study of 1,849 business founders in Germany shows that human capital—education, work, and industry experience—predicts venture longevity (Bruederl et al., 1992). Similar effects regarding human capital were reported by Watson et al. (2003).

Hence, in the interest of ease and straightforwardness and because of the overlap in term of overt expression, the following subsections aggregate human and social capital (including social skills) under the broader umbrella hereinafter called *human skills* (for an extensive review of the social capital construct, see Adler & Kwon, 2002).

In the parlance of social network theory and resource-based view, human skills—the resources embedded in an individual's social and professional network—are valuable because they are difficult to imitate or transfer. Social capital is particularly tricky to document, difficult to identify by third parties, and at times may pass unrecognized by the entrepreneurs themselves. Social capital consists of networks embedded in individuals and may even include perceived prestige and trustworthiness. As with human capital and consistent with the old cliché of "it's not what you know but who you know," research shows that strong social capital is a significant predictor of diverse outcomes in organizational contexts. High human and/or social capital predicts scientists' access to National Science Foundation grants (Feinberg & Price, 2004), predicts finding a job (Granovetter, 1974; Mouw, 2003), and increases wages and occupational prestige (Lin, 1999). Strategic management research also shows that in order to fulfill organizational objectives executives try to exploit interpersonal ties and professional networks (Luo, 2003), and corporations often hire CEOs because of the social and human capital they are believed to possess. Similarly, social capital and human capital—as captured by, respectively, the density and resourcefulness of an individual's contacts and knowledge—predict individual and team performance (Baldwin, Bedell, & Johnson, 1997; Mehra, Kilduff, & Brass, 2001), mentoring and personnel assimilation (Higgins & Kram, 2001), promotions (Burt, 1992; Seibert et al.,

2001), personnel retention (Alvesson, 2000), and venture longevity (Bruederl et al., 1992; Watson et al., 2003). Finally, because social capital and human capital are tied to individuals' knowledge networks, they contribute substantially to the effectiveness and efficiency of individuals and their organizations (Hoegl, Parboteeah, & Munson, 2003). It is clear, then, that human skills are vital in diverse organizational contexts, and, as discussed later, evidence shows that such skills can be considered entrepreneurs' competencies.

Human skills are important entrepreneurial competencies because no venture exists, let alone thrives, in a vacuum, and very few ventures—even among those launched by highly knowledgeable, skilled, and able entrepreneurs—develop in isolation. In other words, launching a new venture require skills in attracting, motivating, and retaining key personnel (e.g., employees and partners) and creating relationships with potential customers, suppliers, and investors.

Diverse sets of skills are particularly important for entrepreneurs when they embed themselves in a dense social and professional network in order to access knowledge and influence others. Recently, Baron and Markman (2003) conducted studies with entrepreneurs working in the cosmetics and high-tech industries to investigate whether entrepreneurs' social skills (e.g., accuracy in perceiving others, impression management, social adaptability, persuasiveness) are related to their financial success. Findings show that regardless of industry, accuracy in perceiving others is positively related to entrepreneurs' financial success. Interestingly, some social skills seem to be industry specific: Adaptability was found to be particularly important for entrepreneurs in the cosmetics industry whereas expressiveness was found to be more important for the entrepreneurs in the high-tech industry.

Additional research shows that scientists' social capital and human capital make it easier to link and embed their ventures into professional networks in the scientific community. In the context of university professors who engage in entrepreneurial activity this is done through a local network of current and former students and advisors and through a wider network of colleagues and coauthors established through collaboration, collegiality, and even competition (Murray, 2004). This suggests that skills and experience in science coupled with human skills can be translated into critical scientific networks in which entrepreneurial firms become embedded.

Human skills, with their related knowledge networks as a primary source of ideas and insights from relations with others (Coleman, 1988), play a particularly important role in entrepreneurship (Chung & Gibbons, 1997; Ibarra, 1993; Yli-Renko, Autio, & Sapienza, 2001; Young, Charns, & Shortell, 2001). Relationships and networks allow transfer of knowledge among individuals, providing opportunities for discovery and learning, while at the same time enabling the creation of new knowledge and enhancing one's ability to innovate (Tsai & Goshal, 1998). Discoveries occur because problem solving involves entrepreneurs seeking and relying on their own experience as well as expertise located outside their emerging organization, such as among suppliers, distributors, customers, or investors. Thus, entrepreneurs' social and human capital can provide access to useful knowledge networks and resources. Such boundary spanning (Ancona & Caldwell, 1992) into knowledge networks and resources is critical, as entrepreneurs seldom have the resources and expertise needed for launching or growing their ventures.

To recap, human skills are important entrepreneurs' competencies because success in any social systems hinges on building, nurturing, and enhancing relationships and networks. Accumulated knowledge and skills—technical, conceptual, and human—are important competencies in entrepreneurship processes, but they too are insufficient without the inclusion of abilities, which is the subject of the following section.

ABILITIES

Entrepreneurs must have an ability to collect, process, apply, and disseminate tacit and explicit knowledge regarding undervalued resources and to deploy and exploit these resources to create new wealth. Indeed, it is a recurrent premise of this chapter that the abilities and skills to capitalize on knowledge are reciprocally dependent on one's ability and skill to absorb, comprehend, and utilize that knowledge. Ability as an entrepreneur's competency, then, is the aptitude to combine assets and resources (including knowledge) in new ways to deploy them to meet customers' needs while maintaining profitability. As noted earlier, knowledge can range from explicit to tacit—when it is difficult to communicate and imitate (Barney, 1991; Polanyi, 1962)—but invariably it requires some skills and abilities (Grant & Baden-Fuller, 1995). Until entrepreneurs codify and coordinate it as a resource to obtain profit, knowledge might remain a mental endowment, usually abstract, dispersed, fragmented, and even contradictory.

To echo Schumpeter (1942), entrepreneurs are those who are *able* to discover new opportunities and disrupt market equilibrium. This suggests that entrepreneurs are able to create and respond to the dis-equilibrium that emerges subsequent to their entry into markets. Using mathematical models, Gifford (1993) predicts that depending on their abilities, individuals choose careers as entrepreneurs, managers, or as employees. Similarly, empirical research shows that the requirement of entrepreneurial work is a curvilinear moderator of the relationship between preownership experience and subsequent venture performance (Chandler, 1996). Other scholars argue that people become entrepreneurs because of low opportunity costs

(Amit & Schoemaker, 1993). Douglas and Shepherd (1998) note that individuals choose between entrepreneurial or employment careers (or a combination of the two) based on expected utility such as income, risk, work, and independence.

To succeed, entrepreneurs must also be able to overcome the difficulties of obtaining capital, labor, raw materials, components, and technology in emerging and existing markets. As such, ventures emerge and thrive when entrepreneurs' abilities are characterized as valuable, rare, and inimitable (Guillen, 2000). Other scholars invoked resource-based theory to conceptualize the cognitive ability of entrepreneurs as a unique resource. According to Alvarez and Busenitz (2001), cognitive resources facilitate entrepreneurs' ability to recognize opportunities, assemble and organize resources, and then to create heterogeneous outputs that are superior to existing market offerings. An interesting question, then is, what kinds of valuable, rare, and difficult to imitate abilities are particularly relevant in entrepreneurial contexts?

Abilities: An Entrepreneur's Competency

Despite the fact that scholars agree that entrepreneurs must be highly able individuals, empirical research to identify the specific abilities is surprisingly limited. Markman and Baron's model of person–entrepreneurship fit (2003) proposes that several personal abilities and skills, including opportunity recognition, human and social capital, social skills, and perseverance, are highly relevant to starting a new venture. Their model suggests that when such attributes are strong, there is a better degree of person– entrepreneurship fit, and thus (a) a stronger likelihood that individuals will choose to become entrepreneurs and (b) a greater ultimate success as entrepreneurs.

The theory that the ability to persevere is important in entrepreneurial contexts is not surprising, given that new business formation is a formidable and daunting task (Aldrich, 1999). Indeed, research based on a random sample of 217 patent inventors in the medical industry shows that entrepreneurs exhibited significantly higher levels of perseverance than did nonentrepreneurs (Markman, Baron, & Balkin, 2005). In fact, the higher the overall perseverance scores of patent inventors, the higher were their annual earnings. Interestingly, the same study shows that high levels of perseverance that presumably help entrepreneurs to overcome setbacks and obstacles are also associated with significant personal costs—the experience of regretful thinking.

Although a few economists note that entrepreneurial ability is not wholly innate (e.g., it might be fostered by education; cf. Schultz, 1993), for many the engine for growth remained largely exogenous to the entrepreneur (Kirzner, 1997). A recent study shows that (a) higher testosterone levels are directly related to prior entrepreneurial experience and (b) this relationship is also mediated by one's propensity toward risk (White, Thornhill, & Hampson, 2004). Put differently, an individual's testosterone is related to involvement in a new venture, and this relationship is also mediated by risk propensity. Whether or not specific biological indicators are related to biological evolution cannot be deduced from this study. However, it may be fascinating to direct research to the question of how much entrepreneurial capabilities are related to biological and to evolutionary processes.

Ability is also necessary when entrepreneurs reallocate resources in response to economic disequilibria, which occurs when circumstances become more dynamic. The ability to reallocate resources is enhanced by knowledge and skills, which in turn improve one's ability to collect and process information, to recognize its implications, and to calculate risk. As with executives and managers (cf. Lane, Lyles, & Salk, 1998), the ability to organize, use knowledge, and marry them with skills and abilities is keenly relevant in entrepreneurial contexts. For example, if entrepreneurs differ in their "absorptive capacity" of managerial knowledge and technical know-how, then those endowed with greater absorptive capacity stand a greater chance of success than those whose absorptive capacity is limited. Absorptive capacity theory might also explain why habitual entrepreneurs stand a greater chance of success; their experience with earlier ventures provides a familiar corridor for additional knowledge, skills, and abilities regarding firm creation. Indeed, Alvarez and Busenitz (2001) speculate that entrepreneurial capabilities are an absorptive capacity to recognize opportunity, continuously innovate, and transform inputs into heterogeneous output. Entrepreneurial experience and high absorptive capacity can also improve the ability to learn and make cognitive connections among knowledge elements thus creating higher level of causal ambiguity that hinders imitators.

Because according to cognitive resource theory (Kanfer & Ackerman, 1989) cognitions connect and unite knowledge, skills, and abilities, the next subsection is devoted to the role of cognitions in entrepreneurship contexts. Despite the parallel links among cognition, knowledge, and skills, the link between cognitions and entrepreneurship is discussed here, under the ability heading, because cognitions are a precursor to action.

Cognitions

Cognitions are the mental process of knowing, including aspects such as awareness, perception, reasoning, and judgment. Although research on the link between cognitive ability and entrepreneurship is rare, general research on cognition and entrepreneurship is growing fast. For example, looking at cognitive ability as a moderator between planning and business success, Escher and her colleagues (2002) report that it does not matter whether high-cognitive-ability business owners plan or not, but low-cognitive-ability owners compensate for their low degree of cognitive ability with detailed planning. Also, if high education is any indication of strong cognitive ability, then it is interesting to note that businesses' founders in Western countries are highly educated (Reynolds, Hay, Bygrave, Camp & Autio, 2000). Busenitz and Barney (1997) suggest that entrepreneurs have the ability to think differently, which allows them to use heuristics and make decisions in fundamentally different ways from managers. Relying on heuristics, entrepreneurs are able to quickly make sense out of uncertain and complex situations, which in turn facilitates unorthodox and forward-looking thinking and accelerates learning (Gavetti & Levinthal, 2000).

Broadly speaking, past research has taken two cognitive-related views: search and recognition. Entrepreneurial alertness (or flashes of superior insight) is the ability to cognitively foresee the utility for and value behind not-yet-invented offerings. Although entrepreneurial discovery theory and alertness stress random search (Kirzner, 1979, 1997), Fiet (2002) posits that the ability to apply systematic search is a more effective technique for discovering opportunities, particularly when coupled with prior knowledge. Indeed, based on a series of studies, Fiet (2002) illustrates that the ability to discover opportunities can indeed be taught. Recognition is the ability of some, but not all, to cognitively frame situations as opportunities (e.g., the deployment of existing offerings in a new market context or a unique way to organize and recombine existing resources). In this respect, Alvarez and Busenitz (2001) note that the ability to rely on heuristic-based logic accelerates entrepreneurs' learning, compresses their reaction time to new changes, and thus increases the chances that they will capitalize on their discoveries. If entrepreneurs are able to spot and exploit discoveries that others missed or chose not to pursue, then a fundamental question in entrepreneurship is why and how some people, but not others, discover, create, and exploit new opportunities. This question is important because despite their popularity, heuristics and other cognitive shortcuts can also lead to errors, missed opportunities, and flat-out failure.

Inimitability of resources depends on the process by which these resources were created or utilized (Diericks & Cool, 1989). In entrepreneurship, such resources may be inimitable because they are based on tacit, idiosyncratic, and complex knowledge, which is specific to the founder(s). Resources may yield advantage and entrepreneurial rents when they hinge on abilities that are difficult to adequately observe, describe, value (Itami & Roehl, 1991), or replicate. Such abilities may include recognizing opportunities and bootstrapping together resources for a venture launch, building trusting relationships with suppliers and distributors, attracting and retaining customer loyalty, and achieving legitimacy among market analysts and regulators. Thus, over and above heuristics, entrepreneurs wishing to obtain above normal returns must be able to consistently discover better opportunities, process knowledge more effectively, and utilize their skills more industriously than others in the same market.

To recap, entrepreneurs' abilities (e.g., perseverance, cognition) combined with knowledge and skills might yield some advantage when such combination is valuable, rare, imperfect, mobile, and costly to imitate or substitute. Once entrepreneurs gain an initial advantage, they should continue to reapply their knowledge, skills, and abilities to secure or use additional resources and "freeze out" rivals. This should lead to an ongoing rent (Doh, 2000). To sustain the exploitation of valuable and rare resources, entrepreneurs must also be able to mount a barrier between themselves and rivals (Wernerfelt, 1989). Hence, sustaining a competitive advantage over a period of time requires not only cognitive heuristics or the ability to build a business, but also the ability to erect isolating mechanisms that prevent imitation or direct incursions (Lippman & Rumelt, 1982).

DISCUSSION AND THE FUTURE FOR ENTREPRENEURSHIP COMPETENCY RESEARCH

What individual differences are relevant to entrepreneurial behavior and why they matter is the focus of a growing research with the general consensus that individuals and individual differences do matter and that the person—the entrepreneur—is a key factor in entrepreneurship. Because not all environments provide equal opportunities and not all individuals are equally endowed with knowledge, skills, and abilities in recognizing, pursuing, and exploiting opportunities, entrepreneurship is frequently described as the nexus of both—lucrative opportunities and enterprising individuals (Shane & Venkataraman, 2000). This and similar views acknowledge environmental/contextual factors and individual-level factors. This chapter focused on the latter. In an effort to develop a theory that describes, explains, and predicts which individual differences play an important role in entrepreneurship, the chapter reviewed the literature on individual difference and suggested that aggregating these into three broad entrepreneurs' competencies—knowledge, skills, and ability—provides clarity and coherence.

Developing a theory of entrepreneurs' competencies is important for several reasons. First, although most entrepreneurs know their strengths and weaknesses, potential investors, suppliers, buyers, partners, and employees generally do not. Providing a framework that aggregates individual differences into entrepreneurs' competencies—knowledge, skills, and ability—gives common language and clarity to what may become a hodge-podge of concepts, constructs, and definitions. For instance, "entrepreneurs' abilities are a critical determinant of the ultimate payoff from the venture investment" (Amit, Glosten, & Muller, 1990, p. 1243), but the absence of clear definitions of and matrixes to assess entrepreneurs' competencies raises a moral hazard and adverse selection problems related to the amount of capital entrepreneurs can raise from investors. Investors may have a good understanding of discoveries and opportunities entrepreneurs disclose to them, a sound knowledge of market and industry contexts, and adequate comprehension of issues related to finance and technology. However, in many cases investors (as researchers) are unclear on how to ascertain and measure the competencies of entrepreneurs. Moral hazard might occur under conditions of information asymmetry when entrepreneurs' behaviors and actions change from frugality and prudence to lavishness and carelessness after they receive investment capital. Adverse selection might occur when entrepreneurs can better predict the future failure of their ventures than investors can. That is, adverse selection might occur when entrepreneurs seek capital because their ventures are failing, rather than thriving. Investors are aware of this information asymmetry, but they do not know ex ante that it is the entrepreneur who capitalizes on this asymmetry most. To remedy this asymmetry and adverse selection, investors may either allocate less capital than requested (essentially claiming larger ownership shares in ventures) or delay and even refuse investments even to quite promising ventures. The main consequence of this asymmetry is that the market fails to allocate capital efficiently and many high-potential ventures remain undercapitalized.

Second, most of the dimensions that comprise entrepreneurs' competencies have been recognized as crucial factors in diverse managerial roles, but to date, entrepreneurship research has largely studied them in isolation and with little recognition of their reciprocal causality. Because all three entrepreneurs' competencies are presumed to play a key function in wealth creation, the framework advanced in this chapter posits that these competencies should be studied together with special effort to test for potential reciprocal causalities among constructs. It is quite possible that certain interactions among the various competencies (knowledge, skills, and abilities) and their respective subcategories (e.g., tacit and codified knowledge, human and technical skills, and perseverance and cognitions) may yield different and even unexpected findings. To illustrate, Markman and his colleagues (2005) suggest that highly perseverant entrepreneurs may experience more regrets than less perseverant entrepreneurs.

Third, much of past research on individual differences in entrepreneurship focused on differences between entrepreneurs and others, with few attempts to link individual differences to firm-level or financial outcomes.

The theory of entrepreneurs' competencies seeks to inspire empirical research on the links between differences at the individual level and performance or success at the firm level.

One area is singled out as needing further study. As mentioned earlier, there is a need to address the problem of the "web of interactions" between and among the various competencies, their subcategories, and their relationship with success—growth and profitability. The priority is to identify the key components, to analyze the interactive relationships between them, and to test predictions about their apparent correlation with income and growth. For example, are there some levels of substitution or trade-offs between codified knowledge and tacit knowledge, skills and abilities, or human capital and social capital? Because time is a key resource needed for the creation of social capital, is human capital a reliable substitute for social capital? Additional research should focus on the link between skills and abilities, especially after providing specificity of and sufficient control for their subcategories.

The issue of tacit knowledge and codification is receiving some attention, but more questions are raised. For example, if knowledge accelerates the degree of information codification (Marsili, 2002), are some entrepreneurs better than others in capitalizing on such acceleration of codification, and if so, why? This is an interesting empirical question that should be settled at the empirical level, but one challenge entrepreneurship (and management) scholars face is how to reliably measure tacit and codified knowledge. If successful, such research would make a solid contribution, as the degrees of knowledge tacitness and codification may not have equivalent importance. First, even if more knowledge were generated, collected, and organized, it is unclear whether greater volumes of data are in themselves of any economic significance (e.g., many universities, including those that pride themselves as "knowledge creators," are at the brink of insolvency). Second, it is also unclear whether codification of information reduces tacit knowledge into elements of clear and explicit knowledge.

Scholars may also contribute by vetting the consequences of codification and what drives the processes of codification in entrepreneurial contexts. For instance, because codification is presumed to allow modularization, separability, repeatability, and specialization of the processes of knowledge production and diffusion (Arora & Gambardella, 1996; Cowan & Foray, 1997), researchers may seek to test whether codification of tacit knowledge reduces the transaction costs implied in the exchange of knowledge between different economic agents. Another challenge is that codification may or may not ease access to knowledge. First, codified knowledge might be proprietary, such as a patent, whereas other knowledge might be in the public domain but remain tacit. Second, because the amount to be learned is always relative to one's prior knowledge, codification and public knowledge mean neither ease of learning nor ease of use. For instance, to an extent, advanced mathematics, genetics, nanotechnology, and biomedicine are codified knowledge, but their learning, use, and transferability are far from trivial.

To better understand the integrative role of entrepreneurs' competencies, research must certainly look further. This integrative view is important because, in essence, entrepreneurs need to have the knowledge, skills, and ability to recognize opportunities and perhaps different knowledge, skills, and abilities to transform opportunities into appropriable new wealth in the face of inevitable uncertainty and adversity. At least part of the theory, as proposed in this chapter, may lie in an understanding that such competencies are dynamic and entail a multitude of higher level interactions among the various dimension comprising knowledge, skills, and abilities. At this point it is also important to apply the concept of *fungibility*, or the extent to which one form of competency can be used as a substitute for another. Knowledge, skills, and abilities are valuable entrepreneurs' competencies precisely because they are not fungible—they cannot be used as costless, perfect substitutes for one another, and having only one or two competencies is probably insufficient. Put bluntly, competitive advantage in entrepreneurship contexts is more likely when individuals are endowed with all three competencies. At the same time, it should also be noted that because each competency is made of several factors, equifinality suggests that different makeup of knowledge, skills, and abilities may still yield highly successful venture.

As this chapter draws to an end, here is a summary of key questions research on entrepreneurs' competencies may seek to address:

- What is link between entrepreneurs' competencies and the amount of capital raised from external investors?
- Assuming all three competencies play a vital role in entrepreneurship, how should reciprocal causalities among knowledge, skills, and abilities (and their subcategories) be assessed? How should these various interactions be linked to firm-level outcomes?
- How frequent are trade-offs or substitution among the entrepreneurs' competencies and to what extent do they occur? For example, can the ability to codify knowledge substitute for the accumulation of tacit knowledge? What skills might compensate for insufficient knowledge or abilities? Or because time is a key resource needed for the creation of social capital, to what extent can strong human capital compensate for low social capital?
- Does absorbent capacity of knowledge accelerate the codification of incoming new information? Are some entrepreneurs indeed better

than others in capitalizing on such acceleration of codification, and if so, why?

- What measures and how should they be used to capture entrepreneurs' competencies? When studying knowledge, how should scholars operationalize tacit and codified knowledge?
- To reduce imitation and protect their discoveries, how and to what extent can entrepreneurs conceal the codification of tacit knowledge? Alternatively, because codification of tacit knowledge facilitates modularization, separability, repeatability, and specialization of knowledge-based processes, do entrepreneurs actually use codification to seek advantage (e.g., reduce transaction costs implied in the exchange of knowledge between different economic agents)?
- To what extent are the knowledge, skills, and ability to recognize and create opportunities different from the knowledge, skills, and abilities used to appropriate rents from these opportunities through new ventures?
- To what extent are knowledge, skills, and abilities fungible competencies?

In closing, the chapter echoes Thomas Edison, who once said that genius is 1% inspiration and 99% perspiration, and John D. Rockefeller,[3] who said, "Every right implies a responsibility, every opportunity an obligation, every possession a duty." Echoing both an inventor and entrepreneur is important because research on individual differences in entrepreneurship tends to emphasize either the former (e.g., insights, discoveries, and opportunity recognition) or the later (e.g., execution, exploitation, and appropriation). This chapter suggests that a fundamental hurdle to theory development in the field of entrepreneurship is hidden in capturing "new combinations"—in appreciating and testing the interactions between insights and their execution, discoveries and their exploitation, opportunities and their appropriation. The notion that entrepreneurship entails inherent responsibilities, obligations, and duties is important because starting a business is constrained by time and resources, and it entails substantial adversity. At the extreme, insights, discoveries, and opportunity recognition are a costless mental exercise or a cognitive workout in wishful thinking that cannot produce—by themselves—new businesses. Still, recognizing opportunities is clearly imperative (i.e., opportunities are unlikely to be pursued in the absence of recognition). Thus, the framework of entrepreneurs' competencies advanced here advocates a concurrent focus on knowledge, skills, and abilities that make the discovery of opportunities and appropriation of new wealth highly achievable.

---

[3]Quoted from a commemorative inscription outside Rockefeller Center in New York City.

REFERENCES

Ackerman, P. L. (1988). Determinants of individual differences during skill acquisition: Cognitive abilities and information processing. *Journal of Experimental Psychology, 117,* 288–318.

Adler, P. S., & Kwon, S. (2002). Social capital: prospects for a new concept. *Academy of Management Review, 27*(1), 17–40.

Aldrich, H. (1999). *Organizations evolving.* Thousand Oaks, CA: Sage.

Alvarez, S. A., & Busenitz, L. W. (2001). The entrepreneurship of resource-based theory. *Journal of Management, 27*(6), 755–775.

Alvesson, M. (2000). Social identity and the problem of loyalty in knowledge-intensive companies. *Journal of Management Studies, 37,* 1101–1123.

Amit, R., & Schoemaker, P. J. H. (1993). Strategic assets and organizational rent. *Strategic Management Journal, 14,* 33–46.

Amit, R., Glosten, L., & Muller, E. (1990). Entrepreneurial ability, venture investments, and risk sharing. *Management Science, 36*(10), 1232–1246.

Ancona, D. G., & Caldwell, D. F. (1992). Bridging the boundary: External activity and performance in organizational teams. *Administrative Science Quarterly, 37,* 634–665.

Ardichvili, A., Cardozo, R., & Ray, S. (2003). A theory of entrepreneurial opportunity identification and development. *Journal of Business Venturing, 18*(1), 105–124.

Arora, A., & Gambardella, A. (1990). Complementarity and external linkages: The strategies of large firms in biotechnology. *Journal of Industrial Economics, 38,* 361–379.

Arora, A., & Gambardella, A. (1996). The changing technology of technological change: General and abstract knowledge and the division of innovative labor. *Research Policy, 23,* 523–532.

Bain, J., (1956). *Barriers to new competition.* Cambridge, MA: Harvard University Press.

Baker, W. (2000). *Achieving success through social capital: Tapping the hidden resources in your personal and business networks.* San Francisco, CA: Jossey-Bass.

Baldwin, T. T., Bedell, M. D., & Johnson, J. L. (1997). The social fabric of a team-based M.B.A. program: Network effects on student satisfaction and performance. *Academy of Management Journal, 40,* 1369–1397.

Barney, J. (1991). Firm resources and sustained competitive advantage. *Journal of Management, 17,* 99–120.

Baron, R. A., & Markman, G. D. (2003). Beyond social capital: The role of entrepreneurs' social competence in their financial success. *Journal of Business Venturing, 18*(1), 41–60.

Baron, R. A., & Markman, G. D. (in press). Toward a process view of entrepreneurship: The changing impact of individual level variables across phases of new venture development. In M. A. Rahim, R. T. Golembiewski, & K. D. Mackenzie, (Eds.), *Current topics in management* (Vol. 9). New Brunswick, NJ: Transaction.

Baum, J. R., Locke, E. A., & Smith, K. G., (2001). A multidimensional model of venture growth. *Academy of Management Journal, 44*(2), 292–303.

Bird, B. (1988). Implementing entrepreneurial ideas: The case of intentions. *Academy of Management Review, 13*(3), 442–453.

Boyatzis, R. E. (1982). *The competent manager; A model for effective performance.* New York: John Wiley & Sons.

Bruederl, J., Preisendoerfer, P., & Ziegler, R. (1992). Survival chances of newly founded business organizations. *American Sociological Review, 57,* 222–242.

Burt, R. S. (1992). *Structural holes: The social structure of competition.* Cambridge, MA: Harvard University Press.

Busenitz, L., & Barney, J. (1997). Differences between entrepreneurs and mangers in large organizations: Biases and heuristics in strategic decision-making. *Journal of Business Venturing, 12,* 9–30.

Chandler, G. N., & Jansen, E. (1992). The founder's self-assessed competence and venture performance. *Journal of Business Venturing, 7*, 223–236.

Chandler, G. N. (1996). Business similarity as a moderator of the relationship between pre-ownership experience and venture performance. *Entrepreneurship Theory and Practice, 20*(3), 51–65.

Chung, L. H., & Gibbons, P. T. (1997). Corporate entrepreneurship: The role of ideology and social capital. *Group and Organization Management, 22*, 10–30.

Ciavarella, M. A., Bucholtz, A. K., Riordan, C. M., Gatewood, R. D., & Stokes, G. S. (2004). The big five and venture success: Is there a linkage? *Journal of Business Venturing*.

Cohen, W. M., & Levinthal, D. A. (1990, March). Absorptive capacity: A new perspective on learning and innovation. *Administrative Science Quarterly, 35*(1), 128–152.

Coleman, J. S. (1988). Social capital in the creation of human capital. *American Journal of Sociology, 94*, S95–S120.

Cowan, R., & Foray, D. (1997). The economics of codification and the diffusion of knowledge. *Industrial and Corporate Change, 6*, 595–622.

Davidsson, P., & Honig, B. (2003). The role of social and human capital among nascent entrepreneurs. *Journal of Business Venturing, 18*(3), 301–331.

Diericks, I., & Cool, K. (1989). Asset stock accumulation and sustainability of competitive advantage. *Management Science, 35*, 1504–1511.

Doh, J. P. (2000). Entrepreneurial privatization strategies: Order of entry and local partner collaboration as sources of competitive advantage. *Academy of Management Review, 25*(3), 551–571.

Dosi, G., (1982). Technological paradigms and technological trajectories. A suggested interpretation of the determinant and direction of technological change. *Research Policy, 11*, 147–162.

Douglas, E. J., & Shepherd, D. A. (2000, May). Entrepreneurship as a utility maximizing response. *Journal of Business Venturing, 15*(3), 231.

Eisenhardt, K., & Schoonhoven, C. B. (1990). Organizational growth: Linking founding team, strategy, environment, and growth among U.S. semiconductor ventures, 1978–1988. *Administrative Science Quarterly, 35*, 504–529.

Eisenhardt, K., Schoonhoven, C. B., & Bird, C. (1996). Resource-based view of strategic alliance formation: Strategic and social effects in entrepreneurial firms. *Organization Science, 7*(2), 136–150.

Ensley, M. D., Carland, J. W., & Carland, J. C. (2000). Investigating the existence of the lead entrepreneur. *Journal of Small Business Management, 38*(4), 59–77.

Escher, S., Grabarkiewicz, R., Frese, M., van Steekelenburg, G., Lauw, M., & Friedrich, C. (2002). The moderator effect of cognitive ability on the relationship between planning strategies and business success of small-scale business owners in South Africa: A longitudinal study. *Journal of Developmental Entrepreneurship, 7*(3), 305–308.

Feinberg, R. M., & Price, G. N. (2004). The funding of economics research: Does social capital matter for success at the national science foundation? *Review of Economics and Statistics, 86*(1), 245–252.

Fiet, J. O. (2002). *The systematic search for entrepreneurial discoveries.* Westport, CT: Quorum Books.

Fleishman, E. A., & Quaintance, M. K. (1984). *Taxonomies of human performance: The description of human tasks.* New York: Academic Press.

Gavetti, G., & Levinthal, D. (2000). Looking forward and looking backward: Cognitive and experimental search. *Administrative Science Quarterly, 45*, 113–137.

Gifford, S. (1993). Heterogeneous ability, career choice and firm size. *Small Business Economics, 5*(4), 249–259.

Granovetter, M. (1974). *Getting a job.* Chicago: University of Chicago Press.

Granovetter, M. (1985). Economic action and social structure: The problem of embeddedness. *American Journal of Sociology, 91*(3), 481–510.

Grant, R. M., & Baden-Fuller, C. (1995). A knowledge-based theory of inter-firm collaboration. *Academy of Management Best Paper Proceedings*, pp. 17–21.

Guillen, M. F. (2000). Business groups in emerging economies: A resource-based view. *Academy of Management Journal*, 43(3), 362–380.

Hansen, M. T. (1999). The search-transfer problem: The role of weak ties in sharing knowledge across organization subunits. *Administrative Science Quarterly*, 44, 82–111.

Hayek, F. A. (1945, September). The use of knowledge in society. *American Economic Review*, 35(4), 519.

Higgins, M. C., & Kram, K. E. (2001). Reconceptualizing mentoring at work: A developmental network perspective. *Academy of Management Review*, 20, 254–288.

Hoegl, M., Parboteeah, K. P., & Munson, C. L. (2003). Team-level antecedents of individuals' knowledge networks. *Decision Sciences*, 34(4), 741–770.

House, R. J., & Aditya, R. N. (1997). The social scientific study of leadership: Quo vadis? *Journal of Management*, 23(3), 409–473.

Ibarra, H. (1993). Network centrality, power, and innovation involvement: Determinants of technical and administrative roles. *Academy of Management Journal*, 36, 471–501.

Itami, H., & Roehl, T. W. (1991). *Mobilizing invisible assets*. Cambridge, MA: Harvard University Press.

Kanfer, R., & Ackerman, P. L. (1989). Motivation and cognitive abilities: An integrative/aptitude-treatment interaction approach to skill acquisition. *Journal of Applied Psychology*, 74, 657 690.

Kirzner, I. (1979). *Perception, opportunity, and profit*. Chicago: University of Chicago Press.

Kirzner, I. (1997). Entrepreneurial discovery and the competitive market process: An Austrian approach. *Journal of Economic Literature*, 35, 60–85.

Kogut, B., & Kulatilaka, N. (2004). Real options pricing and organizations: The contingent risks of extended theoretical domains. *Academy of Management Review*, 29(1), 102–110.

Lane, P. J., & Lubatkin, M. (1998, May). Relative absorptive capacity and interorganizational learning. *Strategic Management Journal*, 19(5), 461.

Lane, P. J., Lyles, M. A., & Salk, J. E. (1998). Relative absorptive capacity, trust, and interorganizational learning in international joint ventures. In M. Hitt, J. Ricart, & R. Nixon (Eds.) *Managing strategically in an interconnected world* (pp. 373–398). New York: John Wiley.

Lin, N. (1999). Social networks and status attainment. *Annual Review of Sociology*, 25, 467–487.

Lippman, S. A., & Rumelt, R. (1982). Uncertain irritability: An analysis of interfirm differences in efficiency under competition. *Bell Journal of Economics*, 13, 418–438.

Louis, K. S., Blumenthal, D., Gluck, M. E., & Stoto, M. A. (1989). Entrepreneurs in academe: An exploration of behaviors among life scientists. *Administrative Science Quarterly*, 34(1), 110–131.

Luo, Y. (2003). Industrial dynamics and managerial networking in an emerging market: The case of China. *Strategic Management Journal*, 24(13), 1315–1327.

Markman, G. D., Balkin, D. B., & Baron R. A. (2002, Winter). Inventors and new venture formation: The effects of general self-efficacy and regretful thinking. *Entrepreneurship Theory & Practice*, pp. 149–165.

Markman, G. D., & Baron, R. A. (2003). Person-entrepreneurship fit: Why some people are more successful as entrepreneurs than others. *Human Resource Management Review*, 134, 1–21.

Markman, G. D., Baron R. A., & Balkin, D. B. (2005). Are perseverance and self-efficacy costless? Assessing entrepreneurs' regretful thinking. *Journal of Organizational Behavior*, 26(1), 1–19.

Marsili, O. (2002). Technological regimes and sources of entrepreneurship. *Small Business Economics*, 19(3), 217–231.

Matthews, G., Jones, D. M., & Chamberlain, A. G. (1992). Predictors of individual differences in mail-coding skills and their variation with ability level. *Journal of Applied Psychology*, 77(4), 406–418.

McClelland, D. C. (1961). *The achieving society*. New York: Van Nostrand Reinhold.

Mehra, A., Kilduff, M., & Brass, D. J. (2001). The social network of high and low self-monitors: Implications for workplace performance. *Administrative Science Quarterly, 46,* 121–146.

Mischel, W. (1973). Toward a cognitive social learning reconceptualization of personality. *Psychological Review, 80,* 252–283.

Mouw, T. (2003). Social capital and finding a job: Do contacts matter? *American Sociological Review, 68*(6), 868–898.

Murray, F. (2004). The role of academic inventors in entrepreneurial firms: Sharing the laboratory life. *Research Policy, 33*(4), 643–659.

Peteraf, M. (1993). The cornerstones of competitive advantage: A resource-based view. *Strategic Management Journal, 14,* 179–192.

Piazza-Georgi, B. (2002). The role of human and social capital in growth: Extending our understanding. *Cambridge Journal of Economics, 26,* 461–479.

Polanyi, M. (1962). *Personal knowledge: Towards a post-critical philosophy.* Chicago: University of Chicago Press.

Reynolds, P. D., Carter, N. M., Gartner, W. B., & Greene, P. G. (2004). The prevalence of nascent entrepreneurs in the United States: Evidence from the panel study of entrepreneurial dynamics. *Small Business Economics, 23*(4), 263–284.

Roure, J. B., & Madique, M. A. (1986). Linking prefunding factors and hightechnology venture success: An exploratory study. *Journal of Business Venturing, 1*(3), 295–306.

Sarasvathy, D. K., Simon, H. A., & Lave, L. (1998, January). Perceiving and managing business risks: Differences between entrepreneurs and bankers. *Journal of Economic Behavior & Organization, 33*(2), 207.

Schultz, T. W. (1993). *Origins of increasing returns.* Oxford: Blackwell.

Schumpeter, J. A. (1942). *Capitalism, socialism, and democracy.* New York: Harper. (Reprinted by Harper Colophon, 1975)

Seibert, S. E., Kraimer, M. L., & Liden, R. C. (2001). A social capital theory of career success. *Academy of Management Journal, 44,* 219–237.

Shane, S. (2000, July/August). Prior knowledge and the discovery of entrpreneurial opportunities. *Organization Science: A Journal of the Institute of Management Sciences, 11*(4), 448.

Shane, S. (2001, February). Technological opportunities and new firm creation. *Management Science, 47*(2), 205.

Shane, S., & Venkataraman, S. (2000). The promise of entrepreneurship as a field of research. *Academy of Management Review, 25,* 217–226.

Shepherd, D. A. (2003). Learning from business failure: Propositions of grief recovery for the self-employed. *Academy of Management Review, 28*(2), 318–328.

Simon, D. G., & Hitt, M. A. (2003). Managing resources: Linking unique resources, management, and wealth creation in family firms. *Entrepreneurship Theory and Practice, 27*(4), 339–358.

Spencer, J. A., & Spencer, B. J. (1983). Strategic commitment to R&D: The symmetric case. *Bell Journal of Economics, 14*(1), 225–236.

Tsai, W., & Goshal, S. (1998). Social capital and value creation: The role of intrafirm networks. *Academy of Management Journal, 41,* 464–476.

Venkataraman, S. (1997). *The distinctive domain of entrepreneurship research. Advances in entrepreneurship, firm emergence and growth.* Katz (Eds.) 3: 119–138. Greenwich, CT: JAI Press Inc.

Watson, W., Stewart, W. H., Jr., & BarNir, A. (2003). The effects of human capital, organizational demography, and interpersonal processes on venture partner perceptions of firm profit and growth. *Journal of Business Venturing, 18*(2), 145–164.

Wernerfelt, B. (1989, Spring). From critical resource to corporate strategy. *Journal of General Management, 14*(3), 4–12.

White, R. E., Thornhill, S., & Hampson, E. (2004). *Entrepreneurs and evolutionary biology: The relationship between testosterone and new venture creation.* Working Paper, Richard Ivey School of Business, University of Western Ontario, London, Ontario, Canada.

Yli-Renko, H., Autio, E., & Sapienza, H. J. (2001). Social capital, knowledge acquisition, and knowledge exploitation in young technology-based firms. *Strategic Management Journal, 22,* 587–613.

Young, G. J., Charns, M. P., & Shortell, S. M. (2001). Top manager and network effects on the adoption of innovative management practices: A study of TQM in a public hospital system. *Strategic Management Journal, 22,* 935–951.

Zacharakis, A., Reynolds, P. D., & Bygrave, W. D. (1999, June). National Entrepreneurship Assessment: United States of America 1999 Executive Report. *Global Entrepreneurship Monitor,* Kansas City, MO, Kauffman Center for Entrepreneurial Leadership. (http://www.gemconsortium.org/download/1139419675140/GEM1999USA.pdf

5

Entrepreneurial Motivation

Edwin A. Locke
J. Robert Baum

Motivation energizes, directs, and sustains action. It is based on the individual's needs, values, desires, goals, and intentions, as well as incentives and rewards that affect those internal mechanisms (Steers & Porter, 1991). Dr. Thomas Chialastri, founder of American Orthopedic Devices, LLC, invented a surgical device to reduce back pain. His dream of a significant and financially successful company, passion for surgical tools, fierce energy, and confidence drove him through multiple challenges to his goal to create a premier orthopedic devices company. A person may have sufficient technical skill and money to start a business, but without motivation nothing happens.

Entrepreneurship researchers study both cognition and motivation. In normal human action, motivation (e.g., desire) and cognition (e.g., knowledge, belief) always operate together. Knowledge or belief in the absence of motivation leads nowhere, and motivation in the absence of knowledge and belief leads to random or unproductive action (Locke, 2000).

Entrepreneurial motivation involves motivation that is directed toward entrepreneurial goals (e.g., goals that involve the recognition and exploitation of business opportunities). Gartner, Bird, and Starr (1992) characterized entrepreneurial motivation as the forces within individuals that drive nascent entrepreneurs to and through the process of venture emergence and growth.

We begin this chapter with a review of current entrepreneurship motivation models, and follow with an exploration of motivating factors (traits, values, motives, goals, etc.) that impact entrepreneurial motivation. We end by posing some unanswered research questions.

ENTREPRENEURSHIP MOTIVATION MODELS

Entrepreneurship researchers Gartner, Bird, and Starr (1992) reviewed Landy and Becker's (1987) five categories of motivation theory—needs, reinforcement, equity, expectancy, and goal theory—and concluded that expectancy theory (Guest, 1984; Vroom, 1964) and goal theory (Locke & Latham, 2002) offered useful structures for understanding entrepreneurs' motivation. They noted that expectancy theory provides a framework for understanding why and how some people choose to be entrepreneurs and suggested that entrepreneurs' outcome arrays are more complex and the probabilities of each outcome are smaller than for others. To explain the relevance of expectancy theory, Gartner, Bird, and Starr suggested that entrepreneurs may be attracted to high-uncertainty situations or be able to make choices when they face equivocal options because, compared with managers of established businesses, they are more tolerant of uncertainty.

Goal theory's fundamental proposition is that specific challenging goals (given adequate commitment, feedback, and knowledge) result in high performance (Locke & Latham, 2002). Thus, goal theory offers a more direct explanation of entrepreneurial motivation than expectancy theory, suggesting that entrepreneurs set higher entrepreneurship goals than those who do not start businesses. To explain, Gartner et al. (1992) suggested that goal theory was promising (and testable) in terms of predicting entrepreneurship performance:

> Studies of goals (e.g., making the first sale, obtaining venture capital, developing the prototype) set by entrepreneurs as well as studies of the goals entrepreneurs establish for other individuals involved in the emerging organization may reveal that entrepreneurs who set higher goals are more likely to enable their emerging organizations to survive and grow larger than entrepreneurs with lower goals. (p. 25)

Surprisingly, Gartner et al. (1992) did not include social-cognitive theory (Bandura, 1986) in their list of potentially useful theories. Social cognitive theory's core concept, self-efficacy (Bandura, 1997), has important applications to the field of entrepreneurship. (In 1998, Chen, Greene, and Crick published the first of many studies of entrepreneurial self-efficacy in entrepreneurship research journals.)

Naffziger, Hornsby, and Kuratko (1994) proposed a theoretical model of entrepreneurial motivation that included perceptions and equity theory comparisons as proposed by Adams (1965) and others. With the exception of goals and self-efficacy, the models just mentioned have stimulated little research about entrepreneurial motivation.

Other motivating concepts that have been studied by entrepreneurship researchers are intentions and perseverance. Shepherd and Krueger (2002) and Krueger (2003) advanced the study of entrepreneurship motivation through application of social cognition theory (Ajzen, 1991) to the entrepreneurship domain. They point to entrepreneurial intentions and perceptions of desirability and feasibility to explain new venture (and corporate entrepreneurship) behaviors. Ajzen has proposed that intentions reflect the motivational factors that influence behavior. Intentions indicate how much effort they are planning to exert in order to get to their goal. The stronger the intentions, the stronger is the effort (Ajzen, 1991, p. 181).

Markman and Baron (2002) utilized several motivation components (perseverance and self-efficacy) to create a model of who will choose to start a new venture. They argued that to the extent entrepreneurs are high on individual differences that relate to the entrepreneurs' situation, there will be a greater likelihood or magnitude of the entrepreneurs' successes.

ENTREPRENEURSHIP MOTIVATION FACTORS

Entrepreneurship starts with a good business idea. This core idea is usually referred to as the entrepreneurial vision. Vision, of course, is primarily cognitive, although, as we discuss later, it has motivating aspects too. After acknowledging the role of situational factors, we discuss vision, because, as we noted, motivation without cognition is useless. Then we consider general motivational values, traits, and motives, including independence, general self-confidence, achievement motivation, drive, egoistic passion, and tenacity. We follow with consideration of three situationally specific motivators: self-efficacy, goals, and vision. We offer a reminder that goal setting is a process that is fully integrated with the other factors; indeed, self-set goals emerge from simultaneous consideration of all of the other motivational factors.

Situational Factors

It is tempting to focus solely on factors within the individual when explaining human action but situational factors play a role too. Entrepreneurial activities lead to various degrees of profitability and growth and many new ventures fail completely. The factors contributing to success or failure include the environment, characteristics of the new organization, and attributes of the entrepreneur (Baum, Locke, & Smith, 2001). Outside factors, even if favorable, do not directly cause entrepreneurial activity. They only set the stage for it (or prevent it if the factors are unfavorable). *The most direct cause of entrepreneurship is the entrepreneur.* Like all individuals, the entrepreneur possesses volitional choice and is, therefore, the agent of his or her own actions (Binswanger, 1991).

However, external factors, such as economic freedom and market forces, can limit or discourage or they can facilitate and encourage entrepreneurial activity. The most important context element in entrepreneurship is economic freedom. True entrepreneurs cannot even arise in socialist, communist, or fascist economies. Even in mixed economies, those with limitations on freedom, political pull may have profound effects on "entrepreneurial" success (Folsom, 1991). The second set of context characteristics is market forces. These can affect the initiation and success of entrepreneurial ventures; examples include the state of the economy, technology, population demographics, availability of labor (including skilled labor), industry structure, and the availability of investment capital (Shane, Locke, & Collins, 2003).

Rational entrepreneurs take account of these external factors when formulating their product or service ideas and their business plans. Such factors both limit what they can do and provide opportunities; for example, potential entrepreneurs living in state-oriented economies try to emigrate to freer countries; those with limited capital do not start automobile companies; those in countries with rapidly aging populations may look for emerging opportunities among senior citizens.

Vision

The essence of vision, as noted, is that it is the idea of the business. Specifically, it is the leader's concept of what the business will be and what will make it attractive to customers and investors.

Vision should not be confused with vision statements. The vision statement is a shorthand summary usually formulated for the purpose of inspiring others (e.g., we will make the best quality cars in the world). The full vision, however, is inside the entrepreneur's head and is much more detailed than any one statement. By detailed, however, we do not mean highly complex, but rather something more elaborate than a slogan. Great wealth creators do not "complexify," they simplify (Locke, 2002). The entrepreneur defines the nature of the business, sees the parts, sees the whole, and sees how each part relates to the whole. Entrepreneurs bring order out of seeming chaos. They do not get overwhelmed by minutiae, and they think in terms of principles (Locke, 2002).

Formulating successful business principles requires inductive reasoning ability. The entrepreneur must look at hundreds or thousands of concrete facts, decide which ones are important, observe how they are connected, and integrate these observations into a small number of key ideas. Jack Welch used to say that all you need to manage a business is three measurements: customer satisfaction, employee satisfaction, and cash flow. Of course, he knew very well it was not really that simple, but he had a genius for picking out, from the morass of information he was faced with, what was important and essential. Sam Walton only had one fundamental idea—one that he got from others—discount retailing. But he was still a visionary genius, because he figured out how to do it better than any retailer in the world (e.g., through information sharing with employees, buying directly from manufacturers, implementing new policies rapidly, the use of technology).

Entrepreneurs must make inferences from their observations and integrations. The key element in being visionary is having foresight (Locke, 2000). Foresight is the ability to see beyond the immediate moment, to see past what is working now, to see what will work in the future. It's the ability to see not just actuality but potentiality. Steve Jobs saw the potential of the PC when no one else did and started a whole new industry.

How does one see potentiality? By looking at the facts that are known and from projecting future possibilities—usually in the form of "what if ...?" What if we could make a computer than works electronically (IBM)? What if we doubled the speed of the computer chip and then doubled it again and again (Intel)? What if we could write software that could be sold along with PCs (Microsoft)? What if we could offer airfares that were much cheaper than other airlines (Jet Blue)? What if we combined the feature of a car and a minivan into a new type of vehicle (the SUV)? What if we would offer high-quality steaks with ambience at good prices (Outback Steak House)? To be successful, such projections, of course, must be more than just wishes; they must be grounded in reality.

Successful visionaries know what businesses to be in and what businesses not to be in. Jack Welch was a genius at knowing which existing GE businesses to sell and which new ones—those with growth potential—to buy. As Warren Buffet has said, even the most brilliant business leader cannot make a lousy business work.

Motivational Traits, Values, and Motives[1]

Independence. By definition, entrepreneurs are independent. They value being able to run their companies, whether it be an existing company or one that they have founded. Often they are people who have been frustrated by working for other people—bosses who they think know less than the aspiring entrepreneurs do or who have thwarted their attempts to change, grow, or improve an existing business. They want to be able to make key decisions themselves. Furthermore, entrepreneurs do things that no one has done before or do them in a way that has not been done before. This means they often go against the status quo, defy tradition, or do what others claim is foolish, crazy, or impossible. Entrepreneurs, therefore, must

---

[1]The values, traits, and motives material presented here is based to a considerable extent on Locke (2000), a qualitative study of 80 great wealth creators. However, quantitative, empirical studies or reviews of such studies are cited where relevant.

not only be in charge, they must be independent thinkers. Regardless of whom they consult, they must rely in the end on their own judgment. The buck stops with them. Dependent, follower types cannot operate in such a role and do not seek to (Timmons, 2000).

True independence does not mean independence from reality or acting blindly on feelings. Nor does it mean acting in the opposite way others do just to be different (negative conformity). It is not irrationalism. It means using one's best rational judgment.

Nor does being independent mean the refusal to listen to good ideas from others. A rational entrepreneur will be delighted to get as many good ideas from others as possible, but, in the end, an independent judgment has to be made as to the validity of others' ideas.

General Self-Confidence.   There are two types of self-confidence: general and task-specific. We discuss the latter type below. General confidence or efficacy means that one believes one can deal with the world, meet life's challenges, overcome obstacles, and achieve the goals one sets for oneself. Generalized self-confidence is an aspect of self-esteem. Self-esteem is the conviction that one is generally worthy and efficacious. Often confidence is developed from childhood experiences in which one undertakes independent projects (e.g., running a paper route, building a computer and selling it), masters difficulties, and succeeds. Confidence may also stem from one's awareness of one's own cognitive abilities. Many successful entrepreneurs have strong mathematical ability, which is obviously important in many businesses (Locke, 2000).

Confidence is essential in entrepreneurship, because running or starting a business and making it successful is usually a very difficult undertaking. There are many stages involved in, for example, starting a new business, including formulating the basic vision, finding investors, hiring competent people, finding a suitable location, making the product, finding customers, building a sales force, beating out competitors, dealing with lawsuit and government regulations, and overcoming setbacks at every phase. Entrepreneurship is not a career for the fainthearted.

Entrepreneurship researchers have quantitative evidence that general business or entrepreneurial self-efficacy (a concept half-way between life confidence and task-specific confidence) predicts new venture creation (startup) (Boyd & Vozikis, 1994; Krueger & Brazeal, 1994; Markman, Balkin, & Baron, 2002; Markman, Baron, & Balkin, 2003). Chandler and Jansen (1992) found a significant relationship between entrepreneurial self-confidence and early stage venture performance. Chen, Greene, and Crick (1998) defined entrepreneurial self-efficacy (ESE) as "the strength of a person's belief that he or she is capable of successfully performing the various roles and tasks of entrepreneurship." It consisted of five factors: innovation, risk taking, marketing, management, and financial control. The total ESE score for the founders was significantly higher than the score for managers of established firms.

General self-efficacy may be most important in the earliest stages of new venture creation when uncertainty is highest, and nascent entrepreneurs tend to be alone with their entrepreneurial vision and strategies (Baron & Markman, 2005; Chen, Greene, & Crick, 1998; Tierney & Farmer, 2002).

Overconfidence, the unrealistically high belief in the efficacy of one's own judgments, may cause problems for entrepreneurs. This can make them susceptible to the illusion of control (Amit, MacCrimmon, Zietsma, & Oesch, 2001; Busenitz & Barney, 1997). The illusion of control is the unjustified belief in the capacity to influence the outcomes that one faces (Simon, Houghton, & Aquino, 2000).

Similarly, most people believe that entrepreneurs value risk taking; however, this is not exactly true (Shane et al., 2003). First, there is some evidence that entrepreneurs are actually risk avoidant, although the literature is contradictory (Miner & Raju, 2004; Miner, Smith & Bracker, 1989). Of course, the fewer risks they take, the better are their chances of succeeding. Second, even if it is objectively the case that a large number of entrepreneurial ventures fail, entrepreneurs do not experience their ventures as highly risky, as compared, say, to how an outsider would experience it. This is because entrepreneurs have high self-confidence; in relation to *their* perceived ability the venture may not seem risky. And if they posses genuine ability, the venture may not be objectively risky for them. Population statistics, for example, regarding venture success/failure ratios, are only averages, which may not apply to a given individual. This is clearly a topic that requires further research.

Achievement Motivation. Achievement motivation means the desire to achieve standards of excellence, for example, to improve, and to attain goals. Because entrepreneurship (and any business) involves goal-directed activity, it makes sense that entrepreneurs would value the process of pursuing goals. Two different methods have been used to measure achievement motivation. David McClelland (1961) used a projective technique, the Thematic Apperception Test (TAT), which involves people writing stories in response to pictures; the stories are then scored for achievement imagery. McClelland claimed that this method measures achievement motivation at the subconscious level. A second approach asks people to answer direct questions about their motivation (self-report personality tests). This approach measures conscious achievement motivation. A recent meta-analysis of studies using both approaches by Collins, Hanges, and Locke (2004) found that both types of measures were significantly associated with (a) choice of an entrepreneurial occupation and (b) success in entrepreneurship. It must be noted that the two types of measures, projective and self-report, although equally valid, have been found not to be correlated; thus, they must be getting at two different yet relevant aspects of achievement motivation.

Drive[2]: Proactivity, Ambition, and Energy.   Proactivity is an element of drive (Bird, 1989; Chandler & Jansen, 1992). Entrepreneurs are not ivory-tower intellectuals who are content to sit and dream. They want things to happen. They want to make the vision real. They are impatient for results. They show initiative. They are proactive rather than passive.

Another element of drive is ambition. Ambition literally means a strong desire to achieve or improve something; in this respect it sounds similar to achievement motivation, but ambition has the added connotation of moving ahead toward a distant and high goal.

Ambition has a negative moral connotation in many peoples' minds, because the high goals many people seek are things like power and fame. Some ambitious people are neurotically obsessed with impressing others. Such people lack independence and self-esteem and are simply trying to feel that they look good to other people's eyes. Further, some ambitious people have no moral scruples and do not care how they reach their goal as long as they reach it.

However, there is such a thing as healthy ambition. The Sam Waltons and Bill Gateses are not out to impress others in order to relieve self-doubt but to build a business because they enjoy creating something great. They want to build it for themselves. And many ambitious people have high moral standards; they don't just want the result, they want to earn it fair and square.

People differ enormously in their degree of ambition. Great entrepreneurs are highly ambitious people. Sam Walton said, "I have been overblessed with drive and ambition since I hit the ground" (Locke, 2000, p. 88). One of his earliest ambitions was to make his "little Newport store to be the best, most profitable variety store in Arkansas within five years" (p. 88). Reaching that goal encouraged him to set his sights even higher—and the rest is history.

Wrongly formulated ambitions can be damaging. If one's ambition exceeds one's cognitive capacity, failure is assured. Furthermore, ambitions that are too large in scope can lead to errors in judgment, such as overly rapid expansion so that costs exceed cash flow.

---

[2]In Locke (2000) the drive concept encompassed the drive to action, ambition, energy, tenacity, and setting high goals. Here tenacity is put in a separate trait category and goals are discussed under situationally specific motivators.

Another aspect of drive is energy. Entrepreneurs usually have to work long hours, especially during the startup phase. Work weeks may exceed 100 hours at times. Extensive travel may be required. There may be too little time to get adequate sleep. Only people with high energy and stamina can manage such demands.

Egoistic Passion. For many people, egoism, like ambition, has nothing but negative connotations. To them, to be egoistic is to be arrogant, boastful, vain, self-obsessed, and amoral. People like this are asserted to have "big egos," but in fact, they have inflated egos; their real egos are small and riddled with self-doubt. Their self-preoccupation is an attempt to relieve that doubt. People with genuine self-esteem do not need constant attention, approval, and worship. They do not constantly compare themselves with others. Nor does egoism mean doing whatever you feel like doing, regardless of the rights of others or the dictates of reason. The actual meaning of *egoism* is, acting in one's own interest. The term does not specify what one's interests are or how one discovers them.

Ayn Rand explained that to discover what is in one's self-interest requires the use of reason and long-range thinking (Peikoff, 1991). For example, it is in one's self interest to possess moral virtues such as rationality, honesty, and integrity (Locke, 2000; Locke & Woiceshyn, 1995; Peikoff, 1991).

Rational egoism (Rand, 1964) holds that one's own happiness is one's highest moral purpose. If so, it follows that it is in one's self-interest to work at a job or profession that one loves. Because one spends a considerable part of one's life earning a living, full happiness would be impossible without a career that one enjoys. Furthermore, it would be virtually impossible to sustain a serious, long-range focus in one's career if one did not passionately enjoy it.

Entrepreneurs and great wealth creators do, in fact, selfishly love their work. They do not act on the premise of altruism (self-sacrifice). They don't say, "I really hate the food business, but people need to eat so it is my duty to provide them with food, regardless of what I want to do with my life." They may put their work before other priorities, but that is no sacrifice if their work is more important to them than those other values. Entrepreneurs feel joy in the process of creation. Warren Buffet, who has bought many companies that continue to be successful year after year, put it this way: "Find the leader who loves his business" (Locke, 2000, p. 113). Southwest Airlines founder Herb Kelleher would agree: "I love it, I love it—I sure as heck do" (p. 113). Quantitative data (Baum & Locke, 2004; Baum, Locke & Smith, 2001) support the contention that passion for the work is a significant contributor to successful venture growth.

An important qualification is needed regarding passion: Passion without reason and knowledge, that is, pure emotionalism, will not work. Passion is the driver, but reason is needed to make sure one knows what to do. As Michael Dell put it, "[Many companies] started with little more than passion and a good idea. There are also many that failed …. The difference is that the thriving companies gathered the knowledge that gave them a substantial edge on their competition …. Those that didn't simply didn't make it" (Dell, 1999, p. 206).

Tenacity.   Nearly all entrepreneurs at some point in their careers will confront difficult obstacles (e.g., barriers to entry) or will have setbacks (e.g., a product that does not work as planned, cost overruns) or will even fail completely (and have to start over). If making a new business succeed or making an existing business grow were easy, then almost anyone would be able to do it. In fact, only a relatively small number of people are successful entrepreneurs. One trait that sets them apart from others is that they do not give up when things go wrong. They are tenacious and persistent. Shaver and Scott (1991) note that successful entrepreneurs pick themselves up after failure, in part because they attribute failure to bad luck or insufficient effort on their part. They assume that if they work harder, they will succeed. In a study of 217 inventors, those who had a higher adversity quotient (able to recover from bad news) founded more businesses (Markman, Balkin, & Baron, 2002). Baum and Locke (2004) found that the trait of tenacity contributed to venture growth even with a 6-year time lag between the measurement of the trait and subsequent performance.

There are many examples of tenacity among entrepreneurs. FedEx was on the verge of bankruptcy for 3 years until Fred Smith made it work. Mary Kay Ash staggered through the death of two husbands, the failure of her first beauty show, and a disastrous sales decline before making her beauty products company a huge international success. It took Bill Gates and Microsoft 7 years to develop a viable Windows operating system. Sam Walton failed with a drug chain, a home improvement center, two Hypermarts, and some disastrous store openings, but he made it big in the end with Wal-Mart.

It can be asked: Where does a successful entrepreneur draw the line between productive tenacity and foolish persistence? Sometime it is hard to tell until after the fact, especially in the case of an entirely new product, but one common type of foolish persistence is to stick to a strategy that worked in the past even in the face of mounting evidence that the competitive environment is radically changing. Consider Henry Ford's refusal to abandon the Model T—which had been a best-selling car for 19 years—in the face of threats from General Motors. By the time Ford developed new models, GM had snatched away Ford's position as the number one car company in the world—a position that Ford never regained. One guideline then is that the entrepreneur should keep close tabs on the outside world when deciding whether or not to retain abandon a strategy or product. If the product is totally new, the entrepreneur has to decide if there is enough cash flow to keep the project going.

Situationally Specific Motivators

We have just presented *general* motivational value, trait, and motive concepts; however, all action is taken with respect to a specific task and a specific situation. Thus there have to be some means by which general concepts are applied to specific tasks and situations. In the realm of motivation, there is evidence for at least three situationally specific motivators: self-efficacy, vision, and goals.

Situationally Specific Self-Efficacy. Situationally specific self-efficacy contrasts with self-esteem, which involves a more generalized type of confidence. Thus, one may feel one can handle life's challenges, but this is different from one's confidence in being able to raise $5 million for a business venture, get an A in a statistics course, or run a 10-mile marathon in 1 hour. Self-efficacy is a self-regulatory motivational variable that is "concerned with judgments of how well one can execute a course of action required to deal with prospective situations" (Bandura, 1982, p. 122) and "beliefs in one's capabilities to mobilize the motivation, cognitive resources and course of action needed to meet given situational demands" (Wood & Bandura, 1989, p. 370). Put simply, self-efficacy is task-specific self-confidence (Bandura, 1997).

Self-efficacy is affected most strongly by past accomplishments (and less strongly by social factors such as persuasion and role models), but it is not simply a summary of one's past achievements. People reach different estimates about capability from what they accomplished in the past, based on such factors as how hard the previous accomplishment was and whether they attribute what they did in the past to skill or luck. The evidence is clear that self-efficacy has causal efficacy (Bandura & Locke, 2003); it affects subsequent performance independently of past performance.

Self-efficacy is best measured by asking people to rate their confidence in being able to attain various outcomes levels (e.g., sales increases of 5% or more; 10% or more; 15% or more; 20% or more, etc.) and then summing the confidence ratings across all levels. It is rated most accurately when people have been given feedback regarding their performance on the same task.

Baum et al. (2001) found that the chief executive officer (CEO) self-efficacy (as part of a larger specific motivation factor) was significantly related to the growth of early stage ventures within the same industry for the 2 years following measurement. In a follow-up study of the same entrepreneurs, CEO self-efficacy was used as a single variable and was significantly related to growth over the subsequent six years (Baum & Locke, 2004).

Situationally specific self-efficacy can be measured more generally than specifying a graduated series of performance levels (e.g., "How confident are you that you can successfully expand your business?"). Sometimes this is necessary because no relevant quantitative outcomes can be specified, although one would expect that the validities of these less precise measures would be somewhat lower than those using quantitative outcome levels.

Can situationally specific efficacy be too high just as with general efficacy? Yes. A slight degree of overconfidence is not harmful, but marked overconfidence is a genuine psychological hazard. It means that the entrepreneur is not in touch with reality, due either to ignorance or to denying or evading real risks that need to be considered. Overconfidence is often connected to arrogance, which usually combines excess confidence in oneself with a gross underestimation of risk, including the ability of one's competitors. We are reminded of a story told in the 1980s. A top U.S. auto executive was asked by a friend if he should buy a Toyota dealership. The executive replied with something like, "No, don't buy it; we are going to push them into the sea." Toyota went on to become far more successful than the Big 3 automobile company that that executive worked for. This means that the entrepreneur is not in touch with reality, either due to ignorance or to denying or evading real risks that need to be considered. Overconfidence is often connected to arrogance, which usually combines excess confidence in oneself with a gross underestimation of risk, including the ability of one's competitors.

In an experiment, Audia, Locke, and Smith (2000), for example, using a business simulation, found that people with high self-efficacy (along with high goals and satisfaction) based on past success were less likely to change strategies in the face of a radical environmental change than those with lower efficacy which had been associated with lower past success. This led to lower subsequent performance for those with high self-efficacy. This result stresses the need to pay attention to feedback from the environment to insure that efficacy levels are appropriate. Furthermore, people with very high efficacy may work less hard than people with low efficacy if the task is not seen as highly challenging.

Situationally Specific Goals.   Goal-setting theory (Locke & Latham, 2002) has shown that specific, difficult goals lead consistently to higher performance than vague and/or easy goals. Goal setting works most effectively when people are committed to their goals and have feedback regarding their progress in relation to their goals. As tasks become more complex, goal effects may become smaller because some people may not have the knowledge required to achieve the goals.

Goals help motivate people to use suitable task strategies or to search for suitable strategies if they lack the knowledge they need. However, hard goals can sometimes lead to dysfunctional strategy searches and thereby undermine performance. When faced with new complex tasks, it may be best to strive not for performance outcome goals but rather for learning goals (Locke & Latham, 2002).

Most goal-setting studies have been conducted with individuals and groups but two studies mentioned earlier found that they affect performance when set at the (small) firm level too. In the Baum et al. (2001) study, goals, along with self-efficacy, were an element of the motivation factor that had a direct affect on firm growth. In the Baum and Locke (2004) study, CEO goals for the company had a direct effect on venture growth in the 6-year follow up. In another study, Tracy, Locke, and Renard (1999) found significant relationships between the financial, growth, and innovation goals of entrepreneurs in the printing business and corresponding performance measures obtained 2 years later.

Goals at the firm level may not have such a strong influence on outcomes of larger firms. In small companies, the CEO often has relatively direct control over the actions that lead to goal accomplishment. In larger firms, there are more layers and most of the work has to be delegated. Furthermore, firm strategies in large organizations may be more complex than those in smaller companies and thus more prone to error. Complex strategies are also less easily and less rapidly changed when problems occur. Finally, problems in the economy and legal issues may affect large firms (e.g., automobile manufacturers) more than smaller ones. (e.g., ice cream makers). This is a subject for further study.

Situationally Specific Vision. Previously we discussed visions from a cognitive viewpoint (the nature of the business, business strategy). However, visions can also have motivational elements. Recall Sam Walton's early vision to make his variety store the best store in Arkansas within 5 years. A less ambitious individual might have as a goal "to survive for the next 2 years." Baum, Locke, and Kirkpatrick (1998) coded the written vision statements of the entrepreneurs used in the Baum et al. (2001) and Baum and Locke (2004) studies. They coded both for vision attributes (e.g., brevity, clarity, future orientation, stability, ability to inspire) and growth imagery. Both measures predicted venture growth. These effects were partially mediated by vision communication (whether the vision was communicated as reported by a subordinate).

The Relationship Between General Traits and Situationally Specific Motivation

If there are both general and situationally specific motivators of entrepreneurial performance, how should they be combined to best predict success? There are two possibilities: They should be used as simultaneous predictors, or the situationally specific motivators should mediate (or partially mediate) the effects of the general traits. The latter model makes the most sense logically in that general variables would be "applied" to situations through their effects on specific variables.

The mediation model has generally been supported. The better fitting model from the Baum et al. (2001) study is shown in Fig. 5.1. Observe that the two general variables in that study, traits (composed of tenacity, proactivity and passion for the work) and the cognitive variable, general competencies (composed of organization skill and opportunity skill), did not have any direct effects on venture growth. They operated through their effects on specific variables, namely, situationally specific motivation (goals and efficacy and vision), specific competencies (industry skill and technical skill), and competitive strategies (focus [negative], low cost [negative], and differentiation). Motivational traits were strongly related to specific motivation and strategies and even to general competencies. This suggests that traits can motivate the development of business skills as well as the direct motivation to perform.

The mediation model was also supported in Baum and Locke (2004), as shown in Fig. 5.2. Passion, tenacity, and new resource skill (a general cogni-

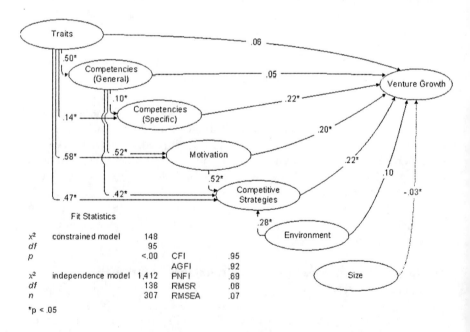

Figure 5.1. Structural equation model for indirect and direct effects; from Baum et al. (2001, Fig. 2).

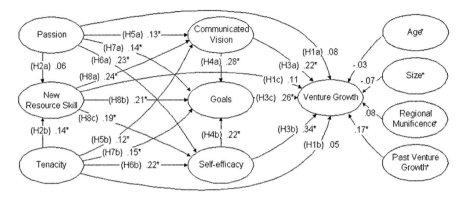

Structural equation results: entrpreneurial traits, skill, and motivation to subsequent venture growth model. Fit statistics: $\chi^2 = 66.12$, degrees of freedom = 28, $p \leq .00$; χ^2 (independence model) = 1241.16, degrees of freedom = 49, $n = 229$; goodness of fit index = .93; adjusted goodness of fit index = .90; root-mean-square error = .049; root-mean-square error of approximation = .067; expected cross-validation index = .89.
Plus signs indicate control variables, and asterisks indicate significance at $*p < .05$.

Figure 5.2.   Structural equations model from Baum and Locke (2004, Fig. 1).

tive variable) affected 6-year venture growth solely through their effects on communication vision, self-efficacy, and growth goals. All three general variables were significantly related to each of the three specific variables. Observe also that growth goals partly mediated the effects of vision and self-efficacy.

These results help explain why entrepreneurship researchers and commentators have often been disappointed by the results of trait studies (e.g., Low & MacMillan, 1988). If general traits have mainly or only indirect effects, then their ties to performance outcomes would not show up or would not show up strongly unless the mediating variables were also included in the studies. Future studies of entrepreneurs that include trait measures would do well to include both general and situationally specific variables in their research models. Skills such as being able to find capital, organizing the enterprise, selling and marketing the product, and developing teamwork should be included as well.

CONCLUSION

A summary of the key motivation variables discussed in this chapter is shown in Fig. 5.3. Based on previous findings, we show general trait measures being mediated by specific measures. Fig. 5.3 does not include cognitive variables, although these would, of course, be critical to a full model of entrepreneurial success or venture growth. Cognitive variables may interact with motivation variables, or there may be a mediated relationship between them when predicting performance.

It should be noted that independence as a value may be most relevant to the prediction of who will start a business than to business success, although the cognitive aspect of independence, thinking for oneself, would be relevant to success at any stage.

It is obvious that there is some conceptual overlap between some of our trait measures (e.g., achievement motivation, drive, egoistic passion), so it will take further study to see if each of these traits explains independent variance in outcome measures (directly or indirectly).

It appears that projective measures (of subconscious motivation) would have to be kept separate from self-report measures because the two types are not correlated. To make matters worse, Collins et al. (2004) also looked at the validity of a second type of projective measure, the Incomplete Sentence Blank (ISB), used by Miner, Smith, and Bracker (1989). It was also was a significant correlate of entrepreneurial career choice and success, but Tracy et al. (1999) found that the two types of projective measures of achievement motivation (TAT and ISB) were not correlated with each other.

In conclusion, it is worth comparing what we have said about entrepreneurial motivation with what Jim Collins (2001) reports in his best-selling book *Good to Great*. Collins tracked eleven companies that had moved from being good or average companies to great companies. The great companies he studied averaged cumulative stock market returns 6.9 times greater (i.e.,

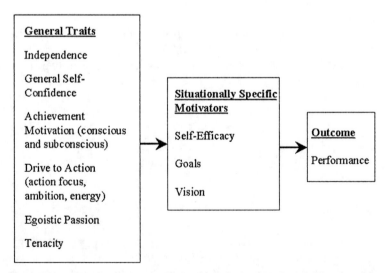

Figure 5.3.   Summary of motivational traits and situationally specific motivators.

close to 700%) than the general market and sustained this performance for a period of no less than 15 years.

Although Collins has a strong, self-admitted bias against the importance of leadership, his research team and his data reluctantly forced him to concede that it was important. The traits and motivators he mentions are very consistent with those that we have described above. Collins (2001) describes the leaders of these companies as independent, in that "they never defined their strategies, principally, in response to what others were doing" (p. 160); "fearless" (p. 22); having "faith" (i.e., confidence, p. 86), in that they never doubted their ability to succeed (p. 32); "fierce" and "ferocious" (p. 18); "fanatically driven" (p. 30); "ambitious" (p. 21); "passionate" (p. 61); tenacious ("we will persist for a hundred years if that's what it takes," p. 82); "demanding" (they were completely intolerant of low-performing executives, which implies they pushed for high goals; p. 127); and wanting to be the "best in the world" (p. 96). This list covers virtually everything in our list except vision, although that is implicit in wanting to be the best in the world.

Collins also asserts that the leaders of his great companies were not vain, boastful, power-lusting, publicity-seeking showoffs, but modest and unassuming, people who loved their work rather than perks and publicity. This agrees with what we found in my study of great wealth creators (Locke, 2000).

However, we believe that Collins goes overboard in stressing the trait of humility[3]—although it did seem that some of his CEOs suffered from false modesty, because they were often shy and because they did not want to be seen as vain "big shots." They also did not want to unfairly hog all the credit for their companies' successes, because they had many outstanding people working for them. Collins argues that his CEOs' "ambition is first and foremost for the institution, not themselves" (p. 21). But this is a misleading dichotomy. If you love your work and your company, you are automatically working for yourself and your company at the same time. There is no bifurcation between the two. If your company succeeds, you succeed, and you have the right to feel proud of what *you* did and to get paid handsomely as a result. The way we would have put it is that his CEOs did not want to get credit and rewards they did not deserve *at the expense of* the company and its employees (cf, Enron). In other words, they wanted to be just.

PROPOSED RESEARCH QUESTIONS

Are the traits we listed in Fig. 5.3 exhaustive or are there additional ones that contribute to entrepreneurial success?

---

[3]There is one respect in which humility on the part of CEOs is valid: It is being humble before the facts of reality, which means taking facts seriously and not acting just on wishes. Both Locke (2000) and Collins (2001) stress the importance of never putting ego ahead of reality.

Do different traits play stronger or weaker roles during different stages of the evolution of a new business?

Do the mediation models shown in Figs. 5.1 and 5.2 apply in industries other than the one used for these studies?

How important is conscious versus subconscious motivation in determining entrepreneurial success?

REFERENCES

Adams, J. S. (1965). Injustice in social exchange. In L. Berkowitz (Ed.), *Advances in experimental social psychology* (Vol. 2, pp. 214–226). New York: Academic Press.

Ajzen, I. (1991). The theory of planned behavior. *Organizational Behavior & Human Decision Processes, 50,* 179–211.

Amit, R., MacCrimmon, K. R., Zietsma, C., & Oesch, J. M. (2001). Does money matter? Wealth attainment as the motive for initiating growth-oriented technology ventures. *Journal of Business Venturing, 16,* 119–143.

Audia, P., Locke, E. A., & Smith, K. G. (2000). The paradox of success: An archival and a laboratory study of strategic persistence following a radical environmental change. *Academy of Management Journal, 43,* 837–853.

Bandura, A. (1982). Self-efficacy mechanism in human agency. *American Psychologist, 37,* 747–755.

Bandura, A. (1986). *Social foundations of thought and action: A social cognitive view.* Englewood Cliffs, NJ: Prentice Hall.

Bandura, A. (1997). *Self-efficacy: The exercise of control.* New York: Freeman.

Bandura, A., & Locke, E. A. (2003). Negative self-efficacy and goal effects revisited. *Journal of Applied Psychology, 88,* 87–99.

Baron, R. A., & Markman, G. D. (2005). Toward a process view of entrepreneurship: The changing impact of individual level variables across phases of new venture development. In M. A. Rahim, R. T. Golembiewski, & K. D. Mackenzie (Eds.), *Current topics in management* (Vol. 9, pp. 45–64). New Brunswick, NJ: Transaction Publishers.

Baum, J. R., & Locke, E. A. (2004). The relationship of entrepreneurial traits, skill and motivation to subsequent venture growth. *Journal of Applied Psychology, 89,* 587–598.

Baum, J. R., Locke, E. A., & Kirkpatrick, S. (1998). A longitudinal study of the relation of vision and vision communication to venture growth in entrepreneurial firms. *Journal of Applied Psychology, 83,* 43–54.

Baum, J. R., Locke, E. A., & Smith, K.G. (2001). A multidimensional model of venture growth. *Academy of Management Journal, 44,* 292–303.

Binswanger, H. (1991). Volition as cognitive self-regulation. *Organizational Behavior and Human Decision Processes, 50,* 154–178.

Bird, B. J. (1989). *Entrepreneurial behavior.* Glenview, IL: Scott, Foresman.

Boyd, N. G., & Vozikis, G. S. (1994). The influence of self-efficacy on the development of entrepreneurial intentions and actions. *Entrepreneurship Theory and Practice, 18,* 63–90.

Busenitz, L. W., & Barney, J. B. (1997). Differences between entrepreneurs and managers in large organizations: Biases and heuristics in strategic decision-making. *Journal of Business Venturing, 12,* 9–30.

Chandler, G. N., & Jansen, E. (1992). The founder's self-assessed competence and venture performance. *Journal of Business Venturing, 7,* 223–236.

Chen, C. C., Greene, P. G., & Crick, A. (1998). Does entrepreneurial self-efficacy distinguish entrepreneurs from managers? *Journal of Business Venturing, 13,* 395–316.

Collins, C. J. (2001). *Good to great: Why some companies make the leap … and others don't.* New York: Harper Business.

Collins, C. J., Hanges, P. J. & Locke, E. A. (2004). The relationship of need for achievement to entrepreneurship: A meta analysis. *Human Performance, 17,* 95–117.

Dell, M. (1999). *Direct from Dell.* New York: Harper Business.

Folsom, B. (1991). *The myth of the robber barons.* Herndon, VA: Young America's Foundation.

Gartner, W. B., Bird, B. J., & Starr, J. A. (1992, Spring). Acting as if: Differentiating entrepreneurial from organizational behavior. *Entrepreneurship Theory and Practice,* pp. 13–31.

Guest, D. (1984, May). What's new in motivation. *Personnel Management,* pp. 20–23.

Krueger, N. F., Jr. (2003). The cognitive psychology of entrepreneurship. In Z. Acs & D. B. Audretsch (Eds.), *Handbook of entrepreneurial research* (pp. 105–140). London: Kluwer Law International.

Krueger, N., & Brazeal, D. (1994). How believing in ourselves increased risk taking. *Decision Sciences, 25*(3), 385–400.

Landy, F. J., & Becker, W. S. (1987). Motivation theory reconsidered. In L. L. Cummings & B. M. Staw (Eds.), *Research in Organizational Behavior* (Vol. 9, pp. 1–38). New York: Elsevier.

Locke, E. A. (2000). *The prime movers: Traits of the great wealth creators.* New York: AMACOM.

Locke, E. A. (2002). The epistemological side of teaching management: Teaching through principles. *Academy of Management Learning and Education, 1,* 195–205.

Locke, E. A., & Latham, G. P. (2002). Building a practically useful theory of goal setting and task motivation: A 35-year odyssey. *American Psychologist, 57,* 705–717.

Locke, E. A., & Woiceshyn, J. (1995). Why businessmen should be honest: The argument for rational egoism. *Journal of Organizational Behavior, 16,* 405–414.

Low, M .B., & MacMillan, I. C. (1988). Entrepreneurship: Past research and future challenges. *Journal of Management, 14,* 139–151.

Markman, G. D., Balkin, D. B., & Baron, R. A. (2002, Winter). Inventors and new venture formation: The effects of general self-efficacy and regretful thinking. *Entrepreneurship Theory and Practice,* pp. 149–165.

Markman, G. D., & Baron, R. A. (2002). Individual differences and the pursuit of new ventures: A model of person–entrepreneurship fit. In J. Katz & T. M. Welbourne, (Eds.), *Advances in entrepreneurship, firm emergence, and growth* (Vol. 5, pp. 23–53). Greenwich, CT: JAI Press.

Markman, G. D., Baron, R. A., & Balkin, D. B. (2003). The role of regretful thinking, perseverance, and self-efficacy in venture formation. In J. Katz & D. A. Shepherd (Eds.), *Cognitive approaches to entrepreneurship research* (pp. 73–104). New York: Elsevier Science.

McClelland, D. (1961). *The achieving society.* New York: Free Press.

Miner, J. B., & Raju, N. S. (2004). Risk propensity differences between managers and entrepreneurs and between low- and high-growth entrepreneurs: A reply in a more conservative vein. *Journal of Applied Psychology, 89,* 3–13.

Miner, J. B., Smith, N. R., & Bracker, J. S. (1989). Role of entrepreneurial task motivation in the growth of technologically innovative firms: Interpretations from follow-up data. *Journal of Applied Psychology, 79,* 627–630.

Naffziger, D. W., Hornsby, J. S., & Kuratko, D. F. (1994). A proposed research model of entrepreneurial motivation. *Entrepreneurship Theory and Practice, 18*(3), 29–42.

Peikoff, L. (1991). *Objectivism: The philosophy of Ayn Rand.* New York: Dutton.

Rand, A. (1964). *The virtue of selfishness.* New York: Signet.

Shane, S., Locke, E. A., & Collins, C. J. (2003). Entrepreneurial motivation. *Human Resources Management Review, 13,* 257–279.

Shaver, K. G., & Scott, L. R. (1991, Winter). Person, process, choice: The psychology of new venture creation. *Entrepreneurship Theory and Practice,* pp. 23–45.

Shepherd, D. A., & Krueger, N. F. (2002, Winter). An intentions-based model of entrepreneurial teams' social cognition. *Entrepreneurship Theory and Practice,* pp. 167–185.

Simon, M., Houghton, S. M., & Aquino, K. (2000). Cognitive biases, risk perceptions, and venture formation: How individuals decide to start companies. *Journal of Business Venturing, 19,* 189–202.

Steers, R. M., & Porter, L. W. (1991). *Motivation and work behavior.* New York: McGraw-Hill.

Tierney, P., & Farmer, S. M. (2002). Creative self-efficacy: Potential antecedents and its relationship to creative performance. *Academy of Management Journal, 45,* 1137–1148.

Timmons, J. A. (2000). *New venture creation: Entrepreneurship 2000* (5th ed.). Homewood, IL: Irwin.

Tracy, K., Locke, E. A., & Renard, M. (1999, August). *Conscious goal setting versus subconscious and motives: Longitudinal and concurrent effects on the performance of entrepreneurial firms.* Paper presented at the Academy of Management meeting, Chicago.

Vroom, V. (1964). *Work and motivation.* New York: McGraw-Hill.

Wood, R. E., & Bandura, A. (1989). Social cognitive theory of organizational management. *Academy of Management Review, 14,* 361–384.

6

Entrepreneurs as Organizational Products Revisited

Pino G. Audia
Christopher I. Rider

Macro studies of entrepreneurship emphasize how environmental conditions—social, economic, and political—facilitate the creation of new organizations. Examples include how periods of political turbulence create favorable conditions for the emergence of new organizations (e.g., Delacroix & Carroll, 1983), how market concentration driven by the movement of generalist organizations favors the emergence of specialist organizations (e.g., Carroll, Dobrev, & Swaminathan, 2002), and how dissolutions of organizations influence the emergence of new ones (e.g., Delacroix & Carroll, 1983). Because individuals rather than local conditions actually create organizations, this perspective is often criticized for lacking a theory of agency (e.g., Shane, Locke, & Collins, 2003; Thornton, 1999). However, in recent years, a strand of macro research has emerged that promises to address, at least in part, this problem and offers stronger links to micro research on entrepreneurship. This body of work focuses on organizations as key components of the environment and proposes that organizations are social contexts within which individuals acquire many of the critical psychological and social resources necessary to create new organizations (e.g. Aldrich & Wiedenmayer, 1993; Freeman, 1986; Romanelli, 1989; Sorenson & Audia, 2000). To use Freeman's (1986) felicitous expression, the key idea underlying this line of work is that *entrepreneurs often are organizational products*.

The origins of this idea can be traced in the organizational literature to Stinchcombe's (1965) seminal piece on social structure and organizations,

113

Cooper's (1973, 1985) work on high-technology firms, and Brittain and Freeman's (1980, 1986) research on organizational life cycles, and in economics the origins can be traced to Jacobs's (1969) study of the economy of cities and Beesley's (1955) analysis of entrepreneurs in England's West Midlands region. Nonetheless, it is only recently that a body of theoretical and empirical work has begun to accumulate (e.g., Dobrev & Barnett, 2005; Gompers, Lerner, & Scharfstein, 2005; Shane & Khurana, 2003; Sorenson & Audia, 2000). This chapter reviews the progress made in this line of inquiry. We begin by delineating the micro processes linking organizational contexts to individuals' motivations and abilities to create new organizations. We then review empirical evidence supporting the view of entrepreneurs as organizational products. We conclude by identifying gaps between the theory and the empirical evidence and by highlighting directions for future research.

THEORY

The notion of entrepreneurs as organizational products is that, in comparisons between otherwise similar people, those employed by existing organizations are more likely to become entrepreneurs. Organizational contexts increase the probability that individuals may start a new organization in three related ways. First, organizations create opportunities for individuals to build confidence in their ability to create new organizations (Sorenson & Audia, 2000). Second, organizational contexts provide varying access to broad industry knowledge and fine-grained information about entrepreneurial opportunities, neither of which is readily available to outsiders (Freeman, 1986; Romanelli, 1989). Third, organizations help individuals form social networks that facilitate resource mobilization (Freeman, 1986; Aldrich & Zimmer, 1986).

Confidence

Confidence in "judgment and disposition" is essential to performing the entrepreneurial function (Knight, 1964, p. 268). Creating a new organization is a time-consuming, complex process that discourages many individuals from trying and also causes many motivated individuals who do try to give up after they start. New organizations usually start small, and small companies suffer from liabilities of smallness (Freeman, Carroll, & Hannan, 1983) and high rates of abandonment (Aldrich & Auster, 1986). The difficulties inherent in creating a new organization render confidence, one's belief in the ability to perform a task (Bandura, 1986), a critical differentiating factor between persons who start a business and those who do not. The reason is that confidence provides individuals with the psychological strength necessary not only to initiate activities preceding organizational creation but also to persist in the face of obstacles and uncertainty. Empirical evidence that confidence is a critical factor in organizational creation comes from several studies. Cooper, Woo, and Dunkelberg (1988) found that 95% of entrepreneurs surveyed perceived their own business's chances of success to be better than or equal to the chances of any similar business. In a laboratory study, Camerer and Lovallo (1999) found evidence of excess market entry—entry into crowded markets that offered slim success chances—ostensibly instigated by individuals who held biased (e.g., overconfident) assessments of their competitive abilities. Additionally, Markman, Balkin, and Baron (2001) found confidence to be a strong predictor of whether or not patent holders chose to start a new venture or to license their invention.

How do individuals develop confidence in their ability to create new organizations? Bandura's (1986, 1994) social cognitive theory suggests that the social context plays a critical role in fostering or hindering the development of confidence and implies that organizations may increase individuals' confidence through mastery and vicarious experiences (Sorenson & Audia, 2000). Individuals accumulate *mastery experiences* through success on tasks important to organizational functioning, thereby building coping skills and forming a belief in their abilities to exercise control in the face of potential threats (Bandura, 1994). As individuals achieve success on organizational tasks, especially tasks similar to those performed in the role of entrepreneur, confidence rises. For example, drawing upon past success at Apple, Steve Jobs founded NeXT in 1988 with confidence that the NeXT computer would "change the world of computing" (Barker, 2000). When questioned on the delayed launch date of his product, Jobs is said to have responded, "Late? This computer is five years ahead of its time" (Barker, 2000). Such self-confidence in the face of obstacles like a delayed product launch may be attributed, at least partially, to Jobs's mastery experiences at Apple and Atari.

Vicarious experiences, on the other hand, occur as individuals observe social models that they perceive as similar (i.e., their organizational peers) succeeding through sustained effort (Bandura, 1986). Successful individuals serve as proficient models and transmit knowledge, vicariously, to other employees. Exposure to successful entrepreneurs of similar social and occupational backgrounds may stimulate individuals to entertain notions of also becoming entrepreneurs. For example, Saxenian (1994, p. 19) quotes a founder of a minicomputer firm: "Those guys [entrepreneurs] were just like you and me. There was nothing unique or special about them. I figured if they can do it, why can't I?" In short, the role of organizations in enhancing employees' confidence is critical in preparing individuals for entrepreneurship. These opportunities to build confidence are less available to those not employed by organizations.

Information About Entrepreneurial Opportunities

The motivation to create a new organization is strengthened not only by an individual's confidence in his or her abilities to succeed but also by access to information about entrepreneurial opportunities (Burt, 1992; Kirzner, 1973; Shane, 2000; Stinchcombe, 1965; Venkataraman, 1997). In micro terms, Vroom's (1964) expectancy theory suggests that specific and timely information about entrepreneurial opportunities might increase an individual's expectation that entrepreneurial effort will lead to entrepreneurial rewards, thereby increasing entrepreneurial motivation. Much of this information originates within existing organizations and is not easily available to outsiders (Freeman, 1986; Romanelli, 1989). Consequently, individuals employed by organizations in a particular industry will have greater access to this information than individuals located elsewhere in the social structure. For example, as vice-president of engineering at Grid Systems, Jeff Hawkins met frequently with Grid's customers— vending machine route salespeople—who used Grid's devices to record sales data on-site. These customers expressed an interest in similar devices for personal use (Brush, Greene, & Hart, 2001). Shortly thereafter, Hawkins founded Palm Computing to commercialize just such a device. As Romanelli (1989) notes and as this example illustrates, organizational contexts filter information on markets, technologies, and resources to employees.

Individuals employed by existing organizations enjoy an additional advantage. Recognizing an opportunity requires knowledge of the business, and such knowledge is often acquired through work experience (Venkataraman, 1997) and the repetitive activities of employment. For example, customers may express their frustration regarding the functionality of existing products (e.g., Von Hippel, 1986), but only individuals who have in-depth knowledge of the business may view this information as indicative of an entrepreneurial opportunity. Shane (2000), in a field study of eight business opportunities conceived to exploit a patented MIT invention, found that knowledge of specific businesses gleaned from prior employment and education conditioned individuals' abilities to envision uses for the invention. This is because individuals obtain *blueprints* (Hannan & Freeman, 1977) or *mental models* (Burton, 2001; Schoonhoven & Romanelli, 2001) from their employing organizations related to appropriate and, often, inappropriate ways of organizing and conducting business. Individual career trajectories, then, constrain the activities and processes that compose individuals' body of knowledge (Shane & Khurana, 2003; Sorenson & Audia, 2000). Possession of this knowledge increases individuals' abilities to recognize entrepreneurial opportunities and, as a result, increases the probability that those individuals will create a new organization.

Empirical studies support the contention that knowledge of opportunity is often obtained via employers. A study of 201 firms with at least eight employees found that 58% of the ventures' founders listed the source of their business idea as a "prior job" (Cooper, Woo, & Dunkelberg, 1989). Similarly, a survey of 100 founders of the 1989 *Inc.* 500 fastest growing companies found that 71% of the founders sampled "replicated or modified an idea encountered through previous employment" (Bhide, 1994, 2000). In addition, Klepper and Sleeper's (2000) study of 465 producers in the U.S. commercial laser industry indicates that entrepreneurs in that industry tended to draw on highly specific information from parent organizations. In summary, information about entrepreneurial opportunities strengthens the motivation to create a new organization, and this information is more easily available and more easily recognized by individuals employed by existing organizations.

Social Ties to Resource Providers

Information on entrepreneurial opportunity is typically accessed via social ties formed through employment and is most useful when knowledge of the opportunity is specific and timely (Burt, 1992; Granovetter, 1974). By providing access to information, cohesive social ties are instrumental in providing the psychological resources (i.e., motivation) necessary for new venture creation. However, the creation of a new organization is not conditioned solely by confidence and information about entrepreneurial opportunity; entrepreneurs must also bring their idea to market (Schumpeter, 1934). To that end, entrepreneurs rely on social relationships not only for gaining access to information on entrepreneurial opportunities, but also for mobilizing resources to build new organizations (Aldrich & Zimmer, 1986; Burt 1992; Freeman, 1986). Especially critical are social ties to people who are well connected within the particular industry into which the potential entrepreneur intends to enter. These ties provide access to information that increases the probability of knowing how to pitch the venture in a way that is appealing to potential customers, suppliers, and other resource providers, as well as the probability of identifying the most appealing individuals to pitch. Such ties also provide a basis for referrals to customers, suppliers, and potential employees, who are more likely to back the new organization if the reliability of the potential entrepreneur can be substantiated by trusted informants. Finally, network ties, based on the trust that arises from long-term relationships, can buffer the potential entrepreneur from opportunistic behavior and make it possible for him or her to count on the support of resource providers in challenging situations.

Established organizations provide a social context that allows would-be entrepreneurs to develop the social ties critical to the creation of a new venture because of the relationship between physical proximity, interaction, and friendship (e.g., Festinger, Schachter, & Back, 1950). Regular interactions with colleagues, customers, and suppliers enable would-be entrepreneurs to develop social relationships in the course of everyday employment. Resource providers are generally reluctant to back strangers. However, the intertwined social and economic aspects of the relationships established during prior employment motivate parties to act fairly, to trust one another, and to respect a general sense of obligation in the exchange (Granovetter, 1985; Gulati, 1995). Other social ties link the potential entrepreneur to key resource providers through third parties who have strong ties to both. These so-called weak ties (Granovetter, 1974) help potential entrepreneurs overcome resource provider reluctance by facilitating the flow of reputational information that mitigates the uncertainty inherent in the new venture.

The empirical evidence supports the importance of social ties in the entrepreneurial process. Ruef, Aldrich, and Carter (2003) analyzed multi-industry data from the Panel Study of Entrepreneurial Dynamics (PSED) and found that trust and familiarity are more critical to founding team composition than are complementary skill sets. The importance of trust, familiarity, and cohesion of founding teams was also noted in a study of semiconductor companies that found that prior joint work experience of top management teams contributes to higher growth in new ventures (Eisenhardt & Schoonhoven, 1990). The empirical evidence shows that, in addition to leveraging networks to attract employees, nascent entrepreneurs rely on network ties to attract financing. For example, venture capitalists rely on information from network contacts in deciding which startup companies to fund and in monitoring pursued investments (Florida & Kenney, 1988; Freeman, 1999). In a sample of 202 seed-stage investors, Shane and Cable (2002) found that both direct and indirect ties between entrepreneurs and investors positively influenced investors' decisions about which ventures to finance. Finding that entrepreneurs' reputations mediate the effects of both types of ties, the authors concluded that network ties function primarily as a mechanism for information transfer. In addition, Sorenson and Stuart's (2001) findings of geographic concentration in venture capital (VC) investing also support the importance of social ties in sourcing and monitoring investments. Organizational contexts, then, provide opportunities for employees to form social ties to the critical resource providers, who enable nascent entrepreneurs to pursue entrepreneurial opportunities.

EMPIRICAL EVIDENCE

Three distinct bodies of work support the notion of entrepreneurs as organizational products: (1) *career history studies* that focus on individuals' experiences prior to entrepreneurship; (2) *spatial distribution studies* that focus on the location of entrepreneurial activity; and (3) *differential fertility studies* that explore whether certain organizations are more conducive to generating new entrepreneurs than others. Next, we review representative studies within each stream of research.

Career History Studies

Career history studies share a focus on the educational and professional experiences of entrepreneurs prior to formation of a new organization. The key finding is that a large proportion of founders of new organizations come from the ranks of preexisting organizations operating in similar businesses. Cooper found that 70% of 890 founders from a cross section of industries started businesses closely related to their prior employment and that 85% of 250 technical entrepreneurs did the same (Cooper, 1970; Cooper & Dunkelberg, 1981). In a subsequent study of 161 new firms, Cooper (1985) found that in most technical industries entrepreneurs started businesses related to their previous employment. For example, 78% of 46 founders of electronics and computer ventures had previous employment in electronics and computer industries.

Other studies examine how organizations promote regional development by expanding the pool of potential entrepreneurs. For example, in a longitudinal study of 73 business and research organizations, Mitton et al. (1990) analyzed the patterns of proliferation and growth in the San Diego area biotech industry. This study found that the founders of 13 spin-off companies were previously employed by Hybritech, while a sizeable number of other companies were created by individuals linked to local research institutions (e.g., Scripps and UCSD) and other local biotech firms. Neck et al. (2004), using surveys and semistructured interviews in a study of the Boulder County, Colorado, region, traced the roots of local high-tech spin-off organizations to seven primary incubator organizations.

Additional career history studies examine the role of prior experience in conditioning an individual's ability to recognize and exploit entrepreneurial opportunities. For example, in a study of all 1,397 U.S. patents assigned to MIT from 1980 to 1996, Shane and Khurana (2003) estimated the effects of inventors' career experiences on the likelihood that an invention would lead to commercialization via the founding of a new organization. For 363 founding events, the authors found that valuable information acquired over the course of one's career influenced the motivations of individuals to found new organizations as well as the motivations of resource providers to support the new organizations. The impact of career histories was found to be substantial even when controlling for factors related to the industry and the technology.

Other career history studies observe the effects of management teams' joint work experience. For example, a study by Eisenhardt and Schoonhoven (1990) examined 102 new entrants in the semiconductor industry between 1978 and 1985 and found that management teams with prior joint work experience achieved greater sales growth. The authors attributed their findings to the notion that these strong teams "appeared to move more quickly, get more done, and make fewer mistakes than other teams" (Eisenhardt & Schoonhoven, 1990, p. 525). Additionally, Higgins and Gulati (2003) analyzed the career histories of over 3,000 top management teams from 1961 to 1994 and found that the executives' prior employment relationships were crucial in gaining the endorsement of the investment banks that underwrite initial public offerings (IPOs). In a separate study, Higgins (2005) found that in 23% of the biotech firms that went public in the period 1979–1996, at least one member of the IPO team had previous employment at Baxter, a prominent biotech firm. In the biotech industry, Baxter gained a prominent reputation for producing entrepreneurs (Higgins, 2005), as former Baxter employees were management team members of 29 venture-backed startups from 1986 to 1999 (Gompers, Lerner, & Scharfstein, 2005). Higgins refers to *career imprinting* as the process by which certain organizations such as Baxter can cultivate employees' capabilities, connections, and confidence to pursue emerging industry opportunities.

Other research in this vein examines the development of industries and market niches. For example, Rindova and Fombrun (2001, pp. 244–245) examined the emergence of the specialty coffee industry and described how the founders of Starbucks Coffee Company, Coffee Connection, and other key firms learned from Alfred Peet (founder of Peet's Coffee and Tea Company) how to select, define, roast, and distinguish specialty coffees from mainstream coffee. Additionally, several studies of the hard-disk-drive industry (e.g., Agarwal et al., 2004; Christensen & Bower, 1996; Franco & Filson, 2000) document the high degree of intraindustry mobility of employees from existing to new firms. This pattern of entry by firms started by ex-employees of preexisting firms was accompanied by repeated introductions of disruptive innovations (Christensen, 1993; Christensen & Bower, 1996) that created new market niches such as the specialty coffee niche documented by Rindova and Fombrun (2001). Career history studies like these, and those discussed earlier, highlight the role that existing organizations play in exposing individuals, via professional experiences, to the confidence-building tasks, information on entrepreneurial opportunities, and social contacts that often lead to the production of entrepreneurs. In the process, industries are shaped and transformed. The available evidence, though, is not limited to studies tracing the work histories of founders. Macro-level studies also provide strong evidence for the role of existing organizations in ongoing entrepreneurial activity.

Spatial Distribution Studies

Spatial distribution studies demonstrate geographical areas that have a greater number of organizations of a certain kind tend to generate a greater number of new firms of that same kind. Researchers explain this spatial relationship by noting that existing organizations expand the pool of potential entrepreneurs available in a locale by employing individuals in organizational roles conducive to acquiring information about entrepreneurial opportunities and to developing the social contacts necessary for resource mobilization. Because entrepreneurs rely on supportive social structures in creating new organizations (Stinchcombe, 1965) and because those individuals tend to develop social networks that are geographically localized (Festinger, Schachter, & Back, 1950), they are more likely to start new organizations in close proximity to their homes and their current organizations of employment (e.g., Cooper & Dunkelberg, 1987; Johnson & Cathcart, 1979; Katona & Morgan, 1952; Mueller & Morgan, 1962). For example, a study of Portuguese manufacturing plants found a significant *home bias*—the tendency to locate new organizations in the founders' region of residence—such that Portuguese entrepreneurs were willing to accept labor costs three times higher than in alternative locations to locate the new businesses in their current geographic areas (Figueiredo, Guimaraes, & Woodward, 2002). This geographical inertia is typically attributed to the presumably high costs, both social and financial, faced by entrepreneurs who relocate in pursuit of entrepreneurial opportunity; such entrepreneurs must simultaneously form new social ties and a new organization. For many organizational researchers, then, the constraints that space poses on individuals' positions within the social structure coupled with the role of existing organizations in preparing individuals for entrepreneurship justify an empirical focus on the role that the spatial distribution of organizations plays in promoting entrepreneurial activity.

Sorenson and Audia (2000) examined the constraints that the existing spatial distribution of production poses on entrepreneurial activity in the U.S. footwear industry from 1940 to 1989. Their analyses of the founding rate of shoe manufacturers by state showed that greater local density (number of plants in the state) substantially increased the rate of founding events. Sorenson and Audia argued that the current geographic distribution of production places important constraints on entrepreneurial activity because nascent entrepreneurs need existing organizations to build confidence, acquire knowledge of the business, and establish social ties. Stuart and Sorenson (2003a) replicated this finding in another industry (biotech) and at a finer geographic unit of analysis (ZIP code). The authors analyzed 644 biotech firm founding events over the period 1978–1995 to investigate potential explanations for spatial heterogeneity in firm founding rates.

Their analyses demonstrate that new biotech firms were more likely to be founded when proximity to other biotech firms, venture capital firms, and research universities was greater.

Cattani, Pennings, and Wenzel (2003) found additional evidence that the local density of organizations increases the emergence of new organizations of the same kind in a study of Dutch accounting firms from 1880 to 1986. They argued that founding rates were spatially constrained by existing subpopulations because new organizations relied on existing organizations (and the knowledge and social ties those organizations offer individuals) for *cognitive legitimacy* (Aldrich & Fiol, 1994), which is the social recognition of the new organizations' existence. However, they also found that interregional movement of individuals provided an important vehicle for the diffusion of organizational forms from one region to another. Collectively, these spatial distribution studies suggest that the creation of new organizations is constrained by the geographic distribution of existing organizations. Given such findings, many researchers find it natural to concentrate their empirical focus on existing organizations as influential in the production of entrepreneurs.

Differential Fertility Studies

Differential fertility studies focus on organizational characteristics to explain employees' motivation to pursue entrepreneurial opportunities. Organizational contexts are treated as fundamentally different in terms of their propensity to produce entrepreneurs. Two findings emerging from this body of work provide indirect evidence regarding the micro-level processes that govern new venture creation. First, technological innovation appears to make organizations more fertile grounds for entrepreneurs. This is consistent with the view that organizations operating at the technological frontier are more likely to provide their employees with greater access to valuable entrepreneurial opportunities. In a study of the semiconductor industry from 1955 to 1981, Brittain and Freeman (1986) found that firms that were the first entrant in a primary product group were more likely to generate spin-offs. Franco and Filson's (2000) study of 192 firms in the rigid-disk-drive industry from 1977 to 1997 found that firms with greater technical know-how (i.e., superior technology) and early-mover know-how (i.e., first to introduce a new product) provided richer training grounds for entrepreneurs. Similarly, Gompers, Lerner, and Scharfstein (2005), in a study of publicly traded firms between 1987 and 1999, found that firms spawned more venture-capital-backed startups if they had higher quality patents. The number of citations received evidenced patent quality.

The second finding emerging from this body of work is that younger and smaller firms are more conducive to the emergence of new entrepreneurs. This evidence too seems consistent with the micro processes discussed earlier. Arguably, employees of small, young firms are more likely to be exposed to entrepreneurial opportunities because they have greater access to information regarding the entire business. They are also more likely to develop strong ties to colleagues in different functional areas, who may join them in the new venture, and to have more opportunities to establish contacts with key resource providers. Finally, they can more easily build confidence in their ability to create a new organization because they fulfill a broader number of roles crucial to the operations of entrepreneurial organizations.

Evidence regarding the greater fertility of young and small organizations comes from Sørensen's (2004) systematic investigation of individual transitions to self-employment (entrepreneurship). Sørensen used data representative of both the population of individuals and the population of employers in the Danish labor market from 1970 to 1997. He found that the rate of entrepreneurship declined with the size of the individual's employer—employees of large firms were less likely to become entrepreneurs. This effect was fairly robust, holding up to alternative explanations when controlling for individual characteristics such as occupational category (i.e., white-collar, blue-collar), educational level and major, and financial status (i.e., income, assets, debt). Sørensen's analysis also indicates that younger firms were more likely to produce entrepreneurs than older firms. Although Sørensen's study is probably the most systematic differential fertility study to date, his results are consistent with at least two additional studies of less representative samples of U.S. organizations. Dobrev and Barnett (2005) used career survey data from 5,283 Stanford MBA graduates to advance a multilevel model of individuals' transitions to entrepreneurship. Analyzing the effects of individual, organizational, and environmental characteristics on entrepreneurial transitions, they found that organizational members were *less* likely to become entrepreneurs as their organizations grew larger and older, although founders were *more* likely to become entrepreneurs as their organizations aged. Gompers, Lerner, and Scharfstein (2005) also found that younger firms were more likely to spawn new firms in their study of venture-capital-backed startups founded by individuals employed by public corporations.

Together, these fertility studies provide fine-grained evidence that links organizational contexts to the emergence of entrepreneurs. Furthermore, by providing evidence linking specific features of the organizational context to members' propensities to create new organizations, these studies help to shed light on the micro-level processes that govern new venture creation.

FUTURE RESEARCH

We can conclude from this review that a large volume of empirical studies supports the notion of entrepreneurs as organizational products. Important gaps, however, remain. Empirical evidence linking the experiences of employment to the microprocesses highlighted in the theory outlined herein is still limited and often indirect. Studies tracing how work experiences influence the development of the psychological and social resources that facilitate entrepreneurial activity would help provide not only a direct test of the theory but also a better understanding of the conditions under which organizations are more likely to be conducive to generating entrepreneurs. These studies might ask which organizational contexts are more likely to provide the mastery and vicarious experiences that help build confidence in one's ability to create a new organization and, in so doing, might establish a microfoundation for future differential fertility research. For example, Baron and Markman (2000) suggest that many sales and customer relations employees develop social skills, through training programs, that help entrepreneurs persuade financiers, customers, and potential cofounders to support their new ventures. Building on their argument, future research on mastery and vicarious learning experiences might investigate the influences of organizational training programs in producing entrepreneurs.

Much of the recent evidence supporting the notion of entrepreneurs as organizational products concerns the effects of organizational characteristics such as size, age, and technical innovation (i.e., Gompers, Lerner, & Scharfstein, 2005; Sørensen, 2004). In addition, the study of Dobrev and Barnett (2005) emphasizes an individual's organizational role in assessing the likelihood of engaging in entrepreneurial activity. Although this work provides insights to macro researchers regarding research topics such as bureaucracy, generalism versus specialism, technical innovation, and role theory, micro researchers have much to add to this emerging body of evidence. For example, one challenge for investigators in the entrepreneurs-as-organizational-products tradition is accounting for individual self-selection into the types of organizations and organizational roles most conducive to producing entrepreneurs (Sørensen, 2004). By investigating the individual constructs that predict employment with certain types of organizations (i.e., small vs. large, hierarchical vs. flat, young vs. old, product vs. service, etc.) and in certain organizational roles (i.e., externally vs. internally oriented, sales vs. finance vs. engineering, etc.), micro researchers may contribute profoundly to entrepreneurship research by separating organizational characteristics from the effects of self-selection.

Our understanding of entrepreneurial outcomes may be further advanced by identifying the micro-level mediators of entrepreneurial action as it relates to the work settings argued to be so important in providing information and motivation to would-be entrepreneurs. In explaining the relationship between social networks and entrepreneurial activity, Burt (1992, p. 35) argues that structural position is "simultaneously an indicator of entrepreneurial opportunity and of motivation" that both pulls and pushes individuals to entrepreneurship. Micro-level researchers seem best equipped to untangle the effects of structural position and individual cognitions and motivations. For example, network researchers have investigated the relationship between personality characteristics and network centrality (Klein et al., 2004) as well as the relationship between personality and individuals' perceptions of networks (Casciaro, 1998). Furthermore, studies have found that individuals possessing more accurate cognitions of formal networks tend to be viewed as more powerful by their peers (Krackhardt, 1990). Identifying the network positions most conducive to enabling entrepreneurial behavior as well as the individual-level determinants (i.e., personality traits, cognitive styles, etc.) of attaining such positions seems to be a promising avenue for future micro research. This research strategy might also shed light on the specific aspects of prior experience that condition individual abilities to recognize and exploit entrepreneurial opportunities (i.e., Shane, 2000). At the least, such a multi-level approach suggests new directions for traits-based research.

Another surprising gap in the available literature is the paucity of studies that compare the likelihood of individuals who are employed in established organizations becoming an entrepreneur to the likelihood of individuals who are not. Such studies require drawing samples of individuals from the entire population, which is often difficult for researchers to accomplish. Data limitations may be assuaged by the PSED, a large-scale effort to collect data on nascent entrepreneurs as well as an appropriate comparison set from the general population. The PSED may allow future researchers to examine not only the probability of these two groups of individuals (employed and unemployed) becoming nascent entrepreneurs, but also the impact that work experiences have on different stages of the process leading to the creation of a new organization. For example, the research program on nascent entrepreneurs (e.g., Carter, Gartner, & Reynolds, 1996; Carter et al., 2003; Gartner, 1985) differentiates the stage at which individuals initiate activities aimed at the creation of a new organization and the stage at which a new full-fledged organization becomes operational. Researchers could investigate whether the psychological and social resources that individuals acquire through their work experiences might have varying effects at these different stages. The theory, for example, implies that social ties to industry insiders play a critical role in the transition from being a nascent entrepreneur to creating the new organization. How different types of ties (i.e., direct, indirect) vary in importance as a new venture grows is an open empirical question.

Future researchers might also investigate how the identity and/or reputation of nascent entrepreneurs' prior employers affect resource providers' impressions of entrepreneurs. In a stratified sample of 173 Silicon Valley companies, Burton, Sørensen, and Beckman (2002) argue that entrepreneurial networks differentially situate potential entrepreneurs, based on the prominence of their employer, to receive crucial information and valuable reputation benefits. They find that those with prior experience at more prominent employers possess advantages in attracting the social and financial resources necessary for pursuing new ventures. Their measure of employer prominence is endogenous to their data (the number of startups in the data set generated by a focal employer), and their findings, by the authors' own admission, would be strengthened by a better understanding of "the criteria by which members of the entrepreneurial community rank existing firms" (Burton, Sørensen, & Beckman, 2002, p. 254). Therein lies an empirical opportunity for micro researchers: What employer characteristics make resource providers more or less likely to support a new venture? Elaborating the micro foundations of employer prominence would contribute to the theory underlining both career history and differential fertility studies.

Another promising avenue for future research lies in asking under what conditions organizational members prefer to create a new organization as opposed to seeking to create a new division or product group within the existing organization. The potential for innovation need not imply the potential for a spin-off organization (Garvin, 1983). Leaving an existing organization to create a new one requires not only the motivation and the ability to be an entrepreneur but also the motivation to leave one's employer. The existing theory specifies how individuals' work settings enhance the motivation and the ability to create a new organization but says less regarding the organizational factors that influence the motivation to leave. Resource allocation processes and political processes may play an important role. For example, critical moments in the life cycles of parent or incubator organizations (i.e., chief executive officer [CEO] succession, acquisition, or bankruptcy) have been found to give rise to spin-offs (Brittain & Freeman, 1986; Neck et al. 2004; Romanelli & Schoonhoven, 2001; Stuart & Sorenson, 2003b). One possible explanation for these observations is that resource allocation processes have inherent limits for absorption of employee-led initiatives and that critical moments alter the "rules of the game" that govern internal resource allocation. A second possible explanation for these observations is that organizational change creates greater uncertainty and therefore greater politicization of the decision-making processes that govern resource allocations for new initiatives (Cyert & March, 1963; Maritan, 2001).

In conclusion, research on entrepreneurs as organizational products is alive and well. The distinctive contribution of this body of research to the entrepreneurship literature lies in emphasizing the importance of organizations as social contexts conducive to the development of the psychological and social resources necessary for entrepreneurial activity and in providing a link between micro and macro explanations of entrepreneurial action. Promising opportunities exist for micro researchers to strengthen the theory that guides this growing body of research.

REFERENCES

Agarwal, R., Echambadi, R., Franco, A., & Sarkar, M. B. (2004). Knowledge transfer through inheritance spinout generation, development and survival. *Academy of Management Journal, 47*(4), 501–522.

Aldrich, H. E., & Auster, E. (1986). Even dwarfs started small: Liabilities of age and size and their strategic implications. In B. Staw & L. L. Cummings (Eds.), *Research in organizational behavior* (Vol. VIII, pp. 165–198). Greenwich, CT: JAI Press.

Aldrich, H. E., & Fiol, C. M. (1994). Fools rush in? The institutional context of industry creation. *Academy of Management Review, 19*(40, 645–670.

Aldrich, H. E., & Wiedenmayer, G. (1993). From traits to rates: An ecological perspective on organizational foundings. *Advances in Entrepreneurship, Firm Emergence, and Growth, 1,* 145–195.

Aldrich, H. E., & Zimmer, C. (1986). Entrepreneurship through social networks. In D. Sexton & R. Smilor (Eds.), *The art and science of entrepreneurship* (pp. 3–23). New York: Ballinger.

Bandura, A. (1986). *Social foundations of thought and action: A social cognitive theory.* Englewood Cliffs, NJ: Prentice Hall.

Bandura, A. (1994). Self-efficacy. In V. S. Ramachaudran (Ed.), *Encyclopedia of Human Behavior* (Vol. 4, pp. 71–81). New York: Academic Press.

Barker, C. (2000). *NeXT computer: When cool wasn't enough.* Accessed February 28, 2006, www.vnunet.com/vnunet/features/2129861/computer-cool-wasn-enough

Baron, R. A., & Markman, G. D. (2000). Beyond social capital: How social skills can enhance entrepreneurs' success. *Academy of Management Executive, 14*(1), 106–116.

Beesley, M. E. (1955). The birth and death of industrial establishments: Experience in the West Midlands Conurbation. *Journal of Industrial Economics, 4*(1), 45–61.

Bhide, A. V. (1994, March–April). How entrepreneurs craft strategies that work. *Harvard Business Review,* pp. 150–161.

Bhide, A. V. (2000). *The origin and evolution of new businesses.* Oxford, UK: Oxford University Press.

Brittain, J. W., & Freeman, J. (1980). Organizational proliferation and density dependent selection. In J. R. Kimberley & R. Miles (Eds.), *The organizational life cycle* (pp. 291–338). San Francisco, CA: Jossey Bass.

Brittain, J. W., & Freeman, J. (1986). *Entrepreneurship in the semiconductor industry.* Unpublished manuscript. August.

Brush, C., Greene, P. G., & Hart, M. M. (2001). From initial idea to unique advantage: The entrepreneurial challenge of constructing a resource base. *Academy of Management Executive, 15*(1), 64–80.

Burt, R. (1992). *Structural holes: The social structure of competition.* Cambridge, MA: Harvard University Press.

Burton, M. D. (2001). The company they keep: Founders' models for organizing new firms. In C. B. Schoonhoven & E. Romanelli (Eds.), *The entrepreneurship dynamic* (pp. 13–39). Stanford, CA: Stanford University Press.

Burton, M. D., Sørensen, J. B., & Beckman, C. (2002). Coming from good stock: Career histories and new venture formation. In M. Lounsbury & M. Ventresca (Eds.), *Social structure and organizations revisited* (pp. 229–262). Oxford, UK: Elsevier JAI Press.

Camerer, C., & Lovallo, D. (1999). Overconfidence and excess entry: An experimental approach. *American Economic Review, 89*(1), 306–318.

Carroll, G. R., Dobrev, S. D., & Swaminathan, A. (2002). Organizational processes of resource partitioning. In B. M. Staw and R. M. Kramer (Eds.), *Research in organizational behavior* (Vol. 24, pp. 1–40). Greenwich, CT: JAI Press.

Carter, N. M., Gartner, W. B., & Reynolds, P. D. (1996). Exploring start-up event sequences. *Journal of Business Venturing, 11*, 151–166.

Carter, N. M., Gartner, W. B., Shaver, K. G., & Gatewood, E. J. (2003). The career reasons of nascent entrepreneurs. *Journal of Business Venturing, 18*, 13–39.

Casciaro, T. (1998). Seeing things clearly: Social structure, personality, and accuracy in social network perception. *Social Networks, 20*, 331–351.

Cattani, G., Pennings, J. M., & Wenzel, F. C. (2003). Spatial and temporal heterogeneity in founding patterns. *Organization Science, 14*(6), 670–685.

Christensen, C. M. (1993). The rigid disk drive industry: A history of commercial and technological turbulence. *Business History Review, 67*, 531–588.

Christensen, C. M., & Bower, J. L. (1996). Customer power, strategic investment, and the failure of leading firms. *Strategic Management Journal, 17*(3), 197–218.

Cooper, A. C. (1970). *The founding of technologically-based firms.* Milwaukee, WI: Center for Venture Management.

Cooper, A. C. (1973). Technical entrepreneurship: What do we know? *Research and Development Management, 3*, 3–18.

Cooper, A. C. (1985). The role of incubator organizations in the founding of growth-oriented firms. *Journal of Business Venturing, 1*, 75–86.

Cooper, A. C., & Dunkelberg, W. C. (1981). A new look at business entry: Experiences of 1805 entrepreneurs. In K. Vesper (Ed.), *Frontiers of entrepreneurship research* (pp. 1–20). Wellesley, MA: Babson Center for Entrepreneurial Studies.

Cooper, A. C., & Dunkelberg, W. C. (1987). Entrepreneurial research: Old questions, new answers and methodological issues. *American Journal of Small Business, 11*, 11–23.

Cooper, A. C., Woo, C., & Dunkelberg, W. C. (1988). Entrepreneurs' perceived chances of success. *Journal of Business Venturing, 3*, 97–108.

Cooper, A. C., Woo, C., & Dunkelberg, W. C. (1989). Entrepreneurship and the initial size of firms. *Journal of Business Venturing, 4*, 317–332.

Cyert, R., & March, J. G. (1963). *A behavioral theory of the firm.* Englewood Hills, NJ: Prentice Hall.

Delacroix, J., & Carroll, G. R. (1983). Organizational foundings: An ecological study of the newspaper industries of Argentina and Ireland. *Administrative Science Quarterly, 28*, 274–291.

Dobrev, S. D., & Barnett, W. P. (2005). Organizational roles and transitions to entrepreneurship. *Academy of Management Journal, 48*(3), 433Œ449.

Eisenhardt, K. M, & Schoonhoven, C. B. (1990). Organizational growth: Linking founding team, strategy, environment, and growth among U.S. semiconductor ventures, 1978–1988. *Administrative Science Quarterly, 35*(3), 504–529.

Festinger, L., Schachter, S., & Back, K. (1950). *Social pressures in informal groups: A study of human factors in housing.* New York: Harper.

Figueiredo, O., Guimaraes, P., & Woodward, D. (2002). Home-field advantage: Location decisions of Portuguese entrepreneurs. *Journal of Urban Economics, 52*(2), 341–361.

Florida, R., & Kenney, M. (1988). Venture capital, high technology and regional development. *Regional Studies, 22*(1), 33–48.

Franco, A. M., & Filson, D. (2000). *Knowledge diffusion through employee mobility.* Staff Report 272. Federal Reserve Bank of Minneapolis.

Freeman, J. H. (1986). Entrepreneurs as organizational products: Semiconductor firms and venture capital firms. *Advances in the Study of Entrepreneurship, Innovation, and Economic Growth, 1*, 33–52.

Freeman, J. H. (1999). Venture capital as an economy of time. In S. M. Gabbay & R. T. A. J. Leenders (Eds.), *Corporate social capital and liability* (pp. 460–482). Boston, MA: Kluwer Academic.

Freeman, J. H., Carroll, G. R., & Hannan, M. T. (1983). The liability of newness: Age dependence in organizational death rates. *American Sociological Review, 48*(5), 692–710.

Gartner, W. B. (1985). A conceptual framework for describing the phenomenon of new venture creation. *Academy of Management Review, 10*(4), 696–706.

Garvin, D. A. (1983). Spin-offs and the new firm formation process. *California Management Review, 25*(2), 3–20.

Gompers, P., Lerner, J., & Scharfstein, D. (2005). Entrepreneurial spawning: Public corporations and the formation of new ventures, 1986–1999. *Journal of Finance, 60,* 577–614. (Earlier version distributed as National Bureau of Economic Research Working Paper No. 9816.)

Granovetter, M. S. (1974). *Getting a job: A study of contacts and careers.* Cambridge, MA: Harvard University Press.

Granovetter, M. S. (1985). Economic action and social structure: The problem of embeddedness. *American Journal of Sociology, 91,* 481–510.

Gulati, R. (1995). Does familiarity breed trust? The implications of repeated ties for contractual choice in alliances. *Academy of Management Journal, 38*(1), 85–112.

Hannan, M. T., & Freeman, J. H. (1977). The population ecology of organizations. *American Journal of Sociology, 82,* 829–864.

Higgins, M. C. (2005). *Career imprints: Creating leaders across an industry.* San Francisco: Jossey-Bass.

Higgins, M. C., & Gulati, R. (2003). Getting off to a good start: The effects of upper echelon affiliations on underwriter prestige. *Organization Science, 14,*(3), 244–263.

Jacobs, J. (1969). *The economy of cities.* New York: Vintage.

Johnson, P. A., & Cathcart, D. G. (1979). New manufacturing firms and regional development: Some evidence from the Northern region. *Regional Studies, 13,* 269–280.

Katona, G., & Morgan, J. N. (1952). The quantitative study of factors determining business decisions. *Quarterly Journal of Economics, 66,* 67–90.

Kirzner, I. M. (1973). *Competition and entrepreneurship.* Chicago: University of Chicago Press.

Klein, K. J., Lim, B. C., Saltz, J. L., & Mayer, D. M. (2004). How do they get there? An examination of the antecedents of centrality in team networks. *Academy of Management Journal, 47*(6), 952–963.

Klepper, S., & Sleeper, S. (2000). *Entry by spinoffs.* Mimeo. Pittsburgh: Carnegie Mellon University.

Knight, F. (1964). *Risk, uncertainty and profit* (pp. 269–275). New York: Augustus Kelley.

Krackhardt, D. (1990). Assessing the political landscape: Structure, cognition, and power in organizations. *Administrative Science Quarterly, 35,* 342–369.

Maritan, C. A. (2001). Capital investment as investing in organizational capabilities: An empirically grounded process model. *Academy of Management Journal, 44*(3), 513–531.

Markman, G. D., Balkin, D. B., & Baron, R. A. (2001, August). *Inventors' cognitive mechanisms as predictors of new venture formation.* Paper presented at the meetings of the Academy of Management, Washington, DC.

Mitton, D. G., Churchill, N. C., Bygrave, W. D., Hornaday, J. A., Muzyka, D. F., Vesper, K. H., Wetzel Jr., J. A. (1990). Bring on the clones: A longitudinal study of the proliferation, development, and growth, of the biotech industry in San Diego. In N. C. Churchill et al. (Eds.), *Frontiers of entrepreneurship research* (pp. 344–358). Wellesley, MA: Babson College.

Mueller, E., & Morgan, J. N. (1962). Location decision of manufacturers. *American Economic Review, 52,* 204–217.

Neck, H. M., Meyer, G. D., Cohen, B., & Corbett, A. C. (2004). An entrepreneurial system view of new venture creation. *Journal of Small Business Management, 42*(2), 190–208.

Rindova, V. P., & Fombrun, C. J. (2001). Entrepreneurial action in the creation of the specialty coffee niche. In C. B. Schoonhoven & E. Romanelli (Eds.), *The entrepreneurship dynamic* (pp. 236–261). Stanford, CA: Stanford University Press.

Romanelli, E. (1989). Organization birth and population variety: A community perspective on origins. *Research in Organizational Behavior, 11*, 211–246.

Romanelli, E., & Schoonhoven, C. B. (2001). The local origins of new firms. In C. B. Schoonhoven & E. Romanelli (Eds.), *The entrepreneurship dynamic* (pp. 40–67). Stanford, CA: Stanford University Press.

Ruef, M., Aldrich, H. E., & Carter, N. (2003). The structure of organizational founding teams: Homophily, strong ties, and isolation among U.S. entrepreneurs. *American Sociology Review, 68*(2), 195–222.

Saxenian, A. (1994). *Regional advantage: Culture and competition in Silicon Valley and Route 128.* Cambridge, MA: Harvard University Press.

Schoonhoven, C. B., & Romanelli, E. (2001). Emergent themes and the next wave of entrepreneurship research. In C. B. Schoonhoven & E. Romanelli (Eds.), *The entrepreneurship dynamic* (pp. 383–408). Stanford, CA: Stanford University Press.

Schumpeter, J. (1934). *Theory of economic development.* Cambridge, MA: Harvard University Press.

Shane, S. (2000). Prior knowledge and the discovery of entrepreneurial opportunities. *Organization Science, 11*(4), 448–469.

Shane, S., & Cable, D. (2002). Network ties, reputation, and the financing of new ventures. *Management Science, 48*(3), 364–381.

Shane, S., & Khurana, R. (2003). Bringing individuals back in: The effects of career experience on new firm founding. *Industrial and Corporate Change, 12*(3), 519–543.

Shane, S., Locke, E. A., & Collins, C. J. (2003). Entrepreneurial motivation. *Human Resource Management Review, 13*, 257–279.

Sørensen, J. B. (2004). *Does bureaucratization cause entrepreneurship?* Working Paper. Cambridge, MA: Massachusetts Institute of Technology.

Sorenson, O., & Audia, P. G. (2000). The social structure of entrepreneurial activity: Geographic concentration of footwear production in the United States, 1940–1989. *American Journal of Sociology, 106*(2), 424–462.

Sorenson, O., & Stuart, T. E. (2001). Syndication networks and the spatial distribution of venture capital investments. *American Journal of Sociology, 106*(6), 1546–1588.

Stuart, T. E., & Sorenson, O. (2003a). The geography of opportunity: Spatial heterogeneity in founding rates and the performance of biotechnology firms. *Research Policy, 32*, 229–253.

Stuart, T. E., & Sorenson, O. (2003b). Liquidity events and the geographic distribution of entrepreneurial activity. *Administrative Science Quarterly, 48*(2), 175–201.

Stinchcombe, A. L. (1965). Social structure and organizations. In J. G. March (Ed.), *The handbook of organizational behavior* (pp. 142–193). Chicago: Rand McNally.

Thornton, P. H. (1999). The sociology of entrepreneurship. *Annual Review of Sociology, 25*, 19–46.

Venkataraman, S. (1997). The distinctive domain of entrepreneurship research: An editor's perspective. In J. Katz & R. Brockhaus (Eds.), *Advances in entrepreneurship, firm emergence, and growth* (Vol. 3, pp. 119–138). Greenwich, CT: JAI Press.

Von Hippel, E. (1986). Lead users: A source of novel product concepts. *Management Science, 32*(7), 791–805.

Vroom, V. (1964). *Work and motivation.* New York: Wiley and Sons.

7

Cognition and Capabilities in Entrepreneurial Ventures

Lowell W. Busenitz
Jonathan D. Arthurs

The exploring of entrepreneurial opportunities is about the development of new ideas and the building of those ideas into thriving businesses. But to develop new business opportunities, various resources and capabilities are needed to bring the new ideas to reality. Starting a new business usually involves dealing with very limited human and capital resources to the extent that bootstrapping often starts ventures. Furthermore, entrepreneurship usually occurs in complex and dynamic environments, so it is a nontrivial challenge for researchers to constructively make inroads in addressing this important issue. Given these challenges, it is both fascinating and important to probe why some people and not others choose to pursue and develop a potential opportunity. Indeed, the skills and capabilities utilized in pursuing a new venture and developing its full potential tend to be unique and demanding.

The resources and capabilities required for starting a new venture are obviously quite substantial and often exceed those of the founder(s) very quickly. Furthermore, environments shift, and early perceptions about where the actual opportunities exist may not be accurate or may be changing. Of course, this suggests that ventures often need to adjust resources and adapt to environmental changes and an increasingly evident reality. Dynamic capabilities are unarguably an important part of a venture if it is to succeed over the longer term. Dynamic capabilities help entrepreneurs change and adjust, and the effective use of networks can facilitate this ability to adjust. It is also argued that entrepreneurial skills and capabilities are the primary premise of a venture. Additionally, the distinction between individual-level capabilities and dynamic capabilities is oftentimes blurred.

This chapter seeks to accomplish several things. We seek to more carefully articulate the role of entrepreneurial cognition and how it facilitates the development of the capabilities consistent with starting a new venture. We argue that entrepreneurial capabilities can be a potential source of competitive advantage. We then address how entrepreneurial cognition tends to impact the decisions that entrepreneurs make and the firms they create leading to a potential source of competitive advantage. Finally, we explore the meaning of dynamic capabilities in the entrepreneurship context. By addressing both entrepreneurial cognition and dynamic capabilities in the entrepreneurship context, we add clarity to the distinction between them, adding clarity to a literature that heretofore has been plagued by ambiguity (Helfat & Peteraf, 2003; Winter, 2003).

THE COGNITIVE APPROACH IN THE STUDY
OF ENTREPRENEURSHIP

The resurgence of the study of interindividual differences of entrepreneurs that started in the 1990s took the cognitive approach, rather than the trait approach used earlier. Two articles, by Busenitz and Barney (1997) and Baron (1998), in particular provided an important premise. Although these two articles where not the first in entrepreneurship to take a cognitive perspective (e.g., Katz, 1992), their acceptance seemed to signal that the winds were shifting. Busenitz and Barney (1997) took a cognitive decision-making approach to examine potential differences between entrepreneurs and managers in large organizations. Their findings suggest that entrepreneurs rely on heuristics more extensively than do managers in large organizations. Heuristics are mental shortcuts, and every human mind uses them. However, the assumption here is that some individuals use them more extensively than others. The identified biases and heuristics are many (for more extensive reviews see Bazerman, 1990; Hogarth, 1987; Tversky & Kahneman, 1974).

Baron (1998) published a theoretical paper that called attention to the cognitive mechanisms that are likely to be at work among entrepreneurs. These include counterfactual thinking, affect infusion, attributional style, the planning fallacy, and self-justification. Baron specifically explored the impact that each one of these mechanisms is likely to be reflected in the way entrepreneurs think. Now articles with a cognitive perspective are appearing regularly in the top entrepreneurship journals. Furthermore, *Entrepreneurship Theory and Practice* (2002, volume 27(2)) and *Journal of Business Venturing* (2004, volume 19(2)) both recently published special issues on cognition and entrepreneurship, with another special issue in *Entrepreneur-*

ship Theory and Practice forthcoming. The number of dissertations now being conducted with a cognitive perspective is also increasing.

The recent growth in the use of the cognitive perspective in the entrepreneurship domain merits further explanation. This signals that the cognitive perspective is quite constructive in studying entrepreneurship. I offer several explanations here. First, understanding the entrepreneurial process is obviously quite varied and at times extremely complex (Baron, 2004). Societies and environments change, and sometimes one or a few people see a specific opportunity where most just see a world that is changing and adjustments that need to be made. Risks have to be taken if an opportunity is going to be pursued and relationships managed. Baron argues that when one considers the complexity of the entrepreneurial process, the cognitive perspective becomes suitable for probing entrepreneurship-related phenomena.

Second, the cognitive approach usually allows researchers to get closer to the actual phenomenon being investigated. The observation of issues such as information processing, the seeing of potential opportunities where most do not, decision making with limited information, and operating in substantial uncertainty are all examples of phenomena of great interest to entrepreneurship researchers. Conceptually, the examination of personality factors leaves researchers at more of a distance, sometimes at the expense of misunderstanding the actual phenomenon. For example, one of the most commonly researched personality factors in the entrepreneurship domain is risk taking. This is also the characteristic that is commonly associated with entrepreneurship by those outside the academic community. Given the high failure rate of entrepreneurial ventures, entrepreneurship clearly involves a great deal of risk. Yet the empirical findings on risk taking among entrepreneurs are mixed, leading some researchers to conclude that entrepreneurs are managers of risk more than actual risk takers (e.g., Ray, 1994). However, this paradox can be resolved by examining entrepreneurial risk through the lens of cognitive psychology and decision making. Entrepreneurial risk may be explained by recognizing that entrepreneurs utilize heuristics more extensively in their decision making, which is likely to lead them to perceive less risk in a given decision situation (Busenitz, 1999). It is not that entrepreneurial situations are equally as risky as other business opportunities; it is just that the perspective of entrepreneurs (high optimism and heuristic-based decision making) leads to a different perspective in the risk actually involved in starting a new venture.

In sum, these issues point toward the cognitive approach showing much promise in the study of entrepreneurs, an approach that should enable the study of interindividual differences to get closer to the phenomenon itself as well as to be of more benefit in teaching future entrepreneurs. From this foundation, the following section explicitly develops the concept of entrepreneurial capabilities from a cognitive perspective. Finally, we develop the concept of dynamic capabilities in an entrepreneurial setting. The cognitive or entrepreneurial capabilities are seen as constructive and necessary but not sufficient to successfully pursue an entrepreneurial venture. Thus, this chapter seeks to push the frontiers of entrepreneurial cognition forward, as well as to discuss the necessary and complementary nature of additional capabilities.

ENTREPRENEURIAL AND DYNAMIC CAPABILITIES

When firms have resources that are valuable, rare, inimitable, and nonsubstitutable, resource-based theory suggests that they will "conceive and implement a value-creating strategy not simultaneously being implemented by any current or potential competitors" (Barney, 1991, p. 102). If other firms are unable to obtain the same resources and capabilities to implement the same strategy, a sustainable competitive advantage should result (Barney, 1991). The resource-based perspective seems very appropriate for entrepreneurial firms because much of entrepreneurship involves the development and implementation of undervalued assets or undervalued strategic factors (Barney, 1986, p. 1991). The resource-based perspective, from an entrepreneurship perspective, begins with the identification of an opportunity in the product market and proceeds with investment in the strategic factors necessary to pursue the opportunity or, more broadly, to implement the value-creating strategy. This investment in undervalued strategic factors can be the result of accurate managerial perceptions concerning the future or it can be the result of luck (Barney, 1986).

Entrepreneurial capabilities can be seen as the ability to identify new opportunities and develop the resource base needed to start a venture firm. *Dynamic capabilities* are broadly defined as the ability to reconfigure the firm's resource base to meet changing demands (Eisenhardt & Martin, 2000). Although the identification of a new opportunity and the subsequent investments to the resource base are the hallmark of entrepreneurial capabilities, the integration and reconfiguration of the resource base in conjunction with an extant opportunity have been characterized as dynamic capabilities (Teece, Pisano, & Shuen, 1997). Both are similar insofar that they represent investments to the organization's resource base. However, entrepreneurial capabilities are primarily linear with the opportunity positioned as the reference point for decision makers. That is, decision makers identify the opportunity and begin building the resource base that they deduce is necessary for the given opportunity. Dynamic capabilities, on the other hand, are primarily recursive in that they combine knowledge concerning the organization's performance against its aspired level of performance in the product market, along with the search for new strategic inputs and recombinations that would permit the organization to meet its performance expectations. Falling short of aspirations is a common motivator for change and the need for dynamic capabilities. As such, the focal point with dynamic capabilities fluctuates among an examination of external influencers of performance in the product market, the target customer base, an examination of the organization's capabilities vis-à-vis any potential competitors for the customer base, and an examination of the strategic factors market for potential undervalued strategic inputs.

The distinction between the two is more clearly specified when we consider the nature of the opportunity and the nature of the organization. We characterize entrepreneurial capabilities as being associated with new opportunities. When the opportunity is new and is pursued in the context of a new organization (e.g., one without an established resource base), the organization's decision makers have greater flexibility in building the resource base to equip the organization in the pursuit of the new opportunity. This is similar to the group of entrepreneurs who recognize an opportunity and work together to build a product and develop an organization to pursue the opportunity. If successful, the entrepreneurs will be able to take their company public and reap the rewards of their entrepreneurial capabilities. The more developed organization with an established resource base is likely to have inherent rigidities (Leonard-Barton, 1992) that arise as the result of the aggregation of stocks of capabilities (Diericks & Cool, 1989) in connection with the pursuit of a former opportunity. These rigidities, which are path dependent and occur over time (Nelson & Winter, 1982), alter the future search of the organization and impede future entrepreneurial capabilities (Hill & Rothaermel, 2003). For example, because knowledge is path dependent and shapes the lens and search patterns in the organization, decision makers' alertness for seeing new entrepreneurial opportunities will narrow in accordance with organizational experience. Furthermore, the range of possibilities that decision makers consider becomes much more limited once the organization has developed an established resource base. Thus, as an entrepreneurial venture advances, the need for dynamic capabilities becomes apparent as organizational adjustments to its resource base and changes in the broader environment come into play. Dynamic capabilities do not replace entrepreneurial capabilities, but rather they serve as a potentially important complement to the earlier foundation.

Figure 7.1 presents the initial entrepreneurial capabilities as the initial opportunity identification and resource base development (e.g., strategic factor investments) and subsequent product market performance. The dynamic capabilities are represented in the feedback loop. The feedback loop represents an assessment of the elements in the external environment and internal environment that impact product market performance and how they impact that performance. Furthermore, this loop represents an evalua-

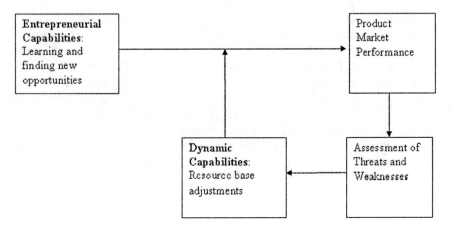

Figure 7.1.   Entrepreneurial cognition and dynamic capabilities.

tion of the product market performance versus competitors, an examination of the nature of the opportunity as it is now becoming clearer, and an evaluation of the resource base that the organization currently possesses versus that which is deduced necessary to meet performance expectations in the future (given the competitor resource bases). These multiple evaluations become the basis for making adjustments to the resource base, which can include purchasing new strategic inputs as well as reconfiguring the existing resource base.

ENTREPRENEURIAL COGNITION AS A RESOURCE

We now develop in more depth the entrepreneurial capabilities dimension specified in Fig. 7.1. More specifically, we focus on entrepreneurial cognition as a potentially valuable resource for starting a new venture. We define *entrepreneurial cognition* as an individual-level resource that enables some individuals to recognize previously undiscovered opportunities and to launch a business in the face of opposition and scarce resources in pursuit of those opportunities. If some individuals are better at recognizing new opportunities and are more likely to develop them into new opportunities, then it follows that their cognitive approaches and the tendencies they facilitate are likely to have strengths and weaknesses in various competitive environments and are a potential source of competitive advantage (Barney, 1991).

Most decision research has generally assumed that individuals tend to make decisions in a similar fashion, and in terms of heuristics, they are susceptible to common errors. However, recent research on cognition indicates that entrepreneurs use heuristics in their decision making more than do their managerial counterparts in large organizations (Busenitz & Barney, 1997; Forbes, 1999). Consequently, entrepreneurs often make significant leaps in their thinking, leading to innovative ideas that are not always very linear or factually based. This research stream is now starting to recognize that entrepreneurs' more extensive use of heuristics in their decision making is at least a partial extension of who they are as individuals (e.g., Simon, Houghton, & Aquino, 2000). Without attention to these cognitive processes, our understanding of entrepreneurs is significantly limited. This has particular implications for entrepreneurs because they regularly find themselves in situations that tend to maximize the potential impact of various heuristics (Baron, 1998).

From a utility function perspective, these cognitive processes are thought to have some substantial benefits as well as weaknesses (Alvarez & Busenitz, 2001). Entrepreneurs typically have to operate in highly ambiguous and highly uncertain environments in the pursuit of a new venture. Thus, the willingness and confidence to readily rely on heuristics to piece together limited information to make convincing decisions may be the only way to move forward with a business opportunity (Busenitz & Barney, 1997). The use of a more factual-based logic in the pursuit of new opportunities becomes too overwhelming and very costly if not impossible to pursue. In essence, the window of opportunity for a new venture closes by the time enough information becomes available for the factual decision maker to decide. The decision-making contexts facing entrepreneurs also tend to be very complex. The heuristic-based logic can have a great deal of utility in enabling entrepreneurs to make decisions that exploit brief windows of opportunity (Tversky & Kahneman, 1974), whereas the elaborate policies, procedural routines, and structural mechanisms common to those with more of a managerial cognition (characteristic of managers in large organizations) are likely to erect barriers in the pursuit of innovative activities.

Learning is clearly a central part of entrepreneurship process. When encountering new information, entrepreneurs seek to achieve new levels of understandings, interpretations and insights. However, for entrepreneurs, the process seems different than learning all that there is to know about A and then moving on to learn about B, and so on. Learning by those with an entrepreneurial cognition may have important associations with the use of heuristics in decision making. Sources of competitive advantage are thought to potentially evolve around knowledge creation and decision-making capabilities (Barney, 1991). Lower level learning tends to be single-loop in nature, stemming from repetitious observations and routinized learning. Such learning tends to be short-term and temporary (Fiol & Lyles, 1985). Consistent with the notion of single-loop learning, there are few changes in underlying policies or values (Argyris & Schon, 1978). Such learning modes tend to be slower and more imitable (Lei, Hitt, & Bettis, 1996), in part because decision makers usually build on results from repeated outcomes of success or failure to reach their decisions. Higher level learning involves the use of heuristics and intuition to generate new insights and solving ambiguous problems (Lei et al., 1996). Such learning tends to create new insights and directions for solving problems. Although the more extensive use of heuristic may be less systematic and less accurate, use of individual-specific clusters of knowledge facilitates quick adjustments to emerging trends (Krabuanrat & Phelps, 1998).

The more extensive use of heuristics in decision making may have some interesting implications for the learning process in the entrepreneurial context. The more extensive use of heuristics may enable entrepreneurs to more quickly make sense out of uncertain and complex situations. Such decision styles can lead to forward-looking approaches (Gavetti & Levinthal, 2000), perceiving new opportunities, faster learning, and unorthodox interpretations (innovations). Given that some people use heuristics more extensively and given the potential advantages as well as disadvantages such a decision style, entrepreneurial cognition can be a source of competitive advantage. If the insights and decisions reached with the more extensive use of heuristics are potentially valuable in the market, if they are indeed rare, if they are difficult to imitate, and if the generated ideas are exploited by the entrepreneurs, then these entrepreneurial insights and decisions are a resource that can potentially lead to a competitive advantage.

The way some people think and make decisions with the more extensive use of heuristics allows them to function more effectively in the pursuit of entrepreneurial endeavors. Given that individual characteristics and decision styles are at least partially embedded in our personalities, they cannot be readily transferred to those who might want to be entrepreneurs when they do not have the personal capabilities. Consequently, it becomes apparent that they are sources of competitive advantage in the entrepreneurial domain. By extension, then, we suggest that not only can those with an entrepreneurial cognition make faster decisions, but they may also learn more quickly and be more likely to think differently about things sometimes leading such individuals to have innovative insights. Thus, an entrepreneurial cognition can facilitate a potential competitive advantage in several important ways. From this premise, we now move our discussion to address how an entrepreneurial cognition can positively impact the pursuit of an entrepreneurial venture. We specifically address the areas of opportunity recognition and entrepreneurial cognition, opportunity recognition and social interactions, and the acquiring of critical resources.

Opportunity Recognition and Entrepreneurial Cognition

As indicated earlier, those with an entrepreneurial cognition perspective tend to use heuristics more extensively as opposed to more fact-based decision making. Such decision styles can lead to seeing things in new ways and perceiving opportunities that have previously gone undetected. More fact-based decision styles often build from proven information and progress with a new opportunity; the preponderance of information and evidence needs to be available and in support of the identified idea. However, new inventions and opportunities are much less likely to evolve from the minds of those who make decisions based more on facts. Furthermore, those with a more structured decision style tend to become very frustrated by situations involving nonlinearity. It is not that information is less important to those who use heuristics more extensively; rather, it is that some information quickly becomes much more salient than others, and it is often assembled in a nontraditional manner. Instead of a more linear $A \rightarrow B \rightarrow C$ type logic, it is more like thinking characterized by leaps, as in a $A \rightarrow G \rightarrow P$ type logic. Information tends to be selectively chosen, and information tends to be recombined in some unusual ways, leading to innovative outcomes.

The recognition of new opportunities is an area of research that is starting to attract a growing amount of attention (e.g., Fiet, 2002; Gaglio & Katz, 2001; Shane & Venkataraman, 2000). We argue here that entrepreneurial cognition has particular relevance for the recognition of new opportunities. In the context of environmental change, those with an entrepreneurial cognition orientation often see new opportunities where others tend to be concerned with pending changes and protecting themselves from possibly developing threats. We suspect that an entrepreneurial cognition may enable an entrepreneur to see an emerging opportunity instead of a pending threat. Instead of viewing new information as problematic and inconsistent with the linear models that have evolved from historic information, entrepreneurial cognition allows one to make leaps and project certain hypotheses about where new opportunities are likely to reside. This is consistent with recent arguments suggesting that the mental structures that individuals possess are associated with the patterns that they see in the world around them (Skuse et al., 1997). The pursuit of new opportunities invariably involves addressing gaps and changes in the context of incomplete information. Some individuals are very reluctant to address new opportunities until more thorough information becomes available. Entrepreneurs, on the other hand, willingly move forward in the face of limited information by connecting the information gaps with inferences consistent with their mental structures. Their mental structures are developed from experience, individual capabilities, and decision style. These mental structures or capabilities at the individual level may be a heterogeneous resource that can be used to organize other resources.

Austrian economists have posited that the search for new opportunities should focus on the process side of discovery. More explicitly, Kirzner (1979) developed the term *entrepreneurial alertness*, the ability to see where products (or services) do not exist or have unexpectedly emerged as valuable. Alertness exists when one individual has an insight into the value of a given resource when others do not. From this perspective, entrepreneurial alertness is associated with "flashes of superior insight" that enable one to recognize an opportunity when it presents itself (Kirzner, 1997). In distinguishing between entrepreneurial alertness and the knowledge expert, Kirzner (1979) argues that the knowledge expert does not fully recognize the value of his or her knowledge or how to turn that knowledge into a viable business opportunity. The entrepreneur may also have the specific knowledge similar to an expert (such as a technological expert), but it is the entrepreneur who can extend or make connections between pieces of knowledge and expertise and the potential application and business opportunity they may have in the workplace.

In entrepreneurship, the knowledge that precipitates the recognition of an opportunity is the connection or relationship between two or more issues that has not been previously made. One or more of these relationships is likely to involve an environmental shift and developing change. The more extensive use of heuristics allows one to make substantial leaps in logic and to make approximations regarding the future direction of a specific market. In reality, the market typically is making changes and shifts; obviously, sometimes these shifts vary a great deal whereas at other times there is more stability. Those who extrapolate more from past events are essentially looking for patterns and trends—something akin to a weighted moving average line. Such decision styles and reasoning can be quite effective in predicting the future during stable periods but can become very inaccurate during more volatile times or with the emergence of a new trend. Those with a decision style that uses heuristics more extensively can be more erratic and ineffective during stable times but potentially quite beneficial during times of transition. Responses to very early variations during stable times is likely to lead one down errant paths and the pursuit of new opportunities for which there is no room. However, such logic can be quite beneficial during periods of transition. The more extensive use of heuristics allows one to make substantial leaps in estimating where the market is likely to be heading. Of course, most estimates are not going to be precise and accurate, but if they are in the general area of the new environmental shift, they open up the possibility of quicker learning in identifying the new opportunities. In sum, these arguments attempt to help clarify how the more extensive use of heuristics helps to enable entrepreneurs to see new discoveries more readily than their counterparts. The more extensive use of heuristics appears to give entrepreneurs a competitive advantage in quickly learning about new changes and what the implication of those changes are for the development of specific discoveries.

Opportunity Recognition and Social Interactions

When a firm's resources and capabilities are socially complex they are likely to be sources of sustained heterogeneity (Barney, 1995). Socially complex resources may be difficult to imitate because they are complex phenomena that are hard to systematically manage and influence. Because new ventures typically start with a founder, the socially complex phenomena by definition occur outside the firm. The interaction between those with entrepreneurial cognition and the broader society creates an interesting context in which to understand how learning transpires reflecting a socially complex asset.

The resource-based view of the firm draws attention to assets that are inimitable because of socially complex properties. In the entrepreneurship domain, tacit socially complex assets are often specific to the founder and the organizations they create. These assets that are often intangible tend to be difficult to observe, describe, and value but have a significant impact on a firm's competitive advantage (Itami, 1987). For example, some of these assets may include an entrepreneurial cognition that recognizes and generates new opportunities, builds trusting relationships with other individuals and firms, and bootstraps together the necessary resources for a venture to successfully launch. Two characteristics of these and other related assets are that they tend to be characterized by social complexity and path dependence.

Given that entrepreneurs tend to be highly motivated individuals who use heuristics more extensively in their thinking, these differences may lead to the development of some unique social interactions as well. The social cognition literature, which focuses on mental processes involved in social interactions, can offer some direction in probing entrepreneurs. In processing information about all the complexities of life, individuals (some more than others) attempt to effectively reduce the complexities by structuring, imposing their mental models and integrating information (Johnston & Hawley, 1994; McClelland, McNaughton, & O'Reilly, 1995). In making sense of social environments, individuals typically construct and use categorical representations to simplify and streamline the person-perception process, sometimes referred to as *categorical thinking* (Macrae & Bodenhousen, 2000). Given the cognitive limitations of human actors in the midst of a complex and stimulating world, actors need ways to simplify and structure the person perception process. Once implemented, categorical thinking can have a profound effect on what one perceives and recollects of others. Furthermore, to move forward in a purposive manner, actors must possess stable internal representations of their environment (McClelland et al., 1995). "Knowing what to expect—and exactly where, when, and from whom to expect it—is information that renders the world a meaningful, orderly, and predictable place" (Macrae & Bodenhousen, 2000, p. 94).

For entrepreneurs, we suspect that their A → G → P type logic along with their distinct mental models and categorical thinking often leads them to put together information in unique ways and draw clues and conclusions from some nontraditional associations. Their more extensive categorical thinking provides them with the confidence to trigger some new leaps and potential opportunities. Information is undoubtedly an important part of the new venture process. Furthermore, information that entrepreneurs use in the discovery process and in starting new ventures is often nonlinear in nature. We suspect that involvement by entrepreneurs in distant and varied social interactions facilitates the gathering of diverse, unusual, and sometimes specific information. Their weak ties gives them exposure to chaotic bits of information that sometimes get combined in unusual ways and sometimes lead them to see new opportunities.

Assembling and Combining Resources

Starting a new venture generally requires the accumulation of a variety of resources with very limited financial resources (Brush, Greene, & Hart, 2001). Here again, we suspect that the unique ways in which entrepreneurs think and confidently develop their own mental categories helps to facilitate the accumulation of the necessary and sometimes rare resources. Rare resources that an entrepreneur uses to create heterogeneous outputs may often be construed from rarely used assets, and their availability becomes known through the entrepreneur's diverse cross section of acquaintances. Stated differently, the bootstrapping of resources in an economical fashion is so often necessary for a startup with time constraints and limited budgets.

The bootstrapping of resources, itself a potentially rare and valuable resource, can be made sense of through how entrepreneurs think, especially their categorical thinking. Because they tend to know what to expect from whom and when (Macrae & Bodenhausen, 2000), they confidently and often aggressively move forward with obtaining the critical resources. This assertion is in contrast to the perspective that entrepreneurs have bigger networks or have the right connections to garner the appropriate resources (e.g., Aldrich & Zimmer, 1986). Actually, we suspect that, on average, entrepreneurs do not have bigger networks and may even be more selective with whom they network. More importantly, it may be their confidence in what they know and from whom to expect it that makes their network activity important. Individuals with resources respond to those with confidence about the opportunities that they see; thus, entrepreneurs are more likely to have people respond to them with some of the much-needed resources for the venture.

Resource-based theory extends the product market view to include factor markets and suggests that firms wishing to obtain expected above normal returns from implementing factor market strategies must have better insights about the future value of the necessary resources compared to other firms in the same market (Barney, 1986). In the bundling of resources, entrepreneurs use their available insights to make decisions to produce a product that utilizes the available resources in a definitive manner. Consistent with strategic market theory, often strategic resources are purchased at a cheaper price because the full value of those resources has yet to be recognized. The information and its application and know-how are available to the entrepreneur through previous learning and projected insights. The knowledge that entrepreneurs have about resources and socially complex issues tends to be deeply embedded in their mental models and categorical thinking. By simplifying their world, often in dramatic ways, they development mental models about how the venture will develop and the resources that are needed to bring the venture fruition.

ACTIVE DEVELOPMENT OF CAPABILITIES

To this point we have argued that entrepreneurial capabilities are important for the identification and pursuit of new opportunities. However, such capabilities are rarely sufficient for the long-term success of the organization. At some particular point, the more extensive use of heuristics in decision-making can lead to the development of blind spots, which may create a situation of unintended escalation. These blind spots can arise if systems have not been put into place to systematically capture, analyze, understand, and act on the ensuing reality of the competitive environment. When an entrepreneur begins to pursue a new idea and to develop a resource base and a concomitant product or service, the environment is largely unknown and ill developed (Daft & Weick, 1984). That is, there may be no similar products on the market and no consumer awareness; there may be no extant competitors if the entrepreneur's product is radically new; there may be no suppliers with the ability to immediately supply the inputs to the product; and there may be no employees with the necessary skills to help develop and produce the product. The entrepreneur no doubt has a vision for what the market wants and therefore goes about enacting that vision (Sarasvathy, 2003). If the entrepreneur is successful at developing the product and offering it in the marketplace, environmental elements such as customers, suppliers, competitors, employees, and governmental forces (to name just a few) begin to interact around this entrepreneurial offering. The result is the creation of a reality, which will naturally deviate (to varying degrees) from the entrepreneur's original vision. Ultimately, new threats will develop in the environment from competitor actions as well as from changes in customers' preferences. Furthermore, suppliers and employees may seek to appropriate any rents, which may have begun to accrue to the entrepreneurial venture (Shane & Venkataraman, 2000) as a result of the earlier success. These weaknesses and threats require that the organization develop routines and processes to deal with these elements. For example, compensation and monitoring and performance systems may need to be developed to provide the necessary inducements and safeguards to avoid any potential agency problems. Furthermore, new capabilities may need to be contracted or developed to deal with government legislation and legal liability. In short, the organization must be able to adjust the resource base as needed. This adjustment may require recombining resources as well as finding new, exogenous resources. For example, the venture's products may require customer-desired changes, which might demand additional R&D knowledge not currently resident in the organization. This identification of weaknesses and threats and adjusting the resource base accordingly are the essence of dynamic capabilities. Notice that dynamic capabilities are necessary in order for the organization to incrementally evolve, whereas entrepreneurial capabilities are necessary for the organization to be created. Dynamic capabilities allow the organization to better understand and react to the given reality of the competitive situation. These dynamic capabilities motivate the establishment of routines to systematically collect, analyze, and act on environmental information.

Unfortunately, the entrepreneurial capabilities that are necessary in the early years are rarely sufficient later in the life of a new venture when dynamic capabilities take on greater importance. The skills and decision style appropriate for the early stages may also become dysfunctional in later stages (Busenitz & Barney, 1997; Komisar, 2001). The nonlinear entrepreneurial cognition so useful when the market is new or unstable may miss critical market information regarding the reality of the market. For example, once the dominant technological design has been established (Teece, 1987), and market demand has become predictable, success for the organization requires greater focusing and consolidation to service the market (Sorenson, 2000). Failure to do so may allow second movers the opening to capture critical market share (Lieberman & Montgomery, 1988, 1998). Additionally, the entrepreneur's social networks, which earlier provided key knowledge and resources for the nascent organization, may no longer provide access to the types of inputs and resources more needed in a burgeoning organization. Other types of networks associated with professional organization and greater bureaucracy become critical, and access to these networks allows the organization to acquire additional resources at a lower price. For example, venture capital backing appears to provide new ventures with access to professional management as well as access to institutional funding, which are both necessary to establish organizational legitimacy and reliability.

The point at which dynamic capabilities take on greater importance in the life of a new venture is not easily identified. It would seem that the initial public offering (IPO) provides a potentially expedient demarcation for researchers (cf. Arthurs & Busenitz, in press). Firms going through the IPO seek to raise equity capital in order to pursue additional growth and to leverage the earlier success. The post-IPO period represents an era in which the transition from entrepreneurial leadership to professional management requires the application and development of new skills to deal with SEC requirements, new government regulations, investor demands, and increasing competitor activity as the result of increasing visibility. These new skills help the organization to establish legitimacy and reliability and result in a transition away from charismatic leadership arising from the employment of entrepreneurial capabilities to more of a bureaucratic leadership arising from the employment of dynamic capabilities. In this situation, greater comprehensiveness in decision making becomes important, and a heuristics-based decision style that overgeneralizes from a limited knowledge base poses a severe threat for the venture. Unfortunately, many entrepreneurs lack the managerial skills needed in a larger, more developed organization. Furthermore, entrepreneurs may lack specific technical skills as the demands for increased specialization arise. Finally, entrepreneurs may pose an impediment to their organization in that they may continue their involvement in all parts of the business instead of transitioning to the more strategic aspects of top management.

In summary, entrepreneurial ventures and their managers must adjust their resource base as the venture grows and faces new environmental threats in the life cycle of the organization. This situation poses a unique problem in that entrepreneurial capabilities and dynamic capabilities require different types of cognition. The former tends to be characterized by enacting, whereas the latter can be characterized as reacting. That is, entrepreneurial cognition tends to result in decisions arising from the entrepreneur's vision, which includes an estimation of opportunities in the environment but focuses more on the reality in the mind of the entrepreneur. On the other hand, the cognition needed to develop dynamic capabilities produces decisions, which arise through the focus on the reality of the developing competitive environment. This cognition tends to develop and reside around the routines established in the organization. Therefore, this type of cognition is not likely to reside in any single individual within the organization. Rather, it is more likely the sum total of several inputs. Given the diverse cognition involved in each, it is no wonder that entrepreneurs tend to make poor managers. Ideally, entrepreneurs would identify the weaknesses and emerging threats and adjust the resource base accordingly. Unfortunately, this can be extremely difficult, especially when the earlier decision style (e.g., entrepreneurial cognition) is a strength in one stage of the firm but a weakness in another.

Our view here is not that entrepreneurial capabilities and dynamic capabilities are mutually exclusive. Indeed, we believe that one without the other will ultimately result in the demise of the organization. Yet we would argue that their importance tends to fluctuate, so that it may appear at times that they are mutually exclusive. Organizations that lose their entrepreneurial capabilities ultimately lose the capacity for radical innovation. Alternatively, those that lack dynamic capabilities (or never develop them) may never attain any great size and success. Importantly, our focus on cognition tends to paint the picture of entrepreneurial capabilities as being resident in people (e.g., entrepreneurs) and dynamic capabilities as being resident within the organization (through its developed routines). Our analysis would present entrepreneurial capabilities as preceding dynamic capabilities. And because dynamic capabilities are developed in light of the former entrepreneurial capabilities, they tend to create path rigidities, which impede new entrepreneurial capabilities. Thus, although they are not mutually exclusive, the two types of capabilities tend to resist one another.

DISCUSSION AND CONCLUSION

Entrepreneurship research has placed considerable focus on the individual entrepreneur over the decades, with some debate over the usefulness of examining interindividual differences of entrepreneurs (Gartner, 1988; Sarasvathy, 2004). Sarasvathy (2004) noted that some individuals are highly likely to start their own business no matter what, whereas other are highly unlikely to start their own business no matter what, but the large majority are in the middle group, whose entrepreneurial behavior is contingent on numerous other factors. The implications of the arguments developed in this chapter move the focus in another direction. The focus has been on the individual-level resources that are typically necessary to start and grow an entrepreneurial firm. It has been argued that the resources that are necessary to get a venture up and running are quite different from those that are needed for a firm once it reaches the more mature phases and develops into a larger business enterprise. The question then becomes, "Does a given individual have the capabilities that will allow him or her to excel in the startup phases of starting a new venture?"

To help address this question, we have sought to further develop the entrepreneurial cognition concept. If a person can recognize and develop previously unrecognized opportunities and is able to launch a business pulling together enough scarce resources, then the person has done something that the majority of people have not done. If someone starts multiple new ventures, that person becomes a habitual entrepreneur (Rosa, 1998). The ability to make fast decisions with limited information and in a context of much uncertainty tends to be extremely beneficial for starting ventures that are pursuing new opportunities. The presence of a heuristic-based logic and categorical thinking allows entrepreneurs to readily navigate through all the twists and turns of starting a new business and to do so with confidence. This confidence is a helpful communication tool that can enable entrepreneurs to bring together the necessary resources and human capital to build the venture. In sum, we have argued that these cognitive abilities have the potential to give some individuals a competitive advantage in starting new ventures. We have taken what we hope will be a more fruitful line of inquiry that seeks to identify the skills and capabilities that are most germane to the starting of a new venture. If these cognitive abilities offer some individuals but not others a competitive advantage in starting a new venture, then they merit further inquiry.

Furthermore, our arguments recognize that entrepreneurial ventures change and go through various stages and that once a venture gets through some of the initial stages, changes will need to occur. Skills and capabilities very relevant during the early stages may not be so relevant in the later stages. If the venture is to grow and expand over time, dynamic capabilities will usually be needed as an integrative part of the venture. The firm's resource base will need to be reconfigured and adjusted to accommodate needed changes and to ameliorate resource-base weaknesses created as the result of misperceptions concerning the market. In this sense, entrepreneurial capabilities and dynamic capabilities are complementary. A new venture pursues a new opportunity with the resources and capabilities of the founding team and whatever other resources that are deemed necessary and can be garnered. Entrepreneurs typically have a firm track on where the venture is going. At some point, the venture is likely to encounter a different reality from what was perceived, at which point dynamic capabilities are very much required to help the firm launch into subsequent phases.

One of the benefits of looking at both entrepreneurial and dynamic capabilities in the context of entrepreneurial ventures is that we are able to better articulate the nature of dynamic capabilities. The dynamic capabilities literature has sometimes struggled because of ambiguities in our understanding of its meaning (Helfat & Peteraf, 2003; Winter, 2003). Although making firm-level adjustments to fit with the environment has been an anchor of the dynamic capabilities literature, what parts of those adjustments are specific to dynamic capabilities and which ones are a regular part of organizational life has been less clear. The model developed here is able to draw a firmer distinction between the entrepreneurial and dynamic capabilities.

REFERENCES

Aldrich, H. E., & Zimmer, C. (1986). Entrepreneurship through social networks. In D. L. Sexton and R. W. Smilor (Eds.), *The art and science of entrepreneurship* (pp. 3–23). Cambridge, MA: Ballinger.

Alvarez, S. A., & Busenitz, L. W. (2001). The entrepreneurship of resource-based theory. *Journal of Management, 27*, 755–775.

Argyris, C., & Schon, D. (1978). *Organizational learning: A theory of action perspective.* Reading, MA: Addison-Wesley.

Arthurs, J. D., & Busenitz, L. W. (in press). Dynamic capabilities and venture performance: The effects of venture capitalists. *Journal of Business Venturing.*

Barney, J. B. (1986). Strategic factor markets: Expectations, luck and business strategy. *Management Science, 42*, 1231–1241.

Barney, J. B. (1991). Firm resources and sustained competitive advantage. *Journal of Management, 17*, 99–120.

Barney, J. B. (1995). Looking inside for competitive advantage. *Academy of Management Executive, 9*, 49–61.

Baron, R. (1998). Cognitive mechanisms in entrepreneurship: Why and when entrepreneurs think differently than other people. *Journal of Business Venturing, 13*, 275–294.

Baron, R. (2004). Potential benefits of the cognitive perspective: Expanding entrepreneurship's array of conceptual tools. *Journal of Business Venturing, 19*, 169–172.

Bazerman, M. H. (1990). *Judgment in managerial decision making* (2nd ed.). New York: John Wiley and Sons.

Brush, C. G., Greene, P. G., & Hart, M. M. (2001). Creating wealth in organizations: The role of strategic leadership. *Academy of Management Executive, 15*(1), 64–78.

Busenitz, L. W. (1999). Entrepreneurial risk and strategic decision making: It's a matter of perspective. *Journal of Applied Behavioral Science, 35*(3), 325–340.

Busenitz, L., & Barney, J. (1997). Differences between entrepreneurs and managers in large organizations: Biases and heuristics in strategic decision-making. *Journal of Business Venturing, 12*, 9–30.

Daft, R., & Weick, K. (1984). Toward a model of organizations as interpretation systems. *Academy of Management Review, 9*(2), 284–295.

Dierickx, I., & Cool, K. (1989). Asset stock accumulation and sustainability of competitive advantage. *Management Science, 35*, 1504–1511.

Eisenhardt, K. M., & Martin, J. (2000). Dynamic capabilities: What are they? *Strategic Management Journal, 21*, 1105–1121.

Fiet, J. O. (2002). *The systematic search for entrepreneurial discoveries.* Westport, CT: Quorum.

Fiol, C. M., & Lyles, M. A. (1985). Organizational learning. *Academy of Management Review, 10*, 803–813.

Forbes, D. (1999). Cognitive approaches to new venture creation. *International Journal of Management Review, 1*, 415–439.

Gaglio, C. M., & Katz, J. A. (2001) The psychological basis of opportunity identification: Entrepreneurial alertness. *Small Business Economics, 16*, 95–111.

Gartner, W. B. (1988). Who is an entrepreneur? is the wrong question. *American Journal of Small Business, 12*(4), 11–32.

Gavetti, G., & Levinthal, D. (2000). Looking forward and looking backward: Cognitive and experimental search. *Administrative Science Quarterly, 45*, 113–137.

Helfat, C. E., & Peteraf, M. A. (2003). The dynamic resource-based view: Capability lifecycles. *Strategic Management Journal, 24,* 997–1010.

Hill, C. W. L., & Rothaermel, F. T. (2003). The performance of incumbent firms in the face of radical technological innovation. *Academy of Management Journal, 28,* 257–274.

Hogarth, R. M. (1987). *Judgment and choice: The psychology of decisions.* New York: John Wiley and Sons.

Itami, H. (1987). *Mobilizing invisible assets.* Cambridge, MA: Harvard University Press.

Johnston, W. A., & Hawley, K. J. (1994). Perceptions inhibition of expected inputs: The key that opens closed minds. *Psychometric Bulletin Review, 1,* 56–72.

Katz, J. A. (1992). A psychosocial cognitive model of employment status choice. *Entrepreneurship Theory and Practice, 17*(1), 29–37.

Kirzner, I. (1979). *Perception, opportunity, and profit.* Chicago: University of Chicago Press.

Kirzner, I. (1997). Entrepreneurial discovery and the competitive market process: An Austrian approach. *Journal of Economic Literature, 35,* 60–85.

Komisar, R. (2001). *The monk and the riddle.* Boston: Harvard Business School Press.

Krabuanrat, K., & Phelps, R. (1998). Heuristic and rationality in strategic decision making: An exploratory study. *Journal of Business Research, 41,* 83–93.

Lei, D., Hitt, M. A., & Bettis, R. (1996). Dynamic core competences through meta-learning and strategic context. *Journal of Management, 22*(4), 549–569.

Leonard-Barton, D. (1992). Core capabilities and core rigidities: A paradox in managing new product development. *Strategic Management Journal, 13,* 111–125.

Lieberman, M. B., & Montgomery, D. B. (1988). First-mover advantages. *Strategic Management Journal, 9,* 41–58.

Lieberman, M. B., & Montgomery, D. B. (1998). First-mover (dis)advantages: Retrospective and link with the resource-based view. *Strategic Management Journal, 19,* 1111–1125.

Macrae, C. N., & Bodenhausen, G. V. (2000). Social cognition: Thinking categorically about others. *Annual Review of Psychology, 51,* 93–120.

McClelland, J. L., McNaughton, B. L., & O'Reilly, R. C. (1995). Why there are complementary learning systems in the hippocampus and neocortex: Insights from the success and failure of connectionist models of learning and memory. *Psychology Review, 102,* 419–457.

Nelson, R. R., & Winter, S. G. (1982). *An evolutionary theory of economic change.* Cambridge, MA: Harvard University Press.

Ray, D. M. (1994). The role of risk-taking in Singapore. *Journal of Business Venturing, 9*(2), 157–177.

Rosa, P. (1998). Entrepreneurial processes of business cluster formation and growth by "habitual" entrepreneurs. *Entrepreneurship Theory and Practice, 22*(4), 43–62.

Sarasvathy, S. D. (2003). Entrepreneurship as a science of the artificial. *Journal of Economic Psychology, 24,* 203–230.

Sarasvathy, S. D. (2004). The questions we ask and the questions we care about: Reformulating some problems with entrepreneurship research. *Journal of Business Venturing, 19,* 707–717.

Shane, S., & Venkataraman, S. (2000). The promise of entrepreneurship as a field of research. *Academy of Management Review, 25*(1), 217–226.

Simon, M., Houghton, S. M., & Aquino, K. (2000). Cognitive biases, risk perception, and venture formation: How individuals decide to start companies. *Journal of Business Venturing, 14*(5), 113–134.

Skuse, D. H., James, R. S., Bishop, D. V., Coppin, D., Dalton, P., Aamodt-Leeper, G., Bacarese-Hamilton, M., Creswel, D., McGurk, R., & Jacobs, P. A. (1997). Evidence from a Turner's syndrome of an imprinted X-linked locus affecting cognitive function. *Nature, 387*(6634), 705–708.

Sorenson, O. (2000). Letting the market work for you: An evolutionary perspective on product strategy. *Strategic Management Journal, 21,* 577–592.

Teece, D. J. (1987). Profiting from technological innovation: implications for integration, collaboration, and public policy. In D. J. Teece (Ed.), *The competitive challenge* (pp. 185–219). Cambridge, MA: Ballinger.

Teece, D. J., Pisano, G., & Shuen, A. (1997). Dynamic capabilities and strategic management. *Strategic Management Journal, 18*(7), 509–533.

Tversky, A., & Kahneman, D. (1974). Judgment under uncertainty: Heuristics and biases. *Science, 185*, 1124–1131.

Winter, S. G. (2003). Understand dynamic capabilities. *Strategic Management Journal, 24,* 991–995.

8

The Psychological Actions and Entrepreneurial Success: An Action Theory Approach[1]

Michael Frese

This chapter starts with a strong assumption: Entrepreneurs' actions are important and should be a starting point for theorizing in entrepreneurship (cf. also McMullen & Shepherd, 2006). I am well aware that not all entrepreneurship theorists share this assumption. Most importantly, ecological theories have left out actions from their theories (Aldrich, 1999). This is surprising for an evolutionary approach because entrepreneurial actions are as important to entrepreneurial outcomes as sexual behavior is to procreation and, therefore, survival of genes and population of genes (Dawkins, 1976). Whether or not an organization occupies a successful niche or whether or not it introduced an innovation is the result of actions and not a purely accidental process. Starting one's business in a market niche and defending the niche is an active process and not passive adaptation. Such an active approach is slowly accepted in entrepreneurship research, as scholars take more seriously that there can be effective and non-effective actions vis-à-vis the market (McMullen & Shepherd, 2006; Sarasvathy, 2001). Most actions are geared towards the environment and take into account environmental conditions. However, the most important feature of entrepreneurial action is not that it is well adjusted to environmental conditions (this is true of behavior that reacts to environmental stimuli and is guided by the stimuli) but that it changes the environment.

[1]I received very valuable comments and insights from Robert Baron, Robert Baum, and Sabine Sonnentag.

In contrast to most other animals, humans are particularly active, as they intervene in the course of nature (e.g., by building scientific models, houses, cities, dams, etc., that change our environment dramatically) and even in the course of their own natural evolution (e.g., producing spectacles and thereby compensating for the biological weakness of shortsightedness; Dolgin, 1985; Schurig, 1985).

Thus, I assume that actions by the entrepreneur make a difference for whether or not an organization sees the light of day and/or whether an entrepreneurial unit becomes successful. Our arguments are in line with the so-called Austrian school of economics (cf. Kirzner, 2001; Von Mises, 1963), as well as Schumpeter's theory of entrepreneurship (Schumpeter, 1935). For Schumpeter, the very hallmark of entrepreneurship was the active approach of the entrepreneur.

The purpose of this chapter is to present a psychological theory of action regulation (which has been developed independently from entrepreneurship research) and to apply it to entrepreneurship. We think that such a theory of action is of particular importance for entrepreneurship research because the nature of entrepreneurship is to proactively produce effective solutions to problems and opportunities (Sarasvathy, 2001; Shane & Venkataraman, 2000). Our theory is based on the so-called action theory or action regulation theory (Frese & Sabini, 1985; Frese & Zapf, 1994; Hacker, 1998; G. A. Miller, Galanter, & Pribram, 1960). Briefly, action theory is a meta-theory that attempts to understand how people regulate their actions to achieve goals actively and how this is done both in routine situations as well as in novel situations. Because it is a molar theory (similar to Lewin's theory), it is a theory that can be applied quite well. As the theory of action regulation is a meta-theory (such as behaviorism or psychoanalysis), much of its "charm" is based on its integrative function. However, we also use action theory as a specific theory that explains certain phenomena, such as psychological action strategies or failures and errors by entrepreneurs. Moreover, it is a theory that is easily applicable and that makes it possible to deduce interventions. Action regulation theory as described here is an individualistic theory. Obviously this theory applies more to the first stages of the development of a firm in which entrepreneurs as individuals largely influence what is happening in their firms. At a later point in the life cycle of a firm, an individual perspective is much less useful, as the entrepreneurial actions are largely leadership actions aimed at improving and aligning the actions of the firms' employees (Van Gelderen, Frese, & Thurik, 2000). In principle, these actions can also be described with the theory, but this is not in the foreground of this chapter (e.g., Tschan, 2002).

In the course of this article, we first describe the building blocks of this theory in a rather abstract way; we then show its integrative function and its function of hypothesis development and research approaches in a few areas of entrepreneurship.

ACTION THEORY—BUILDING BLOCKS

Action is goal-oriented behavior (Frese & Sabini, 1985). Three aspects stand in the foreground to understand how humans regulate their actions: sequence, structure, and focus. Sequence refers to how actions unfold, structure involves levels of regulation, and the focus of an action can be the task, the social context in which the task is done, and the self. Every action can be decomposed into these three components of actions, and therefore a full understanding of entrepreneurs' action has to take all those aspects into consideration.

Sequence

The following steps of the action sequence can be minimally differentiated (cf. Fig. 8.1): goal setting, mapping of the environment, planning, monitoring of the execution, and feedback processing (Frese & Zapf, 1994; cf. also Dörner & Schaub, 1994; Norman, 1986). For the entrepreneurial process this means that a would-be entrepreneur has the goal to found a firm (or *not* to work as an employee), maps out the area in which the firm is supposed to operate (opportunity detection may be one facet), plans how to achieve this goal, monitors the process of executing these ideas, and processes feedback from (potential) customers, banks, business angels, the public, and so on.

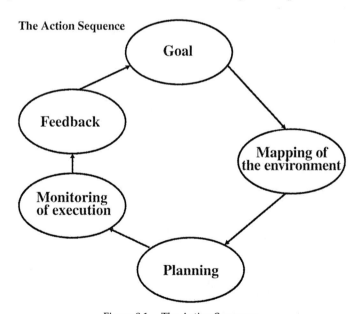

Figure 8.1. The Action Sequence.

Goals

Action is goal-oriented behavior; therefore, goals are of primary importance for actions (Locke & Latham, 1990). Goals are anticipated future action results and they are used as set points (Hacker, 1985). Goals pull the action; therefore, higher goals usually have a higher pull and therefore lead to higher performance (Locke & Latham, 1990). Anticipated results can be visualized and thereby produce motivation (e.g., to sell the first product). A better visualization of a goal probably has a higher pull function and probably leads to higher commitment. One way to develop a clear idea and visualization of a goal is to specify the goal in detail; this has been emphasized in goal setting theory (Locke & Latham, 1990).

Empirical work has differentiated three principal ways in which people think about their goals (Oettingen, Hoenig, & Gollwitzer, 2000). One way is to fantasize about how good it would be to having achieved the goal; another is to worry about not achieving the goal, and a third one is to contrast the goal with the current condition. Although fantasizing about goal achievement and worrying reduce the chances to achieve the goal, contrasting the positive goal fantasies with the current condition is most effective for high achievement (Oettingen et al., 2000). It follows that (would-be) entrepreneurs who mainly fantasize or mainly worry about their goal achievement are less likely to either start a firm or be successful.

A goal can only function as a motivator for performance, if it has regulatory power over the action (Semmer & Frese, 1985). With Heckhausen and Kuhl (1985), we call ineffective goals *wishes*. A wish is something that a person would like to achieve, but he or she is not (yet) doing anything about it. Sometimes, wanting to start a company may not get translated into action (as a matter of fact, there are many "nascent entrepreneurs" who never really start a company; Reynolds, 2000), and frequently owners are happy to talk about "goals" that really do not regulate their behavior. However, goals can be *developed* from wishes. Heckhausen and Kuhl (1985) argued that the factors represented by the acronym OTIUM (opportunity for action, time to do something about it, importance of the goal, urgency of achieving the goal, and means to be able to achieve the goal) are important parameters that produce the translation of a wish into a goal.

Goals can be associated with a higher or lower commitment (Hollenbeck & Klein, 1987). Higher goal commitment leads to higher goal strivings (Locke & Latham, 1990). If goal commitment is high, owners are more likely satisfied with their situation (Maier & Brunstein, 2001).

People usually pursue several goals at once. Some of these goals may be hierarchically related (e.g., starting a firm and getting money to get the patent rights for an invention), some other ones are not related (e.g., planning a leisure time event for a day off and working on a business plan), and some may be conflicting and need to be compromised or in some way negotiated (e.g., helping a specific employee and making sure that there is equitable treatment for all employees). Goals are organized into hierarchies (more on the concept of hierarchy later). This does not mean, however, that we always pay attention to the full hierarchy. As a matter of fact, higher level goals, such as life goals and moral standards, are typically not in the foreground of our attention. Because our working memory has a limited capacity (Kahneman, 1973), we can only attend to those goals that are of immediate action relevance. Long-range life goals are typically of less action relevance than those directly related to daily life. Humans are action-oriented animals. Therefore, intermediate goals are in the foreground of our attention. This is one of the reasons why time management techniques teach people to attend to the important long-range rather than just the urgent short-range goals (Macan, 1996). This leads to the interesting hypothesis that long-range goals often have less regulatory power than short- or medium-range goals even if they are deemed to be more important. Moreover, contradictions between medium-range goals and long-range goals are not always detected.

Recently, social psychology has argued that there are two types of goals: goals to achieve something (promotion focused) and goals to prevent something (prevention focused) (Higgins, 1997). There are a number of ramifications of this differentiation. Prevention-focused goals are more anxiety related; the strategy that is pursued is more of avoiding things than to achieve certain things. Combining this with risk taking as described by prospect theory (Kahneman, Slovic, & Tversky, 1982) leads to the interesting hypothesis that anxious owners may take more risks. In contrast, promotion-focused owners who are more strongly oriented toward achieving positive goals (e.g., combining a hobby with starting a firm) are less anxious and take less risks (cf. Baron, 2004).

Mapping of the Environment

Owners have to know the environment or acquire knowledge of the environment in which they (plan to) operate. There is a large literature on mental models in cognitive psychology that has looked at how people understand their environment (Gentner & Stevens, 1983). The following issues are of importance: (a) realism of mental model, (b) broad signal inventory, including opportunity recognition and the function of quick detection of complex signals (chunking), (c) developing a map of the environment that has operative value, and (d) the right level of decomposition to understand an environment.

There is an interesting debate as to the functionality of realism: Some argue that people are more motivated and persistent if they are more optimistic than objectively called for (Taylor, 1989). On the other hand, people may be overoptimistic, which may lead to wrong decisions and negative effects (Vancouver, Thompson, & Williams, 2001). Even venture capitalists are overconfident in the likelihood of success of business ventures that they give money to (Zacharakis & Shepherd, 2001). This may be particularly important in dynamic environments, which punish wishful thinking (Fenton-O'Creevy, Nicholson, Soane, & Willman, 2005). However, a recent publication suggests that optimism may vary at different points of time in the action sequence. Illusions of optimism were lower in a preactional state, before one has developed an action plan or has started acting, whereas illusionary optimism was higher once a person actually started to act to achieve a certain goal (Taylor & Gollwitzer, 1995), protecting the action from perturbing thoughts. In addition, there is evidence that interpretations of the environment are often self-serving (Crocker & Park, 2004) and related to cognitive biases (Shaver & Scott, 1991).

Experts usually have a broader inventory of signals that tell them which kinds of actions are called for in which situations. Signals are developed through a process of prototyping, which is often tacit and without conscious awareness. With experience, we tend to develop an average concept of similar situations—a so-called prototype (Glass & Holyoak, 1986). Also, with experience, we tend to grasp complex patterns more quickly—expertise research suggests that this so-called chunking helps to understand complex signals faster, which also tends to facilitate high performance (Chase & Simon, 1973; G. A. Miller, 1956). Because experts are faster in detecting complex signals (chunking) and have a larger inventory of signals, we can hypothesize that experts actually take less time analyzing environmental factors but that they still develop more adequate ideas about this environment. Therefore, it follows that expert entrepreneurs would understand complex situations more rapidly and more adequately than nonexpert entrepreneurs. However, it is not easy to know what an expert entrepreneur is. Some have suggested that repeat entrepreneurs (who have started several firms) are experts; however, simple repetition does not seem to produce expert status—rather, the breadth and depth of experience are important for expertise (Sonnentag, 1998). This implies that those entrepreneurs who have a high breadth of experience in various areas of relevance for entrepreneurship should have more economic success than novice entrepreneurs.

The mapping of the environment has to have operative value. Not every mental model is action oriented (Gentner & Stevens, 1983). Abstract and general mental models may be unrelated to one's actions. Action theory assumes that only action-oriented knowledge is useful for entrepreneurs. Mapping is as often the result of action (experimentation) and the feedback the actor receives as a result of that action. Thus, we do not really get to know an environment without acting on the environment. Moreover, action orientation implies that mapping ought to be parsimonious, that people sometimes jump to action prematurely, and that the model is sketchy. As a matter of fact, experts regard problem analysis as highly important and they emphasize the importance. However, they do not necessarily spend much time getting oriented, because they can quickly get the most relevant information and are able to differentiate important from non-important and are, therefore, more quickly ready for action (Sonnentag, 1998; Sonnentag & Kleine, 2000). As environments are often dynamic and their factors are interrelated, better mental models are able to adequately predict future states of the environment from a limited set of predictors (Dörner, 1996). Action orientation is also an individual difference variable that is related to performance in various fields (Diefendorff, 2004).

Entrepreneurs need to map an environment on the right level of decomposition (Dörner, 1996). For example, entrepreneurs sometimes experience the environment as one that emphasizes only good inventions but do not perceive the importance of marketing. Marketing typically operates on a different level of decomposition than inventions (the level of perceived needs by market participants rather than the newness of the invention). One of the functions of good entrepreneurship is that different levels of decomposition are taken into account and it may be one of the most important competencies of entrepreneurs to be able to think on these different levels of decomposition—a competency that has not been studied (cf. chap. 4 by Markman, this volume).

Plans

For G. A. Miller et al. (1960), plans are the bridges between thoughts and actions as they transfer a goal into executable sequences of operations. Plans order the sequence of operations that need to be performed (G. A. Miller et al., 1960). Plans (or action programs) are not to be confused with their everyday meaning; the latter often implies plans that include relatively elaborate blueprints. Entrepreneurship research often uses planning in the sense of formalized plans of business plans or strategic plans. We go beyond formal planning (e.g., Schwenk & Shrader, 1993) in our approach. We think of plans in the psychological sense that one has some kind of order of operations for the next few seconds, minutes, months, or years. Some plans are relatively elaborate, some others just consists of a general idea of how to proceed, and finally some plans are automatized schemata or frames (e.g., for talking to a customer; cf. G. A. Miller et al., 1960). The detailedness of plans may differ. Some plans stipulate many aspects of operations before one starts the action (detailed planning); other plans develop the details during the execution phase (nondetailed planning) (Frese, Stewart, & Hannover, 1987). Detailed planning also includes backup plans in case something goes wrong. This form of planning may be particularly useful in uncertain environments (Honig, 2004). Some plans are related to events in the long-term future, whereas other plans deal only with imminent actions (long-term vs. short term-orientation) (Frese et al., 1987).

Action theory suggests that planning should help owners to be successful. Planning increases the likelihood that people get started by translating their goals into actions and mobilizes extra effort. As Gollwitzer (1996) showed, a plan leads to an implementation intention and to a higher degree of checking the environment for opportunities to be able to achieve a goal. It follows from this theory that planning may be one of the more important factors to recognize entrepreneurial opportunities and to take advantage of them (without a plan, we would not automatically recognize relevant signals for actions in our environment—but remember, this is not a formal plan). Planning helps a person to stay on track and ensures that the goal is not lost or forgotten (Gollwitzer, 1996). Planning also amplifies persistence or decreases distraction (Diefendorff & Lord, 2004). Moreover, planning produces better knowledge of contingency conditions and time allocation to tasks, and leads to a clearer focus on priorities (Tripoli, 1998). It follows that entrepreneurs who plan less, will get distracted more from their goals and they will have a lower focus on important issues. Planning usually involves thinking of things that might go wrong. Planning motivates the owners to deal with additional problems, and prepares them to have a ready-made answer if something goes wrong; therefore, actions run more smoothly (Berg, Strough, Calderone, Meegan, & Sansone, 1997). Planning allows the person to cope with the inherent insecurities of being a business owner by making good use of scarce resources (Rauch & Frese, 1998). Finally, there is also the problem of premature actions, which are made less likely if the owner plans well, because planning makes premature triggering of an action less likely (Kuhl & Kazen, 1999). One of the most important success factors of planning may be that planning leads to better feedback systems and that people who plan better gain flexibility because they detect changing circumstances and adjust their actions appropriately (contingency planning) (cf. also Scott & Delmar, 2004).

It follows from action theory that more successful entrepreneurs have more ready-made plans available. That may lead to the paradoxical result that effective entrepreneurs actually plan less at any given moment, because they already have plans available that have been stored in memory some time ago. Because action plans can be conscious or unconscious, owners may actually tell an observer that they do not consciously plan at all and that they just follow intuition, when they actually follow previously routinized plans of action (more on this later).

Planning is not free of costs. The more conscious planning is and the more formalized it is (writing it down, using certain planning techniques, etc.) and the more one thinks about long-term future events, the higher are the costs in terms of time (and sometimes money). Another important cost is that owners tend to stick to plans, which implies a certain amount of rigidity. It follows that there are certain situations where planning may be dysfunctional, for example, chaotic situations in which every prediction turns out to be wrong (however, note that slightly chaotic situations actually require more planning, because one needs to take potential problems into account—contingency planning and a plan B). Another prediction from action theory is that people can learn to put flexibility into the plan (more contingency planning, more flexibility to replan when ones plans did not work out); we assume that training for flexibility (importance of being flexible), and the development of expertise as a result of having acted in heterogeneous situations with very different types of plans (Sonnentag, 1998) may be important factors that contribute to flexibility.

Monitoring of the Execution

Actually, the concept of *plan* already implies execution—it is the bridge between cognition and action (G. A. Miller et al., 1960). Nevertheless, we sometimes store plans in a sort of pipeline waiting to be called upon. In these cases, one can distinguish a phase called *executing*. Monitoring of execution draws heavily on the working memory processes; therefore, omission errors appear here (Reason, 1997). Important parameters in this execution phase are speed, flexibility, whether or not plans are coordinated with others, and whether one uses a time-sharing overlapping plan execution mode or not. Because working memory is so important in the monitoring phase, the question is how to overcome its limitations. The most important strategy is to chunk several issues into one bit of information (G. A. Miller, 1956).

Feedback

Without feedback one would not know where one stands with regard to a goal (Erez, 1977; Locke & Latham, 1990; G. A. Miller et al., 1960). On the other hand, feedback may trigger self-related thoughts and thereby divert attention from the task, actually producing negative performance effects (Kluger & DeNisi, 1996). Important parameters with regard to feedback are process vs. outcome feedback, the degree of realism versus self-serving interpretations (Dörner & Schaub, 1994), feedback search rate, and how active this search for feedback is (Ashford, 1989). It is one of the assumptions in economics that small firms are faster to process and to react to feedback than larger firms (Chen & Hambrick, 1995) because information processing is faster in small organizations due to lack of complicated hierarchical procedures. However, one of the prerequisites of this hypothesis is that the small firm owner actually recognizes the significance of the feedback signal (mental model) and that he or she finds the right response to this feedback. We also assume that feedback increases the rate of learning of firm owners, at least if the feedback comes from the task itself and if it does not involve too many self-related thoughts (Kluger & DeNisi, 1996).

It is commonplace to talk about entrepreneurs' need to deal with situations of high complexity and little predictability. This implies that feedback needs to be actively constructed and is not "out there." Complex feedback needs to be interpreted. Take the example of a chef who owns a restaurant and who notices that the income of the restaurant is slowly decreasing. It is a matter of interpretation whether he is alarmed by this feedback or whether he interprets this to be "just one of those months." When he is alarmed he has to seek feedback actively (Ashford & Tsui, 1991)—for example, by asking for customer feedback, by analyzing leftovers on the plate for changes in taste, by analyzing the amount of expensive or inexpensive wine bottles ordered for changes in income available for restaurants, by analyzing the composition of his customers in terms of age, dress, and so on. Only this process of active feedback seeking and construction will lead to adequate strategies to deal with the problems of this restaurant owner.

Unpredictability of feedback (and events) can be differentiated into unpredictability of when or under what circumstances an event will occurs, what kind of event will occur, or whether a certain event will occur at all (S. Miller, 1981). Entrepreneurs may not be able to predict any of these events and feedbacks and, therefore, have to be prepared.

Action theory maintains that the most useful feedback is probably negative feedback, because it accentuates the fact that the actor has not yet achieved the goal (Frese & Zapf, 1994). Positive feedback—the goals have been achieved—may have motivational function to do a certain action again, but little learning occurs. In contrast, under negative feedback conditions, a high amount of learning occurs under certain circumstances (we talk about that later in this chapter).

The Interplay of the Steps in the Action Sequence

The action steps are not as regular as the description just given and Fig. 8.1 may suggest. Actions are inherently messy and do not always follow a neat sequence. People sometimes rethink their goals after they develop some action plans; they invariably go back and forth between starting an action and rethinking plans and doing some more search in the environment. Thus, we do not want to suggest that the sequence is invariable; however, we believe that every one of the steps is necessary for effective actions, and if one of the steps is missing, actions will become incomplete and inefficient (or outright impossible). A case in point is that actions without feedback lead to disarray (G. A. Miller et al., 1960). Similarly, there must be goal setting and some kind of planning in actions. Although planning and subgoaling are sometimes equated, there is a function of planning that does not exist in producing subgoals: Planning implies that entrepreneurs do a mental simulation of their actions ("*Probehandlung*").

One set of evidence for the differential importance of goal setting and planning comes from the Rubicon theory (Gollwitzer, Heckhausen, & Ratajczak, 1990; Heckhausen, 1987). Different processes exist before one crosses the Rubicon and afterward. It is planning that makes people cross the Rubicon (the Rubicon concept was named after the famous quote from Caesar that "the dice have fallen" after he had traversed the river Rubicon—he implied that one cannot go back on one's decision after one has started to act). Before crossing the Rubicon, the intention is developed within a rational decision-making model of goal choice. Once people plan (i.e., think about when and how to put an intention into action), the intention is transformed into an implementation intention. Once an implementation intention is formed, the Rubicon is traversed and the person is then in the phase of willing. Here automatic processes may take over to push the person into action (Gollwitzer, 1993).

One important implication of this theory is that rational processes of understanding a situation and setting one's goals are dominant before the Rubicon; thus, we can understand owners in this phase with rational choice models quite well (e.g., valence–expectancy–instrumentality models; Vroom, 1964). Once an owner has crossed the Rubicon, psychological processes change. Then the owner is less likely to ask whether or not a certain goal is useful—scrutinizing and analyzing the goal is unlikely to happen in this phase. People in this phase are implementation oriented and just want to achieve the goal. Therefore, in this phase, owners often become unrealistic (Gollwitzer, 1993). New information is only registered if it helps to achieve the goal; in contrast, new information is not taken up and used well if it could call into question whether or not the goal was useful in the first place. The phenomenon of escalation of commitment—throwing good money after bad money (Staw & Ross, 1987)—and the development of rigid strategies under threat (threat-rigidity phenomenon; Staw, Sandelands, & Dutton, 1981) can be explained by this theory. Instead of a cool analysis of the pros and cons, information processing in the willing phase is only used to support actions to overcome barriers and problems. In this phase, difficulties and barriers of goal achievement increase the motivation (in contrast to the phase before the Rubicon, where high difficulties may lead to giving up the goal): The more difficulties turn up after the Rubicon, the more owners develop the will to overcome them.

Action regulation theory may be combined with the approach by McMullen and Shepherd (2006), which puts actions into the center of the theory. McMullen and Shepherd (2006) argue that entrepreneurial actions are always done under uncertainty (perceived uncertainty and willingness to bear uncertainty). From an action regulation theory perspective, we would argue that there are uncertainties for every step of the action sequences and that in each case, uncertainty means something different—uncertainty with regard to an action goal implies that there is uncertainty between a goal and further long-term goals of the entrepreneur. Uncertainty with regard to mapping the environment may be related to the complexity of the situation; uncertainty with regard to the plans related to how uncertain it is that the plan will work out; and uncertainty with regard to feedback may be uncertainty on whether one gets the feedback, when one gets it, or which kind of feedback one is likely to get.

ACTION STRUCTURE

The action structure is concerned with the hierarchical cognitive regulation of behavior. The structure constitutes a sort of "grammar" for action. The notion of hierarchy is needed to understand well-organized behaviors that achieve higher level goals (e.g., launching a new product) by using lower level behaviors (e.g., uttering a sentence, typing a word, or using the appropriate muscles to strike a key) (cf. Carver & Scheier, 1982; G. A. Miller et al., 1960). The higher levels of the hierarchy of action regulation are conscious, thought oriented, and more general; the lower levels consist of routines; they are specific; and they frequently involve muscle movements. This hierarchy is not neatly organized but has potential reversals. Such a reversal is most pronounced in the example of a capture error (Norman, 1981); a routine takes over and leads to action errors (as in the example that someone wants to buy bread on the way home but the routine of going home takes over and he or she finds him- or herself at home without bread). Therefore, we call this hierarchy a *weak hierarchy* (with Turvey, 1977).

The Four Levels of Regulation

We differentiate three task-oriented levels of regulation and one metacognitive level.

The Skill Level of Regulation.   The lowest level of regulation (called skill level, by Rasmussen, 1982; sensorimotor level of regulation, by Hacker,

1998; psychomotor, by Ackerman, 1988; automatized, by Shiffrin & Schneider, 1977; or procedural knowledge, by Anderson, 1983) regulates situationally specific automatized or routinized skills. Information on this level is parallel, rapid, effortless, and without apparent limitations. However, it is difficult to substantially modify action programs. In order to change them, they have to be lifted to a higher level of regulation, so that some conscious form of (effortful) processing can be applied. The skill level of regulation is the preferred level of regulation (March & Simon, 1958), particularly when there is high load (Kahneman, 2003).

Level of Flexible Action Patterns. Well-trained schematic action patterns (Norman, 1981) dominate here. These ready-made action programs are available in memory but must be flexibly adjusted to situationally defined parameters. Perceptual processes of action signals are important here (Ackerman, 1988; Hacker, 1998). The two—skill level and level of flexible action patterns—are often subsumed under the term of mindlessness (Fiol & O'Connor, 2003).

Conscious Level. This level is concerned with conscious regulation of goal oriented behavior (variously called "knowledge based," by Rasmussen, 1982; "declarative knowledge," by Anderson, 1983; "controlled," by Shiffrin & Schneider, 1977; "cognitive," by Ackerman, 1992; "intellectual level," by Hacker, 1998, and Frese & Zapf, 1994; or "system 2 reasoning," by Kahneman, 2003). Although the term *consciousness* has had a checkered history in psychology, it seems to be a good umbrella term to mean that people are aware of how they go about a certain action (or are aware of the important parameters of the action). Consciousness or awareness does not necessarily imply that a thought is verbalizable but can also mean that a person can image it—in the sense of a vivid thought that is simulating a certain action (e.g., mental simulation; Shephard & Metzler, 1971). Conscious processing implies effort (Kahneman, 1973); it is slow, it is constrained by limited resources of the central (conscious working memory) processor (Baddeley, 1986), and it works in a serial mode. These are the task-oriented levels of regulation.

Level of Metacognitive Heuristics. We do not have only conscious strategies to deal with the world; we also have some knowledge on how we ourselves use these strategies (knowledge about our cognitive regulation; cf. Brown, 1987). Moreover, people self-reflect about how they go about their actions (Brown, 1987). The issue of metacognition has been studied in training (Ford, Smith, Weissbein, Gully, & Salas, 1998; Keith & Frese, 2005). People often know how much they will be able to learn (Metcalfe, 1993), what they do not know (Kruger & Dunning, 1999), and what kind of strategies they use (Gleitman, 1985; Weinert & Kluwe, 1987). Metacognitive heuristics are also related to the steps of the action sequence discussed above; people have general heuristics of how they set goals, get information, plan, monitor, and process feedback (Frese et al., 1987). These general heuristics can be processed either consciously or automatically (Brown, 1987; Flavell, 1987), and they may be highly generalized or specific. Generalized and automatic heuristics with regard to action regulation are called *action styles* and function as equivalents to personality traits (Frese et al., 1987). They affect directly how one regulates actions on the conscious level of regulation (cf. also Busenitz & Arthurs, chap. 7, this volume).

The highest level—the meta-level—is usually not implicated when we receive an outside task for which some solution is known. Because these types of tasks dominate our working life, this is one reason why we typically do not think about our life goals, moral issues, or general procedures of how we deal with things, in our everyday activities.

Automaticity and the Levels of Regulation.   Routines are developed when the environment is redundant and when satisfactory results can be achieved with the routine. With practice, automatization is achieved (an overlearning process). Experts have more routines than novices. Whenever possible, lower levels of regulation are preferred because processing on this level is less effortful and the action is smoother. Another advantage is that the higher levels of regulation are freed from the constraints on working memory and are free to do other things (e.g., scan the environment for opportunities to satisfy other goals, or to preparatorily solve a problem that might appear in the future or to do pleasurable things like daydreaming).

Routines do not only develop for sensorimotor acts but also for thoughts. The use of theories can be such a routinized skill. For example, people raised in the tradition of the ecological theory of entrepreneurship will automatically think about the importance of environmental issues. This is one reason why theories have a life of their own and it is difficult (and effortful) to change them. The automatic use of the theory presents an impulse to the person on how he or she should orient him- or herself with regard to a scientific question.

Because routines are developed in redundant environments, expectations are high that is possible to use one's routines. Frustration appears when the lower level routines cannot be used (Amsel, 1958). People react negatively when their usual routines do not work any longer. Moreover, people are motivated to reestablish the routine (a sort of reactance effect; Wicklund 1974).

Keeping routines makes people conservative (therefore, older firms with established routines are more conservative than newer firms). People have a tendency to stick to their routines, even against a certain amount of environmental pressure. This goes for thought routines (e.g., using a certain theory and keeping this theory even when there are actually better alternatives available) as well as for sensorimotor routines (e.g., use a certain approach to selling that is kept up even though better alternatives are available). Therefore, entrepreneurs who have done well in the past may have problems when the environment changes, when continuous improvement is necessary, when innovations have to be speedily implemented (e.g., "not-invented-here-syndrome"), or when team composition is changed quickly (e.g., in project work) (Audia, Locke, & Smith, 2000).

On the other hand, if actions are only routine-driven (thus, the higher levels of regulation are under occupied), boredom ensues. However, boredom does not necessarily lead to higher level processing on a particular task. Rather the higher levels are then in search of some other tasks. This may lead to daydreaming or to radical changes (e.g., founding a new company). Thus, if routines get interrupted, people react with negative emotions, but if people's actions are reduced only to routines there are negative effects (Hacker, 1998), as well.

The activities of entrepreneurs are of high complexity and they often have to act within unknown and unpredictable environments. Therefore, entrepreneurs will tend to need to regulate more tasks on the conscious level of regulation than other occupations. Because new tasks appear for entrepreneurs again and again as the firm unfolds, conscious regulation of action is likely to be important for several years in contrast to most other jobs. From this follow a number of interesting implications: First, cognitive ability should be more important for entrepreneurs than for other occupations (note, however, that there may be reduced variance in Western countries because of a selection effect—people low on cognitive ability do not usually become entrepreneurs or are selected out quickly). Because cognitive ability is a limiting factor of working memory and attention allocation and because conscious processing is done because new tasks appear frequently, entrepreneurs are required to use a large reservoir of cognitive resources (which is cognitive ability) (Ackerman, 1988). Second, entrepreneurs work under high cognitive load more frequently than people in other occupations (Baron, 1998); therefore, more errors in planning and feedback interpretation on a conscious level happen to entrepreneurs (Zapf, Brodbeck, Frese, Peters, & Prümper, 1992). Third, because of this overload, entrepreneurs may be tempted to prematurely delegate regulation to lower (less conscious) levels of regulation—one implication is that wrong actions may be routinized (e.g., in the area of leadership) that are difficult to break up later on. Finally, the learning curve will be steep for entrepreneurs.

Learning and the Hierarchy. Learning can take place in two ways. The first avenue is to learn something directly on the lower and unconscious levels of regulation—so-called tacit learning (Myers & Davids, 1993). The second avenue is to first learn to perform an action consciously and with practice to transfer the regulation more and more to the lower levels of regulation. Consciousness does not imply that the action regulation can be verbalized—sometimes we can only visualize it consciously (e.g., when a person mentally simulates how to ride a bicycle). The second form of learning is the more efficient avenue because conscious regulation has the advantage that people learn principles of action as well and that a person can learn rapidly (cf. Kahneman, 2003, on a similar point). Such explicit knowledge can help to adjust one's skills more flexibly to changing circumstances than does tacit learning (Myers & Davids, 1993). Note, however, that both avenues of learning may take place at the same time: People adjust their behaviors that were once learned consciously to the specific circumstances on lower levels of regulation. The most obvious example of tacit learning is pattern recognition or prototyping (Posner & Keele, 1970). In the basic experiment, people look at a series of dots that are random variations of a prototype. Although the prototype itself is not shown, it is readily accessible and memory for it is particular good in comparison to the random variations that actually have been shown to the people. "Implicit knowledge is likely to develop in complex tasks containing many irrelevant variables but where key relationships are not obvious" (Myers & Davids, 1993, p. 127). Note, however, that categorization can also be done on a conscious level (Sloman, 1996).

Crossing Sequence and Structure

Some regulation theories are primarily concerned with the action sequence (Dörner & Schaub, 1994; Gollwitzer, 1993; Locke & Latham, 1990), and some other ones primarily with the action structure in terms of hierarchical regulation (Carver & Scheier, 1982; Lord & Levy, 1994). It makes sense to combine these two perspectives and cross action sequence and the levels of regulation (cf. Table 8.1). The dimension of consciousness reaches from nonconscious to conscious (similarly, the meta-level includes conscious and nonconscious processing). Goals, information mapping, plans, monitoring, and feedback processing are regulated based on knowledge from long-term memory (called *knowledge base* in Table 8.1).

Two interesting implications of crossing action structure and sequence are: Certain theories used in entrepreneurship research restrict themselves to processes on a conscious level of regulation, for example, expectancy × value (Vroom, 1964) and choice theories (Naylor, Pritchard, & Ilgen, 1980). Further, as Ackerman (1988) has pointed out, predictors related to performance regulated on a high level may be related to cognitive ability, whereas lower levels may be less so. Cognitive ability is the limiting factor for the resources available to an individual when the tasks are processed con-

TABLE 8.1

A Model of Levels of Regulation and Structure

Structure	Skill level	Level of flexible action pattern	Conscious level	Meta-level	
Consciousness of regulation	Unconscious; normally no access to consciousness necessary	Access to consciousness possible, but not necessary	Conscious representation to heuristics	Both conscious and automatic use of heuristics	
Elements of the knowledge base	Movement-oriented schemata;	Flexible action schemata	Complex, problem-oriented knowledge base	Generalized heuristics, possibly automatized	
Sequence	Goals	Triggered, by higher level or situational cues	Subgoals	Goals	Standards and metagoals, life goals
Mapping	Orientation reflex of environment	Schema	Conscious, prognosis	How much knowledge necessary to feel equipped to act	
Action programs / plans	Blueprints of elementary movement patterns and cognitive routines	Well-known action patterns with situational specifications	Conscious complex plans, strategies	Metaplans, heuristics	
Feedback / signals	Stereotype test programs, unconscious processing of kinesthetic and pro-prioceptive feedback signals	Processing of known signals / feedback	Analysis and synthesis of new information	Abstract (nonobject-oriented) checks, logical inconsistencies, heuristics for feedback processing	

(Adapted from Frese & Zapf, 1994, p. 285)

sciously. Cognitive ability should have a stronger impact on those processes that are regulated on the conscious level and much less so on processes regulated on the skill level. Because in the beginning of a learning process more tasks need to be processed consciously, and because learning implies that people increasingly rely on routines, cognitive ability should have a more important effect on people in the beginning of their learning. Therefore, cognitive ability should predict the performance of entrepreneurs in their first years more than in later years or should predict better the performance of those entrepreneurs who operate in highly changing environments (with the demand on consciously dealing with those changes) than those in stable environments (Kanfer & Kantrowitz, 2002).

The Relationship Between Upper and Lower Level Processing

Evidence for the differentiation of levels of regulation comes primarily from training studies and reaction time tasks (Shiffrin & Schneider, 1977). Ackerman (1988) showed that cognitive ability predicts performance better in the beginning of the training process (when processing is done consciously); perceptual speed is a good predictor in the middle (when processing is on the level of flexible action patterns); and psychomotor predictors are good at the end of the training (when the task is handled routinely).

The function of the higher levels of regulation is to give input into the lower levels. Lord and Levy (1994, p. 340) summarize this by arguing that "moving up one level explains *why* an action is done (to reduce discrepancies in higher-level systems), and moving down a level explains *how* discrepancies are reduced (by the operation of lower-level systems)." The input from a higher level may be a goal in a negative feedback loop (Carver & Scheier, 1982). Additional inputs on the higher levels may be triggering conditions (when should an action or operation be set into motion), selection of strategies of how to proceed, sensibilization for detecting certain feedback and signals, or protecting the action from interference (Hacker, 1985). Lord and Levy (1994) see the important function of higher level processes to guide attention and to protect the functioning of the lower levels from interference. In contrast, the lower levels should detect discrepancies and send information upwards.

Actions are regulated on a higher level when barriers, opportunities for new goals, or environmental pressures appear. *Barriers* are, for example, problems that are difficult to solve, errors, or an objective no-go situation. The consequence of moving up the level of regulation is that one is forced to think consciously about the problem. This may be frustrating because one's plans of action are interrupted (Mandler, 1964), but it can also lead to new conscious learning (Frese, 1995). *Opportunities* lead to a higher level regulation when they can satisfy current concerns (e.g., when an entrepreneur talks to a customers and notices that there might be an opportunity present for additional work, he or she might start to think more consciously about these talks than when the conversation takes place as an everyday event). In such a case, people tend to focus consciously on the task and decide whether to finish it or to use the opportunity as a trigger of new actions. Sometimes entrepreneurs may develop routines to search for opportunities—for example, giving a business card to every potential new customer. But once an important new opportunity is detected, action processing is more likely conscious. Because conscious processing is limited by capacity levels of the conscious processor (Norman & Bobrow, 1975), new opportunity recognition should be easier for entrepreneurs who have been in business for some time (because they can regulate most other things on a lower level of regulation) than for somebody who has just started a firm. But note that this tendency is offset by the tendency of entrepreneurs to stick to their routines once they are developed. Thus, with increasing routinization of work there are two processes taking place that have opposing effects on opportunity pursuit: On the one hand, as a cognitive process, people are, in principle, able to deal with additional demands (such as pursuit of new opportunities); on the other hand, motivationally, people feel comfortable to stick with their routines and are therefore less open to new ideas once they have developed their routines. Thus, cognitively people are able to see new ideas, but motivationally they are not necessarily open to them.

Environmental pressures can produce actions because people know that they have to do certain things (e.g., be friendly to a preferred customer is sometimes done with a conscious strategy). If environmental pressure makes it necessary to produce actions that are not well rehearsed, it is necessary to process these actions on a higher level of regulation. An example is writing a business plan—here the would-be owners are forced to consciously think about the plans of actions. Therefore, if environmental pressure is high, there are fewer differences of how people proceed with their actions than in situations where environmental pressure is lower.

Some scholars have argued that *mindfulness*—just another term for processing information on the conscious level of regulation—has mainly positive consequences (Fiol & O'Connor, 2003; Langer & Piper, 1987) for individuals and organizations. Although action theory shares the argument that processing is more thorough, realistic, and often more appropriate if done on higher levels of regulation, there is an important caveat: Entrepreneurs and organizations can only be mindful in their processing of a limited number of actions. If these actions are the important ones and if the environment is nonredundant, it pays off to be mindful, as long as other important issues are processed nonconsciously (i.e., mindless). If an entrepreneur attempted to be mindful for every action or operation, he or she would be incapacitated (e.g., hardly any sentence could be produced in a sale pitch, because of mindful attention to the grammar). Action theory also suggests that there are advantages to lower level (mindless) processing (mainly related to issues of load on the restricted processing capacity of higher levels of regulation; cf. Norman & Bobrow, 1975).

When moving up the level of regulation, certain problems appear: Higher level processing overloads processing capacity, and it is more difficult; the actions are less elegant and smooth. *Overload* is the direct result of having more things to do on the upper levels of regulation (Kahneman, 1973). Shifting to higher level processing is *difficult*; experts often report that to work against one's routines is more difficult, and earlier routines may interrupt the process and habit errors occur (Kimble & Perlmuter, 1970; Prümper, Zapf, Brodbeck, & Frese, 1990). Especially frustrating is the lower degree of performance *elegance* and *smoothness* when people are asked to consciously control routinized actions (Kimble & Perlmuter, 1970).

Learning can (and has to) take place on all levels of regulation; however, learning implies different things on different levels. Learning on the lowest level implies that one's skills are adjusted to the particulars of a situation and to increase the coordination of muscles and between different skills—skill execution become smoother and the various operations of the skills become better coordinated. Moreover, some motor skills or cognitive patterns, such as prototyping, are probably only learned on this level (Broadbent, 1977; Myers & Davids, 1993). However, learning on this level is highly situation specific and there is little transfer to other situations. In contrast, learning on the conscious level has high transfer potential because it is based on developing insights. Of course, even if learning is originally done on a high level of regulation, with practice the regulation of action moves downward so that less conscious attention is needed (Kanfer & Ackerman, 1989; Sloman, 1996).

An important corollary is the necessity to practice the relationship between the levels of regulation (Semmer & Frese, 1985). Not every conscious or abstract thought has regulatory power over one's actions. Only if thoughts are related to lower levels of regulation do thoughts control action. Therefore, it is necessary that a new insight is entrained to relate to action. Most people know that learning something new, for example, bookkeeping in a university course, does not imply that one is able to use it—some transfer (transfer with lower levels of regulation) needs to be done. Bookkeeping may well continue to be an abstract concept. The learner might be good at reproducing the knowledge on bookkeeping in a test, but this knowledge may still not have regulatory power, unless the entrepreneur has learned how to use it in specific practical situations. This can only be done by engaging all levels of regulation. Therefore, training and teaching have to involve all levels of regulation.

Another corollary to the preceding reasoning is that people may misunderstand their own action regulation. For example, entrepreneurs argue quite frequently that they decide things without much thought—in the sense of intuitive decision making. For action theory, intuition implies that the action (including a cognitive action) is regulated on lower levels. Intuition exists and may be efficient under these conditions: First, the entrepreneur has been in those situations before and routinized how to deal with them. Second, the deep-level characteristics of the situation must be the same as other situations that the entrepreneur has mastered before (sometimes the surface characteristics may be the same, but not the deep-level characteristics—this may lead to wrong decisions on the basis of intuition or routines [Adelson, 1984]). Third, the entrepreneur must know the right signals (or other cues) that tell him or her which kinds of actions are adequate in this situation. Finally, the entrepreneur must be skilled at using feedback on the lower level of regulation (which again implies prior exposure and practice with this feedback). It follows that whenever a new situation requires new decision making, intuition is probably bad advice.

Limits to Good Performance: Cognitive Misers, Satisficing Strategy, and Action Styles

Our discussion so far could be misunderstood as saying that there is an inherent tendency toward optimal performance (because people get feedback and improve their actions as a result of them). Any good theory must come to grips with the fact that there are limits to good performance and that there are people who do not learn quickly and well enough to deal with difficult situations. Psychologists have tended to argue against optimistic concepts in economics that allowed people to become highly knowledgeable participants in the market—the most important concept being "bounded rationality" (March & Simon, 1958). From an action theory view, five processes are responsible for continuous suboptimal performance: First, people are cognitive misers (Taylor, 1981). This means that they normally prefer to use automatic, stereotypical responses rather than to put high effort into goal analysis, orienting themselves fully, developing well-thought-out plans, or developing new feedback signals (Dörner, 1996; Fiol & O'Connor, 2003; Reither & Staeudel, 1985). High cognitive effort will only be used if there are good reasons to use it. Serious errors, difficult problems, obvious opportunities, and environmental pressures constitute good reasons. Actors use conscious, effortful approaches only if they assume that the routine responses do not function well (Frese & Zapf, 1994).

Second, a similar issue relates to the aspiration level of performance. As March and Simon (1958) noted, people most often use satisficing and not necessarily optimizing action strategies. This means that the "next best" solution is preferred rather than an unknown optimal solution. Obviously, this puts limits on the development of high performance, and many modern organizational interventions are geared to increase the use of optimizing strategies (total quality management, lean production, etc.).

Third, suboptimal, subsatisficing performance may be kept up even against evidence because of the function of action styles (Frese et al., 1987). Action styles are automatic heuristics that regulate how we set goals, map our environment, plan, monitor, and process feedback. For example, some people tend to make precise and long-term plans even for actions that do not need to be planned out well. Others tend to do the opposite, even for actions that would certainly profit from a high degree of planfulness. Because these action styles are automatic and general (i.e., they apply to a wide variety of action areas), we do not typically think about them. Rather, whenever we get some specific feedback, we use a specific response and learn something rather specific. Thus, a person will say in a particularly case, "I should have known better, I should have really planned out in detail what I needed to do." Thus, for this specific problem, the person will have learned to use a higher degree of prior planning. However, with a somewhat different situation, this person will use the old approach of little planning. Thus, because people do not reconsider their general approach to, for example, planning, only specific instances are optimized, but generally suboptimal action styles are kept up. The problem of action styles is aggravated when people (like entrepreneurs) have many different tasks to do; this makes it unlikely that they spend enough time to develop nonroutine approach to problems. A similar argument can be made for regulatory focus, that is, whether people are promotion or prevention focused (Brockner, Higgins, & Low, 2004).

Fourth, environmental pressures often suggest a certain amount of urgency. In an urgent situation (e.g., signs of immediate danger), people use the first automatic or routinized approach that appears to be appropriate at first sight (Reason, 1990).

Fifth, heuristic processing produces fast results. However, under certain circumstances heuristic processing leads to negative effects—for example, if the task is not adjusted to the functioning of human beings. Famous examples imply heuristics in statistical reasoning (Kahneman et al., 1982) (cf. chap. 7 by Busenitz & Arthurs, this volume).

THE FOCUS: TASK, SOCIAL, AND SELF

Much of our discussion of entrepreneurial performance in this chapter assumed an individual task—thus, the focus on the task. This is certainly useful for small business owners who determine to a large extent what is happening in the firm, but it probably applies less and less as a firm grows. Achievement in work is often based on some sort of collective activities.

Therefore, high firm performance is based on how well the social and organizational context in which task performance takes place is regulated (cf. Borman & Motowidlo, 1993; Organ, 1988). In this case, the regulatory focus is the social context. A third focus of regulation can be the self, for example, in the sense of self-regulation or self-management (Bandura, 1997; Karoly, 1993). Thus, all of our concepts developed can be applicable for regulating with the three foci of performance—the task, the social context, and the self.

The Task as Focus of Regulation

The task as focus of regulation has been discussed at length and does not need to be repeated here. It is of obvious importance and any diversion from the task probably leads to lower success. As a matter of fact, the problems of neuroticism may lie in its effect of diverting attention away from the task to one's individual anxieties (Judge, Higgins, Thoresen, & Barrick, 1999). An interesting finding in the expertise literature shows that experts and nonexperts alike may get diverted from the task, but experts are more quickly task oriented again than nonexperts (Sonnentag, 1998).

The Social Context as Focus of Regulation

Entrepreneurship is a social endeavor—as a matter of fact, starting an organization is per se a social endeavor because it implies that other people are involved. Therefore, to be successful, entrepreneurs have to regulate the social contexts of task performance. The following are important mechanisms of why a social focus is important (Organ, 1988):

1. The entrepreneur needs to hold up the smooth functioning of the organization.
2. Sometimes employees need help and support to work well (Borman & Motowidlo, 1993).
3. The technical and production equipment has to be kept up and serviced. This implies that production methods have to be continually improved.
4. Organizational objectives need to be defended and supported (Borman & Motowidlo, 1993; Van Scotter & Motowidlo, 1996).

We propose that it is possible to analyze actions focused on the social side of the enterprise with the same concepts as discussed for the regulation of task performance. Thus the steps in the sequence—goal, mapping, plan, monitoring of execution, and feedback processing—are relevant here, as well. There is one major difference for task performance, however: Social focus actions are primarily based on interactions—thus, the other people are also acting back—in the form of communicative actions or in terms of other actions. Thus, interactions of people stand in the foreground.

The Self as the Focus of Regulation

High performance requires regulating oneself effectively—self-management (including personality management), self-efficacy, and switch from self to task. Whenever attention is turned to a higher level of regulation, the self system is potentially implicated (Carver & Scheier, 1982). This is particularly so after failure (Mikulincer, 1989).

Self-management implies that the self is managed and regulated. This implies that one knows one's weaknesses and works consciously (and with time automatically) against them and that one knows one's strengths and capitalizes on them. Self-management also implies some meta-cognitive questions: Which long-range goals does an entrepreneur pursue? What kind of approaches does he or she typically take? What has gone wrong and why, and what has gone right and why?

One specific approach to the self, the concept of self-efficacy, has been suggested by Bandura (1997). *Self-efficacy* means that a person believes that he or she can do well on a task. Thus, it asks the relational question: How well is this task suited to my self and how well am I suited to the task? Bandura's self-efficacy should have an influence on all of the steps of the sequence (goal, plan, feedback processing, etc.). In terms of hierarchical regulation, there are two important issues. First, we assume that consistent self-efficacy can generalize and can therefore have an influence on heuristics of setting goals, information collection, and so on. Second, self-efficacy should have a higher influence on consciously regulated task performance than on routinized activities. Thus, self-efficacy should be more highly related to performance in novel actions; therefore, in the startup phase of a business self-efficacy should be more important because novel actions are consciously regulated. Self-efficacy issues should also come up more frequently when task performance needs to be regulated on higher levels, for example, because of errors, difficulties, failures, or opportunities.

The self system is regulated on the meta-level. However, attending to the self implies often that one is consciously thinking about whether or not one is doing well. Reflection on the self is therefore an additional load on the working memory. Thus, attention to the self leads to quick enhancement of achievement in an easy task but, at least in the short term, to a reduction of achievement in a difficult task (Mikulincer, Glaubman, Ben-Artzi, & Grossman, 1991).

Some goals, particularly life and self-presentational goals, are more intimately related to the self than to other goals. It is sometimes argued that emotions are the result of self-regulation (e.g., Kluger & DeNisi, 1996). Although we do not disagree that the self is a good candidate to influence emotions, we do not think that the self is necessarily implied when developing emotions from work (cf. Pekrun & Frese, 1992, for a fuller discussion).

APPLICATIONS IN ENTREPRENEURSHIP

Two applications of action theory to entrepreneurship research should be briefly described: personal initiative as an active approach, and planning.

Active Approach: Personal Initiative

Bandura (1986) argued against control theory because it does not understand increases in goal levels after a prior goal has been reached. Action theory does not suffer from the same problems as control theory does. One of the assumptions of action theory is that people (and many other organisms) are inherently active (White, 1959). White (1959) argued that an effectance motive made organisms constantly searching for new mastery experiences. The effectance motive is tied to the biological survival value of being active. In the language of action theory, people have inherent heuristics of how to approach goals (higher, faster, more far-reaching, better, etc.) that imply that one wants to achieve higher goals in task areas of high importance (as in any inherent tendency, there are interpersonal differences, as manifested in achievement motives; McClelland, 1987). Action theory assumes that it is an ontological given that humans are active because activity increases the chance for procreation and for keeping the offspring alive. Action theory assumes that many people become more active with time, because they learn that an active approach increases chances to learn, to control the environment, to reach one's goals, and to reach positive consequences. Active approaches are powerful because they can influence events before they appear (proactivity). One can prevent negative events from happening and/or can prepare for opportunities. An active entrepreneur is actively (systematically or unsystematically) searching for opportunities (cf. Baron, chap. 2, this volume). Active approaches make it possible to adjust the task to one's knowledge, skills, and aptitudes. Thus, the environment is made to fit the person better. An active approach can institute changes more easily because actions are less driven by the situation and more by long-range goals. Finally, natural tasks do not always present optimal feedback. Active approaches make it possible to tune and develop feedback signals that are optimal for learning.

Entrepreneurs are typically more active than the general population. We have introduced the concept of personal initiative to describe this active orientation (Frese & Fay, 2001). This concept allows us to understand why and how people change their environment both inside and outside a firm. *Personal initiative* is defined as self-starting, proactive, and persistent behavior (Frese, Kring, Soose, & Zempel, 1996). Personal initiative can be divided into facets of goal setting, information mapping, planning, monitoring, and feedback processing (Frese & Fay, 2001). Self-starting implies that entrepreneurs develop self-set goals and that they actively explore the environment and do experiments in it (to get good information). In the area of planning, self-starting means to develop an active strategy (i.e., a strategy that changes the environment and actively intervenes rather than that takes things for granted or just reacts to situational cues), and in monitoring and feedback processing, self-starting means to self-develop feedback signals and to actively search for feedback. To be proactive implies that future problems and opportunities are anticipated and converted into goals, cognitive models, plans, and feedback processes now. Finally, to be persistent means to protect one's goals, information search, plans, and feedback processing against frustration and too high complexity and to overcome barriers when they occur.

Small-scale entrepreneurs exhibit a higher degree of initiative (Crant, 1996; Frese, Fay, Leng, Hilburger, & Tag, 1997). Moreover, personal initiative is related to success in small business people (Crant, 1995; Koop, De Reu, & Frese, 2000; Zempel, 1999). Finally, small to medium-sized firms are more successful if their chief executives scanned the environment proactively when if managers did not do that (Daft, Sormunen, & Parks, 1988). In entrepreneurship research, the concept that comes closest to personal initiative is the proactive stance in entrepreneurial orientation. One facet of entrepreneurial orientation is proactiveness, which has been shown to be related to both the decision to pursue an entrepreneurial career and to success (Frese, Brantjes, & Hoorn, 2002; Krauss, Frese, & Friedrich, 2005; Lumpkin & Dess, 1996; Miller & Friesen, 1982; Rauch, Wiklund, Frese, & Lumpkin, 2005).

Planning

In order to be able to show a high degree of proactiveness, it is necessary to plan. A plan describes the sequence of actions to achieve a goal. A plan is proactive if it is long-term oriented. Planning for long-term events (opportunities or threats) implies that I prepare for these events today. This usually includes some kind of plan B (alternative plan in case the developed plan does not work out). In entrepreneurship, planning is more important than for other occupations, because there is nobody else who structures the goals and the ways to achieve those goals for the entrepreneur. He or she, therefore, has to bet on the unpredictable future and develop plans to achieve those bets.

Although there is a high degree of literature on formal planning in entrepreneurship (e.g., Schwenk & Shrader, 1993), planning from an action theory perspective is concerned with everyday planning. Interestingly, everyday action planning has not been in the foreground of research in entrepreneurship (Sarasvathy, 2001). We differentiate four different characteristics of how entrepreneurs (Frese et al., 2000) structure their approaches to a goal: comprehensive planning, critical-point planning, opportunistic, and reactive. These characteristics can be differentiated along the lines of goal orientation, long-term planning, knowledge base, proactiveness, and situational responsiveness.

Comprehensive planning means that owners develop and implement strategies with high goal orientation, high long-term planning, high knowledge, and high proactiveness. The goals and plans are developed with a long-term perspective. The owners who plan frequently develop a good knowledge base. Long-term planning is an active strategy because it proactively looks at future events, predicts future problems and opportunities, and changes the environment to prepare for these future events. Using complete planning has many advantages because it actively structures the situation and makes it possible to work with long-term anticipation and knowledge. However, there are also disadvantages, as planning is time-consuming and costly. Once one has a developed a plan, one is likely not to change it and not to respond quickly to the situation (thus, situational responsiveness is low).

Critical-point strategy plans for the most salient issue first and then plans out other issues after this issue has been dealt with (Zempel, 2003). It can be described as a an economic way of main-issue planning (Sonnentag, 1996), meaning that the person has one clear goal in mind and concentrates on the main issues to achieve this goal. Thus, it is goal oriented, not very long term, and it does not deal with potential future problems and opportunities as much as comprehensive planning. Critical-point strategy has the advantage of allowing a certain degree of situational responsiveness because the owners have invested less into their plans.

An *opportunistic* strategy actively scans the environment for business opportunities and acts on new opportunities (cf. Hayes-Roth & Hayes-Roth, 1979). Once an opportunity is found, the respective person easily deviates from his or her prior plans and goals. Thus, situational responsiveness and activeness are high but planning and goal setting are low. The major differences from complete planning and critical-point planning are that opportunistic planning leads people to plan little, to have a low future orientation, and to be easily distracted from a plan of action.[2] People characterized by opportunistic strategy might put aside a plan quickly and might not plan enough to stay on course in a difficult environment because they are attracted by newly perceived opportunities. An opportunistic owner might, for example, detect a cheap product and would therefore change the business focus to include it.

A *reactive* strategy characteristic implies that the owner is driven by the situation and there is no or little proactive and planned use of information. Thus, this strategy encompasses little planning and little proactiveness. There is little goal orientation, no long-term planning, and the knowledge base is not well developed because feedback cannot be understood, because these owners do not have hypotheses (as part of their plan) about what might go right or wrong. There is, however, a high degree of situational responsiveness. In contrast to opportunistic planning, owners with a reactive strategy are not actively searching for opportunities and other environmental changes; rather, they stumble on these changes or are made aware by their competitors or other people. No systematic search of feedback is done, and therefore the information is often too late or lacking enough detail to be useful. Therefore, a reactive strategy would only be useful in a completely random environment (which, however, does not exist in reality).

Empirically, the reactive strategy is negatively related to success in most environments, whereas planning is positively related to success (Frese et al., 2006; Frese, Brantjes, & Hoorn, 2002). With planning, there is better knowledge of the situation and the plans include back-up plans for potential problems (plan B). Proactively structuring and influencing the situation should also have a positive impact on success. To be proactive means that the owner can change the situation, knows potential future difficulties, and deals with them in anticipation. Complete planning and critical-point planning imply both planning and proactiveness and are therefore more highly related to success than opportunistic planning, which is only proactive (Frese et al., 2002).

An opportunistic strategy is proactive as it searches for opportunities; however, it is also reactive because the opportunities govern the owners' actions. There is little proactiveness in the sense of developing forethought about potential future problems. Because of the little preplanning involved, a person deviates easily from the pursuit of one goal when other opportunities arise. Therefore, business owners might lose sight of their long-term plans and goals, which might mean that they do not put enough effort into the long-term development of their firm. This also means that opportunistic

---

[2]A potential misunderstanding of the term *opportunistic strategy* is that it is confused with the search and exploitation of opportunities as a general characteristic of all entrepreneurship (Shane & Venkataraman, 2000). It should be carefully distinguished. In our view, entrepreneurs are well advised to carefully plan and anticipate opportunities to be able to exploit them. An opportunistic strategy is an active approach but because it implies that the entrepreneur gets easily diverted from a goal, opportunities may not be as carefully searched and as well exploited with an opportunistic approach than with some kind of planning. As a matter of fact, we considered alternative concepts to opportunistic strategy like "easy fix/opportunistic" or "easy win" in the sense of "pick the low-hanging fruits."

owners do not actively *develop* opportunities; they may not be persistent enough; rather, they just attempt to exploit the obvious opportunities (Ardichvili, Cardozo, & Ray, 2003). An opportunistic approach is often characterized by the lack of a clear business vision and by lack of focus (Inkpen & Choudhury, 1995). Nigerian business owners who were opportunistic were shown to be less successful in the long run than nonopportunistic owners (Wilfert, 1992), because they switched their type of business too often. Thus, an opportunistic strategy has advantages and disadvantages, depending on the specifics of the situation. Following this line of reasoning, overall, the pros and cons of this strategy may cancel each other out.

A reactive approach means that there is no planning and no proactiveness. There are no clear-cut goals, and this keeps business owners from dealing with potential problems before they occur. A reactive strategy is a passive adaptation and does not attempt to influence the situation. All of this suggests that a reactive strategy is dysfunctional for success. Empirically, it has been shown that this strategy is negatively related to success in various studies, in contrast to the two planning strategies of comprehensive planning and critical point planning (Frese, 2000; Frese et al., 2002; Frese, Friedrich, & Hass, 2004; Frese, van Gelderen & Ombach, 2000). This is also true of a longitudinal study showing that planning leads to success and is positively influenced by success (van Gelderen et al., 2000).

Another approach was to study the effects of training entrepreneurs to be less reactive and more active/planning. We have empirically validated a training program derived from action theory and from personal initiative theory for small scale business owners. Entrepreneurs who participated in this training were more successful than entrepreneurs who were in a comparison group (Frese et al., 2004; Glaub, Gramberg, Friedrich, & Frese, 2006).

CONCLUDING REMARKS

We suggested that entrepreneurial performance should be considered from three perspectives: sequence, structure, and regulatory focus. Sequence has the following dimensions: goal development, orientation, planning, execution and monitoring, and feedback processing. Structure is related to a hierarchical regulation of action with four levels: skill level, level of flexible action patterns, conscious level, and metacognitive heuristics. Finally, the regulatory focus differentiates the areas of task and contextual performance, and the role of the self. Our goal with this article was to provide an integrative framework that allows one to pinpoint which aspect of performance one is studying in detail.

Obviously, our presentation is only a first sketch of a complete theory of entrepreneurial performance. This kind of theory promises to fill the gap between performance predictors and action. For example, expectancies have been taken to be important predictors of performance (Vroom, 1964). However, it is interesting to ask how expectancies affect the action—for example, via goals, orientations, and plans.

There is some need to explicate the role of motivation and emotion within the theory. Motivation is directly linked to goals (Locke & Latham, 1990) and to feedback (Kluger & DeNisi, 1996). Thus far, motivation is easily incorporated. However, there may be motivational and emotional processes directly linked to each part of the action sequence (Klinger, 1985; Pekrun & Frese, 1992). Moreover, people may regulate their emotions in order to develop better performance strategies; for example, when an entrepreneur has to present his or her products, he or she may actually attempt to make him- or herself anxious so that he or she prepares better for this important event. The result is that the presenter gets physiologically aroused before the event (Nitsch & Allmer, 1979). These processes have to be explicated.

The relationship between the self and the sequence, structure, form, and content also awaits clarification. Further, entrepreneurial performance at work is often done within teams. Group regulatory processes have to be tackled as well, and may be partly similar to the ones described for the individual (Tschan, 1995). In spite of these problems, we hope that our contribution can be useful as a framework that helps to decipher what aspects of entrepreneurial actions are important.

There are a number of research questions that follow from this theory. First, the overarching importance of action follows from this theory. That means how actions change the environment, how actions interact with the environment, and how they are influenced by environmental conditions are important issues. Second, although there is evidence that active approaches are more successful in entrepreneurship, there may be exceptions, for example, in chaotic environments. In certain situations, adjustment is more important than active influence (e.g., in a situation in which an entrepreneur is highly dependent on others, such as dependent on banks). Third, each aspect of the action sequence may be the focus of research. Goal setting has been studied best, although self-developed goals were not in the foreground. All the other aspects of the action sequence have not been studied, such as the development of the mental model, how realistic and detailed it needs to be (and under which conditions, this is positively or negatively related to entrepreneurial performance), which signals and prototypes are developed by entrepreneurs and within the context of innovation, and so on. Similarly, the action orientation of mental models has not been explicitly developed (and also the personality variable action orientation has not been studied systematically within entrepreneurship research). Finally, it has not been studied in the field, where thinking on different levels of decomposition is important (cf. Dörner, 1996).

Planning has been studied to a certain extent, but there are many details that still need to be worked out. What kind of planning is too much for an entrepreneur? How are planning and active orientation related? Can there be an active approach without planning that is completely opportunistic (driven by opportunities rather than exploiting opportunities), and under which conditions can this approach have positive effects (Frese et al., 2000)?

The issues of information overload in entrepreneurs has received surprisingly little attention (exception Baron, 1998), although the executive function of working memory is of high importance in somebody who has to deal with various task domains as small business owners typically do. An obvious parameter here is cognitive ability, and another is how strongly actions are regulated by automatized or routinized schemata.

Surprisingly, feedback processes have been little studied in entrepreneurship, although feedback is one of the most important facets of learning processes.

Further, it would pay to take the differentiation between levels of regulation seriously in entrepreneurship research. Too often the different levels of regulation have been used as opposites and not as complementary. For example, scholars seem to argue about whether decision making is primarily intuitive or deliberate, rather than acknowledging that these belong to different phases of the learning process and environmental redundancy (the more practice a person has in redundant environments, the more automatic and intuitive are actions). Further, neither of these levels of regulation can be called more effective or efficient than the other, because this depends on the task structure. New tasks need deliberate and conscious regulation. On the other hand, it is efficient to routinize and delegate tasks to lower levels of regulation if they repeat themselves. Whenever, an environment changes, the person with old routines geared toward a different environment has more difficulties relearning. However, if the environment stayed the same, we would call this person an expert because of his or her routines. Obviously, there are many issues here that have not been resolved. One question is: How can training increase the flexibility to go from one level to the other? (We tend to think that a training device we developed —error management training—helps with that, but this has not yet been empirically proven; cf. Frese, 1995.)

In general, action regulation theory is useful because it allows to start with cognitive concepts that are directly related to actions—regulation processes. Cognitive models applied to entrepreneurship have been often in the area of pre-action cognitions, such as expectancy × value models (e.g., Krueger, 2000) or in areas of understanding statistical information or general decision making. Although we think that these models are useful, we also think that cognitions that directly regulate actions may be more important for entrepreneurship research. Action regulation theory has overcome the bias of cognitive theories to be contemplative rather than dealing directly with cognitive action regulation. We therefore think that it is a useful theory for entrepreneurship.

REFERENCES

Ackerman, P. L. (1988). Determinants of individual differences during skill acquisition: Cognitive abilities and information processing. *Journal of Experimental Psychology: General, 117*(3), 288–318.

Ackerman, P. L. (1992). Predicting individual differences in complex skill acquisition: Dynamics of ability determinants. *Journal of Applied Psychology, 77,* 598–614.

Adelson, B. (1984). When novices surpass experts: The difficulty of a task may increase with expertise. *Journal of Experimental Psychology: Learning, Memory, and Cognition, 10,* 483–495.

Aldrich, H. E. (1999). *Organizations evolving.* London: Sage.

Amsel, A. (1958). The role of frustrative nonreward in non-continuous reward situations. *Psychological Bulletin, 55,* 102–119.

Anderson, J. R. (1983). *The architecture of cognition.* Cambridge, MA: Harvard University Press.

Ardichvili, A., Cardozo, R., & Ray, S. (2003). A theory of entrepreneurial opportunity identification and development. *Journal of Business Venturing, 18,* 105–123.

Ashford, S. J. (1989). Self-assessments in organizations: A literature review and integrative model. *Research in Organizational Behavior, 11,* 133–174.

Ashford, S. J., & Tsui, A. S. (1991). Self-regulation for managerial effectiveness: The role of active feedback seeking. *Academy of Management Journal, 34*(2), 251–280.

Audia, P. G., Locke, E. A., & Smith, K. G. (2000). The paradox of success: An archival and laboratory study of strategic persistence following radical environmental change. *Academy of Management Journal, 43,* 837–853.

Baddeley, A. D. (1986). *Working memory.* New York: Basic.

Bandura, A. (1986). *Social foundations of thought and action.* Englewood Cliffs, NJ: Prentice Hall.

Bandura, A. (1997). *Self-efficacy: The exercise of control.* New York: Freeman.

Baron, R. A. (1998). Cognitive mechanisms in entrepreneurship: Why and when entrepreneurs think differently than other people. *Journal of Business Venturing, 13,* 275–294.

Baron, R. A. (2004). The cognitive perspective: A valuable tool for answering entrepreneurship's basic "why" questions. *Journal of Business Venturing, 19,* 221–240.

Berg, C. A., Strough, J., Calderone, K., Meegan, S. P., & Sansone, C. (1997). Planning to prevent everyday problems from occurring. In S. L. Friedman & E. K. Scholnick (Eds.), *The developmental psychology of planning: Why, how, and when do we plan?* (pp. 209–236). Mahwah, NJ: Lawrence Erlbaum Associates.

Borman, W. C., & Motowidlo, S. J. (1993). Expanding the criterion domain to include elements of contextual performance. In N. Schmitt & W. C. Borman (Eds.), *Personnel selection in organizations* (pp. 71–98). San Francisco: Jossey-Bass.

Broadbent, D. E. (1977). The hidden preattentive process. *American Psychologist, 32,* 109–118.

Brockner, J., Higgins, E. T., & Low, M. B. (2004). Regulatory focus theory and the entrepreneurial process. *Journal of Business Venturing, 19,* 203–220.

Brown, A. L. (1987). Metacognition, executive control, self-regulation, and other more mysterious mechanism. In F. E. Weinert, & R. H. Kluwe, (Eds.), *Metacognition, motivation, and understanding* (pp. 65–116). Mahwah, NJ: Lawrence Erlbaum Associates.

Carver, C. S., & Scheier, M. F. (1982). Control theory: A useful conceptual framework for personality, social, clinical, and health psychology. *Psychological Bulletin, 92,* 111–135.

Chase, W. G., & Simon, H. A. (1973). The mind's eye in chess. In W. G. Chase (Ed.), *Visual information processing* (pp. 215–281). New York: Academic Press.

Chen, M.-J., & Hambrick, D. (1995). Speed, stealth, and selective attack: How small firms differ from large firms in competitive behavior. *Academy of Management Journal, 38*, 453–482.

Crant, J. M. (1995). The proactive personality scale and objective job performance among real estate agents. *American Psychologist, 80*, 532–537.

Crant, M. J. (1996). The proactive personality scale as a predictor of entrepreneurial intentions. *Journal of Small Business Management, 34*(3), 42–49.

Crocker, J., & Park, L. E. (2004). The costly pursuit of self-esteem. *Psychological Bulletin, 130*, 392–414.

Daft, R. L., Sormunen, J., & Parks, D. (1988). Chief executive scanning, environmental characteristics, and company performance: An empirical study. *Strategic Management Journal, 9*, 123–139.

Dawkins, R. (1976). *The selfish gene*. New York: Oxford University Press.

Diefendorff, J. M. (2004). Examination of the roles of action-state orientation and goal orientation in the goal-setting and performance process. *Human Performance, 17*, 375–395.

Diefendorff, J. M., & Lord, R. G. (2004). The volitional and strategic effects of planning on task performance and goal commitment. *Human Performance, 16*, 365–387.

Dolgin, K. G. (1985). An action-theory perspective of the tool-using capacities of chimpanzees and human infants. In M. Frese & J. Sabini (Eds.), *Goal directed behavior: The concept of action in psychology* (pp. 35–47). Hillsdale, NJ: Lawrence Erlbaum Associates.

Dörner, D. (1996). *The logic of failure*. Reading, MA: Addison-Wesley.

Dörner, D., & Schaub, H. (1994). Errors in planning and decision-making and the nature of human information processing. *Applied Psychology: An International Review, 43*, 433–454.

Erez, M. (1977). Feedback: A necessary condition for the goal setting–performance relationship. *American Psychologist, 62*, 624–627.

Fenton-O'Creevy, M., Nicholson, N., Soane, E., & Willman, P. (2005). *Traders: Risks, Decisions, and Management in Financial Markets*. Oxford, UK: Oxford University Press.

Fiol, C. M., & O'Connor, E. J. (2003). Waking up! Mindfulness in the face of bandwagons. *Academy of Management Review, 28*, 54–70.

Flavell, J. H. (1987). Speculations about the nature and development of metacognition. In F. E. Weinert & R. H. Kluwe (Eds.), *Metacognition, motivation, and understanding*. Hillsdale, NJ: Lawrence Erlbaum Associates.

Ford, J. K., Smith, E. M., Weissbein, D. A., Gully, S. M., & Salas, E. (1998). Relationships of goal orientation, meta-cognitive activity, and practice strategies with learning outcomes and transfer. *American Psychologist, 83*, 218–233.

Frese, M. (1995). Error management in training: Conceptual and empirical results. In C. Zuchermaglio, S. Bagnara, & S. U. Stucky (Eds.), *Organizational learning and technological change* (pp. 112–124). Berlin: Springer.

Frese, M. (Ed.). (2000). *Success and failure of microbusiness owners in Africa: A psychological approach*. Westport, CT: Quorum Books.

Frese, M., Brantjes, A., & Hoorn, R. (2002). Psychological success factors of small scale businesses in Namibia: The roles of strategy process, entrepreneurial orientation and the environment. *Journal of Developmental Entrepreneurship, 7*, 259–282.

Frese, M., & Fay, D. (2001). Personal Initiative (PI): A concept for work in the 21st century. *Research in Organizational Behavior, 23*, 133–188.

Frese, M., Fay, D., Leng, K., Hilburger, T., & Tag, A. (1997). The concept of personal initiative: Operationalization, reliability, and validity in two German samples. *Journal of Occupational and Organizational Psychology, 70*, 139–161.

Frese, M., Friedrich, C., & Hass, L. (2004). *Training entrepreneurs for higher efficiency and effectiveness: A psychological training study*. University of Giessen, German Report.

Frese, M., Krauss, S., Keith, N., Escher, S., Grabarkiewicz, R., Unger, J., & Friedrich, C. (2006). *Business owners' action planning and its relationship to business success in three African countries*. Giessen: Department of Psychology, submitted for publication.

Frese, M., Kring, W., Soose, A. & Zempel, J. (1996). Personal initiative at work: differences between East and West Germany. *Academy of Management Journal, 39*, 37–63.

Frese, M. & Sabini, J. (Eds.) (1985). *Goal-directed behavior: The concept of action in psychology.* Hillsdale, NJ: Lawrence Erlbaum Associates.

Frese, M., Stewart, J., & Hannover, B. (1987). Goal orientation and planfulness: Action styles as a personality concepts. *Journal of Personality and Social Psychology, 52*, 1182–1194.

Frese, M., van Gelderen, M., & Ombach, M. (2000). How to plan as a small scale business owner: Psychological process characteristics of action strategies and success. *Journal of Small Business Management, 38*(2), 1–18.

Frese, M., & Zapf, D. (1994). Action as the core of work psychology: A German approach. In H. C. Triandis, M. D. Dunnette, & J. M. Hough (Eds), *Handbook of industrial and organizational psychology* (Vol. 4, 2nd ed., pp. 271–340). Palo Alto, CA: Consulting Psychology Press.

Gentner, D. R., & Stevens, A. L. (Eds.). (1983). *Mental models.* Hillsdale, NJ: Lawrence Erlbaum Associates.

Glass, A. L., & Holyoak, K. J. (1986). *Cognition.* New York: Random House.

Glaub, M., Gramberg, K., Friedrich, C., & Frese, M. (2004). *Personal initiative training for small business owners in South Africa: Evaluation study of a 3-day training program.* Giessen: University of Giessen.

Gleitman, H. (1985). Some trends in the study of cognition. In S. Koch & D. E. Leary (Eds.), *A century of psychology as science: Retrospections and assessments* (pp. 420–436). New York: McGraw-Hill.

Gollwitzer, P. M. (1993). Goal achievement: The role of intentions. In W. Stroebe & M. Hewstone (Eds.), *European review of social psychology* (Vol. 4, pp. 141–185). London: Wiley.

Gollwitzer, P. M. (1996). The volitional benefits of planning. In P. M. Gollwitzer & J. A. Bargh (Eds.), *The psychological of action* (pp. 287–312). New York: Guilford Press.

Gollwitzer, P. M., Heckhausen, H., & Ratajczak, H. (1990). From weighing to willing: Approaching a change decision through pre- and postdecisional mentation. *Organizational Behavior and Human Decision Processes, 45*, 41–65.

Hacker, W. (1985). Activity: A fruitful concept in industrial psychology. In M. Frese & J. Sabini (Eds.), *Goal directed behavior: The concept of action in psychology* (pp. 262–284). Hillsdale, NJ: Lawrence Erlbaum Associates.

Hacker, W. (1998). *Allgemeine Arbeitspsychologie* [General Work Psychology]. Bern: Huber.

Hayes-Roth, B., & Hayes-Roth, F. (1979). A cognitive model of planning. *Cognitive Science, 3*, 275–310.

Heckhausen, H. (1987). Perspektiven einer Psychologie des Wollens [Perspectives of a psychology of wanting]. In H. Heckhausen, P. M. Gollwitzer, & F. E. Weinert (Eds.), *Jenseits des Rubikon: Der Wille in den Humanwissenschaften* (pp. 121–142). Berlin: Springer.

Heckhausen, H., & Kuhl, J. (1985). From wishes to action: The dead ends and short cuts on the long way to action. In M. Frese & J. Sabini (Eds.), *Goal-directed behavior: The concept of action in psychology* (pp. 134–160). Hillsdale, NJ: Lawrence Erlbaum Associates.

Higgins, E. T. (1997). Beyond pleasure and pain. *American Psychologist, 52*, 1280–1300.

Hollenbeck, J. R., & Klein, H. J. (1987). Goal commitment and the goal-setting process: Problems, prospects, and proposals for future research. *American Psychologist, 72*, 212–220.

Honig, B. (2004). Entrepreneurship education: Toward a model of contingency-based business planning. *Academy of Management Learning and Education, 3*, 258–273.

Inkpen, A., & Choudhury, N. (1995). The seeking of strategy where it is not: Towards a theory of strategy absence. *Strategic Management Journal, 16*, 313–323.

Judge, T. A., Higgins, C. A., Thoresen, C. J., & Barrick, M. R. (1999). The Big Five personality traits, general mental ability, and career success across the life span. *Personnel Psychology, 52*(3), 621–652.

Kahneman, D. (1973). *Attention and effort.* Englewood Cliffs, NJ: Prentice Hall.

Kahneman, D. (2003). A perspective on judgment and choice: Mapping bounded rationality. *American Psychologist, 58*, 697–720.

Kahneman, D., Slovic, P., & Tversky, A. (Eds). (1982). *Judgment under uncertainty: Heuristics and biases.* Cambridge: Cambridge University Press.

Kanfer, R., & Ackerman, P. L. (1989). Motivation and cognitive abilities: An integrative/aptitude-treatment interaction approach to skill acquisition. *American Psychologist, 74*, 657–690.

Kanfer, R., & Kantrowitz, T. M. (2002). Ability and non-ability predictors of job performance. In S. Sonnentag (Ed.), *Psychological management of individual performance* (pp. 27–50). Chichester, UK: Wiley.

Karoly, P. (1993). Mechanisms of self-regulation: A systems view. *Annual Review of Psychology, 44*, 23–52.

Keith, N., & Frese, M. (2005). Self-regulation in error management training: Emotion control and metacognition as mediators of performance effects. *Journal of Applied Psychology, 90*, 677–691.

Kimble, G. A., & Perlmuter, L. C. (1970). The problem of volition. *Psychological Review, 77*, 361–384.

Kirzner, I. M. (2001). Entrepreneurial discovery and the competitive market approach: An Austrian approach. *Journal of Economic Literature, 35*, 60–85.

Klinger, E. (1985). Missing links in action theory. In M. Frese & J. Sabini (Eds.), *Goal directed behavior: The concept of action in psychology* (pp. 311–321). Hillsdale, NJ: Lawrence Erlbaum Associates.

Kluger, A. N., & DeNisi, A. (1996). The effects of feedback interventions on performance: A historical review, a meta-analysis and a preliminary feedback intervention theory. *Psychological Bulletin. 119*, 254–284.

Koop, S., De Reu, T., & Frese, M. (2000). Sociodemographic factors, entrepreneurial orientation, personal initiative, and environmental problems in Uganda. In M. Frese (Ed.), *Success and failure of microbusiness owners in Africa: A psychological approach* (pp. 55–76). Westport, CT: Quorum.

Krauss, S. I., Frese, M., Friedrich, C., & Unger, J. (2005). Entrepreneurial orientation and success: A psychological model of success in Southern African small scale business owners. European *Journal of Work and Organizational Psychology, 14*, 315–344.

Krueger, N. F. (2000, Spring). The cognitive infrastructure of opportunity emergence. *Entrepreneurship: Theory and Practice*, pp. 5–23.

Kruger, J., & Dunning, D. (1999). Unskilled and unaware of it: How difficulties in recognizing one's own incompetence lead to inflated self-assessments. *Journal of Social and Personality Psychology, 77*, 1121–1134.

Kuhl, J., & Kazen, M. (1999). Volitional facilitation of difficult intentions: Joint activation of intention memory and positive affect removes Stroop interference. *Journal of Experimental Psychology: General, 128*, 382–399.

Langer, E., & Piper, A. I. (1987). The prevention of mindlessness. *Journal of Personality and Social Psychology, 53*, 280–287.

Locke, E. A., & Latham, G. P. (1990). *A theory of goal setting and task performance.* Englewood Cliffs, NJ: Prentice Hall.

Lord, R. G., & Levy, P. E. (1994). Moving from cognition to action: A control theory perspective. *Applied Psychology: An International Review, 43*, 335–366.

Lumpkin, G. T., & Dess, G. G. (1996). Clarifying the entrepreneurial orientation construct and linking it to performance. *Academy of Management Review, 21*, 135–172.

Macan, T. H. (1996). Time management training: Effects on time behaviors, attitudes and job performance. *Journal of Psychology, 130*, 229–236.

Maier, G. W., & Brunstein, J. C. (2001). The role of personal work goals in newcomers' job satisfaction and organizational commitment: A longitudinal analysis. *American Psychologist, 86*, 1034–1042.

Mandler, G. (1964). The interruption of behavior. In D. Levine (Ed.), *Nebraska Symposium on Motivation* (pp. 163–219). Lincoln, NE: University of Nebraska.

March, J., & Simon, H. A. (1958). *Organizations*. New York: Wiley.

McClelland, D. C. (1987). *Human motivation*. Cambridge, England: Cambridge University Press.

McMullen, J. S., & Shepherd, D. A. (2006). Entrepreneurial action and the role of uncertainty in the theory of the entrepreneur. *Academy of Management Review, 31,* 132–152.

Metcalfe, J. (1993). Novelty monitoring, metacognition, and control in a holographic associative recall model: Implications for Korsakoff amnesia. *Psychological Review, 100,* 3–22.

Mikulincer, M. (1989). Cognitive interference and learned helplessness: The effects of off-task cognitions on performance following unsolvable problems. *Journal of Personality and Social Psychology, 57,* 129–135.

Mikulincer, M., Glaubman, H., Ben-Artzi, E., & Grossman, S. (1991). The cognitive specificity of learned helplessness and depression deficits: The role of self-focused cognitions. *Anxiety Research, 3,* 273–290.

Miller, G. A. (1956). The magical number seven, plus or minus two: Some limits on our capacity for processing information. *Psychological Review, 63,* 81–97.

Miller, G. A., Galanter, E., & Pribram, K. H. (1960). *Plans and the structure of behavior*. London: Holt.

Miller, S. (1981). Predictability and human stress: Toward a clarification of evidence and theory. In L. Berkowitz (Ed.), *Advances in experimental social psychology* (Vol. 14, pp. 203–256). New York: Academic Press.

Miller, D., & Friesen, P. (1982). Innovation in conservative and entrepreneurial firms: Two models of strategic momentum. *Strategic Management Journal, 3,* 1–25.

Myers, C., & Davids, K. (1993). Tacit skill and performance at work. *Applied Psychology: An International Review, 42,* 117–137.

Naylor, J. C, Pritchard, R. D., & Ilgen, D. R. (1980). *A theory of behavior in organization*. New York: Academic Press.

Nitsch, J., & Allmer, H. (1979). Naive psychoregulative Techniken der Selbstbeeinflussung im Sport [Naive psychoregulative techniques of self-regulation in sport]. *Sportwissenschaft, 9,* 143–163.

Norman, D. A. (1981). Categorization of action slips. *Psychological Review, 88,* 1–15.

Norman, D. A. (1986). Cognitive engineering. In D. A. Norman & S. W. Draper (Eds.), *User centered system design* (pp. 31–61). Hillsdale, NJ: Lawrence Erlbaum Associates.

Norman, D. A., & Bobrow, D. G. (1975). On data-limited and resource-limited processes. *Cognitive Psychology, 7,* 44–64.

Oettingen, G., Hoenig, G., & Gollwitzer, P. M. (2000). Effective self-regulation of goal attainment. *Educational Research, 33,* 705–732.

Organ, D. (1988). *Organizational citizenship behavior: The good soldier syndrome*. Lexington, MA: Lexington Books.

Pekrun, R., & Frese, M. (1992). Emotions in work and achievement. In C. L. Cooper & I. T. Robertson (Eds.), *International review of industrial and organizational psychology 1992* (Vol. 7, pp. 153–200). Chichester, UK: Wiley.

Posner, M. L., & Keele, S. W. (1970). Retention of abstract ideas. *Journal of Experimental Psychology, 83,* 304–308.

Prümper, J., Zapf, D., Brodbeck, F. C., & Frese, M. (1990). *Errors of novices and experts: Some surprising differences from computerized office work* (Vol. 4). Zwischenbericht an das Bundesministerium für Forschung und Technologie (HdA). Munich: University.

Rasmussen, J. (1982). Human errors: A taxonomy for describing human malfunction in industrial installations. *Journal of Occupational Accidents, 4,* 311–335.

Rauch, A., & Frese, M. (1998). A contingency approach to small scale business success: A longitudinal study on the effects of environmental hostility and uncertainty on the relationship of planning and success. In P. D. Reynolds, W. D. Bygrave, N. M. Carter, S. Manigart, C. M. Mason, G. D. Meyer, & K. G. Shaver (Eds.), *Frontiers of entrepreneurship research* (pp. 190–200). Babson Park, MA: Babson College.

Rauch, A., Wiklund, J., Frese, M., & Lumpkin, G. T. (2005). *Entrepreneurial orientation and business performance: Cumulative empirical evidence.* Giessen: University of Giessen. Submitted for publication.

Reason, J. T. (1990). *Human error.* New York: Cambridge University Press.

Reason, J. T. (1997). *Managing the risks of organizational accidents.* Aldershot, England: Ashgate.

Reither, F., & Staeudel, T. (1985). Thinking and action. In M. Frese & J. Sabini (Eds.), *Goal directed behavior: The concept of action in psychology* (pp. 110–122). Hillsdale, NJ: Lawrence Erlbaum Associates.

Reynolds, P. D. (2000). National panel study of U.S. business startups: Background and methodology. *Databases for the Study of Entrepreneurship, 4,* 153–227.

Sarasvathy, S. D. (2001). Causation and effectuation: Toward a theoretical shift from economic inevitability to entrepreneurial contingency. *Academy of Management Review, 26,* 243–263.

Schumpeter, J. (1935). *Theorie der wirtschaftlichen Entwicklung* [Theory of economic development] (4th ed.). Munich, Germany: Von Duncker & Humblot.

Schurig, V. (1985). Stages in the development of tool behavior in the chimpanzee (*Pan troglodytes*). In M. Frese & J. Sabini (Eds.), *Goal directed behavior: The concept of action in psychology* (pp. 20–34). Hillsdale, NJ: Lawrence Erlbaum Associates.

Schwenk, C. R., & Shrader, C. B. (1993, Spring). Effects of formal strategic planning on financial performance in small firms: A meta-analysis. *Entrepreneurship: Theory and Practice,* pp. 53–64.

Scott, S., & Delmar, F. (2004). Planning for the market: Business planning before marketing and the continuation of organizing efforts. *Journal of Business Venturing, 19,* 767–785.

Semmer, N., & Frese, M. (1985). Action theory in clinical psychology. In M. Frese & J. Sabini (Eds.), *Goal directed behavior: The concept of action in psychology* (pp. 296–310). Hillsdale, NJ: Lawrence Erlbaum Associates.

Shane, S., & Venkataraman, S. (2000). The promise of entrepreneurship as a field of research. *Academy of Management Review, 25,* 217–226.

Shaver, K. G., & Scott, L. R. (1991, Winter). Person, process, choice: The psychology of new venture creation. *Entrepreneurship: Theory and Practice,* pp. 23–45.

Shephard, R. N., & Metzler, J. (1971). Mental rotation of three-dimensional objects. *Science, 171,* 701–703.

Shiffrin, R. M., & Schneider, W. (1977). Controlled and automatic human information processing: II. Perceptual learning, automatic attending, and a general theory. *Psychological Review, 84,* 127–190.

Sloman, S. A. (1996). The empirical case for two systems of reasoning. *Psychological Bulletin, 119,* 3–22.

Sonnentag, S. (1996). Planning and knowledge about strategies: their relationship to work characteristics in software design. *Behaviour and Information Technology, 15,* 213–225.

Sonnentag, S. (1998). Expertise in professional software design: A process study. *American Psychologist, 83,* 703–715.

Sonnentag, S., & Kleine, B. M. (2000). Deliberate practice at work: A study with insurance.

Staw, B. M., & Ross, J. (1987). Behavior in escalation situations: Antecedents, prototypes and solutions. *Research in Organizational Behavior, 9,* 39–78.

Staw, B. M., Sandelands, L. E. & Dutton, J. E. (1981). Threat-rigidity effects in organizational behavior: A multilevel analysis. *Administrative Science Quarterly, 26,* 501–524.

Taylor, S. E. (1981). The interface between cognitive and social psychology. In J. Harvey (Ed.), *Cognition, social behavior, and the environment.* Hillsdale, NJ: Lawrence Erlbaum Associates.

Taylor, S. E. (1989). *Positive illusions. Creative self-deception and the healthy mind.* New York: Basic Books.

Taylor, S. E., & Gollwitzer, P. M. (1995). Effects of mindset on positive illusions. *Journal of Personality and Social Psychology, 69*, 213–226.

Tripoli, A. M. (1998). Planning and allocating: Strategies for managing priorities in complex jobs. *European Journal of Work and Organizational Psychology, 7*, 455–475.

Tschan, F. (1995). Communication enhances small group performance if it conforms task requirements: The concept of the ideal communication cycles. *Basic and Applied Social Psychology, 17*, 371–393.

Tschan, F. (2002). Ideal cycles of communication (or cognitions) in triads, dyads, and individuals. *Small Group Research, 33*, 615–643.

Turvey, M. T. (1977). Preliminaries to a theory of action with reference to vision. In R. Shaw & J. Bransford (Eds.), *Perceiving, acting and knowing. Toward an ecological psychology*. Hillsdale, NJ: Lawrence Erlbaum Associates.

Vancouver, J. B., Thompson, C. M., & Williams, A. A. (2001). The changing signs in the relationships among self-efficacy, personal goals, and performance. *Journal of Applied Psychology, 86*(4), 605–620.

van Gelderen, M., Frese, M., & Thurik, R. (2000). Strategies, uncertainty and performance of small business startups. *Small Business Economics, 15*, 165–181.

Van Scotter, J. R., & Motowidlo, S. J. (1996). Interpersonal facilitation and job dedication as separate facets of contextual performance. *Journal of Applied Psychology, 81*, 525–531.

Von Mises, L. (1963). *Human action: A treatise on economics*. (3rd ed.). Chicago: Henry Regnery.

Vroom, V. H. (1964). *Work and motivation*. New York: John Wiley.

Weinert, F. E., & Kluwe, R. H. (Eds.). (1987). *Metacognition, motivation, and understanding*. Hillsdale, NJ: Lawrence Erlbaum Associates.

White, R. W. (1959). Motivation reconsidered: The concept of competence. *Psychological Review, 66*, 297–333.

Wilfert, A. (1992). *Die Strategien nigerianischer Unternehmer bei wechselnden ökonomischen Rahmenbedingungen* [Strategies of Nigerian entrepreneurs in changing economic conditions]. Fuchsstadt, Germany: Wilfer.

Wicklund, R. A. (1974). *Freedom and reactance*. New York: Wiley.

Zacharakis, A. L., & Shepherd, D. A. (2001). The nature of information and overconfidence on venture capitalists' decision making. *Journal of Business Venturing, 16*, 311–332.

Zapf, D., Brodbeck, F. C., Frese, M., Peters, H., & Prümper, J. (1992). Errors in working with computers: A first validation of a taxonomy for observed errors in a field setting. *International Journal of Human-Computer Interaction, 4*, 311–339.

Zempel, J. (1999). Selbstaendigkeit in den neuen Bundeslaendern: Praediktoren, Erfolgsfaktoren und Folgen—Ergebnisse einer Laengsschnittuntersuchung [Independence in the newly formed German states: Predictors, success factors and outcomes—Results of a longitudinal study]. In K. Moser, B. Batinic, & J. Zempel (Eds.), *Unternehmerisch erfolgreiches Handeln* (pp. 69–91). Goettingen, Germany: Verlag fuer Angewandte Psychologie.

Zempel, J. (2003). *Strategien der Handlungsregulation (Strategies of action regulation)*. Unpublished doctoral thesis, Giessen University, Giessen.

9

Entrepreneurship and Leadership

John Antonakis
Erkko Autio

Throughout much of its history, the domain of entrepreneurship has attempted to identify the enterprising individual. This chapter encourages psychology and entrepreneurship researchers to build on past leadership studies for development of entrepreneurship theory and methodology. We begin with a reminder that entrepreneurs do not need to convince only themselves when starting a new business: Perhaps even more importantly, they need to convince their customers, external resource holders, and their employees of the viability, worthiness, and value of their vision. Entrepreneurs need to paint a vision that is uplifting, convincing, and resonates with the desires of those who need to comply with their vision. Entrepreneurs need to use this vision to inspire internal and external followers. Entrepreneurs need to project and inspire confidence that the vision is achievable. Finally, entrepreneurs need to manage the process of organizational emergence in such as way as to achieve the transfer from a vision to an ongoing, institutionalized mode of transacting within a given social and economic context. These objectives cannot easily be attained by relying solely on the force of one's own personality traits, one's desire for achievement, or one's tendency to overestimate one's own strengths and underestimate risks, nor can they be easily attained through sheer persistence, tenaciousness, or low vulnerability. Something more is required—qualities that are projected through behaviors in daily encounters: leadership.

In this chapter, we suggest that entrepreneurial leadership is critical for the achievement of entrepreneurial goals, and that it may also be a neglected theme in entrepreneurship research. Drawing on both entrepreneurship and leadership literatures, we seek to identify commonalities between the two domains, with a particular focus on what entrepreneurship could gain from a more explicit incorporation of ideas from leadership research. On the basis of this review, we propose a speculative model of entrepreneurial leadership that gives explicit consideration to context as a moderator of entrepreneurial leadership behaviors and entrepreneurial task outcomes.

PAST ENTREPRENEURSHIP AND LEADERSHIP RESEARCH

The entrepreneurship trait research tradition described in chapters 1 and 3 has reflected, but lagged, leadership research. Indeed, the lagged relationship between the two domains has included many study design issues over 50 years. We believe that entrepreneurship researchers will gain once again by following leadership researchers in terms of concepts studied and models employed. For example, we encourage entrepreneurship researchers to recognize that the same set of personality traits and personal characteristics does not predict entrepreneurial outcomes in similar ways during all stages of the new firm organizing process. In his review of entrepreneurship studies from the leadership perspective, Vecchio (2003, p. 305) makes a similar point: "The trait approach to leadership (after failing to establish strong associations) was recognized as being limited because of its exclusion of contextual factors. At present, leadership research acknowledges the importance of (and seeks the integration of) individual-level factors with contextual-level factors in explaining differences in effectiveness. A similar approach seems essential for the study of entrepreneurship." Reviewing recent studies in the "trait" vein of entrepreneurship studies, there indeed appears to be a gradual progression toward more comprehensive models that also incorporate contextual factors. So far, however, there have been no systematic reviews of the links between contextual factors and potential outcomes of entrepreneurial leadership behaviors.

The lag between leadership and entrepreneurship research is not great. Indeed, some entrepreneurship researchers were frustrated with weak findings from their trait studies, and they advocated a more explicit focus on the process of organizational emergence (Gartner, 1985, 1989, 1990; Gartner, Bird, & Starr, 1992; Katz & Gartner, 1988), a reflection of research movement in leadership studies. Because of its focus on the process of organizational emergence, and on related behaviors, this stream of entrepreneurship research appears closest to leadership research. In this stream, attention is focused on the interrelationships between the individual, his or her environment, the process of organizational founding, and the emerging organization (Gartner, 1985). Justification for doing so was sought from received experience in leadership studies (Van de Ven, 1980, p. 86, and cited by Gartner, 1989):

Researchers wedded to the conception of entrepreneurship for studying the creation of organizations can learn much from the history of research on leadership. Like the studies of entrepreneurship, leadership research began by investigating the traits and personality characteristics of leaders. However, no empirical evidence was found to support the expectation that there are a finite number of characteristics or traits of leaders and that these traits differentiate successful from unsuccessful leaders. More recently, research into leadership has apparently made some progress by focusing on the behavior of leaders (that is, on what they do instead of what they are) and by determining what situational factors or conditions moderate the effects of their behavior and performance.

Gartner continued his focus on the emergence process (Gartner et al., 1992, p. 23) by shifting attention to the motivation of followers:

From an organizational behavior perspective, the antecedent factors that influence the motivation of entrepreneurs have typically been explored ... the primary question asked was: what motivates entrepreneurs to start businesses? ... However, when viewing organizational phenomena though the lens of emergence, the entrepreneur is likely to be the independent variable because the entrepreneur is critical to the process of changing the equivocality of interactions among a number of different individuals into the non-equivocal interaction of an organization. In emergence, the motivation equation is reversed. The question becomes: how do entrepreneurs motivate others?

The question of motivating others speaks directly to leadership. This is the direction to which they propose entrepreneurship research. They called for more explicit attention to understanding entrepreneurship, not from the perspective of mere outcomes, but as a process through which those outcomes are materialized. The focus of this analysis should be on the network of social relations, both internal and external to the firm, in which the firm is embedded. This shifts the focus from the entrepreneurs characteristics, motivations, and needs to the motivations and needs of those whose compliance is required for making the firm happen: "Instead of the profile of the needs of the entrepreneur, research could be directed to providing profiles of the needs of investors, new employees, suppliers, and buyers. Research might also explore how entrepreneurs go about discovering and satisfying each stakeholder's array of needs" (Gartner et al., 1992, p. 24). According to Gartner et al., to understand organizational emergence, it is important to understand how the emerging organization can achieve a sufficient level of social acceptance so as to secure the compliance and support of external stakeholders, such as customers, resource providers, and other external stakeholders. This legitimization process requires understanding of the varied needs of the external stakeholders, as well as an ability to craft a valuable, feasible, and uplifting vision of the tasks, roles, and contributions that the emerging organization and its various stakeholders should accommodate in order to make the new business model a reality. Internally, important roles of the entrepreneur (in addition to those already listed) include the management of expectations, morale, and the sense of equity in a situation in which the entrepreneur is going to reap the lion's share of the economic benefits if the emerging firm is successful. Thus, the entrepreneur needs to construct and manage a varied range of sometimes even conflicting visions and motivations regarding the structure, social relations, and tasks of the new venture. From this perspective, the entrepreneur can be seen as an agent of social construction who steers the process through leadership behaviors:

> We suggest that entrepreneurs create a constellation of different motivational systems to involve different stakeholder groups in the organizing process. Entrepreneurs suggest ... that certain outcomes ... will occur from the organizing process. Entrepreneurs, therefore, both seek out, as well as develop, motivations that will enable organizations to emerge. (Gartner et al., 1992, p. 25)

A similar outcome-based focus on the study of entrepreneurship is in evidence also in other models of strategic opportunity pursuit. In their model of "strategic entrepreneurship," Ireland, Hitt, and Sirmon (2003) explicitly evoked entrepreneurial leadership as a central component. In their model, an entrepreneurial mind-set, combined with entrepreneurial culture and entrepreneurial leadership, gave rise to strategic management of resources, and eventually to competitive advantage and wealth creation. They defined entrepreneurial leadership as the ability to influence others to manage resources strategically in order to emphasize both opportunity-seeking and advantage-seeking behaviors. Following Covin and Slevin (2002), they defined six "imperatives" for entrepreneurial leadership: (a) nourishing an entrepreneurial capability; (b) protecting innovations threatening the current business model; (c) making sense of opportunities; (d) questioning the dominant logic; (e) revisiting deceptively simple questions; and (f) linking entrepreneurship and strategic management. However, only two of these behaviors are framed as an interaction between a leader and followers: Entrepreneurs openly share information with organizational members to describe disruptive innovations' organizational benefits, and entrepreneurial leaders are able to communicate the value of opportunities and how exploiting them contributes to the firm's overall goals as well as to individuals' goals.

As a conclusion to our review of entrepreneurship and leadership research, we note many commonalities, especially where the study of individual-level behavioral effectiveness in organizational emergence situations is concerned. However, there also appear to be few direct links between the two domains at the conceptual level. Our review suggests that micro-level entrepreneurial behaviors constitute an area of study that may have received insufficient attention from entrepreneurship researchers. Given that micro-level behaviors are an important determinant of the success of entrepreneurial efforts, a more detailed study of this area might help shed light on the determinants of entrepreneurial failure—an issue that may not have received sufficient attention from entrepreneurship researchers thus far. Thus, the domain of entrepreneurship might benefit from a closer integration with leadership research, as suggested recently by leadership scholars (Cogliser & Brigham, 2004; Vecchio, 2003). To guide industrial/organizational (I/O) psychologists who wish to translate leadership research thinking to the entrepreneurship domain, we begin with fundamental definitions of leadership and review current leadership research.

A DEFINITION OF LEADERSHIP

Many definitions of leadership exist. One current definition that captures what we believe is the essence of leadership describes it as

> the nature of the influencing process—and its resultant outcomes—that occurs between a leader and followers and how this influencing processes is explained by the leader's *dispositional characteristics* and *behaviors, follower perceptions* and *attributions* of the leader, and the *context* in which the influencing process occurs. (Antonakis, Cianciolo, & Sternberg, 2004, p. 5, italics added)

Thus, to understand the leadership process, one has to study the context in which the influencing process occurs, along with the traits of the leader, how the leader behaves, and the perceptions of those the leader is attempting to influence. Ignoring any of these important components of the process will invariably lead to confusion and contradictory findings. For example, contextual factors affect the types of traits that might matter for successful leadership (see Zaccaro, Kemp, & Bader, 2004; Zaccaro & Klimoski, 2001). Similarly, the traits and behaviors that predict entrepreneurial success might change depending on the context in which entrepreneurship is found (e.g., traits like extraversion will matter more in the "expansion" phase than in the "startup" phase). Furthermore, supervisory leadership (in the "startup" phase) and strategic leadership (in the "expansion" phase) entail different processes associated with follower perceptions and how the leader is legitimized (Antonakis & Atwater, 2002). Thus, follower perceptions and attributions of entrepreneur actions are critical in understanding the types of actions that are linked to or representative of entrepreneurial success (e.g., see Gartner et al., 1992). This information-processing perspective has been fruitful in explaining why certain leaders' behaviors are effective by examining (a) what followers consider as being prototypically effective leadership and (b) how leader prototypes vary by context (see Brown, Scott, & Lewis, 2004).

CONTEMPORARY LEADERSHIP RESEARCH

Contemporary thinking about leadership was established by House (1977) and others (e.g., Bass, 1985; Bennis & Nanus, 1985; Burns, 1978) who introduced charismatic and visionary leadership to the domain. The full-range leadership theory, based on the original theorizing of Bass, currently dominates the leadership research landscape (Hunt, 1999; Lowe & Gardner, 2000). Furthermore, as discussed later, leadership research has come full circle, currently including elements of trait, behavior, and contingency theories in what can be termed hybrid or process theories.

Bass's (1985) theory is essentially a behavioral theory of leadership that focuses on three major classes of leader behavior: (a) transformational leadership, which explains value-based, visionary, emotional, and charismatic leader actions, which are predicated on the leader's symbolic power[1]; (b) transactional leadership, a quid pro quo influencing process utilizing reward and coercive power; and (c) laissez-faire leadership, a form of no leadership in which the leader abdicates his or her responsibility and is highly avoidant (for the development of the theory, refer to Avolio & Bass, 1991; Avolio, Waldman, & Yammarino, 1991; Bass, 1998; Bass & Avolio, 1993, 1994; Hater & Bass, 1988). Transformational and transactional leadership consist of various dimensions (i.e., nine factors constitute the model); however, for purposes of parsimony, we focus on the broad classes of behaviors. Although Bass specified certain individual differences predictors of the full-range model as well as contextual factors that might inhibit or support the emergence of certain styles, researchers largely focused on the effects of the full-range behaviors on leader outcomes.

Support for the theory, in terms of its predictive validity, is very robust, as indicated by the results of several meta-analyses (DeGroot, Kiker, & Cross, 2000; Dumdum, Lowe, & Avolio, 2002; Gasper, 1992; Judge &

---

[1]Charisma is, at times, associated with negative consequences, but it need not necessarily be the case. Charisma can be manifested in a "personalized" way (e.g., Hitler) or "socialized" (e.g., Gandhi) way (Howell, 1988; McClelland, 1975). The former refers to the use of power for personal gain and the exploitation of followers who are dependent on the leader; the latter refers to the use of power to serve the greater good with a focus on developing and empowering followers. This beneficial enactment of power is demonstrated by leaders who have "concern for group goals, for finding those goals that will move [followers], for helping the group to formulate them, for taking initiative in providing means of achieving them, and for giving group members the feeling of competence" (McClelland, 1975, p. 263). Furthermore, charisma in and of itself—even if demonstrated in a prosocial manner—might be detrimental to the organization. The "bad" side of "good" charisma would be prevalent in the case where the leader, or his or her top management team, is lacking instrumental or domain-relevant expertise, and by the power of persona convincingly leads the organization "up the garden path" (Antonakis & House, 2004, p. 9).

Piccolo, 2004; Lowe, Kroek, & Sivasubramaniam, 1996). That is, transformational leadership is strongly associated with leader outcomes. Elements of active transactional leadership are also positively related to outcomes, but less so than are the transformational leader factors. Finally, passive-avoidant leadership is negatively related to outcomes.

Bass's theory is not without fault (Yukl, 1999) and fails to address instrumental leader behavior. Antonakis and House (2002, 2004) recently argued and found that instrumental leadership, a form of leader expertise centered on the strategic and work facilitation functions of leadership, would predict variance in outcomes above and beyond transformational and transactional leadership. This form of leadership is essential for organizational and follower performance because it is centered on actions that ensure organizational adaptability, reification of vision, and facilitation of follower work outcomes.

In particular, strategic leadership (i.e., environmental monitoring and strategy formulation and implementation) addresses the "leadership of" as opposed to "leadership in" organizations (see Hunt, 1991). Antonakis and House (2002) also specified contextual factors and suggested that individual difference motives (e.g., need for power) would predict the various classes of leader behaviors. They recently found that the "big five" personality factors (i.e., extraversion, neuroticism, openness, agreeableness, and conscientiousness) accounted for a substantial portion of variance in the leadership factors (21%, 24%, and 28% of the variance in transformational, instrumental, and passive-avoidant leadership, respectively; see Antonakis & House, 2004; see also Bono & Judge, 2004). Implicit in this finding is that traits predict leaders' styles and behaviors, which in turn predict outcomes.

The success of the entrepreneurial firm depends, in part, on the ability of the leader to influence followers (i.e., stakeholders—employees, investors, suppliers, customers). Stakeholders must identify with and trust the leader, particularly because the entrepreneurial startup reflects equivocal and turbulent situations or "elaborate fictions of proposed possible future states of existence" (Gartner et al., 1992). According to Antonakis and Atwater (2002), trust in the leader is based on whether the leader (a) has domain-relevant expertise (i.e., instrumental leadership); (b) exhibits values that are congruent to those of the stakeholders, challenges the status quo for the better, demonstrates conviction that collective goals are achievable (i.e., transformational leadership); and (c) is honest and reliable in terms that fulfill his or her transactional obligations (i.e., transactional leadership).

Critical to the success of the leader and a foundational element of transformational leadership is vision, or the ability to "construct the future first mentally and then behaviorally" (Sashkin, 2004, p. 186). The vision is usually a very distal and general end state (see Shamir, House, & Arthur, 1993).

To have vision, a leader must be expert in the system—that is, the leader has a complex causal model of the operating environment and understands condition–action links (Cianciolo, Antonakis, & Sternberg, 2004). Entrepreneurship researchers have addressed some of these aspects of leadership (e.g., see Baum, Locke, & Kirkpatrick, 1998). However, being expert in the system and having a vision that is communicated and understood is not enough. Followers must identify with the leader.

Psychological theories of charisma explain why leader behavior, and in particular transformational and instrumental leadership, matters for organizational effectiveness. The first psychological theory of charisma was presented by House (1977), who build on the work of Weber (1924/1947). Weber (p. 358) referred to charismatic leaders as being attributed with "supernatural, superhuman, or at least specifically exceptional powers or qualities." These leaders emerged in equivocal and distressing situations and had "specific gifts of the body and spirit not accessible to everybody" (Weber, 1968, p. 19). For House, the charismatic leader appealed to followers by virtue of projecting an ideal future state. These leaders are courageous and have moral conviction. They are confident in themselves and their followers and set high expectations for themselves and their followers. Because the leader takes a risk by not following established norms, he or she is idealized by followers and seen as courageous. The leader then becomes a symbol to emulate for followers.[2]

This identification process is nicely explained by Conger and Kanungo (1998) through a three-step and not a necessarily sequential process (see also Sashkin, 2004). First, leaders assess the status quo, determine the needs of followers, evaluate organizational/human capital resources (all instrumental leader processes), and arouse follower interest by articulating a compelling and realistic argument for change (i.e., they use metaphor, symbolic actions, impression management, all elements of transformational leader behavior). Second, like prophets, leaders articulate a vision of the future that inspires follower action (transformational leadership). The idealized vision creates follower identification and affection for the leader, because the vision embodies a future state of affairs that is valued by followers (transformational leadership). Third, leaders create an aura of confidence and competence by demonstrating conviction that the mission is achievable (transformational leadership), by leading by example (transformational leadership), by carving the vision into strategic and tactical plans (instrumental leadership), and by providing technical expertise (instru-

---

[2]Note that although we draw on literature using Weberian definitions of charisma, the manifestation of charisma in organizations occurs in a more subdued fashion. Consistent with most neo-charismatic scholars we are discussing a "tamer" form of charisma or what could be termed "organizational" instead of "revolutionary" charisma (see Antonakis & House, 2002; House, 1999; Shamir, 1999). In its subdued form, charismatic-transformational leadership is evident in organizations and, when measured, correlates strongly with leadership outcomes.

mental leadership) and socioemotional support (transformational leadership). Thus, the self-fulfilling prophecy occurs. As the prophecy occurs, followers further legitimize the leader by associating and attributing outcomes to the leader (i.e., followers view favorable outcomes and other performance cues that are representative of successful leadership as proof of the leader's ability and gift; see Antonakis & Atwater, 2002; Shamir, 1995).

The charismatic leader is thus seen as powerful and confident and, as Weber surmised, blessed with a special gift. For House (1977), however, "the 'gift' is likely to be a complex interaction of personal characteristics, the behavior the leader employs, characteristics of followers, and certain situational factors prevailing at the time of the assumption of the leadership style" (p. 193). This is the complex process of leadership that we investigate next.

A PROCESS MODEL OF ENTREPRENEURIAL LEADERSHIP

Traits that have shown promise for their predictive utility for leadership include IQ or general mental ability (Judge, Colbert, & Ilies, 2004), extraversion and openness (Judge, Bono, Ilies, & Gerhardt, 2002), and need for power (with a lower need for affiliation and achievement; see Antonakis & House, 2002, for a review). However, simply looking at traits would be very limiting, given the complex nature of leadership. It thus seems reasonable to assume that modeling the leadership phenomenon will require a complex theory that includes traits (e.g., implicit motives, personality, and cognitive ability), important mediatory processes (e.g., skills, competencies, behaviors), and moderator and contextual variables (see Fig. 9.1). Our thinking follows recent theorizing (Zaccaro et al., 2004) and empirical tests (Lim & Ployhart, 2004), which suggest that the effects of traits are mediated by context-specific skills and abilities.

The model just described suggests that distal "traits" will predict proximal "states," which in turn will be linked to outcomes in certain contexts. In the first, and to our knowledge the only, test of such a leadership theory, Lim and Ployhart (2004) showed that the "big five" personality traits accounted for 28% of the variance in transformational leadership. Furthermore, the context moderated the extent to which transformational leadership was related to performance. (Note: This type of theorizing in entrepreneurship research is also rare. Laudable exceptions include Baron and Markman [2005] and Baum and Locke [2004].)

In a bolder theoretical initiative, Zaccaro et al. (2004) suggested that combinations of traits (i.e., configurations or patterns linked to leader outcomes; see Smith & Foti, 1998) should be examined as distal predictors of leader outcomes. Essentially the argument is that a specific combination of leader characteristics is necessary for leader success (see Foti, 2003). Also,

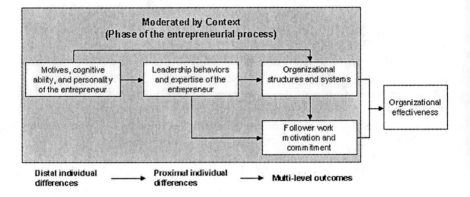

Figure. 9.1.   An integrated process model of entrepreneurial leadership.

Foti noted that taking a configurational approach captures persons as units of analysis; the units of analysis are not the traits spread across individuals. Important to note is that using this perspective entails classifying individuals according to their traits and testing a *specific* interaction using *individuals* as objects of study. Taking a variable perspective (i.e., using moderated multiple regression) would be limiting because the number of groups analyzed would equal the number of subjects (see Sharma, Durand, & Gur-Arie, 1981). Moderated multiple regression thus does not test a specific type of moderation effect, but a general moderation effect across subjects, depending on the distribution of variables across subjects.

Smith and Foti (1998), for instance, showed that when leaders high on dominance, general self-efficacy, and intelligence were compared to leaders low on these attributes, the grouping factor (i.e., the high, high, high, vs. the low, low, low leaders) accounted for almost 45% of the variance in leader emergence. The predictive power of such an approach seems to be more powerful than looking at bivariate or interaction models.

Combinations of traits, should however, be linked to contextual factors, as also argued by Vecchio (2003). For example, in the "startup phase" it is unlikely that extraversion will play a strong role in predicting entrepreneurial effectiveness because in that phase, entrepreneurs do not have to exercise "leadership" but have to use intellectual arguments as to the merits of their discovery. Thus, in the "startup" phase, traits like intelligence and self-efficacy might be very important. Similarly, need for achievement might matter to a large extent in the startup phase; however, when the leader has to delegate and influence others (i.e., during the "expansion" phase), achievement orientation might actually be detrimental to leader success (see Antonakis & House, 2002; Miller & Toulouse, 1986).

Thus, consistent with scholars of leadership (e.g., Cogliser & Brigham, 2004; Vecchio, 2003) as well as scholars of entrepreneurship (e.g., Baron & Markman, 2005), we propose that the traits and behaviors of successful entrepreneurship must be rooted in the context in which they are likely to matter, as we specify in Table 9.1. Important to note here is that mixing contexts (i.e., sampling entrepreneurs from different phases of the entrepreneurial process and not grouping subjects according to phase) will create pooled data that are not causally homogeneous (see Antonakis, Avolio, & Sivasubramaniam, 2003). Samples have to be causally homogeneous to ensure that the "relations among their variable attributes are accounted for by the same causal relations" (Mulaik & James, 1995, p. 132). If they are not causally homogeneous, it is highly likely that results will be conflicting or null (e.g., if achievement is positively associated with effectiveness in phase 1 but negatively associated with effectiveness in phase 2, and if the sampling units are equally drawn from phase 1 and phase 2, the researcher is sure to find null or close to nonsignificant results). We speculate that a potential reason for the current impasse in entrepreneurship research regarding traits might be due, in part, to the use of nonhomogeneous samples (for similar arguments and empirical results, refer to Baron & Markman, 2005).[3]

Table 9.1 is purposefully speculative and based on selective and cursory interpretation of previous research. The variables that we have selected should not be thought of in terms of a predictive theory but as an exploratory process model useful for viewing entrepreneurship in terms of a process model. What is important to understand here is that entrepreneurial tasks vary according to the context (i.e., phase), as might the types of leader behaviors, as well as the traits linked to them. Furthermore, processes should be identified that theoretically predict entrepreneurial outcomes (i.e., the traits → skills/behaviors → outcomes).

For example, in Phase 0, there is no direct leadership per se because the entrepreneur does not have followers in the traditional sense. In this situation, the entrepreneur has to convince external constituents as to the viability of the entrepreneurial opportunity. To that effect, certain elements of transactional and transformational leadership would be useful. Equally

---

[3]Another problem potentially plaguing entrepreneurial research is the fact that research samples are typically based on individuals that are practicing entrepreneurs (and thus relatively successful). As a consequence, failed entrepreneurs are undersampled, leading to the sample selection problem (see Denrell, 2003). When sampling on the dependent variable (i.e., studying only cases of success), it becomes difficult to disentangle associations between independent and dependent variables because of the lack of variation in the dependent variable. Furthermore, finding characteristics that are common across cases of success does not mean that those characteristics have caused the success—those characteristics might well be prevalent in failed cases as well. Thus, apart from controlling for the various phases across the entrepreneurial process, as we suggest previously, researchers should also strive to obtain data across ranges of the dependent variable (or to design longitudinal studies wherein all cases of success and failure have been tracked).

TABLE 9.1

Model of Entrepreneurial Contexts and Associated Leadership Behaviors

Context	Traits	Entrepreneurial Tasks		Leadership Behaviors
Phase 0: Precreation	Openness to experience Conscientiousness (achievement motivation) General intelligence Self-efficacy Locus of control	Internal Opportunity evaluation Planning Team building	External Opportunity recognition Resource identification Resource access	"Leadership of External Constituents" **Transactional** - deal making; contingent rewards and sanctions **Transformational** - intellectual stimulation - idealized influencing - inspirational motivation
Phase 1: Start-up	Conscientiousness (achievement motivation) General intelligence Self-efficacy Locus of control Extraversion Risk taking	Planning Motivation Team building Resource building	Resource access Resource mobilization Legitimization	"Leadership in" Instrumental - strategy formulation - strategy implementation **Transactional** - contingent rewards and sanctions **Transformational** - inspirational motivation - idealized influence - intellectual stimulus - individualized consideration
Phase 2: Consolidation	Need for power greater than achievement motivation Need for power greater than need for affiliation Extraversion General intelligence Self-efficacy Locus of control	Planning Motivation Coordination Delegation	Resource consolidation Environmental monitoring Competitive response	"Leadership of: Distant leadership" **Instrumental** - environmental monitoring - strategy implementation **Transformational** - idealized influence - symbolic communication - vision communication

useful would be individual difference factors that predict success in the startup phase (e.g., see Cogliser & Brigham, 2004, from which we selectively drew traits that are theoretically related to the behaviors and tasks). Note that we have added general mental ability (IQ) because it is strongly related to work outcomes across a variety of contexts (Salgado et al., 2003a, 2003b; Schmidt & Hunter, 1998) and to leader emergence and effectiveness (Judge et al., 2004; Lord, De Vader, & Alliger, 1986).

In Phase 1, the entrepreneur has to take on leadership roles leading "in" the organization (i.e., close or direct leadership; see Antonakis & Atwater, 2002; Hunt, 1991). The leader needs to be extraverted in this case, because this trait is correlated with effective leader behavior (Antonakis & House, 2004; Judge et al., 2002). In this case, the leader is legitimized by virtue of what he or she does, because followers have direct access with the leader (Antonakis & Atwater, 2002; Shamir, 1995). In Phase 2, however, where leading and delegating are important, the personality profile changes again in terms of achievement motivation, which is now unlikely to yield positive outcomes (see Antonakis & House, 2002). Leaders at top organizational levels must not be overtly concerned with their personal achievement but by influencing others; thus, need for power is probably the best predictor of success (Antonakis & House, 2002).

Theorizing in terms of processes should not be limited to what we have proposed. Other types of process models could be investigated, including the impact of leader individual differences on organizational structure (e.g., see Hambrick & Mason, 1984; Miller, Kets de Vries, & Toulouse, 1982), or the impact of leadership on the top management team (Peterson, Smith, Martorana, & Owens, 2003). Thus, researchers should consider multilevel consequences of their theories. Evident here is that constructs may operate at one or more levels of analysis (e.g., individual, dyad, group, department, organizations; see Rousseau, 1985). Studying entrepreneurship thus becomes complex because the construct may operate at various levels, which if not accounted for statistically might lead to incorrect conclusions (see Dansereau, Alutto, & Yammarino, 1984; Dansereau & Yammarino, 1998; Klein, Dansereau, & Hall, 1994).

Leadership researchers have been increasingly investigating the multilevel consequences of leadership (see Antonakis, Schriesheim, Donovan, Gopalakrishna-Pillai, Pellegrini, & Rossomme, 2004; see also a special issue in the *Leadership Quarterly*, 2002, Volume 13, Number 1)—an element of research that has hitherto been largely overlooked by entrepreneurship researchers (Cogliser & Brigham, 2004). For example, in this issue of the *Leadership Quarterly*, Bliese, Halverson, and Schriesheim (2002) showed that incorrect conclusions that might be made if levels were not taken into account (e.g., a moderation effect might not operate—hence not be detected—at the individual level but on the group level of analysis). However, the moderation effect was detected when using the appropriate multilevel procedures (see Bliese & Halverson, 2002; Gavin & Hofmann, 2002; Markham & Halverson, 2002). Finally, looking at the traits depicted in Table 9.1, begs the following two questions: "Can one person have *all* the traits that are likely to correlate with effectiveness outcomes across all phases?" and "Can a person *learn* to behave in different ways?" As regards the first question, we think it is unlikely that one can change his or her personality (Costa & McCrae, 1992) or his or her cognitive ability in adulthood (Gottfredson, 2002). We acknowledge that there is controversy surrounding this point, however. Sternberg (1998), for example, argues that abilities are forms of developing expertise and are thus malleable. Also, studies show that changes in personality can occur, particularly in affective personality states (see Vaidya, Gray, Haig, & Watson, 2004). We leave it up to future research to determine whether fundamental changes in cognitive functioning or personality will be observable longitudinally in entrepreneurs across the various phases of the entrepreneurial process. As regards the second question, recall that traits predict a substantial part but not all of the variance in behaviors. Thus, the answer is yes, it is possible to learn leader behaviors, as has been demonstrated empirically by several researchers (Avolio & Bass, 1991; Barling, Weber, & Kelloway, 1996; Dvir, Eden, Avolio, & Shamir, 2002).

CONCLUSION

Entrepreneurship as a domain of research is haunted by a nagging question: why do most entrepreneurial attempts fail? The Panel Study of Entrepreneurial Dynamics suggests that less than 50% of all startup attempts are carried to conclusion (Gartner, Shaver, Carter, & Reynolds, 2004). If entrepreneurship as a domain of study focuses on the question of how, by whom, and with what effects opportunities to create future goods and services are discovered, evaluated, and exploited (Shane & Venkataraman, 2000; Venkataraman, 1997), then it would seem important to recognize that most such attempts do not lead to either the creation of new firms or to the creation of new business activities within existing firms. We argued earlier that this omission may be due to the fact that most definitions of entrepreneurship, as well as the bulk of entrepreneurship research, have focused on the predictors of entrepreneurial outcomes, or they have tended to define entrepreneurial behaviors themselves in terms of outcomes of individual-level influencing behaviors, while sidestepping the study of what those individual-level influencing behaviors might be. This is where leadership studies might contribute best to the study of entrepreneurship. In order to truly understand organizational emergence, it is important to extend the scope of studies beyond the outcomes of micro-level behaviors to those behaviors themselves. Clearly, the field of entrepreneurship could benefit significantly from a closer integration of ideas from leadership theories and empirical research.

As a field of study, leadership has a much longer history than entrepreneurship has. Our review suggests, consistent with other recent reviews, that the domain of leadership studies has developed greater theoretical and methodological sophistication and could therefore provide a rich source of inspiration for entrepreneurship research. In this review, we have highlighted three tangible contributions: (a) a more explicit adoption of multilevel theories and models; (b) a more explicit consideration of moderating (contextual) and mediating (processes) influences on entrepreneurial outcomes; and (c) the adoption of taxonomic trait structures when studying entrepreneurial individuals. The first two points are illustrated in our speculative model of entrepreneurial contexts and associated leadership behaviors. We speculate that the effectiveness of entrepreneurial leadership behaviors is influenced by the context of their application—in this case, the phase of the startup process. The direct implication of this model is that if context matters, then pooled samples that do not control for context will mask the influences of interest. Another important implication is that as the process gathers momentum, the level of analysis becomes increasingly important, because the pertinent theoretical constructs may operate at different levels. What starts as an individual-level behavior may result in a highly complex organization.

Our general argument has been that entrepreneurship could stand to gain from a closer integration with leadership research. How far, then, should this integration be taken? Some have suggested that entrepreneurship is nothing more than leadership in a specific context: that of an entrepreneurial firm (Vecchio, 2003). We think that such a position would probably overemphasize the behavioral aspects of entrepreneurship, much the same way as current economics- and outcome-based definitions tend to ignore the pertinence of micro-level behaviors. Entrepreneurship is a hugely important economic phenomenon, and many economic structures (e.g., the venture capital) are directly adapted to this kind of economic activity. Although a more explicit consideration of micro-level behaviors would likely add valuable new insight into the entrepreneurial process, a myopic focus on micro-level behaviors might deflect attention from the broader economic and strategic implications of these processes. In this review, we have suggested that the greatest opportunities offered by leadership studies might be found in advancing theoretical and empirical sophistication of entrepreneurship studies, as outlined earlier. We hope that our speculative model will inspire further, more sophisticated attempts to understand the multilevel and context-dependent influences on, and outcomes of, entrepreneurial processes.

REFERENCES

Antonakis, J., & Atwater, L. (2002). Leader distance: A review and a proposed theory. *Leadership Quarterly, 13*, 673–704.

Antonakis, J., & House, R. J. (2002). An analysis of the full-range leadership theory: The way forward. In B. J. Avolio & F. J. Yammarino (Eds.), *Transformational and charismatic leadership: The road ahead* (pp. 3–33). Amsterdam: Elsevier Science/JAI.

Antonakis, J., & House, R. J. (2004, June). *On instrumental leadership: Beyond transactions and transformations.* Paper presented at the Gallup Leadership Institute Conference, University of Nebraska.

Antonakis, J., Avolio, B. J., & Sivasubramaniam, N. (2003). Context and leadership: An examination of the nine-factor Full-Range Leadership Theory using the Multifactor Leadership Questionnaire (MLQ Form 5X). *Leadership Quarterly, 14*, 261–295.

Antonakis, J., Cianciolo, A. T., & Sternberg, R. J. (2004). Leadership: Past, present, and future. In J. Antonakis, A. T. Cianciolo, & R. J. Sternberg (Eds.), *The nature of leadership* (pp. 3–15). Thousand Oaks, CA: Sage.

Antonakis, J., Schriesheim, C. A., Donovan, J. A., Gopalakrishna-Pillai, K., Pellegrini, E. K., & Rossomme, J. L. (2004). Methods for studying leadership. In J. Antonakis, A. T. Cianciolo, & R. J. Sternberg (Eds.), *The nature of leadership* (pp. 48–70). Thousand Oaks, CA: Sage.

Avolio, B. J., & Bass, B. M. (1991). *The full range leadership development programs: Basic and Advanced manuals.* Binghamton, NY: Bass, Avolio & Associates.

Avolio, B. J., Waldman, D. W, & Yammarino, F. J. (1991). Leading in the 1990's: Towards understanding the four I's of transformational leadership. *Journal of European Industrial Training, 15*(4), 9–16.

Barling, J., Weber, T., & Kelloway, E. K. (1996). Effects of transformational leadership training on attitudinal and financial outcomes: A field experiment. *Journal of Applied Psychology, 81*, 827–832.

Baron, R. A., & Markman, G. D. (2003). Beyond social capital: The role of entrepreneurs' social competence in their financial success. *Journal of Business Venturing, 18*, 41–60.

Baron, R. A., & Markman, G. D. (2005). Toward a process view of entrepreneurship: The changing impact of individual-level variables across phases of new firm development. In M. A. Rahim, R. T. Golembiewski, & K. D. Mackenzie (Eds.), *Current topics in management* (Vol. 9, pp. 45–64). New Brunswick, NJ: Transaction Publishers.

Bass, B. M. (1985). *Leadership and performance beyond expectations.* New York: Free Press.

Bass, B. M. (1998). *Transformational leadership: Industrial, military, and educational impact.* Mahwah, NJ: Lawrence Erlbaum Associates.

Bass, B. M., & Avolio, B. J. (1993). Transformational leadership: A response to critiques. In M. M. Chemers & R. Ayman (Eds.), *Leadership theory and research: Perspectives and directions* (pp. 49–80). San Diego: Academic Press.

Bass, B. M., & Avolio, B. J. (Eds.). (1994). *Improving organizational effectiveness through transformational leadership.* Thousand Oaks, CA: Sage.

Baum, J. R., & Locke, E. A. (2004). The relationship of entrepreneurship traits, skill, and motivation to subsequent venture growth. *Journal of Applied Psychology, 89*, 587–598.

Baum, J. R., Locke, E. A., & Kirkpatrick, S. A. (1998). A longitudinal study of the relation of vision and vision communication to venture growth in entrepreneurial firms. *Journal of Applied Psychology, 83*, 43–54.

Bennis, W., & Nanus, B. (1985). *Leaders: The strategies for taking charge.* New York: Harper & Row.

Bliese, P. D., & Halverson, R. R. (2002). Using random group resampling in multilevel research: An example of the buffering effects of leadership climate. *Leadership Quarterly, 13*, 53–68.

Bliese, P. D., Halverson, R. R., & Schriesheim, C. A. (2002). Benchmarking multilevel methods in leadership: The articles, the model, and the data set. *Leadership Quarterly, 13*, 3–14.

Bono, J. E., & Judge, T. A. (2004). Personality and transformational and transactional leadership: A meta-analysis. *Journal of Applied Psychology, 89,* 901–910.

Brown, D. J., Scott, K. A., & Lewis, H. (2004). Information processing and leadership. In J. Antonakis, A. T. Cianciolo, & R. J. Sternberg (Eds.), *The nature of leadership* (pp. 125–147). Thousand Oaks, CA: Sage.

Burns, J. M. (1978). *Leadership.* New York: Harper & Row.

Cianciolo, A. T., Antonakis, J., & Sternberg, R. J. (2004). Practical intelligence and leadership: Using experience as a "mentor." In D. V. Day, S. J. Zaccaro, & S. M. Halpin (Eds.). *Leader development for transforming organizations* (pp. 211–236). Mahwah, NJ: Lawrence Erlbaum Associates.

Cogliser, C. C., & Brigham, K. H. (2004). The intersection of leadership and entrepreneurship: Mutual lessons to be learned. *Leadership Quarterly, 15,* 771–799.

Conger, J. A., & Kanungo, R. N. (1998). *Charismatic leadership in organizations.* Thousand Oaks, CA: Sage.

Costa, P. T., & McCrae, R. R. (1992). *NEO-PI professional manual.* Lutz, FL: Psychological Assessment Resources.

Covin, J. G., & Slevin, D. P. (2002). The entrepreneurial imperatives of strategic leadership. In M. A. Hitt, R. D. Ireland, S. M. Camp, & D. L. Sexton (Eds.), *Strategic entrepreneurship: Creating a new mindset* (pp. 309–327). Oxford: Blackwell.

Dansereau, F., Alutto, J. A., & Yammarino, F. J. (1984). *Theory testing in organizational behavior: The variant approach.* Englewood Cliffs, NJ: Prentice Hall.

Dansereau, F., & Yammarino, F. J. (Eds.). (1998). *Leadership: The multiple-level approaches* (part A, part B). Stamford, CT: JAI Press.

DeGroot, T., Kiker, D. S., & Cross, T. C. (2000). A meta-analysis to review organizational outcomes related to charismatic leadership. *Canadian Journal of Administrative Sciences, 17,* 356–371.

Denrell, J. (2003). Vicarious learning, undersampling of failure, and the myths of management. *Organization Science, 14,* 227–243.

Dumdum, U. R., Lowe, K. B., & Avolio, B. J. (2002). A meta-analysis of the transformational and transactional leadership correlates of effectiveness and satisfaction: An update and extension. In B. J. Avolio & F. J. Yammarino (Eds.), *Transformational and charismatic leadership: The road ahead* (pp. 35–66). Amsterdam: JAI Press.

Dvir, T., Eden, D., Avolio, B. J., & Shamir, B. (2002). Impact of transformational leadership on follower development and performance: A field experiment. *Academy of Management Journal, 45,* 735–744.

Foti, R. J. (2003). *Patterns and variables: Evidence from leadership emergence and effectiveness.* Manuscript submitted for publication.

Gartner, W. (1985). A conceptual framework for describing the phenomenon of new venture creation. *Academy of Management Review, 10,* 696–706.

Gartner, W. (1989). "Who is an entrepreneur?" is the wrong question. *Entrepreneurship Theory and Practice, 13,* 47–68.

Gartner, W. (1990). What are we talking about when we talk about entrepreneurship? *Journal of Business Venturing, 5,* 15–28.

Gartner, W. B., Bird, B. J, & Starr, J. A. (1992, Spring). Acting as if: Differentiating entrepreneurship from organizational behavior. *Entrepreneurship Theory and Practice,* pp. 13–31.

Gartner, W. B., Shaver, K. G., Carter, N. M., & Reynolds, P. D. (2004). *Handbook of Entrepreneurial Dynamics.* Thousand Oaks, CA: Sage.

Gasper, J. M. (1992). Transformational leadership: An integrative review of the literature. *Dissertation Abstracts International* DAI-A53/08, p. 2619. (University Microfilms No. 9234203).

Gavin, M. B., & Hofmann, D. A. (2002). Using hierarchical linear modeling to investigate the moderating influence of leadership climate. *Leadership Quarterly, 13,* 15–33.

Gottfredson, L. S. (2002). Where and why g matters: Not a mystery. *Human Performance, 15,* 25–46.

Hambrick, D. C., & Mason, P. (1984). Upper echelons: The organization as a reflection of its top managers. *Academy of Management Review, 9,* 193–206.

Hater, J. J., & Bass, B. M. (1988). Superiors' evaluations and subordinates' perceptions of transformational and transactional leadership. *Journal of Applied Psychology, 73,* 695–702.

House, R. J. (1977). A 1976 theory of charismatic leadership. In J. G. Hunt & L. L. Larson (Eds.), *Leadership: The cutting edge* (pp. 189–207). Carbondale: Southern Illinois University Press.

House, R. J. (1999). On the taming of charisma: A reply to Janice Beyer. *Leadership Quarterly, 10,* 541–553.

Howell, J. M. (1988). Two faces of charisma: Socialized and personalized leadership in organizations. In J. A. Conger & R. N. Kanugo (Eds.), *Charismatic leadership: The elusive factor in organizational effectiveness* (pp. 213–236). San Francisco: Jossey-Bass.

Hunt, J. G. (1991). *Leadership: A new synthesis.* Newbury Park, CA: Sage.

Hunt, J. G. (1999). Transformational/charismatic leadership's transformation of the field: An historical essay. *Leadership Quarterly, 10,* 129–144.

Ireland, R. D., Hitt, M. A., & Sirmon, D. G. (2003). A model of strategic entrepreneurship: The construct and its dimensions. *Journal of Management, 29*(6), 963–989.

Judge, T. A., Bono, J. E., Ilies, R., & Gerhardt, M. W. (2002). Personality and leadership: A qualitative and quantitative review. *Journal of Applied Psychology, 87,* 765–780.

Judge, T. A., Colbert, A. E., & Ilies, R. (2004). Intelligence and leadership: A quantitative review and test of theoretical propositions. *Journal of Applied Psychology, 89,* 542–552.

Judge, T. A., & Piccolo, R. F. (2004). Transformational and transactional leadership: A meta-analytic test of their relative validity. *Journal of Applied Psychology, 89,* 755–768.

Katz, J., & Gartner, W. (1988). Properties of emerging organizations. *Academy of Management review, 13,* 429–441.

Klein, K. J., Dansereau, F., & Hall, R. J. (1994). Levels issues in theory development, data collection, and analysis. *Academy of Management Review, 19,* 195–229.

Lim, B. C., & Ployhart, R. E. (2004). Transformational leadership: Relations to the five-factor model and team performance in typical and maximum contexts. *Journal of Applied Psychology, 89,* 610–621.

Lord, R. G., De Vader, C. L., & Alliger, G. M. (1986). A meta-analysis of the relation between personality traits and leadership perceptions: An application of validity generalization procedures. *Journal of Applied Psychology, 71,* 402–410.

Lowe, K. B., & Gardner, W. L. (2000). Ten years of *The Leadership Quarterly*: Contributions and challenges for the future. *Leadership Quarterly, 11,* 459–514.

Lowe, K. B., Kroek, K. G., & Sivasubramaniam, N. (1996). Effectiveness correlates of transformational and transactional leadership: A meta-analytic review of the literature. *Leadership Quarterly, 7,* 385–425.

Markham, S. E., & Halverson, R. R. (2002). Within- and between-entity analysis in multilevel research: A leadership example using single level analyses and boundary conditions (MRA). *Leadership Quarterly, 13,* 35–52.

McClelland, D. C. (1975). *Power: The inner experience.* New York: Halsted Press.

Miller, D., Kets de Vries, M. F., & Toulouse, J.-M. (1982). Top executive locus of control and its relationship to strategy-making, structure, and environment. *Academy of Management Journal, 25,* 237–253.

Miller, D., & Toulouse, J.-M. (1986). Chief executive personality and corporate strategy and structure in small firms. *Management Science, 32,* 1389–1409.

Mulaik, S. A., & James, L. R. (1995). Objectivity and reasoning in science and structural equation modeling. In R. H. Hoyle (Ed.), *Structural equation modeling: Concepts, issues, and applications* (pp. 118–137). Thousand Oaks, CA: Sage.

Peterson, R. S., Smith D. B., Martorana, P. V., & Owens, P. D. (2003). The impact of chief executive officer personality on top management team dynamics: One mechanism by which leadership affects organizational performance. *Journal of Applied Psychology, 88,* 795–808.

Rousseau, D. M. (1985). Issues of level in organizational research: Multi-level and cross-level perspectives. In L. L. Cummings & B. M. Staw (Eds.), *Research in Organizational Behavior* (Vol. 7, pp. 1–37). Greenwich, CT: JAI Press.

Salgado, J. F., Anderson, N., Moscoso, S., Bertua, C., & de Fruyt, F. (2003a). International validity generalization of GMA and cognitive abilities: A European community meta-analysis. *Personnel Psychology, 56,* 573–605.

Salgado, J. F., Anderson, N., Moscoso, S., Bertua, C., de Fruyt, F., & Rolland, J. P. (2003b). A meta-analytical study of general mental ability validity for different occupations in the European Community. *Journal of Applied Psychology, 88,* 1068–1081.

Sashkin, M. (2004). Transformational leadership approaches. In J. Antonakis, A. T. Cianciolo, & R. J. Sternberg (Eds.), *The nature of leadership* (pp. 171–196). Thousand Oaks, CA: Sage.

Schmidt, F. L., & Hunter, J. E. (1998). The validity and utility of selection methods in personnel psychology: Practical and theoretical implications of 85 years of research findings. *Psychological Bulletin, 124,* 262–274.

Shamir, B. (1995). Social distance and charisma: Theoretical notes and an exploratory study. *Leadership Quarterly, 6,* 19–47.

Shamir, B. (1999). Taming charisma for better understanding and greater usefulness: A response to Beyer. *Leadership Quarterly, 10,* 555–562.

Shamir, B., House, R. J., & Arthur, M. B. (1993). The motivational effects of charismatic leadership: A self-concept based theory. *Organization Science, 4,* 577–594.

Shane, S., & Venkataraman, S. (2000). The promise of entrepreneurship as a field of research. *Academy of Management Review, 35,* 217–226.

Sharma, S., Durand, R. M., & Gur-Arie, O. (1981). Identification and analysis of moderator variables. *Journal of Marketing Research, 18,* 291–300.

Smith, J. A., & Foti, R. J. (1998). A pattern approach to the study of leader 7emergence. *Leadership Quarterly, 9,* 147–160.

Sternberg, R. J. (1998). Abilities as forms of developing expertise. *Educational Researcher, 27,* 11–20.

Vaidya, J. G., Gray, E. K., Haig, J., & Watson, D. (2002). On the temporal stability of personality: Evidence for differential stability and the role of life experiences. *Journal of Personality and Social Psychology, 83,* 1469–1484.

Van de Ven, A. (1980). Early planning, implementation, and performance of new organizations. In J. Kimberly & R. Miles (Eds.), *Encyclopedia of entrepreneurship* (pp. xxxi–xxxviii). Englewood Cliffs, NJ: Prentice Hall.

Vecchio, R. P. (2003). Entrepreneurship and leadership: Common trends and common threads. *Human Resource Management Review, 13,* 303–327.

Venkataraman, S. (1997). The distinctive domain of entrepreneurship research: An editor's perspective. In J. Katz & R. Brockhaus (Eds.), *Advances in entrepreneurship, firm emergence, and growth* (Vol. 3, pp. 119–138). Greenwich, CT: JAI Press.

Weber, M. (1947). *The theory of social and economic organization* (T. Parsons, Trans.). New York: Free Press. (Original work published 1924)

Weber, M. (1968). *Max Weber on charisma and institutional building* (S. N. Eisenstadt, Ed.). Chicago: University of Chicago Press.

Yukl, G. (1999). An evaluation of conceptual weaknesses in transformational and charismatic leadership theories. *Leadership Quarterly, 10,* 285–305.

Zaccaro, S. J., Kemp, C., & Bader, P. (2004). Leader traits and attributes. In J. Antonakis, A. T. Cianciolo, & R. J. Sternberg (Eds.), *The nature of leadership* (pp. 101–123). Thousand Oaks, CA: Sage.

Zaccaro, S. J., & Klimoski, R. J. (2001). The nature of organizational leadership. In S. J. Zaccaro, & R. J. Klimoski (Eds.), *The nature of organizational leadership* (pp. 3–41). San Francisco: Jossey-Bass.

10

Education and Training in Entrepreneurship

Jerome A. Katz

"Can entrepreneurship be taught?" is a classic question in interviews of self-made entrepreneurs. The classic answer is, "No. Entrepreneurs are born." However, ask the question of more than 5,000 entrepreneurship professors worldwide, or their millions of students, or the tens of thousands of consultants in small business development or microenterprise development, or their millions of clients, and you would get a very different answer.

The fact is that training and education in entrepreneurship represents one of the earliest and most significant successes of the modern postsecondary educational system. The impact is evident today in terms of the numbers of people taking entrepreneurship education or training. In the United States alone, nearly 125,000 individuals annually take entrepreneurship classes in colleges or universities. Another 125,000 each year take collegiate courses in the related area of small business. In terms of training, in fiscal year 2003, 687,000 people were trained or given one-on-one counseling by the Small Business Development Centers,[1] while 473,000 more received help from the Service Corps of Retired Executives.[2]

This effort in America contributes to more than 1 million new businesses a year being created, but, more to the point, such entrepreneurship education and training efforts are intended to help more of those businesses survive and profit. Although evidence is widely dispersed and unintegrated, the effort does seem to work, and that recurring result makes entrepreneurship education a key factor not only in business education but also in economic development and job creation.

---

[1] http://www.sba.gov/sbdc
[2] http://www.score.org/pdf/AnnualReport03.pdf

The purpose of this chapter is to introduce the concept of entrepreneurship education and explain its background, track record, and delivery
methods. Once this foundation is laid, a more intense and critical look is
taken at one form of entrepreneurship education—academic programs in
postsecondary institutions.

BACKGROUND

This enormous effort in training and formal education for entrepreneurship was the brainchild of pioneering researchers in college-level education, and from those roots, now more than a century old, has spread to a
worldwide network of training and formal educational institutions, who
by and large can claim one of the most closely observed and rigorously
evaluated arenas in all of educational outcome assessment.

Although the theoretical underpinnings of entrepreneurship come from
economics, with theorists such as Schumpeter, the intellectual underpinnings of entrepreneurship education come from agriculture. Small farms
have been the modal form of small business since time immemorial, and
the success of nations still hinges in large measure on the success of their
farms. Realizing that successful farms are the basis for a successful economy, 19th-century university pioneers such as Philipp Emanuel von
Fellenberg of Bern, Switzerland, developed the model we now call Agricultural Extension (AgEx).

The AgEx model was based on university classes held during the winter
for the children of farmers, with summers reserved for faculty research, and
consulting by "outreach" faculty (itinerant agricultural teachers or
Wanderlehrer) to get farmers to try the latest techniques (Jones & Garforth,
1997). Inspired by the European model, America passed the Morrill Act of
1862, creating publicly funded universities of agriculture and the "me-
chanic arts," the original land-grant universities, and the Hatch Act, which
created a formal Agricultural Extension Service. The AgEx Service was the
successful template for the U.S. Small Business Administration in 1953, and
later the Small Business Institute (SBI program) in 1972, and the Small Business Development Center (SBDC) program in 1977 (Katz, 2003). Variants of
this approach exist in the standard form for microenterprise interventions
around the world.

This approach pioneered in agricultural extension became the model for
university-based technology diffusion: a model still working largely unchanged more than 160 years later. For entrepreneurship, there are faculty
doing research and developing new approaches. There are entrepreneurship centers, incubators, and small business development centers providing various forms of outreach through expert advice grounded in research.
There are formal classes and majors. One innovation of the current ap-

proach is the development of support networks (of alumni, mentors, angels, and venture capitalists) to complement the educational and outreach efforts.

What we are talking about here is training for the *profession* of entrepreneurship. This sort of training is intended to make a person a more competent and a more professionalized business owner, as opposed to making the individual into a native entrepreneur. It is the difference between Microsoft's Bill Gates and Steve Ballmer. Gates may have been the visionary, and vision is not easy to teach, but Ballmer (the third person hired at Microsoft) was the one who organized the business to be an aggressive competitor and a small business that would relatively smoothly grow to be one of the world's largest firms.

WHY ENTREPRENEURSHIP TRAINING
AND EDUCATION IS IMPORTANT

Study after study shows that small business startups are highly risky. The current best thinking about survival rates is that about 50% of all business startups die off within 4 (Headd, 2003) or 5 (Birch, 1987) years. These statistics reflect the entire population of firms. However, when the population is narrowed to those seeking help through entrepreneurship training programs or entrepreneurship majors in academic programs, the results are significantly different.

Survival

Small businesses receiving assistance from American SBDCs reported survival rates of 90.4% after 3 years, and 81.5% after 5 years (Chrisman, 1999; Chrisman & McMullen, 2000). This study has been replicated in several states with SBDC programs using the same methodology (R. X. Cutler, memorandum to State Senator Mae Yih, Oregon Small Business Development Center, Eugene, 2001).

In one study (Charney & Liebcap, 2000), MBA entrepreneurship program graduates were three times more likely than other MBA graduates to be involved in the creation or ownership of a new venture than their compatriots in other majors (27.2% to 9%). Teresa Menzies (2003) summarized research this way:

> Eighty-seven percent of graduates from the entrepreneurship program at Swinburne University in Australia started their own business or were intrapreneurs (McMullan & Gillin, 1998). Graduates with a degree in entrepreneurship were found to have a higher venturing rate than graduates from other disciplines (Kolvereid & Moen, 1997). Another study found that several years after graduation, 40% of entrepreneurship graduates had started their

own firms, 30% worked in a family business, and 30% worked for a corporation (Upton, Sexton, & Moore, 1995). (p. 6)

In Menzies's own studies the effect of entrepreneurship courses is clear. Students taking one entrepreneurship course were compared to a stratified, random sample comparison group. Although only 26% of the comparison group had become business owners at any time since graduation, the ownership rate for course alums was 48% (Menzies & Paradi, 2002), although the business characteristics of the two groups once in the firms were little different (Menzies & Paradi, 2003).[3]

The potential for self-selection bias in these studies is very real, and finding a way to study entrepreneurship programs impacts within the natural problems of an ongoing educational program is a challenge that perhaps psychologists interested in entrepreneurship can solve. In the meantime, however, it makes sense to put some credence in these studies' results. The reason is that the control educational intervention is a reasonable first approximation of what one would expect in a well-designed study. For studies done in business school settings, both entrepreneurship and nonentrepreneurship students take the same core courses in business, which is a reasonable basis for going into business.

Growth

Although population estimates put the number of "gazelles" (firms growing 20% a year or more) at around 3% (Birch interview; see Chrisman & McMullen, 2000), the number of SBDC clients achieving such levels of growth is 38.4% over a 3-year period and 12.5% over a 5-year period. This study also has been replicated in several states with SBDC programs using the same methodology (R. X. Cutler, memorandum, 2001).

In American SBDCs, every dollar spent on the program generates $22.96 of sales growth. In the Charney and Liebcap (2000) study, MBA entrepreneurship program graduates had personal assets twice as large as nonentrepreneurship majors, and their firms had sales and employment growth five times that of nonentrepreneurship graduates.

Studies have shown that during an 8-year period, among the poorest in Bangladesh with no credit service of any type, only 4% pulled themselves above the poverty line. But with individuals and families with credit and advice from Grameen Bank, more than 48% rose above the poverty line.[4]

---

[3]The results reported here apply specifically to North America, and work reasonably well for Asian countries. The exception to date has been Europe, where entrepreneurship education has had what can be described at best as an uneven set of results (Chrisman and McMullen, 2004; Davidsson, 2002; Fleming, 1996).

[4]http://www.gdrc.org/icm/data/d-snapshot.html

Although the popular media focuses on famous entrepreneurs who did not have a college education, such as Bill Gates (who dropped out of Harvard), the fact is that most of the supersuccesses of the popular press take on someone with conventional business education as part of the startup team. For Bill Gates and his partner Paul Allen (who dropped out of Washington State University), it was Steve Ballmer, who double majored at Harvard in economics and mathematics. For Pierre Omidyar of eBay, it was Jeff Skoll, who started two companies with his bachelor's in electrical engineering and then went on to get a Stanford MBA before getting tapped as the business-side brains behind eBay. For Sam Walton of Wal-Mart, it was an economics degree from the University of Missouri,[5] supplemented with ownership of franchised Ben Franklin stores to learn the practical side of operations. The point is that education's contribution to entrepreneurship is often overlooked.

HOW ENTREPRENEURSHIP EDUCATION IS STRUCTURED

In this section we describe the four major types of structures: academic programs, training programs, peer coaching, and individual coaching/counseling. The section ends with a discussion of two very common hybrid forms, those based on providing financial supports and those providing locational supports.

Academic Programs

The typical academic entrepreneurship program consists of a core of two courses. One of these is an introductory course, which provides an overview of the functional areas of business (accounting, finance, marketing, management) refocused on the needs of new and small firms. This course is often taught using a textbook, occasionally with cases, but often with outside speakers (Katz, 1995) and some form of project or experiential component (Gundry & Buchko, 1996). The second course focuses on the completion of a business plan, often one presented to outside judges for evaluation.

Student entrepreneur groups (Students in Free Enterprise or Collegiate Entrepreneurs Organization are the biggest ones), a university-based entrepreneurship center, and often alumni groups of supporters typify the components of a modern entrepreneurship program. Part of the goal for these social groups is to connect entrepreneurship students to individuals who can offer individual advice, support and contacts.

Entrepreneurship Training

Group training is often short-term, from 2 hours to 2 days, and specific to one topic. The typical technique is lecture–discussion, with some experien-

---

[5]http://www.stfrancis.edu/ba/ghkickul/stuwebs/bbios/biograph/walton1.htm

tial exercises to supplement this. There are few consistent models for such programs, which are offered through government agencies (such as the Small Business Administration, www.sba.gov; and the Cooperative State, Research, Education, and Extension Service of the U.S. Department of Agriculture (http://www.csrees.usda.gov/), nongovernmental organizations (NGOs) such as the Kauffman Foundation (www.emkf.org), commercial organizations, and individual consultants.

Although the government programs undergo periodic evaluations and reviews, it is rare for commercial or individual providers to do so. This lack of review, coupled with the lack of accreditation or licensing standards in the area, means that the quality of training can vary widely and uncertainly.

Longer programs are not uncommon, with the FastTrac programs of the Kauffman Foundation (http://www.fasttrac.org) being the preeminent providers of longer programs focused around feasibility studies and business plans. One advantage of the FastTrac program for psychologists is that it is one of the best designed and most rigorously evaluated of the training approaches in the United States, making it one of the easiest programs to understand, apply, evaluate, and study.

Peer Coaching

One of the most common forms of training and education comes from peer groups. Organized peer groups are very common in business. Practice, trade and professional associations exist in large part to help entrepreneurs learn more about business in general and their industry, trade, or profession in particular. Often these organizations commission research and arrange for training and education programs tailored to the specifics of the group.

In addition to these larger organizations, entrepreneurs often band together into smaller peer groups to offer mutual advice. These can be formalized through programs such as the Fast Company's Company of Friends (which has online and in-person activities at http://www.fastcompany.com/cof), the President's Resource Organization (www.propres.com), or The Alternative Board (http://www.tabboards.com).

Although networking has been shown to be a powerful factor for entrepreneurial success (Aldrich & Zimmer, 1986; Alvarez & Barney, 2001; Larson, 1992; Larson & Starr, 1993), the specific activities or structures within peer networks that lead to success remain largely unaccounted. Interestingly, although peer counseling has received significant research attention in clinical psychology and counseling (Levenson & Dwyer, 2002; Murr, Miller, & Papadakis, 2002; Paulson et al., 1999), the methods and evaluations developed to improve peer counseling in clinical situations has not been applied to peer networking groups in entrepreneurship.

Individual Coaching/Counseling

One-on-one counseling and advising services remain a mainstay of entrepreneurship education and training, as they have since the creation of the extension approach. Today the foremost provider of such services to the public in the United States is the U.S. Small Business Administration (www.sba.gov) with the Small Business Development Center program (http://www.sba.gov/sbdc is the main site, although training information is best found at http://sbdcnet.utsa.edu) and the Service Corps of Retired Executives (SCORE at www.score.org) being the major vehicles for such delivery.

There remains considerable innovation and variety in this area, with techniques such as student teams consulting to businesses through programs such as the Small Business Institute (http://www.smallbusinessinstitute.org) or similar service programs (Gundry & Buchko, 1996).

Hybrid Forms

Financial Hybrids. The most typical hybrid is to include educational/training and peer and individual services with financial support. At the highest end, venture capitalists (VCs) rarely just invest money in firms. They become involved in aspects of the firm where their expertise or contacts can help assure the business's success (Gompers & Lerner, 1999). And throughout the venturing process, the VCs are coaching recipients on ways to improve their business and its returns.

At the other extreme are microenterprise operations, where small loans are made to individuals seeking to start one-person firms in depressed areas (Balkin, 1989; Daley-Harris, 2003). Here again, research has shown that loans with advising or training services are more likely to get repaid, and the associated firms are more likely to profit than firms receiving loans without training or individual coaching. Typically, peer networks are developed as an integral part of providing businesses with a business-to-business customer base.

Locational Hybrids. The most typical locational hybrid is the incubator, where startup or small firms can obtain space at subsidized rates. Incubators also include coaching services and offer training programs, access to peer, alumni, and expert networks, and even preferred access to government loans or tax incentives. As with other forms of outcome assessment, providing the training services with incubator space produces superior results to simply providing the incubator space alone.

HOW ENTREPRENEURSHIP IS DIFFERENT

An often-heard argument about entrepreneurship is that it is not a discipline in its own right, but really just a specific application of X, where X is most often economics or strategy. However, entrepreneurship's theoretical underpinnings involve four key ideas, which are at odds with the older disciplines. These differences are why entrepreneurship is in fact studying a different process and population, with different dynamics than those other disciplines. The four differentiating ideas are moderate/controlled risk taking, entrepreneurial/small business differentiation, opportunity as a controllable process, and creation as a goal.

Moderate/Controlled Risk Taking.   Economists classically thought of entrepreneurs as risk-takers, but David McClelland (1961)[6] suggested and Robert Brockhaus found that showed entrepreneurs in reality had only a moderate risk-taking propensity. Entrepreneurs don't take risks; they manage them.

Entrepreneurial/Small Business Differentiation.   Economists think of every firm smaller than the *Fortune 500* as alike, but research clearly shows two types of smaller firms: the classic small business, which provides a substitute income to employment by others, with modest prospects for growth, and high-growth ventures that start small but grow into major firms like Google or Microsoft.[7] In fact, MBA-level entrepreneurship education is based on teaching how to create and manage the high-growth business (Nesheim, 2000; Stevenson & Gumpert, 1985; Stevenson, Roberts, Grousbeck, & Bhide 1998; Timmons & Spinelli, 2004).

Opportunity as a Controllable Process.   To economists and strategists, opportunities are found, usually through a process of luck. However, entrepreneurship researchers today generally believe that opportunity recognition and exploitation are (like risk) things that can be managed and can benefit from management.[8] Pioneered by Venkataraman (1997), the opportunity approach also has led to distinctive pedagogical models (Fiet, 1996, 1997, 2001; Fiet, Piskounov, & Gustavsson, 2000; Fiet & Samuelsson, 2000; Gaglio, 1997; Gaglio & Katz, 2001).

---

[6]He did not use entrepreneurs in his 1961 book *The Achieving Society*; he did use them (or at least potential entrepreneurs) in his 1969 study with David Winter, but he did not test this group for risk-taking propensity (McClelland & Winter, 1969).

[7]See Smith (1967), Collins and Moore (1970), Churchill and Lewis (1983), Carland, Hoy, Boulton, and Carland (1984), Begley and Boyd (1987), Gartner, Carland, Hoy, and Carland (1988), Fesser and Willard (1990), Eggers, Leahy, and Churchill (1994), Begley (1995), Schein (1978, 1996), and Stewart, Watson, Carland, and Carland (1999).

[8]See Shane (2000, 2003), Shane and Venkataraman (2000, 2001), Gaglio and Taub (1992), Gaglio (1997), Gaglio and Katz (2001), Hills and Schrader (1998), Shepherd and DeTienne (2001), Sarasvathy (2001), Sarasvathy, Dew, Velamuri, and Venkataraman (2003) and Oviatt and McDougall (2005).

Creation as a Goal.   To economists and strategists, firm creation is a nearly magical event. Thinking in terms of an economy or industry, firms may *look* like they magically emerge, but the process is hardly random. The major environmental and individual factors in firm creation are known (Gartner, 1985, 1988; Katz & Gartner, 1988), and are different from those necessary for the growth of existing businesses. Today the dominant model, used in the Global Entrepreneurship Monitor (Reynolds et al., 2004) or GEM studies, tracks this across more than 40 nations, using a consistent methodology. Firm creation is the major source of job creation, which as we show later is the major force in economic well-being (Birch, 1987).

By the way, opportunity and creation compete as dominant models for defining entrepreneurship, but they share two points of commonality: enactment and resources. Several authors note that opportunities are enacted by the individual from cues in the environment (Gaglio & Katz, 2001; Gartner, 1993; Katz & Peters, 2001; Oviatt & McDougall, 2005). These enactments, called *intentions* in the Katz and Gartner model, include the opportunity to be pursued. Similarly, resources are one of the four necessary and sufficient preconditions for firm creation in the Katz and Gartner (1988) model, and the enabling factor for converting opportunities into business realities.

The advantage of the firm creation definition is that it is easily observed, robust, and has high face validity. For psychologists, this approach has a long-established pedigree, including works by McClelland and Winter (1969) for personality theory, as well as by Sarason (1972) and Katz (1992) for systems theory. The advantage of the opportunity approach is that it readily opens entrepreneurship to a large body of work, primarily in economics, which helps define opportunity, but has been in need of empirical demonstration. For psychologists, opportunity has been studied using a variety of cognitive approaches (DeKoning, 2003; McMullen & Shepherd, 2003; Ucbasaran, Wright, Westhead, & Busenitz, 2003). The entrepreneurial setting provides exactly the opportunity to take this component of modern economics and extend it in ways that make opportunity unique to the field of entrepreneurship.

With these four ideas distinguishing the managerial approach to entrepreneurship from the economic one, the field went on to develop a distinctive domain for research and education. As a discipline, entrepreneurship's fundamental conceptual underpinnings, although adapted from other disciplines, integrates them in a way that is unlike the contributing disciplines. Hence entrepreneurship intellectually proves its distinctiveness as a discipline. Even if others accept the distinctiveness, however, there is still another hurdle to cross, and that is the hurdle of legitimacy.

STANDARDIZATION/LEGITIMIZATION OF A NEW APPROACH

One way to think about the legitimization of a discipline is as seeing whether the theoretical models of the discipline change the practices in the larger world. It is evident in two ways that the discipline of entrepreneurship has contributed a different understanding of business startups. These two areas are the recognition of a high-growth model for firms in the financial sector and the focus on job generation as a benefit of entrepreneurship in the political sector.

VC/High-Growth Model

The intention in entrepreneurship classes is to posit the high-growth firm as the goal of the firm creation effort. This high-growth firm is characterized by annual growth rates of 50% or more, profit levels of 20% (preferably 40%) or more, and a strategy for dominating the market, or at least the chosen niche of the firm. Often these firms are financed with venture capital (VC) monies at some point in their existence, and the ultimate goal for the founder and the venture capitalists is the eventual sale of stock in the firm on the major markets through an initial public offering (IPO).

Venture capital describes a portion of the financing industry that focuses on providing financial support and expertise to businesses that offer the potential for extraordinary growth and returns—typically 10 times the amount invested in 5 years (a 58.5% annual return).

In practice, these high-growth firms (called *gazelles* by David Birch) are posited to represent somewhere between 1% to 5% of all businesses, depending on the stringency of the defining model. They are the true pool of firms coveting venture capital, and a disproportionate number of them come from university entrepreneurship programs.

Consider this: The VC industry is a multibillion-dollar one, with some $788 billion raised worldwide and $660 billion invested in companies to date. In the United States, there were 2,715 deals worth $18,200,000,000 in 2003 alone (PricewaterhouseCoopers, 2004). But these 2,715 deals were done among 20.9 million businesses, so that 0.00015% of all firms received venture capital funding. For startups, VC funding is only slightly better. Of the more than 1 million startups in 2003, less than 200 (0.0002%) received VC funding.

However, these rates are significantly higher among entrepreneurship programs. Although not tracked to date, reviewing the web sites of the major business plan competitions at universities suggests that around 10% of the firms making it to the competitions receive venture funding, a level substantially higher than the general population. At my own school, the rate has been 1.25% for all business plans presented, and our program has not had explicit VC involvement.

Thus for academic programs the model of entrepreneurship education emphasizing venture capital as an outcome is highly aspirational and probably intended to be highly inspirational. But these programs appear to have an exceptionally high rate of VC involvement, which supports the rare but recurring nature of this highly visible type of funding. There are several reasons that entrepreneurship course plans are more likely to receive VC funding:

- Universities often use entrepreneurship majors to develop the business plans to commercialize university technologies, and these technologies have above-average likelihoods of VC funding.
- Universities often involve venture capitalists in evaluating business plans in classes, giving their students increased exposure and feedback to VCs, and increasing the likelihood of inclusion.
- Universities often involve VCs in networking events in order to increase opportunities for funding.
- Student developed plans face evaluation and revision by faculty and expert judges, which helps winnow out projects unsuitable for VCs, and refine those potentially suitable for VCs, in effect "prescreening" ideas for VCs.

VC funds and academic entrepreneurship programs have a synergistic mutuality. The programs train future entrepreneurs to deliver the kinds of strategic orientations and even business plans that VC firms prefer to see. Entrepreneurship programs are routinely raided by VC firms seeking analysts for themselves and staff for businesses in their portfolios. This effort is supported by classes in VC and even by specialized VC competitions such as the University of North Carolina's Venture Capital Investment Competition, where MBA students compete to see which teams can perform VC-type analyses best.

In return, VC firms establish, nourish, and support ties to the entrepreneurship programs, offering expertise, contacts, and, on occasion, funding to students' startups. The rate for VC funding opportunities in entrepreneurship programs can easily be 1,000 times more likely than in the general business world, which shows the value entrepreneurship education has in the eyes of fund managers.

Job Creation as Outcome

Job creation is the modern mantra for the old concept of having employees. It has been known since the 1960s that one of the best indicators of business survival has been the presence of employees (Mayer & Goldstein, 1961; McClelland & Winter, 1969). David Birch, then an MIT professor, came up with the phrase "job generation" as a key benefit of small business startups in his 1987 book *Job Creation in America*. Birch's phrasing was critical to the growth of the field. Politicians quickly recognized that job creation meant adding taxpaying businesses and, more importantly, employees to the local rolls. Job generation became the key benefit of small business to the community and the larger economy. It became the shorthand for evaluating the state of the economy in a way that Republican and Democrat, owner and worker could understand and agree.

As a result, the modern entrepreneurship course looks at creating a multiperson organization. This can be done initially with a startup team (Stewart, 1989) of managers, or with owners assisted by a network of advisors, or a virtual firm with activities outsourced (Katz, Safranski, & Khan, 2003), or the more conventional models of family businesses or employer–employee firms. But common to all is that the entrepreneur is part of a group, even if the business looks legally like a one-person organization (Katz, 1984; Star, 1979).

NEW ACADEMIC STANDARDS

Entrepreneurship education has converged on a set of educational practices that define the fundamental approach to the discipline. These five educational elements are in some cases truly distinctive of the discipline, whereas others reflect the specific application of common practices in business schools to the specifics of the entrepreneurial process. The five elements are: business plans as modeling and entry tool; networking into local, industry, finance, and university cohorts; getting/giving expert help; team entrepreneurship; and leveraging academic knowledge.

Business Plans as Modeling and Entry Tool

Perhaps nothing is as distinctive to entrepreneurship education today as the creation of a business plan. It is widely expected that a graduate of an entrepreneurship program will create a business plan for any creation, purchase, or expansion of a business. Bankers, investors, lawyers, and even some business consultants will demand a plan before taking an entrepreneur seriously.

Today there are textbooks (Stevenson et al., 1998; Timmons & Spinelli, 2004) and courses (Solomon, Duffy, & Tarabishy, 2002) devoted to business plans, and a series of school-wide, regional, national, and even international competitions for the best business plans.[9] Business planning is one of the most popu-

---

[9]For a listing of such competitions, look at http://dir.yahoo.com/Education/Academic_Competitions/College_and_University/Business_Plans or http://50k.mit.edu/gsw/global-bplan.html

lar types of courses offered in entrepreneurship majors, and is a central component of even introductory courses and texts in entrepreneurship.

The business plan has only recently come under scrutiny in terms of its contribution to business success, with contradictory results to date (Delmar & Shane, 2003; Honig & Karlsson, 2004). But researchers admit that the business plan has established its institutional place in entrepreneurship education.

Leveraging Know How

Another key idea from entrepreneurship research that defined the contemporary practices in entrepreneurship education is the concept of the embedded entrepreneur. Although the entrepreneurial mythos has long been that of the solitary owner (Collins & Moore, 1970; Nelson, 1968; Shapero, 1975; Smith, 1967; Zaleznik & Kets deVries, 1975), entrepreneurship education has espoused a different model, one in which even sole proprietorships are organized as part of an extended network of relationships, and where entrepreneurial teams (Stewart, 1989)—be they informal or formal—are the norm. This approach takes four forms:

1. The development of "Know Who" (Bechard & Toulouse, 1998[10]), which focuses on the highly valuable process (Aldrich & Zimmer, 1986) of getting the entrepreneurship student networked into local, industry, finance, and university cohorts. Through involvement of these outsiders in the entrepreneurship programs as presenters, mentors, and judges, the students grow into their entrepreneurial role with a ready-made set of relationships.
2. The giving of expert help, which helps increase the student's understanding of entrepreneurship, their network of contacts, and their track record and legitimacy as business professionals (Gundry & Buchko, 1996). Foremost of these efforts has been the efforts to have students consult with small businesses as a classroom activity. Originated as the Small Business Institute program of the SBA in 1972 (Katz, 2003), the program moved entirely into the private realm in

---

[10]There are five potential contributing kinds of knowledge for entrepreneurship education and training: know-how, know-when, know-who, know-what and know-why (Johannisson, 1991; Lipparini & Sobrero, 1994; Malecki, 1994, 1997): (a) know-why: a form of explicit knowledge that entails the scientific or technological underpinning of the business; (b) know-what: a form of explicit knowledge about the method for applying know-why to business. This parallels Argyris's concept of "espoused theory"; (c) know-how: tacit knowledge about business processes, which comes from learning how to integrate know-why and know-what. This parallels Argyris's concept of "theory-in-use"; (d) know-when: tacit knowledge about market moves, timing, and costs (opportunity and financial). (f) know-who: tacit knowledge about key contacts in an industry, business community, and market.

1996, and today continues both as a formal program and as a set of parallel but unaffiliated consulting efforts.

3. Team entrepreneurship, in which the contemporary entrepreneur operates as a member of a team. This can be as a formal team as in the case of top management or founder groups—a situation called team entrepreneurship (Stewart, 1989)—or as a subcontracted network consisting of the entrepreneur and his or her related professionals (e.g. lawyer, certified public accountant [CPA], marketing consultant, etc.), or even as an informal network with the entrepreneur as the nexus and unpaid or equity-paid advisors providing assistance and advice. The modern model suggests that no successful entrepreneur is an island.

4. Leveraging academic knowledge specific to the needs of entrepreneurs is also fairly standardized. For example, students in collegiate entrepreneurship programs routinely use resources such as the Risk Management Association's *Annual Statement Studies* to provide benchmarks for the assessment of financial ratios and balance sheets for small businesses in hundreds of surveyed industries. The vast majority of small business owners are unaware that such detailed and comprehensive data exist, and are often shocked when students seem to know many of the most closely guarded numbers of the business. This information was long available to bankers and financiers, but self-taught entrepreneurs rarely learn about it. Graduates of entrepreneurship programs routinely not only know about such resources, but also are taught how to use and even extend them.

Taken together, these four characteristics of modern entrepreneurship education point to a model of entrepreneurship that is consistent, grounded in research, and in many cases distinct from entrepreneurship as practiced by those without the benefit of entrepreneurship education. Even for students who do not apply all of these elements, the four elements define the subtext of contemporary entrepreneurship education.

THE FAQS OF ENTREPRENEURSHIP EDUCATION

One lesson of the Internet boom is that for many people the most important part of a web site is the FAQs or "frequently asked questions." Entrepreneurship education comes with its own distinctive set of FAQs, and this section covers them. Although up until this point the chapter has attempted to operate as a resource, explaining the "what" of entrepreneurship education, and providing supporting research to help the reader document (and if necessary disconfirm) the points being made, this section is more opinionated.

Can Entrepreneurship Be Taught?

This is the most popular of the FAQs in entrepreneurship education. Many entrepreneurs believe that it cannot. No less a luminary than David Birch, who has taught in entrepreneurship classes, contends that only entrepreneurs can teach entrepreneurs (Aronsson, 2004). However, by that reasoning, wouldn't we require a clinical psychologist to have been psychotic or neurotic before practicing? Or require an oncologist to survive cancer or an obstetrician to have a baby first or a cardiologist to survive a heart attack? Does it make sense to require a lawyer to have been a criminal before practicing?

The proven answer is that entrepreneurship *can* be taught, and a wide range of people can teach it. As noted earlier in the chapter, microenterprise programs produce tremendous improvements in the success of people starting businesses. Most microenterprise trainers have never been entrepreneurs. They have been taught how to teach a model that works. Most SBDC consultants have not owned their own business, but their success rate in helping businesses start, survive, and grow is phenomenal.

Formal entrepreneurship education follows this pattern in the United States at least. Entrepreneurship professors in fact developed many of the consulting and training models used in microenterprise and SBDC training. They also developed the modern for-credit courses that launch hundreds of new, high-tech, high-growth businesses a year from our business schools. The proof that nonentrepreneurs can successfully teach entrepreneurship is evident in the annually evaluated training, consulting, and educational programs.

To be sure, entrepreneurship education can be improved through the inclusion of practicing entrepreneurs in all phases of the educational process (Katz, 1995). Many entrepreneurship professors have owned highly successful businesses—including famous professors such as Robert Hisrich of Case Western and Dale Meyer of Colorado. But virtually all entrepreneurship professors can point to dozens or even hundreds of businesses they have worked with in the classroom and the real world.

In anticipation of a model popularized by the Price–Babson Fellows Program,[11] I have taught my business-planning course with an entrepreneur as a coteacher for 18 consecutive years. In practice, there have been few times when we have been in disagreement. For example, one of my coteachers got onto the subject of "usefully passing the buck," getting others to do your work. When we started talking about it (in front of the students, who rarely see discussions among faculty), it turned out he was talking about two ideas the students were taught. One of these was bootstrapping—doing

---

[11]The website for this program is http://www3.babson.edu/ESHIP/programs/ BabsonSEE/PriceBabson/default.cfm

things on the cheap, for example, borrowing a machine instead of buying or renting one. The other was externalizing costs, where you get others to do things you would otherwise have to pay for. Fast food restaurants externalize the cost of wait staff by getting the customers to order, carry, and clean up their own food. I admit I have sought "thoughtful entrepreneurs"[12] as my coteachers, but most of the established ideas entrepreneurs work with have been operationalized and given a theoretical foundation by business researchers over the past 50 years.

There is no question that a thoughtful entrepreneur who has been hugely successful and is also steeped in the academic model can be one of the most outstanding entrepreneurship educators possible. Someone like Andy Grove, who brought Intel to dominance, wrote about *Tough-Minded Management*, and taught for years at Stanford, is clearly an example. Steven Spinelli, cofounder of Jiffy Lube, coauthor of *New Venture Creation*, and head of Babson's internationally recognized entrepreneurship program, is another.

Consider oncologists once again. Dr. Maria Hugi[13] is a Canadian physician and cancer survivor. Her knowledge of the two worlds makes her uniquely qualified to teach doctors about oncology and the process of cancer. However, the vast majority of oncologists are cancer free. Does this lack of personal experience mean they are incapable of teaching about how to treat cancer? One finding from the peer counseling literature is worth bringing up here. Studies like that of Paulson et al. (1999), mentioned earlier, have pointed out that peer counselors and professional counselors do different things. In the Paulson et al. study, peer counselors qualitatively focused on "being there" for the client, whereas professionals focused on getting done the tasks of counseling. The former provide emotional support and practical advice; the latter move toward the core problem and ameliorating it. Ideally, counselors would offer both, and both have value, but both have been shown to work. If this were similarly true for the specific case of entrepreneurship education,[14] it could serve as a starting hypothesis worthy of research.

The point of creating a discipline (and one hopes, eventually, a science) is that it makes possible a tremendous multiplier effect, so that people can

---

[12]A term for which I thank Bill Gartner.

[13]See http://www.medicalpost.com/mpcontent/article.jsp?content=/content/EXTRACT/RAWART/3718/40A.html. Other examples include *Diagnosis Cancer: Your Guide Through the First Few Months*, by Wendy S. Harpham, MD (New York: Norton, 1992). Dr. Harpman is also a cancer survivor, as is Geoffrey Kurland, MD, who recently published the book *My Own Medicine: A Physician's Life as a Patient*.

[14]The certainty of this is not clear-cut but is defended by some entrepreneurship educators such as Katz (1995), Carlock (1996), and Meyer (2001). However, some entrepreneurship researchers, such as Fiet (2001), would dispute this is possible. Again, it is a great opportunity for some research with a ready audience.

learn how to apply the lessons of the discipline to help others. The discipline of entrepreneurship has been created, tested in the real world, and found to work effectively. Learned and applied conscientiously, it can help people start, continue, and grow businesses, regardless of the particular personal background of the instructor. That is part of what creating a discipline is all about.

Can You Teach Someone to Be the Next Bill Gates (Oprah Winfrey, Sam Walton, Richard Branson, etc.)?

For most of its history, collegiate entrepreneurship education would resignedly say, "No." Although the strategic thinking and organizational skills necessary to build a multibillion-dollar empire *could* be taught, the ability to recognize and exploit the opportunity leading to that windfall was not possible. Generally the golden opportunity was seen as a complex interplay of luck and energy.

Today the answer has two parts and both are positive. First, entrepreneurship education can minimize the down side. Many great visionaries have faltered because they did not supplement their vision with the necessary business acumen. Although Bill Gates and Paul Allen of Microsoft got their friend (and Harvard economics graduate) Steve Ballmer to handle the business necessities, their biggest competitor, Gary Kildall of Digital Research, foundered on his own (Cringley, 1996), lacking the skills to professionalize and grow the business, especially in the face of mounting competition from Microsoft.

Entrepreneurship education *can* prepare individuals to develop and manage businesses in ways that minimize the chances of failure. If the person comes into the class with an idea, and is willing to take the help offered, it *is* possible to help the person bring his or her business to fruition. Without the business-side acumen, great ideas will falter, often petering out before they hit their stride.

Second is recognizing or creating opportunities. Gates, Winfrey, Walton, and Branson all distinguished themselves by identifying opportunities others did not (and then exploiting them with skill, but that was the prior point). The issue has been whether this kind of skill could be taught. For a long time, the answer remained "No." Many economic models said it was impossible to teach because it involved so much luck. But since 1997, various entrepreneurship researchers have rigorously and successfully explored the nature of opportunity, and their work is beginning to move from the field into the classroom. As noted earlier, the works of Gaglio (1997; Gaglio & Katz, 2001), Fiet (1996, 1997, 2001; Fiet & Samuelsson, 2000; Fiet, Piskounov, & Gustavsson, 2000), and Shane (2003; Shane & Baron, 2005) have articulated the nature and process of opportunity in ways that take the lead in translating opportunity research into educational practice. It is too early to declare the issue handled, but in the next 5 years, outcome assessments of the growing number of educational efforts in opportunity recognition will tell if the traditional, unteachable crux of entrepreneurship is finally susceptible to educational interventions.

Is a Business Plan Absolutely Essential?

A business plan is a document designed to detail the major characteristics of a firm—its product or service, its industry, its market, its manner of operating (production, marketing, management), and its financial outcomes, with an emphasis on the firm's present and future (Katz & Green, 2007). It is arguably the hallmark of modern postsecondary entrepreneurship education. MBA entrepreneurship majors have made the business plan the capstone of their programs, even enshrining these institutionally through annual campus-wide and even international competitions for business plans.

One result of this is that the business plan has become essential for the legitimate pursuit of entrepreneurship by business school graduates. Bankers, investors, lawyers and consultants often ask to see the business plan before being willing to take the business school-trained entrepreneur seriously. From the standpoint of social expectation, it is essential—for legitimacy and entry.

What has only recently become an issue is whether the business plan is *functionally or educationally* essential. The traditional thinking has been that plans are educationally needed. Students who do plans learn better than those who do not. By extension, businesses started by students who have underlying business plans should do better than businesses started by students who did not have underlying plans.

This latter comparison has started to be debated in the literature. Honig (2004; Honig & Karlsson, 2004) has argued that a formal written plan is not necessarily tied to success, following an observation by Duchesneau and Gartner (1990), whereas Delmar and Shane (2003) have argued that business plan presence does help predict success, following a pattern noted by Orser, Hogarth-Scott, and Riding (2000), Perry (2001), Gibson and Cassar (2002), and Upton, Teal, and Felan (2001). At this early stage in the formulation of samples, a clear winner is not evident, but it is a question that is certain to face increasing scrutiny in the future.

The idea of challenging one of the foundations of entrepreneurship education demonstrates the extent to which the discipline is results driven. This stands to reason in a discipline where the quality of the educational program can be measured by outcomes as straightforward as starting and maintaining a business. This particular situation also shows the close interaction of entrepreneurship academics and practitioners. Parallel to this debate, one of the foremost proponents of business plan development, David Gumpert—a former *Harvard Business Review* editor and author of several top-selling trade books on business plan development—published *Burn Your Business Plan* (Gumpert, 2003), which argues that there are situations where a full business plan does not make sense.

Do You Have to Be in a Business School (or Have a Business Background) to Benefit From Entrepreneurship Education?

Simply put, the answer is no. Today many programs offer two or three distinct educational tracks. Typically the most elite (and business focused) of these is the entrepreneurship track, focused on the high-growth multiperson firm. Aside from an occasional technological bent, the business model for such classes is generalist, that is, it is intended for nearly any sort of high-growth firm.

The second track is also generalist, but focuses on the general case of a conventional firm. The classes in this track are often called "small business" or a similar name. The intended businesses will typically be self-funded by the founder, often starting with no employees, and often starting part-time. These businesses generally are aiming for stable income substitution as a minimal goal, with variations of a "solid income" as the ultimate goal. For a few small businesses, eventual growth to a larger firm is the intention. The purpose of classes in this topical area is to help students apply the basic skills learned in other business courses to the specific case of a smaller and more resource poor firm. Often this involves relearning concepts intended for a large business. For example, although large firms have sufficient cash reserves and borrowing power to be able to operate for months or years with a negative cash flow, small businesses survive not by profits, but by having the cash on hand to pay bills. Big businesses managers learn to focus on profits, whereas small business owners need to learn to focus on cash flow.

The third track differs insofar as it is a specialist track. Increasingly, entrepreneurship is being recognized as a missing element in training for many disciplines. For example, many engineers are finding that they lack the business skills to build a firm around their inventions or consulting skills. For them, engineering entrepreneurship courses are being taught. The same is true for doctors, lawyers, and therapists, where practice management skills need to be learned. Even artists are learning that freelancing in graphic design or writing involves running businesses, and books such as Lee Caplin's *The Business of Art* (1998) have spawned for-credit courses that apply these entrepreneurship skills to the specific industry or profession. The example for psychology is the concept of practice management (e.g., Bennett, Bryant,

VandenBos, & Greenwood, 1990, or see the American Psychological Association [APA] Practice Directorate at www.apapractice.org).

This "entrepreneurship across the curriculum" sort of thinking has even spawned new efforts, such as a massive $25 million grant program in 2004 to sponsor such entrepreneurial curricula, by the Ewing Marion Kauffman Foundation of Kansas City. Similarly, the University of Rochester developed a new associate provost position to promote entrepreneurship across the university. In such efforts, what seems to be typical is the creation of local varieties of entrepreneurship or small business classes.

CONCLUSION: PSYCHOLOGY AND THE FUTURE OF ENTREPRENEURSHIP EDUCATION

Emotionally and politically, my mentor was the great organizational psychologist Stan Seashore. One of his lessons to me was the value of patience. The lesson has served me well, because I came into the field of entrepreneurship as a psychologist at the end of a time of great involvement by psychologists. Today there is a revitalization of interest among psychologists and those in other disciplines who favor a psychological approach to thinking.

Entrepreneurship is unusual because it requires the individual or small group to come into being. Because of this, psychological processes are central to the process of entrepreneurship. As such, people with varied backgrounds intuitively look to psychological methods to explain entrepreneurship. This is so prevalent that the careful reader will quickly discover whole volumes dedicated to psychological topics in entrepreneurship, such as cognitive models of entrepreneurship (Katz & Shepherd, 2003) or human resource models of entrepreneurship (Katz & Welbourne, 2002).

This chapter talks of opportunity, and many academics are entrepreneurs as they seek and exploit opportunities for professional, personal and disciplinary advancement. Entrepreneurship offers a forum with a considerable international audience of researchers, educators, practitioners, consultants, and policymakers. Rigorous and useful results get quickly disseminated and used. That provides a powerful incentive to gain mind share.

Additionally, entrepreneurial academics have created an exceptionally large and rich infrastructure. There are more than 45 referred English language journals in entrepreneurship, more than 150 centers, and more than 560 endowed positions in the field.[15] The opportunities for publishing or doing research in entrepreneurship can eclipse those in psychology.

The fact is also that, despite two decades of low numbers, those few psychologists in entrepreneurship have established an enviable reputation for theoretical and research acumen. Social psychologist Kelly Shaver, then of

---

[15]These infrastructural elements are tracked by the author of this chapter. The results are available online at http://eweb.slu.edu

William and Mary College, was central to the Panel Study of Entrepreneurial Dynamics, the largest longitudinal study of firm creation ever conducted. Robert Baron of Renssalaer and Michael Morris of Syracuse have made outstanding contributions translating psychological theory into critical tests of entrepreneurial dynamics. David McClelland's work still remains revered, and the career works of Edgar Schein define a major approach in modern entrepreneurship.

What can a psychologist contribute to entrepreneurship? Probably the most powerful contribution is the psychologist's disciplinary bias toward theory construction and testing. Psychologists typically have more training in theory development than business schools offer. Second, psychologists bring a set of techniques and theories that are novel and distinctive. These range from restricted availability personality tests to advanced grouping analyses and even laboratory methods.

The third contribution is a strong sense of ethics. The ethical base for the discipline of entrepreneurship comes from the Academy of Management.[16] Although clearly a good start, any psychologist would be amazed at the brevity of the academy's ethics statement and at its general lack of detail. Entrepreneurship is in many ways fraught with the ethical complexities of clinical psychology, with researchers also having knowledge that could help participants, or having complex and multifaceted relationships with companies that can be research subjects, direct employers, employers of students, network access points, and endowment contributors all at once. In such situations, not even the APA's voluminous materials on ethics provide specific answers, but psychologists are typically steeped in the requirement to consider and structure the ethical dimension of involvement from the beginning. That can only help the discipline of entrepreneurship to grow in responsibility.

For a psychologist who would recognize the opportunity presented by entrepreneurship, what should be the next step? If you've carefully followed the preceding modeling, two possibilities should be evident. One is to secure an exceptionally large amount of money for venture capital and let several schools know you're willing to have their students try for it.

Perhaps, however, an easier approach suggested by the earlier ideas is to network into the field of entrepreneurship. This is remarkably easy. Most entrepreneurship gatherings number in the hundreds of participants, a far cry from the monumental gatherings of the APA or Association for Psychological Science (APS). The major organizations are the Entrepreneurship Division of the Academy of Management (http://www.usfca.edu/alev/aom/EntprDiv.htm) and the International Council for Small Business (www.icsb.org) or its American affiliate the U.S. Association for Small Busi-

---

[16]The code can be found at: http://www.aomonline.org/aom.asp?ID=&page_ID=54

ness and Entrepreneurship (www.usasbe.org). The academy's Entrepreneurship Division has an online discussion group ENTREP-L, which is open to everyone, and can help the psychologist-as-aspiring-entrepreneurship-researcher to get oriented to the people and topics.

A final word of caution. Psychologists and others coming to entrepreneurship gatherings often marvel at the openness and friendliness of entrepreneurship researchers. This makes getting into the discipline remarkably easy, much easier than psychology. Talking to the leading researchers and educators is as simple as walking up and introducing yourself. I did this myself some 25 years ago, asking Frank Hoy, then the head of the entrepreneurship group at the Academy of Management, "Is there something I could do?" Frank smiled, and in 25 years I have not had a moment's quiet or a lack of opportunity for ideas to develop, questions to answer, or outreach efforts to undertake. To my surprise, today's newcomers report the field is nowhere near its limits. Looking back, I would argue it is an opportunity worth pursuing. Rebuttals are welcome.

ACKNOWLEDGMENTS

Support for this chapter came from the Coleman Foundation Chair in Entrepreneurship and the Mary Louise Murray Endowed Professorship in Management, John Cook School of Business, Saint Louis University.

REFERENCES

Aldrich, H., & Zimmer, C. (1986). Entrepreneurship through social networks. In D. L. Sexton & R. W. Smilor (Eds.), *The art and science of entrepreneurship* (pp. 3–23). Cambridge, MA: Ballinger.

Alvarez, S. A., & Barney, J. B. (2001). How entrepreneurial firms can benefit from alliances with large partners. *Academy of Management Executive, 15,* 139–148.

Aronsson, M. (2004). Education matters—But does entrepreneurship education? An interview with David Birch. *Academy of Management Learning and Education, 3*(3), 289–292.

Balkin, S. (1989). *Self-employment for low income people.* New York: Praeger-Greenwood.

Bechard, J.-P., & Toulouse, J.-M. (1998). Validation of a didactic model for the analysis of training objectives in entrepreneurship. *Journal of Business Venturing, 13,* 317–332.

Begley, T. M. (1995). Using founder status, age of firm, and company growth rate as the basis for distinguishing entrepreneurs from managers of smaller businesses. *Journal of Business Venturing, 10*(3), 249–263.

Begley, T. M., & Boyd, D. P. (1987). Psychological characteristics associated with performance in entrepreneurial firms and smaller businesses. *Journal of Business Venturing, 2*(1), 79–93.

Bennett, B. E., Bryant, B. K., VandenBos, G. R., & Greenwood, A. (1990). *Professional liability and risk management.* Washington, DC: APA.

Birch, D. (1987). *Job creation in America.* New York: Free Press.

Caplin, L. (1998). *The business of art* (3rd ed.). Englewood Cliffs, NJ: Prentice Hall.

Carland, J. W., Hoy, F., Boulton, W. R., & Carland, J. C. (1984) Differentiating entrepreneurs from small business owners: A conceptualization. *Academy of Management Review, 9*(2), 354–359.

Carlock, R. A. (1996). *The adjunct and new instructor's guide to teaching entrepreneurship.* Homewood, IL: Irwin.

Charney, A., & Liebcap, G. (2000). *Impact of entrepreneurship education.* Kansas City, MO: Kauffman Center for Entrepreneurial Leadership.

Chrisman, J. J., (1999). The influence of outsider-generated knowledge resources on venture creation. *Journal of Small Business Management, 37*(4), 42–58.

Chrisman, J. J., & McMullen, W. E. (2000). A preliminary assessment of outsider assistance as a knowledge resource: The longer-term impact of new venture counseling. *Entrepreneurship Theory and Practice, 24*(3), 37–53.

Chrisman, J. J., & McMullen, W. E. (2004). Outsider assistance as a knowledge resource for new venture survival. *Journal of Small Business Management, 42*(3), 229–244.

Churchill, N. C., & Lewis, V. L. (1983). The five stages of small business growth. *Harvard Business Review, 83*(3), 3–12.

Collins, O., & Moore, D. G. (1970). *The organization makers: A behavioral study of independent entrepreneurs.* New York: Appleton.

Cringley, R. X. (1996). *Accidental empires: How the boys of silicon valley make their millions, battle foreign competition, and still can't get a date.* New York: HarperInformation.

Daley-Harris, S. (2003). *State of the Microcredit Summit Campaign report 2003.* New York: United Nations Capital Development Fund. http://www.microcreditsummit.org/pubs/reports/socr/2003/SOCR03-E[txt].pdf, accessed February 4, 2006.

Davidsson, P. (2002). What entrepreneurship research can do for business and policy practice. *International Journal of Entrepreneurship Education, 1*(1), 1–20.

DeKoning, A. (2003). Opportunity development: a socio-cognitive perspective. In J. A. Katz & D. Shepherd (Eds.), *Advances in entrepreneurship, firm emergence and growth* (Vol. 6, pp. 265–314).Greenwich, CT: JAI Press.

Delmar, F., & Shane, S. (2003). Does business planning facilitate the development of new ventures? *Strategic Management Journal, 24*(12), 1165.

Duchesneau, D. A., & Gartner, W. B. (1990). A profile of new venture success and failure in an emerging industry. *Journal of Business Venturing, 5*(5), 297–312.

Eggers, J. H., Leahy, K. T., & Churchill, N. C. (1994). Stages of small business revisited: Insights into growth path and leadership/management skills in low- and high-growth companies. In W. D. Bygrave, S. Birley, N. C. Churchill, E. Gatewood, F. Hoy, R. H. Keeley, & W. E. Wetzel (Eds.), *Frontiers of Entrepreneurship Research, 1994* (pp. 20–39). Wellesley, MA: Center for Entrepreneurial Studies.

Fesser, H., & Willard, G. (1990). Founding strategy and performance: A comparison of high and low growth high-tech firms. *Strategic Management Journal, 11*, 87–98.

Fiet, J. O. (1996). The informational basis for entrepreneurial discovery. *Small Business Economics 8*, 419–430.

Fiet, J. O. (1997, June). Education for entrepreneurial competency: A theory-based activity approach. *Proceedings of IntEnt97*, International Conference on Entrepreneurship Education, Monterey, CA, pp. 25–27.

Fiet, J. O. (2001). The theoretical side of teaching entrepreneurship. *Journal of Business Venturing 16*, 1–24.

Fiet, J. O., Piskounov, A., & Gustavsson, V. (2000, May). *How to decide how to search for entrepreneurial discoveries.* Paper presented at the Babson/Kaufman Research Conference, Wellesley, MA.

Fiet, J. O., & Samuelsson, M. (2000). Knowledge-based competencies as a platform for firm formation. In P. Reynolds, E. Autio, C. G. Brush, W. D. Bygrave, S. Manigart, H. J. Sapienze, & K. G. Shaver (Eds.), *Frontiers of Entrepreneurship Research* (pp. 166–178). Wellesley, MA: Babson College.

Fleming, P. (1996). Entrepreneurship education in Ireland: A longitudinal survey. *Academy of Entrepreneurship Journal, 2*(1), 95–119.

Gaglio, C. M. (1997). Opportunity identification; Review, critique and suggested research directions. In J. A. Katz (Ed.), *Advances in entrepreneurship, firm emergence and growth* (Vol. 3, pp. 139–202). Greenwich, CT: JAI Press.

Gaglio, C. M., & Katz, J. A. (2001). The psychological basis of opportunity identification: Entrepreneurial alertness. *Small Business Economics, 16*(2), 95–111.

Gaglio, C. M., & Taub, R. P. (1992). Entrepreneurs and opportunity recognition. In N. C. Churchill, S. Birley, W. D. Bygrave, D. F. Muzyka, C. Wahlbin, & W. E. Wetzel, Jr. (Eds.), *Frontiers of entrepreneurship research* (pp. 136–147). Wellesley, MA: Babson College.

Gartner, W. B. (1985). A conceptual framework for describing the phenomenon of new venture creation. *Academy of Management Review, 10*, 696–706.

Gartner, W. B. (1988). Who is an entrepreneur? is the wrong question. *American Journal of Small Business, 12*, 11–32.

Gartner, W. B. (1993). Words lead to deeds: Towards an organizational emergence vocabulary. *Journal of Business Venturing, 8*, 231–239.

Gartner, W. B., Carland, J. W., Hoy, F., & Carland, J. A. C. (1988). "Who is an entrepreneur?" is the wrong question. *Entrepreneurship Theory & Practice, 12*(4), 11–33.

Gibson, B., & Cassar, G. (2002). Planning behavior variables in small firms. *Journal of Small Business Management, 40*(3), 171–186.

Gompers, P., & Lerner, J. (1999) *The venture capital cycle.* Cambridge, MA: MIT Press.

Gumpert, D. E. (2003). *Burn your business plan: What investors really want from entrepreneurs.* Needham, MA: Lauson.

Gundry, L., & Buchko. A. (1996). *Field casework: Methods for consulting to small and startup businesses.* Thousand Oaks, CA: Sage.

Headd, B. (2003). Redefining business success: Distinguishing between closure and failure. *Small Business Economics, 21*(1), 51–61.

Hills, G. E., & Shrader, G. E. (1998). Successful entrepreneurs' insights into opportunity recognition. In P. D. Reynolds, W. D. Bygrave, N. M. Carter, S. Manigart, G. D. Meyer, & K. G. Shaver (Eds.), *Frontiers of entrepreneurship research 1988* (pp. 30–49). Wellesley, MA: Babson College/De Vlerick School voor Management.

Honig, B. (2004). Entrepreneurship education: Toward a model of contingency based business planning. *Academy of Management Learning and Education, 3*(3), 258–273.

Honig, B., & Karlsson, T. (2004). Institutional forces and the written business plan. *Journal of Management, 30*(1), 29–48.

Johannisson, B. (1991). University training for entrepreneurship: Swedish approaches. *Entrepreneurship and Regional Development, 3*, 67–82.

Jones, G. E., & Garforth, C. (1997). The history, development, and future of agricultural extension. In B. E. Swanson, R. P. Bentz, & A. J. Sofranko (Eds.), *Improving agricultural extension. A reference manual.* Rome: Food and Agriculture Organization of the United Nations. http://www.fao.org/docrep/W5830E/w5830e03.htm, accessed February 4, 2006.

Katz, J. A. (1984). One-person organizations: a resource for researchers and practitioners. *American Journal of Small Business, 8*(3), 24–30.

Katz, J. A. (1992). A psychosocial cognitive model of employment status choice. *Entrepreneurship: Theory and Practice, 17*(1), 29–37.

Katz, J. A. (1995). Managing practitioners in the entrepreneurship class. *Simulation & Gaming, 26*(3), 361–375.

Katz, J. A. (2003). The chronology and intellectual trajectory of American entrepreneurship education. *Journal of Business Venturing, 18*, 283–300.

Katz, J. A., & Gartner, W. B. (1988). Properties of emerging organizations. *Academy of Management Review, 13*(3), 429–441.

Katz, J. A., & Green, R. P. (2007). *Entrepreneurial small business.* Burr Ridge, IL: McGraw-Hill.

Katz, J. A., & Peters, S. (2001). Understanding the entrepreneur in the growth process of SMEs. *International Journal of Entrepreneurship and Innovation Management, 1*(3/4), 366–380.

Katz, J. A., Safranski, S. R., & Khan, O. (2003). Virtual instant global entrepreneurship: Cybermediation for Born International Service Firms. *Journal of International Entrepreneurship*, *1*, 43–57.

Katz, J. A., & Shepherd, D. A. (2003). *Advances in the study of entrepreneurship firm emergence and growth, Vol. 6, Cognitive Approaches to Entrepreneurship Research*. Amsterdam: Elsevier/JAI Press.

Katz, J. A., & Welbourne, T. (Eds.). (2002). *Advances in the study of entrepreneurship firm emergence and growth, Vol. 5, Managing People in Entrepreneurial Organizations*. Greenwich, CT: JAI Press.

Kolvereid, L., & Moen, O. (1997). Entrepreneurship among business graduates: Does a major in entrepreneurship make a difference? *Journal of European Industrial Training, 21*(4), 154–160.

Larson, A. (1992). Network dyads in entrepreneurial settings: A study of the governance of exchange relationships. *Administrative Science Quarterly, 37*, 76–104.

Larson, A. & Starr, J. A. (1993). A network model of organization formation. *Entrepreneurship Theory & Practice, 1993*, 5–15.

Levenson, R. L., Jr., & Dwyer, L. A. (2002). Peer Support in law enforcement: Past, present, and future. *International Journal of Emergency Mental Health, 5*(3), 147–152.

Lipparini, A., & Sobrero, M. (1994). The glue and the pieces: Entrepreneurship and innovation in small-firm networks. *Journal of Business Venturing, 9*, 125–140.

Malecki, E. (1994). Entrepreneurship in regional and local development. *International Review of Regional Science, 16*(1–2), 119–153.

Malecki, E. (1997). Entrepreneurs, networks, and economic development: A review of recent research. In J. A. Katz (Ed.), *Advances in entrepreneurship, firm emergence and growth* (Vol. 3, pp. 57–118). Greenwich, CT: JAI Press.

Mayer, K. B., & Goldstein, S. (1961). *The first two years: Problems of small firm growth and survival*. Washington, DC: Small Business Administration.

McClelland, D. (1961). *The achieving society*. New York: Free Press.

McClelland, D., & Winter, D. (1969). *Motivating economic achievement*. New York: Free Press.

McMullan, W. E., & Gillin, L. M. (1998). Entrepreneurship education: Developing technological start-up entrepreneurs. A case study of a graduate entrepreneurship programme at Swinburne University. *Technovation, 18*(4), 275–286.

McMullen, J. S., & Shepherd, D. A. (2003). Extending the theory of the entrepreneur using a signal detection framework. In J. A. Katz & D. Shepherd (Eds.), *Advances in entrepreneurship, firm emergence and growth* (Vol. 6, pp. 139–180).Greenwich, CT: JAI Press.

Menzies, T. V. (2003). 21st Century pragmatism: Universities and entrepreneurship education and development, Keynote address. *Proceedings of the ICSB 48th World Conference*, Belfast. http://www.sbaer.uca.edu/Research/ICSB/2003/papers/10.doc, accessed February 4, 2006.

Menzies, T. V., & Paradi, J. C. (2002). Encouraging technology-based ventures: Entrepreneurship education and engineering graduates. *New England Journal of Entrepreneurship, 5*(2), 57–64.

Menzies, T. V., & Paradi, J. C. (2003). Entrepreneurship education and engineering students: Career path and business performance. *International Journal of Entrepreneurship and Innovation, 6*(2), 85–96.

Meyer, G. D. (2001, February). *Major unresolved issues and opportunities in entrepreneurship education*. Coleman White Paper Address. Presented at the 2001 USASBE/SBIDA Joint National Conference, Orlando, FL. http://www.usasbe.org/pdf/CWP-2001-meyer.pdf, accessed February 4, 2006.

Murr, A. H, Miller, C., & Papadakis, M. (2002). Mentorship through advisory colleges. *Academic Medicine, 77*(11), 1172–1173.

Nelson, J. I. (1968). Participation and integration: The case of the small businessman. *American Sociological Review, 33*(3), 427–438.

Nesheim, J. L. (2000). *High tech start up: The complete handbook for creating successful new high tech companies*. New York: Free Press.

Orser, B. J., Hogarth-Scott, S., & Riding, A. L. (2000). Performance, firm size, and management problem solving. *Journal of Small Business Management, 38*(4), 42–58.

Oviatt, B. M., & McDougall, P. P. (2005). Toward a theory of international new ventures. *Journal of International Business Studies, 36,* 29–41.

Paulson, R., Herinckx, H., Demmler, J., Clarke, G., Cutler, D., & Birecree, E. (1999). Comparing practice patterns of consumer and non-consumer mental health service providers. *Community Mental Health Journal, 35*(3), 251–269.

Perry, S. C. (2001). The relationship between written business plans and the failure of small businesses in the U.S. *Journal of Small Business Management, 39*(3) 201–209.

PricewaterhouseCoopers. (2004). *MoneyTree Survey, Full-year and Q4 2003 results—US report.* http://www.pwcmoneytree.com/exhibits/Q403MoneyTreeReport.pdf, accessed

Reynolds, P. D., Bygrave, W. D., Autio, E., Arenius, P., Fitzsimons, P., Minniti, M., Murray, S., O'Goran, C., & Roche, F. (2004). *Global Entrepreneurship Monitor 2003 executive report.* Wellesley, MA: Babson College. http://www.gemconsortium.org/download/1091049929218/FINALExecutiveReport.pdf, accessed February 4, 2006.

Sarason, S. B. (1972). *The creation of settings and the future societies.* San Francisco: Jossey-Bass.

Sarasvathy, S. (2001). Causation and effectuation: towards a theoretical shift from economic inevitability to entrepreneurial contingency. *Academy of Management Review, 26*(2), 243–288.

Sarasvathy, S., Dew, N., Velamuri, R., & Venkataraman, S. (2003). Three views of entrepreneurial opportunity. In Z. J. Acs & D. B. Audretsch (Eds.), *Handbook of entrepreneurship research* (pp. 141–160). Dordrecht: Kluwer.

Schein, E. H. (1978). *Career dynamics: Matching individual and organizational needs.* Reading, MA: Addison-Wesley.

Schein, E. H. (1996). Career anchors revised: Implications for career development in the 21st century. *Academy of Management Executive, 10*(4), 80–88.

Shane, S. (2000). Prior knowledge and the discovery of entrepreneurial opportunities. *Organizational Science, 11,* 448–469.

Shane, S. (2003). *A general theory of entrepreneurship: The individual–opportunity nexus.* Cheltenham, UK: Edward Elgar.

Shane, S. A., & Baron, R. A. (2005). *Entrepreneurship: A process perspective.* Mason, OH: Southwestern/Thompson.

Shane, S., & Venkataraman, S. (2000). The promise of entrepreneurship as a field of research. *Academy of Management Review, 25*(1), 217–226.

Shane, S., & Venkataraman, S. (2001). Entrepreneurship as a field of research: A response to Zahra and Dess, Singh, and Erikson. *Academy of Management Review, 26*(1), 13–16.

Shapero, A. (1975). The displaced, uncomfortable entrepreneur. *Psychology Today, 9,* 83–88.

Shepherd, D., & DeTienne, D. (2001). Discovery of opportunities: Anomalies, accumulation and alertness. In W. D. Bygrave, E. Autio, C. G. Brush, P. Davidsson, P. G. Greene, P. D. Reynolds, & H. J. Sapienza (Eds.), *Frontiers of entrepreneurship reseach (2001)* (pp. 138–148). Wellesley, MA: Babson College.

Smith, N. R. (1967). *The entrepreneur and his firm: The relationship between man and type of company.* East Lansing: Michigan State University.

Solomon, G., Duffy, S., & Tarabishy, A. (2002). The state of entrepreneurship education in the United States: A nationwide survey and analysis. *International Journal of Entrepreneurship Education, 1,* 1–22. http://www.senatehall.com/paper.php?article=19, accessed February 4, 2006.

Star, A. D. (1979). Estimates of the number of quasi and small businesses, 1948 to 1972. *American Journal of Small Business, 4*(2), 44–52.

Stevenson, H. H., & Gumpert, D. E. (1985, March–April). The heart of entrepreneurship. *Harvard Business Review*, pp. 85–94.

Stevenson, H. H., Roberts, M. J., Grousbeck, H. I., & Bhide, A. V. (1998). *New business ventures and the entrepreneur* (5th ed.). Burr Ridge, IL: Irwin Press.

Stewart, A. (1989). *Team entrepreneurship.* Newbury Park, CA: Sage.

Stewart, W. H., Jr., Watson, W. E., Carland, J. C., & Carland, J. W. (1999). A proclivity for entrepreneurship: a comparison of entrepreneurs, small business owners, and corporate managers. *Journal of Business Venturing, 14*(2), 189–214.

Timmons, J. A., & Spinelli, S. (2004). *New venture creation: Entrepreneurship for the 21st century* (6th ed.). Burr Ridge, IL: Irwin McGraw-Hill.

Ucbasaran, D., Wright, M., Westhead, P., & Busenitz, L. (2003). The impact of entrepreneurial experience on opportunity identification and exploitation: habitual and novice entrepreneurs. In J. A. Katz & D. Shepherd (Eds.), *Advances in entrepreneurship, firm emergence and growth* (Vol. 6, pp. 231–264).Greenwich, CT: JAI Press.

Upton, N. B., Sexton, D. L., & Moore, C. (1995). Have we made a difference? An examination of career activity of entrepreneurship majors since 1981 (Abstract). In *Frontiers of entrepreneurship research, 1995 Edition* (pp. 727–728).

Upton, N., Teal, E. J., & Felan, J. T. Strategic and business planning practices of fast growth family firms. *Journal of Small Business Management, 39*(1), 60–72.

Venkataraman, S. (1997). The distinctive domain of entrepreneurship research. In J. A. Katz (Ed.), *Advances in entrepreneurship, firm emergence and growth* (Vol. 3, pp. 119–138).Greenwich, CT: JAI Press.

Zaleznik, A., & Kets de Vries, M. F. R. (1975) *Power and the corporate mind.* Boston: Houghton Mifflin, 1975.

11

Intrapreneurship and Innovation[1]

G. Tom Lumpkin

Although the term *entrepreneurship* is usually associated with new ventures and organizational start-ups, it is also used to represent an important function within existing organizations (Stevenson & Jarillo, 1990). Before entrepreneurship emerged as a distinct research domain, strategy scholars Miles and Snow (1978) noted that the "entrepreneurial problem" faced by many going concerns was to address the basic question of what new directions a firm should consider and what new businesses it should enter. The answer to this question helped determine the firm's domain and guided its product–market relationships and resource deployments. Such efforts are essential because they propel firms forward by providing new opportunities for growth and development. Thus, corporate entrepreneurship (Guth & Ginsberg, 1990) and internal corporate venturing (Burgelman, 1983) represent important strategic activities within the context of existing firms.

In 1985, Gifford Pinchot coined the word *intrapreneuring* to represent this type of within-firm entrepreneurial activity. Pinchot described intrapreneurs as "those who take hands-on responsibility for creating innovation of any kind within an organization" (p. xi). Thus the term *intrapreneurship* has been linked to innovation since the word first came into use. Innovation and intrapreneurship are similar in that they both involve processes in which resources are combined to create something new and the intent of both is to generate profits. They differ, in part, in terms of level of analysis. That is, intrapreneurship typically represents an organizational-level effort to organize and manage an internally generated venture. An innovation, by contrast, is usually more specific in that it refers to the radical departure or significant improvement of a product or process. Thus, company-wide or

[1]The author thanks Greg Dess and Lou Marino for their helpful suggestions on earlier drafts of this chapter.

departmental-level intrapreneurial efforts are often aimed at launching or implementing new innovations that arise from the research and development efforts of individuals or teams.

Innovation involves using new or existing knowledge to transform organizational processes or create commercially viable products and services (Damanpour, 1991; Utterback & Abernathy, 1975). The sources of new knowledge may include the latest technology, the results of experiments, creative insights, or competitive information. Innovation may also involve using existing knowledge in new combinations such as applications of existing technologies in new domains. However it comes about, innovation occurs when new combinations of ideas and information can be used to meet customer needs or the demands of new and emergent markets in ways that are commercially viable (Christensen & Bower, 1996; Tushman & O'Reilly, 1997).

The emphasis on newness is a central point. The root of the word innovation is the Latin *novus*, which means new. It is the element of newness that makes innovation something more than mere change (Johannessen, Olsen, & Lumpkin, 2001). Innovation involves introducing or changing to something new.

The innovation process keeps firms alert by exposing them to new technologies, making them aware of marketplace trends, and helping them evaluate new possibilities. Intrapreneurial firms use the fruits of the innovation process to help firms build new sources of competitive advantage and renew their value propositions (Brown & Eisenhardt, 1998; Hamel, 2000). Just as innovation helps firms make positive improvements, corporate entrepreneurship helps firms identify opportunities and launch new ventures.

The focus of this chapter is on the links between innovation and entrepreneurship within existing organizations. First, the impediments to innovation are considered, including three common barriers—systemic, behavioral, and political—as well as five dilemmas of innovation identified by Sharma (1999). Then several activities that firms use to overcome barriers and resolve innovation dilemmas are introduced. Next, the role of entrepreneurial orientation (EO) in improving the effectiveness of intrapreneurial firms is addressed. This section also examines how five management roles and/or practices—product champions, organizational learning, opportunity recognition, "exit" champions, and real options analysis—can enhance a firm's intrapreneurial efforts. Finally, avenues for future research in innovation and intrapreneurship are discussed.

IMPEDIMENTS TO EFFECTIVE INNOVATION

Innovation is essential to sustaining competitive advantages (Stopford & Baden-Fuller, 1994). The extent and success of a company's innovation efforts are also indicators of its overall performance (Tushman & O'Reilly, 1997). Thus, only those companies that actively pursue innovation, even though it is often difficult and uncertain, will get a payoff from their innovation efforts (Hamel, 2000).

As with change, however, firms are often resistant to innovation (Christensen, 1997; Leonard-Barton, 1992; Van de Ven, 1986). In addition, managing innovation can be very challenging. What makes innovation so difficult? Clearly, the uncertainty about outcomes is one factor. Companies are often reluctant to invest time and resources into activities with an unknown future. Innovation also requires organizations to make tough choices, and firms often develop internal barriers to change that make those choices even more difficult. As former Pfizer chairman and chief executive officer (CEO) William Steere (Steere & Niblack, 1997) put it, "Managing innovation is analogous to breaking in a spirited horse. You are never sure of success until you achieve your goal. In the meantime, everyone takes a few lumps" (p. 128).

Innovation is demanding in part because it requires organizations to focus on the external environment and stay attuned to technological trends, competitive advances, and shifts in consumer demands. Often, however, organizations that want to innovate and/or grow via intrapreneurship face powerful internal impediments that block their progress. In the next two subsections, two different impediments to effective innovation are discussed. First, three types of organization barriers are addressed—systemic, behavioral and political. Then, five innovation dilemmas that organizations confront when faced with alternative innovation choices are presented.

Barriers to Innovation

Organizations often develop high levels of competency in a few key areas (D. Miller, 1990, 1993). Their ability to perform well in a particular market segment or to leverage a technology provides a competitive advantage, at least temporarily. They may establish organization routines and production efficiencies in support of their competitive strengths (Nelson & Winter, 1982). Power relationships are formed and internal alliances are instituted (Burgelman & Doz, 2001; Ibarra, 1993). These factors affect individuals, teams, departments, and whole organizations.

Over time, however, such organizations often develop a sort of inertia that makes it difficult to break out of their "comfort zone" and try new things. As a result, barriers to innovation and intrapreneurship develop (Lorange & Murphy, 1984). Even companies that are trying to make good decisions and act responsibly often make choices that obstruct their ability to innovate (Christensen, 1997). Here, several of these barriers to effective innovation are addressed.

Systemic Barriers.   The systems that determine how business is conducted in an organization often become bogged down. For example, the reporting requirements and/or authority relationships that stem from an organization's structure may impede the flow of information. This, in turn, slows down information processing or prevents entities within an organization from getting information that might be useful to effective decision making (Kanter, 1983; Tushman & Nadler, 1978). Another consequence is that becoming bogged down impairs or prevents organizational learning, which may inhibit innovation or cause organizations to repeat the same mistakes (McGrath, 1999; Lant, Milliken, & Batra, 1992).

Bureaucratic rules and outdated procedures can also create conditions that make it difficult for organizations to change (Galbraith, 1982; Lawler, 1996). As a result, the mechanisms of innovation, which rely on communication flows and interaction across organization boundaries to draw together insights from many domains, may be inhibited even in organizations where there is a strong impetus to pursue intrapreneurial goals.

Behavioral Barriers.   Innovation is often impeded when organization members view situations from a biased or limited perspective. For example, "silo thinking" is a kind of bias that occurs when managers and workers in a particular functional area tend to focus exclusively on the role(s) they perform without taking other important functions into consideration (Tucker, 2002). These views may be related to the education, work experience, or values that organizational members bring to a situation. But they also may be the result of work routines that make it difficult for employees to break out of traditional processes or patterns of activity (Ghemawat & Costa, 1993).

Cognitive biases often manifest in intrapreneurial situations that involve a high degree of novelty, uncertainty, and/or time pressure (Baron, 1998). Such biases may create behavioral barriers, but may also encourage intrapreneurial efforts. On the one hand, prior research suggests that biases such as overconfidence or representativeness (which involves drawing conclusions on the basis of limited information) may influence entrepreneurs to "take the plunge" (Busenitz & Barney, 1997). Such biases may actually benefit entrepreneurs by enabling them to take precipitous actions that others might avoid. On the other hand, the willingness to act on biased or limited information may also inhibit effective innovation (Simon, Houghton, & Aquino, 2000).

Another type of behavioral barrier that affects intrapreneurship is career risk or threat of job loss associated with participating in a failed project (e.g., Baron, Davis-Blake, & Bielby, 1986). For example, managers may be reluctant to back a risky project, and employees may feel that innovation projects will require new skill sets that they don't have. Either situation can create anxiety about being passed over for promotion or replaced. Such factors contribute to the limits that behavioral barriers place on innovation efforts.

Political Barriers.   Conflicts arising from power relationships and issues of control and authority can limit the progress of intrapreneurial efforts (Kanter, North, Bernstein, & Williams, 1990). For example, managers who have vested interests in existing projects may resist new initiatives. Because they fear that their pet projects will be sidelined or cannibalized when attention shifts to a new venture initiative, they may refuse to share information or find excuses not to cooperate. Another tactic is to withhold resources that may be needed for a program of innovation to proceed (Kanter, 1985).

Power struggles may also arise over who is in charge of an intrapreneurial project (Vandermerwe & Birley, 1997). Division leaders and/or strategic managers may jockey for position so they can take credit for—or at least "bask in the sun" of—a promising new innovation effort. Conversely, managers may attempt to shift the blame for or distance themselves from intrapreneurial projects that are headed for failure. Such political maneuvering may actually inhibit the success of innovation efforts in the long run.

These and other barriers can plague the most well-intentioned organizations. For example, many companies have implemented programs to increase the quality and efficiency of their operations. These include process management programs such as Total Quality Management (TQM), the ISO 9000 series, and Six Sigma. Efforts to achieve productivity gains and increase efficiency, however, may limit an organization's ability to innovate (Abernathy, 1978). Recent research notes that process management techniques are now being used to select and develop technological innovations (e.g., Brown & Duguid, 2000). Yet practices that make routines more efficient are often inappropriate for innovation projects. Benner and Tushman (2003) argue that placing too much emphasis on exploiting innovations efficiently can act as a barrier to the kind of exploratory activities that are needed to keep a company balanced and open to new innovation-based opportunities.

Cost-cutting efforts may not only inhibit development of innovation technologies but also be a barrier to the effective marketing of an innovation (Kelley, Neck, O'Connor, & Paulson, 2002). For example, traditional market research techniques such as conducting surveys or focus groups may provide inaccurate information about breakthrough innovations. Customers may not understand the uses of the innovation or the company may have initially targeted the wrong niche. Instead of focus groups, prototype trials in which potential customers' behavior can be observed may be needed instead. But cost-cutting initiatives may prevent these or other more effective types of market research from being used.

It is not difficult to understand why barriers to innovation develop. Relationships are established and structural arrangements become fixed in ways that make it difficult to break out of old patterns and/or try new things. It is also not unusual—most companies face such barriers. In addition, organizations that want to innovate face numerous choices about how best to proceed. These choices pose several dilemmas, and it is that subject we turn to next.

Five Innovation Dilemmas

Recent research has provided a wake-up call to established firms that are pursuing innovation goals. In his book *The Innovators's Dilemma*, Harvard Professor Clayton Christensen (1997) made a startling conclusion: "From the simplest to the most radical, the firms that led the industry in every instance of developing and adopting disruptive [radical] technologies were entrants to the industry, not its incumbent leaders" (p. 9). One reason new entrants outperform incumbents, according to Christensen, is that new entrants usually do not face a dilemma that incumbents face, namely, being so occupied with meeting customers' current needs that they fail to take steps to meet future needs. As it turns out, this is only one of several dilemmas that organizations face when making decisions about what innovation path to follow.

A dilemma is defined as "a situation involving choice between equally unsatisfactory alternatives" (*Webster's Dictionary*). Clearly, one of the factors that make managing innovation difficult is that the innovation process involves so many choices. These choices require organizations that pursue innovation goals to select from alternatives that may be equally unsatisfactory or equally compelling. Rarely is there "one right answer." This proves to be an impediment to innovation for many firms. In the subsections that follow, we address five common innovation dilemmas introduced by Sharma (1999).

"Seeds" Versus "Weeds."   Most companies have an abundance of innovative ideas. They must decide which of these is most likely to bear fruit—the "seeds"—and which should be cast aside—the "weeds." This is an ongoing dilemma that is often complicated by the fact that some innovation projects require a considerable level of investment before a firm can fully evaluate whether they are worth pursuing. As a result, firms need a mechanism with which they can choose among various innovation projects.

Experience Versus Initiative.   Companies must decide who will lead an innovation project. Senior managers may have experience and credibility but tend to be more risk averse. Midlevel employees, who may be the innovators themselves, may have more enthusiasm because they can see firsthand how an innovation would address specific problems. As a result, firms need to support and reward organizational members who bring new ideas to light.

Internal Versus External Staffing.   Innovation projects need competent staffs to succeed. People drawn from inside the company may have greater social capital and know the organization's culture and routines. But this knowledge may actually inhibit them from thinking outside the box. Staffing innovation projects with external personnel requires that project managers justify the hiring and spend time recruiting, training, and relationship building. As a result, firms need to streamline and support the process of staffing innovation efforts.

Building Capabilities Versus Collaborating.   Innovation projects often require new sets of skills. Firms can seek help from other departments and/or partner with other companies that bring resources and experience as well as share costs of development. However, such arrangements can create dependencies and inhibit internal skills development. Further, struggles over who contributed the most or how the benefits of the project are to be allocated may arise. As a result, firms need a mechanism for forging links with outside parties to the innovation process.

Incremental Versus Preemptive Launch.   Companies must manage the timing and scale of new innovation projects. An incremental launch is less risky because it requires fewer resources and serves as a market test. But a launch that is too tentative can undermine the project's credibility. It also opens the door for a competitive response. A large-scale launch requires more resources but it can effectively preempt a competitive response. As a result, firms need to make funding and management arrangements that allow for projects to hit the ground running and be responsive to market feedback.

These dilemmas may inhibit a firm's ability to move forward with innovation projects and halt its intrapreneurial efforts. Often the solution is not as simple as picking one alternative over another. For example, the decision whether to enlist the support of innovation partners or hire/promote from within may involve a complex combination of both. The dilemmas and barriers to innovation identified in this section highlight why the innovation process can be daunting even for highly successful firms. Next, we turn to research that addresses how firms have dealt with these impediments.

OVERCOMING THE OBSTACLES TO INNOVATION

Despite the numerous challenges just identified, many firms have overcome the impediments to innovation and successfully launched intrapreneurial ventures. In this section, three broadly defined management practices and techniques used by organizations to deal with the obstacles are addressed: balancing exploration and exploitation, overcoming external barriers, and managing external relationships.

Balancing Exploration and Exploitation

One way to address barriers and dilemmas is to recognize that innovation activities have different objectives. These can be understood, according to one framework, by the type of innovation a company chooses to pursue. There are several frameworks for assessing different types of innovation. Traditionally, innovation has been depicted on a continuum that extends from incremental to radical (Damanpour, 1991; Hage, 1980). *Radical innovation* refers to breakthrough innovations that produce fundamental changes in existing practices; *incremental innovations* represent evolutionary applications that result in small improvements in products and processes (Leifer et al., 2000).

The type of innovation pursued, however, may provide only a partial answer. Another issue is choosing between and/or balancing an organization's exploration and exploitation activities (Levinthal & March, 1993). *Exploration* is associated with complex search processes, risk taking and experimenting with new knowledge and technologies (March, 1991). Firms that aim to expand their domain of activity or capitalize on a strong resource base to develop new initiatives may prefer to explore opportunities for new innovation directions. In contrast, *exploitation* refers to systematic search, risk aversion and improving existing capabilities (March, 1991). Firms that have innovative capabilities that can be used to enhance existing product lines or applied to the development of a more efficient internal process may prefer to exploit such opportunities and postpone investments in new innovations. Successfully managing this trade-off as industry and competitive conditions evolve often requires that firms be ambidextrous, that is, capable of simultaneously pursuing both exploration and exploitation objectives (Benner & Tushman, 2003; He & Wong, 2004).

Developing policies that clarify the balance between exploration and exploitation provides firms with a means to focus their innovation efforts (e.g., Ghemawat & Costa, 1993; Leonard-Barton, 1992). One technique used to balance exploration and exploitation activities is "strategic enveloping," which involves defining the scope of an organization's innovation efforts to ensure that its efforts are not wasted on projects that are highly uncertain or outside the firm's domain of interest (Sharma, 1999). Strategic enveloping sets forth the range of acceptable projects and creates a firm-specific view of innovation that defines how a firm can create new knowledge and learn from an innovation initiative even if the project fails (e.g., McGrath, 1999).

Although such limitations might seem overly constraining, they also give direction to a firm's innovation efforts that helps separate seeds from weeds and builds internal capabilities.

Overcoming Internal Barriers

Creating flexibility within organizational structures and using new forms for organizing work are two solutions companies are implementing to overcome internal barriers to intrapreneurship. At the core of both efforts is an attempt to improve information flows through organizations and to enhance the management of knowledge. One way to achieve this is by creating "boundaryless" organizations (Ashkenas, Ulrich, Jick, & Kerr, 2002). Within most organizations, vertical boundaries separate hierarchical levels, horizontal boundaries separate functional areas, and external boundaries separate firms from customers, suppliers, and other stakeholders (Ashkenas, 1997).

Boundarylessness aims to make those boundaries more permeable by emphasizing cross-functional coordination, facilitating the exchange of information, and increasing the depth of employee involvement in planning and decision making (Devanna & Tichy, 1990; Barringer & Bluedorn, 1999). Such practices not only address the systemic and structural impediments that inhibit innovation but also create situations where decisions are challenged and decision makers have to defend their proposals, thus addressing political and behavioral barriers (D. Miller, 1987).

New organizational forms are also being used to break down barriers, increase efficiency, and speed the innovation process (Dess, Rasheed, McLaughlin, & Priem, 1995). Virtual organizations, increasingly common in the Internet era, allow for rapid communication and knowledge sharing among multiple organizational partners (Doz & Hamel, 1998). Because they are virtual, such organizations may not be subject to the trappings of power that are often associated with physical locations (e.g., headquarters vs. branch; "top floor" vs. "shop floor"). Modular or "cellular" organizations, consisting of autonomous business units that interact around themes of innovation and continuous improvement, have also emerged as a way to organize innovation efforts more effectively (Miles, Snow, Mathews, Miles, & Coleman, 1997). Many of these alternative forms are designed to empower multifunctional teams that can cross functional boundaries and work cohesively to commercialize new knowledge and successfully launch innovative products and services (Ancona & Caldwell, 1992; Wenger & Snyder, 2000).

Rewards and incentives, because of their role in motivating and controlling behavior, provide another method to overcoming internal barriers to innovation (Kanter, 1994). For example, rewards are often used to encourage collective action by rewarding team-level outcomes rather than individual performance (Rodengen, 1997). In general, reward and incentive systems need to reinforce company goals and commitments by being fair, visible, and clearly linked to performance and desired behaviors (Rappaport, 1999). To support intrapreneurship, rewards and incentives must also encourage and not constrain creativity and risk taking as well as independent and "out-of-the-box" thinking (Kanter, 1994; Schuler, 1986). Poorly designed reward and incentive systems may inhibit intrapreneurial behavior (Balkin & Logan, 1988). Problems with internal barriers are worsened when the activities that employees are rewarded for are counter to or misaligned with company aspirations and create confusion, inefficiencies, and improper behavior (Kerr & Slocum, 1987). When designed with an overall vision in mind, however, rewards and incentives can build strong commitments, create synergies among innovative teams, and help make tough staffing decisions go over more smoothly.

Managing External Relationships

Two of the dilemmas discussed earlier involve selecting innovation partners. The dilemma of internal versus external staffing is concerned with identifying and selecting the best personnel to staff an innovation project; building capabilities versus collaborating involves the decision to invest in internal development versus sourcing solutions or seeking support from outside partners. These dilemmas are intensified if political and/or systemic barriers impede clear decision making. Research indicates that companies that overcome these dilemmas by effectively drawing on external resources and building alliances with collaboration partners are among the strongest intrapreneurial performers (Chesbrough, 2003; Doz, 1996; Kogut, 1988; Leifer et al., 2000).

Within organizations, it is rare for any one work group or department to have all the information it needs to carry an innovation from concept to commercialization (Kanter, 1985; Mitchell & Singh, 1996). Even a company that is highly competent with its current operations usually needs new capabilities to achieve new results. External innovation partners can provide the skills and insights that are often needed to make innovation projects succeed (Cooper, 2002; Doz & Hamel, 1998). To choose partners, firms need to ask what competencies they are looking for and what the innovation partner will contribute. These contributions might include knowledge of markets, technology expertise, or contacts with key players in an industry. Innovation partnerships also typically need to specify how the rewards of the innovation will be shared and who will own the intellectual property that is developed.

Collaborating with multiple partners and the speed and ease with which partners can network are changing the way innovation is conducted, according to Harvard professor Henry Chesbrough (2003). In an era when new knowledge and fresh ideas abound, the old way of innovating no longer seems to be bearing fruit. New technologies and the speed of innovation are creating new demands on companies to look beyond their traditional boundaries and share their intellectual property. The innovation process itself, according to Chesbrough, needs innovating. In his book *Open Innovation*, he argues that today's leading innovators are disclosing intellectual property, crossing organization boundaries, drawing on the knowledge and resources of competitors as well as other strategic partners, and allowing others to share the wealth. Such activities can only occur if organizations are willing to challenge traditional systemic and political barriers.

As this section indicates, managing innovation is an important and challenging organizational activity. For it to be successful, the innovation process has to stay focused on its ultimate purpose—to introduce new products and/or deploy new processes that build competitive advantages and make the company profitable. Another approach to overcoming barriers and resolving dilemmas, as well as pursuing intrapreneurial goals in general, is to adopt an entrepreneurial orientation.

THE ROLE OF ENTREPRENEURIAL ORIENTATION IN FOSTERING INTRAPRENEURSHIP AND INNOVATION

Innovation involves a company-wide commitment, in part because the results of innovation affect every part of the organization (Hamel, 2000; Porter, 1985). Innovation requires both an entrepreneurial skill set and an entrepreneurial mind-set to be effective (McGrath & MacMillan, 2000). Firms that exhibit a strong entrepreneurial orientation (EO) may have an advantage when it comes to undertaking innovation initiatives. EO refers to the strategy-making practices and processes that managers engage in to identify and create venture opportunities. EO has five dimensions, autonomy, innovativeness, proactiveness, competitive aggressiveness, and risk taking, which permeate the decision-making styles of organizational members (Covin & Slevin, 1991; Lumpkin & Dess, 1996). Many firms that are successful innovators attribute much of their success to an entrepreneurial orientation (e.g., Hamel, 1999, 2000).

An entrepreneurial orientation may be especially useful to firms endeavoring to balance the exploration–exploitation trade-off. Prior research has suggested that firms are often strong in some aspects of EO but exhibit only moderate or low levels of other EO dimensions (e.g., Lumpkin & Dess, 2001). In a similar way, different strengths are needed to pursue the different aims of exploration and exploitation. Thus, the various dimensions of EO may contribute to the exploration and exploitation process differently.

The dimensions of innovativeness and autonomy are well matched to the task of exploration. Innovativeness refers to a willingness to introduce newness and novelty by relying on creativity and experimentation (D. Miller & Friesen, 1984). Autonomy refers to independent action by individuals or teams who are free to investigate possibilities without the pressure of strategic norms or organizational traditions that may impede them (Burgelman, 1983, 2001). Such activities are necessary for firms that are exploring opportunities for entrepreneurial development. Proactiveness, which involves a forward-looking, opportunity-seeking perspective (D. Miller, 1983), may also contribute to a firm's exploration efforts. Therefore, firms that are high in innovativeness, autonomy, and proactiveness will more effectively pursue innovation via exploration.

Two other dimensions of entrepreneurial orientation—risk taking and competitive aggressiveness—are well suited to the task of exploiting innovation opportunities.

Risk taking involves making decisions and taking action in the face of uncertainty and/or competitive threats (Baird & Thomas, 1985; Shapira, 1995). Competitive aggressiveness requires intense action aimed at protecting earlier gains and defending against competitive threats (Venkataraman, 1989). Proactiveness, which involves seizing opportunities by acting ahead of competitors (D. Miller, 1983) may also strengthen a firm's ability to exploit innovation opportunities. Therefore, organizations that are high in risk taking, competitive aggressiveness, and proactiveness will more effectively pursue innovation via exploitation.

As a caveat, it surely can be argued that all five EO dimensions could be strongly related to both exploration and exploitation. For example, innovativeness could involve both the development and introduction of an organization's major new products and services, as well as relatively minor activities that improve one of the activities in a firm's value chain (Porter, 1985). Clearly, the former would focus on exploration and the latter would represent exploitation. Even so, the links between exploration and exploitation and the five dimensions of EO may provide important insights regarding how best to apply an entrepreneurial mindset in an intrapreneurial context. In the subsections that follow, each of the dimensions of EO will be described in terms of how they relate to innovation.

Autonomy

In the context of intrapreneurship, autonomous work units are often used to leverage a firm's existing strengths, identify opportunities that are beyond the organization's current capabilities, and encourage development of new ventures or improved business practices (Kanter, 1983; Pinchot, 1985). Autonomy refers to a willingness to work independently in order to act on an opportunity or implement an entrepreneurial vision (Lumpkin & Dess, 1996). Independent action by an individual or team often provides the impetus needed to bring forth a business concept or vision and carry it through to completion (Bird, 1988; Burgelman, 1983).

Organizations that rely on innovation and new venture creation to grow must make an extra effort to foster entrepreneurial behavior (Burgelman & Sayles, 1986; Kanter, 1983). Often this involves freeing organizational members—both individuals and teams—to operate outside an organization's existing norms and strategies where they can think and act more freely. Companies often develop autonomously operated new ventures or independent work units called "skunkworks" to separate employees from their usual routines and practices and encourage creative thinking. In a 4-year study of innovation in American, European, and Japanese firms, the most innovative companies all used some form of skunkworks (Quinn, 1988). Christensen (1997), who found that new entrants were better innovators than established firms, advocated physical separation from headquarters and other strong forms of autonomy to help incumbent firms reverse that trend. Although corporations that have created separate entities to manage new ventures have often been successful (e.g., Kanter, Kao, & Wiersema, 1997), research also indicates that too much separation without taking care to integrate autonomous ventures with ongoing operations can be detrimental to a company's intrapreneurial aspirations (Day, Mang, Richter, & Roberts, 2001).

In the context of internal corporate venturing, both "top-down" and "bottom-up" approaches may be used to encourage intrapreneurial thinking (Quinn & Spreitzer, 1997). Companies with an overall entrepreneurial mission use a top-down approach to stimulate entrepreneurial activity (Birkinshaw, 1997). That is, in organizations such as 3M, Nokia, and the Virgin Group, top managers support programs and incentives that foster a climate of entrepreneurship. Many of the best ideas for new corporate ventures, however, come from the bottom up. In some organizations, even the best ideas are not welcome by top management (Dougherty & Hardy, 1996). Therefore, within many corporations, extra effort and special incentives may be needed to develop and build support for an entrepreneurial venture (Helgesen, 1996). Research indicates that fostering individual-level autonomy not only increases job satisfaction and employee performance but can also increase the competitiveness and effectiveness of firms (Block, 2003; Kanter, 1983).

The Important Role of Product Champions

Prior research suggests that the autonomous action of key individuals is often needed to foster innovation and/or launch intrapreneurial ventures

(Greene, Brush, & Hart, 1999; Kanter, 1983). This may be especially important in smaller firms where the energetic efforts of individuals with good ideas may informally influence new venture initiatives. New venture projects must pass through two critical stages or they may never get off the ground—project definition and project impetus (Burgelman, 1983, 2001). Project definition refers to justifying an opportunity in terms of its attractiveness in the marketplace and how well it fits with the corporation's other strategic objectives. Project impetus refers to the support a new project must obtain from senior managers who have experience with similar projects. For a project to advance through these stages of definition and impetus, a product champion is often needed to generate support and encouragement (Maidique, 1980).

Product champions are especially important during the time after a new project has been defined but before it gains momentum. They form a link between the definition and impetus stages of internal intrapreneurial development (Burgelman, 1983). They do this by procuring resources and stimulating interest for the product among potential customers. For a corporate venture to have a strategic and economic impact, it is often necessary for it become an embryonic business with its own organization and budget (Block & MacMillan, 1995). Thus, in a corporate setting, product champions play an important entrepreneurial role by scavenging for resources and encouraging others to take a chance on promising new ideas (Greene et al., 1999).

Innovativeness

Innovativeness is one of the major components of an intrapreneurial strategy. It refers to a firm's efforts to find new opportunities and novel solutions (Damanpour, 1991). Innovation was discussed at the beginning of this chapter; here the focus is on *innovativeness*, that is, a firm's attitude toward innovation and willingness to innovate.

Innovation involves creativity and experimentation that result in new products, new services, or improved technological processes (Johannessen et al., 2001). Research indicates that innovativeness is associated with strong performance in many contexts (Hamel, 2000; Kanter, 1983). For example, Deshpande and Farley (2004) found in a multicountry study that innovativeness had a stronger effect on performance than either market orientation or organizational culture across the countries in their study. A similar study found that innovativeness in small firms was associated with higher levels of performance than either market orientation or innovative product features (Verhees & Meulenberg, 2004). Although innovativeness does not always lead to strong performance and may be more important as a learning tool than as a way to improve profitability (McGrath, 1999), numerous studies report that the innovative efforts of intrapreneurial firms account for positive financial outcomes (e.g., Kanter et al., 1997; Kuczmarski, 1996).

Innovations come in many different forms (Hage, 1980; Leifer, et al., 2000; Slappendel, 1996). The radical–incremental continuum of innovativeness was identified earlier. Technological innovativeness consists primarily of research and engineering efforts aimed at developing new products and processes. Product–market innovativeness includes market research, product design, and innovations in advertising and promotion. Administrative innovativeness refers to novelty in management systems, control techniques, and organizational structure.

Many corporations owe their success to an active program of innovation-based corporate venturing (Hamel, 1999, 2000). Innovativeness can be a source of great progress and strong corporate growth. As indicated earlier, however, the job of managing innovativeness can be very challenging (Van de Ven, 1986). Expenditures on R&D aimed at identifying new products or process can be a waste of resources if the effort does not yield results. Nevertheless, inventions and new ideas need to be nurtured even when their benefits are unclear. Therefore, even though innovativeness is an important means of internal corporate venturing, it also involves major risks because investments in innovations may not payoff.

The Important Role of Organizational Learning

Although only a few studies have explored the connections between organizational learning and innovation, the entrepreneurship literature suggests that there are important links between recognizing innovative opportunities and successful corporate venturing (Lumpkin & Lichtenstein, 2005). Organizational learning, for example, emphasizes improving practices and expanding into new arenas by creating new knowledge (Senge, 1990), building new understandings (Fiol & Lyles, 1985), and detecting and correcting misapplied decisions (Argyris, 1990). Because these qualities may strengthen efforts to be more intrapreneurial, organizational learning has important implications for how firms create wealth by converting innovative breakthroughs and intrapreneurial insights into strategic advantage.

Moreover, the same attributes used to distinguish a learning organization—"an organization skilled at creating, acquiring, and transferring knowledge, and at modifying its behavior to reflect new knowledge and insights" (Garvin, 1993, p. 81)—are among the qualities needed to effectively recognize and pursue intrapreneurial opportunities. Thus, the relationship between learning and intrapreneurship parallels the literature that has connected individual creativity with organizational innovation through the rubric of learning and action (e.g., Crossan, Lane, & White, 1999; Dougherty, 1992; Nonaka, 1994). The more elements of creativity and innovation a venture or firm expresses—that is, the higher or more intense its capacity for organizational innovation—the more opportunities it may identify (cf. Barringer & Bluedorn, 1999). Thus, in a practical way, the more learning that a firm or an intrapreneur can enact, the more likely it is that new opportunities will be leveraged for strategic advantage.

Proactiveness

Proactiveness refers to an organization's efforts to seize new opportunities. Proactive firms monitor trends, identify the future needs of existing customers, and anticipate changes in demand or emerging problems that can lead to new venture opportunities (D. Miller, 1983). Proactiveness involves a forward-looking perspective that not only recognizes opportunities but is willing to act on those insights ahead of the competition (Lumpkin & Dess, 1996). Highly proactive firms such as Dell and Sony have not only succeeded financially but also changed the competitive landscape in their industries (Collins & Porras, 1997; Evans & Wurster, 2000).

The benefits gained by firms that are the first to enter new markets, establish brand identity, implement administrative techniques, or adopt new operating technologies in an industry are called first mover advantages (Lieberman & Montgomery, 1988). First movers frequently have several advantages. First, industry pioneers, especially in new industries, often capture unusually high profits because there are no competitors to drive prices down. Second, first movers that establish brand recognition are usually able to retain their image and hold on to the market share gains they earned by being first. Sometimes these benefits also accrue to other early movers in an industry (A. Miller & Camp, 1985), but, generally speaking, first movers have an advantage that can be sustained until firms enter the maturity phase of an industry life cycle (Lambkin, 1988).

Among all the dimensions of EO, proactiveness is the element that is most consistently associated with strong performance (see Rauch, Wiklund, Lumpkin & Frese, 2004). Although first movers are not always more successful than early followers or imitators (e.g., Robinson, Fornell, & Sullivan, 1992), there is convincing evidence that proactiveness is consistently associated with high firm performance (e.g., Lieberman & Montgomery, 1988, 1998; D. Miller, 1987). Several studies focused on national differences found that proactively oriented cultural attributes were more likely to be associated with entrepreneurial behavior (Kreiser, Marino, & Weaver, 2002a, 2002b; Swierczek & Ha, 2003). Interestingly, proactivity as a personality dimension is an individual-level measure that has been linked with the success of entrepreneurial startups (Becherer & Maurer, 1999) as well as career success generally (Seibert, Crant, & Kraimer, 1999).

The Important Role of Opportunity Recognition

One of the primary reason firms act proactively is to identify and act on entrepreneurial opportunities. Thus, effective opportunity recognition (OpR) plays a key role in the success of new venture initiatives. Opportunity recognition involves identifying good ideas and transforming them into business concepts that add value and generate revenues (Gaglio & Taub, 1992). Proactiveness suggests a willingness to pursue opportunities. For proactive behaviors to bear fruit, however, they must be matched with key OpR capabilities.

Recently, several models of entrepreneurial opportunity recognition have been suggested (e.g., Ardichvili, Cardozo, & Ray, 2003; Fiet, 2002). A creativity-based approach proposed by Lumpkin, Hills, and Shrader (2004) identified key factors that could also enhance a firm's proactiveness. The model suggested that opportunity recognition involves both discovery of potential opportunities and the formation of such prospects into viable new ventures. Discovery refers to activities that firms use to identify potential opportunities. It includes firm-level activities such as scanning and monitoring as well as the cognitive processes that individuals and teams use. The outcome of discovery is an insight that "breaks the mean–ends framework" (Gaglio & Taub, 1992), that is, elicits new understanding of the nature of a venture opportunity and how it might be pursued. This leads to the next phase, formation, which refers to the selection, evaluation, and refinement processes involved in organizing opportunities. The outcome of the formation phase is go/no-go decision about whether to proceed. Firms that use discovery and formation techniques and other creativity-enhancing practices to identify and pursue opportunities can develop and/or advance their level of proactiveness.

Competitive Aggressiveness

Competitive aggressiveness refers to a firm's efforts to outperform its industry rivals. It is characterized by a combative posture or an aggressive response aimed at improving position or overcoming a threat in a competitive marketplace (D'Aveni, 1994; A. Miller & Camp, 1985). Entrepreneurial managers can use competitive aggressiveness to combat industry trends that threaten their survival or market position. Sometimes firms need to be forceful in defending the competitive position that has made them an industry leader (Smith, Ferrier, & Grimm, 2001; Venkataraman, 1989).

As an avenue of firm development and growth, competitive aggressiveness may involve being very assertive in leveraging the results of other entrepreneurial activities such as innovativeness or proactiveness (D. Miller, 1987; D. Miller & Friesen, 1984). Unlike innovativeness and proactiveness, however, which tend to focus on market opportunities, competitive aggressiveness is directed toward competitors. The dimensions of SWOT analysis—strengths, weaknesses, opportunities, and threats—provide a useful way to distinguish these different approaches to intrapreneurship. Proactiveness is a response to opportunities—the O in SWOT; competitive aggressiveness, by contrast, is a response to threats—the T in SWOT. Research indicates that proactiveness and competitive aggressiveness are distinct dimensions of EO that are differentially related to performance (Lumpkin & Dess, 2001; Rauch, Wiklund, Frese, & Lumpkin, 2004).

A competitively aggressive posture is important for firms that seek to enter new markets and/or excel in the face of intense rivalry (Chen & Hambrick, 1995; D'Aveni, 1994). Companies with an aggressive orientation are willing to "do battle" with competitors. They might slash prices and sacrifice profitability to gain market share, or spend aggressively to obtain manufacturing capacity (Venkataraman, 1989). Not only does such aggressiveness threaten large firms, but also smaller firms often suffer when competitors aggressively enter markets with drastically lower prices. Because the larger firms usually have deep pockets, they can afford to cut prices without being seriously damaged by an extended period of narrow margins. Competitive aggressiveness may not always lead to competitive advantages, however. Some companies (or their CEOs) have severely damaged their reputations by being overly aggressive (e.g., Anthes, 1998). By contrast, individual-level perceptions of subjective rivalry may constrain how managers perceive the competitive environment and cause them to underestimate the need to act competitively to maintain a strategic advantage (Porac & Thomas, 1994).

The Important Role of "Exit Champions"

Although a culture of championing venture projects is advantageous for stimulating an ongoing stream of entrepreneurial initiatives, many—in fact, most—of the ideas will not work out. At some point in the process, a majority of initiatives will be abandoned. Sometime, however, companies wait too long to terminate a new venture and do so only after large sums of resources are used up, or worse, result in a marketplace failure. How can companies avoid these costly and discouraging defeats? Royer (2003) suggests that one way is to support a key role in the intrapreneurial process—"exit champions." An exit champion is one who aggressively challenges new venture initiatives and often puts a stop to projects that appear to lack viability. By demanding hard evidence and challenging the belief system that is carrying an idea forward, exit champions hold the line on ventures that appear shaky.

Both product champions and exit champions must be willing to energetically stand up for what they believe and put their reputations on the line. But they also differ in important ways. Product champions deal in uncertainty and ambiguity; exit champions reduce ambiguity by gathering hard data and developing a strong case for why a project should be killed. Product champions are often thought to be willing to violate procedures and operate outside normal channels; exit champions, by contrast, often have to reinstate procedures and reassert the decision-making criteria that are supposed to guide venture decisions. Although product champions often emerge as heroes, exit champions run the risk of losing status by opposing popular projects. Thus, the role of exit champion may seem unappealing. But it is one that could save a company both financially and in terms of its reputation in the marketplace by helping firms engaged in doomed intrapreneurial projects to cut their losses and move on (Chesbrough, 2003; Leifer et al., 2000).

Risk Taking

Risk taking refers to an organization's willingness to make decisions and take action without certain knowledge of probable outcomes—to act boldly without knowing the consequences (D. Miller, 1983; Sitkin & Pablo, 1992). To be successful through intrapreneurship, firms usually have to take on riskier alternatives, even if it means forgoing the methods or products that have worked in the past. To obtain high financial returns, firms take such risks as assuming high levels of debt, committing large amounts of firm resources, introducing new products into new markets, and investing in unexplored technologies (Baird & Thomas, 1985).

Risk taking as the term is often used in entrepreneurship research is, in many ways, closer to Knight's (1921) concept of "acting under conditions of uncertainty" because it refers primarily to unsystematic risk (as opposed to the more strictly defined systematic risk found in financial analysis). Even so, the parlance of entrepreneurial risk taking includes several different types of risks that organizations might take:

- *Business risk taking* involves venturing into the unknown without knowing the probability of success. This is the risk associated with entering untested markets or committing to unproven technologies.
- *Financial risk taking* requires that a company borrow heavily or commit a large portion of its resources in order to grow. In this context, risk is used to refer to the risk/return logic, which suggests that the more

risky a project is, the more likely it is to generate high returns and the more likely it is to fail.

- *Personal risk taking* refers to the risks that an executive assumes in taking a stand in favor of a strategic course of action. Executives who take such risks stand to influence the course of their whole company and their decisions can also have significant implications for their careers.

It is noteworthy that entrepreneurship scholars often report that, despite their reputation for being risk takers, entrepreneurs usually take only calculated risks based on careful analyses aimed at reducing uncertainty (Bhide, 2000). The empirical evidence supporting that claim is mixed, however. On the one hand, research indicates that only about half of all intrapreneurial ventures are likely to be financially successful (Block & MacMillan, 1995). Further, higher levels of risk taking are not consistently related to stronger performance (Bromiley, Miller, & Rau, 2001). On the other hand, risk perceptions often differ among entrepreneurs (Busenitz & Barney, 1997). Entrepreneurs tend to be subject to a number of biases that cause them to perceive opportunities more positively than nonentrepreneurs (Palich & Bagby, 1995) or to overestimate the extent to which they have effectively evaluated a venture opportunity (Simon et al., 2000). These biases are often present in an intrapreneurial context because of pressure to grow companies based on innovation and venture initiatives.

The Important Role of Real Options Analysis

One way that entrepreneurs can effectively manage the uncertainty associated with intrapreneurial ventures is by making risk taking more incremental and, to some extent, experimental. This can be achieved by using real options analysis. Real options are created whenever a company begins to explore a new venture concept by making initial investments such as conducting market tests, building prototypes, or forming venture teams (Amran & Kulatilaka, 1999). These small investments bestow an option similar to a financial option, which gives the owner the right but not the obligation to engage in certain financial transactions. Options give a firm the flexibility to decide whether to invest additional funds to grow or accelerate the intrapreneurial activity, perhaps delay further investing in order to learn more, to shrink the scale of activity, or even to abandon it.

The process of evaluating intrapreneurial ideas at successive stages in the venture creation process helps firms reduce uncertainty (McGrath, 1999). Janney and Dess (2004) have identified four different types of decisions that entrepreneurs may face—immediate entry, immediate exit, delayed entry, and delayed exit. They suggest that, at different stages of the intrapreneurial launch process, these decision options might be used not only to reduce uncertainty but also to collect information (e.g., about the competitive environment) and/or create new knowledge that influences the innovation process (e.g., developing industry standards) (Janney & Dess, 2004). Thus, even though nearly all intrapreneurial decisions are potentially risky, real options analysis can help firms separate winning ideas from losers in a way that minimizes risks.

DISCUSSION

The topics of intrapreneurship and innovation present numerous promising and worthwhile research questions that warrant future research. For example, what psychological and cognitive factors contribute to the barriers to innovation? Are there elements specific to intrapreneurship and the innovation process that make these barriers more or less difficult to surmount? A similar question could be posed regarding the dilemmas that companies face when making decisions about how to grow via intrapreneurship. How might the cognitive biases that both propel entrepreneurs and also cause them to potentially misinterpret information (e.g., Baron, 1998) affect how they deal with the dilemmas suggested by Sharma (1999)? Such research might also help scholars understand how entrepreneurs perceive risk and their willingness to bear perceived uncertainty (McMullen & Shepherd, 2006).

Regarding EO, scholars could explore what factors may enhance (or inhibit) the strength of the relationship between EO and firm performance. For example, under what conditions would otherwise strong cultures cause core rigidities (Hamel & Prahalad, 1996) and, subsequently, erode innovation and discourage risk taking? How might a leader's emotional intelligence (Goleman, 1998) improve an organization's willingness to take risks and engage in more proactive behaviors? And how do reward systems (e.g., behavioral based or outcome based) facilitate (or retard) such behaviors? Further, researchers could also incorporate different perspectives on risk taking given the increasing role of knowledge in the global economy. For example, firms that judiciously experiment with new products and processes may be able to subsequently turn initial failures into new resource combinations (McGrath, 1999) that thus enable them to create new "learning platforms" (Grenadier & Weiss, 1997) for future value creating endeavors. Capturing such dynamics and their outcomes involves a closer look at dependent variables, which go beyond traditional short-term economic indicators.

Research endeavors should also be directed at assessing and refining the EO construct itself. For example, Lyon, Lumpkin, and Dess (2000) have addressed the relative advantages and disadvantages associated with three alternate approaches—managerial perceptions, firm behaviors, and resource allocations. Ideally, when taken in combination, these approaches should enhance the reliability and validity of EO research. Another avenue for research might involve reconciling individual and firm levels of analysis in EO research. For example, proactiveness has been used to measure both individual- and firm-level behaviors. A future research question might involve comparing firm-level proactiveness with individual-level proactivity. Finally, much can be learned by studying "best practices" of leading-edge organizations. Studies that focused on the relationship between EO and best practices could help researchers to inductively derive theory that can later be tested to confirm or disconfirm extant knowledge. Thus, the viability of descriptive and normative EO theory would be advanced.

REFERENCES

Abernathy, W. J. (1978). *The productivity dilemma*. Baltimore, MD: Johns Hopkins University Press.

Amram, M., & Kulatilaka, N. (1999). *Real options: Managing strategic investments in a uncertain world*. Boston: Harvard Business School Press.

Ancona, D., & Caldwell, D. F. (1992). Bridging the boundary: External activity and performance in organizational teams. *Administrative Science Quarterly, 37*, 634–665.

Anthes, G. H. (1998). Rear view mirror. *Computerworld, 32*(9), 63–65.

Ardichvili, A., Cardozo, R., & Ray, S. (2003). A theory of entrepreneurial opportunity identification and development. *Journal of Business Venturing, 18*, 105–123.

Argyris, C. (1990). *Overcoming organizational defenses*. Boston: Allyn and Bacon.

Ashkenas, R. (1997). The organization's new clothes. In F. Hesselbein, M. Goldsmith, & R. Beckhard (Eds.), *The organization of the future* (pp. 99–108). New York: HarperCollins.

Ashkenas, R., Ulrich, D., Jick, T., & Kerr, S. (2002). *The boundaryless organization. Breaking the chains of organization structure*. San Francisco, CA: Jossey-Bass.

Baird, I. S., & Thomas, H. (1985). Toward a contingency model of strategic risk taking. *Academy of Management Review, 10*(2), 230–243.

Balkin, D. B., & Logan, J. W. (1988). Reward policies that support entrepreneurship. *Compensation and Benefits Review, 20*, 18–25.

Baron, R. A. (1998). Cognitive mechanisms in entrepreneurship: Why and when entrepreneurs think differently than other people. *Journal of Business Venturing, 13*(4), 275–294.

Baron, J. N., Davis-Blake, A., & Bielby, W. T. (1986). The structure of opportunity: How promotion ladders vary within and among organizations. *Administrative Science Quarterly, 31*, 248–273.

Barringer, B. R., & Bluedorn, A. C. (1999). The relationship between corporate entrepreneurship and strategic management. *Strategic Management Journal, 20*, 421–444.

Becherer, R., & Maurer, J. G. (1999). The proactive personality disposition and entrepreneurial behavior among small company presidents. *Journal of Small Business Management, 37*(1), 28–36.

Benner, M. J., & Tushman, M. L. (2003). Exploitation, exploration, and process management: The productivity dilemma revisited. *Academy of Management Review, 28*(2), 238–256.

Bhide, A. V. (2000). *The origin and evolution of new businesses*. New York: Oxford University Press.

Bird, B. (1998). Implementing entrepreneurial ideas: The case for intention. *Academy of Management Review, 13*(3), 442–453.

Birkinshaw, J. (1997). Entrepreneurship in multinational corporations: The characteristics of subsidiary initiatives. *Strategic Management Journal, 18*(3), 207–229.

Block, D. M. (2003). Autonomy of individuals and organizations: Towards a strategy research agenda. *International Journal of Business and Economics, 2*(1), 57–73.

Block, Z., & MacMillan, I. C. (1995). *Corporate venturing.* Boston: Harvard Business School Press.

Bromiley, P., Miller, K. D., & Rau, D. (2001). Risk in strategic management research. In M. A. Hitt, R. E. Freeman, & J. S. Harrison, (Eds.) *Blackwell handbook of strategic management* (pp. 259–288). Oxford, UK: Blackwell.

Brown, J. S., & Duguid, P. (2000). *The social life of information.* Boston: Harvard Business School Press.

Brown, S. L., & Eisenhardt, K. M. (1998). *Competing on the edge: Strategy as structured chaos.* Boston: Harvard Business School Press.

Burgelman, R. A. (1983). A process model of internal corporate venturing in the diversified major firm. *Administrative Science Quarterly, 28,* 223–244.

Burgelman, R. A. (2001). *Strategy is destiny: How strategy-making shapes a company's future.* New York: Free Press.

Burgelman, R. A., & Doz, Y. L. (2001). The power of strategic integration. *MIT Sloan Management Review, 42*(3), 28–38.

Burgelman, R. A., & Sayles, L. R. (1986). *Inside corporate innovation: Strategy, structure and managerial skills.* New York: Free Press.

Busenitz, L., & Barney, J. (1997). Biases and heuristics in strategic decision making: Differences between entrepreneurs and managers in large organizations. *Journal of Business Venturing, 12,* 9–30.

Chen, M. J., & Hambrick, D. (1995). Speed stealth and selective attack: How small firms differ from large firms on competitive behavior. *Academy of Management Journal, 38,* 453–482.

Chesbrough, H. (2003). *Open innovation.* Boston: Harvard Business School Press.

Christensen, C. M. (1997). *The innovator's dilemma.* Boston: Harvard Business School Press.

Christensen, C. M., & Bower, J. L. (1996). Customer power, strategic investment, and the failure of leading firms. *Strategic Management Journal, 17,* 197–218.

Collins, J. C., & Porras, J. I. (1997). *Built to last.* New York: HarperBusiness.

Cooper, A. C. (2002). Networks, alliances, and entrepreneurship. In M. A. Hitt, R. D. Ireland, S. M. Camp, & D. L. Sexton (Eds.), *Strategic entrepreneurship* (pp. 203–222). Oxford, UK: Blackwell.

Covin, J. G., & Slevin, D. P. (1991). A conceptual model of entrepreneurship as firm behavior. *Entrepreneurship Theory and Practice, 16,* 7–24.

Crossan, M., Lane, H., & White, R. (1999). An organizational learning framework: From intuition to institution. *Academy of Management Review, 24,* 522–537.

Damanpour, F. (1991). Organizational innovation: A meta-analysis of effects of determinants and moderators. *Academy of Management Journal, 34,* 555–590.

D'Aveni, R. (1994). *Hypercompetition.* New York: Free Press.

Day, J. D., Mang, P. Y., Richter, A., & Roberts, J. (2001). The innovative organization: Why new ventures need more than a room of their own. *McKinsey Quarterly, 2,* 20–31.

Deshpande, R., & Farley, J. U. (2004). Organizational culture, market orientation, innovativeness and firm performance: An international research odyssey. *International Journal of Research in Marketing, 21,* 3–22.

Dess, G. G., Rasheed, A., McLaughlin, K. J., & Priem, R. L. (1995). The new corporate architecture. *Academy of Management Executive, 9*(3), 7–20.

Devanna, M. A., & Tichy, N. (1990, Winter). Creating the competitive organization of the 21st century: The boundaryless corporation. *Human Resource Management,* pp. 455–471.

Dougherty, D. (1992). A practice-centered model of organizational renewal through product innovation. *Strategic Management Journal, 13,* 77–92.

Dougherty, D., & Hardy, C. (1996). Sustained product innovation in large, mature organizations: Overcoming innovation-to-organization problems. *Academy of Management Journal, 39*(5), 1120–1153.

Doz, Y. L. (1996). The evolution of cooperation in strategic alliances: Initial conditions or learning processes? *Strategic Management Journal, 17*, 55–83.

Doz, Y. L., & Hamel, G. (1998). *Alliance advantage: The art of creating value through partnering.* Boston: Harvard Business School Press.

Evans, P., & Wurster, T. S. (2000). *Blown to bits.* Boston: Harvard Business School Press.

Fiet, J. O. (2002). *The systematic search for entrepreneurial discoveries.* Westport, CT: Quorum Books.

Fiol, C. M., & Lyles, M. A. (1985). Organizational learning. *Academy of Management Review, 10*, 803–813.

Gaglio, C. M., & Taub, P. (1992). Entrepreneurship and opportunity recognition. In *Frontiers of entrepreneurship research, 1992* (pp. 136–147). Babson Park, MA: Babson College.

Galbraith, J. R. (1982). Designing the innovating organization. *Organizational Dynamics, 11*, 5–25.

Garvin, D. (1993, July–August). Building a learning organization. *Harvard Business Review*, pp. 78–91.

Ghemawat, P., & Costa, J. E. (1993). The organizational tension between static and dynamic efficiency. *Strategic Management Journal, 14*, 59–73.

Goleman, D. (1998). What makes a leader? *Harvard Business Review, 76*, 92–105.

Greene, P. G., Brush, C. G., & Hart, M. M. (1999). The corporate venture champion: A resource-based approach to role and process. *Entrepreneurship Theory & Practice, 23*(3), 103–122.

Grenadier, S. R., & Weiss, A. M. (1997). Investment in technological innovations: An option pricing approach. *Journal of Financial Economics, 44*, 397–416.

Guth, W. D., & Ginsberg, A. (1990). Guest editors' introduction: Corporate entrepreneurship. *Strategic Management Journal, 11*, 5–15.

Hage, J. (1980). *Theories of organizations.* New York: Wiley.

Hamel, G. (1999). Bringing Silicon Valley inside. *Harvard Business Review, 77*(5), 70–84.

Hamel, G. (2000). *Leading the revolution.* Boston: Harvard Business School Press.

Hamel, G., & Prahalad, C. K. (1996). Competing in the new economy: Managing out of bounds. *Strategic Management Journal, 17*, 232–242.

He, Z., & Wong, P. (2004). Exploration vs. exploitation: An empirical test for the ambidexterity hypothesis. *Organization Science, 15*(4), 481–494.

Helgesen, S. (1996). Leading from the grass roots. In F. Hesselbein, M. Goldsmith, & R. Beckhard (Eds.), *Leader of the future* (pp. 19–24). San Francisco, CA: Jossey-Bass.

Ibarra, H. (1993). Network centrality, power, and innovation involvement: Determinants of technical and administrative roles. *Academy of Management Journal, 36*, 471–501.

Janney, J. J., & Dess, G. G. (2004). Can real options analysis improve decision making? Promises and pitfalls. *Academy of Management Executive, 18*(4), 60–76.

Johannessen, J.-A., Olsen, B., & Lumpkin, G. T. (2001). Innovation as newness: What is new, how new, and new to whom? *European Journal of Innovation Management, 4*(1), 20–31.

Kanter, R. M. (1983). *The change masters: Innovation and entrepreneurship in the American corporation.* New York: Simon & Schuster.

Kanter, R. M. (1985). Supporting innovation and venture development in established companies. *Journal of Business Venturing, 1*, 47–60.

Kanter, R. M. (1994). *Innovative reward systems for the changing workplace.* New York: McGraw-Hill.

Kanter, R. M., Kao, J., & Wiersema, F. (1997). *Innovation: Breakthrough thinking at 3M, DuPont, GE, Pfizer, and Rubbermaid.* New York: HarperCollins.

Kanter, R. M., North, J., Bernstein, A. P., & Williams, A. (1990). Engines of progress: Designing and running entrepreneurial vehicles in established companies. *Journal of Business Venturing, 5*(6), 415–430.

Kelley, D., Neck H. M., O'Connor, G. C., & Paulson, A. (2002). Developing radical innovation capabilities: Opposing forces from the corporate entrepreneurship and organizational systems. In *Frontiers of Entrepreneurship Research, 2002* (pp. 210–213). Babson Park, MA: Babson College.

Kerr, J., & Slocum, J. W. (1987). Managing corporate culture through reward systems. *Academy of Management Executive, 1*(2), 99–107.

Knight, F. (1921). *Risk, uncertainty, and profit*. New York: Harper and Row.

Kogut, B. (1988). Joint ventures: Theoretical and empirical perspectives. *Strategic Management Journal, 9*(4), 319–332.

Kreiser, P. M., Marino, L., & Weaver, K. M. (2002a, January). *Correlates of entrepreneurship: The impact of national culture on risk-taking and proactiveness in SMEs*. Paper presented at annual USASBE Conference, Reno, NV.

Kreiser, P. M., Marino, L. D., & Weaver, K. M. (2002b). Assessing the psychometric properties of the entrepreneurial orientation scale: A multicountry analysis. *Entrepreneurship Theory & Practice, 26*, 71–95.

Kuczmarski, T. (1996). *Innovation: Leadership strategies for the competitive edge*. Chicago: NTC Publishing Group.

Lambkin, M. (1988). Order of entry and performance in new markets. *Strategic Management Journal, 9*, 127–140.

Lant, T. K., Milliken, F. J., & Batra, B. (1992). The role of managerial learning and interpretation in strategic persistence and reorientation: An empirical exploration. *Strategic Management Journal, 13*(8), 585–608.

Lawler, E. E. III. (1996). *From the ground up: Six principles for building the new logic corporation*. San Francisco, CA: Jossey-Bass.

Leifer, R., McDermott, C. M., O'Connor, G. C., Peters, L. S., Rice, M., & Veryzer, R. W. (2000). *Radical innovation*. Boston: Harvard Business School Press.

Leonard-Barton, D. (1992). Core capabilities and core rigidities: A paradox in managing new product development. *Strategic Management Journal, 13*, 111–125.

Levinthal, D., & March, J. G. (1993). The myopia of learning. *Strategic Management Journal, 14*, 95–112.

Lieberman, M. B., & Montgomery, D. B. (1988). First mover advantages. *Strategic Management Journal, 9*, 41–58.

Lieberman, M. B., & Montgomery, D. B. (1998). First mover (dis)advantages: Retrospective and link with resource-based view. *Strategic Management Journal, 19*(12), 1111–1125.

Lorange, P., & Murphy, D. (1984). Considerations in implementing strategic control. *Journal of Business Strategy, 5*, 27–35.

Lumpkin, G. T., & Dess, G. G. (1996). Clarifying the entrepreneurial orientation construct and linking it to performance. *Academy of Management Review, 21*(1), 135–172.

Lumpkin, G. T., & Dess, G. G. (2001). Linking two dimensions of entrepreneurial orientation to firm performance: The moderating role of environment and industry life cycle. *Journal of Business Venturing, 16*(5), 429–451.

Lumpkin, G. T., & Lichtenstein, B. M. (2005). The role of organizational learning in the opportunity recognition process. *Entrepreneurship Theory & Practice, 29*(4), 451–472.

Lumpkin, G. T., Hills, G. E., & Shrader, R. C. (2004). Opportunity recognition. In H. P. Welsch (Ed.), *Entrepreneurship: The way ahead* (pp. 73–90), London: Routledge.

Lyon, D. W., Lumpkin, G. T., & Dess, G. G. (2000). Enhancing entrepreneurial orientation research: Operationalizing and measuring a key strategic decision making process. *Journal of Management, 26*, 1055–1085.

Maidique, M. A. (1980, Winter). Entrepreneurs, champions, and technological innovation. *Sloan Management Review*, pp. 59–76.

March, J. G. (1991). Exploration and exploitation in organizational learning. *Organization Science, 2*, 71–87.

McGrath, R. G. (1999). Falling forward: Real options reasoning and entrepreneurial failure. *Academy of Management Review, 24*, 13–30.

McGrath, R. G., & MacMillan, I. C. (2000). *The Entrepreneurial Mindset.* Boston: Harvard Business School Press.

McMullen, J. S., & Shepherd, D. A. (2006). Entrepreneurial action and the role of uncertainty in the theory of the entrepreneur. *Academy of Management Review, 31*(1), 132–152.

Miles, R., & Snow, C. (1978). *Organizational strategy, structure, and process.* New York: McGraw-Hill.

Miles, R., Snow, C., Mathews, J., Miles, G., & Coleman, H. (1997). Organizing in the knowledge age: Anticipating the cellular form. *Academy of Management Executive, 11*(4), 7–20.

Miller, A., & Camp, B. (1985). Exploring determinants of success in corporate ventures. *Journal of Business Venturing, 1*(2), 87–105.

Miller, D. (1983). The correlates of entrepreneurship in three types of firms. *Management Science, 29*, 770–791.

Miller, D. (1987). Strategy making and structure: analysis and implications for performance. *Academy of Management Journal, 30*(1), 7–32.

Miller, D. (1990). *The Icarus paradox.* New York: HarperCollins.

Miller, D. (1993). The architecture of simplicity. *Academy of Management Review, 18*, 116–138.

Miller, D., & Friesen, P. H. (1984). *Organizations: A quantum view.* Englewood Cliffs, NJ: Prentice Hall.

Mitchell, W., & Singh, K. (1996). Survival of businesses using collaborative relationships to commercialize complex goods. *Strategic Management Journal, 17*(3), 169–195.

Nelson, R. R., & Winter, S. G. (1982). *An evolutionary theory of economic change.* Cambridge, MA: Belknap Press.

Nonaka, I. (1994). A dynamic theory of organizational knowledge creation. *Organization Science, 5*, 14–37.

Palich, L. E., & Bagby, D. R. (1995). Using cognitive theory to explain entrepreneurial risk-taking: Challenging conventional wisdom. *Journal of Business Venturing, 10*(6), 425–438.

Pinchot, G. (1985). *Intrapreneuring.* New York: Harper & Row.

Porac, J. F., & Thomas, H. (1994). Cognitive categorization and subjective rivalry among retailers in a small city. *Journal of Applied Psychology, 79*(1), 54–66.

Porter, M. E. 1985. *Competitive Advantage.* New York: Free Press.

Quinn, J. B. (1988). *Intelligent Enterprise.* New York: Free Press.

Quinn, R. C., & Spreitzer, G. M. (1997). The road to empowerment: Seven questions every leader should consider. *Organizational Dynamics, 25*, 37–49.

Rappaport, A. (1999). New thinking on how to link pay to performance. *Harvard Business Review, 77*(2), 91–105.

Rauch, A., Wiklund, J., Lumpkin, G. T., & Frese, M. (2004). Entrepreneurial orientation and business performance: Cumulative empirical evidence. *Frontiers of Entrepreneurship Research*, pp. 164–177.

Robinson, W. T., Fornell, C., & Sullivan, M. (1992). Are market pioneers intrinsically stronger than later entrants? *Strategic Management Journal, 13*(8), 609–624.

Rodengen, J. L. (1997). *The legend of Nucor Corporation.* Fort Lauderdale, FL: Write Stuff Enterprises.

Royer, I. (2003, February). Why bad projects are so hard to kill. *Harvard Business Review*, pp. 48–56.

Schuler, R. S. (1986). Fostering and facilitating entrepreneurship in organizations: Implications for organization structure and human resource management practices. *Human Resource Management, 25*(4), 607–629.

Seibert, S. E., Crant, J. M., & Kraimer, M. L. (1999). Proactive personality and career success. *Journal of Applied Psychology, 84*(3), 416–427.

Senge, P. M. (1990). *The fifth discipline.* New York: Doubleday/Currency.

Shapira, Z. 1995. *Risk taking: A managerial perspective*. New York: Russell Sage Foundation.

Sharma, A. (1999). Central dilemmas of managing innovation in large firms. *California Management Review, 41*(3), 147–164.

Simon, M., Houghton, S. M., & Aquino, K. (2000). Cognitive biases, risk perception, and venture formation: How individuals decide to start companies. *Journal of Business Venturing, 14*, 113–134.

Sitkin, S. B., & Pablo, A. L. (1992). Reconceptualizing the determinants of risk behavior. *Academy of Management Review, 17*(1), 9–38.

Slappendel, C. (1996). Perspectives on innovation in organizations. *Organization Studies, 17*(1), 102–129.

Smith, K., Ferrier, W., & Grimm, C. (2001). King of the hill: Dethroning the industry leader. *Academy of Management Executive, 15*(2), 59–70.

Steere, W. C., Jr., & Niblack, J. (1997). Pfizer, Inc. In R. M. Kanter, J. Kao, & F. Wiersema (Eds.), *Innovation: Breakthrough thinking at 3M, DuPont, GE, Pfizer, and Rubbermaid* (pp. 123–145). New York: HarperCollins.

Stevenson, H. H., & Jarillo, J. C. (1990). A paradigm of entrepreneurship: Entrepreneurial management. *Strategic Management Journal, 11*, 17–27.

Stopford, J. M., & Baden-Fuller, C. (1994). Creating corporate entrepreneurship. *Strategic Management Journal, 15*(7), 521–536.

Swierczek, F. W., & Ha, T. T. (2003). Entrepreneurial orientation, uncertainty avoidance and firm performance. *Entrepreneurship and Innovation, 4*(1), 46–57.

Tucker, R. B. (2002). *Driving growth through innovation*. San Francisco, CA: Berrett-Koehler.

Tushman, M. L., & Nadler, D. A. (1978). Information processing as an integrating concept in organizational design. *Academy of Management Review, 3*, 613–624.

Tushman, M. L., & O'Reilly, C. (1997). *Winning through innovation*. Boston: Harvard Business School Press.

Utterback, J. M., & Abernathy, W. J. (1975). A dynamic model of process and product innovation. *Omega, 3*(6), 639–656.

Van de Ven, A. H. (1988). Central problems in the management of innovation. In M. L. Tushman & E. L. Moore (Eds.) *Readings in the management of innovation* (pp. 103–122). Boston: Ballinger.

Vandermerwe, S, & Birley, S. (1997). The corporate entrepreneur: Leading organizational transformation. *Long Range Planning, 30*(3), 345–352.

Venkataraman, S. (1989). Strategic orientation of business enterprises: The construct, dimensionality, and measurement. *Management Science, 35*(8), 942–962.

Verhees, F., & Meulenberg, M. (2004). Market orientation, innovativeness, product innovation, and performance in small firms. *Journal of Small Business Management, 42*(2), 134–154.

Wenger, E. C., & Snyder, W. M. (2000). Communities of practice: The organizational frontier. *Harvard Business Review, 78*(1), 139–145.

12

Cross-Cultural Entrepreneurship: The Case of China[1]

Rosalie L. Tung
Jan Walls
Michael Frese

Before we look at China in more detail (major hypotheses, findings, and cases), we need to make some general remarks that relate entrepreneurship and cross-cultural approaches. Up to 1990 there were few studies on cross-cultural entrepreneurship, but recently there has been an upsurge of studies that compare entrepreneurship across cultures or nations (the Global Entrepreneurship Monitor [GEM] study), and the number of studies on cross-cultural entrepreneurship has increased dramatically. It is not necessary to give a complete overview of cross-cultural entrepreneurship because there is an excellent review of cross-cultural entrepreneurship research by Hayton, George, and Zahra (2002). These seem to be the main conclusions of the Hayton et al. review: First, most studies on national culture base their estimates of the cultures to be studied on Hofstede's seminal research (Hofstede, 1991). Second, individualism is probably positively, power distance negatively, and uncertainty avoidance negatively correlated with entrepreneurship and related constructs (such as innovativeness). Third, there are relationships between national culture and interpersonal differences (that are, in turn, related to entrepreneurship, such as achievement motive or entrepreneurial "scripts"). Finally, national

---

[1]Work by Michael Frese on this article was facilitated by the grant on "Psychological Factors of Entrepreneurial Success in Germany and China" by the Deutsche Forschungsgemeinschaft (FR 638/23-1); this is gratefully acknowledged.

culture is related to corporate entrepreneurship and specific strategies related to corporate entrepreneurship, for example, investing in greenfield sites or acquisitions as strategies of expansion.

SOME THEORETICAL PROPOSITIONS

The most basic hypothesis on culture and entrepreneurship suggests that different nations have different startup, success, or failure rates. Startup rates across nations were described by Reynolds, Bygrave, Autio, Cox, and Hay (2002); the relationship to failure has surprisingly not been empirically studied much. Obviously, it is not just culture that plays a role here because other factors (such as climate, being a neighbor to a strong or an unstable economy, incidental laws [laws not based on culture], differential economic cycles in different nations, etc.) may be as important as cultural factors. Therefore, from a cultural perspective, it is not enough to find national differences; the research also has to prove that cultural dimensions are related to startup rates, success rates, and failure rates. By and large, empirical studies in this area have yielded only very small and inconsistent relationships (Hayton et al., 2002). One requirement is to match the cultural constructs to the entrepreneurial constructs—for example, uncertainty avoidance and power distance are correlated with lack of innovation, and individualism may be related to innovativeness of cultures (Davidsson, 1995; Davidsson & Wiklund, 1997; Shane, 1993).

It is not surprising that simple relationships between cultural variables and entrepreneurial success variables are not high and not very stable: There are many compensatory mechanisms that may play a role here. Take the example of innovation strategies (Shane, Venkataraman, & MacMillan, 1995).

> The more uncertainty accepting a society is, the more people in it prefer champions to overcome organizational inertia to innovation by violating organizational norms, rules and procedures .... The more power distant a society is, the more people in it prefer champions to make those in authority the locus of support for efforts to overcome resistance to innovative ideas. (Shane et al., 1995, pp. 945, 946)

The more uncertainty avoidant a culture is, the more planning becomes a relevant success factor in entrepreneurship (Rauch, Frese, & Sonnentag, 2000). Thus, we should not assume a simple relationship between a cultural variable and startup, success, or failure rates but should go beyond these simple notions by looking at compensatory mechanisms and strategies of how to deal with the requirements of entrepreneurship in different cultures.

In principle, there are three plausible hypotheses with regard to cross-cultural differences in entrepreneurial success. The first hypothesis ne-gates cultural differences and argues that good entrepreneurship is the same across all cultures—entrepreneurial requirements are the same across cultures and, therefore, general laws of entrepreneurship prevail (Mitchell et al., 2002). Maybe this hypothesis can also be restated that entrepreneurship itself is a subculture in societies: The notion of entrepreneurship implies a certain kind of subculture endorsed by entrepreneurs across different cultures (Mitchell et al., 2002). Entrepreneurs may be different from the main culture and that may be one of the success factors. For example, if the national culture is nonentrepreneurial, those entrepreneurs who are different from the culture may survive better. In other words, this hypothesis implies that cultural adjustment may be detrimental to entrepreneurial success under conditions in which the society is nonentrepreneurial.

The second hypothesis—the match hypothesis—requires a good match to exist between an entrepreneur's behavioral tendencies, attitudes, and values and the culture around the entrepreneur. An example is the study by Rauch et al. (2000) alluded to earlier. Irish business owners showed a different relationship between formal planning and success than East and West Germans. Ireland is lower on uncertainty avoidance than both East and West Germany (Sully de Luque & Javidan, 2004), and therefore the correlation between formal planning by business owners and success was negative in Ireland; in contrast, this relationship was positive in both parts of Germany (Rauch et al., 2000). Planning is one way to overcome the negative feelings of uncertainty avoidance (Hofstede, 2001). Entrepreneurs who live in an environment in which planning is emphasized would do well to adjust to the culture and also plan more to be successful (Germany). In contrast, in a less uncertainty-avoidant environment (Ireland), people should emphasize a higher degree of flexibility and at the same time show little formal planning if they want to be successful.

The third general hypothesis makes use of the concept of niche: Entrepreneurs may be successful precisely because they occupy niches that are culturally different from the main culture. For example, people who participated in the minority movement of the Greens in Germany occupied some niches (e.g., wooden hand-carved toys, wind turbines, bicycle shops, restaurants, collectivistic production methods, etc.) against the societal consensus and turned out to be successful with them. Thus, here the very difference from the main culture is one of the factors that make entrepreneurs successful in niches.

These three hypotheses are not diametrically opposed to each other. Different groups of entrepreneurs may follow different models; therefore, different hypotheses may be correct for different groups, different dependent variables, and different cultural variables.

SOME METHODOLOGICAL ISSUES OF CROSS-CULTURAL ENTREPRENEURSHIP

Scholars too often restrict their research to mean differences. Mean differences imply that cross-cultural differences directly affect how entrepreneurs work. Relationship differences imply that there are different correlations in different cultures (in other words, culture is conceptualized as a moderator). The latter is probably more interesting.

Recently, cross-cultural studies have come under attack from methodological points of view. One methodological problem relates to the "ecological fallacy" or "reverse ecological fallacy": Culture-level differences are assumed to also apply to the individual level or individual-level differences are assumed to also exist on the cultural level (Hofstede, 2001). Individual decisions, such as the decision to start a company, should not necessarily be related to culture-level constructs (Mitchell, Smith, Seawright, & Morse, 2000); this is just one instance of the level of analysis issue (Klein, Dansereau, & Hall, 1994). A related problem is that many cultural questionnaires are not made to be used on the individual level and lose reliability there (Hofstede, 2002; Spector, Cooper, & Sparks, 2001). Scholars have to present theoretical ideas—why the ecological variables are useful as culture variables and how they influence individual actions and vice versa. Moreover, the items have to be formulated for the appropriate level (referring to a society for cultural level scales). Also, we can only assume that relationships between cultural variables and outcome variables are due to culture if we find the equivalent correlations between individual variables that are equivalent to the cultural variables and the respective outcome variables (Triandis, 1994). An alternative is to test differences between equivalent subcultures within one country. For example, Chinese-American entrepreneurs should show similar differences (although probably smaller ones) compared to White Americans as native Chinese to White Americans (Tan, 2002). The two methods—showing that the individual value of culture leads to the same relationships as cultural variation and testing relevant subgroups—are unfortunately not often utilized by studies in cultural entrepreneurship.

Moreover, there is a renewed debate on some of the methodological issues related to response scales in cross-cultural psychology (Kitayama, 2002; Oyserman, Coon, & Kemmelmeier, 2002). Which reference groups do people use as comparison group when they answer an item on collective values that this is "true to a high extent"? The issue of reference group is not a trivial question in cross-cultural research (Heine, Lehman, Peng, & Greenholtz, 2002). For example, if a German entrepreneur uses France as a reference group, he or she may respond to the statement: "Entrepreneurs are well accepted in our society" with a high degree of agreement; however, if he or she uses the United States as a comparison society, the response would probably be "no." Here are some suggested improvements for studies on cross-cultural entrepreneurship: First, scholars should ask themselves whether they want to develop or use non-Likert type scales to reliably assess individual cultural tendencies. For this reason, some of us are currently developing scenario-based questionnaires to study entrepreneurs' cultural orientation (with the focus of looking at their own cultural practices in their firms) (Koenig, Frese, Steinmetz, Rauch, & Wang, in preparation). Second, it may be useful to explicitly describe the comparison group to participants when they describe their own society. Third, scholars need to argue theoretically for their choice of cultures to be studied. This also applies, of course, to monoculture studies. For example, scholars have to argue explicitly why their particular research question and theoretical model should be studied in a certain study—all too often people use their home country as a starting point without adequate theoretical reasoning (e.g., comparing a country with the United States). Fourth, cross-cultural studies have to show empirically that their measures are equivalent across cultures (Triandis, 1994). Finally, the issue of differential response styles in different cultures needs to be taken into consideration within cross-cultural research and new approaches need to be considered (Hanges, Dickson, & Sipe, 2004). For example, people in Asian countries are often characterized as avoiding extreme answer possibilities and tend to choose the middle of a scale.

Culture is often defined by being a construct characterized by societal practices and values (House, Hanges, Javidan, Dorfman, & Gupta, 2004). These two aspects of the definition are often not clearly distinguished, and therefore measures of cultural dimensions often confound the practice and value dimensions (e.g., Hofstede, 2001). Any confounding in this area has been shown to be a problem, not only for the reliability of the scales but also because the practices scales and the value scales are by and large negatively correlated (Hanges, 2004; Hanges & Dickson, 2004). This means that operationalizing culture as societal practices may lead to opposite conclusions on relationships with other relevant variables than a concept of culture operationalized as values.

The final methodological/theoretical issue is particularly important for cross-cultural entrepreneurship. There is always the danger that researchers reify cultural differences when in reality differences between countries may be the results of economic differences, differences in knowledge about entrepreneurship, or differences in national wealth (Busenitz, Gómez, & Spencer, 2000; Hofstede, 2001).

CROSS-CULTURAL ENTREPRENEURSHIP: THE CASE OF CHINA

To make our task more manageable, we concentrated our discussion on one country in a bit more detail. We decided to use China as an example, because we all do research in China or with Chinese collaborators and because we think China is a interesting case for entrepreneurship: First there has been a dramatic increase of entrepreneurship within the last few years; however, China is not the emerging nation with the highest entrepreneurial activities. Second, there are numerous entrepreneurs in the diaspora—as a matter of fact, the Chinese diaspora is one of the larger economic powers in the world (cf. later comments). Moreover, entrepreneurs who work within a diaspora are probably less well adjusted to the local culture than "local" entrepreneurs. Thus, they are more likely to be niche players (third general hypothesis discussed earlier) or the culture they come from is a culture that leads to "better" entrepreneurship (first universal hypothesis given earlier). Third, entrepreneurship is often deemed to be an individualistic enterprise (Mitchell et al., 2000), and entrepreneurship in China is an example of entrepreneurship within a collectivistic setting. Finally, Chinese entrepreneurship may show specific advantages and disadvantages that are due to its collectivistic setting.

China shows a high degree of entrepreneurial activities, both in terms of "necessity-based" startup activities in China and "opportunity-based" entrepreneurial activities (Reynolds et al., 2002). Such a picture is typical of developing countries; in developing countries, there are more people who start a firm because they see entrepreneurship as a last resort, because of unemployment or because employment options are not satisfactory. In contrast, opportunity-based entrepreneurship elects "to start a business as one of several possible career options" (Reynolds et al., 2002, p. 15). Although China demonstrates high startup activities in comparison to other parts of the world, startup activities are lower there than in other countries in Asia (notably, Thailand shows a higher degree of entrepreneurial activities than China) (Reynolds et al., 2003).

The People's Republic of China (China, in short) has been one of the fastest growing economies during the past two decades and China is projected to become the world's second largest economy, after the United States, by 2030 (Newton & Subbaraman, 2002). Entrepreneurship, both from the diaspora and within Mainland China, was one of the factors behind this enormous growth. Entrepreneurs, who were once denounced and reviled under a socialist planned economy, are now welcomed as members of the Chinese Communist Party. According to the Asian Development Bank Country Assistance Plan for China, the private sector in China now produces about 24% of the country's gross domestic product (GDP), compared with 0.9% share in 1979 (http://www.adb.org/Documents/CAPs/PRC/0306.asp).

Comparison of China With Other Countries

The following discussion is based on Table 12.1, which describes the results of the recently published GLOBE study (House et al., 2004). The GLOBE

TABLE 12.1

Dimensions of Societal Practices of the GLOBE Study

	United States	West Germany	Canada, English	China	Thailand
Performance orientation	A	B	A	A	B
Future orientation	B	B	A	C	C
Assertiveness	A	A	B	B	B
Institutional collectivism	B	C	B	A	B
Ingroup collectivism	C	C	C	A	A
Gender egalitarianism	B	B	A	B	B
Humane orientation	C	D	B	B	A
Power distance	B	B	B	B	A
Uncertainty avoidance	B	A	B	A	C

Note. Letters A–D represents meaningful country groups for the scales A > B > C > D. A means highest cluster of countries, and D means lowest cluster of countries (in some categories, there are only three clusters: A, B, C) (House et al., 2004).

study is based on Hofstede's seminal work (Hofstede, 2001) but provides important methodological improvements; the GLOBE study differentiated between "As is" (societal practices) and "Should be" (values) and used more concepts. Table 12.1 provides the data on societal practices for China, Canada (the English-speaking part of Canada, which also has a large Chinese diaspora), West Germany, and the United States. The reasons for concentrating on these are pragmatic, because they are the countries the authors live in, and we use the United States because many people know that culture. In addition, we included Thailand because it is an Asian country with a high degree of entrepreneurship and with its Buddhist culture is different from China (Thailand also has a large and successful diaspora of Chinese entrepreneurs).

China is high on performance orientation (similar to the United States and Canada), low on future orientation, middle on assertiveness, high on both forms of collectivism (institutional and in-group collectivism), middle on gender egalitarianism, middle on humane orientation (like Canada) and power distance, and high on uncertainty avoidance (similar to Germany). A number of interesting hypotheses follow from these similarities and differences. Because we are less interested in finding direct relationships between the cultural values and entrepreneurship variables, we would rather develop hypotheses on how cultural variables change how entrepreneurs have to deal with the challenges of entrepreneurship. In the interest of saving space, we present just a few hypotheses. Any number of additional hypotheses can be developed.

The high performance orientation in China may lead to attempts of fast and efficient changes in Chinese firms to increase quality and quantity of performance. Performance pay schemes may motivate employees more in China than in Thailand or Germany.

The low future orientation in China (and Thailand) probably decreases the amount of long-term planning in these countries (particularly compared to Canada). Probably things are finished at the last minute in China. Employees will change jobs whenever they get higher income somewhere else—long-range issues, such as where to get better qualifications, may be less important. Time management makes a difference between urgent tasks and (often long-range) important tasks. Entrepreneurs will have a tendency to go for the urgent rather than for the important tasks. If going for important tasks (e.g., long-range strategy, long-range qualification of personnel, long-range innovation) is important for entrepreneurial success, time management courses may be particularly useful for Chinese entrepreneurs (although these courses have a lower usefulness in Canada—but they should be more popular in Canada because long-range orientation is more important there).

Assertiveness is lower in China and Thailand (although not very low). This implies that to build a network, entrepreneurs should not be seen to aggressively push their agenda or to put their person into the foreground. Dominance may have an unimportant or even negative effect on success in China, whereas it would be positively related in the United States or in Germany.

Collectivism is higher in China. Even a meta-analysis that has been critical of the notion of an undifferentiated concept of collectivism finds a higher degree of collectivism in China (Oyserman et al., 2002). The GLOBE differentiation between institutional collectivism (collective actions and collective distributions of resources) and in-group collectivism (loyalty and pride to in group, particularly family) is useful from this perspective. The correlation between institutional collectivism and in-group collectivism is low (Hanges, 2004). The fact that Thailand is lower on institutional collectivism shows that Asia cannot be assumed to be collectivistic throughout. Loyalty to the firm should be lower in Thailand than in China (and much lower in Germany). It follows that cross-cultural studies should not be approached with a simple-minded formula that individualism leads to higher entrepreneurship. Rather, it follows from in-group collectivism that entrepreneurship in China should be more family-based or group-based than in the United States, Germany, and Canada. Moreover, Chinese firms tend to invest more into relationships before they start a firm and investments into relationships pay off more highly in China than in the United States, Germany, and Canada. As a matter of fact, the Chinese have a telling concept of Guanxi that is of high importance and that implies that relationships with other businesses and the government are cultivated (Tung & Worm, 2001). Finally, to motivate Chinese employees may require a collective vision more than to motivate German employees.

Whether institutional collectivism is higher than in-group collectivism or vice versa may be of high importance. For example, Japan (and to a lesser extent South Korea) exhibits much lower in-group collectivism than institutional collectivism (the highest cultures on institutional collectivism are Sweden, South Korea, and Japan) (Gelfand, Bhawuk, Hishi, & Bechtold, 2004). In contrast, institutional collectivism in China is lower than in-group collectivism. We discuss later the issue of why there is a lack of large networks of companies in China (and in the Chinese diaspora) in contrast to Japan (and South Korea).

Gender egalitarianism should lead to higher chances for success for female entrepreneurs in Canada than in the other countries (corrected for industry; there are large industry effects, and women tend to be owners in industries with smaller return rates; cf. Mead & Liedholm, 1998).

Humane orientation is higher in China than in Germany. It should be easier for entrepreneurs to deal with organizational members on a one-on-one basis because compassion is higher. Employees in China will expect a more moralistic and compassionate orientation in their entrepreneurs than in Germany (and this is even more true in Thailand). Organizational changes will be more easily adjusted to individual likes and dislikes in China than in Germany (Brodbeck, Frese, & Javidan, 2002).

Power distance is similar across the countries (except being higher in Thailand) and is surprisingly low in China. Most cross-cultural observers of China would probably maintain that there is a higher power distance in China than observed in the GLOBE data (Brockner et al., 2001; Hofstede, 2001; McGrath, MacMillan, Yang, & Tsai, 1992) We agree with these researchers and assume that power distance is higher in China. This implies that employees are more likely to obey their employer without reservations in China than in the United States, Canada, and Germany. If this were true, entrepreneurs' decisions in China (and Thailand) would be criticized much less in China than in the other countries. This implies that decisions may be implemented more quickly (by giving orders) but that there is also less feedback to learn for the entrepreneurs in the high power distant countries. Also, participatory strategies should work less well in China (and Thailand) than in the other countries (Brockner et al., 2001). Finally, leadership skills may be more important in a low power distant country than in a high-power distant country—thus, the correlation between leadership skills and success should be lower in China than in countries with lower power distance.

Uncertainty avoidance is highest in Germany and China; thus, the decision to become an entrepreneur is much more difficult in these two countries (at least for opportunity-based entrepreneurship) and will therefore take more time and preparation than in the other countries. China is an exception as uncertainty avoidance is high but future orientation is not high (normally these two dimensions correlate highly) (Hanges, 2004). Because planning for the future is a function of future orientation and of uncertainty avoidance, it is unclear whether planning is effective in China or not.

Chinese Diaspora

According to the *Encyclopedia of the Chinese Overseas* (Pan, 1999), there are approximately 55 million ethnic Chinese living outside of China (50.3 million in East and Southeast Asia, and the rest in Canada, the United States, Latin and South America, Europe, and Africa). The economic output of ethnic Chinese in East and Southeast Asia has been estimated at $500 billion (Zutshi, 1997). According to Backman (1999, p. 207), although ethnic Chinese constitute anywhere from 2% to 15% of the population in Indonesia, Malaysia, Thailand, Philippines and Myanmar, they control an estimated 50% to 80% of those countries' corporate, private and domestic capital. Between 1987 and 1990, emigrants from Hong Kong and Taiwan to Canada brought in an estimated C$14.3 billion and created 48,000 jobs (Pan, 1999). After China's open door policy began in the late 1970s, many of these overseas Chinese networks entered or returned to the China market to explore opportunities there.

The overseas Chinese have maintained a fairly low public profile for at least three major reasons: One is the traditional penchant for secrecy/privacy. Two, following the Confucian principle of "moderation," there is a cultural tendency toward modesty. Because many Chinese believe in the cyclical nature of events (such as fortune and misfortune), they feel that it is best to downplay one's accomplishments (Tung, 1994). Finally, discrimination against them and envy of their economic power exist.

The Jewish and Chinese Diasporas

The economic success and sharp business acumen of the Chinese have often been compared to those of the Jews (Zhang, 2002). Reid (cited in Zhang, 2002, pp. 6–7) asserted that the Chinese and Jews are comparable "in their creative and vulnerable role as 'outsiders at the center.'" Both groups have been able to downplay their "political disadvantage" (by virtue of the fact that they are often the target of discrimination in many host societies that they have settled in) and focus instead on economic achievement, particularly in the areas of trade and finance (Zhang, 2002, p. 8). Both

Jews and Chinese share certain cultural characteristics that have enabled them to succeed in their economic pursuits, including the emphasis placed on literacy and education, hard work, and pride in one's cultural heritage (Zhang, 2002). The Chinese base their "Chineseness" on ethnicity. Typically, many Chinese, regardless of religion, years of residency abroad, and nationality (as determined by passport), will continue to perceive themselves as exclusively Chinese. Like the Jews, personal relationship-based connections are of paramount importance in the formation of Chinese networks. In the case of the Chinese, such relationships are based on family, ancestral village, and school ties. In commercial/business circles, for example, many come from Jiangsu and Zhejiang provinces, more specifically the Shanghai/Ningbo/Wenzhou region. Individuals who trace their ancestral roots to this region are reputed to be savvy and astute, in terms of business.

Chinese firms vis-à-vis Japanese Keiretsu and South Korean Chaebols

Despite some problems in the Japanese and South Korean economies, the significant roles that the *keiretsus* (in the case of Japan) and *chaebols* (in the case of South Korea) have played in the phenomenal growth of their respective countries' economies cannot be denied. *Keiretsus* and *chaebols* both refer to "financial cliques." In the West, the closest equivalent to such "financial cliques" is conglomerates; however, Western conglomerates are often no match to the *keiretsus* and *chaebols* in terms of the magnitude and scope of their operations. Usually, a *keiretsu* or *chaebol* engages in a diverse range of business activities, including banking, trading, petrochemicals, automobile manufacturing, steel manufacturing, aerospace manufacturing, and so on (Cho, 1999; Morris, 1999). To date, no Chinese network has approached the size and diversity of operations of the leading Japanese *keiretsus* and Korean *chaebols*. In the 2002 "Fortune Global 500," 88 Japanese companies made the ranks and 12 Korean companies made the list. Twelve companies from Greater China made the list, as well: ten state-owned enterprises from China and two from Taiwan. Despite the larger size (in terms of population) and foreign reserves of Greater China in comparison to Japan and South Korea, Chinese firms accounted for less than 2% of revenues generated by Fortune's Global 500 companies. This raises an interesting question as to why so few Chinese companies have made it to the "Fortune Global 500" list.

At the risk of oversimplification, three primary factors have inhibited the growth of Chinese enterprises. These are: first, absence of generous government incentives (such as interest-free or low interest loans, subsidies, duty-free import of raw materials); second, the general cultural attitude toward business/commerce; and third, characteristics of Chinese entrepreneurial networks. In comparison, the first two factors are present in Japan and South Korea. In the case of Japan, the relationship between business and government has been close ("Japan Inc.") (Abegglen & Stalk, 1985). This has often been cited as one reason for Japan's economic miracle. In addition, the merchant class has been accorded a relatively high status in Japanese society (just below the samurai class in premodern times). Thus, there was already a thriving merchant community in place when Japan embarked on its modernization/industrialization program. In the case of Korea, under the influence of Confucianism, commerce was despised until fairly recently. Under Confucianism, the traditional hierarchy, from top down, is monarch, intellectuals, artisans, peasants, and merchants. This accounts for the recent history of the Korean *chaebols*. For example, the four leading *chaebols* were all established within the past 70 years (the earliest being Samsung in 1938). However, once the South Korean government decided on industrialization as the path for economic development, it provided very generous incentives to support the growth of the *chaebols*. In the case of Greater China, these factors were either absent or weak, until very recently. There is a popular Chinese saying, "There is no such thing as a merchant who is not crafty," that is, all merchants are dishonest. The pursuit of wealth was only encouraged under the late Chinese leader Deng Xiaoping, who promoted the slogan, "To be rich is glorious." In the case of Hong Kong, even though it has been characterized as one of the freest economies in the world, it is important to note that although the government (under the British) had not imposed restrictions, it did not provide special incentives either, along the lines of the Japanese and Korean governments. In the case of Taiwan, much attention has been and continues to be focused on noneconomic issues, such as the political status of Taiwan. In short, the absence of a nurturing business environment, including the negative attitude toward commerce under the Confucian value scheme and early decades of communism in China, focus on noneconomic issues in the case of Taiwan, and the lack of government incentives in the case of Hong Kong, has stunted, in part at least, the growth of big businesses in Greater China.

An additional factor that has constrained the development of big business in the Chinese diaspora is the characteristics associated with Chinese entrepreneurial networks. In general, Chinese entrepreneurial networks share four common characteristics. These are (a) family ownership, (b) paternalism, (c) personalism, and (d) particularism (Pan, 1999, p. 89). These characteristics all help in the original development of entrepreneurial units because there is a high amount of help within families. However, in the long run, these characteristics may turn out to be barriers to enlarge companies. Each of these characteristics is explained briefly next.

Family Ownership.   Most Chinese entrepreneurial networks are owned and operated by members of the family. This is related to the high values of in-group collectivism in China. In the case of Formosa Plastics, with over 30,000 people, the owner/founder, Mr. Y. C. Wang, directs the company through an inner circle comprised of fewer than 10 professional managers (i.e., outsiders). The rest of the inner circle belongs to the family. Although there are distinct advantages associated with family-oriented businesses, such as emphasis on self-reliance, hard work, thrift, willingness to undertake risks, willingness to reinvest earnings/profit, and relative speed of decision making, they do suffer from certain liabilities, most serious of which are first, the lack of creativity (arising from the unwillingness of children to challenge the authority of the owner/founder and inbreeding, i.e., general reluctance to utilize professional management from outside), and second, mistrust of outsiders, leading to an inability to form institutionalized networking relationships, along the lines of the Japanese *keiretsus*. This issue is elaborated on further as we consider "personalism."

Paternalism. The owner-founder is typically the primary decision maker in family-run enterprises. Even though the children may have earned advanced degrees in business administration and/or economics from prestigious universities abroad, the owner-founder still makes all key decisions because of the general belief that management is an art rather than a science; hence, advanced degrees cannot substitute for experience. Because of respect for one's elders, the children seldom dare to challenge the decisions made by their fathers. Thus decisions in many of these entrepreneurial networks continue to be made on the bases of instincts and gut feelings rather than economic principles and/or theories. Paternalism is related to the high power distance in China.

Personalism. This refers to the reliance on personal connections. Two factors have contributed to this: economic necessity, and mistrust of outsiders. When many Chinese first settled as ethnic minorities in foreign lands, as noted earlier, they experienced discrimination and were denied access to bank credit. Hence they had to rely on their own networks to secure sources of funding for their projects. Furthermore, as a result of political upheavals and natural disasters, a "familial life-raft mentality" has developed among many Chinese (Kao, 1993). This family orientation is consistent with Confucian teachings that family interest takes precedence over that of nation-state. Both family orientation and mistrust toward outsiders are an outgrowth of ingroup collectivism (Gelfand et al., 2004). Because of mistrust of outsiders, recruitment into and promotion within the organization are based on connections rather than merit. This has also led to the general criticism that employees who are nonfamily members and minority shareholders in these companies are often abused, thus contributing to inefficiencies and allegations of corruption (Backman, 1999).

Although the Korean *chaebols* are still directed by the owner/founder of these companies and their families, since the 1980s they have embarked on an active campaign to recruit professional managers into their senior management ranks, particularly ethnic Koreans who have received doctorates in business administration and/or economics from universities abroad, especially from U.S. universities. Both *chaebols* and *keiretsus* are examples of institutional collectivism, which is higher in Japan and South Korea. We assume that whenever ingroup collectivism is higher than institutional collectivism (as in China), growth barriers because of family orientation eventually appear; in contrast, whenever institutional collectivism is higher than ingroup collectivism (as in Japan and South Korea), larger companies can grow and develop.

Particularism.   This refers to ties based on ancestral village/region. When two Chinese first meet, one of the first pieces of information exchanged between the parties is which ancestral village/region they come from. In response to the question "Where do you come from?" most North Americans would cite the place of birth. In contrast, however, the Chinese would typically state the ancestral village in China, even if they have never visited the place before. If two Chinese come from the same ancestral village, even though there is no family relationship between them, an immediate affinity is struck between the parties. On the down side, however, there is often rivalry and animosity between Chinese from different clans and/or provinces. The Chinese from the north, for example, are often critical of those from central and southern China, and vice versa. Max Weber has pointed to "particularism" among Chinese business circles as a primary reason for China's inability to develop "economically 'rational' associations" (Pan, 1999, p. 91). This tendency to form economic associations based on village/ancestral ties serves to explain why most of Hong Kong's investment in China is primarily in Guangdong and most of Taiwan's investment in China is concentrated in Fujian province. Particularism is related to the fact that ingroup collectivism is higher than institutional collectivism. If institutional collectivism is higher than ingroup collectivism, it allows developing larger institutional units that also command high loyalty and respect, such as the Japanese *keiretsus* and Korean *chaebols*.

Although connections continue to play an important role in the Japanese *keiretsus* and Korean *chaebols*, because of the size and magnitude of these groups and the predominant use of professional managers in their organizations, as compared to the Chinese entrepreneurial groups, they appeared to have overcome the limitations associated with Chinese family-run networks and thus developed successfully into large companies. To approach their Japanese and Korean counterparts in terms of size and, hence, influence and impact on the global economy, Chinese businesses would have to overcome their traditional mistrust of outsiders. Furthermore, many of the existing loose networks among the Chinese have to be developed and/or institutionalized to facilitate more active and efficient collaboration/cooperation among their members.

ENTREPRENEURSHIP IN PRESENT-DAY CHINA

Entrepreneurship was not officially encouraged in traditional China; the business class was ranked at the bottom of the social ladder, beneath the scholar-gentry, the farmers, and the artisans. Under Confucianism, scholarship was revered whereas commerce or commercial undertakings were considered as unworthy pursuits of the scholarly elite class. This stemmed from the fact that in traditional China, commerce was seen as an activity whose primary purpose was to impede, not facilitate, the flow of goods from producers to consumers, and in the process to make a profit for those who play these intermediary roles. In the past, as soon as the Chinese had accumulated enough wealth, they would typically invest it in agricultural land and education, as these were the only two orthodox routes to respectable status in society.

Therefore, it was relatively easy for the Chinese communists when they came into power in 1949 to justify a social ranking that put workers, peasants, and soldiers (the vast majority of the population) at the top of society, and big landlords and big business people at the bottom.

In 1978, when Deng Xiaoping began to dismantle the commune system and gave peasant families a chance to decide for themselves what they would plant and sell on the market, the seeds were sown not only for assuming economic responsibility but also for seeking economic opportunity (Liao & Sohmen, 2001). Deng's actions were thus truly revolutionary, not only within the context of a communist system but, perhaps more importantly, within a long-standing societal culture that has not been receptive to commerce. In almost no time at all, freelance agronomy consultants appeared in the country. Very soon, peasants who had the ambition and managerial talent were allowed to employ contracted labor if their production plans exceeded what could be undertaken by members of one's family. This unleashed an entrepreneurial torrent, and by 1987 the private sector in China was growing at an annual rate of 93%. At the same time, the private sector had extended beyond agriculture to that in service and industrial production (Liao & Sohmen, 2001). Deng's policies have thus allowed those with an entrepreneurial flare to prosper.

THREE CASES

We present three very different examples of entrepreneurship here. These three alternative paths to success capture the essence of what entrepreneurship is all about—that there is no single way of development, but there are, indeed, many diverse and varied approaches, many of which are "off the beaten paths." Perhaps these may be seen as concrete examples of the diversity of approaches Deng Xiaoping encouraged through his exhortation: "It doesn't matter if a cat is black or white as long as it catches mice." These cases also show that there are very different approaches to entrepreneurship but that all of them are embedded in some cultural issues related to China.

Case Study 1: Jianguo Qu and the Shanghai Jianguo Foundation

The first example comes from the Shanghai region, the hub of China's commercial and entrepreneurial activities. Prior to the beginnings of the economic reforms in the 1980s, Mr. Jianguo Qu was a carpenter in the countryside near Shanghai. With the implementation of Deng Xiaoping's reforms, Mr. Qu became vice-mayor of two counties, and then general manager of a large state-owned industrial corporation, the Shenhua Corporation, that employed more than 10,000 employees. He took advantage of the new reform policies to convert the Shenhua Corporation from a debt-ridden, state-owned enterprise to a highly profitable public enterprise, Shenhua, Inc., for which shares are listed on the Shanghai Stock Exchange. Mr. Qu soon became one of the first "baofa hu" (or "windfall wealthy") in postreform China. To repay the society that allowed him to prosper, he used his wealth to establish Shanghai's first officially registered private foundation, the Shanghai Jianguo Foundation. Jianguo—which means "national construction"—is also his first name. Hence, the Jianguo Foundation is intended to further the country's reconstruction efforts. Mr. Qu is reported to have contributed almost 100 million RMB (or US$12.2 million) to the foundation, whose objective is to reduce poverty by supporting schools in economically deprived parts of China.

This case dealt with one entrepreneur's transformation of a large state-owned corporation into a highly successful private enterprise. Because one of China's major challenges is how to deal effectively with some moribund and nonperforming state-owned enterprises, the story of Jianguo Qu could serve as a prototype for restructuring in this area. This case is also an example of a person who seemed to combine a high degree of institutional collectivism with humane orientation (repaying society). This is a good example of a person who matches the culture in which he works.

Yang Li and "Crazy English"

The second example is an extraordinary one of an entrepreneur who works from the perspective of a cultural niche. In the late 1980s, Mr. Yang Li was an undergraduate student in mechanical engineering at Lanzhou University in Northwest China. In Mr. Li's own words, he was "busy failing almost everything in sight …. I flunked 13 courses and almost got thrown out of the university." After a while, Li decided that he should seriously consider his future. He stumbled upon his niche when he realized that although millions of people in China wanted to learn English, many failed. Li became convinced that this was where he could make his mark. However, because Li had problems concentrating in the classroom, he found that learning a new language was as difficult as studying engineering. Li became convinced that one could learn only through action—practice, practice, and more practice. He reasoned that just as it is impossible to learn how to swim by reading about it in the classroom, the only way to learn English was by "shouting English phrases at the top of his voice—instead of reading English, I yelled English" (Lee, 1998, p. 26; "Li Yang a Crazy Talker," 2003). This approach apparently bore fruit: Within four months, he received the second highest score in the Level 4 National English Exam for college students.

Impressed with his own success, Mr. Li developed a "tongue muscle training" technique. Li taught his fellow classmates how to master oral English using this technique. This eventually led to his founding of what is now the best known English language program in China, "Crazy English." Today, some fifteen years after Li's pedagogical discovery, "Crazy English" is offered throughout Greater China, Korea, and Japan, and has a cult following of almost 20 million eager students. Li has trained his staff of 140 teachers in this pedagogical method. These, in turn, teach in major cities throughout East Asia. Through the success of his somewhat unconventional pedagogical approach, Li has become a celebrity and can draw stadium crowds of 20,000 to 30,000 for each of his training sessions.

Li attributed the phenomenal success of his pedagogical method to his ability to sell a "self-help venture based on what he says were the failings of his own parents." He was born in 1969 in Urumqi, the capital city of Xinjiang Province, the westernmost province in China and one of the most underdeveloped regions in the country. Li criticized the "greatest failure of his parents and the Chinese schooling system in general" to "a culture of feeding children a lack of confidence." Through his "tongue muscle training," Li advocates that people can take matters into their own hands by action/practice ("Li Yang a Crazy Talker," 2003).

Li's plans for future expansion include opening "Crazy Chinese" offices in the United States and Europe to capitalize on the growing demand for learning Chinese in these countries. "Crazy Chinese" will essentially use teaching and learning techniques similar to those deployed in "Crazy English." Yang Li has combined right attitude (self-confidence, willingness to make mistakes and learn from them), right learning techniques, plus a stage presence that encompasses the zealous enthusiasm of an evangelist with the popular appeal of a rock star, and turned them into an entrepreneurial success story that has inspired unprecedented self-confidence among millions of Chinese. He has also turned himself into a role model for entrepreneurial gurus in the marketing of self-help services in China.

The case focuses on the development and perpetuation of a "self-help" program that revolved around an unorthodox approach to teaching English. The success encountered by Yang Li highlights the vast potential for the "self-help" market in the most populous country in the world, where the entrepreneurial spirit and entrepreneurial success have only recently come to be encouraged and rewarded. This case is a good example of a person who differentiated himself from the collectivism of the Chinese society and who developed his own self-confidence and was able to foster other people's self-confidence with his highly individualistic approach. Apparently, Yang Li was able to occupy a niche that was not conforming to the Chinese culture (thus, he represents a bad match, but still a highly successful example).

Yongxin Xue and the En'wei Group

The En'wei Group (established 1987), located in Chengdu in Sichuan Province, is one of the most well-known private enterprises in China. It was founded by Mr. Yongxin Xue, a former woodworker, and eight other farming households in the city of Chengdu, with an initial investment of under 100,000 RMB (US$12,000). Within 10 years of its founding, the company has developed into a large, high-technology, multinational enterprise that engages in scientific research, production, and trade in the pharmaceutical industry. Its current fixed and flowing assets amount to 500 million RMB (US$60.98 million) and intangible assets of 1 billion RMB (US$121.95 million). The group employs, both directly and indirectly, more than 200,000 employees throughout China. The En'wei Group has won over 60 prizes, including the "Excellent Star Enterprise in China" (Asian Development Bank, 2003). As for Mr. Xue himself, he has been included in Forbes Global 1999 as one of China's 50 richest entrepreneurs, and listed as one of the "28 Most Generous Magnates in China" by the Chinese journal *Scientific Investment* in 2003.

Perhaps Mr. Xue's accomplishments lay not so much in his success in building a multinational enterprise with very little capital but in his ability to develop a management philosophy that represents a blend of traditional Chinese teachings that emphasizes humanism and modern management methods. Mr. Xue is a believer in the virtues of China's "Three Traditional Teachings" (Confucianism, Taoism, and Buddhism), and encourages all En'wei employees to embrace and practice them as a matter of company management philosophy.

En'wei's strategy is based on the Taoist principles of "Ruling a large kingdom is like cooking small fish" and "Way of 'Non-Ado.'" As translated into practice, the principle of "Ruling a large kingdom is like cooking small fish" means governing according to the laws of nature. "For years, we have not changed our aim to serve society and benefit mankind, and have not changed our pledge: to bring happiness to all living creatures, and good fortune to society. The management ideology of 'governing on the basis of the laws of nature remains unchanged as well'" (http://www.enwei.com.cn/b2b_en, accessed April 14, 2004).

As applied to management, the principle of "Non-ado" does not mean

> random or without intent .... It means that the leaders' actions ought to obey the observable principles of nature and society, and they should make appropriate rules and systems accordingly. They should never change policies casually. Given such rules and systems, people can bring their wisdom and talent into play, and they will bring their best to work. This is called "the way of Non-ado." (http://www.enwei.com.cn/b2b_en, accessed April 14, 2004)

These Taoist principles have served Xue well. In the course of growing his group, he had to face many crises, including patent violations by former research and development (R&D) employees, serious contract violations by the company's Hong Kong joint venture partners, and unsubstantiated charges of tax evasion by the Chinese government taxation authorities (Asian Development Bank, 2003).

This case pertains to a former woodworker who has no formal training in business principles but who went on to develop a management philosophy that sought to combine traditional Chinese principles of humanism with modern management practices developed in the West. This case is a good example of an entrepreneur who maximizes the match to the culture in which he lives. Performance orientation is combined with lack of assertiveness, but high power distance and high ingroup collectivism and humane orientation.

CONCLUSIONS

Using the case of China, this chapter has raised more questions about cross-cultural entrepreneurship than it could answer. The following is a listing of some of the topics that merit further research attention:

- The different hypotheses of the relationship of culture with entrepreneurship (entrepreneurship as subculture, match to dominant culture, and occupying a cultural niche) should be studied in more detail. There are no systematic studies that compare these different approaches.

- There should be more studies on how entrepreneurs deal with cultural issues and how they exploit cultural orientations. For example, it would be interesting to know how entrepreneurs deal with the issue of innovation in various countries (and how they compensate for lack of innovation in some cultures).
- There are a number of methodological issues that need to be studied, appropriate scales have to be developed, and more attention should be paid to appropriate methodology.
- A number of meaningful hypotheses follow from the differences of China from other countries as described by recent studies of cultures, such as the GLOBE study. Most of these hypotheses have never been studied; in particular, comparisons between different developing countries are rare.
- For methodological reasons, it is necessary to measure culture not only better on a collective level but also on an individual level. There are a number of issues that need to be researched here, such as how these individual cultural factors are different from personality dimensions.
- Size has both positive and negative consequences. Chinese entrepreneurs with their higher family and ingroup collectivism may have more difficulties growing to match the size of their counterparts in Korea and Japan (the latter show a higher degree of the institutional form of collectivism). This may have negative effects on resource dependency and market power. On the other hand, the smaller size of Chinese companies may keep them nimble and allow them to seize opportunities rapidly once they arise. Future research can explore the relationship of size to cultural characteristics and how one deals with family collectivism and growth in the Chinese context.
- How does entrepreneurship in East Asia compare with that in the West? The chapter alludes to some of the similarities and differences. These certainly merit further systematic research.
- This chapter provided a brief comparison of the similarities between the Chinese and Jewish diasporas. Another ethnic group whose economic clout has been legendary is that of India. What are the similarities and differences among the Indian, Chinese, and Jewish diasporas?

REFERENCES

Abegglen, J. C., & Stalk, G. (1985). Kaisha, The Japanese corporation. New York: Basic Books.

Asian Development Bank. (2003). *The development of private enterprise in the People's Republic of China.* http://www.adb.org/documents/studies/PRC_Private _Enterprise_Development/ annex.pdf, accessed

Backman, M. (1999). *Asian Eclipse: Exposing the Dark Side of Business in Asia.* Singapore: Wiley.

Brockner, J., Ackerman, G., Greenberg, J., Gelfand, M. J., Francesco, A. M., Chen, Z. X., & Leung, K. (2001). Culture and procedural justice: The influence of power distance on reactions to voice. *Journal of Experimental Social Psychology, 37,* 300–315.

Brodbeck, F. C., Frese, M., & Javidan, M. (2002). Leadership made in Germany: Low on compassion, high on performance. *Academy of Management Executive, 16*(1), 16–29.

Busenitz, L. W., Gómez, C., & Spencer, J. W. (2000). Country institutional profiles: Unlocking entrepreneurial phenomena. *Academy of Management Journal, 43,* 994–1003.

Cho, D. S. (1999). Chaebols. In R. L. Tung (Ed.), *IEBM handbook of international business* (pp. 572–585). London: Thomson Learning.

Davidsson, P. (1995). Culture, structure and regional levels of entrepreneurship. *Entrepreneurship and Regional Development, 7,* 41–62.

Davidsson, P., & Wiklund, J. (1997). Values, beliefs and regional variations in new firm formation rates. *Journal of Economic Psychology, 18,* 179–199.

Gelfand, M. J., Bhawuk, D. P. S., Hishi, L. H., & Bechtold, D. J. (2004). Individualism and collectivism. In R. J. House, P. J. Hanges, M. Javidan, P. W. Dorfman & V. Gupta (Eds.), *Culture, leadership, and organizations: The GLOBE study of 62 societies* (pp. 437–512). Thousand Oaks, CA: Sage.

Hanges, P. J. (2004). Societal-level correlations among GLOBE societal culture scales. In R. J. House, P. J. Hanges, M. Javidan, P. W. Dorfman, & V. Gupta (Eds.), *Cultures, leadership and organizations: A 62 nation GLOBE study* (pp. 733–736). Thousand Oaks, CA: Sage.

Hanges, P. J., & Dickson, M. W. (2004). The development and validation of the GLOBE culture and leadership scales. In R. J. House, P. J. Hanges, M. Javidan, P. W. Dorfman, & V. Gupta (Eds.), *Cultures, leadership and organizations: A 62 nation GLOBE study* (pp. 122–151). Thousand Oaks, CA: Sage.

Hanges, P. J., Dickson, M. W., & Sipe, M. T. (2004). Rationale for GLOBE statistical analyses: Societal ratings and test of hypotheses. In R. J. House, P. J. Hanges, M. Javidan, P. W. Dorfman, & V. Gupta (Eds.), *Cultures, leadership and organizations: A 62 nation GLOBE study* (pp. 219–233). Thousand Oaks, CA: Sage.

Hayton, J. C., George, G., & Zahra, S. A. (2002). National culture and entrepreneurship: A review of behavioral research. *Entrepreneurship: Theory & Practice, 24*(4), 33–52.

Heine, S. J., Lehman, D. R., Peng, K., & Greenholtz, J. (2002). What's wrong with cross-cultural comparisons of subjective Likert scales? The reference-group effect. *Journal of Personality & Social Psychology, 82,* 903–918.

Hofstede, G. (1991). *Cultures and organizations.* London: McGraw-Hill.

Hofstede, G. (2001). *Culture's consequences* (2nd ed.). Thousand Oaks, CA: Sage.

Hofstede, G. (2002). The pitfalls of cross-national survey research: A reply to the article by Spector et al. on the psychometric properties of the Hofstede Values Survey Module 1994. *Applied Psychology: An International Review, 51,* 170–173.

House, R. J., Hanges, P. J., Javidan, M., Dorfman, P. W., & Gupta, V. (Eds.). (2004). *Cultures, leadership and organizations: A 62 nation GLOBE study.* Thousand Oaks, CA: Sage.

Kao, J. (1993, March–April). The worldwide web of Chinese business. *Harvard Business Review,* pp. 24–36.

Kitayama, S. (2002). Culture and basic psychological processes—Toward a system view of culture: comment on Oyserman et al. (2002). *Psychological Bulletin, 128,* 89–96.

Klein, K. J., Dansereau, F., & Hall, R. J. (1994). Levels issues in theory development, data collection, and analysis. *Academy of Management Review, 19*(2), 195–229.

Koenig, C., Frese, M., Steinmetz, H., Rauch, A., & Wang, Z. M. (in preparation). Development and validation of a questionnaire measuring culture in the domain of entrepreneurship. Unpublished manuscript, Giessen.

Lee, E. (1998). Crazy Talk. *Beijing This Month, 59*(October), 26–27.

Li Yang a Crazy Talker. (2003, December 26). In *China Through the Ages.* http://www.china.org.cn/english/ NM-e/83370.htm accessed April 12, 2004.

Liao, D., & Sohmen, P. (2001). The Development of Modern Entrepreneurship in China. *Stanford Journal of East Asian Affairs, 1*, 27–33.

McGrath, R. G., MacMillan, I. C., Yang, E. A.-Y., & Tsai, W. (1992). Does culture endure, or is it malleable? Issues of entrepreneurial economic development. *Journal of Business Venturing, 7*, 441–458.

Mead, D. C., & Liedholm, C. (1998). The dynamics of micro and small enterprises in developing countries. *World Development, 26*, 61–74.

Mitchell, R. K., Smith, B., Seawright, K. W., & Morse, E. A. (2000). Cross-cultural cognitions and the venture creation decision. *Academy of Management Journal, 43*, 974–993.

Mitchell, R. K., Smith, J. B., Morse, E. A., Seawright, K. W., Peredo, A. M., & Mckenzie, B. (2002). Are entrepreneurial cognitions universal? Assessing entrepreneurial cognitions across cultures. *Entrepreneurship: Theory & Practice, 26*(4), 9–33.

Morris, J. (1999). Keiretsu. In R. L. Tung (Ed.), *IEBM handbook of international business* (pp. 605–609). London: Thomson Learning.

Newton, A., & Subbaraman, R. (2002). *China: Gigantic possibilities, present realities.* London: Lehman Brothers.

Oyserman, D., Coon, H. M., & Kemmelmeier, M. (2002). Rethinking individualism and collectivism: Evaluation of theoretical assumptions and meta-analysis. *Psychological Bulletin, 128*, 3–72.

Pan, L. (Ed.). (1999). *The encyclopedia of the Chinese overseas.* Singapore: Archipelago Press.

Rauch, A., Frese, M., & Sonnentag, S. (2000). Cultural differences in planning—success relationships: A comparison of small enterprises in Ireland, West Germany, and East Germany. *Journal of Small Business Management, 38*(4), 28–41.

Reynolds, P. D., Bygrave, W. D., Autio, E., Cox, L. W., & Hay, M. (2002). *Global Entrepreneurship Monitor—2002 Executive report.* London: London Business School.

Reynolds, P. D., Bygrave, W. D., Autio, E., & Others (2003). *Global Entrepreneurship Monitor 2003 executive report.* London: London Business School.

Shane, S. (1993). Cultural influences on national rates of innovation. *Journal of Business Venturing, 8*, 59–73.

Shane, S., Venkataraman, S., & MacMillan, I. (1995). Cultural differences in innovation championing strategy. *Journal of Management, 21*, 931–952.

Spector, P. E., Cooper, C. L., Sparks, K. (2001). An international study of the psychometric properties of the Hofstede Values Survey Module 1994: A comparison of individual and country/province level results. *Applied Psychology: An International Review, 50*, 269–281.

Sully de Luque, M., & Javidan, M. (2004). Uncertainty avoidance. In R. J. House, P. J. Hanges, M. Javidan, P. W. Dorfman, & V. Gupta (Eds.), *Culture, leadership, and organizations: The GLOBE study of 62 societies* (pp. 602–653). Thousand Oaks, CA: Sage.

Tan, J. (2002). Culture, nation, and entrepreneurial strategic orientations: Implications for an emerging economy. *Entrepreneurship: Theory and Practice, 26*, 95–111.

Triandis, H. C. (1994). Cross-cultural industrial and organizational psychology. In H. V. Triandis, M. D. Dunnette, & L. M. Hough (Eds.), *Handbook of industrial and organizational psychology* (Vol. 4, pp. 103–172). Palo Alto, CA: Consulting Psychologists Press.

Tung, R. L. (1994). Strategic management thought in East Asia. *Organizational Dynamics, 22*(1), 55–65.

Tung, R. L., & Worm, V. (2001). Network capitalism: The role of human resources in penetrating the China market. *International Journal of Human Resource Management, 12*, 517–534.

Zhang, L. X. (2002, September). *Jewish and Chinese Diasporas.* Paper presented at the Howard Gilman International Conference on China, Israel and the Jews, Tel Aviv University, Hong Kong.

Zutshi, R. (1997). East Asian SMEs: Learning the technology. *Journal of Enterprising Cultures, 5*(2), 165–191.

13

Method Challenges and Opportunities in the Psychological Study of Entrepreneurship

Per Davidsson

As the title suggests, this chapter discusses a number of method issues that researchers face when doing psychological research on the elusive but important phenomenon we call *entrepreneurship*. To get our bearings right, I should explain up front that these issues are discussed from the perspective of a researcher who has extensive experience from empirical entrepreneurship research on different levels of analysis and using different theoretical points of departure—including psychological studies on the individual level—but with limited formal training in psychology. Although I can claim some expertise as an entrepreneurship researcher and I took my PhD in a unit for economic psychology in a business school, I am not a psychologist. My knowledge of psychology is like an archipelago of islands separated by unknown waters, and there is therefore risk that I am naive or ignorant at times regarding how the research problems and opportunities appear from the perspective of psychology proper. What I can offer in return is multidisciplinary and methodology insights within the specific domain of entrepreneurship research that do not necessarily come with standard research training in psychology.

The topic I address is too broad to be covered exhaustively in a book chapter, and the selection of specific issues is admittedly colored by the author's experience and preferences. It should also be noted that although some of the challenges brought up are decidedly entrepreneurship specific, others have much broader applicability. In terms of organization, the chapter covers first some general design and sampling issues and then turns to challenges and opportunities associated with different research approaches: working with archival data, survey research, in-depth case studies, and laboratory research methods, respectively.

CHOOSING A PERSPECTIVE ON ENTREPRENEURSHIP

Before going into any of that, however, we need to sort out at least roughly what phenomenon we are talking about when we are talking about *entrepreneurship*. There is no shortage of suggestions. On the contrary, the literature is full of discussions of the essence of the entrepreneurship phenomenon (cf. Davidsson, 2004, chap. 1). The good news is that, as many of the differences are but a matter of emphasis, things are not as messy as they may seem. Some scholars may want to highlight a certain aspect as the most central characteristic of entrepreneurship, whereas others acknowledge that aspect but give it a less central role. Some may want to include particular features in the definition that others see as common but not necessary aspects of entrepreneurship; hence, the latter do not regard them as belonging in the definition of the phenomenon. Differences of this kind are natural, probably inescapable, and—I would argue—not very harmful to collective knowledge accumulation.

However, the many views on entrepreneurship arguably boil down not to one, but *two* major, and not fully compatible, perspectives of what entrepreneurship actually is (Davidsson, 2004; Gartner, 1990). The first equates the term with *independent business*: Entrepreneurship is starting and running one's own firm (sometimes including organized not-for-profit activities). According to this view, entrepreneurship research studies *entrepreneurs*, understood as flesh-and-blood business owner-managers. Such people remain entrepreneurs as long as they are running their own business, and any trait, emotion, cognition, behavior, or achievement of such individuals is an issue for entrepreneurship research.

The second view regards entrepreneurship as the *creation of new economic activity* (or, in the most allowing cases, any new activity). The major underlying theme here is that the development and renewal of any society, economy, or organization requires micro-level actors who show the initiative and persistence to make change happen. According to this view, *entrepreneur* is a theoretical abstraction that refers to one or more individuals who in a particular case bring about this change as an individual feat *or* as a team effort *or* in sequence; that is, different individuals may fulfill different roles as an entrepreneurial process unfolds over time. The focus is on the activity, on entrepreneur*ship*. Although this requires individual initiative to happen, it is not necessary to appoint one individual as "the entrepreneur" with regard to a particular entrepreneurial process. Neither is there a particular class of people who are constantly "entrepreneurs" whereas others are not. Rather, entrepreneur is a *role*, which individuals exercise on a temporary basis. As soon as the individual is no longer involved in the creation of new economic activity, that person is no longer an entrepreneur (Schumpeter, 1934).

To further illustrate the difference as well as the overlap, we may note that the creation or emergence of new, independent business is of central interest from both perspectives. A topic like family business succession problems falls naturally within the domain when entrepreneurship is understood as the founding *and running* of independent businesses, whereas this topic has nothing to do with entrepreneurship from the *creation of new economic activity* view—unless the research focuses specifically on, for example, the effect of succession on the firm's ability to innovate. So-called "corporate entrepreneurship"—that is, creation of new economic activities by large, established firms (with dispersed ownership)—is part of the domain from the latter perspective, but is an oxymoron when entrepreneurship is understood as starting and running an independent business.

For a psychologist it would be tempting to go for the first option, which equates entrepreneurship with self-employment. This perspective puts the individual squarely at the center stage of inquiry, and hence the psychologist's theoretical and methodological toolboxes apply to the full without much adaptation. Besides, studying business owner-managers is a worthy cause. Being self-employed implies a radically different risk/reward structure, with a much wider span of financial outcomes, than does employment. The border between work and leisure is also much more fluid for people in that situation. There are many aspects of, for instance, motivation, satisfaction, attributions, and so on that are likely to be different for people who are self-employed and who may also be the employers of others.

However, it is a well-known fact that the majority of independent businesses, once they have established themselves, are relatively stable operations in mature and low to medium value-added industries. Many of them thus score low on other attributes commonly associated with entrepreneurship, such as proactiveness, newness, innovation, risk taking, and value creation (Gartner, 1990; Hornaday, 1990; Lumpkin & Dess, 1996). At the same time, there are certainly firms that are not owner managed, which fulfill the role of creating new economic activity. This begs the question, why we should call any study of business owner-managers "entrepreneurship research"?

There has been a clear drift in the entrepreneurship research community toward emphasizing instead the second major notion of entrepreneurship, that is, that entrepreneurship is about the creation of new economic activity.

This is evident in attempts at formal definitions (Davidsson, 2004; Gartner, 1988; Low & MacMillan, 1988; Lumpkin & Dess, 1996; Shane & Venkataraman, 2000; Stevenson & Jarillo, 1990; Venkataraman, 1997) as well as the contents of outlets for "entrepreneurship research" (Grégoire, Noël, Dery, & Bechard, 2004). Over time, researchers have become aware that practicing business founders may not have all the answers to successful entrepreneurship (Fiet, 2002), that entrepreneurship often is a team effort (Ruef, Aldrich, & Carter, 2003), and that entrepreneurship is best conceived of as a *process* (Baron, this volume; Bhave, 1994; Davidsson, 2004; Gartner & Carter, 2003; Shane, 2003). In this process, different individuals may contribute in slightly different roles over time.

Although this might make entrepreneurship research methodologically more challenging for psychology scholars, I would urge psychologists to consider this latter notion of entrepreneurship. Entrepreneurship scholarship can benefit greatly from the combination of disciplinary knowledge and deep familiarity with the phenomenon (Davidsson, 2003), and if psychologists adopt a contemporary notion of entrepreneurship their contributions will be most welcome and will have an impact not only within their own discipline, but also within the multidisciplinary field and community of entrepreneurship research. Although this means having to deal with intriguing methodological challenges, there is certainly room for psychology. Entrepreneurship requires human agency (Shane, 2003), which highlights the need and opportunity to study the individuals who exercise such agency with the help of the psychologists' toolbox of theories and methods. This becomes particularly apparent if one takes into account research that clearly demonstrates that the profit-maximizing rationality of economic theory is not what solely or even primarily characterizes the individuals who engage in entrepreneurial action (Amit, MacCrimmon, & Zietsma, 2000; Wiklund, Davidsson, & Delmar, 2003). In order to really understand what goes on at the micro level in the entrepreneurial domain, there is every reason to study the emotions, cognitions, behaviors, and other characteristics of the individuals involved. If trained psychologists do not devote their expertise to studying the role of individuals in entrepreneurial processes, others will. In all likelihood, their tools will be less suitable for the task, or less skillfully applied, than if professional psychologists make an effort to study this important domain of human behavior.

ENTREPRENEURSHIP AS CREATION OF NEW ECONOMIC ACTIVITY: SOME GENERAL DESIGN ISSUES

When defined as the creation of new economic activity, it becomes clear that entrepreneurship is something that can be studied on many different levels of analysis. However, in order to qualify as entrepreneurship research, entrepreneurial activity on the chosen level of analysis must be explicitly considered. That is, the middle box in Fig. 13.1 is a must, while the antecedents and outcomes are optional (Davidsson & Wiklund, 2001). Thus, the study of characteristics of small firms as related to their financial performance is entrepreneurship research if and only if creation of new economic activity by the firm is explicitly modeled and assessed as the mechanism that links firm characteristics to performance. On the industry, region, or nation level, we may see numbers of patents and business startups (i.e., *rates*; cf. Aldrich & Wiedenmayer, 1993) as more or less direct measures of entrepreneurial activity. The emerging new activity itself—that is, the business idea and the activity that evolves around it—can also be used as the level of analysis. I have argued elsewhere that this is a particularly relevant but rarely used option (Davidsson & Wiklund, 2001).

What does this tell us about the psychological approach and toolbox? Well, it is *not* restricted to individual level research. On more aggregate levels such as regions and nations, psychological characteristics may be assessed on the individual level and then aggregated to represent cultural traits of the aggregate units, and related to entrepreneurial activity and outcomes assessed on that level (Davidsson, 1995; Hofstede, 1980; Lynn, 1991; McClelland, 1961). On the firm level, it has been popular to assess firms' (propensity for) entrepreneurial activity with the *Entrepreneurial Orientation* (EO) scale (Covin & Slevin, 1986; Lumpkin & Dess, 1996; Wiklund, 1998). Although conceptualized as a firm-level characteristic, EO is typically assessed by the responses of a single individual (e.g., the chief executive officer [CEO]). This is an example of level mix-up where trained psychologists—especially those with experience from group level research—would likely do a better job.

This brings us down to the individual level and to a type of cross-level research that very commonly—and apparently without much reflection on the inherent problems—has been applied in entrepreneurship research, and not only by researchers lacking training in psychology. This is when the design builds on the assumption that (stable or innate) characteristics of the individuals(s) involved are the main, direct explanations for the emergence of a new firm and/or its performance. When we explain firm-level phe-

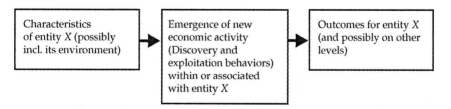

Figure 13.1.   Entrepreneurship research design possibilities.

nomena primarily with individual-level variables, we actually use a type of cross-level model that Kozlowski and Klein (2000) do not even consider in their comprehensive overview of multilevel research. Their models always cross downward, with effects running from, for example, unit level to individual level (Direct Effects Model), from firm, unit, and individual levels to individual level (Mixed Determinants Model), or from firm level to firm, unit, and individual levels (Mixed Effects Model). It should perhaps be taken as a warning sign that they do not discuss an "upward" direct effects model, such as from individual to firm level.

Some might argue that at very early stages of a firm's development it is neither possible nor necessary to separate the emerging firm from the individual. However, Katz and Gartner (1988) already pointed at the possibility, and among other things, the fact that many startups are team efforts (Aldrich, Carter, & Reynolds, 2004; Delmar & Davidsson, 2000) and many individuals are involved in multiple ventures (Scott & Rosa, 1996; Westhead & Wright, 1998) shows this is at least desirable, if not necessary for all research purposes. Over time, the firm and the individual certainly become separate entities. It may in fact be argued that this is how really successful entrepreneurs create their personal wealth: by creating business activities that can continue to live and flourish without their own continued involvement.

For these reasons, I think it advisable for researchers to think of their micro-level study *either* as an individual-level study *or* as a venture-level study (where cases are particular business activities, which in some cases change their association with particular individuals and/or organizations) *or* as a firm-level study (where cases are business organizations that may run several ventures in parallel or in sequence; cf. Davidsson & Wiklund, 2000, 2001). That is, it may be useful to think of one's project as a single-level design before starting to make crossovers. This would mean considering having the core predictor variables and the criterion variable(s) refer to the same level of analysis before one makes an active and informed decision to break away from that pattern.

PSYCHOLOGICAL ENTREPRENEURSHIP RESEARCH ON THE INDIVIDUAL LEVEL

Let us discuss first the individual level. In the early days of empirical entrepreneurship research (meaning roughly the 1960–1990 period) there were many studies that compared the characteristics of entrepreneurs—understood as business founders or business owner-managers—with non-entrepreneurs, which were represented by employed managers or the general population. Baron (chap. 2) offers some of the reasons why the early research with such a focus failed to arrive at strong conclusions: weak theoretical basis, focus on few and/or the wrong person characteristics, and weak measurement. As regards weak theory and wrong variables, the research often attempted to explain "entrepreneur" status with a "home brew" of personality variables or at best dated theory from the psychological discipline. Either way, the person constructs that were used as predictors were typically distal to specific behaviors. They were also rarely of the readily teachable and learnable kind. Therefore, the best one could hope for from that research in terms of practical application was to develop a selection mechanism for educators and investors: "You're the right stuff; you are not." By and large, this project failed.

When you think of it, why should a person scoring high on *need for achievement, tolerance for ambiguity,* and *internal locus of control* (Brockhaus, 1982; Delmar, 2000)—or any of the Big Five personality dimensions (Nicholson, 1998), to make use of more updated personality theory—have a high probability of being a business owner-manager? Obviously, such characteristics do not force the individual's behavior in such specific directions. Over long periods of time we would expect individuals with certain characteristics to be overrepresented in jobs with certain matching characteristics, and self-employment may be one of those alternatives. But work characteristics that appeal to such people are not exclusive to the self-employment career; all self-employment careers do not share the same job characteristics, and in many cases people for some reason fail to find the perfect match between their work and their person. So the relationships between stable, innate characteristics of people on the one hand, and being a firm owner-manager on the other, will be very far from deterministic.

When the research aims at explaining the occurrence of business startups during a specific period (say, within 12 months after the assessment of the person characteristics), successful prediction becomes even more unlikely. Characteristics of this kind may perhaps be somewhat overrepresented among recent business founders, thanks to (unmeasured) interaction with dispositional and situational factors like having family background or work experience that have made striking out on one's own a considered alternative: stumbling over an attractive opportunity and/or losing one's previous job. However, in any one-time period, most people who are high on presumed "entrepreneurial personality traits" would *not* start a new venture because they already have a life situation that is gratifying and/or time-consuming enough, whereas some people who score low on these characteristics are forced by circumstances to go into business for themselves. Hence, stable, innate characteristics of individuals will never be the major explanation of single events like starting a new firm.

More recently, however, researchers pursuing research comparing "entrepreneurs" with "nonentrepreneurs" have dealt successfully with most of these issues. With the influx of trained psychologists, the quality of operationalizations has certainly increased in recent years. As regards the-oretical underpinning and selection of person level constructs, we find ap-plications of more modern and sophisticated theory—especially from cognitive psychology—and use of more proximal variables such as percep-tions, goals, intentions, and self-efficacy (see Delmar, 2000, and Krueger, 2003, for overviews). The findings therefore have more potential for teach-ing and learning. To name a few examples, this goes for research on entre-preneurial scripts by Mitchell, Seawright, and Morse (2000) and on heuristics and biases by Busenitz and Barney (1997) and Simon and Houghton (2000), and for Baron's (1999) work on counterfactual thinking as well as Amit et al. (2000), mentioned earlier, demonstrating that business founders' motivations are far more complex than the assumptions of economic theory suggest.

Despite the marked improvements, there are two major, remaining is-sues with this type of research. The first is that the implicit or explicit as-sumption is that the person characteristics cause "entrepreneur" status. The research is usually not designed in such a way that reversed causality can be ruled out (see, e.g., Shaver, 2003, for discussion of the Busenitz & Barney, 1997, study). The second issue is the nature of the dependent vari-able, "entrepreneur status." Although this can be regarded as career choice and hence an individual-level variable (rather than "venture emergence," a venture-level construct), and although the use of more proximal variables reduces its seriousness, it remains a problem that the dependent variable is dichotomous. We have already noted that stable, innate characteristics of individuals are distal with respect to single events and therefore unlikely to explain much of them (Delmar, 1996; Rauch & Frese, 2000). When, on the other hand, all variables in the model are proximal, we approach a situation where all we can say is something meaningless like "people found busi-nesses because they almost already did," and we revert again to asking what more fundamental factors led to their high scores on, for example, measures of entrepreneurial self-efficacy and intentions. According to Eagly and Chaiken (1993, p. 162), "It is now fairly common knowledge among social scientists that constructing an appropriate aggregative index of behaviors is one way to obtain moderately high correlations between people's behaviors and their tendencies (e.g., attitudes) or dispositions (e.g., personality traits)." Regrettably, it does not appear to have become common knowledge among entrepreneurship researchers.

The pure individual level study, which should be the psychologist's real home turf, offers many other possible dependent variables, which are not di-chotomous. It is therefore somewhat surprising—and an excellent opportu-nity for future research—that this type of study is conspicuous in its absence. With "this type of study" I then mean, first, studies that relate individual characteristics to *individual level* outcomes such as personal financial success, goal achievement, learning, satisfaction, and changes in values, motivation(s), and attitudes (cf. Van Gelderen, Van der Sluis, & Jansen, 2005).

I also mean studies that relate individual characteristics to *all* the entrepreneurial activity that the individual is associated with. If we relate the achievement motivation, or extraversion, or general intelligence of one member of each startup team to the 3-year performance of their ventures, we are not unlikely to find that these factors are insignificant. Would that prove wrong a theory predicting positive effects of IQ, extroversion, and need for achievement (*n*Ach) on performance in entrepreneurial endeavors? No, the result can just as well be interpreted as disclosing poor research design. It is when it comes to explaining repeated patterns of behavior—and associated levels of success—over long periods of time that such factors are likely to show their strength. If these factors were related instead to an individual's cumulative success over several entrepreneurial endeavors, the result would be much more likely to support the theory. More or less idiosyncratic situational and environmental influences may far overshadow the person variables' effects with respect to each individual event, but over the long term and across several ventures these other influences will either cancel out or become diluted, or the individual's skill at choosing his or her environment will shine through. Therefore, for individual-level studies the ideal design would allow the assessment of "entrepreneurial career performance"—that is, the quantity and quality of independent and internal ventures that the individual has been involved with over a longer period of time—or something approaching that idea. In short, *if we are to successfully explain or predict entrepreneurial action and success with (distal) variables on the individual level, then entrepreneurship has to be assessed broadly on the individual level, and preferably over longer periods of time.*

PSYCHOLOGICAL ENTREPRENEURSHIP RESEARCH ON VENTURE OR FIRM PERFORMANCE

Other researchers with a strong interest in the individual do not compare "entrepreneurs" to "nonentrepreneurs" but test instead their hypotheses within a sample of business owner-managers. Typically, person characteristics are related to the success of a specific firm or venture, that is, effectively a cross-level design (Klein & Kozlowski, 2000; Rousseau, 1985). Unlike the dichotomous founder/nonfounder variable, venture or firm performance is in a sense an aggregate of (the consequences of) multiple behaviors, so the theoretical chances for strong explanations should be higher. Yet it remains unlikely that stable, innate, personal characteristics would have strong, direct effects that explain much of the level of performance of a venture during a specific time period (Ciavarella, Buchholtz, Riordan, Gatewood, & Stokes, 2004; Nicholson, 1998; Rauch & Frese, 2000). The fate of a venture or firm is influenced by a broad range of factors, many of which cannot even indirectly be influenced to any meaningful extent by the founder's personality: the inherent qualities of the business idea/market offering; macroenvironmental issues like interest rates and (changes in) regulations; actions by competitors, customers, and resource providers; and so on.

Again, psychologically trained researchers have recently shown examples of drastic improvements from the naive designs that hope for direct effects of distal person variables as main explanations of firm performance. In fact, in my opinion we find in this category studies that are among the strongest contributions of any in entrepreneurship research in the last few years. This has been achieved by selecting more interesting and actionable psychological variables for inclusion in the first place; by including both distal and proximal psychological constructs and modeling the influence of the former as mediated by the latter; by including carefully selected nonperson variables as controls; and by checking also for interactions between person and nonperson variables. As an example of more proximal, actionable variables, mediation, and nonperson controls the study by Baum, Locke, and Kirkpatrick (1998) on the role of vision for venture growth deserves mentioning. Escher et al. (2002) demonstrated an interesting interaction between cognitive ability and planning strategies (a proximal and learnable variable) on small business success, suggesting that owner-managers can make up for weaknesses in cognitive ability by planning. Likewise with data from Africa and dealing with planning, Frese, Brantjes, and Hoorn (2002) showed that planning behaviors and entrepreneurial orientation (learnable and proximal variables) have positive effects on small business success; however, the effect of entrepreneurial orientation is moderated by the characteristics of the (perceived) environment.

Fascinating—although somewhat tentative—are Hmieleski and Ensley's (2004a) results on multiple intelligences and venture success. In short, according to their results, analytical intelligence has no main effect on venture outcomes in the preformation and formation stages, whereas this conventional form of intelligence has a strong positive effect on performance in the presumably more structured and less genuinely uncertain growth stage. For creative and practical intelligence the pattern is the opposite; however, the positive effects of these types of intelligence in the earliest stages are boosted if analytical intelligence is also high. These results accord well with conclusions from other types of research on successful entrepreneurial behavior under varying degrees of uncertainty (Gustavsson, 2004; Sarasvathy, 1999, 2001). Also interesting is the same authors' research on how improvisation behavior interacts with environmental dynamism and the degree of change of the venture idea in determining venture success (Hmieleski & Ensley, 2004b).

Finally, a particularly exemplary recent study is Baum and Locke's (2004) research on psychological determinants of venture growth. They make a novel and interesting selection of "traits" to include, namely, *tenacity* and *passion*—which I would argue are latent qualities that people marshal when they work on ideas they find important, interesting, and challenging. They model these variables' influence as mediated by more proximal psychological constructs, and they also include well selected, nonperson control variables. Further, they apply above-standard checks of the quality of their operationalizations and test their model on a less heterogeneous sample of ventures, and with a higher response rate, than the conventional. Finally, their study is longitudinal, assessing the dependent variable over a period of 6 years.

Although considerable improvement is evident, there are remaining issues with using the (entrepreneurial) qualities of the individual as the focal predictors of performance of a particular venture. The peculiar cross-level nature of this approach leads to two problems. First, we have the issue of team startups. This is no marginal issue; in both the American and the Swedish PSED data sets (discussed later) the team startups slightly outnumber the solo efforts (Aldrich et al., 2004; Delmar & Davidsson, 2000). Clearly, when the startup is a team effort, data on (and preferably from) more than one individual are needed. Second, the qualities of an individual can be used for many purposes other than furthering the performance of a specific venture. The reason why an individual's score on psychological scale X is not reflected in high performance for the selected venture Y may be that the individual in question spends most of his or her time amazing the world in *another* venture that was not selected! Hence, the perils of level mix-up may dilute the results both ways. A third problem is that entrepreneurial tendencies and behaviors do not always translate into favorable venture- or firm-level outcomes such as profit or growth. In stable environments it may be wiser not to rock the boat (Hmieleski & Ensley, 2004b).

Although the latter can to some extent be successfully dealt with through the introduction of person × environment interaction terms, I would recommend that researchers distinguish clearly between *entrepreneurial performance*—measured as an aggregation of entrepreneurial actions, that is, actions geared toward the creation of new business activity—and *business performance*, measured as firm or venture profitability, growth, or the like (cf. Delmar, 1996). Further, I would suggest that researchers wholeheartedly adopt the firm or the venture as the level of analysis wherever the business performance of specific ventures or firms is the ultimate dependent variable in the research design. As explained earlier, another alternative is to go wholeheartedly for the individual level and use a decidedly individual-level dependent variable, preferably something approaching "entrepreneurial career performance."

When the firm or venture is the level of analysis, *human capital* becomes one type of resource that it is natural to link to its performance, along with financial, physical, social, and organizational capital (Davidsson, 2004). This perspective veers away from trying to explain the fate of the firm (predominantly) by the characteristics of one individual. Clearly, *all* the human capital at the firm's disposal is relevant and equally clearly human resources are but one resource type among many. Yet other candidates for explaining performance also exist, such as qualities of the environment and of the business idea itself, and the fit between these elements and the individual(s) involved (Shane, 2003). A consistent emphasis on the venture or firm as the focal unit facilitates viewing the role of individual characteristics and behavior in those terms. Although this approach may appear less psychological, there is ample room for psychologists to contribute, to research on this level, new theoretical approaches as well as better developed and better validated concepts and measures for assessing human capital and entrepreneurial behavior. As regards venture or firm level outcomes, the psychologist should perhaps consider allying him- or herself with a business or economics expert in order to achieve the same quality with regard to the dependent variable—although it should be admitted that the standards are not always what they should be even among these alleged experts on such issues.

PSYCHOLOGICAL ENTREPRENEURSHIP RESEARCH ON TEAMS

The existence of team startups also point at a third micro level of analysis: the team—or group—itself. The present author is no expert on how groups should be sampled or how data from them should be collected and analyzed. However, groups have long been studied in psychology (e.g., Klein & Kozlowski, 2000; Thibaut & Kelley, 1959), and trained psychologists are therefore well equipped to contribute theoretically and methodologically to the study of entrepreneurial teams. In particular, they may be well positioned to break with the cross-level habit of relating team characteristics only to venture- or firm-level outcomes and thus add to the small number of "pure" group-level studies in entrepreneurship (e.g., Ruef et al., 2003; West, 1990).

SAMPLING ISSUES

Unlike opinion polls and industrial quality control, it is never the case in social science research that *the* entire theoretically relevant populations of units such as industries, firms, ventures, or individuals exist in one place at one time. We want our theories to apply to entrepreneurship in another country and in another year as well. Hence, the researcher's task is to obtain a theoretically relevant selection or sample of units on the chosen level of analysis, and to assess the quantity and quality of entrepreneurial activity on that level. We have already noted that research on entrepreneurship can be conducted on different levels of analysis. As this chapter is about psychological research, we focus on sampling of micro-level units. To narrow this further, I continue to concentrate on *individuals* and *ventures* also when we discuss sampling. Although obtaining a theoretically sound sample of *firms* is a more challenging task than one might first think, I refer the reader to Davidsson (2004) for a treatment of sampling on that level.

The level of analysis that is the most difficult to deal with from a sampling perspective is, arguably, the emerging new venture itself. These entities cannot be found in any register. For reasons elaborated on elsewhere (Davidsson, 2003, 2004), I think that the *Panel Study of Entrepreneurial Dynamics* (PSED; see Gartner, Shaver, Carter, & Reynolds, 2004; Reynolds, 2000) is a major leap forward in solving this tricky problem. That study started with a very large, representative sample of households (individuals in the Swedish study; cf. Delmar & Davidsson, 2000). These households were screened for occurrences of individuals involved in ongoing venture startup processes. A few percent qualified, and these were followed over time. This procedure made it possible to study for the first time a large and reasonably representative sample of ongoing business start-ups. Of course, what should be the minimum and maximum criteria for inclusion in the sample had to be determined (Shaver, Carter, Gartner, & Reynolds, 2001). Researchers involved in the project have applied different rules, but a common minimum criterion is that some action has to be taken—mere contemplation or intention does not suffice. As regards the upper limit, positive cash flow for 3 months has been suggested as showing that the startup has now become an up-and-running firm.

There are also other issues with the sampling that could be debated. As the screening sample is based on households or individuals, team startups will be overrepresented relative to solo efforts. This is so because more households or individuals are associated with a team startup. Moreover, startup processes that are of long duration will (in a sense) also be oversampled, and an additional problem is that when they first enter the sample some processes are just started whereas others are close to completion. However, these issues can be satisfactorily remedied with interview data on the other team members and on the occurrence and timing of a large set of "gestation behaviors" (Davidsson, 2004; Gartner et al., 2004).

An unresolved issue in the PSED research is the heterogeneity of venture startups and nascent entrepreneurs, as it aims at a representative sample of all startups and because prestratification on, for example, venture age, size, or industry is not possible. The heterogeneity points at a tricky balance. With a broader sample the results have broader applicability—but may be weak and blurred. My experience has led me to advise that when possible the researcher should try to work with a more homogeneous sample, yet one that represents at least *one* theoretically relevant subpopulation (cf. Baum & Locke, 2004). Broader generalizability, I would suggest, has to grow out of cumulative evidence from different studies, all investigating the relationship in question for some (although not the same) theoretically relevant population. One way of reducing the heterogeneity in a PSED-like sample would be to focus on informants with a particular level and type of education (cf. Delmar, Wiklund, & Sjöberg, 2003).

A PSED-like sampling procedure can also be employed for capturing emerging internal ventures within established firms. Using a large cohort of firms we were already doing research on as the screening sample, we recently developed and employed such a technique with notable success. For further details, see Chandler, Dahlqvist, and Davidsson (2003), and Davidsson (2004).

Turning now to sampling of individuals, the most important sampling implication for entrepreneurship research of adopting the perspective proposed here, that is, that entrepreneurship is the creation of new economic activity, is this: The entrepreneurship research process does *not* start from defining the population of "entrepreneurs" and drawing a sample from that population. As "entrepreneur" is a theoretical abstraction and a transitory role, *a well-defined population of entrepreneurs simply does not exist.* The nonexistence of a reasonably stable population of "entrepreneurs" as opposed to "nonentrepreneurs" leads us to conclude that individual-level studies could start from any population of individuals (in fact, predefining a group of "entrepreneurs" may even involve undesirable sampling on the dependent variable). Following the logic in Fig. 13.1, the researcher would like to assess in this sample each individual's possible antecedents of entrepreneurship, each one's "amount" of entrepreneurial activity, and various outcomes deemed relevant based on the theory that guides the research.

For many purposes, however, it would be impractical to work with a general sample of "individuals." As entrepreneurship is a minority phenomenon, the sample would have to be huge for enough entrepreneurial activity to occur. For a researcher with a descriptive interest in the middle box only—behaviors in the entrepreneurial process possibly expanded also to outcomes of such processes—the PSED type of procedure offers a solution. Only individuals who are currently in the process of starting a firm are theoretically relevant; hence, only "nascent entrepreneurs" should be included in the research (cf. Penrose, 1959, for analogous reasoning on firm growth). I have earlier portrayed the PSED procedure as aiming at sampling emerging new ventures. In actual fact, it was a simultaneous sampling of "firms-in-gestation" and "nascent entrepreneurs" at the time, with more emphasis on the latter. The difference between the levels becomes apparent the hard way when you conduct a follow-up interview 6 months later and the respondent (a) is still trying to start a new firm, but based on an entirely different idea (and possibly with other teammates) than last time, or (b) has abandoned the effort, while other team members are still pursuing it. What is now a valid case? In the Swedish study, we solved this problem by creating two versions of the data set: one that followed original individuals who remained active and one that followed original projects that remained active.

The blurred notion of level or unit of analysis that we had at the time is also reflected in the sampling of a "comparison group" intended to reflect the general population. This aims at comparing people who are in an (infrequent) temporary state with those who are not—somewhat akin to comparing "people on vacation" with the general population (parts of which, obviously, will be on vacation next week). It is not a totally irrelevant comparison, and significant differences are likely to be found. However, the basic logic of the design is better suited for studying "What does being involved in a startup process do to you?" than for "What makes you enter a startup process?"

Although not necessarily thought of such at the design stage, the PSED approach is also a workable strategy for achieving a theoretically relevant sample of entrepreneurial teams (Ruef et al., 2003). The fact that larger teams will be oversampled can be remedied with post weighing if deemed important.

Another way of delimiting the study to people who are in a good position to exercise entrepreneurial behavior is to sample, for example, owner-managers of independent businesses. Importantly, however, with our proposed perspective this would *not* constitute a sample of "entrepreneurs." I would argue that it is more fruitfully conceived of as a sample of theoretically relevant individuals whose level of entrepreneurial activity and success is to be assessed and explained by the study.

This focus on *entrepreneurship* rather than *entrepreneurs* also in individual-level studies saves one from reducing entrepreneurship to a simple dichotomy. Also within a sample of owner-managers it is debatable whether dichotomization and contrasting of "types" of entrepreneurs represents a good research strategy. Categories like novice, habitual (portfolio; serial), craftsman-entrepreneurs and opportunistic-entrepreneurs do not appear in any registers. Consequently, they cannot be targeted for sampling. Moreover, categories like these do not seem to be very distinct empirically (Davidsson, 1988; Woo, Cooper, & Dunkelberg, 1991). Therefore, we can only create those categories by converting one or more higher order variables into a dichotomy by arbitrarily chosen cutoffs. Although contrasting of types may lead to results that are more easily communicated, it is inescapable that potentially valuable information is deliberately thrown away in this process of dichotomization.

Should we stay with predefined categories, I would hold that a more promising contrast than that between habitual and novice "entrepreneurs" is the seemingly similar distinction derived from cognitive psychology between experts and novices in entrepreneurial endeavors (Gustavsson, 2004). The notion of "habitual" is based on experience and or behavior. One reason for the limited results in research on habitual versus novice business founders may be that some people learn from experience whereas others do not. Another reason is that running multiple projects may decrease rather than increase the likelihood of success for any one of them. By contrast, an expert is defined by performance. Establishing that expert entrepreneurs do better is thus not an issue. The purpose of the research is instead to unveil what teachable and learnable skills they have developed that can explain their superior performance. This is a promising avenue for entrepreneurship research, and here I have no qualms about sampling on the dependent variable. However, it is crucially important that it be ascertained that the sampled experts' superior performance really is attributable to their strategic behavior; otherwise, we risk confounding expertise with luck (Demsetz, 1983). It is also important that every effort be made to assure that the empirical categories "expert" and "novice" match as closely as possible the theoretical ideal types they represent. It is never possible to sample "perfect" experts, nor novices that lack every trace of the experience and skills that experts possess. The less strict the researcher is in his or her sampling criteria, the more "contaminated" will the groups be with characteristics typical for the opposite ideal type and hence the greater the risk that good theory will be rejected on the basis of bad data.

Individuals can sometimes be sampled in order to represent a more aggregated level of analysis. This, however, involves an element of cross-level research (Klein & Kozlowski, 2000; Rousseau, 1985), the implications of which one ought to be aware of. For example, does the mean score across a sample of inhabitants on a psychological scale represent a valid estimate of a region's "culture" or "mentality" on that dimension, which we can relate to that region's level of entrepreneurship, measured as the number of business startups (cf. Davidsson, 1995)? This is an example of a "shared unit model" in the terminology of Kozlowski and Klein (2000), which adds the problem of justifying the aggregation from individual to unit level to the problem of justifying causal interpretation of the relationship between the two variables.

The sampling problems involved are tricky. For example, whose data should be aggregated to represent cultural characteristics of spatial units? Everybody who lives there? Those who always lived there? Some select group of opinion leaders? Should people who already founded firms be included in the computation of the culture score? What happens to the logic of the research if that group—included or excluded—is 10% in one region and 50% in another region? Beyond sampling, a mean of 3 could be produced by everybody in that region agreeing on that score, or by having half the population check off a 5 and the other half a 1. Does then the estimate of the mean, the measure of dispersion, both, or neither represent qualities of the aggregate? Questions like these have no self-evident answers, but the researcher should be aware of the problems and alternative solutions— preferably at the design stage already.

In summary, the most important suggestion in this section was that *entrepreneurship research does not start from defining the population of "entrepreneurs,"* and drawing a sample from that population. Any sample of individuals may be relevant, and the entrepreneurial behaviors and success of hitherto "non-entrepreneurial" individuals can be observed as they unfold over time, or are induced and assessed in a laboratory setting. For many research purposes it is more practical to delimit the sample to individuals who are particularly likely to exercise a nonzero level of entrepreneurship, such as internal venture managers, individuals currently involved in a business startup, or owner-managers of independent businesses. However, I would argue that research that examines variation in entrepreneurship within that group holds more promise than does regarding it as a homogeneous group of "entrepreneurs" whose behavior is to be compared to that on "nonentrepreneurs." Yet other studies may want to contrast expert entrepreneurs to novices. For such studies, the premier sampling challenge is to find good empirical representatives for these conceptual categories.

Emerging new ventures are arguably the most difficult units to sample, but the PSED research shows it is feasible to arrive at theoretically relevant samples of ongoing startup efforts, which are also reasonably representative in the statistical sense. Although the ventures are identified through a sample of individuals, the resulting data set can be arranged as a sample of ventures. This implies that when the sampled informant is no longer involved with the startup, it can still be an alive and valid case if others are working on it, whereas should the informant (and all other team members) abandon the idea in order to work on a completely different startup, we no longer have a valid case for continued data collection. It is my conviction that refined versions of the two-stage sampling technique used for PSED will become a standard tool in future entrepreneurship research.

Other studies may aim at more aggregate levels on analysis. Sometimes this nevertheless requires sampling of individuals as informants, whose data are to be aggregated to the focal level. In such cases, one must carefully think through who can represent the more aggregate level, and with what justification.

ARCHIVAL RESEARCH CHALLENGES AND OPPORTUNITIES

Research based on secondary data can be really depressing. As the data were not collected for the purpose for which they are being used, they may show severe undercoverage of the most relevant parts of the population, such as the youngest and smallest ventures (cf. Aldrich, Kalleberg, Marsden, & Cassell, 1989). Further, the data are typically shallow and researchers are forced to use simple, distant proxies in the (vain) hope that they will reflect complex theoretical concepts. I have previously—and justifiably—likened the situation to that of the drunkard who is searching for his lost keys under the streetlight, well aware that this is not where he lost them, but simply because that is the only place where he can possibly find anything at all (Davidsson, 2004).

However, in the same work I explain that some of my best experiences as a social scientist, and some of my strongest research results, emanate from studies based on "secondary" data (Davidsson & Delmar, 1998; Davidsson, Lindmark, & Olofsson, 1994, 1998; Delmar, Davidsson, & Gartner, 2003). As detailed in Davidsson (2004), the trick behind this was careful and thorough work in close collaboration with experts at the statistical organization in order to use and combine the best available data for creating reliable, customized data sets that could actually answer the research questions that we were asking. This, of course, was a costly and time-consuming exercise, thus effectively removing two of the alleged advantages of archival data: easy access and low cost. However, we could retain other important advantages, like working with census rather than sample data, and having a longitudinal data set where each data point had been collected at the right time rather than representing retrospections years in arrears.

Recently, and importantly in the present context, the experiences from this way of developing high-quality, customized data sets from register data have been applied to the individual level of analysis (Delmar et al., 2003). In this work, which at the time of this writing is in an early stage, the entrepreneurial activity of individuals is followed annually over 11 years. More precisely, two (types of) data sets are being created: one that follows individuals in and out of self-employment/firm ownership, and one that gauges the performance over time for the companies these individuals are involved in. Studying the role of human capital is at the core of this project, but its approach creates much other interesting potential. For example:

- By following individuals over many years and across several ventures, it approaches the ideal of assessing "entrepreneurial career performance."
- By creating a link between individuals and *all* ventures they are involved in, it allows analysis of portfolio entrepreneurship (Westhead & Wright, 1998) and overcomes some severe limitations of firm-level analysis (Davidsson, 2004; Scott & Rosa, 1996).
- By following *all* individuals in educational cohorts in and out of entrepreneurship, it can help explore and establish the notion that "entrepreneur" is a transitory role that a large proportion of individuals

take on at some time, rather than being the label for a special breed of people.

- By following the individuals' involvement in several ventures over time, it may help in assessing the longer term effects of "failure" and help establish the notion that venture failure does not necessarily mean individual failure (Sarasvathy, 2004).
- Provided that all individuals in the data set are identifiable by unique codes, this type of data set allows the study of the composition and heterogeneity of teams (as regards gender, age, education, etc.; cf. Ruef et al., 2003), and associated performance effects, as well as the (in)stability of teams across time and different ventures.

In no country is a ready-to-use data set available that can do all of this, and in many countries it would not even be possible to create an individual-level data set that could do any of these. However, in other countries the elements needed for creating a data set that can address at least some of these questions may well be there. It just takes some effort and determination to realize that potential.

A severe limitation of existing statistical register data is that typically the available variables are few and/or assessed with rather crude indicators. This goes for both dependent and independent variables, and means that only relatively simple (all the way down to meaningless) relationships can be investigated. As regards the dependent variable, entering or leaving self-employed status may be the only indicator of entrepreneurship in pure individual level data sets. According to the perspective on entrepreneurship advocated in this chapter, this is not a satisfactory state of affairs. Sometimes individual-level earnings may be available (de Wit & van Winden, 1989). When individual- and firm-level data can communicate, the situation improves, as characteristics of the individuals can be linked to the number of ventures they are involved in, as well as their size, growth, and financial performance (Scott & Rosa, 1996).

From the perspective of psychology, the limitations may be even more severe as regards explanatory variables. Secondary data sets often include personal background data that make them suitable for sociological research (Stanworth, Blythe, Granger, & Stanworth, 1989) but only marginally useful for the psychologist. Some variables may be included from which (social) psychological processes can be inferred, such as having parents who ran their own businesses (Aldrich, Renzulli, & Langton, 1998), or that are at the outskirts of the psychology domain, such as educational attainment. But often this is where the upper limit is. In a few cases researchers have been able to find and use IQ scores and relate them to entrepreneurial behavior over the longer term, but ironically the results have been meager (Delmar, 1996; de Wit & van Winden, 1989).

In rare cases, available data collected for other purposes do include a richer and more validly assessed array of psychological variables (see, e.g., Delmar & Gunnarsson, 1997). However, not even in these cases can an even more fundamental shortcoming of secondary data sets be avoided. This is that entrepreneurship, as understood here, is about emerging phenomena. Ventures typically do not end up in registers while they are still emerging. Likewise, statistical organizations typically do not create identification codes for new industries or organizational populations (Aldrich, 1999) until they have been in existence for quite some time. For this reason, it may be possible to work on the most central research questions in entrepreneurship with archival data only when primary data—and non-standard primary data at that—have been converted into secondary data by being put in the public domain. The PSED data on "nascent entrepreneurs" and ongoing startups is arguably the first large-scale example of such a data set (Gartner et al., 2004; Reynolds, 2000). Although much has been published already from the PSED data, and although the psychological variables are not as carefully assessed as one might have wished for, there are certainly lots of research opportunities left for those who want to make use of this unique data set. Moreover, at the time of this writing the carrying out of a "PSED II" has recently been decided (N. Carter and P. Reynolds, personal communication). If these data are also put in the public domain, even more research opportunities will be created. Hopefully, other "secondary" data sets, which are suitable for addressing the core issues in entrepreneurship, will also be created—preferably those including psychological measures of high quality.

SURVEY RESEARCH CHALLENGES AND OPPORTUNITIES

The questionnaire-based survey approach has many advantages for investigating the complex relationships that signify social phenomena in general and therefore also entrepreneurship. Where experiments can typically only consider the influence of one or a few variables (and hopefully design away some others), surveys can include a broad range of variables of different types. Where psychological variables are lacking completely or have to be approximated with distant single-item proxies in studies relying on secondary data, the survey can include pretested, multiple-item batteries to get at such difficult-to-measure characteristics. Where in-depth case studies have to rely on the researcher's subjective assessments based on cases of unknown generalizability, the survey approach offers (more) objective measures across a large, representative sample. In addition, the survey method achieves all this at reasonable cost. No wonder then that it enjoys such popularity in entrepreneurship research (Aldrich & Baker, 1997; Chandler & Lyon, 2001).

Unfortunately, there is a big caveat as well. Arguably, what is directly measured in questionnaires is not attitudes, intentions, goals, personality traits, or real-world behaviors, and not even experiences, levels of education, or age. What we measure in questionnaires are paper-and-pencil behaviors in response to particular stimuli, namely, the questionnaire items at hand (Pieters, 1988). Questionnaire-based survey approaches are so common that we perhaps reflect too seldom on the rather strong assumptions we make when we believe that the responses correctly reflect the theoretical concepts we are after. Moreover, we make additional strong assumptions when we trust the estimated relationships between these paper-and-pencil behaviors, in particular when we make the inference from cross-sectional survey data that one variable causes variation in the other in the real world.

Hence, huge validity issues are associated with survey research. Admittedly, these problems are not unique to the questionnaire approach but apply equally or even more to other methods that do not involve researcher-manipulated stimuli and/or direct observation of real-world behavior. However, I find the survey context a particularly suitable place to discuss them. This is because entrepreneurship researchers have developed a habit of discussing minor aspects of the validity problem, while remaining silent on more fundamental aspects of it. Psychology is a discipline that is relatively sophisticated regarding these matters, and researchers with a background in psychology can therefore score relatively easily on this dimension when they turn to researching entrepreneurship problems.

Entrepreneurship researchers very frequently provide a maximum of two arguments for the quality of a measure. The first is that it has been used before. Using what is perceived to be "tried and true" measures generally is good advice, even when the existing measure is not the "perfect" measure for the purpose (Davidsson, 2004, chap. 6). Developing a new measure with satisfactory measurement properties is more demanding than one might think, and using an existing one also provides a basis for comparison. However, previous use is obviously not evidence per se that the measure has validity. Only if one can show that previous use directly supports correspondence between the measure and the underlying theoretical concept is this an acceptable validity criterion.

The second common defense of one's measures is Cronbach's alpha coefficient. Researchers proudly state they have measured some tricky unobservable not with a single-item measure, but with a multiple item index, which has reached the magical number .70 (or even .80) on the Cronbach's alpha test for internal consistency (Nunnally, 1967; Nunnally & Bernstein, 1994). Along with the 5% rule for statistical significance, this is one of the great examples of *idola scholae* (blind acceptance of rules) in our type of research. First, the logic behind Cronbach's alpha (and testing factor structure) applies only for *reflective indices*, that is, when it can be assumed that the variance in the items is caused by the underlying latent variable that the index is designed to measure. This would be the case for a measure of "entrepreneurial expertise" consisting of responses to a number of knowledge questions. However, when indicators like having self-employed parents, work-experience from entrepreneurial firms, entrepreneurship-relevant educational attainment, and previous involvement in independent startups are summed, we have a *formative index* of "entrepreneurial expertise" for which high intercorrelations among the indicators is not a logical necessity, and for which the Cronbach's alpha logic therefore does not apply (see further Diamantopoulos & Winklhofer, 2001, on the two types of index).

Many multiple-item measures are reflective in nature, and Cronbach's alpha is thus relevant. But it only proves internal consistency and not validity. Unless the theoretical concept is itself very narrow or easily assessed (such as age or level of education), the only way to approach perfect overlap between concept and measure may be to have an operationalization with quite a large number of items. This is the strategy used in psychological tests of intelligence or aptitude. In survey research on complex phenomena, where we want to capture many different types of variables, we may not afford the space such "perfect" measures demand. The shortcut to a high alpha value with a small number of items is to have items that are very similar. They will then have high intercorrelations and therefore yield a high Cronbach's alpha value. However, *they may be far from exhausting the theoretical concept we are after*. In fact, it is entirely possible to have a high alpha value when measuring with high precision something entirely different from the theoretical concept we were aiming for. It may actually be preferable to have a measure that roughly captures more of the theoretical concept, although with a lower alpha (lower reliability), than one that very precisely covers but a fraction of the theoretical concept.

This illustrates the detrimental effect of a single-eyed concern for internal consistency. Cronbach's alpha is but one of the 13 criteria for evaluation of validity/reliability suggested by Robinson, Shaver, and Wrightsman (1991). These also include, for example, the extent to which prior research in the field is considered and face validity is established; the quality of pilot testing and item development; the composition of the sample; evidence of convergent and discriminant validity, and so on. Psychologists are well equipped for raising the standards of entrepreneurship research by applying more of these criteria to their entrepreneurship research. For an earlier entrepreneurship example see Brown, Davidsson, and Wiklund (2001).

In entrepreneurship research the data are often assumed to represent not just an individual but also a team, a venture, or a firm. Using multiple informants, checking their internal consistency, and deciding on how to combine their responses then become important validity issues. Over and above checking technical criteria, the researcher should also provide evidence that the operationalization is *theoretically sound*—that it has *construct validity*. This is done most effectively by showing that previous research or one's own data prove that the measure is related and unrelated to other variables in accordance with the theory. Of course, the relationships used to support validity have to be other than those the specific piece of research sets out to test.

The truth value of the figure arrived at can be questioned not only for measures but also for estimates of the relationships between them. When two measures originate from the same source (e.g., person) and/or are measured with the same method (e.g., Likert-scale items), it may be suspected that their interrelation is a method artifact. Arguably, the risk for this is particularly pronounced for self-report questionnaire data. The seriousness of this problem is debated. For an informed and balanced account, see Crampton and Wagner (1994), who conclude that general condemnation of self-report methods is not warranted, but that the problem can be serious in domain-specific contexts.

Podsakoff, MacKenzie, Lee, and Podsakoff (2003) take a broader approach to so-called "common method bias" and its sources. They also provide very useful advice for remedy. Importantly, they point out that very strong relationships are typically underestimated, whereas it is weak ones that risk becoming inflated by method artifacts. This is a dilemma for psychological research on complex phenomena such as entrepreneurship, where the sound theory-based expectation may well be a weak—although true—effect for each psychological variable (Rauch & Frese, 2000).

Podsakoff et al. (2003) suggest for all situations that all procedural remedies related to questionnaire design be used. There is an abundance of codified knowledge available on such issues, and it is my experience from extensive survey research that the research craft advice found in the methods literature is generally well worth following (Dillman, 1978, 2000; Fink, 1995). Other than that, Podsakoff et al. (2003) point out obtaining data on the predictor and criterion variables from different sources as the most important remedy. If that cannot be achieved, they offer obtaining the data in different contexts as a second best. One example of this, from which I have positive experiences, is to combine phone and mail questionnaires. As a bonus, this also allows using response formats suitable for each mode. If the source of the bias can be measured, this is a third solution Podsakoff et al. (2003) suggest. In addition to remedies at the data collection stage, they also discuss corrections that can be introduced in the analysis.

Before closing the book on operationalization and validity, it is worth mentioning that a delicate balance to deal with in operationalization is that between the "perfect" operationalization for a specific type of venture, and the most generally applicable operationalization. For example, the best measure of firm size may be the number of vehicles for a taxi company, the number of seats for a restaurant operation, and the quantity of electricity delivered for a power station. However, how are we to compare the firms' growth across these different measures? Sales and number of employees are more generally applicable, but may have other disadvantages (Bolton, 1971; Davidsson & Wiklund, 2000). A similar type of concern may be the reason for weak quantifications (e.g., "a lot," "often," "strong") in questionnaire items. For example, the specific number of innovations you would need to undertake in order to stand out as more entrepreneurial than average is highly industry specific. How would a retailer, a manufacturer, and a consulting firm, respectively, respond to the question "How many new products or services have you introduced over the last *xx* months?"

In developing a scale for measuring "degree of entrepreneurship" or "entrepreneurial performance"—that is, a behavioral aggregate as alternative to the dichotomous firm startup/no firm startup—the less-than-perfect alternatives we are left with seem to be the following:

1. Delimit the study to a narrow and homogeneous subset of ventures/ firms/individuals, and use measures that are suitable for that group.
2. Develop one multiple-item operationalization that is assumed to be applicable to all ventures/firms/individuals. Accept that interesting manifestations of entrepreneurship that clearly apply only to narrow subsets cannot be included in the measure. Also accept as a fact that larger firms and firms in some industries, on average, exercise more entrepreneurship than do smaller firms and firms in certain other industries.
3. Develop one multiple-item operationalization for all ventures/ firms/individuals. However, normalize the score within industry/ size class (or other) groups, and use deviation from the own class mean as the measure of entrepreneurship. This would eliminate what can be regarded as a bias against certain categories when approach (1) is applied, but this comes at the cost of assuming that all subgroups are equally "entrepreneurial." That is, only within-group and not between-group differences will be detected.
4. Develop separate and adapted multiple-item operationalizations for different subgroups (by industry, size class, or otherwise). Standardize these measures, so that comparisons can be made across different operationalizations of entrepreneurship. This would allow including the presumably most relevant indicators for each category in the total sample, but involves a considerable risk of comparing apples and oranges in the analysis.

Similar issues of best versus most generally applicable operationaliz-ations could be discussed with regard to explanatory or outcome variables. As no obviously "right" decision can be made on this kind of issue, a good solution is often to try different approaches within the same study—if space allows.

Quality of operationalization is, of course, not the only challenge of sur-vey research. For example, whom or what to sample is a fundamental issue, but at least some aspects of this have been dealt with in a previous section of the chapter. Closely related to sampling is the issue of (initial) response rate. It is an embarrassing state of affairs that most published survey research is based on effective samples with response rates well below 50%, and even more embarrassing that authors try to portray this as quite okay because their response rate is equal to or higher than that of other published studies. The truth is that substantial nonresponse means that those included in the analyzed sample have not been selected randomly or probabilistically. Therefore, the applicability of statistical inference theory (significance test-ing) can be fundamentally questioned. This remains the case even if one can show that the nonrespondents do not differ systematically from the respon-dents in terms of, for example, demographic characteristics. The fact is ines-capable that the nonrespondents do differ from the respondents on one behavioral measure, namely, their propensity to answer questionnaires, and there is a risk of unknown magnitude that they also differ on the substantive matters of the research in question.

There is relief, though. First, the response rate can be substantially im-proved by applying the cumulative knowledge of the craft of survey re-search (Dillman, 1978, 2000; Fink, 1995). This is equally true regardless of whether one has the privilege of doing one's research in Sweden—where for some peculiar cultural reason respondents are unusually cooperative— or in countries where reaching above 50% remains a vain dream no matter what you do. Second, as we noted in the section on sampling earlier, exact representation of the empirical population in one country at one time is not the most relevant issue. Therefore, what the researcher should do is to show that the analyzed sample, after nonresponse and all, is suitable for the task from a theoretical point of view. Thus, if the research is hypothetico-deduc-tive, the sample should present a fair test of the theory—that is, if the theory is any good, it is reasonable to assume its predictions to be borne out for this sample (as well as in many other, untested samples that may be somewhat differently composed). If the research is theory generating, there should ex-ist now or in the future a population of similar cases that is large enough, so that we have something to which it is worth generalizing the results. As re-gards statistical testing, the sad fact is that it is not the powerful and per-fectly suited tool that social scientists need (and sometimes think it is; cf. Cohen, 1994; Oakes, 1986). However, even though its applicability in a strict sense can almost always be challenged, I would suggest that for lack of better alternatives we are well advised to continue using it in order to safeguard against overinterpreting results that may well have occurred for stochastic reasons.

I have already emphasized the process nature of entrepreneurship. An implication of this, as well as the generally rising quality of entrepreneurship research, is that other than for particular research questions, reviewers and editors of leading scholarly journals will not accept a cross-sectional survey methodology. This points at longitudinal designs (repeated surveys) and additional nonresponse problems. In the worst-case scenario, a combination of natural attrition (dissolution of the venture) and refusal to continue to cooperate may lead to having complete data for such a small sample that no meaningful analyses can be made. As regards natural attrition, this is partly a matter of aiming at a large enough initial sample and partly about applying analysis methods that can handle censoring (cf. Delmar & Shane, 2003; Samuelsson, 2004). Concerning other dropouts, the experience from both the Swedish and the American PSED projects (Delmar & Davidsson, 2000; Gartner et al., 2004) has been that this problem is not as big as one might fear; once the nascent entrepreneurs have decided to participate in the study, many of them actually appreciate the continued contact.

Finally, for internal nonresponse the replacing of missing data with the mean or with a predicted value from a regression may be defensible when only a tiny percentage of the cases are manipulated in this way. However, such techniques reduce the error variance, and therefore it amounts to cheating when the problem of partially missing data is more substantial. To our rescue, method experts have developed more sophisticated techniques for data imputation that can be applied. See, for example, Little and Rubin (1987), Fichman and Cummings (2003), or other contributions to the same special issue of the *Organization Research Methods* journal (Volume 6, Issue 3).

IN-DEPTH CASE STUDY RESEARCH CHALLENGES AND OPPORTUNITIES

As noted earlier, contemporary conceptualizations of entrepreneurship emphasize *behaviors* in the *process* of creation of new economic activity, often highlighting also the intricate interactions among individual, task ("opportunity"), and the environment (Davidsson, 2003, 2004; Gartner, 1988; Shane, 2003). This would seem to make *ethnography* a strong methodological candidate for making progress in entrepreneurship research. Ethnographic case studies are longitudinal in nature and can thus capture processes. They involve direct and rich observation of real behavior, as opposed to the few, barren "facts" in archival data, the paper-and-pencil exercises in survey research, or the researcher-manipulated behavior of laboratory research. Arguably, the closeup character of ethnographic work also allows insights into the interplay between individual(s), tasks, and environmental characteristics—issues that are either designed away or hard to get at with other methods.

Hence, there are frequent calls (but little following) for intense ethnographic study of (super)entrepreneurs of the kind Mintzberg (1974; cf. Kurke & Aldrich, 1983) did in his classical study of managers (Aldrich & Baker, 1997). Such studies can no doubt give new insights. An early refreshing experience I had as a researcher was the reading of the Frank Williams case in Stanworth and Curran (1973). Although this case built on repeated interviews rather than true ethnography, it certainly gave insights into the dynamic nature of the motivations and goals of an ambitious small firm owner-manager. Another early encounter with deep and insightful fieldwork was Barker and Gump's (1964) work on the implications of organization size. Although their work concerned schools, it is easy to see the analogy to the potential for empowerment and innovation in small firms.

All in-depth case approaches share the limitation that statistical generalizability cannot be obtained. What one can hope for is analytical generalizability—the generation of new concepts and suggested contingencies that are worthy of consideration also for cases not investigated. When entrepreneurship is regarded as equal to starting and running an independent business, I have little doubt that ethnographic closeup studies of business owner-managers are an excellent tool for generation of new, tentative insights. When entrepreneurship is regarded as the process of creation of new economic activity, the value of this approach is, regrettably, less than it might first seem. This is because, as we already discussed, entrepreneurship is a process and "entrepreneur" is a transitory role; nobody is an "entrepreneur" all the time. Clearly, an intense but short-in-duration closeup study like Mintzberg's (1974) would not do the trick. Even if focused on an independent businessperson known for repeated success at creating new ventures, there is considerable risk that a week-long observation of that individual would capture many more managerial than entrepreneurial behaviors. Unless the researcher is extremely persistent or lucky, he or she is likely to capture but a fraction of the entrepreneurial process.

In particular, when the entrepreneurial process is conceptually subdivided further into the interrelated processes of *discovery* (development of the business idea) and *exploitation* (resource-acquisition and market-making behaviors to realize the idea; cf. Fig. 13.1; Davidsson, 2003, 2004, and Shane & Venkataraman, 2000), it becomes clear that the ethnographic approach would be inadequate for gaining insights into the *discovery* subprocess. The earliest part of this process—that is, the initial conception of an embryonic business idea—is an infrequent event, unlikely to happen just as the ethnographer is present. Further, it represents cognition rather than being a behavior, and may therefore be missed even if the researcher were lucky enough to be around. The continuation of the discovery process is also cognitive rather than behavioral in nature and may therefore require research approaches other than passive observation (De Koning, 2003; Sarasvathy, 1999). However, if the researcher is careful in the selection of cases and prepared to spend considerable time in the field, the ethnographic approach can be excellent for gaining insights into the exploitation process, and at least adequate for studying certain aspects of the discovery process. Apart from pure ethnography, longitudinal, real-time case studies combining several means of data collection such as observation, interviews, and diaries (cf. Brundin, 2002) may well be worth trying.

Retreating to more conventional case study designs means avoiding some of the hassle and problems inherent in ethnographic approaches—but at considerable cost. When cases are retrospective and interview-based, whole arrays of method issues that fundamentally threaten the validity of the findings come to the fore. Selection (success) bias is likely to become worse, further limiting the generalizability of the findings. Moreover, we are now no longer dealing with direct observation of behaviors, but retrospective self-reports of such. These reports are subject to memory decay, hindsight bias/rationalization after the fact, and impression management/social desirability problems. These shortcomings of interview-based, retrospective case studies are hardly news to trained psychologists, but among management researchers—particularly in Europe—their significance appear grossly underrated. The use of multiple informants and supplementary data from documents may remedy these problems to some extent, but compared to approaches that observe behaviors in real time the retrospective case study arguably remains an inferior alternative.

Yet new ideas (e.g., hypotheses) have to originate somewhere, and for that purpose thorough and at least semisystematic "qualitative" studies are often a superior alternative to armchair reasoning or deductive, quantitative research. However, in this author's opinion the studies that are successful at developing intriguing new ideas (Bhave, 1994; De Koning, 2003; Sarasvathy, 1999; Shane, 2000) tend to be those that include a somewhat greater number of cases (say, half a dozen to a couple of dozen) and focus on a narrower set of issues, rather than those that try to tell everything about one or two in-depth cases.

LABORATORY RESEARCH CHALLENGES AND OPPORTUNITIES

As mentioned earlier, the "first generation" of empirical entrepreneurship research focused largely on the characteristics of "entrepreneurs." The mission for entrepreneurship was to describe how such people differ from others. An underlying assumption was that knowing about real-world entrepreneurs automatically leads not only to descriptively but also prescriptively valid knowledge about entrepreneurship. It is perhaps superfluous to state that such assumptions indicate neither need nor have room for laboratory research, as we cannot readily manipulate the innate characteristics of people.

Many of the changes that have occurred since then have opened up room for contributions from laboratory research such as experiments and simulations. First, entrepreneurship is decreasingly seen as a dichotomous individual disposition, but rather as a result of the interplay between person, task, and environment (Shane, 2003). Tasks and environments are things that experimental psychologists manipulate with great mastery. Further, it is increasingly being agreed that most people under the right circumstances can show some level of entrepreneurship. As noted earlier, this means that not only "practicing entrepreneurs" but almost any sample of individuals can be a relevant group of experimental subjects for studying entrepreneurship (although it must be pointed out that students are often *not* a preferable group). Moreover, it is increasingly understood that those who have set up ventures in the real world do not necessarily have all the right answers, and that researchers should take on the greater challenge of testing theoretically derived success recipes *before* the most successful practitioners have already found them and proved them true (Davidsson, 2002; Fiet, 2002). In other words, in order to arrive at conclusions that are not only descriptively but also normatively valid, the researcher may have to look beyond even the best current practice. To sometimes lead rather than lag practice, empirical entrepreneurship research needs to test what has not yet occurred "out there." This can only happen in the laboratory.

Thus, the increased use of laboratory research methods in entrepreneurship research can be welcomed (Baron & Brush, 1999; Fiet & Migliore, 2001; Gustavsson, 2004; Sarasvathy, 1999). The primary, general strength of such methods is, of course, that they can establish causality in a relatively unambiguous manner. This is no small deal. I once heard a researcher claim her research showed that loan officers discriminated against women entrepreneurs. The empirical basis for this was that in a very small, all-women, nonrandom sample of business founders, some interviewees had been less successful at obtaining loans than they wished to, and a few of them (when prompted) attributed this to the fact that they were women. Obviously, nobody needs to take a claim based on such weak evidence very seriously, and the researcher risks being laughed at—as does, regrettably, the result, even if it happened to be true. Compare this with a systematic, quantitative survey based on representative samples of men and women founders and including most other suspected explanations as control variables in the analysis. If the latter study showed significant gender discrimination it would be hard to disregard—but not impossible for the diehard. There are so many potentially confounding factors that conclusive proof cannot be claimed. Compare that again with obtaining support for gender discrimination in an experimental study where loan officers indicate their willingness to give loans based on written business plans, where the genders of the founding team members are manipulated while absolutely everything else is held constant. In this latter case, it is definitely those who refuse to accept the results that deserve to be laughed—or yelled—at.

The process nature of entrepreneurship is an additional reason to consider simulation or experimentation. Studying real-world processes is a costly and time-consuming endeavor with uncertain rewards. Although the laboratory alternative will never completely substitute for real-world studies, laboratory studies are a valuable complement—and sometimes an acceptable alternative when resource limitations prohibit a longitudinal study in the real setting. Laboratory methods make it possible to compress time and collect multiperiod data—such as in the context of a computer-based business simulation game—without having to wait for ages before any serious analysis work can be done.

Earlier we portrayed entrepreneurship as consisting of two interrelated and (partially) overlapping subprocesses, which we called *discovery* (idea development) and *exploitation* (behaviors that make it happen). Both of those could presumably be induced in the laboratory. However, we noted earlier that the earliest part of the discovery process is the most difficult to study as it happens in the real world. When the researcher controls the stimuli that may lead to discovery of new venture ideas, studying also this central part of the entrepreneurial process becomes viable (Gustavsson, 2004; Sarasvathy, 1999).

Adding *evaluation* to discovery and exploitation, Shane and Venkataraman (2000) actually characterize the entrepreneurial process as consisting of three parts. Assuming the founders' perspective, I here regard evaluation as part of the continued discovery process, as evaluation is cognitive (and affective) rather than behavioral in nature. At any rate, when evaluation tasks can be modeled as the comparison of a finite set of multiattribute alternatives, they lend themselves to experimental manipulation. In experiments or conjoint analysis tasks, subjects can be asked to make holistic judgments that reveal the relative importance of the attributes for arriving at the overall assessment (Shepherd & Zacharakis, 1997). Arguably, this leads to much more credible information on the relative weight of decision criteria than do attribute-by-attribute self-reports of relative importance (Zacharakis & Meyer, 1998). So far, this research option has mainly been applied to external investors' evaluations of proposals or business plans (e.g., Bruns, 2004; Shepherd & Zacharakis, 1997; Zacharakis & Meyer, 1998), but with some creativity it may well be applied to other entrepreneurship research problems as well, such as entrepreneurs' evaluations of alternative venture ideas, their evaluations of any hypothetical future states such as different future sizes of their firms (Davidsson, 1986), or—to turn the conventional line of thinking around—the criteria by which they choose their venture capitalists.

Not all individuals are likely to make evaluations in entrepreneurial contexts in the same way. In particular, experienced and repeatedly successful entrepreneurs, that is, experts, are likely to have developed decision strategies that differ from the novice. As with any other group of experts (Anderson, 1990), this is an area where laboratory methods seem helpful. Assessing how expert entrepreneurs differ from novices in the real setting is difficult first because the population of novices is censored—complete novices do not exercise entrepreneurial behaviors and thus cannot be compared to experts regarding these behaviors—and second because so many nonperson variables vary at the same time. An interesting recent example of a laboratory approach to expert versus novice study in entrepreneurship is a study by Gustavsson (2004). Presenting subjects to hypothetical venture opportunities with varying degree of uncertainty, she was able to confirm the theoretically derived hypothesis that experts much more than novices adapted their decision-making style (on an analysis-to-intuition continuum) to the nature of the task.

The general shortcoming of laboratory research is that the external validity of the findings can always be questioned. What works in the laboratory does not necessarily repeat itself in the field, where loads of other influences also have their say. Further, the laboratory design may force participants to use information they otherwise would not have considered, or to compare alternatives in a parallel and optimizing manner where real-life evaluations typically are sequential and satisficing. If developed into an isolated paradigm, laboratory research on entrepreneurship runs the risk of accumulating knowledge that has nothing to do with how things work in real life. Therefore, laboratory work should preferably be integrated into programs that include also analysis of real-world data, so that the field and the laboratory can inform and inspire one another. Cialdini's (1980) ideas on "full cycle social psychology," which assigns important roles to exploratory case studies as well as to laboratory proof of causality and to broadly based quantitative verification, seem to point out a sensible route to follow.

Laboratory research also has other shortcomings. Experimental control is not as easy to achieve as idealized examples would suggest. For example, in evaluation tasks the systematic variation and combination of attributes may result in having participants evaluate highly unrealistic alternatives. A more fundamental challenge for laboratory research, especially as applied to discovery, is that in real life the creative entrepreneur can use any cues and information from pools that are for all practical purposes limitless, and combine them in innumerable new ways. In the laboratory task, the creativity a participant can show is normally limited to what has already been conceived by the designer of the experiment. A critic can easily argue that if we cannot study entrepreneurial cognition and behavior that is more imaginative than that of the researcher, neither can we get any insights into the more spectacular forms of entrepreneurial breakthroughs.

CONCLUSION

In this chapter I have argued, on the one hand, that researchers with a psychology background can make strong and welcome contributions—on various levels of analysis—to the study of entrepreneurship understood as the creation of new economic activity. On the other hand, I have pointed out quite a number of method challenges that have to be dealt with in such pursuit. These method challenges ranged from sampling challenges stemming from the emerging nature of the entrepreneurship phenomenon and the nonexistence of a well-defined population of "entrepreneurs," to operationalization and analysis problems that signify different methodological approaches. Hopefully, though, I have not conveyed the image that conducting worthwhile entrepreneurship research is prohibitively difficult. It is not—especially not for those equipped with the theoretical and methodological toolboxes of an established discipline, like psychology. "Perfect" research is neither necessary nor possible. All one has to achieve is to do a little better than one's predecessors (along some dimension), and with the help of the tools and experiences others have made and shared, it should in fact be rather easy to reach that goal in this young field. Beyond that, trying to do as much better as possible is actually the type of challenge that makes life as a researcher interesting!

REFERENCES

Aldrich, H. E. (1999). *Organizations evolving*. Newbury Park, CA: Sage.

Aldrich, H. E., & Baker, T. (1997). Blinded by the cites? Has there been progress in the entrepreneurship field? In D. Sexton & R. Smilor (Eds.), *Entrepreneurship 2000* (pp. 377–400). Chicago: Upstart.

Aldrich, H. E., Carter, N. M., & Reynolds, P. D. (2004). Teams. In W. B. Gartner, K. G. Shaver, N. M. Carter, & P. D. Reynolds (Eds.), *Handbook of entrepreneurial dynamics: The process of business creation* (pp. 299–310). Thousand Oaks, CA: Sage.

Aldrich, H. E., Kalleberg, A. L., Marsden, P. V., & Cassell, J. (1989). In pursuit of evidence: Strategies for locating new businesses. *Journal of Business Venturing, 4*(6), 367–386.

Aldrich, H. E., Renzulli, L., & Langton, N. (1998). Passing on privilege: Resources provided by self-employed parents to their self-employed children. In K. Liecht (Ed.), *Research in social stratification and mobility* (pp. 291–317). Greenwich, CT: JAI Press.

Aldrich, H. E., & Wiedenmayer, G. (1993). From traits to rates: an ecological perspective on organizational foundings. In J. Katz & R. Brockhaus (Eds.), *Advances in entrepreneurship, firm emergence, and growth* (Vol. 1, pp. 145–196). Greenwich, CT: JAI Press.

Amit, R., MacCrimmon, K. R., & Zietsma, C. (2000). Does money matter? Wealth attainment as the motive for initiating growth oriented technology ventures. *Journal of Business Venturing, 16*, 119–143.

Anderson, J. R. (1990). *Cognitive psychology and its implications*. New York: Freeman.

Barker, R. G., & Gump, P. V. (1964). *Big school, small school*. Stanford, CA: Stanford University Press.

Baron, R. (1999). Counterfactual thinking and venture formation: The potential effects of thinking about "what might have been." *Journal of Business Venturing, 15*, 79–91.

Baron, R. A., & Brush, C. G. (1999). The role of social skills in entrepreneurs' success: evidence from videotapes of entrepreneurs' presentations. In P. D. Reynolds, W. D. Bygrave, N. M. Carter, S. Manigart, C. M. Mason, G. D. Meyer, & K. G. Shaver (Eds.), *Frontiers of entrepreneurship 1999* (pp. 45–57). Wellesley, MA: Babson College.

Baum, J. R., & Locke, E. A. (2004). The relationship of entrepreneurial traits, skill, and motivation to subsequent venture growth. *Journal of Applied Psychology, 89*, 586–598.

Baum, J. R., Locke, E. A., & Kirkpatrick, S. A. (1998). A longitudinal study of the relation of vision and vision communication to venture growth and performance. *Journal of Applied Psychology, 83*(1), 43–54.

Bhave, M. P. (1994). A process model of entrepreneurial venture creation. *Journal of Business Venturing, 9*, 223–242.

Bolton, J. E. (1971). *Small firms. Report of the Committee of Inquiry on Small Firms*. London: Her Majesty's Stationery Office.

Brockhaus, R. H. (1982). The psychology of the entrepreneur. In C. A. Kent, D. L. Sexton, & K. H. Vesper (Eds.), *Encyclopedia of entrepreneurship* (pp. 39–71). Englewood Cliffs, NJ: Prentice Hall.

Brown, T., Davidsson, P., & Wiklund, J. (2001). An operationalization of Stevenson's conceptualization of entrepreneurship as opportunity-based firm behavior. *Strategic Management Journal, 22*(10), 953–968.

Brundin, E. (2002). *Emotions in motion. Leadership during radical change*. Doctoral dissertation, Jönköping International Business School, Jönköping.

Bruns, V. (2004). *Who receives bank loans? A study of lending officers' assessments of loans to growing small and medium-sized enterprises*. Doctoral dissertation, Jönköping International Business School, Jönköping.

Busenitz, L. W., & Barney, J. B. (1997). Differences between entrepreneurs and managers in small firms: Biases and heuristics in strategic decision-making. *Journal of Business Venturing, 12*, 9–30.

Chandler, G. N., Dahlqvist, J., & Davidsson, P. (2003, August). *Opportunity recognition processes: A taxonomic classification and outcome implications*. Paper presented at the Academy of Management Meeting, Seattle, WA.

Chandler, G. N., & Lyon, D. W. (2001). Methodological issues in entrepreneurship research: The past decade. *Entrepreneurship Theory & Practice, 25*(4), 101–113.

Cialdini, R. B. (1980). Full cycle social psychology. In L. Beckman (Ed.), *Applied social psychology annual* (Vol. 1, pp. 21–48). Beverly Hills, CA: Sage.

Ciavarella, M. A., Buchholtz, A. K., Riordan, C. M., Gatewood, R. D., & Stokes, G. S. (2004). The Big Five and venture survival: Is there a linkage? *Journal of Business Venturing, 19*, 465–483.

Cohen, J. (1994). The earth is round ($p < .05$). *American Psychologist, 47*(12), 997–1003.

Covin, J. G., & Slevin, D. P. (1986). The development and testing of an organizational-level entrepreneurship scale. In R. Ronstadt, J. A. Hornaday, R. Peterson, & K. H. Vesper (Eds.), *Frontiers of entrepreneurship research 1986* (pp. 628–639). Wellesley, MA: Babson College.

Crampton, S. M., & Wagner, J. A. (1994). Percept-percept inflation in microorganizational research: An investigation of prevalence and effect. *Journal of Applied Psychology, 79*(1), 67–76.

Davidsson, P. (1986). *Tillväxt I små företag: En pilotstudie om tillväxtvilja och tillväxtförutsättningar I små företag* [Small firm growth: A pilot study on growth willingness and opportunity for growth in small firms]. Studies in Economic Psychology No. 120. Stockholm: Stockholm School of Economics.

Davidsson, P. (1988). Type of man and type of company revisited: A confirmatory cluster analysis approach. In B. Kirchhoff, W. Long, W. McMullan, K. Vesper, & W. Wetzel (Eds.), *Frontiers of entrepreneurship research 1988* (pp. 88–105). Wellesley, MA: Babson College.

Davidsson, P. (1995). Culture, structure and regional levels of entrepreneurship. *Entrepreneurship & Regional Development, 7,* 41–62.

Davidsson, P. (2002). What entrepreneurship research can do for business and policy practice. *International Journal of Entrepreneurship Education, 1*(1), 5–24.

Davidsson, P. (2003). The domain of entrepreneurship research: Some suggestions. In J. Katz & D. Shepherd (Eds.), *Advances in Entrepreneurship, firm emergence and growth. Cognitive approaches to entrepreneurship research* (Vol. 6, pp. 315–372). Oxford, UK: Elsevier/JAI Press.

Davidsson, P. (2004). *Researching entrepreneurship.* New York: Springer.

Davidsson, P., & Delmar, F. (1998, September). *Some important observations concerning job creation by firm size and age.* Paper presented at the Rencontres St Gall, Elm, Switzerland.

Davidsson, P., Lindmark, L., & Olofsson, C. (1994). New firm formation and regional development in Sweden. *Regional Studies, 28,* 395–410.

Davidsson, P., Lindmark, L., & Olofsson, C. (1998). The extent of overestimation of small firm job creation: An empirical examination of the "regression bias.". *Small Business Economics, 10,* 87–100.

Davidsson, P., & Wiklund, J. (2000). Conceptual and empirical challenges in the study of firm growth. In D. Sexton & H. Landström (Eds.), *The Blackwell handbook of entrepreneurship* (pp. 26–44). Oxford, MA: Blackwell Business.

Davidsson, P., & Wiklund, J. (2001). Levels of analysis in entrepreneurship research: Current practice and suggestions for the future. *Entrepreneurship Theory & Practice, 25*(4), 81–99.

De Koning, A. (2003). Opportunity development: a socio-cognitive perspective. In J. Katz & D. Shepherd (Eds.), *Advances in entrepreneurship, firm emergence and growth. Cognitive approaches to entrepreneurship research* (Vol. 6, pp. 265–314). Oxford, UK: Elsevier/JAI Press.

Delmar, F. (1996). *Entrepreneurial behavior and business performance.* Stockholm: Stockholm School of Economics.

Delmar, F. (2000). The psychology of the entrepreneur. In S. Carter & D. Jones-Evans (Eds.), *Enterprise & small business: Principles, practice and policy* (pp. 132–154). Harlow: Financial Times.

Delmar, F., & Davidsson, P. (2000). Where do they come from? Prevalence and characteristics of nascent entrepreneurs. *Entrepreneurship & Regional Development, 12,* 1–23.

Delmar, F., Davidsson, P., & Gartner, W. (2003). Arriving at the high-growth firm. *Journal of Business Venturing, 18*(2), 189–216.

Delmar, F., & Gunnarsson, J. (1997, September). *Predicting group membership among entrepreneurs, nascent entrepreneurs and non-entrepreneurs using psychological data and network activities.* Paper presented at the IAREP XXII Conference, Valencia, Spain.

Delmar, F., & Shane, S. (2003). Does business planning facilitate the development of new ventures? *Strategic Management Journal, 24,* 1165–1185.

Delmar, F., Wiklund, J., & Sjöberg, K. (2003). *The involvement in self-employment among the Swedish science and technology labor force between 1990 and 2000* (No. a2003:017). Stockholm: Swedish Institute for Growth Policy Studies.

Demsetz, H. (1983). The neglect of the entrepreneur. In J. Ronen (Ed.), *Entrepreneurship* (pp. 271–280). Lexington, MA: Lexington Books.

de Wit, G., & van Winden, F. A. A. M. (1989). An empirical analysis of self-employment in the Netherlands. *Small Business Economics, 1,* 263–272.

Diamantopoulos, A., & Winklhofer, H. M. (2001). Index construction with formative indicators: An alternative to scale development. *Journal of Marketing Research, 38*(2), 269–277.

Dillman, D. A. (1978). *Mail and telephone surveys: The total design method.* New York: Wiley-Interscience.

Dillman, D. A. (2000). *Mail and internet surveys: The tailored design method.* New York: Wiley.

Eagly, A. H., & Chaiken, S. (1993). *The psychology of attitudes.* Orlando, FL: Harcourt Brace Jonanovich.

Escher, S., Grabarkiewicz, R., Frese, M., Steekelenburg, G., Lauw, M., & Friedrich, D. (2002). The moderator effect of cognitive ability on the relationship between planning strategies and business success of small scale business owners in South Africa: A longitudinal design. *Journal of Developmental Entrepreneurship, 7*(3), 305–325.

Fichman, M., & Cummings, J. N. (2003). Multiple imputation for missing data: Making the most of what you know. *Organizational Research Methods, 6*(3), 282–308.

Fiet, J. O. (2002). *The search for entrepreneurial discoveries.* Westport, CT: Quorum Books.

Fiet, J. O., & Migliore, P. J. (2001). The testing of a model of entrepreneurial discovery by aspiring entrepreneurs. In W. D. Bygrave, E. Autio, C. G. Brush, P. Davidsson, P. G. Greene, P. D. Reynolds, & H. J. Sapienza (Eds.), *Frontiers of entrepreneurship research 2001* (pp. 1–12). Wellesley, MA: Babson College.

Fink, A. (Ed.). (1995). *The survey kit.* Thousands Oaks, CA: Sage.

Frese, M., Brantjes, A., & Hoorn, R. (2002). Psychological success factors of small businesses in Namibia: The role of strategy process, entrepreneurial orientation, and the environment. *Journal of Developmental Entrepreneurship, 7*(3), 259–282.

Gartner, W. B. (1988, Spring). "Who is an entrepreneur" is the wrong question. *American Small Business Journal,* pp. 11–31.

Gartner, W. B. (1990). What are we talking about when we are talking about entrepreneurship? *Journal of Business Venturing, 5,* 15–28.

Gartner, W. B., & Carter, N. (2003). Entrepreneurial behavior and firm organizing processes. In Z. J. Acs & D. B. Audretsch (Eds.), *Handbook of entrepreneurship research* (pp. 195–221). Dordrecht: Kluwer.

Gartner, W. B., Shaver, K. G., Carter, N. M., & Reynolds, P. D. (2004). *Handbook of entrepreneurial dynamics: The process of business creation.* Thousand Oaks, CA: Sage.

Grégoire, D., Noël, M., Dery, R., & Bechard, J.-P. (2004). *Is there conceptual convergence in entrepreneurship research? An empirical analysis.* Unpublished manuscript. Boulder: University of Colorado.

Gustavsson, V. (2004). *Entrepreneurial decision-making.* Doctoral dissertation, Jönköping International Business School, Jönköping.

Hmieleski, K. M., & Ensley, M. D. (2004a, June). *An investigation of the linkage between entrepreneur intelligence and new venture performance.* Paper presented at the Babson College/Kauffman Foundation Entrepreneurship Research Conference, Wellesley, MA.

Hmieleski, K. M., & Ensley, M. D. (2004b, June). *An investigation of improvisation as a strategy for exploiting dynamic opportunities.* Paper presented at the Babson College/Kauffman Foundation Entrepreneurship Research Conference, Wellesley, MA.

Hofstede, G. (1980). *Culture's consequences: International differences in work-related values.* Beverly Hills, CA: Sage.

Hornaday, R. V. (1990). Dropping the E-words from small business research: An alternative typology. *Journal of Small Business Management, 28*(4), 22–33.

Katz, J., & Gartner, W. B. (1988). Properties of emerging organizations. *Academy of Management Review, 13*(3), 429–441.

Klein, K. J., & Kozlowski, W. J. (2000). *Multilevel theory, research, and methods in organizations.* San Francisco: Jossey-Bass.

Kozlowski, W. J., & Klein, K. J. (2000). A multilevel approach to theory and research in organizations. In K. J. Klein & W. J. Kozlowski (Eds.), *Multilevel theory, research, and methods in organizations* (pp. 3–80). San Francisco: Jossey-Bass.

Krueger, N. F. (2003). The cognitive psychology of entrepreneurship. In Z. Acs & D. Audretsch (Eds.), *Handbook of entrepreneurship research: An interdisciplinary survey and introduction* (pp. 105–140). Dordrecht: Kluwer.

Kurke, L. B., & Aldrich, H. E. (1983). Mintzberg was right!: A replication and extension of the nature of managerial work. *Management Science, 29*(8), 975–984.

Little, R. J. A., & Rubin, D. B. (1987). *Statistical analysis with missing data.* New York: Wiley.

Low, M. B., & MacMillan, I. C. (1988). Entrepreneurship: Past research and future challenges. *Journal of Management, 14,* 139–161.

Lumpkin, G. T., & Dess, G. G. (1996). Clarifying the entrepreneurial orientation construct and linking it to performance. *Academy of Management Review, 21*(1), 135–172.

Lynn, R. (1991). *The secret of the miracle economy. Different national attitudes to competitiveness and money.* London: The Social Affaires Unit.

McClelland, D. C. (1961). *The achieving society.* Princeton, NJ: Van Nostrand.

Mitchell, R. K., Seawright, K. W., & Morse, E. A. (2000). Cross-cultural cognition and the venture creation decision. *Academy of Management Journal, 43*(5), 974–993.

Mintzberg, II. (1974). *The nature of managerial work.* New York: Harper & Row.

Nicholson, N. (1998). Personality and entrepreneurial leadership: A study of the heads of the UK's most successful independent companies. *European Management Journal, 16,* 529–538.

Nunnally, J. C. (1967). *Psychometric theory.* New York: McGraw-Hill.

Nunnally, J. C., & Bernstein, I. H. (1994). *Psychometric theory* (3rd ed.). New York: McGraw-Hill.

Oakes, M. (1986). *Statistical inference: A commentary for the social and behavioural sciences.* Chichester: Wiley.

Penrose, E. (1959). *The theory of the growth of the firm.* Oxford: Oxford University Press.

Pieters, R. G. M. (1988). Attitude–behavior relationships. In W. F. van Raaij, G. M. van Veldhoven & K.-E. Wärneryd (Eds.), *Handbook of economic psychology* (pp. 108–142). Dordrecht, the Netherlands: Kluwer.

Podsakoff, P. M., MacKenzie, S. B., Lee, J.-Y., & Podsakoff, N. P. (2003). Common method biases in behavioral research: A critical review of the literature and recommended remedies. *Journal of Applied Psychology, 88*(5), 879–903.

Rauch, A., & Frese, M. (2000). Psychological approaches to entrepreneurial success: A general model and an overview of findings. In C. L. Cooper & I. T. Robertson (Eds.), *International Review of Industrial and Organizational Psychology* (Vol. 15, pp. 101–141). Chichester: Wiley.

Reynolds, P. D. (2000). National panel study of US business start-ups. Background and methodology. In J. A. Katz (Ed.), *Advances in entrepreneurship, firm emergence and growth* (Vol. 4, pp. 153–227). Stamford, CT: JAI Press.

Robinson, J. P., Shaver, P. R., & Wrightsman, L. S. (1991). Criteria for scale selection and evaluation. In J. P. Robinson, P. R. Shaver, & L. S. Wrightsman (Eds.), *Measures of personality and social psychological attitudes* (pp. 1–16). San Diego, CA: Academic Press.

Rousseau, D. M. (1985). Issues of level in organizational research: multi-level and cross-level perspectives. *Research in Organizational Behavior, 7,* 1–37.

Ruef, M., Aldrich, H. E., & Carter, N. M. (2003). The structure of organizational founding teams: Homophily, strong ties, and isolation among U.S. entrepreneurs. *American Sociological Review, 68*(2), 195–222.

Samuelsson, M. (2004). *Creating new ventures: A longitudinal investigation of the nascent venturing process.* Doctoral dissertation, Jönköping International Business School, Jönköping.

Sarasvathy, S. (1999). *Decision making in the absence of markets: An empirically grounded model of entrepreneurial expertise.* Seattle: School of Business, University of Washington.

Sarasvathy, S. (2001). Causation and effectuation: Towards a theoretical shift from economic inevitability to entrepreneurial contingency. *Academy of Management Review, 26*(2), 243–288.

Sarasvathy, S. (2004). The questions we ask and the questions we care about: Reformulating some problems in entrepreneurship research. *Journal of Business Venturing, 19*(5), 707–720.

Schumpeter, J. A. (1934). *The theory of economic development.* Cambridge, MA: Harvard University Press.

Scott, M., & Rosa, P. (1996). Opinion: Has firm level analysis reached its limits? Time for a rethink. *International Small Business Journal, 14*(4), 81–89.

Shane, S. (2000). Prior knowledge and the discovery of entrepreneurial opportunities. *Organization Science, 11*(4), 448–469.

Shane, S. (2003). *A general theory of entrepreneurship: The individual–opportunity nexus.* Cheltenham, UK: Edward Elgar.

Shane, S., & Venkataraman, S. (2000). The promise of entrepreneurship as a field of research. *Academy of Management Review, 25*(1), 217–226.

Shaver, K. G. (2003). The social psychology of entrepreneurial behavior. In Z. Acs & D. Audretsch (Eds.), *Handbook of entrepreneurship research: An interdisciplinary survey and introduction* (pp.). Dordrecht: Kluwer.

Shaver, K. G., Carter, N. M., Gartner, W. B., & Reynolds, P. D. (2001). Who is a nascent entrepreneur? Decision rules for identifying and selecting entrepreneurs in the panel study of entrepreneurial dynamics (PSED) [summary]. In W. D. Bygrave, E. Autio, C. G. Brush, P. Davidsson, P. G. Greene, P. D. Reynolds & H. J. Sapienza (Eds.), *Frontiers of entrepreneurship research 2001* (p. 122). Wellesley, MA: Babson College.

Shepherd, D., & Zacharakis, A. (1997). Conjoint analysis: A window of opportunity for entrepreneurship research. In J. Katz & R. H. Brockhaus (Eds.), *Advances in entrepreneurship, firm emergence, and growth* (Vol. 3, pp. 203–248). Greenwich, CT: JAI Press.

Simon, M., & Houghton, S. M. (1999). Cognitive biases, risk taking, and venture formation: How individuals decide to start companies. *Journal of Business Venturing, 15*, 113–134.

Stanworth, J., Blythe, S., Granger, B., & Stanworth, C. (1989). Who becomes an entrepreneur. *International Small Business Journal, 8*, 11–22.

Stanworth, J., & Curran, J. (1973). *Management motivation in the smaller business.* Epping, Essex: Gower Press.

Stevenson, H. H., & Jarillo, J. C. (1990). A paradigm of entrepreneurship: Entrepreneurial management. *Strategic Management Journal, 11*, 17–27.

Thibaut, J. W., & Kelley, H. H. (1959). *The social psychology of groups.* New York: Wiley.

Van Gelderen, M., Van der Sluis, L., & Jansen, P. (2005). Learning opportunities and learning behaviors of small business starters: relations with goal achievement, skill development, and satisfaction. *Small Business Economics, 25*(1), 97–108.

Venkataraman, S. (1997). The distinctive domain of entrepreneurship research: An editor's perspective. In J. Katz & J. Brockhaus (Eds.), *Advances in entrepreneurship, firm emergence, and growth* (Vol. 3, pp. 119–138). Greenwich, CT: JAI Press.

West, M. A. (1990). The social psychology of innovation in groups. In M. A. West & J. L. Farr (Eds.), *Innovation and creativity at work: Psychological and organizational strategies* (pp. 309–333). Chichester: Wiley.

Westhead, P., & Wright, M. (1998). Novice, portfolio, and serial founders: Are they different? *Journal of Business Venturing, 13*, 173–204.

Wiklund, J. (1998). *Small firm growth and performance: Entrepreneurship and beyond.* Doctoral dissertation series No. 3. Jönköping, Sweden: Jönköping International Business School.

Wiklund, J., Davidsson, P., & Delmar, F. (2003). Expected consequences of growth and their effect on growth willingness in different samples of small firms. *Entrepreneurship Theory & Practice, 27*(Spring), 247–269.

Woo, C. Y., Cooper, A. C., & Dunkelberg, W. C. (1991). The development and interpretation of entrepreneurial typologies. *Journal of Business Venturing, 6*, 93–114.

Zacharakis, A., & Meyer, G. D. (1998). A lack of insight: Do venture capitalists really understand their own decision process? *Journal of Business Venturing, 13*(1), 57–76.

14

Psychology, Entrepreneurship, and the "Critical Mess"

William B. Gartner

"You just have to expose yourself to more, and see what the consequences are." —*Robert Rauschenberg.* (Tompkins, 2005, p. 77)

This chapter focuses on what scholars "pay attention" to (Langer, 1989) when we delve into research about entrepreneurship. What we already know brings to the forefront what we will see, or not see. I tend to read entrepreneurship scholarship "backward" by reading the list of references in an article or book first, because prior knowledge is reflected by them, and this prior knowledge provides the basis for the direction of the work (Latour, 1987, 1999; Sargent, 1997). I'm often surprised as to what other entrepreneurship scholars seem to ignore, or be oblivious to, when they create a list of references to serve as the background for their manuscripts. Often, the references cited seem to focus on such a narrow range of theoretical and empirical evidence that I wonder whether these articles reflect an "accurate" sense of the phenomenon explored. I believe that the lack of a more comprehensive and complicated knowledge of entrepreneurship (as reflected in what scholars reference), or the lack of a willingness to recognize a more comprehensive and complicated knowledge of entrepreneurship, may be detrimental to developing "better" (i.e., accurate, plausible, relevant; insightful; and useful to both academics and practitioners) entrepreneurship scholarship.

The chapters in this book make a significant contribution to advancing our knowledge of the intersection of psychology and entrepreneurship, particularly in accumulating and organizing a rather broad and disparate body of scholarship that both touches on psychology and entrepreneurship and works to inform each other's disciplinary perspective. These are difficult tasks that the authors of these chapters have often brilliantly achieved. My concern when reading these chapters (or other scholarly work in the field of entrepreneurship) is about how the use of a more focused disciplinary view in entrepreneurship scholarship (that explains narrow aspects of what the phenomenon of entrepreneurship is, from the discipline, itself) seems to be driving out a more complicated and comprehensive understanding of phenomenon of entrepreneurship.

I liken the use of a narrow disciplinary focus on aspects of entrepreneurship to a "good news/bad news" joke:

> The surgeon comes out of the operating room and says, "I've got good news and bad news. The good news is—the cancer operation was a success! The bad news is—the patient died of a heart attack.

I offer this joke as a metaphor for this conundrum: Scholars can generate right answers to issues germane to their own discipline, yet fail to address broader issues that critically inform these insights. That is, one can do the surgery right, in a narrow sense, but get the wrong outcome, overall. I suppose my concern about academic scholarship in entrepreneurship is about the face validity of generating theory and evidence that seem to focus on a part of entrepreneurship (using a very narrow disciplinary approach) without paying attention to the whole (a "complicated and comprehensive" understanding of the phenomenon.) As I read some of the chapters in this book, I often thought: "Well, yes, these ideas and results make sense because of what has been cited, but if other scholarship had been recognized, or if this scholar had an awareness of practitioner information (i.e., *Inc. Magazine*, autobiographies of entrepreneurs, etc.), this approach and these results would have made less sense." So, without putting certain chapters in this book on the spot, so to speak, as specific examples of this concern, I'll provide the reader with a more general framework regarding this issue. The reader can go back and explore which chapters might benefit from the approach I offer.

I would be the first to admit my own narrow perspective about what I pay attention to when exploring the phenomenon of entrepreneurship (Gartner, 2004). In some respects, then, this chapter is self-reflective, in that it is my challenge to myself to engage in a more complicated and comprehensive understanding of entrepreneurship. This chapter tends to talk about the extremes of two approaches to exploring entrepreneurship. I do not believe that scholars are likely to practice pure forms of either approach. Yet, as a way of comparing and contrasting these two views, the reader might assume that I want to polarize scholars into different camps. This is not my intention.

THE "CRITICAL MESS"

The label I have given to the "complicated and comprehensive" approach to understanding the phenomenon of entrepreneurship is the "critical mess." I came across the label "critical mess" in reading an article on book collecting in *The New Yorker* magazine that Sue Birley and I subsequently used as an analogy for the value of qualitative research in the field of entrepreneurship (Gartner & Birley, 2002). Our meditation on the similarity between the process of book collecting and the process of qualitative research came out as this thought:

> Finally, we offer an insight about the nature of qualitative research which might be considered as a parting trifle, but we believe contains some truth which bears consideration: the "critical mess theory." In qualitative research there is typically an immersion into the muddled circumstances of an entrepreneurial phenomenon that is cluttered and confusing. Part of the difficulty of generating and reporting the findings of a qualitative research effort seems to stem from the experience of being in such an untidy reality. Qualitative researchers seem to get overwhelmed with too much information, rather than too little. Yet, it is in this experience of information overload that a certain knowledge and wisdom often occurs. One can often tell which researchers in our field have spent considerable time intensively involved with entrepreneurs. The knowledge and insights that stem from all of their research just seem to ring a bit truer and clearer. We borrow a label for this sensibility of immersion from a profile of Michael Zinman, a bibliophile and Michael Reese's insights into Zinman's strategy for collecting books:
>
> > You don't start off with a theory about what you're trying to do. You don't begin by saying, 'I'm trying to prove x.' You build a big pile. Once you get a big enough pile together—the critical mess—you're able to draw conclusions about it. You see patterns …. People who have the greatest intuitive feel for physical objects start from a relationship with the objects and then acquire the scholarship, instead of the other way around. The way to become a connoisseur is to work in the entire spectrum of what's available—from utter crap to fabulous stuff. If you're going to spend your time looking only at the best, you're not going to have a critical eye. (Singer, 2001, p. 66)
>
> Qualitative researchers are likely to be the connoisseurs of entrepreneurship scholarship only in that they are more likely to immerse themselves to a greater depth and in a wider variety of situations where entrepreneurship occurs. We encourage all entrepreneurship scholars to develop a critical eye in their efforts to explore entrepreneurship, and hope that more work will be undertaken to utilize qualitative methods for seeking such an understanding. (Gartner & Birley, 2002, p. 394)

I find that scholars who are keen to use a rather narrow disciplinary focus in the field of entrepreneurship often lack this "critical eye." It is all too easy to use the "fabulous stuff" in one's own discipline without attending to the "utter crap" that might be found in other disciplines or in other research findings in one's own discipline, as well. Without a deep and comprehensive understanding and appreciation of the breadth and complexity of entrepreneurship scholarship (as well as other nonscholarly work about entrepreneurship), it is easy to generate results that seem to look right (given the theory and evidence used) yet are wrong to anyone with a broader knowledge of the phenomenon of entrepreneurship, itself.

In somewhat the same vein, Davis (1971) in "That's Interesting!" suggests this conflict is inherent between laypersons with "conventional wisdom" and experts with "esoteric knowledge."

> Intellectual specialties were formed when various groups of self-styled experts began to accept those propositions, which had refuted the assumptions of laymen. As an intellectual speciality developed, what began merely as a proposition which refuted a taken-for-granted assumption of the common-sense world now became a taken-for-granted assumption in its own right. When an intellectual speciality reached maturity—and this is the important point—all propositions generated within it are referred back not to the old baseline of the take-for-granted assumption of the common-sense world, but to the new baseline of the take-for-granted assumption of the intellectual speciality itself. (Davis, 1971, p. 330)

Something gets lost when the focus of research on entrepreneurship sticks too closely to the "esoteric knowledge" of a narrow disciplinary perspective. A finding can be right and interesting to a scholar within a specific theoretical perspective, but wrong or obvious to the practitioner and scholar with a broader, more muddled experience and knowledge of the phenomenon. If scholarship in the field of entrepreneurship emphasizes the search for answers using narrow disciplinary approaches, we may find ourselves irrelevant to the issues facing those persons involved in the broader phenomenon of entrepreneurship, itself.

I offer the idea of the "critical mess," therefore, as an alternative approach to pursuing scholarship about entrepreneurship compared to research efforts that tend to use the narrower lens of a particular theory or methodology. The remainder of this chapter: (a) briefly describes the characteristics of the "critical mess" in entrepreneurship, (b) offers some implications for why "critical mess" efforts may be of value for entrepreneurship scholarship as a whole, and (c) suggests how scholars might pursue a "critical mess" research effort in their studies of entrepreneurship.

CHARACTERISTICS OF THE CRITICAL MESS IN ENTREPRENEURSHIP

Imagine all of the journal articles, monographs, books, working papers, and all of the other paraphernalia (such as courses, cases, teaching notes, exercises, newspaper and magazine blurbs and interviews, etc.) that academics generate about the phenomenon entrepreneurship all heaped together. Imagine, as well, all of the other material on entrepreneurship that has been created by government agencies, magazines, newspapers, television programs, biographers, nonfiction writers, fiction writers, and from entrepreneurs. This is the pile, the "critical mess."

The "critical mess" is an overwhelming mass of material about entrepreneurship. I do not want anyone to assume that I believe that any one individual can ever assimilate the "critical mess." And I don't want anyone to assume that I would make any judgments as to the quality of this quantity of material. Most of the critical mess is, by most standards of scholarship (even most of the scholarly work) and by most standards of practice, often wrong and misinformed, that is, "utter crap." The "critical mess," from the standards of both "conventional wisdom" and "esoteric knowledge," will be full of material that is useless, stupid, ill-informed, wrong, idiotic, bad, and of no redeeming quality whatsoever. But, there will be those rare finds that will surface for those who devote time to sorting through it.

As another way to imagine the "critical mess," I offer this quote from *Lord Jim*:

> Yes! Very funny this terrible thing is. A man that is born falls into a dream like a man who falls into the sea. If he tries to climb out into the air as inexperienced people endeavor to do, he drowns—nicht wahr? … No! I tell you! The way is to the destructive element submit yourself, and with the exertions of your hands and feet in the water make the deep, deep sea keep you up. (Conrad, 1900/1992, p. 165)

"To the destructive element submit yourself" is what scholars face when they look beyond the narrow confines of a narrow disciplinary perspective. There is an ocean of stuff about entrepreneurship that one can easily drown in, if one jumps into it. A discipline, and the scholarship that represents the exemplars for that field, tend to keep one away from all of the bad scholarship and bad ideas: the destructive element. A discipline keeps one from falling into the sea. What could possibly be of value for those who would dive into such a miasma?

THE VALUE OF THE "CRITICAL MESS"
FOR ENTREPRENEURSHIP SCHOLARSHIP

To wade into the critical mess would appear to be an inherently inefficient method for gaining knowledge. Rather than only reading the "good stuff" from one's own discipline—in fact, rather than only reading the *really* good stuff from one's own discipline—the critical mess approach asks one to read all of the bad stuff too! The paradox of the critical mess approach is that those who refuse to wade into all of the "utter crap" in the field of entrepreneurship are less likely to create fabulous insights and ideas. Exploring the critical mess is vastly time-consuming, yet, I believe, only through understanding the meaning and essence of bad scholarship (or bad practitioner advice) can one actually begin to see what great scholarship might be. The point, then, of the critical mess approach is not to seek out the exemplars of one's own discipline, but to wade into all of the scholarship and information about the phenomenon of entrepreneurship, and thereby uncover the exemplars of scholarship in one's own discipline that provides insights into the phenomenon of entrepreneurship. The critical mess approach is the process of being undiscriminating in one's exploration of what constitutes knowledge in the entrepreneurship field.

One of the reasons I can suggest the critical mess approach for entrepreneurship scholars is that scholarly training will inherently point out what are considered as the exemplars of ones discipline. Focusing on great scholarship is somewhat like a diet of only one kind of food, and I think that for one's own health, there should be variety to one's cuisine (assuming that the "critical mess" isn't all junk food.) I suppose that the need for variety, then, moves toward Weick's arguments for the value of requisite variety (Weick, 1979), in that complex and complicated phenomena require complex and complicated ways of seeing, which seem to only be gained through his aphorism: "Complicate yourself." I believe that delving into the critical mess is likely to achieve this.

PURSUING THE "CRITICAL MESS" IN ENTREPRENEURSHIP SCHOLARSHIP

I suggest that there are a number of ways that scholars can study entrepreneurship through a "critical mess" approach. First, scholars studying entrepreneurship should recognize multiple audiences for their work. By far the broadest range of audiences is likely to be the dichotomy between academic approaches and practitioner interests. An example of how scholars might engage in this dialogue between scholars and practitioners is to read the *Journal of Business Venturing*. In their guide for authors, the editors ask that "all articles should be prefaced by a minimum two-page Executive Summary which discusses the essence of the paper for a lay reader." Merely by requesting an Executive Summary for lay readers, scholars have to consider what practitioners are likely to know. A scholar, therefore, must explore conventional wisdom by reading what practitioners write. Writing for the lay reader puts one in the critical mess. Second, entrepreneurship scholars would be wise to recognize (cite) research from other scholarly disciplines. I offer this advice particularly for scholars who tend to use scholarship from economics or psychology. I have found that there is nearly always a parallel research stream in another discipline that should be acknowledged. Therefore, I tend to find entrepreneurship articles that fail to look for scholarship beyond a specific discipline to be suspect, only in that there are likely to be others who are exploring nearly similar ideas and issues. I find that scholars are never alone in their research efforts. There is always someone, somewhere, who is pursuing similar research, albeit from some other perspective or discipline. Our challenge is to find them and engage in a dialogue with them (and citations provide the way that such connections are made). Overall, entrepreneurship scholars need to consider a more comprehensive and complicated view of their community. Our audience is beyond the colleagues in our discipline or those in academics. Entrepreneurship research should have some connection to the larger world of entrepreneurs and the community of individuals involved with entrepreneurship (public policymakers, government administrators, consultants, and service providers). So, in order to speak to them, we must also seek to find out what they are saying as well.

Another way that entrepreneurship scholars can pursue the critical mess approach is to focus more effort on generating facts (Gartner, 2004):

> I do not believe that efforts to build theory in entrepreneurship can progress until there is more information upon which new theory can be generated. The "critical mess theory" suggests that scholars sort through a lot of data in order to make sense of what makes sense as theory about the phenomenon: the collection of evidence is necessary before theory development may occur. And, in the entrepreneurship field, there simply isn't enough evidence. This might seem surprising, but entrepreneurship scholars seem to have such a limited view of what would be "a relevant fact" that the field sorely needs more information about the phenomenon. (p. 207)

By "facts" I mean evidence that may, or may not, be about causality among variables in a phenomenon. There has been an ongoing bias in the entrepreneurship field toward assuming that increasing methodological sophistication is an important characteristic of a mature scholarly domain (Chandler & Lyon, 2001; Low & MacMillan, 1988; Wortman, 1987). For example, Chandler and Lyon (2001) end their overview of the entrepreneurship field with: "Hence, though progress has been made, Low and MacMillan's (1988) admonition to move away from exploratory studies and towards causality remains relevant" (p. 112). The kinds of relevant facts that appear to be of more interest in the entrepreneurship field are those facts tied to some kind of theoretical construct, that is, "theoretical facts": Facts that offer some sense of "why" something occurred are to be preferred.

I suggest that the entrepreneurship field needs more descriptive research, rather than less. Descriptive facts may or may not have an ability to answer "Why?" but these facts do provide more information about the phenomenon itself. I believe one of the reasons that the field of entrepreneurship might not be a "mature" field is because we know so little about what entrepreneurship is, as a phenomenon. It surprises me how little we actually know, for example, about organizational emergence, although most universities have courses or programs that teach this topic of new venture creation. Most students want to know about the process of organization formation—how it occurs, the kinds of behaviors necessary for business startup, the ways in which these behaviors occur—and little evidence can actually be provided from scholarly research about what entrepreneurs actually do (Gartner & Carter, 2003). I do not believe that the most effective way to understand the process of organization formation is to develop a theory about how and why this process occurs *before* attempting to actually observe how this process actually occurs.

Theory does not necessarily provide the kinds of details that portray the details of the phenomenon. Theoretical facts seem to provide a plausible explanation of a way to make sense of aspects of entrepreneurship, yet these theoretical facts often seem to leave out so much of what, on face validity, would be sufficient for understanding the process.

I believe the theoretical development makes sense in the field of entrepreneurship in situations where there is an abundance of information (the critical mess) that can then be better understood by identifying the more critical elements that are better able to explain the phenomenon. Theory, in this sense, helps to sort through a very rich and complex understanding of the phenomenon, rather than acting as a lens that narrows our vision and experience of what is actually occurring.

CONCLUSIONS

I think the reason that more scholars are engaged in generating information that is labeled as entrepreneurship scholarship is because the topic area of entrepreneurship (however you want to define it) is interesting and important. As both Venkataraman (1997) and Davidsson (2003) have so aptly demonstrated, much of a society's ability to create wealth and well-being occurs through entrepreneurial activity. An activity with such an important outcome should not be ignored. The concern I express using the label "critical mess" has been in regard to how scholars should pay attention to this area.

I believe that scholars interested in the phenomenon of entrepreneurship must look beyond their own disciplinary perspective in order to have a reasonable grasp of what entrepreneurship "is." I don't think the competitive advantage of entrepreneurship, as an emerging field of scholarship, will come about, initially, because of the development of new theory. I think entrepreneurship will have a competitive advantage vis-à-vis other scholarly domains when it creates new evidence. I would like more efforts to be put on generating "descriptive" evidence, rather than "theoretical" evidence. We need more facts about the entrepreneurial phenomenon, rather than theoretical speculation. I believe that those scholars who are willing to immerse themselves in a "critical mess" of information about entrepreneurship are those scholars who are more likely to make important and lasting contributions to the field. I think the "theories that matter" (Weick, 1999) in the field of entrepreneurship will be derived from those individuals who have really developed a critical eye about the phenomenon. I believe this critical eye will occur when there is a willingness to look at a wider variety of sources of information: autobiographies, newspaper and magazine articles, personal interviews, and so on. And, as scholars, we should be reading more of each other's work. I humbly admit my ignorance of the entrepreneurship scholarship appearing in European journals and conferences, for example.

I think that one of the reasons that the entrepreneurship field has been so slow to emerge, as a recognizable scholarly domain, has been the failure, collectively, of scholars in the field to read and cite each other's work. I find a certain ahistorical quality to many entrepreneurship journal articles: articles that tend to ignore previous efforts to grapple with similar issues and problems. Although much of the prior research in entrepreneurship might not meet current methodological and theoretical "standards" for quality scholarship, I find prior work in the field to offer information and insights that are invaluable and important. I think the entrepreneurship field needs to begin with what currently exists as entrepreneurship scholarship, rather than tossing all of it out. My caution to young scholars entering the entrepreneurship field with new approaches and ideas is that in the not too distant future your new ideas and approaches will also be outdated. A scholarly domain grows when researchers build on prior work, all of the "good" and the "bad" research efforts. Achieving critical mess occurs when we see value in, and use, all of our efforts (scholarship across many different disciplines as well as information from nonacademic sources) to understand the phenomenon.

REFERENCES

Chandler, G. N., & Lyon, D. W. (2001). Issues of research design and construct measurement in entrepreneurship research: The past decade. *Entrepreneurship Theory and Practice, 25*(4), 101–113.

Conrad, J. (1992). *Lord Jim.* New York: Everyman's Library. (Original work published 1900)

Davidsson, P. (2003). The domain of entrepreneurship research: Some suggestions. In J. A. Katz & D. Shepherd (Eds.), *Advances in entrepreneurship, firm emergence, and growth* (Vol. 6, pp. 315–372). Greenwich, CT: JAI Press.

Davis, M. S. (1971). That's interesting! Towards a phenomenology of sociology and a sociology of phenomenology. *Philosophy of Social Science, 1*, 309–344.

Gartner, W. B. (2004). Achieving "critical mess" in entrepreneurship scholarship." In J. A. Katz & D. Shepherd (Eds.), *Advances in entrepreneurship, firm emergence, and growth* (Vol. 7, pp. 199–216). Greenwich, CT: JAI Press.

Gartner, W. B., & Birley, S. (2002). Introduction to the special issue on qualitative methods in entrepreneurship research. *Journal of Business Venturing, 17*(5), 387–395.

Gartner, W. B., & Carter, N. M. (2003). Entrepreneurial behavior and firm organizing processes. In Z. J. Acs & D. B. Audretsch (Eds.), *Handbook of entrepreneurship research* (pp. 195–221). Boston: Kluwer Academic.

Langer, E. J. (1989). *Mindfulness*. Cambridge, MA: Perseus Books.

Latour, B. (1987). *Science in action*. Cambridge, MA: Harvard University Press.

Latour, B. (1999). *Pandora's hope: Essays on the reality of science studies*. Cambridge, MA: Harvard University Press.

Low, M. B., & MacMillan, I. C. (1988). Entrepreneurship: Part research and future challenges. *Journal of Management, 14,* 139–161.

Sargent, R. M. (1997). The social construction of scientific evidence. *Journal of Constructivist Psychology, 10*(1), 75–96.

Singer, M. (2001, February 5). The book eater. *The New Yorker,* pp. 62–71.

Tompkins, C. (2005, May 23). Everything in Sight. *The New Yorker,* pp. 68–77.

Venkataraman, S. (1997). The distinctive domain of entrepreneurship research: An editor's perspective. In J. Katz & J. Brockhaus (Eds.), *Advances in entrepreneurship, firm emergence, and growth* (Vol. 3, pp. 119–138). Greenwich, CT: JAI Press.

Weick, K. E. (1979). *The social psychology of organizing* (2nd ed.). New York: Random House.

Weick, K. E. (1999). That's moving: Theories that matter. *Journal of Management Inquiry, 8*(2), 134–142.

Wortman, M. S. (1987). Entrepreneurship: An integrating typology and evaluation of the empirical research in the field. *Journal of Management, 13,* 259–279.

15

C2D2: Psychological Methods In Entrepreneurship Research

Kelly G. Shaver

No, it isn't R2D2's younger sibling. Or a character from a forgotten episode of Star Trek. Rather, it is a shorthand reference to principles of psychological research that are fundamental to the progress psychology has made as a discipline. The principles are *concepts, comparisons, definitions,* and *data.* Unfortunately, these principles are only rarely found together in a single piece of research on entrepreneurial behavior.

In the history of psychology as a separate field of inquiry, advances in method have arguably been as important as advances in theory. Any Introductory Psychology student knows that Wilhelm Wundt founded the first psychological research laboratory, in Leipzig, in 1879. Perhaps more importantly, people who had been Wundt's doctoral students founded many of the early psychological laboratories in the United States between 1888 and 1900. This list includes Catholic University, Columbia, Cornell, Harvard, New York University, Northwestern, Stanford, Smith College, Wesleyan College, Yale, and the Universities of California at Berkeley, of Nebraska, and of Pennsylvania (Hilgard, 1987). Skinner's behaviorism is as much about method as it is theory (indeed, Skinner would not have wanted it called "theory"). Where would the study of attitudes be without the contributions of Thurstone, Likert, and, more recently, Fishbein and Ajzen? Most of the serious controversies regarding human intelligence involve its measurement, or ways to determine heritability. Without factor analysis and other multivariate techniques, modern personality theory would look quite different. Moving closer to home, Lewin taught us the value of action research, the Hawthorne studies reminded us that what people think is happening in research might be every bit as important as the objective changes in environmental manipulations, and Rosenthal made us worry that what we find in research might be due to what we expect. All of this methodological history is part of the stock in trade for experimental, social, and organizational psychologists, regardless of whether our *current* research interest is "hot cognition," interpersonal influence, or entrepreneurial behavior. For those whose intellectual traditions do not include such an extensive concentration on the human relationship between investigator and research participant, this chapter outlines four broad principles that, if adhered to, might well improve the study of entrepreneurship.

CONCEPTS

A good friend and former colleague of mine was notorious among thesis and dissertation students for asking—regardless of the topic of the work being defended—"What does this have to do with behaviorism?" In response to the question, the poorer students simply stammered something like, "but I'm studying *attributions of blame!*" The better students recognized the larger meaning of the question: If psychologists believe that they are engaged in a scientific endeavor, they recognize that science is both incremental and *cumulative*. Science involves data statements, theoretical statements, and meta-theoretical assumptions. Watsonian behaviorism's underlying suspicion of anything not directly observable thus provides a metatheoretical challenge to any research involving cognitive processes like attributions.

In the present context, the notion of a cumulative science imposes two requirements on entrepreneurship researchers. The first requirement is to know, and trace, the intellectual ancestry of the concepts we employ in our research. The consequences of failing to follow this requirement can be illustrated with three examples. I once reviewed an entrepreneurship manuscript that attempted to use Festinger's (1957) theory of cognitive dissonance as an explanation for why an entrepreneur might put still more money and time into a venture that any outside observer would say should simply be abandoned. To anyone familiar with the proselytizing behavior of the Seekers following their failure to be taken by spaceship to Clarion (described in Festinger, Riecken, & Schachter's *When Prophecy Fails*, 1956), cognitive dissonance does seem a plausible explanation for the behavior of some entrepreneurs whose ventures are failing. Unfortunately, the author had not also read the more recent revision of dissonance theory published in 1984 by Cooper and Fazio. Incorporating all of the qualifications that had become necessary, Cooper and Fazio pointed out that a critical precursor to dissonance arousal was perceived *personal responsibility* for the negative consequences that occurred. Now it might be that the *founder* of a venture could feel some personal responsibility for the venture's failure, although even this assertion is open to debate. What is clear, however, is that a person who is only a *manager* of a firm, not its founder, ought to be dissonance free. But the sample of participants included both founders and managers who were not founders. This fatal methodological flaw might have been avoided with more careful attention to the past and present status of the concept presumably being employed.

The second requirement is to know, and state, how the concept presently under consideration is *different from* (if not also superior to) ideas that might appear to be similar. Here I am forced to admit that I am also among the guilty. Consider the concepts of locus of control (Rotter, 1966; Strickland, 1989), achievement motivation (Fineman, 1977; McClelland, Atkinson, Clark, & Lowell, 1953), expectancy (Gatewood, Shaver, Powers, & Gartner, 2002; Vroom, 1964), and self-efficacy (Bandura, 1997; Krueger & Dickson, 1994). There are clear differences among these four at a conceptual level. The original Rotter locus of control scale was designed to assess locus of control *of reinforcement*, that is, the person's beliefs about how—in many domains of action—outcomes get distributed. Specifically, what is the person's *generalized* belief: Do people control events and processes, or do these just happen? In contrast to this generalized belief about the way the world works, achievement motivation has typically been conceptualized as an internal motivational state produced by two opposing processes. One of these processes is the desire for success; the other is the fear of failure. Achievement motivation is the resultant of the difference between the two, often corrected by the perceived probability of each outcome (success or failure). Similar to aspects of achievement motivation, expectancy involves subjective probabilities: the probability that one can successfully perform an action, the probability that doing so will produce a desired outcome, and so forth. Unlike achievement motivation, however, expectancy theory considers action to be the product of a chain of several expectancy-value propositions, rather than a single underlying motive. Finally, where achievement motivation and locus of control are relatively generalized, self-efficacy is even more domain specific than expectancy. Alone among the four, self-efficacy is both an individual difference variable and a variable whose underlying value can be altered with appropriate training.

Even this cursory review has methodological implications for entrepreneurship research. For example, as I have noted earlier (Gatewood, Shaver, & Gartner, 1995), the original Internal-External (I-E) locus-of-control scale routinely produces several dimensions when factor analyzed. Only the "personal efficacy" dimension seems particularly relevant for entrepreneurship, so the domain-general form of the I-E scale should probably not be used to assess entrepreneurial behavior. Tests for the achievement motivation of entrepreneurs should probably include items designed to measure fear of failure, as well as items designed to measure desire for success. Expectancy theory-based work with entrepreneurial samples should include, at a minimum, measures of the effort–performance link, the performance–outcome link, and the presumed valence of those outcomes. Measures of self-efficacy should be domain specific and should concentrate on mastery. Unfortunately, it is all too easy to find a single item or two that might have a bearing on any of the four concepts. Thus, a convincing case that one (and only one) of the underlying concepts has been tested is very likely to require *multiple* items, the set of which collectively allows a clear conceptual interpretation.

COMPARISONS

Nearly everyone has read an inspiring story of one entrepreneur or another. You know the way it goes: Arising from humble beginnings and overcoming substantial barriers, the hero or heroine perseveres, creating a multimillion-dollar company from little more than a vision of how to do something better or new. This is heartwarming, but it is biography, not science. Journalism can afford to be content with *what*; science needs to know *how* or *why*. As I have argued elsewhere (Shaver, 1985), the modern scientific understanding of causality is rooted in the "regularity theory" of Hume, the "necessity theory" of Kant, the notion of person-as-agent presented by Thomas Reid (1863), and especially the methods proposed in Mill's *A System of Logic* (1888). And as Cook and Campbell (1979) have noted, the essence of causal inference is the *comparison* between one set of conditions and another. The deliberate variation in treatments is the heart of experimentation, but it is also a central feature of the numerous quasi-experimental designs described in detail by Cook and Campbell (1979).

The key point in all of this literature is that no inferences of causality are possible without some sort of comparison. In entrepreneurship research, the requirement for comparison does not mean that every research design need be experimental, or even quantitative. An exceedingly detailed case study that reported the operations of an entrepreneurial firm before the firm received its first round of funding, and repeated the same observations after funding, would satisfy the requirement for comparison. On the other hand, a case description devoid of comparison is not a scientific study of entrepreneurial behavior, no matter how valuable the case might be as a springboard for class discussion.

Interestingly, having a built-in comparison might also be problematic if the comparison is inappropriate or misinterpreted. Let me illustrate this with a principle from social psychology. For years, the attitude literature supported the conclusion that people with similar attitudes would be attracted to one another. Indeed, the finding was so robust that Byrne (1971) called it the "law of attraction." Experimental subjects in this line of research first indicated their own attitudes on a series of social issues. Then they were shown what was described as another person's answers on the same items. After reviewing the "other person's" answers, research participants expressed their liking for the other as a person and as a potential work partner. Typically, expressed liking increased as a positive linear function of the number of attitude items on which the bogus stranger agreed with the research participant. Hence, the "law of attraction."

This research always included a comparison, but as Rosenbaum (1986) pointed out, there was a comparison missing. Specifically, research participants were never asked to indicate their liking for a stranger whose attitudes they did not know. When Rosenbaum included this critical comparison group, he found that liking for the attitude-free stranger was essentially identical to the liking expressed for the attitudinally similar other. So it then appeared that instead of similarity breeding attraction, *dis*similarity was breeding rejection. Rosenbaum's findings were immediately challenged by Byrne and his colleagues (e.g., Smeaton, Byrne, & Murnen, 1989), and other studies have identified still more variables that might be involved (e.g., Pilkington & Lydon, 1997). On the other hand, for present purposes the important point is that some of the most recent work on similarity and attraction (e.g., Montoya & Horton, 2004) has followed Rosenbaum's methodological lead—by employing a similarity condition, a dissimilarity condition, and a control condition—even without citing Rosenbaum's work.

There is a parallel to Byrne's original studies in entrepreneurship research. Numerous studies compare entrepreneurs with corporate managers, often finding the entrepreneurs to be higher in achievement motivation, or desire for financial success, or need for control—or pick your favorite result. My purpose here is not to provide a detailed critique of the several flaws in the entrepreneur–manager design, but rather to comment on the nature of the comparison.

In a review of the achievement motivation research in entrepreneurship, Johnson (1990) concluded that higher achievement motivation was likely to be associated with entrepreneurial behavior. This very careful article identified all of the studies, samples, and measures used. Eight of the studies described contained a comparison group of nonentrepreneurs (typically managers of one sort or another); seven of the eight studies found entrepreneurs to score higher than the managers. By the time this finding reaches textbooks, it is taken so for granted that many books state unequivocally that entrepreneurs are higher in achievement motivation (often without mentioning any particular comparison group). Indeed, more than a few books actually include questions designed to assess the achievement strivings in sections designed to give students an idea of whether they "have what it takes" to be entrepreneurs.

But there is a problem. The Panel Study of Entrepreneurial Dynamics (PSED) is the only data set that contains the right comparison. In that study, described in detail by Gartner, Shaver, Carter, and Reynolds (2004), a nationally representative group of nascent entrepreneurs (people who were *starting* businesses, not who already had those businesses up and running) were compared to a nationally representative group of people who were *not* starting businesses. The data for the PSED are publicly available from the Institute of Social Research at a University of Michigan web site (http://psed.isr.umich.edu/main.php). No differences in achievement motivation emerged. Now, one reason might be that achievement motivation was measured by a limited number of items. So many different conceptual variables were included in the PSED that none could be assessed with anything like a whole psychological scale. Still, there were conceptual variables, such as expectancies, measured with fewer items than were used for achievement motivation, that showed very clear differences between nascents and the comparison group. What are we to make of the past studies that found entrepreneurs "higher" in achievement motivation? The parallel to Rosenbaum's work is instructive: In the cold light cast by the PSED, it suddenly appears that the prior differences might have occurred because the *managers were lower than average* in achievement motivation, whereas entrepreneurs are the same as other people who are not managers. Perhaps it is the "organization man" who is different, not the entrepreneur. Whatever account ultimately turns out to be correct, the lesson for researchers is clear: Use comparison groups, but choose them very wisely.

DEFINITIONS

Suppose for a moment that you are a behavioral neuroscientist. Your work involves the determination of which areas of the cortex are involved in the solving of mathematical reasoning problems. You present your research participants with a timed array of mathematical problems to solve. Remaining true to the principle of comparison, you also present the participants with several other cognitive and perceptual tasks that require attention, concentration, memory, and the verbal production of an answer. As the participant performs these various cognitive tasks, he or she is undergoing fMRI—*functional* magnetic resonance imaging. At the most basic level, your data are the pictures generated by the MRI machine. Current analysis methods, however, permit these individual pictures to be treated as a time-based stream of images. There are MRI-generated "maps" of the human brain, so if you simply specify the equipment you are using and the detailed research protocol, you can actually talk about what was going on in the participant's head, with no fear that an "anonymous reviewer" will say "Why did you do the study *that* way?" You have controlled as much extraneous variability as you can, you have followed the standard procedure for this sort of research, you have specified the characteristics of all of the equipment. You have given us an *operational definition* of the concept known as "problem solving." Any other neuroscientist can replicate what you did, and can do so exactly.

That would be a pleasant world to live in, but as entrepreneurship researchers, we're simply not there. Except for the PSED (and the PSED2 now underway), our research participants are not randomly selected from the population. The entrepreneurs available to us are typically on one or another list—tax rolls, telephone directory entries, membership lists for organizations like the National Federation of Independent Business (NFIB) or the Chamber of Commerce, or the *Inc.* 500. To be clear, it is typically not a *person* who is on such lists, but rather a business founded by the person of interest. Next, the entire list, or at least a large portion of it, is contacted to participate. Some people agree to do so, and some do not. Those who do will be interviewed on the telephone or in person, or will be sent some form of research instrument (notice that this could be an experimental task just as easily as it could be a survey) through the mail. Not everyone who receives the materials will complete them (or continue participating until an interview is finished). Even those who do complete the research protocol will do so under the following conditions:

- They will know they are participating in research.
- They will have some personal impression of the institution or organization with which the investigator is associated.
- They may know the investigator.
- Without conscious awareness, they will be affected by several cognitive biases: hindsight (interpreting events after knowing the outcome), self-serving bias (taking too much credit for successes and too little responsibility for failures), and their assumptions concerning the "real" interests of the investigator.

Finally, if the research format is at all open-ended, the investigator's own expectations can produce the desired behavior, or lead to the omission of information that does not agree with the investigator's cognitive schemata.

If conducting relatively "clean" research on entrepreneurial behavior begins to look challenging at best, well, it is. There are often several participant selection biases—the effects of which are compounded by their sequential nature. There are what the methodologists would regard as "instrumentation" issues, because no small set of interview items or research questions can hope to encompass all of the subtleties of the concepts being tested. And then there are all of the impression-management issues that arise whenever two human beings engage in a social interaction. The solution to this set of problems is to document, document, document. Recognize that no matter what an investigator's choice of method might be, some other investigator (or some editorial reviewer) will be able to think of several *other* ways that the conceptual question might have been investigated. So make every methodological choice explicit and be prepared to defend them all. The result will be a series of *operational definitions* that are detailed enough to permit exact replication. Do not say, "Attitudes were measured," without describing the scale and the way in which items were combined into the scores that were analyzed. Do not say that "in-depth interviews" were conducted without providing a thorough list of the questions asked, a description of the conditions under which the interviews were done, and a list of the people involved (if there were any other than the researcher and a single participant). Do not say that entrepreneurs were "shadowed" for portions of several days without providing a codebook of the behaviors to be recorded, an indication of how frequently each code was generated, and a description of the specific way in which individual actions might have been aggregated prior to analysis. The real value of such detailed operational definitions is that they permit the discipline to distinguish *real* (read, behaviorally important) differences across research projects from spurious differences generated by alterations in method. The validity of a study's conclusions is limited by the reliability of its methods.

DATA

In one recent year a major entrepreneurship journal published 34 articles. Five of these contained no data at all, another 15 presented data derived from an archived database collected for some purpose other than the purpose envisioned by the researchers, and only 14 presented data from individuals or companies first contacted by the study authors. Yes, it's true: One cannot study initial public offerings (IPOs) by contacting individuals and asking about their process of going public. On the other hand, the archival research problems of selective sampling, selective deposit, and selective survival, coupled with the fact that the scholars who ultimately used the databases had no hand in designing them, should give us pause. So taking this particular journal-year as the example, fewer than 50% of the published articles contained data collected by the investigators who designed the data structure. Similar results are reported by Ireland, Reutzel, and Webb (2005), who examined the "entrepreneurship" research papers published in the *Academy of Management Journal* between 1963 and 2005. They found 50 such papers, 29 of which reported analyses of secondary data. This presents tremendous barriers to choices of topics for study: The research questions are too often dictated by what analyses are possible. Moreover, the resulting literature is top-heavy, with too many papers, over too many years, relying on slightly different analyses conducted on entirely too few databases.

Whatever else one may say about research in social psychology (and plenty *has* been said), the vast majority of its empirical research is conducted with participants recruited *de novo* for the study at hand. It is certainly true that too many of social psychology's experimental contributions have been based on data obtained from college sophomores. On the other hand, at most universities nearly every liberal arts student (and most preprofessional students as well) takes Introductory Psychology (the typical source for research participants). Thus, there is essentially no self-selection involved, save that which accompanies being in college as opposed to not being in college. And if, as is typically the case, research participants are randomly assigned to experimental treatments, whatever self-selection biases might have been present are effectively filtered out within the study. By contrast, in research on entrepreneurial behavior, self-selection is not merely the way participants are obtained; it is also how they become "assigned" to groups to be compared.

There is nothing like recounting all of the potential problems in gathering data to make a reader want to say, "Forget this data stuff, I'll simply write conceptual pieces." This appears to be a popular choice in entrepreneurship. Even the Babson–Kauffman Entrepreneurship Research Conference, which formerly insisted on the inclusion of data, has now begun permitting submission of conceptual pieces. The typical "model" presented in entrepreneurship imports principles derived from some other discipline, suggests how those principles might apply in an entrepreneurial context, and offers "propositions" concerning ways in which entrepreneurs might be distinguished from nonentrepreneurs, or ways in which successful firms might be differentiated from less successful ones.

There are three important problems inherent in this typical approach. The first problem is that without data, almost any carefully constructed conceptual article will sound plausible. Let me give you a brief illustration. We know that one of the success factors for adult entrepreneurial behavior is having had entrepreneurial parents as a child. Whether the intergenerational transfer of capital is financial, human, social, or some combination of the three is not yet clearly understood. But the transfer is real. From this well-known piece of information, one could plausibly state the following proposition: Entrepreneurs are more likely than other people to respect and build on the family's traditions. So far, so good. Unfortunately, the data get in the way. Specifically, data from the PSED show that the opposite is true. The PSED included items relating to personal motivations for job and career (items Qg1a through Qg1r in the first wave of data). And a detailed comparison of nascents to others on the six motive factors showed that, in fact, entrepreneurs were *lower* than nonentrepreneurs in their expressed desires to follow in a family tradition (Carter, Gartner, Shaver, & Gatewood, 2003). For present purposes, the real problem is not that the data contradict the "proposition." Rather, the problem is that—*now that we know the outcome*—we could just as easily construct a line of reasoning that would produce a prediction that entrepreneurs, desiring to "strike out on their own," would be less likely than others to express fealty to outmoded family traditions. Conceptual arguments alone can suggest what entrepreneurs *might* do, but only data can tell us for certain.

A second difficulty inherent in the field's overreliance on conceptual papers harks back to our notion of comparisons. Even on the theoretical side, the typical "model" paper does not adequately compare its preferred model to any number of competing possibilities. To use a social cognition example, is a statement concerning one person's presumed characteristics a stereotype, a prototype, the specification of an exemplar, or an instance of a schema? There are differences among these concepts, just as there are differences among achievement motivation, locus of control, optimism, and expectancy. But far too few entrepreneurship "models" take the extra—and essential—step of identifying the conceptual close cousins and saying in what way the presented model is both different and superior. Ask yourself how many models you have seen that contain a box labeled with some version of "external environmental conditions," or one labeled with some version of "individual characteristics of the entrepreneur." What is the real value added by these models? Why are only some of their boxes described in detail, whereas other boxes remain literally and metaphorically black?

The third problem is that there is only a slim chance that the existing data available to the field can be used to test the model's predictions. As we have seen, only a minority of empirical articles include data from primary, rather than secondary, sources. The precise wordings specified by the model are not likely to appear in exactly that way in some existing database. Moreover, although it might be possible to exclude cases to "purify" the definition of an entrepreneur, it is less likely that the database will contain any reasonable comparison group, or appropriate indications of success and failure. Without being able to point to prior data-driven results obtained by others, the authors of a model are, effectively, in the position of saying to the research community, "Here is what we *think*. We don't want to go to the trouble to test it ourselves, but we encourage you to test it." Given the structure of the academic incentive system (more publications are better), and the time and effort needed to collect artifact-free data on entrepreneurs, this implicit assertion can be seen as annoyingly condescending. An equitable caste system in entrepreneurship research would reserve the upper class for those who present the data to test their model's predictions.

Especially in the last few years, entrepreneurship has made significant strides as a field of inquiry. There are well-respected national and international journals. There are large undergraduate enrollments and strong doctoral programs. Membership in the predominant professional society practically doubled from 2000 to 2005. As of this writing (fall 2005), the PSED2 is underway and building on the foundation that is the PSED. For all of these reasons, the study of entrepreneurial behavior is poised—as are many entrepreneurial companies—to go "to the next level." That promised potential will be achieved more quickly if entrepreneurship scholars rededicate themselves to the four core principles of concepts, comparisons, definitions, and data.

REFERENCES

Bandura, A. (1997). *Self-efficacy: The exercise of control.* New York: W. H. Freeman.

Byrne, D. (1971). *The attraction paradigm.* New York: Academic Press.

Carter, N. C., Gartner, W. B., Shaver, K. G., & Gatewood, E. J. (2003). The career reasons of nascent entrepreneurs. *Journal of Business Venturing, 18,* 13–39.

Cook, T. D., & Campbell, D. T. (1979). *Quasi-experimentation: Design and analysis issues for field settings.* Chicago: Rand-McNally.

Cooper, J., & Fazio, R. H. (1984). A new look at dissonance theory. In L. Berkowitz (Ed.), *Advances in experimental social psychology* (Vol. 17, pp. 229–266). New York: Academic Press.

Festinger, L. (1957). *A theory of cognitive dissonance.* Stanford, CA: Stanford University Press.

Festinger, L., Riecken, H. W., & Schachter, S. (1956). *When prophecy fails.* Minneapolis: University of Minnesota Press.

Fineman, F. (1977). The achievement motive construct and its measurement: Where are we now? *British Journal of Psychology, 68,* 1–22.

Gartner, W. B., Shaver, K. G., Carter, N. M., & Reynolds, P. D. (Eds.). (2004). *The handbook of entrepreneurial dynamics: The process of business creation.* Thousand Oaks, CA: Sage.

Gatewood, E. J., Shaver, K. G., & Gartner, W. B. (1995). A longitudinal study of cognitive factors influencing start-up behaviors and success at venture creation. *Journal of Business Venturing, 10,* 371–391.

Gatewood, E. J., Shaver, K. G., Powers, J. B., & Gartner, W. B. (2002). Entrepreneurial expectancy, task effort, and performance. *Entrepreneurship Theory & Practice, 27*(2), 187–206.

Hilgard, E. (1987). *Psychology in America: A historical survey.* San Diego: Harcourt, Brace, Jovanovich.

Ireland, R. D., Reutzel, C. R., & Webb, J. W. (2005). Entrepreneurship research in AMJ: What has been published and what might the future hold? *Academy of Management Journal, 48,* 556–564.

Johnson, B. R. (1990). Toward a multidimensional model of entrepreneurship: The case of achievement motivation and the entrepreneur. *Entrepreneurship Theory & Practice, 14*(3), 39–54.

Krueger, N., Jr., & Dickson, P. R. (1994). Risk taking: Perceived self-efficacy and opportunity recognition. *Decision Sciences, 25,* 385–400.

McClelland, D. C., Atkinson, J. W., Clark, R. A., & Lowell, E. L. (1953). *The achievement motive.* New York: Appleton-Century-Crofts.

Mill, J. S. (1888). *A system of logic.* New York: Harper & Row.

Montoya, R. M., & Horton, R. S. (2004). On the importance of cognitive evaluation as a determinant of interpersonal attraction. *Journal of Personality and Social Psychology, 86,* 696–712.

Pilkington, N. W., & Lydon, J. E. (1997). The relative effect of attitude similarity and attitude dissimilarity on interpersonal attraction: Investigating the moderating roles of prejudice and group membership. *Personality and Social Psychology Bulletin, 23,* 107–122.

Reid, T. (1863). Of the liberty of moral agents. In W. Hamilton (Ed.), *The works of Thomas Reid, D.D.* (6th ed., Vol. 2, pp. 599–636). Edinburgh: Machlachlan & Stewart.

Rosenbaum, M. E. (1986). The repulsion hypothesis: On the nondevelopment of relationships. *Journal of Personality and Social Psychology, 51,* 1156–1166.

Rotter, J. B. (1966). Generalized expectancies for internal versus external control of behavior. *Psychological Monographs, 80,* 1–28.

Shaver, K. G. (1985). *The attribution of blame: Causality, responsibility, and blameworthiness.* New York: Springer-Verlag.

Smeaton, G., Byrne, D., & Murnen, S. K. (1989). The repulsion hypothesis revisited: Similarity irrelevance or dissimilarity bias? *Journal of Personality and Social Psychology, 56,* 54–59.

Strickland, B. R. (1989). Internal–external control expectancies: From contingency to creativity. *American Psychologist, 44,* 1–12.

Vroom, V. H. (1964). *Work and motivation.* New York: Wiley.

16

Research Gains: Benefits of Closer Links Between I/O Psychology and Entrepreneurship

Robert A. Baron
Michael Frese
J. Robert Baum

This is an unusual book. It is a cooperative endeavor of authors from the areas of entrepreneurship and industrial and organizational psychology (in short, I/O psychology)—to our knowledge, it is the only book of this kind. A major goal of this book is the promoting of closer ties between the fields of I/O psychology and entrepreneurship. The basic rationale behind this goal can be stated succinctly: *Increased cooperation between the two fields can be highly beneficial to both.* In particular, we believe that the findings, methods, principles, and theories of I/O psychology can assist entrepreneurship in answering several of its most basic questions. Conversely, we suggest that the field of entrepreneurship, with its focus on new ventures, can provide I/O psychology with a novel and potentially valuable arena for testing and extending its findings and theories, most of which have been developed in the context of large, mature organizations.

One issue is to overcome prejudices across the two disciplines. Many entrepreneurship researchers seem to think that personality traits might be the only important contribution by I/O psychology (if any), whereas many I/O psychologists seem to think that entrepreneurship research can only contribute the dependent variable—success—to the equation (if there is any thought on this at all; as Eden, 1973, pointed out some time ago, self-employment and entrepreneurship are not well-developed subfields of I/O psychology).

We focus on the research gains that appear from a closer cooperation and from the chapters assembled in this book. An organizing figure for this discussion is developed here as a variant of the Giessen–Amsterdam model (Rauch & Frese, 2000) (cf. Fig. 16.1). This figure represents what the book chapters show: One can differentiate distal and proximal factors to success (Kanfer, 1992). The distal factors relate to personality traits (chap. 3), cognitive ability (chap. 4), and experience and knowledge/skills/abilities (KSA) (chap. 4) and learning (chap. 10), which contribute to more proximal factors, such as motivation (chap. 5), leadership (chap. 9), cognitions (chap. 7), and actions (chap. 8), which contribute to changes in the environment and to success. Moreover, innovation contributes to success (chap. 11), as well as social networks (one aspect of the environment, which in turn interacts with personality; chap. 6). There are a number of general issues that relate to all of the constructs described in Fig. 16.1: entrepreneurial process (chap. 2), issues of definition and issues of intrapreneurship (chaps. 1, 11, & 13), national culture (chap. 12), and methodological issues (chap. 13).

The remainder of this chapter focuses on the nature of the reciprocal benefits for the two fields, describing (a) ways in which I/O psychology can contribute to answering key questions concerning entrepreneurs and entrepreneurship (e.g., Why do some persons but not others adopt this role? Why are some much more successful in it than others?), and (b) ways in

Entrepreneurship and Psychological Factors

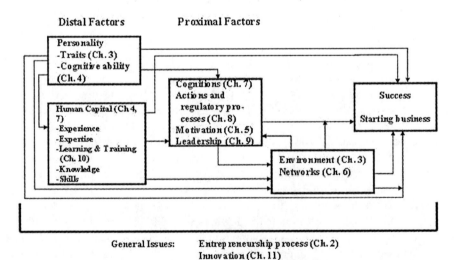

FIG. 16.1. Entrepreneurship and psychological factors.

which the methods and findings of entrepreneurship can contribute to progress in I/O psychology (e.g., by providing a new and potentially valuable setting for conducting research, by offering insights into how innovation occurs not just in new ventures, but in existing organizations, etc.)

THE FUNCTION OF HUMAN CAPITAL AND EXPERTISE FOR BUSINESS CREATION AND SUCCESS

The area of human capital includes experience and expertise, including knowledge and skills, as well as learning and training, as described in Figure 1. These issues are discussed by Markman (chap. 4) Busenitz and Arthurs (chap. 7), and Katz (chap. 10).

Entrepreneurship research commonly accepts that knowledge, skills, and abilities (KSAs) are necessary to be an effective entrepreneur. Markman (chap. 4) develops a competency analysis in the tradition of Fleishman and Quaintance (1984) and McClelland (1973) for the "job" of the entrepreneur.

Markman discusses also social capital or social skills. These skills include impression management, accuracy in perceiving others (social perception), effectiveness at communication generally and persuasion in particular, expressiveness (the ability to express one's emotions clearly), and social adaptability (the ability to adapt to a wide range of social contexts). Such skills have been found to play an important role in many organizational processes and in individual success as well as in entrepreneurs (e.g., Baron & Markman, 2003; Wayne, Liden, Gran, & Ferris, 1997). This suggests that efforts to enhance entrepreneurs' social competence may contribute measurably to their success—a possibility well worth investigating.

In addition, recent research suggests that more general aptitudes or abilities, such as what Sternberg (2004) and other researchers (e.g., Baum & Bird, 2004) describe as *practical intelligence,* and certain aspects of emotional competence (e.g., Law, Wong, & Song, 2004) may play a role in entrepreneurs' success. To date, the specific effects of such abilities and aptitudes have not been investigated in the context of entrepreneurship, so this appears to represent a potentially valuable focus for future research.

Busenitz and Arthurs (chap. 7) use the concept of entrepreneurial and dynamic capabilities as their starting point: They "combine knowledge concerning the organization's performance against its aspired level of performance" (p. 134). Entrepreneurial capabilities are related to new opportunities and dynamic capabilities related to working with one's (restricted) resource base. Examples of entrepreneurial capabilities are

For Busenitz and Arthurs it is of particular importance that entrepreneurial capabilities and dynamic capabilities are both needed but may be at times in some kind of dialectic relationship to each other, where the entrepreneurial capabilities may lead to problems with adjusting one's knowledge base (in the sense of dynamic capabilities), particularly when the firm grows over time. Busenitz and Arthurs include interesting and at times controversial hypotheses: For example, they argue that entrepreneurs perceive opportunities where others perceive threats. This implies that there is a consistent leaning toward higher risks in entrepreneurs. Entrepreneurs are able to combine expertise in an area with market knowledge—this is again an interesting hypothesis, because it implies that both are needed to start a company, to grow it and to be successful. Also, it follows from their chapter that entrepreneurs use more complexity reducing heuristics than other people but that they tend to concentrate on unusual thoughts.

Katz (chap. 10) maintains that it is possible to train important competencies to (would-be) entrepreneurs. He also points out how little the training and education programs in entrepreneurship have been evaluated. Sophisticated evaluation designs are uncommon, and this is clearly an area in which a stronger orientation toward I/O psychology would enhance the field. Two recent I/O psychology textbooks on training discuss techniques that help to maximize learning and to improve evaluation designs (Goldstein & Ford, 2002; Wexley & Latham, 2002). There is also little reference in entrepreneurship research to the cumulative knowledge in management training (Burke & Day, 1986).

On the other hand, I/O psychology is surprisingly silent on the major focus of entrepreneurship education, the function of developing a business plan for the survival and business growth. From Katz's chapter, a number of interesting questions can be developed with regard to business plans. Is developing a business plan a rite of passage that legitimizes entrepreneurs (e.g., vis-à-vis banks or venture capitalists), a cognitive exercise that helps to develop knowledge of markets, opportunities, and products, a cognitive tool that allows a person to really think through the implications of being starting a firm, a self-selection instrument in the sense of a realistic job preview (Wanous, Poland, Premack, & Davis, 1992) that provides a rational decision tool for making the decision to become an entrepreneur or not, because risks are correctly estimated, a compensatory tool that helps to slow down entrepreneurs who would have taken undue risks and followed too instinctively their heuristic thinking and their optimistic projections into the future? Thus, additional questions appear: Is a business plan useful for all people or only for certain people? Is a business plan useful at every stage of the entrepreneurship process—in other words, is it useful to start out immediately with a business plan or should it be rather developed a little later in the startup process? Is it useful to make it a habit of developing written business plans for every year as an entrepreneur? Are there interactions with other human capital variables, such as school education, social skills, and so on?

If opportunity detection and exploitation, innovativeness, and personal initiative (proactivity) are central factors in entrepreneurship, how can teaching them be made more effective? These are central questions that are interesting for I/O psychology as much as for entrepreneurship research.

Finally, the whole area of learning a multifaceted skill and knowledge pattern that is necessary for entrepreneurship is in its own right an important issue (cf. chap. 7). We must assume that entrepreneurs have to be generalists in comparison to nearly all occupations, which have a much more specialist orientation—this is true even of managers who typically have some division of labor. The literature on expertise has been much more concerned with special knowledge and skills of certain professions or artistic and athletic skills (Ericsson & Lehmann, 1996; Sonnentag, 1998; Tesluk & Jacobs, 1998). Can this literature be applied to the much more general skills and knowledge that are required of entrepreneurs (Unger, Keith, Frese, Hilling, & Gielnik, 2005)?

THE FUNCTION OF PERSONALITY FACTORS AND COMPETENCIES FOR BUSINESS CREATION AND SUCCESS

Writing almost 40 years ago, Baumol (1968) stated, "Trying to understand entrepreneurship without considering entrepreneurs is like trying to understand Shakespeare without including Hamlet in the discussion" (p. 67) We agree with this sentiment and contend that this book shows that person factors do indeed play a crucial role in the process of entrepreneurship (Shane, Locke, & Collins, 2003; Shane & Venkataraman, 2000). To the extent this is so, it is only reasonable to attempt to understand the characteristics, skills, motives, and abilities of entrepreneurs, and to ask how they influence the founding and subsequent growth of new ventures (e.g., Amit, McCrimmon, Zietsma, & Oesch, 2000) and the chapters by Busenitz and Arthurs (chap. 7), Markman (chap. 4), and Rauch and Frese (chap. 3).

Given the interest in personality factors in traditional entrepreneurship research, it is all the more surprising that the dominant consensus in entrepreneurship research currently maintains that personality factors are quite unimportant for our understanding of business creation and success. We hope that the chapters 3, 4, and 7 of this book may have convinced even the skeptics that this consensus needs to be revisited. Both Rauch and Frese and Markman in this book argue forcefully that this is not the case. Rauch and Frese base their chapter on three meta-analyses that show that, indeed, personality factors do play a role in the explanation of business creation and success. These correlations are in the same range as the correlations reported by I/O psychology (Barrick & Mount, 1991) in personality factors contributing to performance: They are typically in the range of $r = .20$ to $r = .40$. These correlations are all the more important as the correlations between personality factors and business success are systematically under-estimated for methodological reasons. Because there is a correlation between personality and business creation, there is reduced variance in the personality variables among entrepreneurs leading to reduced correlations.

I/O psychology has shown that meta-analyses have had consequences for the design of studies. Journal editors and reviewers demand, for example, that selection studies should include a set of basic proven predictors (such as mental ability and conscientiousness), and scholars are expected to prove additional explained variance whenever a new variable is introduced. Entrepreneurship research might want to move in this direction as well. Once further studies (and meta-analyses) have shown which personality traits explain both business creation as well as success, these traits should be routinely introduced in all those studies that attempt to introduce new concepts in explaining entrepreneurial success and venture creation.

Rauch and Frese argue that meta-analyses have shown that personality traits are all the more predictive when they are measured more specifically to entrepreneurship. Specific personality factors are those factors that have a plausible match with the requirements that appear in entrepreneurship; an example is achievement motivation. In the words of Rauch and Frese (chap. 3, this volume):

> Specific traits showed higher relationships with business creation and success than the broad traits .... Broad personality traits are highly aggregated across time and situations, and, therefore do not predict specific behaviors in specific situations. Therefore, there is only a weak albeit significant relationship between broad personality traits and entrepreneurial success .... A similar effect of specificity was found for employee performance as well (Tett, Steele, & Beaurgard, 2003). It is noteworthy that the specificity issue discussed above is not restricted to the personality variable but also to the criterion variable. (Hattrup & Jackson, 1996)

Markman (chap. 4) takes this type of argument to the next logical step as he does what I/O psychology has always demanded to do in the description of relevant job situations for people: a KSA (knowledge, skill, and ability) analysis of entrepreneurship. It follows from his chapter that entrepreneurship should more frequently analyze situations and differentiate between weak and strong situation; competencies are more important in weak situations. This implies that entrepreneurship researchers should look at the issues of the situation—for example, whether there are tight policy controls that regulate an industry (e.g., pharmacological industry) versus few controls that restrict the freedom do develop different ways of doing things.

Rauch and Frese, as well as Markman, suggest that entrepreneurship research ought to take a much closer look at issues of match or fit between person and environment. There is ample research in I/O psychology that could be used to model good new research in entrepreneurship. Issues that come to mind are person–industry fit, person–economic cycle fit, person–business cycle or business process phase fit (cf. Baron, chap. 2), person– opportunity fit, or person–culture fit (cf. Edwards, 1991).

Both chapters (Rauch and Frese, and Markman) argue that broadband distal personality variables may be important in the prediction of success and business creation, but to maximize explained variance more proximal factors, such as motivational, cognitive, action styles and strategies, and leadership approaches, may be more important. This is in line with newer personality theory as well: Mischel and Shoda (1998) argued that personality research has never been and should be not be reduced to just studying traits, but should include personality process variables, such encoding, expectancies and beliefs, affects, goals and values, competencies, and self-regulatory plans. Many if not most of these are described as proximal variables in Fig. 16.1 and are discussed next.

THE FUNCTION OF COGNITION, MOTIVATION, ACTIONS AND REGULATORY PROCESSES, AND LEADERSHIP FOR BUSINESS CREATION AND SUCCESS

Busenitz and Arthurs (chap. 7), Frese (chap. 8), Locke and Baum (chap. 5), and Antonakis and Autio (chap. 9) deal with these issues.

Cognitive Factors

Becoming an entrepreneur is a major career decision, fraught with potential economic danger for those who make it. Often people give up secure employment in a mature and thriving organization for the uncertainties of starting a new venture. These considerations raise an intriguing question: What factors lead some individuals, but not others, to become entrepreneurs? Initially, entrepreneurship research sought to answer this question largely in terms of career experience (Cooper et al., 1988) and economic factors (e.g., Evans & Leighton, 1989). For example, Levesque, Evans, and Shepherd (2002) view the decision to become self-employed rather than retain employment in an existing organization in the context of a *utility-maximizing model*. This model suggests that people choose to be self-employed (e.g., to become entrepreneurs) when the combination of income, risk, work effort required, and the independence provided by being self-employed provides greater utility than does the corresponding combination offered by the best organizational employment available to them. Levesque, Shepherd, and Douglas (2002) extended this model by noting that the utility and disutility weights for these factors (i.e., income, work effort, risk, and independence) frequently change over time. For instance, although people are generally work averse (they have a disutility weight for work effort), this disutility increases with age. (Note, however, that there is ample evidence in I/O psychology that lack of work—in the sense of unemployment—leads to strong ill-health effects; cf. Murphy & Athanasou, 1999.) Similarly, Levesque et al. (2002) suggest that the disutility weight for risk and the utility weight for income both decrease with age.

An underlying assumption of such economic models is that people make a rational choice between being self-employed and working for an organization, and that such choices are based on the tendency to maximize utility—to obtain outcomes that are positively valued and to avoid outcomes that are negatively valued. Although this is certainly true up to a point, such models fail to take account of a large number of additional factors that may also influence this choice (e.g., factors pertaining to the characteristics of entrepreneurs and to the persons with whom they have long-term relationships, such as their friends and family). Further, these economic-centered models generally ignore the fact that human cognition is often far from rational; on the contrary, the cognitive processes that provide the foundation for decision making are often influenced by factors that lead individuals to select options different from those that would be predicted by utility-maximizing models (e.g., their affective or emotional reactions; Forgas, 1995; Plous, 1993).

First, consider heuristics. Cognitive scientists have recently drawn a clear distinction between two modes or styles of thought: *systematic processing*, which involves careful, analytic thinking, and *heuristic processing*, a contrasting style in which information is processed quickly and effortlessly, in accordance with various simple heuristics (e.g., "If it comes from a good source, then I will believe it; if not, I will reject it"; Petty & Cacioppo, 1990). It seems reasonable to suggest that entrepreneurs, as a group, show a preference for heuristic thinking: They are, after all, action oriented and strongly prefer making things happen to merely thinking about them (e.g., Amit et al., 2000). Busenitz and Arthurs (chap. 7) argue that entrepreneurs show a preference for basing their decisions on heuristics because they are under constant overload of information and need to make risky decisions in a complex environment and at the same time need to be innovative. This carries risks but it also affords the advantages of flexibility and speed. In this way, Busenitz and Arthurs go back to the original definition of heuristics—as helping the decision-making process—as first discussed by Gestalt theoreticians (Duncker, 1935), and overcome some modern restrictions that reduce the concept of heuristics to biases (cf. Frese, chap. 8).

On the other hand, because entrepreneurs are, by definition, breaking new ground in terms of the products or services their companies provide, they must also engage in careful analysis of situations and events and formulate strategic plans for developing their companies. This reasoning suggests that perhaps successful entrepreneurs are ones who can restrain their own preference for heuristic thinking and for "forging ahead," at least to a degree (cf. chap. 8). In other words, they can indeed think carefully and strategically when the need arises. In contrast, less successful entrepreneurs may be less adept at making this change, and may retain their preference for heuristic thinking even in situations where more systematic thought would be beneficial. In addition, it is possible that successful entrepreneurs are more proficient than less successful ones at formulating effective heuristics—mental aids for making fast but accurate decisions. Entrepreneurship researchers may well wish to investigate these predictions, derived from research in I/O psychology and closely related fields.

Successful entrepreneurs may be less prone to cognitive biases than less successful ones (e.g., Baron, 1998; Busenitz & Barney, 1997; Simon, Houghton, & Aquino, 2000). There is a wealth of information in I/O psychology on the effects of cognitive biases on decision making and many related processes; drawing on this work may provide the field of entrepreneurship with important insights into the "mind of the entrepreneur." And understanding how entrepreneurs think, in turn, can shed important light on why some are more successful than others.

Second, consider perceptions of risk. Most new ventures fail within a few years—that is a basic fact. Yet most entrepreneurs are confident of their own success. In a sense, they suffer from a strong *optimistic bias* (e.g., Shepperd, Ouellette, & Fernandez, 1996), believing that their likelihood of experiencing positive outcomes is much higher than objective facts actually suggest. One important basis for this unwarranted optimism is the tendency of persons who choose to become entrepreneurs to underestimate the amount of risk involved in starting a new venture. When compared to other persons, entrepreneurs do not appear to be "riskier"—they do *not* have a higher overall propensity or tolerance for risk (e.g., Kahneman & Lovallo, 1993). But because of additional cognitive tendencies (e.g., an inflated illusion of control; Simon, Houghton, & Aquino, 2000), they tend to perceive existing risks as smaller than they are, and smaller in magnitude than other persons do. It seems reasonable to suggest that entrepreneurs' perceptions of risk are one factor that can influence their decision "take the plunge" and start a new venture.

Third, consider learning. Because entrepreneurs have to make decisions in uncertain situations and because even under the best of circumstances they can never be prepared for everything that they will encounter, learning is important (cf. Busenitz & Arthurs, chap. 7). Learning can take place on several levels of regulation—on a more intuitive and automatic level and on a more conscious level (Frese, chap. 8). Because learning is situationally based and situationally constrained, learning has a nonimitable component in it, which helps entrepreneurs to stay ahead of their competitors and larger firms. Learning processes can be enhanced or constrained by the learner, and some learners are actively seeking (negative) feedback and will be able to gain competitive advantage (Busenitz & Arthurs, chap. 7; Frese, chap. 8). Topics such as learning from others (model learning) (Bandura, 1977), learning from feedback (cf. Frese, chap. 8), cognitive processes of skill acquisition (Anderson, 1987), learning emotional relationships (classical conditioning), and learning mental models (Gentner & Stevens, 1983), as well as interaction of learning with cognitive ability (aptitude–treatment interaction; Kanfer & Ackerman, 1989), need to be considered.

The Special Case of Opportunity Perception

There is no question that opportunity identification and exploitation lie at the heart of entrepreneurship (cf. Baum et al., chap. 1)—at least in the beginning of the entrepreneurial process (cf. Baron, chap. 2). In fact, entrepreneurs' decisions to found a new venture often stem from their belief that they have identified an opportunity no one else has yet recognized, one that they can successfully develop. Opportunity recognition has long been a central concept in the field of entrepreneurship, but until recently, little effort has been made to approach it from a behavioral perspective. (Recent work by Gaglio and Katz [2001] and Gaglio [2004] is one important exception to this general pattern.) It is clear, however, that opportunity recognition must, in several respects, involve basic aspects of human behavior.

When an entrepreneur identifies an opportunity (assume for the moment that the opportunity does in fact exist), this implies that there is "something" out there to notice—some kind of stimulus or stimulus configuration that is noticed or perceived. The question is what stimulus configuration constitutes an opportunity. This basic question has, to date, been largely ignored.

Recent efforts to understand opportunity recognition in the context of perception (e.g., Baron, 2004) have focused on the possibility that opportunity recognition is closely related to *pattern recognition*—the process through which perceivers recognize patterns in the stimuli to which they are exposed in a given environment (e.g., Matlin, 2002). Although many theories of pattern identification exist, two seem most relevant to the identification of opportunities for new ventures: prototype models and exemplar fit models. Prototype models (cf. Frese, chap. 8) suggest that through experience, we construct *prototypes*, mental representations of specific sets of categories of objects (or patterns). Such prototypes comprise our basic ideas of what a specific object or pattern is like—its essential nature. They are, in a sense, mental models of the best or most central instance of this object or pattern—a model or prototype for it.

Applying prototype models to opportunity recognition, it may be the case that entrepreneurs compare ideas for new products or services with their existing prototype for "opportunity"—a mental abstraction acquired through experience. Such a prototype might encompass a combination of attributes such as newness, potential economic value, desirability, plus novelty, practicality, likelihood of competition, and so on. According to such models, opportunity recognition would involve comparison of ideas for something new (new products, services, markets, etc.) with existing prototypes of opportunity. The closer the match, the more likely would entrepreneurs be to conclude that an idea for a new product or service does indeed constitute an opportunity worth pursuing (cf. Craig & Lindsay, 2001).

Other models of pattern recognition emphasize the importance of specific knowledge rather than idealized, highly typical prototypes. Such *exemplar models* (Hahn & Chater, 1997) suggest that as individuals encounter new events or stimuli, they compare them with specific examples (exemplars) of relevant concepts already stored in memory. For instance, an individual's concept of "business opportunity" would not consist solely of an idealized representation of the most typical "business opportunity" he or she can imagine (a prototype); rather, it would be composed of numerous examples of business opportunities this person has actually encountered, exemplars that vary in many respects (e.g., exemplars of excellent business opportunities and exemplars of very poor ones). Exemplar models seem especially relevant to opportunity recognition because they do not require an *abstraction process* through which defining features are identified (as required by feature-comparison models) or prototypes constructed (as required by prototype theories). Rather, individuals simply compare newly encountered events or stimuli with examples of a given concept already present in memory. This fits well with entrepreneurs' reports that they "just know a good opportunity when they see it" and do not have to engage in complex processing to reach this conclusion.

Additional models of object or pattern recognition exist (e.g., Biederman, 1995), via chunking, expertise, organized knowledge, and so on (Ericsson & Charness, 1994; Glass & Holyoak, 1986).

All of these models call attention to the following basic question: What patterns of discernible stimuli are recognized by entrepreneurs as constituting opportunities? In other words, what, from the perspective of perceptual processes, are the essential features of opportunities? A related question involves the role of previous experience in this process. If opportunity recognition does indeed involve a kind of pattern recognition, then it can be conceived as a "connect the dots" problem, in which the past training and experience of specific persons would, presumably, equip them with the mental frameworks necessary for recognizing connections between seemingly disparate events and trends—changes in technology, government policies and regulations, markets, and so on. Recognizing such links (and the patterns they suggest) would, in turn, play a key role in opportunity recognition. Investigating these and related questions may provide valuable insights into the nature of opportunity recognition, and this, in turn, can contribute greatly to progress in the field of entrepreneurship.

In this task, several frameworks and theories long utilized by I/O psychologists may well prove extremely helpful. For instance, one that is well known and has been validated in many different contexts is *signal detection theory*. This theory is concerned with the basic issue of how individuals decide that they have indeed perceived a given stimulus or stimulus configuration. Entrepreneurs face this task in determining whether an opportunity they have identified qualifies as a bona fide opportunity—one worth pursuing vigorously. Perception itself is always a probabilistic process; therefore, individuals will be uncertain as to whether they have, or have not, identified a veridical stimulus—especially ones involving complex patterns or configurations. The theory further notes that many factors determine the relative rate at which an individual's experience hits (correct identification or correct rejection), misses (failing to recognize), and has false alarms (erroneously perceiving an opportunity) in any given situation. Some of these relate to the properties of the stimuli themselves (e.g., the stronger the stimulus, in physical terms, the easier it is to be certain that it is present; in this example, the better the player's performance, the more likely it is that he or she possesses real talent). Other factors, however, relate to the current state of the perceiver (e.g., is this person fatigued? highly or weakly motivated to be correct?). Additional factors involve the *subjective criteria* perceivers apply to the task. For instance, consider the situation faced by an entrepreneur who believes that she has identified an opportunity for a profitable new venture. The venture is one that she can start in her spare time and for which little or no capital is needed. As a result, she may set her subjective criterion for concluding "This is a good business opportunity" quite low: The costs of a false alarm are minimal (wasted time and effort) relative to the potential gains of a hit.

Applying signal detection theory to the task of opportunity recognition offers several valuable insights into the nature of this process. First, it suggests that in seeking to recognize opportunities, entrepreneurs face a complex and difficult task. Few opportunities are so obvious that there is little doubt they exist; on the contrary, many are in a gray area: The pattern of changes perceived by the entrepreneur might constitute a real opportunity, or it might not. Entrepreneurs, of course, want only hits: They want to correctly identify bona fide opportunities. But they face serious risks of misses (overlooking real opportunities) and serious costs associated with false alarms (concluding that opportunities exist when in fact they do not).

Opportunity perception also presents an interesting theoretical area because different theories argue for different processes that take place, for example, pattern recognition that is largely unconscious, signal detection that is largely conscious. Action theory as discussed in chapter 8 would argue that opportunity recognition would be an interplay between pattern recognition and actions (a sort of action cycle; cf. Neisser, 1985).

Motivation

An overview is given by Locke and Baum (chap. 5). What aspects of motivation play a role in the decision to become an entrepreneur? Basic factors are independence, self-efficacy, achievement motive, proactivity and tenacity, as well as egoistic passion (Locke & Baum, chap. 5). Empirical evidence on goals and vision, on generalized self-efficacy, on achievement motive is massive. These more general motivational "traits" have to be translated into more specific motivators, such as specific self-efficacy and goals vision. Overall, the findings discussed in chapter 5 suggest that human motivation does indeed play an important role in entrepreneurship. Therefore, major theories of human motivation developed by I/O psychologists may prove very useful in terms of understanding the reasons why specific persons choose to become entrepreneurs. Newer theories of (self-)regulation are of particular importance here (Latham & Pinder, 2005).

Regulation

Regulation or self-regulation theories belong to a class of theories that deal with the issues of how people regulate their own actions, how actions are determined by cognitive processes, and how motivational processes determine actions via direction, energizing, and sustaining. Regulation theories are, therefore, both motivational and cognitive theories (cf. also Brockner, Higgins, & Low, 2004). Action theory is a particularly useful regulation theory because it takes an active perspective of people, and it assumes that actions are the starting point to think about entrepreneurship (Frese, chap. 8). Cognitive models applied to entrepreneurship often restrict themselves to those cognitions that precede actions (e.g., expectancy × value models, understanding statistical information, decision making). Thereby, they do not examine those factors that determine success or founding a firm, namely, actions. Two categories that stem from this theory and have been applied to the field of entrepreneurship are personal initiative (self-starting, proactive, and overcoming barriers) and everyday action planning.

Personal initiative is a central category for entrepreneurship because entrepreneurs do not usually have a clear structure in which they operate. Therefore, they need to self-start their actions to a much larger extent. Because it is *future* opportunities and potential problems that need to be taken care off, rather than those that present themselves now, the proactive component of personal initiative is central for entrepreneurship as well. Finally, entrepreneurs have to deal with problems and barriers because whenever unknown paths have to be taken, barriers will appear. Thus, the concept of personal initiative that was originally developed as a self-regulatory model for I/O psychology (Frese & Fay, 2001) and applied to entrepreneurship only later may be highly useful for entrepreneurship research.

The second area of application of action theory is everyday action planning. This is an interesting issue that may stimulate some controversy. On the one hand, there is ample evidence for the importance of formal business plans for success (Schwenk & Shrader, 1993), and business plans are still the backbone of entrepreneurship courses at business schools (Katz, chap. 10). However, psychology has often be invoked by entrepreneurship researchers who are critical of conscious planning to point our that entrepreneurship is characterized by chaos, bricolage (Baker, Miner, & Eesley, 2003), and experimentation (Benner & Tushman, 2003), as well as nonconscious approaches of intuition or practical intelligence (Sternberg, 2004) rather than conscious planning.

Planning as a psychological variable in the sense of everyday planning is not the same as developing a business plan. Planning implies to have an idea of when, where, and how one wants to put an intention into effect (Gollwitzer, 1999), and it implies that one mentally simulates how one is to achieve one's goals (Taylor, Pham, Rivkin, & Armor, 1998). Planning can be and should be combined with experimenting or improvising. Often it is useful to develop somewhat sketchy plans and then to improvise the rest— a sort of moderate form of action planning (Frese, van Gelderen, & Ombach, 2000). Planning helps to develop explicit mental models of how to achieve goals (via mental simulation). This allows one to develop explicit hypotheses and to think of the relevant parameters of how the action should proceed and how the environment should react. This helps to get more feedback, and thus, learning is stimulated. The entrepreneur is only able to recognize if he or she is on the "right track" if there has been a certain amount of planning. Because planning implies mental simulation, it can be used to think of why actions went well or not. Planning also helps the businessperson to concentrate and stay focused (Armor & Taylor, 2003). Planning is also related to acting on opportunities: "Good opportunities often present themselves only for a short time …. When goal pursuit is planned, goal directed behaviours could be initiated immediately once a relevant situation is encountered" (Gollwitzer, 1999, p. 494). Thus, scholars should test the hypotheses on the specifics of planning—for example, in which situations do owners plan too little and where to they plan too much? And what kinds of plans have positive and what kind of plans negative consequences on flexibility and learning from feedback?

Thus, a number of interesting research questions appear, among others issues of how everyday planning is related to the quality of the business plan (maybe there are no correlations because business plans have been taught so frequently and are so formalized?), how planning is related to risk taking and overconfidence, and to the use of heuristics, and whether it contradicts or complements practical intelligence and intuition. Other questions concern whether there are interactions of planning with cognitive ability (Escher et al., 2002) and with the stage of the entrepreneurship process (cf. Baron chap. 2).

Leadership

Opportunity exploitation often implies that the entrepreneur has to deal with others; therefore, leadership is involved. Interestingly, as pointed out by Antonakis and Autio in chapter 9, the history of leadership research shows a certain similarity with entrepreneurship research during the last 50 years (e.g., how personality was first glorified, then rejected, and then later was resurrected). One of the most important questions in this area is certainly whether there is a specific type of leadership: entrepreneurial leadership (Gupta, MacMillan, & Surie, 2004). For Gupta et al. (2004, p. 242) entrepreneurial leadership is distinct from other behavioral forms of leadership and consists of a combination of "creating a vision and building a cast of competent and committed supporters."

A number of fascinating issues arise at the intersection of leadership and entrepreneurship research (cf. Cogliser & Brigham, 2004): In which phase of the business cycle is charismatic leadership needed (right in the beginning, second phase, later on, when there are more employees)? When is the time to introduce systematic human resource management into the development of the firm? McClelland (1987) argued that leadership was primarily based on task-based achievement motive in entrepreneurs, whereas good managers were more strongly power motivated. Does this mean that in the beginning of the entrepreneurial process, task orientation is more important than being able to play politics? There are many case studies that show that leadership of entrepreneurial units must change from a more charismatic leadership to more bureaucratic processes. I/O psychology tends to be nondynamic in its leadership theories—entrepreneurship theory points to the importance of a dynamic development of leadership over time across the changes that take place in the firm.

Other issues involve the function of certain aspects of leadership: for example, issues of trust and authenticity. Leadership for entrepreneurs may imply much more leadership of nonemployees, for example, colleagues in a network, customers, and suppliers. Do the same factors of leadership apply in this case as for managers of a firm?

Antonakis and Autio suggest that leadership researchers have learned much about successful leadership through a focus on leader behavior and through conduct of multilevel studies. They encourage psychology researchers to do the same.

ENVIRONMENT AND SOCIAL NETWORKS

In entrepreneurship research, the environment is mainly seen as a determiner of success or failure. This is most clearly true of an evolutionary theory (Aldrich, 1999, p. 21), which thinks of the emergence of organizations to be determined by the factors "variation, selection, retention and diffusion, and the struggle over scarce resources." Up to this point, there is very little research that actually pits an evolutionary perspective against a more person-oriented concept and tests which set of variables can explain success (and business creation) better. Some psychological theories (such as personal initiative theory) argue that entrepreneurs can change the environment. But this has also not been proven for important aspects of the environment.

I/O psychology conceptualizes environment mainly as a factor that conditions or moderates the relationships between people and performance or success (aptitude–treatment interaction)—a position that has been taken since the classical formulation of Lewin that behavior is a function of the person and the environment. This is the position that is taken by Rauch and Frese in chapter 3. Such a framework suggests that we systematically observe whether environmental factors moderate the impact of entrepreneurial variables on success (e.g., it has been shown that entrepreneurial orientation is more important in difficult environments; Frese, Brantjes, & Hoorn, 2002). Much more work needs to be done in this area, and we suggest that researchers should discuss in much more specific terms how industry requirements and environments interact with psychological predictors of success (e.g., an obvious hypothesis is that extraversion and social skills are more important in social industries or in industries with a high interpersonal service component).

SOCIAL NETWORKS

In chapter 6, Audia and Rider suggest that organizational contexts give birth to entrepreneurship because organizations provide entrepreneurs with opportunities to develop psychological and social resources that are necessary for new venture creation. Further, they suggest that through political turbulence, market concentration, and organization dissolution, individuals are motivated to leave their organization with their newly acquired assets to create their own organization. In short, entrepreneurs are often organization products.

Audia and Rider support this theory by exploring three mechanisms that may inspire startup: confidence building, information gathering about opportunities, and development of social ties. They provide sufficient evidence to support these views, but point to several gaps in our understanding.

For example, little is known about how work experiences create psychological skills that are relevant for successful entrepreneurship. There may be answers in social cognitive theory and self-selection theory. Antonakis and Audia (chap. 9) suspect that prior employers' reputations may impact the success of follow-on venture creation, and they encourage I/O psychologist to identify specific prior employer characteristics that may be predictors of success.

Social networks discussed in chapter 6 may be influenced by personal initiative. Thus, entrepreneurs high on initiative may be better in developing a niche and influencing the specific environment in which they work. One application of this theory is to look at how much entrepreneurs are able to influence their social networks—one specific area of the environment. Zhao and Frese (2005) combined this approach (espoused by Frese in chap. 8) with social network theory discussed in chapter 6 in an empirical study that shows that socially oriented initiative relates to network building, which in turn relates to success, at least in a collectivist nation.

Additional insights into the question of why some persons but not others choose to become entrepreneurs are provided by I/O psychology research focused on the issues of *prejudice* and *discrimination*. Heilman and Chen (2003) emphasized the relevance of these factors to entrepreneurship. They note that women and minorities often choose to found their own ventures because they face barriers to success in large organizations. At present, such barriers no longer center around overt discriminatory practices; these have been made illegal in many countries. Rather, they reflect more subtle—but often equally harmful—processes. For instance, Heilman, Wallen, Fuchs, and Tamkins (2004) recently reported that women who were highly successful in fields viewed as more appropriate for men than women were indeed perceived to be competent, but were simultaneously down-rated in terms of personal characteristics (e.g., they were viewed as less likable than men who performed at the same levels). Moreover, this was true regardless of whether the people who evaluated them were female or male. Similarly, maintaining an effective balance between work and family life may pose a greater burden for women than men (Stroh & Reilly, 1999). Perhaps even worse, women and minorities are often excluded from informal networks and experience greater difficulties in obtaining mentors than do other persons (e.g., Powell, 1999; Ragins, 1999).

As a result of encountering these and other relatively subtle barriers, women and minorities may well be drawn to entrepreneurship: When one is the chief executive officer (CEO) of one's own company, these obstacles and barriers are no longer applicable. On the other hand, if they opt for the role of entrepreneur, women and minorities may well face additional problems. They may be perceived as less competent than other entrepreneurs or as less suited to running a business, especially in certain industries (e.g., high-tech, manufacturing; e.g., Baron, Markman, & Hirsa, 2001). Yet despite such problems, the lure of entrepreneurship remains high for these groups, and this, in turn, poses a serious dilemma for existing organizations. After all, it may be the most talented women and minority group members who choose to become entrepreneurs—the very persons large organizations most want to retain. Clearly, vigorous action to redress lingering barriers to advancement by women and minorities is necessary if this situation is to be reversed. In any case, it is apparent that research in I/O psychology dealing with the issue of discrimination in work settings may indeed offer added, and perhaps unexpected, insights into the question, "Why do some persons but not others choose to become entrepreneurs?"

GLOBAL ENTREPRENEURSHIP FACTORS: PROCESS, INNOVATION, NATIONAL CULTURE, AND METHODOLOGICAL ISSUES

In this section we comment on global entrepreneurship factors covered in this book. Global factors affect the whole entrepreneurship process and are, therefore, at the bottom of Fig. 16.1. Robert A. Baron (chap. 2) reminded us that entrepreneurship is a process and that the stage of the process is a global variable that matters for our study of the causes of entrepreneurship success. He also noted that other global factors such as innovation, business conditions, and national culture impact entrepreneurship. Research methodology is also a global entrepreneurship research factor because optimal methods are somewhat dependent on the factors and the stage of development studied.

Baron explained that the entrepreneurship process includes large variances in conditions across stages and that we must include these conditions in our studies or at least employ conditional controls. For example, entrepreneurs' personal characteristics, including their preferred behaviors, have the greatest impact on entrepreneurship in the early stages. During this nascent period, entrepreneurs refine their vision to create a venture and take initial steps to create product and service prototypes, test markets, and organize. They may join with others, partnering to gain confidence or resources, but the nascent stage is a solitary time for would-be entrepreneurs. Even if would-be entrepreneurs partner with others, outcomes are almost totally within the control of the lead entrepreneur. Studies conducted during this period may find large variances in outcomes (intellectual property benchmarks, resource gather benchmarks, decisions to continue or not) and significant direct relationships between individual entrepreneurs' personal characteristics such as experience, knowledge, energy, motivation, perseverance, organizing skill, and outcome variables (Baum, 2003).

As the entrepreneurs join with partners, employees, or advisors, the direct effects between venture outcomes and "the entrepreneur" are diluted. As teams develop, studies of personal characteristics must deal with team aggregates. The startup or emergence phase of entrepreneurship further dilutes the direct link with the entrepreneur's personal characteristics as the forces of outside financing, industry characteristics, local competitive environments, and general financial environments impact outcomes such as revenues, cash flows, and markets penetrated. For example, those entrepreneurs who are skilled at dealing with financiers or who are able leaders of employees have little advantage during the nascent phase versus those entrepreneurs who have product/service technical skills. However, resource acquisition and management skills may dominate technical skills after emergence and during the early stages of venture growth in terms of predicting venture outcomes. All of this suggests that researchers must utilize longitudinal models to achieve a complete explanation of the causes of successful entrepreneurship.

Although the overarching message for researchers from chap. 2 is that we must include venture stage as a research variable, we know little about the specifics of the relationships between entrepreneurship and process. I/O psychology researchers can lead the study of the effects of relevant skills and behaviors across stages. For example, new venture organizing skills (resource aggregation skills) may be definable and measurable to yield interesting information for would-be entrepreneurs about the experience and education that they need to be competent entrepreneurs.

I/O psychology should also differentiate between different companies that they do research in. Entrepreneurial companies may be very different from other ones. In addition, there is entrepreneurship, or entrepreneurial behavior, in established companies. Established companies were entrepreneurial new ventures at some point, but they must continue to be creative and innovative to cope with competitive threats and to take advantage of opportunities. Tom Lumpkin (chap. 11) explored entrepreneurship in established companies, suggesting that an entrepreneurial orientation (EO) consisting of autonomy, innovativeness, proactiveness, competitive aggressiveness, and risk taking was important for success. Early studies support his assertion; however, findings should be generalized beyond the limited samples studied and relationships among the component concepts should be explored. For example, do the components have divergent validity? If so, do some components matter more than others? How do threatening situations impact the relative importance of the components? How can firms develop the necessary elements of entrepreneurial orientation? I/O psychology researchers may be able to apply sophisticated measurement of team characteristics to improve the dimensionality of the EO components and guide us to answers to these important questions.

Lumpkin also discussed the relationship of intrapreneurship and innovation and explored the barriers to innovation in established companies. A set of prescriptions for improving innovation in established companies would be enormously valuable for the business community. It may be that I/O psychologists' studies of individual level entrepreneur innovation behavior could uncover sound advice for corporate research and development (R&D) managers. Why is it that most productive and successful bioscience developments appear in new ventures? Is it that the successful entrepreneurs learned their valuable skills and technical knowledge in established companies, quit, and founded their own companies? Or is it that small companies, free from political and administrative distractions, are simply more efficient than established companies?

Tung et al. discuss cross-cultural research in chap. 12, and culture is another global force that impacts entrepreneurship. Why is it that successful entrepreneurship is valued in some societies and not in others? Cultural/social forces must be powerful predictors of entrepreneurship. Entrepreneurs disturb the status quo. They identify unsatisfied needs and underutilized resources. Their habitual search for imbalance and their joy in uncovering opportunity are special personal orientations that may be culturally inspired, at least in the sense that this orientation is enabled and supported. Research about cultural determination of entrepreneurship continues to follow Hofstede's dimensions and prototypes for analysis. Is it not time for an elaboration or freshening of the dimensions? Researchers in this area can make use of the more recent results of the GLOBE study (House, Hanges, Javidan, Dorfman, & Gupta, 2004). Furthermore, entrepreneurship researchers have identified multiple behaviors that fit new venture creation (adaptation in terms of improvisation, bricolage, and experimentation; organizing skills in terms of human organizing, systems organizing, and financial organizing; etc.). Have these entrepreneurial behaviors been adequately studied across cultures?

In chapter 13, Per Davidsson addresses the challenges and opportunities. He begins with advice about sampling. He recommends that I/O psychologists define their subjects to include nonentrepreneurs to help produce useful differences. We agree, but we also suggest that meaningful differences can be discovered within the would-be entrepreneur subset and certainly within the new venturer subset. Davidsson encourages I/O psychologists to draw on laboratory experiments as well as ethnographic studies. We join Davidsson in encouraging I/O psychology researchers to draw on the data that have been collected by the Panel Study of Entrepreneurial Development. Much of the data has not been studied, and many relationships have not been uncovered.

One of the methodological and theoretical factors discussed at length in I/O psychology is the level-of-analysis issue (Klein & Kozlowski, 2000). Here entrepreneurship process theory meets methodology, because during the entrepreneurship process, the organization grows and the locus of action moves from the individual entrepreneur to the organization. Thus, the issue of on what level the entrepreneurial unit needs to be studied becomes important. It is interesting that neither I/O psychology nor entrepreneurship researchers have really met the challenges here: Although, an individual level of analysis may be useful in a small entrepreneurial unit, an organization-level analysis is required when an organization has achieved a certain size. But we do not know from what size onward, on which issues, an organizational level analysis becomes important for which kind of dependent variables. This should be a major focus for level-of-analysis theory, and, at the same time, it is an area of scientific intersection for both disciplines. Moreover, the methodological implications have not yet been met by the disciplines. For example, many studies on entrepreneurial orientation are based on individual level measures of the CEOs of the respective units. A more cultural or climate approach that looks how widespread the entrepreneurial orientation is in the company may be useful here. Similarly, I/O psychology has been too much involved in studying performance from the perspective of the supervisor, whereas the perspective of how the whole organization is doing may be of much higher importance (and the correct level of analysis in many instances). Here I/O psychology can obviously learn from entrepreneurship research.

The range of potential successful entrepreneurship predictors that have been identified in *The Psychology of Entrepreneurship* presents an enormous research challenge for I/O psychology researchers. The factors are internal and external; they appear within and outside the individual and they appear within and outside the firm. They reflect many levels of analysis (individual, team, firm, industry, global). Some are observable; some are intrapsychic. What is a researcher to do? We think the challenging situation is a good thing because the opportunity to make a difference remains in place, and the opportunity for psychology-based academic research about entrepreneurship is huge.

WHAT ENTREPRENEURSHIP CAN CONTRIBUTE TO RESEARCH IN I/O PSYCHOLOGY

Would closer ties between entrepreneurship and I/O psychology also be beneficial to I/O research? Careful consideration of this issue suggests several compelling reasons for an affirmative answer. First, entrepreneurship researchers focus primarily on relatively new organizations—ones that have only recently been launched and that, in many cases, are growing rapidly. Such organizations offer a unique and potentially valuable context in which I/O psychology can test its major theories—theories that have generally been developed in large, mature organizations. Other variables may not be applicable to startup companies, or may operate very differently in startup companies than in large, mature ones (e.g., reward systems; quality of supervision; assistance with career development, seniority). In short, research conducted in startup companies may provide I/O psychology with important new insights into the causes and effects of work-related attitudes—insights that could not readily be obtained in the usual arena of I/O research.

Similarly, consider two other topics that have received considerable attention in I/O research in recent years: *trust* (e.g., Lewicki, McAllister, & Bies, 1998) and *organizational citizenship behavior* (e.g., Bolino, Turnley, & Bloodgood, 2003; Organ, 1997). Given the small size of most startup companies, and the fact that most employees have direct contact with the founder (or founders), it seems possible that both of these aspects of organizational behavior may stem from different sources, and produce different effects, in startup organizations than in large ones. Research designed to determine whether this is indeed the case might well yield important new insights into the nature and effects of both of these In sum, startup companies, which are the central focus of entrepreneurship, offer I/O psychology a new and in some ways unique setting for research—research that can potentially enrich understanding of many key aspects of organizational behavior.

This is not the only way in which closer links to the field of entrepreneurship can assist I/O psychology, however. Organizational change and development have been major themes in much I/O research in recent years. Where better to study such processes than in startup firms, which, by their very nature, exist in turbulent environments and change at a rapid pace? In contrast, large and mature organizations—even ones that are highly successful—change slowly. In a sense, therefore, new ventures provide I/O with a natural setting in which to examine the ways in which organizations evolve—how their culture emerges, how their management practices and structure reflect rapid growth and are shaped by it.

Finally, from the point of view of practice, there may be valuable lessons for mature organizations—and for I/O psychology—in what the field of entrepreneurship has learned about factors affecting the success of start-up ventures. In particular, some of these findings may contain clues as to how large, mature organizations can encourage *innovation*. This has been a growing theme in entrepreneurship research that has focused increasingly on what has been termed *intrapreneurship* (e.g., Antonic & Hisrich, 2001). This research has gone on largely in isolation from basic findings and principles of I/O psychology, but these could certainly inform such investigations in important way. Additional opportunities for progress offered to I/O psychology by entrepreneurship relate to such topic as *workplace aggression, dysfunctional organizational behavior,* and *organizational politics* (e.g., Griffin & O'Leary-Kelly, 2004; Kacmar & Baron, 1999). Because startup companies are so small, it may be more difficult for persons in them to employ the indirect, disguised techniques used effectively in larger organizations (e.g., Baron, Neuman, & Geddes, 1999). In sum, startup companies, which are the central focus of entrepreneurship, offer I/O psychology a new and in some ways unique setting for research—research that can potentially enrich understanding of many key aspects of behavior in work settings.

In sum, it seems clear that the benefits of closer ties between I/O psychology and entrepreneurship are indeed reciprocal in nature: Both fields can gain measurably from such links. Increased collaboration can help each field to answer important questions, and, moreover, may provide each with new conceptual tools and new methods of research. These benefits, in turn, create substantial opportunities for research—opportunities, we sincerely hope, that growing numbers of investigators in the two fields will recognize. To the extent this occurs, both fields may not only benefit—they may also more effectively avoid the dangers suggested by the following maxim: *"Every time history repeats itself, the cost goes up."* We contend that neither I/O psychology nor entrepreneurship can afford such costs, and that one effective way of avoiding them is greater collaboration between the two fields. Efforts to attain this goal are already well under way (e.g., Baron, 2004; Baum & Locke, 2004), and we fully expect to see continued progress in this regard in the years ahead—with mutual and reciprocal benefits for both fields as the key result.

REFERENCES

Aldrich, H. E. (1999). *Organizations evolving*. London: Sage.

Amit, R., MacCrimmon, K. R., Zietsma, C., & Oesch, J. M. (2000). Does money matter? Wealth attainment as the motive for initiating growth-oriented technology ventures. *Journal of Business Venturing, 16,* 119–143.

Anderson, J. R. (1987). Skill acquisition: Compilation of weak-method problem solutions. *Psychological Review, 94,* 192–210.

Antonic, B., & Hisrich, R. D. (2001). Intrapreneurship: Construct refinement and cross-cultural validation. *Journal of Business Venturing, 16,* 495–527.

Armor, D. A., & Taylor, S. E. (2003). The effects of mindset on behavior: Self-regulation in deliberative and implemental frames of mind. *Personality & Social Psychology Bulletin, 29,* 86–95.

Baker, T., Miner, A., & Eesley, D. (2003). Improvising firms: Bricolage, account giving, and improvisational competency in the founding process. *Research Policy, 32,* 255–276.

Bandura, A. (1977). *Social learning theory.* Englewood Cliffs, NJ: Prentice Hall.

Baron, R. A. (1998). Cognitive mechanisms in entrepreneurship: Why and when entrepreneurs think differently than other people. *Journal of Business Venturing, 13,* 275–294.

Baron, R. A. (2004). Opportunity recognition: Insights from a cognitive perspective. In J. Butler (Ed.)., *Research in entrepreneurship and management* (Vol. 4, pp. 47–73). Greenwich CT: Information Age.

Baron, R. A., & Markman, G. D. (2003). Beyond social capital: The role of entrepreneurs' social competence in their financial success. *Journal of Business Venturing, 18,* 41–60.

Baron, R. A., Markman, G. D., & Hirsa, A. (2001). Perceptions of women and men as entrepreneurs: Evidence for differential effects of attributional augmenting. *Journal of Applied Psychology, 86,* 923–929.

Baron, R. A., Neuman, J. H., & Geddes, D. (1999). Social and personal determinants of workplace aggression: Evidence for the impact of perceived injustice and the Type A behavior pattern. *Aggressive Behavior, 25,* 281–296.

Barrick, M. R., & Mount, M. K. (1991). The big five personality dimensions and job performance: A meta-analysis. *Personnel Psychology, 41,* 1–26.

Baum, J. R. (2003). Entrepreneurs' start-up cognitions and behaviors: Dreams, surprises, shortages, and fast zigzags. In W. D. Bygrave, C. G. Brush, P. Davidsson, J. Fiet, P. G. Greene, R. T. Harrison, M. Lerner, G. D. Mayer, J. Sohl, & A. Zacharakis (Eds.), *Frontiers of entrepreneurship research* (pp. 605–619). Babson Park, MA: Babson College.

Baum, J. R., & Bird, B. J. (2004, August). *Practical intelligence of entrepreneurs: Exploring the "know how" of opportunity exploitation.* Paper presented at the meetings of the Academy of Management, New Orleans, LA.

Baum, J. R., & Locke, E. A. (2004). The relationship of entrepreneurial traits, skill, and motivation to subsequent venture growth. *Journal of Applied Psychology, 89,* 587–598.

Baumol, W. (1968). Entrepreneurship in economic theory. *American Economic Review Papers and Proceedings,* 64–71.

Benner, M. J., & Tushman, M. L. (2003). Exploitation, exploration, and process management: The productivity dilemma revisited. *Academy of Management Review, 28,* 238–256.

Biederman, I. (1995). Visual object recognition. In S. F. Kosslyn & D. N. Osherson (Eds.), *An invitation to cognitive science* (2nd ed., pp. 121–1654). Cambridge, MA: MIT Press.

Bolino, M. C., Turnley, W. H., & Bloodgood, J. M. (2003). Citizenship behavior and the creation of social capital in organizations. *Academy of Management Review, 27,* 505–522.

Brockner, J., Higgins, E. T., & Low, M. B. (2004). Regulatory focus theory and the entrepreneurial process. *Journal of Business Venturing, 19,* 203–220.

Burke, M. J., & Day, R. R. (1986). A cumulative study of the effectiveness of managerial training. *Journal of Applied Psychology, 71,* 232–245.

Busenitz, L. W., & Barney, J. B. (1997). Differences between entrepreneurs and managers in large organizations: Biases and heuristics in strategic decision-making. *Journal of Business Venturing, 12,* 9–30.

Cogliser, C. C., & Brigham, K. H. (2004). The intersection of leadership and entrepreneurship: Mutual lessons to be learned. *Leadership Quarterly, 15,* 771–799.

Cooper, A., Woo, C., & Dunkelberg, W. (1988). Entrepreneurship and the initial size of firms. *Journal of Business Venturing, 3,* 97–108.

Craig, J., & Lindsay, N. (2001). Quantifying "gut feeling" in the opportunity recognition process. In W. D. Bygrave, E. Autio, C. G. Brush, P. Davidsson, P. G. Greene, P. D. Reynolds, & H. J. Sapienza (Eds.), *Frontiers of entrepreneurship research* (pp. 124–135). Babson Park, MA: Center for Entrepreneurial Studies.

Duncker, K. (1935). *Zur Psychologie des produktiven Denkens*. Berlin: Springer.

Eden, D. (1973). Self-employed workers: A comparison group for organizational psychology. *Organizational Behavior and Human Performance, 9*, 186–214.

Edwards, J. R. (1991). Person–job fit: A conceptual integration, literature review, and methodological critique. *International Review of Industrial and Organizational Psychology, 6*, 283–357.

Ericsson, K. A., & Charness, N. (1994). Expert performance: Its structure and acquisition. *American Psychologist, 49*, 725–747.

Ericsson, K. A., & Lehmann, A. C. (1996). Expert and exceptional performance: Evidence of maximal adaptation to task constraints. *Annual Review of Psychology, 47*, 273–305.

Escher, S., Grabarkiewicz, R., Frese, M., van Steekelenburg, G., Lauw, M., & Friedrich, C. (2002). The moderator effect of cognitive ability on the relation between planning strategies and business success of small-scale business owners in South Africa: A longitudinal study. *Journal of Developmental Entrepreneurship, 7*, 305–318.

Evans, D., & Leighton, L. (1989). Some empirical aspects of entrepreneurship. *American Economic Review, 79*, 519–535.

Fleishman, E. A., & Quaintance, M. K. (1984). *Taxonomies of human performance*. London: Academic Press.

Forgas, J. P. (1995). Mood and judgment: The affect infusion model. (AIM). *Psychological Bulletin, 117*, 39–66.

Frese, M., Brantjes, A., & Hoorn, R. (2002). Psychological success factors of small scale businesses in Namibia: The roles of strategy process, entrepreneurial orientation and the environment. *Journal of Developmental Entrepreneurship, 7*, 259–282.

Frese, M., & Fay, D. (2001). Personal initiative (PI): A concept for work in the 21st century. *Research in Organizational Behavior, 23*, 133–188.

Frese, M., Krauss, S., Keith, N., Escher, S., Grabarkiewicz, R., Unger, J., & Friedrich, C. (2006). *Business Owners' Action Planning and Its Relationship to Business Success in Three African Countries*. Giessen: Department of Psychology, submitted for publication.

Frese, M., van Gelderen, M., & Ombach, M. (2000). How to plan as a small scale business owner: Psychological process characteristics of action strategies and success. *Journal of Small Business Management, 38*(2), 1–18.

Gaglio, C. M. (2004). The role of mental simulations and counterfactual thinking in the opportunity identification process. *Entrepreneurship Theory and Practice, 28*, 533–552.

Gaglio, C. M., & Katz, J. (2001). The psychological basis of opportunity identification: Entrepreneurial alertness. *Small Business Economics, 16*, 95–111.

Gentner, D. R., & Stevens, A. L. (Eds.). (1983). *Mental models*. Hillsdale, NJ: Lawrence Erlbaum Associates.

Glass, A. L., & Holyoak, K. J. (1986). *Cognition*. New York: Random House.

Goldstein, I. L., & Ford, J. K. (2002). *Training organizations* (4th ed.). Belmont, CA: Wadsworth.

Gollwitzer, P. M. (1999). Implementation intentions: Strong effects of simple plans. *American Psychologist, 54*, 493–503.

Griffin, R. W., & O'Leary-Kelly, A. M. (Eds.). (2004). *The dark side of organizational behavior*. San Francisco: Jossey-Bass.

Gupta, V., MacMillan, I. C., & Surie, G. (2004). Entrepreneurial leadership: Developing and measuring a cross-cultural construct. *Journal of Business Venturing, 19*, 241–260.

Hahn, U., & Chater, N. (1997). Concepts and similarity. In K. Lamberts & D. Shanks (Eds.), *Knowledge, concepts, and categories* (pp. 43–92). Cambridge, MA: MIT Press.

Hattrup, K., & Jackson, S. E. (Eds.). (1996). *Learning about individual differences by taking situations seriously*. San Francisco, CA: Jossey-Bass.

Heilman, M. E., & Chen, J. J. (2003). Entrepreneurship as a solution: The allure of self-employment for women and minorities. *Human Resource Management Review, 13*, 347–364.

Heilman, M. E., Wallen, A. S., Fuchs, D., & Tamkins, M. M. (2004). Penalties for women who succeed at male gender-typed tasks. *Journal of Applied Psychology, 89*, 416–427.

House, R. J., Hanges, P. J., Javidan, M., Dorfman, P. W., & Gupta, V. (Eds.). (2004). *Cultures, leadership and organizations: A 62 nation GLOBE Study.* Thousand Oaks, CA: Sage.

Kacmar, K. M., & Baron, R. A. (1999). Organizational politics: The state of the field, links to related processes, and an agenda for future research. In G. Ferris (Ed.), *Research in personnel and human resources management* (Vol. 18, pp. 1–40). Greenwich, CT: JAI Press.

Kahneman, D., & Lovallo, D. (1993). Timid choices and bold forecasts: A cognitive perspective on risk taking. In R. P. Rumelt, D. E. Schendel, & D. J. Teece (Eds.), *Fundamental issues in strategy: A research agenda* (pp. 71–96). Boston, MA: Harvard Business School Press.

Kanfer, R. (1992). Work motivation: New directions in theory and research. In C. L. Cooper & I. T. Robertson (Eds.), *International review of industrial and organizational psychology* (Vol. 7, pp. 1–54). Chichester: Wiley.

Kanfer, R., & Ackerman, P. L. (1989). Motivation and cognitive abilities: An integrative/aptitude-treatment interaction approach to skill acquisition. *Journal of Applied Psychology, 74*, 657–690.

Klein, K. J. & Kozlowski, S. W. J. (Eds.). (2000). *Multilevel theory, research, and methods in organizations* (pp. 512–553). San Francisco: Jossey-Bass.

Latham, G. P., & Pinder, C. C. (2005). Work motivation theory and research at the dawn of the 21st century. *Annual Review of Psychology, 56*, 485–516.

Law, K. S., Wong, C. S., & Song, L. J. (2004). The construct and criterion validity of emotional intelligence and its potential utility for management studies. *Journal of Applied Psychology, 89*, 483–496.

Levesque, M., Shepherd, D. A., & Douglas, E. J. (2002). Employment or self-employment; A dynamic utility-maximizing model. *Journal of Business Venturing, 17*, 189–210.

Lewicki, R. J., McAllister, D. J., & Bies, R. J. (1998). Trust and distrust: New relationships and realities. *Academy of Management Review, 23*, 438–458.

Matlin, M. W. (2002). *Cognition* (5th ed.). Fort Worth, TX: Harcourt.

McClelland, D. C. (1973). Testing for competence rather than for "intelligence." *American Psychologist, 28*, 1–14.

McClelland, D. C. (1987). *Human motivation.* Cambridge, England: Cambridge University Press.

Mischel, W., & Shoda, Y. (1998). Reconciling processing dynamics and personality dispositions. *Annual Review of Psychology, 49*, 229–258.

Murphy, G. C., & Athanasou, J. A. (1999). The effects of unemployment on mental health. *Journal of Occupational and Organizational Psychology, 72*, 83–99.

Neisser, U. (1985). The role of invariant in the control of movement. In M. Frese & J. Sabini (Eds.), *Goal directed behavior: The concept of action in psychology* (pp. 97–109). Hillsdale, NJ: Lawrence Erlbaum Associates.

Organ, D. W. (1997). Organizational citizenship behavior: It's construct clean-up time. *Human Performance, 10*, 85–98.

Petty, R. E., & Cacioppo, J. T. (1990). Involvement and persuasion: Tradition versus integration. *Psychological Bulletin, 107*, 367–374.

Plous, S. (1993). *The psychology of judgment and decision-making.* New York: Mc Graw-Hill.

Powell, G. N. (1999). Reflections on the glass ceiling: recent trends and future prospects. In G. N. Powell (Ed.), *Handbook of gender and work* (pp. 325–234). Thousand Oaks, CA: Sage.

Ragins, B. R. (1999). Gender and mentoring relationships. In G. N. Powell (Ed.), *Handbook of gender and work* (pp. 347–370). Thousand Oaks, CA: Sage.

Rauch, A., & Frese, M. (2000). Psychological approaches to entrepreneurial success: A general model and an overview of findings. *International Review of Industrial and Organizational Psychology, 15*, 101–142.

Schwenk, C. R., & Shrader, C. B. (1993, Spring). Effects of formal strategic planning on financial performance in small firms: A meta-analysis. *Entrepreneurship: Theory and Practice*, pp. 53–64.

Shane, S., Locke, E. A., & Collins, C. J. (2003). Entrepreneurial motivation. *Human Resource Management Review, 13*, 257–280.

Shane, S., & Venkataraman, S. 2000. The promise of entrepreneurship as a field of research. *Academy of Management Review, 25,* 217–226.

Shepperd, J. A., Ouellette, J. A., & Fernandez, J. K. (1996). Abandoning unrealistic optimistic performance estimates and the temporal proximity of self-relevant feedback. *Journal of Personality and Social Psychology, 70,* 844–855.

Simon, M., Houghton, S. M., & Aquino, K. (2000). Cognitive biases, risk perception, and venture formation: How individual decide to start companies. *Journal of Business Venturing, 15,* 113–134.

Sonnentag, S. (1998). Expertise in professional software design: A process study. *Journal of Applied Psychology, 83,* 703–715.

Sternberg, R. J. (2004). Successful intelligence as a basis of entrepreneurship. *Journal of Business Venturing, 19,* 189–201.

Stroh, L. K., & Reilly, A. J. H. (1999). Gender and careers: Present experiences and emerging trends. In G. N. Powell (Ed.), *Handbook of gender and work* (pp. 307–332). Thousand Oaks, CA: Sage.

Taylor, S. E., Pham, L. B., Rivkin, I. D., & Armor, D. A. (1998). Harnessing the imagination: Mental simulation, self-regulation, and coping. *American Psychologist, 53,* 429–439.

Tesluk, P. E., & Jacobs, R. R. (1998). Toward an integrated model of work experience. *Personnel Psychology, 51,* 321–355.

Tett, R. P., Steele, J. R., & Beaurgard, R. S. (2003). Broad and narrow measures on both sides of the personality–job performance relationship. *Journal of Organizational Behavior, 24,* 335–356.

Unger, J. M., Keith, N., Frese, M., Hilling, C., & Gielnik, M. (2005). *Deliberate practice in entrepreneurship: Relationships with education, cognitive ability, knowledge, and success.* Giessen: University of Giessen, submitted for publication.

Wanous, J. P., Poland, T. D., Premack, S. L., & Davis, K. S. (1992). The effects of met expectations on newcomer attitudes and behaviors: A review and meta-analysis. *Journal of Applied Psychology, 77,* 288–297.

Wayne, S. J., Liden, R. C., Gran, I. K., & Ferris, G. R. 1997. The role of upward influence tactics in human resource decisions. *Personnel Psychology, 50,* 979–1006.

Wexley, K. N., & Latham, G. P. (2002). *Developing and training human resources in organizations* (3rd ed.). Upper Saddle River, NJ: Prentice Hall.

Zhao, X., & Frese, M. (2005). *Dynamic network building and business success in China: The function of social skills, proactive and elaborate social strategies and relationship-oriented personal initiative.* Giessen: University of Giessen, submitted for publication.

Author Index

Subject Index

A

Abilities, 75, 79–83, *see also* Competencies, entrepreneurs'
Absorptive capacity theory, 81
Academic entrepreneurship programs, 213, 218–219
Academy of Management, 229
Academy of Management Journal, 342
Achievement motivation
  conceptual overlap with other traits, 108, 337–338
  correlates of, 50, 56, 361
  and cross-cultural studies, 265
  and extreme situations, 9
  and history of entrepreneurship research, 3, 4, 10–11, 24, 45
  measurement of, 61, 99–100
  predictive power of, 293, 295, 352
  and process model of entrepreneurship, 197–201
  research reviews of, 49, 54, 339–340
Achieving Society, The (McClelland), 4, 10, 12, 216fn
Action programs, *see* Planning
Action regulation, 151–153, 179–182, 359–361
  entrepreneurship applications, 175–179
  focus, 172–175
  interplay of steps, 160–162
  levels of, 162–166, 168–171
  performance limits, 171–172

sequence of steps, 153–160
structure, 166–168
Action styles, 172
Affect infusion, 132
Affiliation, need for, 197, 200
Agreeableness, 48
Agricultural Extension (AgEx), 210
Agriculture, U.S. Department of, 214
Aitken, H. G. J., 10
Alertness, entrepreneurial, 82, 140, *see also* Opportunity recognition
Allen, Paul, 213, 225
Alternative Board, The, 214
Ambition, *see* Achievement motivation
American Made (Livesay), 12
American Orthopedic Devices, LLC, 93
American Psychological Association (APA), 229
Annual Statement Studies (Risk Management Association), 222
Anthropology, 11
Apple Computer, 115
APS (Association for Psychological Science), 229
Archival research, 303–306, 342–344
Ash, Mary Kay, 102
Asia, *see also* Bangladesh; China, entrepreneurship in; Japan; South Korea; Thailand
  Chinese diaspora in, 274
  entrepreneurship education in, 212fn
  use of Likert scales in, 269
Asian Development Bank, 270